CHILTON BOOK COMPANY

REPAIR MANUAL

CHEVETTE PONTIAC 1000 1976-88

All U.S. and Canadian models of CHEVROLET Chevette and PONTIAC 1000

CHILTON BOOK COMPANY
Radnor, Pennsylvania
19089

CONTENTS

GENERAL INFORMATION and MAINTENANCE

ENGINE PERFORMANCE and TUNE-UP

ENGINE and ENGINE OVERHAUL

EMISSION CONTROLS

FUEL SYSTEM

CHASSIS ELECTRICAL

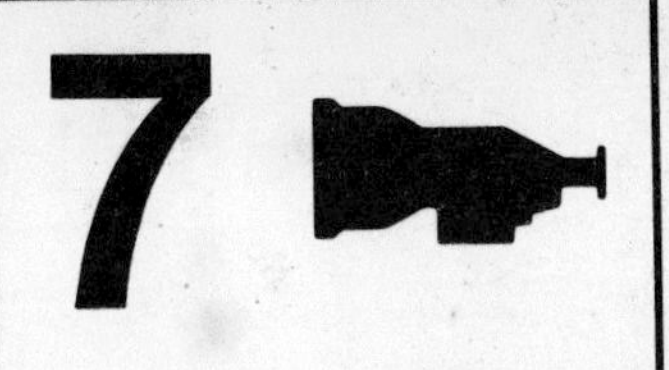

DRIVE TRAIN

SUSPENSION and STEERING

BRAKES

BODY

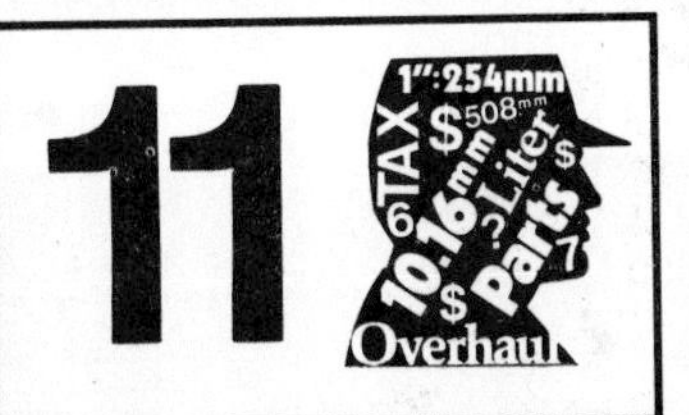

MECHANIC'S DATA

SAFETY NOTICE

Proper service and repair procedures are vital to the safe, reliable operation of all motor vehicles, as well as the personal safety of those performing repairs. This book outlines procedures for servicing and repairing vehicles using safe, effective methods. The procedures contain many NOTES, CAUTIONS and WARNINGS which should be followed along with standard safety procedures to eliminate the possibility of personal injury or improper service which could damage the vehicle or compromise its safety.

It is important to note that repair procedures and techniques, tools and parts for servicing motor vehicles, as well as the skill and experience of the individual performing the work vary widely. It is not possible to anticipate all of the conceivable ways or conditions under which vehicles may be serviced, or to provide cautions as to all of the possible hazards that may result. Standard and accepted safety precautions and equipment should be used during cutting, grinding, chiseling, prying, or any other process that can cause material removal or projectiles.

Some procedures require the use of tools specially designed for a specific purpose. Before substituting another tool or procedure, you must be completely satisfied that neither your personal safety, nor the performance of the vehicle will be endangered.

Although the information in this guide is based on industry sources and is as complete as possible at the time of publication, the possibility exists that the manufacturer made later changes which could not be included here. While striving for total accuracy, Chilton Book Company cannot assume responsibility for any errors, changes, or omissions that may occur in the compilation of this data.

PART NUMBERS

Part numbers listed in this reference are not recommendations by Chilton for any product by brand name. They are references that can be used with interchange manuals and aftermarket supplier catalogs to locate each brand supplier's discrete part number.

SPECIAL TOOLS

Special tools are recommended by the vehicle manufacturer to perform their specific job. Use has been kept to a minimum, but where absolutely necessary, they are referred to in the text by the part number of the tool manufacturer. These tools can be purchased, under the appropriate part number, from Service Tool Division, Kent-Moore Corporation, 1501 South Jackson Street, Jackson MI, 49203—or an equivalent tool can be purchased locally from a tool supplier or parts outlet. Before substituting any tool for the one recommended, read the SAFETY NOTICE at the top of this page.

ACKNOWLEDGMENTS

Chilton Book Company thanks the Chevrolet Motor Division and the Pontiac Motor Division of the General Motors Corporation for assistance in the preparation of this book.

Information has been selected from Chevette and Pontiac 100 Service Manuals.

Published in Radnor, Pennsylvania 19089, by Chilton Book Company

Manufactured in the United States of America
4567890 87654321

Chilton's Repair Manual: Chevette and Pontiac 1000 1976–88
ISBN 0-8019-7845-9 pbk.
Library of Congress Catalog Card No. 87-47930

General Information and Maintenance

1

HOW TO USE THIS BOOK

This book covers all Chevette and Pontiac 1000 models from 1976 through 1987.

The first two chapters will be the most used, since they contain maintenance and tune-up information and procedures. Studies have shown that a properly tuned and maintained car can get at least 10% better gas mileage (which translates into lower operating costs) and periodic maintenance will catch minor problems before they turn into major repair bills. The other chapters deal with the more complex systems of your car. Operating systems from engine through brakes are covered to the extent that the average do-it-yourselfer becomes mechanically involved. This book will not explain such things as rebuilding the differential for the simple reason that the expertise required and the investment in special tools make this task uneconomical. It will give you the detailed instructions to help you change your own brake pads and shoes, tune-up the engine, replace spark plugs and filters, and do many more jobs that will save you money, give you personal satisfaction and help you avoid expensive problems.

A secondary purpose of this book is a reference guide for owners who want to understand their car and/or their mechanics better. In this case, no tools at all are required. Knowing just what a particular repair job requires in parts and labor time will allow you to evaluate whether or not you're getting a fair price quote and help decipher itemized bills from a repair shop.

Before attempting any repairs or service on your car, read through the entire procedure outlined in the appropriate chapter. This will give you the overall view of what tools and supplies will be required. There is nothing more frustrating than having to walk to the bus stop on Monday morning because you were short one gasket on Sunday afternoon. So read ahead and plan ahead. Each operation should be approached logically and all procedures thoroughly understood before attempting any work. Some special tools that may be required can often be rented from local automotive jobbers or places specializing in renting tools and equipment. Check the yellow pages of your phone book.

All chapters contain adjustments, maintenance, removal and installation procedures, and overhaul procedures. When overhaul is not considered practical, we tell you how to remove the failed part and then how to install the new or rebuilt replacement. In this way, you at least save the labor costs. Backyard overhaul of some components (such as the alternator or water pump) is just not practical, but the removal and installation procedure is often simple and well within the capabilities of the average car owner.

Two basic mechanic's rules should be mentioned here. First, whenever the LEFT side of the car or engine is referred to, it is meant to specify the DRIVER'S side of the car. Conversely, the RIGHT side of the car means the PASSENGER'S side. Second, all screws and bolts are removed by turning counterclockwise, and tightened by turning clockwise.

Safety is always the most important rule. Constantly be aware of the dangers involved in working on or around an automobile and take proper precautions to avoid the risk of personal injury or damage to the vehicle. See the section in this chapter, Servicing Your Vehicle Safely, and the SAFETY NOTICE on the acknowledgment page before attempting any service procedures and pay attention to the instructions provided. There are 3 common mistakes in mechanical work:

1. Incorrect order of assembly, disassembly or adjustment. When taking something apart or putting it together, doing things in the wrong order usually just costs you extra time; however it CAN break something. Read the entire procedure before beginning disassembly. Do every-

thing in the order in which the instructions say you should do it, even if you can't immediately see a reason for it. When you're taking apart something that is very intricate (for example a carburetor), you might want to draw a picture of how it looks when assembled at one point in order to make sure you get everything back in its proper position. We will supply exploded views whenever possible, but sometimes the job requires more attention to detail than an illustration provides. When making adjustments (especially tune-up adjustments), do them in order. One adjustment often affects another and you cannot expect satisfactory results unless each adjustment is made only when it cannot be changed by any other.

2. Overtorquing (or undertorquing) nuts and bolts. While it is more common for overtorquing to cause damage, undertorquing can cause a fastener to vibrate loose and cause serious damage, especially when dealing with aluminum parts. Pay attention to torque specifications and utilize a torque wrench in assembly. If a torque figure is not available remember that, if you are using the right tool to do the job, you will probably not have to strain yourself to get a fastener tight enough. The pitch of most threads is so slight that the tension you put on the wrench will be multiplied many times in actual force on what you are tightening. A good example of how critical torque is can be seen in the case of spark plug installation, especially where you are putting the plug into an aluminum cylinder head. Too little torque can fail to crush the gasket, causing leakage of combustion gases and consequent overheating of the plug and engine parts. Too much torque can damage the threads or distort the plug, which changes the spark gap at the electrode. Since more and more manufacturers are using aluminum in their engine and chassis parts to save weight, a torque wrench should be in any serious do-it-yourselfer's tool box.

There are many commercial chemical products available for ensuring that fasteners won't come loose, even if they are not torqued just right (a very common brand is Loctite®). If you're worried about getting something together tight enough to hold, but loose enough to avoid mechanical damage during assembly, one of these products might offer substantial insurance. Read the label on the package and make sure the product is compatible with the materials, fluids, etc. involved before choosing one.

3. Crossthreading. This occurs when a part such as a bolt is screwed into a nut or casting at the wrong angle and forced, causing the threads to become damaged. Crossthreading is more likely to occur if access is difficult. It helps to clean and lubricate fasteners, and to start threading with the part to be installed going straight in, using your fingers. If you encounter resistance, unscrew the part and start over again at a different angle until it can be inserted and turned several times without much effort. Keep in mind that many parts, especially spark plugs, use tapered threads so that gentle turning will automatically bring the part you're threading to the proper angle if you don't force it or resist a change in angle. Don't put a wrench on the part until it's been turned in a couple of times by hand. If you suddenly encounter resistance and the part has not seated fully, don't force it. Pull it back out and make sure it's clean and threading properly.

Always take your time and be patient; once you have some experience, working on your car will become an enjoyable hobby.

TOOLS AND EQUIPMENT

Naturally, without the proper tools and equipment it is impossible to properly service your vehicle. It would be impossible to catalog each tool that you would need to perform each or every operation in this book. It would also be unwise for the amateur to rush out and buy an expensive set of tools on the theory that he may need one or more of them at sometime.

The best approach is to proceed slowly, gathering together a good quality set of those tools that are used most frequently. Don't be misled by the low cost of bargain tools. It is far better to spend a little more for better quality. Forged wrenches, 6 or 12 point sockets and fine tooth ratchets are by far preferable to their less expensive counterparts. As any good mechanic can tell you, there are few worse experiences than trying to work on a car with bad tools. Your monetary savings will be far outweighed by frustration and mangled knuckles.

Begin accumulating those tools that are used most frequently; those associated with routine maintenance and tune-up.

In addition to the normal assortment of screwdrivers and pliers you should have the following tools for routine maintenance jobs (your car, depending on the model year, uses both SAE and metric fasteners):

1. SAE/Metric wrenches, sockets and combination open end/box end wrenches in sizes from 1/8″ (3mm) to 3/4″ (19mm); and a 5/8″ spark plug socket.

If possible, buy various length socket drive extensions. One break in this department is that the metric sockets available in the U.S. will all fit the ratchet handles and extensions you may already have (1/4″, 3/8″, and 1/2″ drive).

2. Jackstands for support

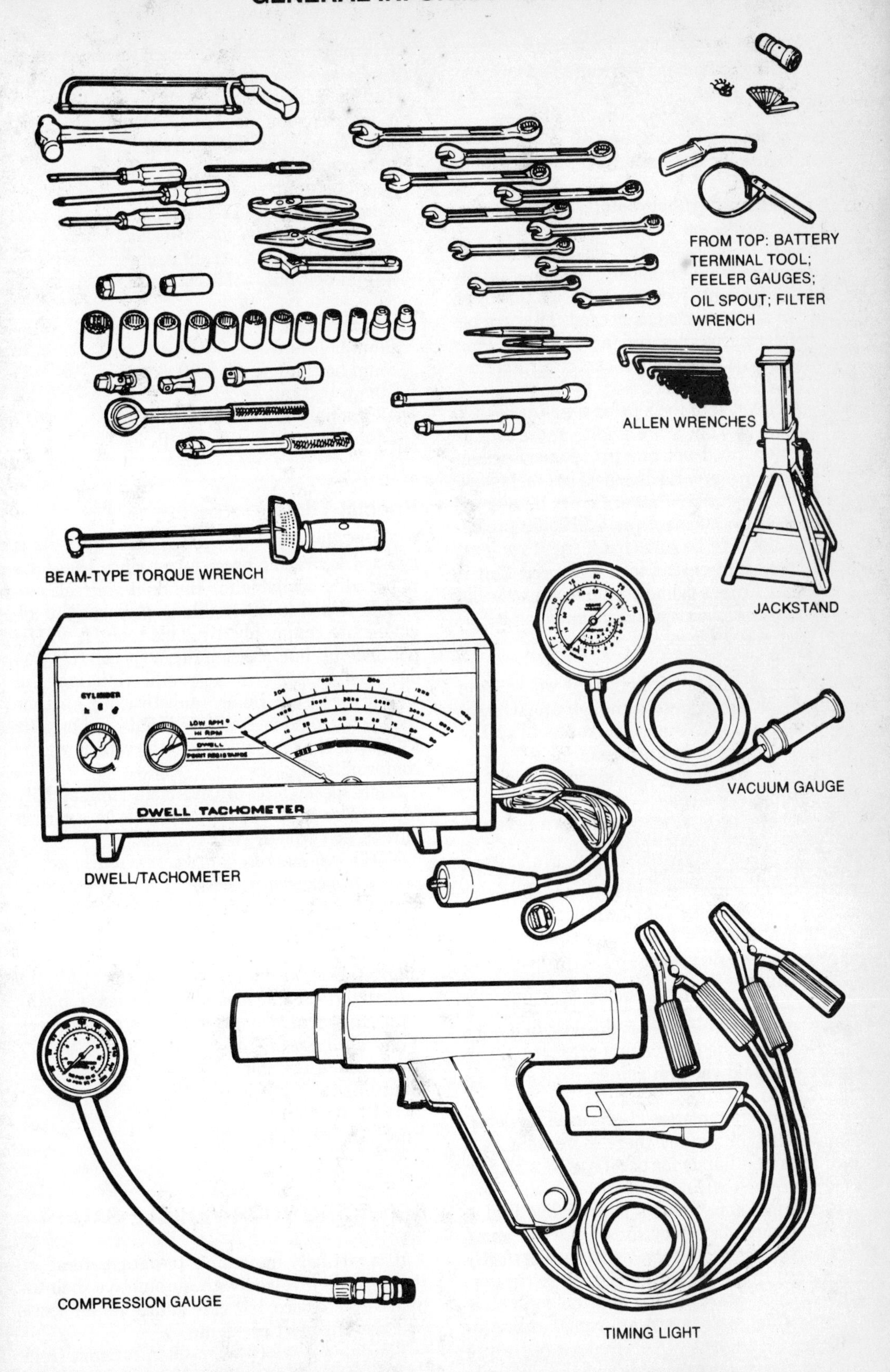

You need only a basic assortment of hand tools and test instruments for most maintenance and repair jobs

3. Oil filter wrench
4. Oil filter spout for pouring oil
5. Grease gun for chassis lubrication
6. Hydrometer for checking the battery
7. A container for draining oil
8. Many rags for wiping up the inevitable mess.

In addition to the above items there are several others that are not absolutely necessary, but handy to have around. These include oil-dry, a transmission funnel and the usual supply of lubricants, antifreeze and fluids, although these can be purchased as needed. This is a basic list for routine maintenance, but only your personal needs and desires can accurately determine your list of necessary tools.

The second list of tools is for tune-ups. While the tools involved here are slightly more sophisticated, they need not be outrageously expensive. There are several inexpensive tach/dwell meters on the market that are every bit as good for the average mechanic as a $100.00 professional model. Just be sure that it goes to at least 1,200-1,500 rpm on the tach scale and that it works on 4, 6 and 8 cylinder engines. A basic list of tune-up equipment could include:

1. Tach-dwell meter
2. Spark plug wrench
3. Timing light (a DC light that works from the car's battery is best, although an AC light that plugs into 110V house current will suffice at some sacrifice in brightness)
4. Wire spark plug gauge/adjusting tools
5. Set of feeler blades.

Here again, be guided by your own needs. A feeler blade will set the point gap as easily as dwell meter will read dwell, but slightly less accurately. And since you will need a tachometer anyway ... well, make your own decision.

In addition to these basic tools, there are several other tools and gauges you may find useful. These include:

1. A compression gauge. The screw-in type is slower to use, but eliminates the possibility of a faulty reading due to escaping pressure
2. A manifold vacuum gauge
3. A test light
4. An induction meter. This is used for determining whether or not there is current in a wire. These are handy for use if a wire is broken somewhere in a wiring harness.

As a final note, you will probably find a torque wrench necessary for all but the most basic work. The beam type models are perfectly adequate, although the newer click (breakaway) type are more precise, and you don't have to crane your neck to see a torque reading in awkward situations. The breakaway torque wrenches are more expensive and should be recalibrated periodically.

Torque specification for each fastener will be given in the procedure in any case that a specific torque value is required. If no torque specifications are given, use the following values as a guide, based upon fastener size:

Bolts marked 6T

6mm bolt/nut – 5-7 ft. lbs.
8mm bolt/nut – 12-17 ft. lbs.
10mm bolt/nut – 23-34 ft. lbs.
12mm bolt/nut – 41-59 ft. lbs.
14mm bolt/nut – 56-76 ft. lbs.

Bolts marked 8T

6mm bolt/nut – 6-9 ft. lbs.
8mm bolt/nut – 13-20 ft. lbs.
10mm bolt/nut – 27-40 ft. lbs.
12mm bolt/nut – 46-69 ft. lbs.
14mm bolt/nut – 75-101 ft. lbs.

Special Tools

Normally, the use of special factory tools is avoided for repair procedures, since these are not readily available for the do-it-yourself mechanic. When it is possible to perform the job with more commonly available tools, it will be pointed out, but occasionally, a special tool was designed to perform a specific function and should be used. Before substituting another tool, you should be convinced that neither your safety nor the performance of the vehicle will be compromised.

Some special tools are available commercially from major tool manufacturers. Others can be purchased through your GM dealer.

NOTE: *Special tools are occasionally necessary to perform a specific job or are recommended to make a job easier. Their use has been kept to a minimum. When a special tool is indicated, it will be referred to by manufacturer's part number, and, where possible, an illustration of the tool will be provided so that an equivalent tool may be used. Manufacturer and addresses follows:*

Service Tool Division
Kent-Moore
29784 Little Mack
Roseville, MI 48066-2298

SERVICING YOUR VEHICLE SAFELY

It is virtually impossible to anticipate all of the hazards involved with automotive maintenance and service, but care and common sense will prevent most accidents.

The rules of safety for mechanics range from "don't smoke around gasoline," to "use the proper tool for the job." The trick to avoiding injuries is to develop safe work habits and take every possible precaution.

Dos

- Do keep a fire extinguisher and first aid kit within easy reach.
- Do wear safety glasses or goggles when cutting, drilling or prying, even if you have 20-20 vision. If you wear glasses for the sake of vision, they should be made of hardened glass that can also serve as safety glasses, or wear safety goggles over your regular glasses.
- Do shield your eyes whenever you work around the battery. Batteries contain sulphuric acid; in case of contact with the eyes or skin, flush the area with water or a mixture of water and baking soda and get medical attention immediately.
- Do use safety stands for any under car service. Jacks are for raising vehicles; safety stands are for making sure the vehicle stays raised until you want it to come down. Whenever the vehicle is raised, block the wheels remaining on the ground and set the parking brake.
- Do use adequate ventilation when working with any chemicals. Like carbon monoxide, the asbestos dust resulting from brake lining wear can be poisonous in sufficient quantities.
- Do disconnect the negative battery cable when working on the electrical system. The primary ignition system can contain up to 40,000 volts.
- Do follow manufacturer's directions whenever working with potentially hazardous materials. Both brake fluid and antifreeze are poisonous if taken internally.
- Do properly maintain your tools. Loose hammerheads, mushroomed punches and chisels, frayed or poorly grounded electrical cords, excessively worn screwdrivers, spread wrenches (open end), cracked sockets, slipping ratchets, or faulty droplight sockets can cause accidents.
- Do use the proper size and type of tool for the job being done.
- Do when possible, pull on a wrench handle rather than push on it, and adjust your stance to prevent a fall.
- Do be sure that adjustable wrenches are tightly adjusted on the nut or bolt and pulled so that the face is on the side of the fixed jaw.
- Do select a wrench or socket that fits the nut or bolt. The wrench or socket should sit straight, not cocked.
- Do strike squarely with a hammer—avoid glancing blows.
- Do set the parking brake and block the drive wheels if the work requires that the engine be running.

Don'ts

- Don't run an engine in a garage or anywhere else without proper ventilation—EVER! Carbon monoxide is poisonous; it takes a long time to leave the human body and you can build up a deadly supply of it in your system by simply breathing in a little every day. You may not realize you are slowly poisoning yourself. Always use power vents, windows, fans or open the garage doors.
- Don't work around moving parts while wearing a necktie or other loose clothing. Short sleeves are much safer than long, loose sleeves and hard-toed shoes with neoprene soles protect your toes and give a better grip on slippery surfaces. Jewelry such as watches, fancy belt buckles, beads or body adornment of any kind is not safe working around a car. Long hair should be hidden under a hat or cap.
- Don't use pockets for toolboxes. A fall or bump can drive a screwdriver deep into you body. Even a wiping cloth hanging from the back pocket can wrap around a spinning shaft or fan.
- Don't smoke when working around gasoline, cleaning solvent or other flammable material.
- Don't smoke when working around the battery. When the battery is being charged, it gives off explosive hydrogen gas.
- Don't use gasoline to wash your hands; there are excellent soaps available. Gasoline may contain lead, and lead can enter the body through a cut, accumulating in the body until you are very ill. Gasoline also removes all the natural oils from the skin so that bone-dry hands will suck up oil and grease.
- Don't service the air conditioning system unless you are equipped with the necessary tools and training. The refrigerant, R-12, is extremely cold and when exposed to the air, will instantly freeze any surface it comes in contact with, including your eyes. Although the refrigerant is normally non-toxic, R-12 becomes a deadly poisonous gas in the presence of an open flame. One good whiff of the vapors from burning refrigerant can be fatal.
- Don't use screwdrivers for anything other than driving screws! A screwdriver used as a prying tool can snap when you least expect it, causing injuries. At the very least, you'll ruin a good screwdriver.
- Don't use a bumper jack (that little ratchet, scissors, or pantograph jack supplied with the car) for anything other than changing a flat! These jacks are only intended for emergency use out on the road; they are NOT designed as a maintenance tool. If you are serious about maintaining your car yourself, invest in a hy-

draulic floor jack of at least 1½ ton capacity, and at least two sturdy jackstands

SERIAL NUMBER IDENTIFICATION

Vehicle Identification Number (VIN)

The VIN (Vehicle Identification Number) is a 13 (1977-80) or 17 (1981 and later) digit number visible through the windshield on the driver's side of the dash and contains the vehicle and engine identification codes. It can be interpreted in the following charts:

Engine

On the gasoline engines the engine identification number is located on a pad on the right side of the cylinder block below the No. 1 spark plug.

On the diesel engines it is located at the left rear of the engine below the exhaust and manifold.

Transmission

The transmission identification number on the 4- or 5-speed manual is centered on a pad on

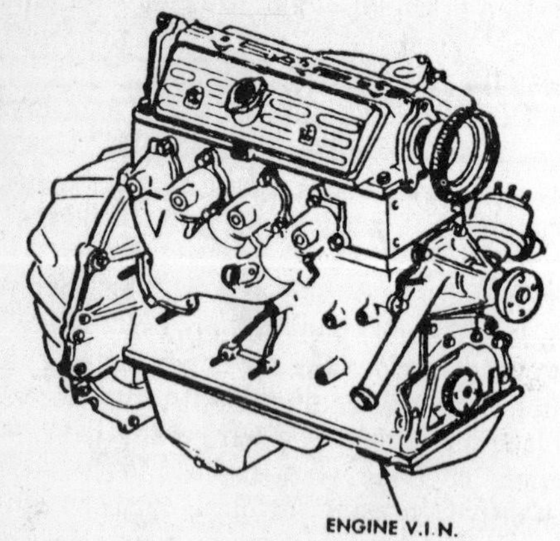

V.I.N. location—1.4 and 1.6 gasoline engine

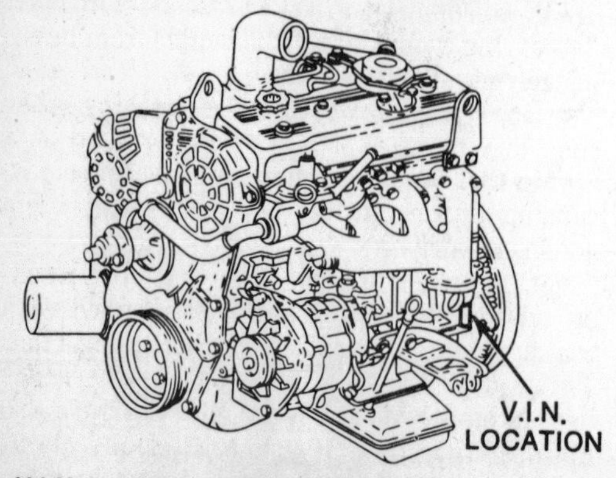

V.I.N. location—1.8 liter diesel engine

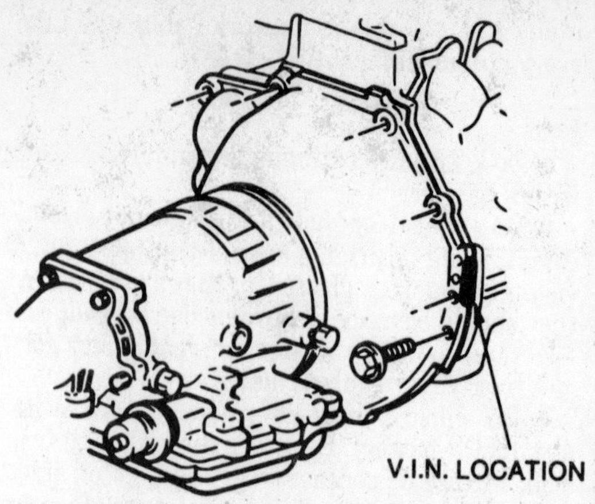

V.I.N. location—automatic transmission

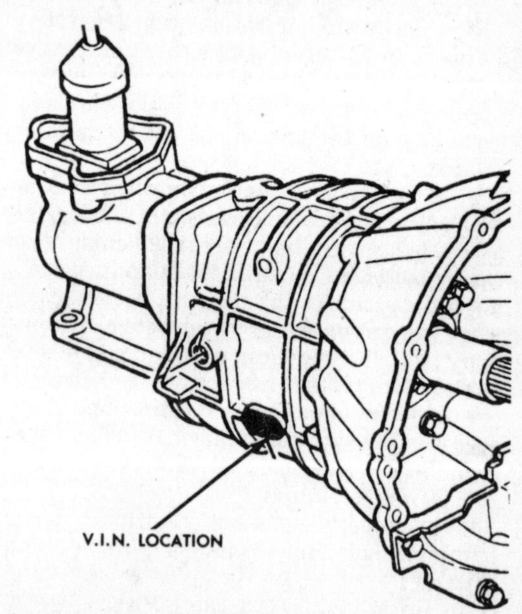

V.I.N. location—4 speed manual transmission

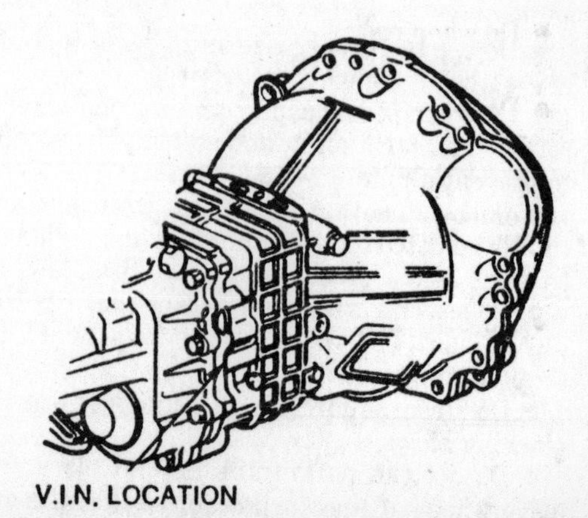

V.I.N. location—5 speed manual transmission

the lower right side of the case. On models with automatic transmissions, the number will be found on a tag on the right side of the transmission.

Drive Axle

The rear axle identification number on all models is on right or left axle tube adjacent to carrier.

ROUTINE MAINTENANCE

Routine maintenance is preventive medicine. It is the single most important process that can be taken in avoiding repairs and extending the life of any automobile. By taking only a minute or so each day to check oil level, tire pressures and coolant level, you'll be saving yourself time and money in the long run.

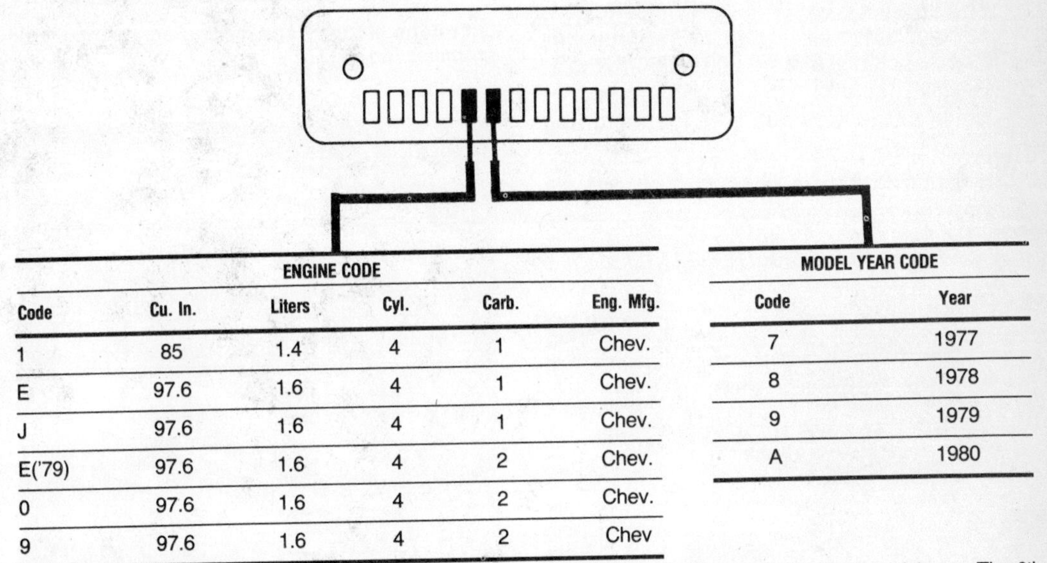

ENGINE CODE					
Code	Cu. In.	Liters	Cyl.	Carb.	Eng. Mfg.
1	85	1.4	4	1	Chev.
E	97.6	1.6	4	1	Chev.
J	97.6	1.6	4	1	Chev.
E('79)	97.6	1.6	4	2	Chev.
0	97.6	1.6	4	2	Chev.
9	97.6	1.6	4	2	Chev

MODEL YEAR CODE	
Code	Year
7	1977
8	1978
9	1979
A	1980

The thirteen digit Vehicle Identification Number can be used to determine engine application and model year. The 6th digit indicates the model year, and the 5th digit identifies the factory installed engine.

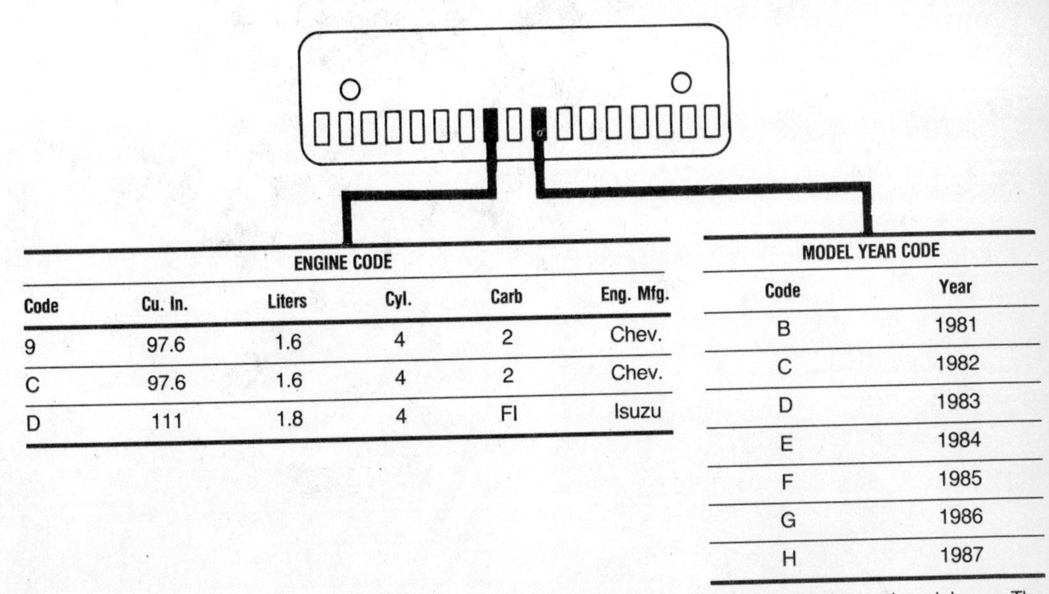

ENGINE CODE					
Code	Cu. In.	Liters	Cyl.	Carb	Eng. Mfg.
9	97.6	1.6	4	2	Chev.
C	97.6	1.6	4	2	Chev.
D	111	1.8	4	FI	Isuzu

MODEL YEAR CODE	
Code	Year
B	1981
C	1982
D	1983
E	1984
F	1985
G	1986
H	1987

The seventeen digit Vehicle Identification Number can be used to determine engine application and model year. The 10th digit indicates the model year, and the 8th digit identifies the factory installed engine.

Air Cleaner

Gasoline Engines

The 1979-87 models have a removable filter element. It is easily replaced by removing the wing nut on top of the air cleaner and placing a new filter in the same position as the old one. GM recommends that the filter be replaced at 50,000 mile intervals when driving under normal conditions. When driving under dusty conditions the filter should be replaced more frequently.

The air cleaner on 1976-78 Chevettes is a welded, non-serviceable unit. GM recommends this filter be changed at 50,000 mile intervals.

To replace the unit:

1. Remove the wing nut from the mounting stud.
2. Pry the retaining bail wire from the air cleaner.

NOTE: *On 1979-87 models, simply remove the air cleaner lid, replace the old filter with a*

The air cleaner wing nut screws off counterclockwise, don't overtighten it when putting it back on

The retaining bail snaps off. Use a screwdriver to pry it off, if it's stubborn

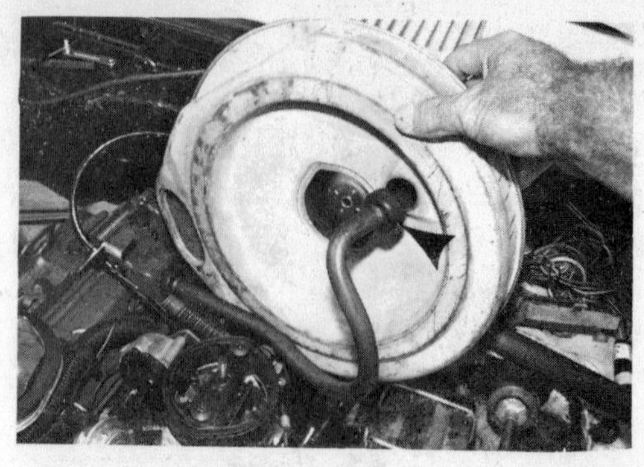

Lift off the old filter and disconnect the hose and grommet (arrow)

This shield keeps direct road dirt from hitting the filter element. Wipe it clean if you are not replacing the filter

Check the rubber gasket that the air cleaner sits on. If it's in bad shape or missing, replace it

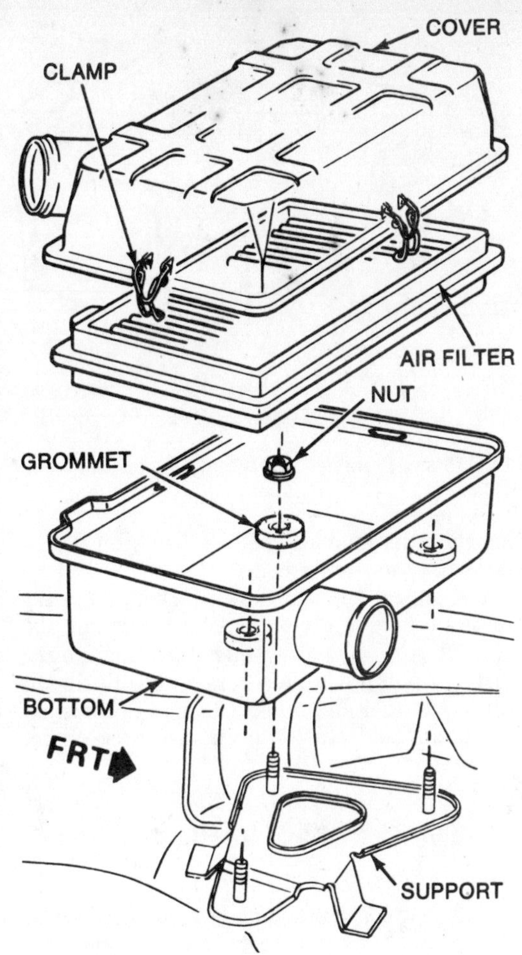

Air cleaner assembly—1.8 liter diesel engine

new one and replace the lid. On 1976-78 models, continue as follows.

3. Disconnect the attaching hose and remove the air cleaner.

4. Position the new air cleaner over the carburetor, attach the hose, reconnect the bail wire, and screw the wing nut back on.

Diesel Engines

GM recommends that the air filter element be replaced at 30,000 mile intervals when driving under normal conditions. When driving under dusty conditions the filter should be changed more frequently.

The air filter element is removed by releasing the 4 top cover retaining clamps. Lift off the top cover and remove the filter. Install the new filter into the air cleaner then replace the top cover and tighten retaining clamps.

NOTE: *Make sure all the air intake hoses are connected properly.*

Fuel Filter

Gasoline Engine

A paper filter element is located behind the carburetor fuel line inlet nut. The filter should be replaced every 12 months or 12,000 miles whichever occurs first. To replace the filter:

On gasoline engines the fuel filter is located behind the inlet fitting in the carburetor

Hold the fitting while loosening the nut to remove the filter

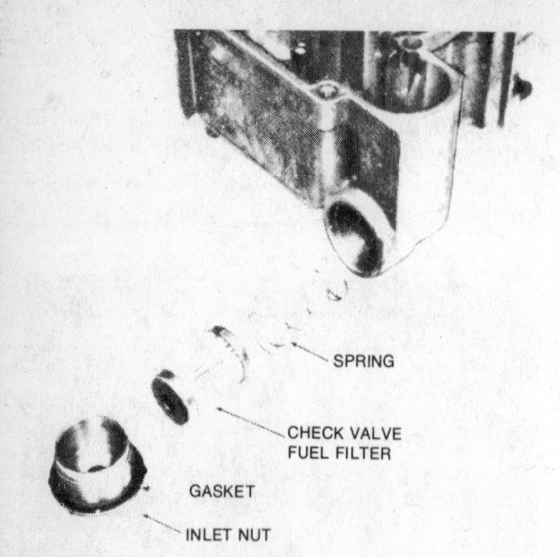

Fuel filter assembly—Gasoline engine

1. Place an absorbent rag beneath the fuel line connection to the carburetor to absorb any spills.
2. Disconnect the small fuel line connection nut, using a flare nut wrench, while holding the large fitting nut with a standard open end wrench.

NOTE: *A flared nut wrench is preferred over a standard open end wrench since it will not slip off and round off the corners of the tubing nut.*

3. Remove the large filter retaining nut from the carburetor. There is a spring behind the filter. Remove the filter and spring.
4. Install the spring and filter gasket.
5. Install the new gasket on the retaining nut and screw it into place. Do not overtighten; the threads are rather soft.
6. Install the fuel line.
7. Discard the gas-soaked rag safely.

Diesel Engine

The fuel filter element should be replaced every 30,000 miles. To replace the filter element:

1. Disconnect the negative battery cable.
2. Disconnect the water sensor lead at the bottom of the filter, then disconnect the water filter to main body hose.
3. Remove the filter element by turning it counterclockwise using a filter strap wrench. Be careful not to spill any fuel.
4. After draining the filter, unscrew the water sensor from the bottom of the element.
5. Install the sensor in the new filter after applying a thin film of diesel fuel to the sensor O-ring.
6. Clean the filter mounting surface, applying a thin film of diesel fuel to the gasket on the new filter and install the filter. Continue turning the filter an additional ⅔ turn after it contacts the filter main body.

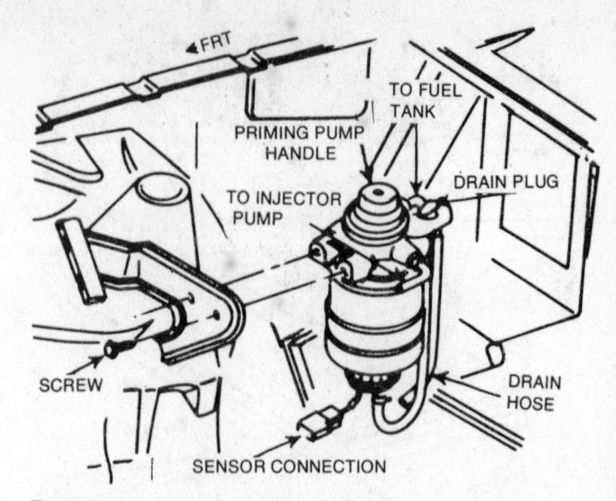

Fuel filter assembly—1.8 liter diesel engine

7. Connect the sensor wire. Disconnect the fuel outlet hose from the injector pump and place in a suitable container, then operate the priming pump handle several times to fill the filter with fuel. Reconnect the hose to the injector pump and start the engine to check for leaks.

Positive Crankcase Ventilation Valve

Gasoline Engines

PCV valve replacement is recommended at 30,000 miles or 2 year intervals. A clogged PCV system will cause poor idle and rough running. To replace the valve:

1. Pull the PCV valve from the valve cover, under the air cleaner.
2. Using a pair of pliers, release the valve retaining clip and remove the valve.
3. Install the new valve and insert it into the valve cover.
4. Inspect all PCV connecting hoses. Replace any cracked or deteriorated hoses.

The PCV valve is located in the valve cover (arrow)

Finally, remove the valve from the connecting hose. Some are retained by a clip which is released by squeezing with pliers

The valve pulls right out of its grommet in the valve cover

Diesel Engines

Periodically check the PCV system for the following:

1. Cracked or plugged hoses.
2. Remove the PCV valve cover and check the diaphragm for deterioration or damage.
3. Broken diaphragm spring.
4. Contamination of the PCV valve body.
5. Make sure the baffle plate located inside the cam cover isn't plugged or contaminated.

To replace the PCV valve:

1. Disconnect the PCV valve connecting hose.
2. Remove the two screws holding the PCV valve to the cam cover.
3. Remove the valve and gasket.
4. Clean the cam cover PCV mounting surface.
5. Use a new gasket and reverse the above to install.

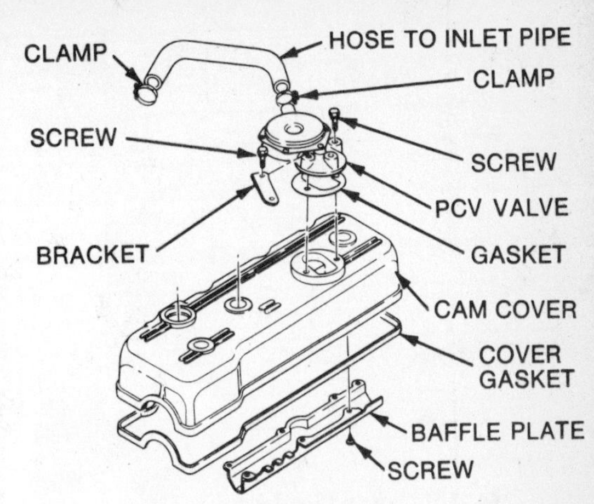

PCV system—1.8 liter diesel engine

Evaporative Canister

On models through 1980 a canister stores carburetor and fuel tank vapors while the engine is off, holding them to be drawn into the

The evaporative canister is located at the front of the engine compartment on the driver's side

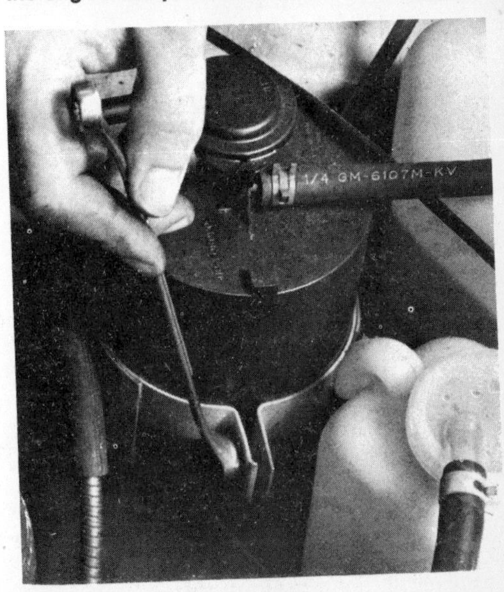

Loosen the bracket retaining screw enough so that you can slip the canister out

Work the old filter out and discard it. The new filter goes in the same way

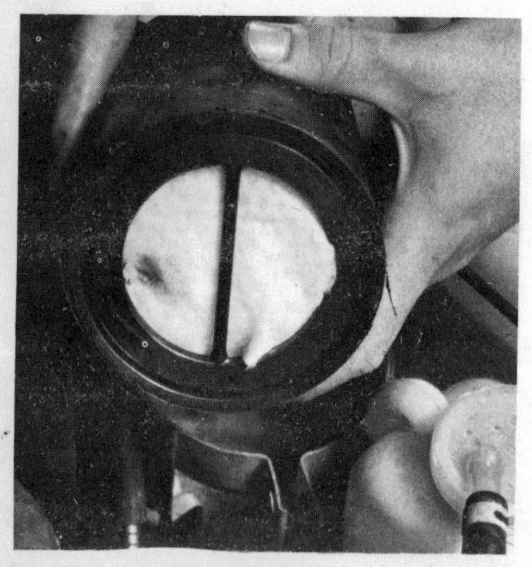

The filter is located in the bottom of the canister

engine and burned when the engine is started. The filter mounted on the bottom of the canister requires replacement at 15,000 mile intervals. To replace the filter:

1. Loosen the screw retaining the canister in its bracket.
2. Lift the canister slightly out of the bracket.
3. Remove the old filter from the bottom of the canister.
4. Install the new filter by working it into the retainers on the bottom of the canister.
5. Lower the canister back into its bracket and tighten the screw.
6. Check all connecting hoses and replace any that are suspect.

Battery

Although the original equipment battery is a sealed unit and does not require added water, it does need periodic cleaning. Any accumulation of dirt or and acid film on the battery may permit current to flow from one terminal to the other, causing the battery to slowly discharge.

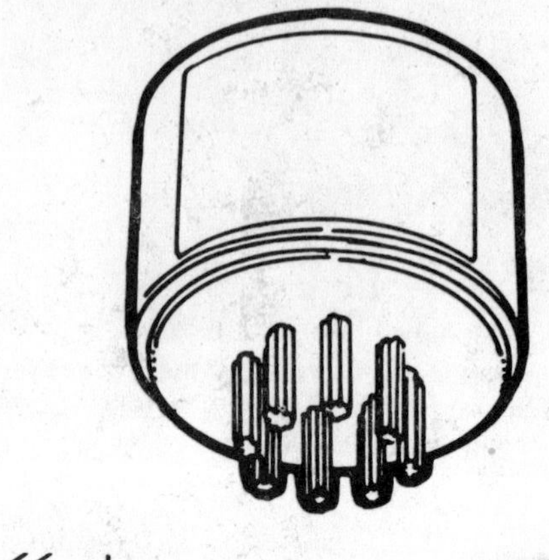

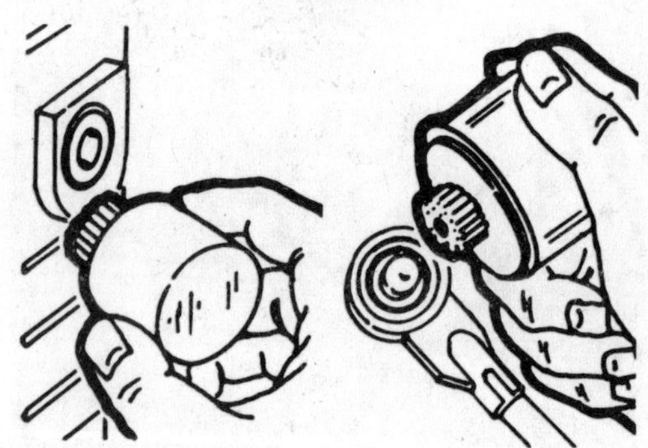

A special tool is available for cleaning the side terminals and clamps

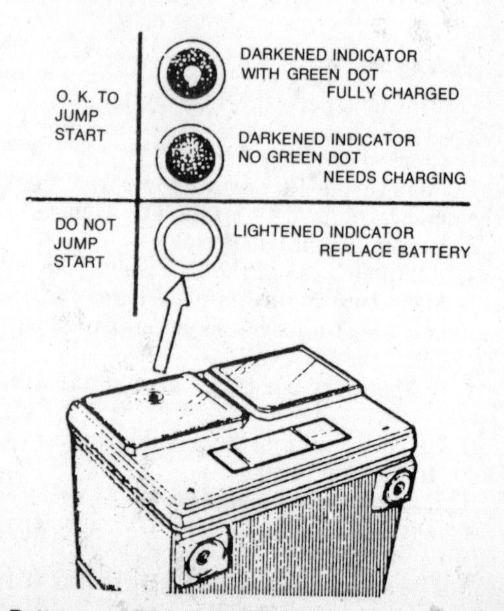

Battery condition indicator

Clean the battery regularly with diluted ammonia and rinse with clean water.

The sealed eye on top of the battery is the charge indicator. When the battery is fully charged the eye will be dark green. If the battery requires recharging, the eye will become a lighter green. When the indicator loses its color the battery must be replaced. Do not attempt to recharge a battery with a lightened indicator. It must be replaced.

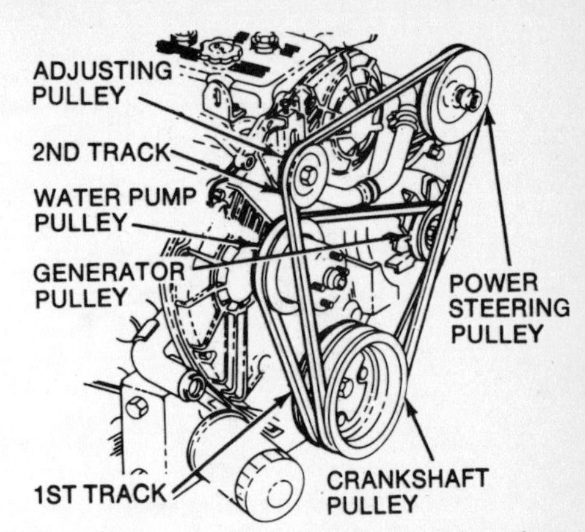

Diesel engine drive belt adjustments and routings

Belts

INSPECTION

The belts which drive the engine accessories such as the alternator or generator, the air pump, power steering pump, air conditioning compressor and water pump are of either the V-belt design or flat, serpentine design. Older belts show wear and damage readily, since their basic design was a belt with a rubber casing. As the casing wore, cracks and fibers were readily apparent. Newer design, caseless belts do not show wear as readily, and many untrained people cannot distinguish between a good, serviceable belt and one that is worn to the point of failure.

It is a good idea, therefore, to visually inspect the belts regularly and replace them, routinely, every two to three years.

ADJUSTING

Belts are normally adjusted by loosening the bolts of the accessory being driven and moving that accessory on its pivot points until the proper tension is applied to the belt. The accessory is held in this position while the bolts are tightened. To determine proper belt tension, you can purchase a belt tension gauge or simply use the deflection method. To determine deflection, press inward on the belt at the mid-point of its longest straight run. The belt should deflect (move inward) 3/8-1/2". Some long V-belts and most serpentine belts have idler pulleys which are used for adjusting purposes. Just loosen the idler pulley and move it to take up tension on the belt.

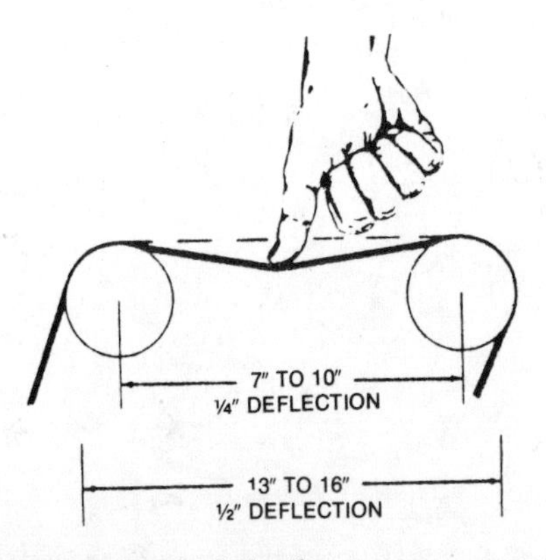

Allowable fan belt deflection

REMOVAL AND INSTALLATION

To remove a drive belt, simply loosen the accessory being driven and move it on its pivot point to free the belt. Then, remove the belt. If an idler pulley is used, it is often necessary, only, to loosen the idler pulley to provide enough slack the remove the belt.

It is important to note, however, that on engines with many driven accessories, several or all of the belts may have to be removed to get at the one to be replaced.

Hoses

REMOVAL AND INSTALLATION

Radiator hoses are generally of two constructions, the preformed (molded) type, which is custom made for a particular application, and the spring-loaded type, which is made to fit several different applications. Heater hoses are all of the same general construction.

Hoses are retained by clamps. To replace a hose, loosen the clamp and slide it down the hose, away from the attaching point. Twist the hose from side to side until it is free, then pull it off. Before installing the new hose, make sure that the outlet fitting is as clean as possible. Coat the fitting with non-hardening sealer and slip the hose into place. Install the clamp and tighten it.

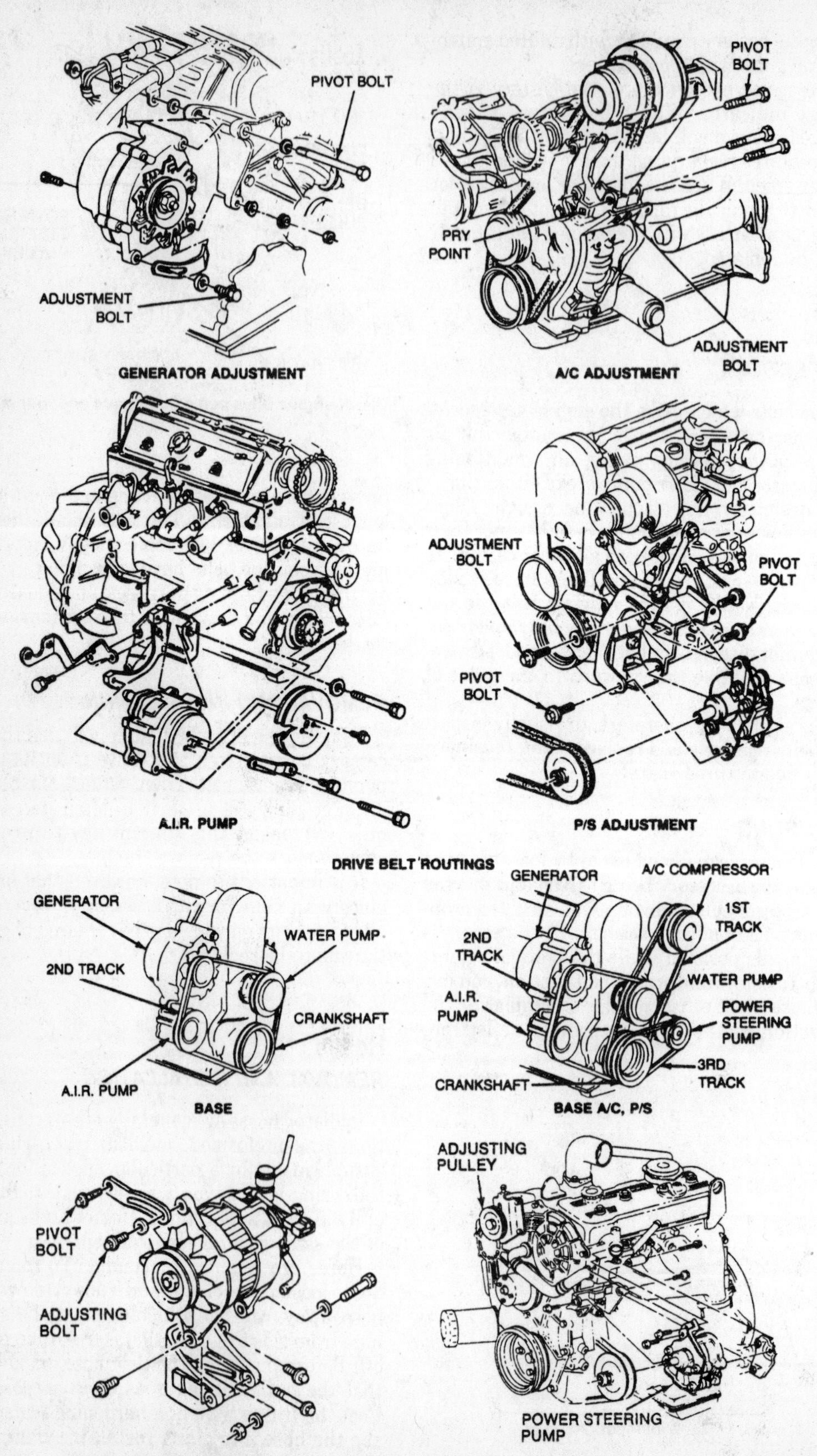

Gasoline engine drive belt adjustments and routings

HOW TO SPOT WORN V-BELTS

V-Belts are vital to efficient engine operation—they drive the fan, water pump and other accessories. They require little maintenance (occasional tightening) but they will not last forever. Slipping or failure of the V-belt will lead to overheating. If your V-belt looks like any of these, it should be replaced.

Cracking or weathering

This belt has deep cracks, which cause it to flex. Too much flexing leads to heat build-up and premature failure. These cracks can be caused by using the belt on a pulley that is too small. Notched belts are available for small diameter pulleys.

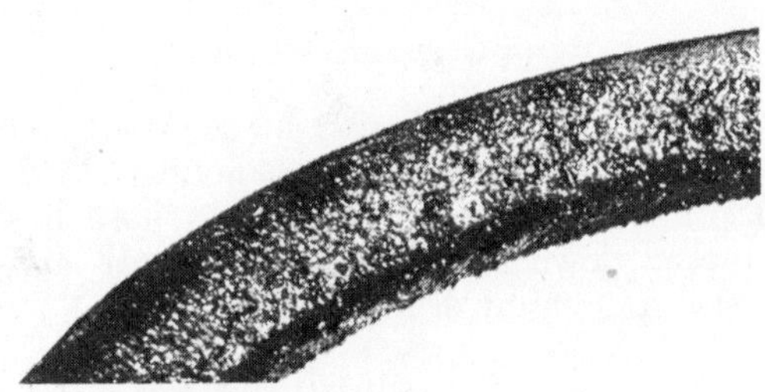

Softening (grease and oil)

Oil and grease on a belt can cause the belt's rubber compounds to soften and separate from the reinforcing cords that hold the belt together. The belt will first slip, then finally fail altogether.

Glazing

Glazing is caused by a belt that is slipping. A slipping belt can cause a run-down battery, erratic power steering, overheating or poor accessory performance. The more the belt slips, the more glazing will be built up on the surface of the belt. The more the belt is glazed, the more it will slip. If the glazing is light, tighten the belt.

Worn cover

The cover of this belt is worn off and is peeling away. The reinforcing cords will begin to wear and the belt will shortly break. When the belt cover wears in spots or has a rough jagged appearance, check the pulley grooves for roughness.

Separation

This belt is on the verge of breaking and leaving you stranded. The layers of the belt are separating and the reinforcing cords are exposed. It's just a matter of time before it breaks completely.

HOW TO SPOT BAD HOSES

Both the upper and lower radiator hoses are called upon to perform difficult jobs in an inhospitable environment. They are subject to nearly 18 psi at under hood temperatures often over 280°F., and must circulate nearly 7500 gallons of coolant an hour—3 good reasons to have good hoses.

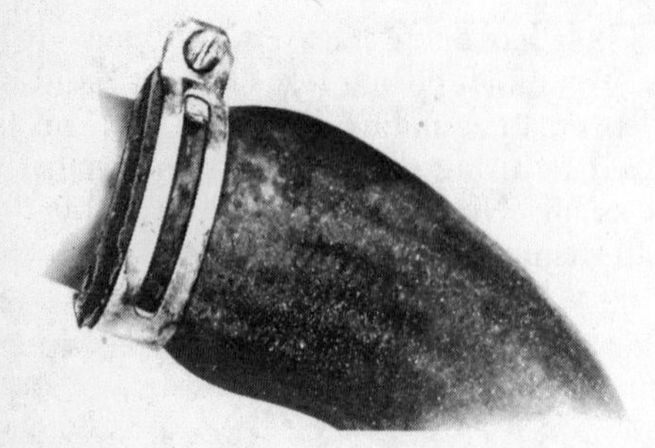

Swollen hose

A good test for any hose is to feel it for soft or spongy spots. Frequently these will appear as swollen areas of the hose. The most likely cause is oil soaking. This hose could burst at any time, when hot or under pressure.

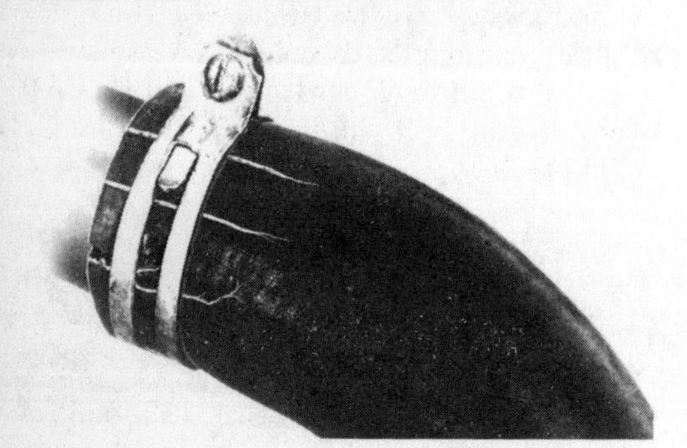

Cracked hose

Cracked hoses can usually be seen but feel the hoses to be sure they have not hardened; a prime cause of cracking. This hose has cracked down to the reinforcing cords and could split at any of the cracks.

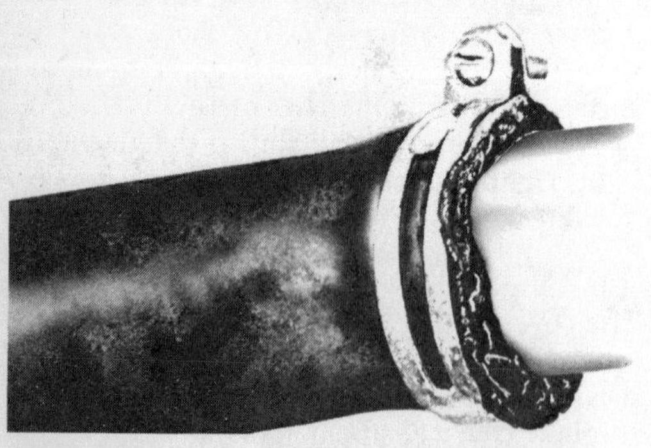

Frayed hose end (due to weak clamp)

Weakened clamps frequently are the cause of hose and cooling system failure. The connection between the pipe and hose has deteriorated enough to allow coolant to escape when the engine is hot.

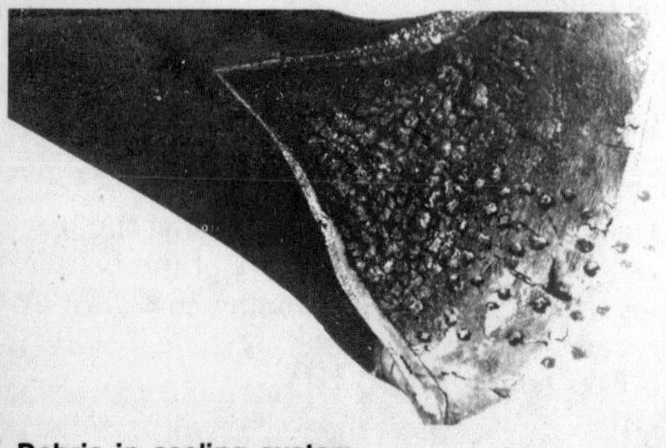

Debris in cooling system

Debris, rust and scale in the cooling system can cause the inside of a hose to weaken. This can usually be felt on the outside of the hose as soft or thinner areas.

Air Conditioning

SAFETY WARNINGS

Because of the importance of the necessary safety precautions that must be exercised when working with air conditioning systems, a recap of the safety warnings are outlined below.

1. Avoid contact with a charged refrigeration system, even when working on another part of the air conditioning system or vehicle. If a heavy tool comes into contact with a section of copper tubing or a heat exchanger, it can easily cause the relatively soft material to rupture.

2. When it is necessary to apply force to a fitting which contains refrigerant, as when checking that all system couplings are securely tightened, use a wrench on both parts of the fitting involved, if possible. This will avoid putting torque on refrigerant tubing. (It is advisable, when possible, to use tube or line wrenches when tightening these flare nut fittings.)

3. Do not attempt to discharge the system by merely loosening a fitting, or removing the service valve caps and cracking these valves. Precise control is possible only when using the service gauges. Place a rag under the open end of the center charging hose while discharging the system to catch any drops of liquid that might escape. Wear protective gloves when connecting or disconnecting service gauge hoses.

4. Discharge the system only in a well ventilated area, as high concentrations of the gas can exclude oxygen and act as an anaesthetic. When leak testing or soldering, this is particularly important, as toxic gas is formed when R-12 contacts any flame.

5. Never start a system without first verifying that both service valves are back-seated, if equipped, and that all fittings throughout the system are snugly connected.

6. Avoid applying heat to any refrigerant line or storage vessel. Charging may be aided by using water heated to less than 125°F (51°C) to warm the refrigerant container. Never allow a refrigerant storage container to sit out in the sun, or near any other source of heat, such as a radiator.

7. Always wear goggles when working on a system to protect the eyes. If refrigerant contacts the eyes, it is advisable in all cases to see a physician as soon as possible.

8. Frostbite from liquid refrigerant should be treated by first gradually warming the area with cool water, and then gently applying petroleum jelly. A physician should be consulted.

9. Always keep refrigerant can fittings capped when not in use. Avoid sudden shock to the can, which might occur from dropping it, or from banging a heavy tool against it. Never carry cans in the passenger compartment of a car.

10. Always completely discharge the system before painting the vehicle (if the paint is to be baked on), or before welding anywhere near refrigerant lines.

SYSTEM INSPECTION

CAUTION: *Do not attempt to charge or discharge the refrigerant system unless you are thoroughly familiar with its operation and the hazards involved. The compressed refrigerant used in the air conditioning system expands and evaporates (boils) into the atmosphere at a temperature of −21.7°F (−29.8°C) or less. This will freeze any surface that it comes in contact with, including your eyes. In addition, the refrigerant decomposes into a poisonous gas in the presence of flame.*

All models utilize C.C.O.T system which does not include a sight glass. The (C.C.O.T) Cycling Clutch Orfice Tube refrigeration system is designed to cycle the compressor on and off to maintain desired cooling and to prevent evaporator freeze.

NOTE: *If your car is equipped with an aftermarket air conditioner, the following system check may not apply. Contact the manufacturer of the unit for instructions on system check.*

1. Run the engine until it reaches normal operating temperature.

2. Open the hood and all doors.

3. Turn the air conditioning on, move the temperature selector to the first detent to the right of COLD (outside air) and then turn the blower on HI.

4. Idle the engine at 1,000 rpm.

5. Feel the temperature of the evaporator inlet and the accumulator outlet with the compressor clutch engaged.

6. Both lines should be cold. If the inlet pipe is colder than the outlet pipe, the system is low on charge.

Air Conditioning Gauges

Most of the service work performed in air conditioning requires the use of a set of two gauges, one for the high (head) pressure side of the system, the other for the low (suction) side.

The low side gauge records both pressure and vacuum. Vacuum readings are calibrated from 0 to 30 inches and the pressure graduations read from 0 to no less than 60 psi.

The high side gauge measures pressure from 0 to at least 600 psi.

Both gauges are threaded into a manifold that contains two hand shut-off valves. Proper manipulation of these valves and the use of the attached test hoses allow the user to perform the following services:

1. Test high and low side pressures.
2. Remove air, moisture, and contaminated refrigerant.
3. Purge the system (of refrigerant).
4. Charge the system (with refrigerant).

The manifold hand valves are designed so they have no direct effect on gauge readings, but serve only to provide for, or cut off, flow of refrigerant through the manifold. During all testing and hook-up operations, the valves are kept in a closed position to avoid disturbing the refrigeration system. The valves are opened only to purge the system of refrigerant or to charge it.

DISCHARGING THE SYSTEM

NOTE: *Perform operation in a well-ventilated area.*

When it is necessary to remove (purge) the refrigerant pressurized in the system, follow this procedure:

1. Operate air conditioner for at least 10 minutes.
2. Attach gauges (low side test hose to service valve that leads to the evaporator located between the evaporator outlet and the compressor) (attach high side test hose to service valve that leads to the condenser) shut off engine and air conditioner.
3. Place a container or rag at the outlet of the center charging hose on the gauge. The refrigerant will be discharged there and this precaution will avoid its uncontrolled exposure.

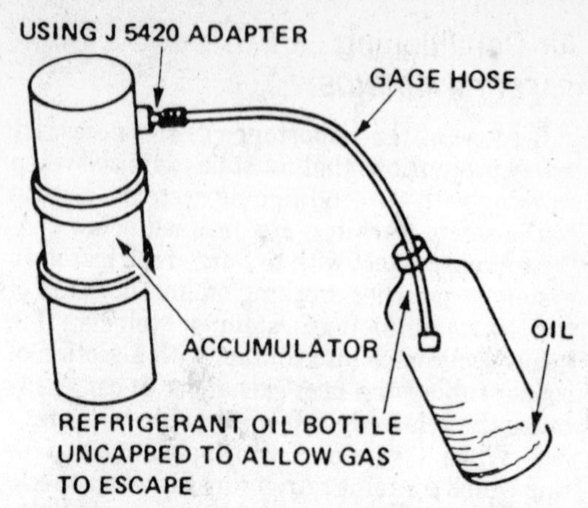

Discharging the C.C.O.T. A/C system without a charging station

4. Open low side hand valve on gauge slightly.
5. Open high side hand valve slightly.

NOTE: *Too rapid a purging process will be identified by the appearance of an oily foam. If this occurs, close the hand valves a little more until this condition stops.*

6. Close both hand valves on the gauge set when the pressures read 0 and all the refrigerant has left the system.

CHARGING THE SYSTEM

CAUTION: *Never attempt to charge the system by opening the high pressure gauge control while the compressor is operating. The*

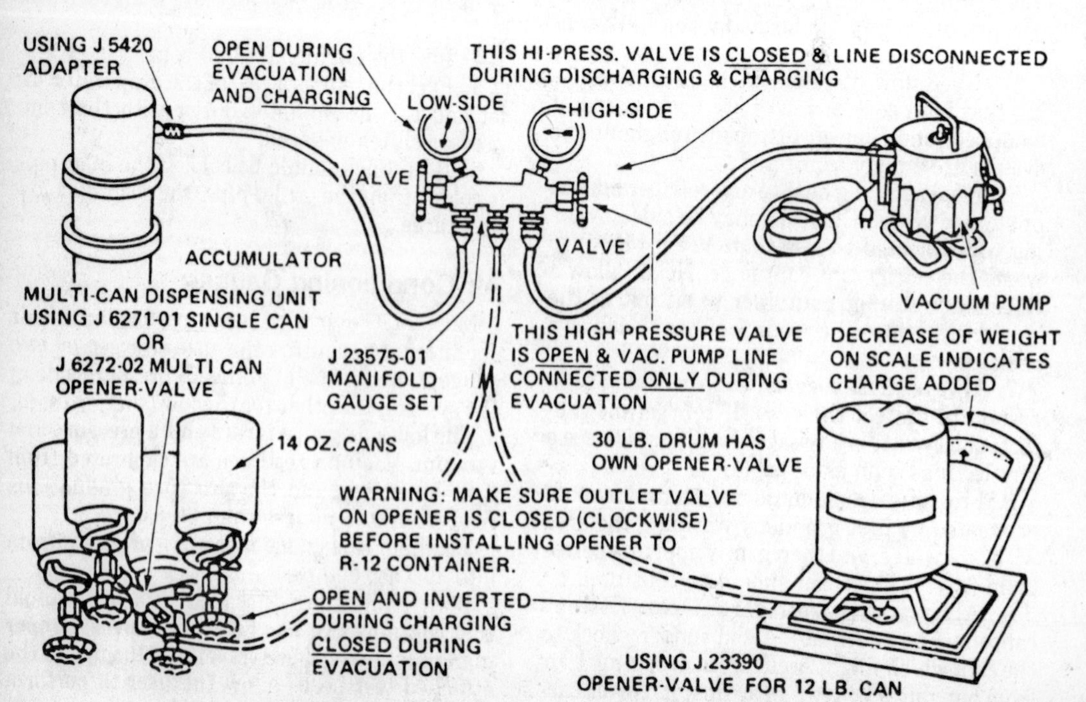

Charging the system with a disposible can or drum

REFRIGERANT CHARGE - 2 LBS. - 4 OZ.					
Temperature of air entering condenser	70 F	80 F	90 F	100 F	110 F
Engine RPM	2000				
Compressor out pressure before expansion tube (psig)	110-140	145-175	185-215	220-250	265-295
Evaporator pressure at accumulator (psig)	24-30	25-31	25-31	26-32	27-33-
Discharge air temp @ right hand outlet*	38 F 44 F	39 F 45 F	39 F 45 F	40 F 46 F	41 F 47 F

System performance temperature pressure data

compressor accumulating pressure can burst the refrigerant container, causing sever personal injuries.

When charging the CCOT system, attach only the low pressure line to the low pressure gauge port, located on the accumulator. Do not attach the high pressure line to any service port or allow it to remain attached to the vacuum pump after evacuation. Be sure both the high and the low pressure control valves are closed on the gauge set. To complete the charging of the system, follow the outline supplied.

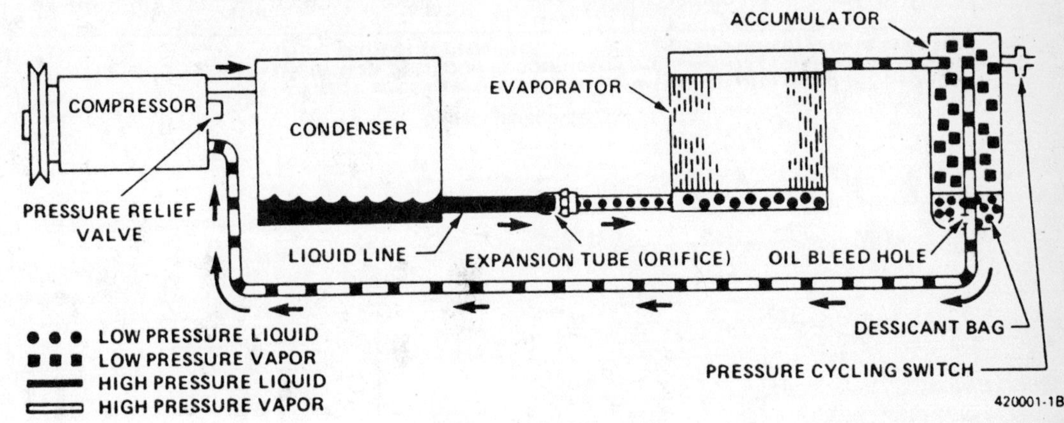

Typical C.C.O.T A/C system

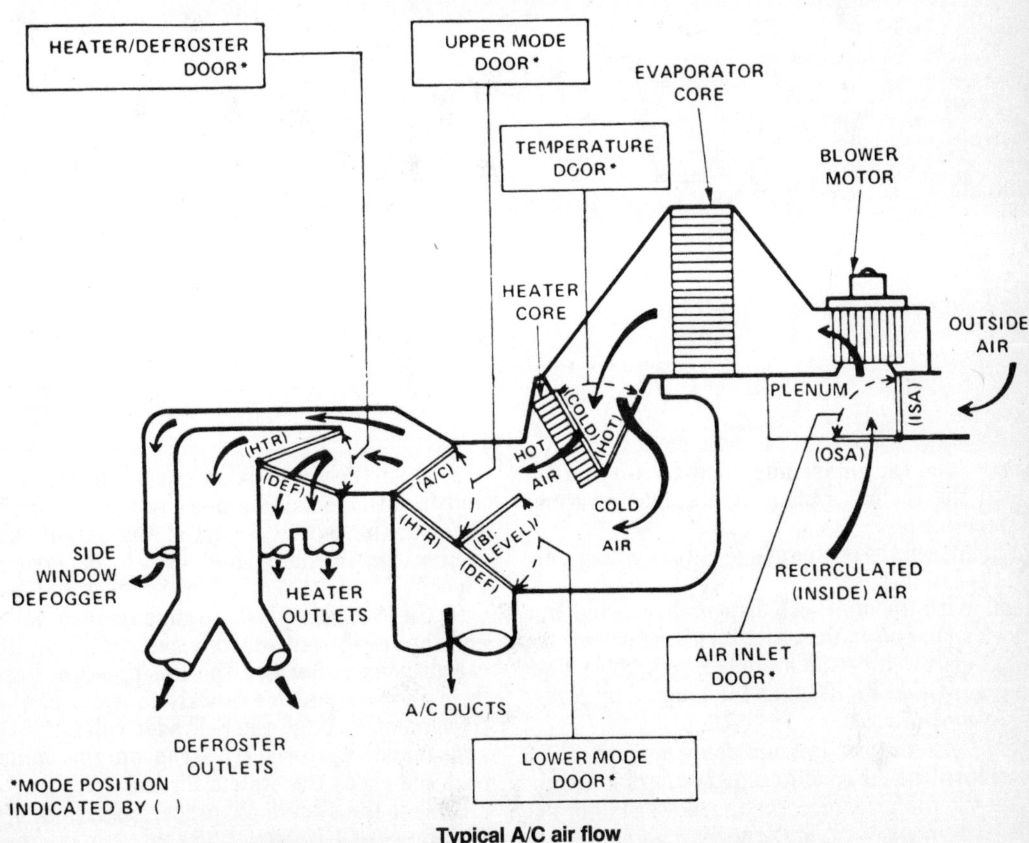

Typical A/C air flow

HEATER AND AIR CONDITIONING

SELECTOR LEVER POSITION	BLOWER SPEEDS AVAILABLE	AIR SOURCE	HEATER DEFROSTER DOOR	A.C DOOR	AIR ENTERS VEHICLE	COMPRESSOR
OFF	ALL	OUTSIDE	OPEN	CLOSED	HEATER AND DEFROSTER OUTLETS	OFF
MAX	HI ONLY	INSIDE %	CLOSED	OPEN	DASH OUTLETS	ON &
NORM	ALL	OUTSIDE	CLOSED	OPEN	DASH OUTLETS	ON &
VENT	ALL	OUTSIDE	CLOSED	OPEN	DASH OUTLETS	OFF
HEATER	ALL	OUTSIDE	OPEN	CLOSED	HEATER OUTLETS*	OFF
DEF	ALL	OUTSIDE	OPEN (TO DEFROST ONLY)	CLOSED	DEFROSTER OUTLETS	OFF

NOTE: *SOME BLEED-BY TO DEFROSTER OUTLETS SOME BLEED-BY TO FLOOR OUTLETS.
% 100% INSIDE AIR IS NOT AVAILABLE. SOME BLEED-THROUGH OF OUTSIDE AIR IS ALLOWED.
& PROVIDING THE DISCHARGE PRESSURE SWITCH PRESSURE IS ABOVE APPROX. 42 PSI.

A/C functional testing

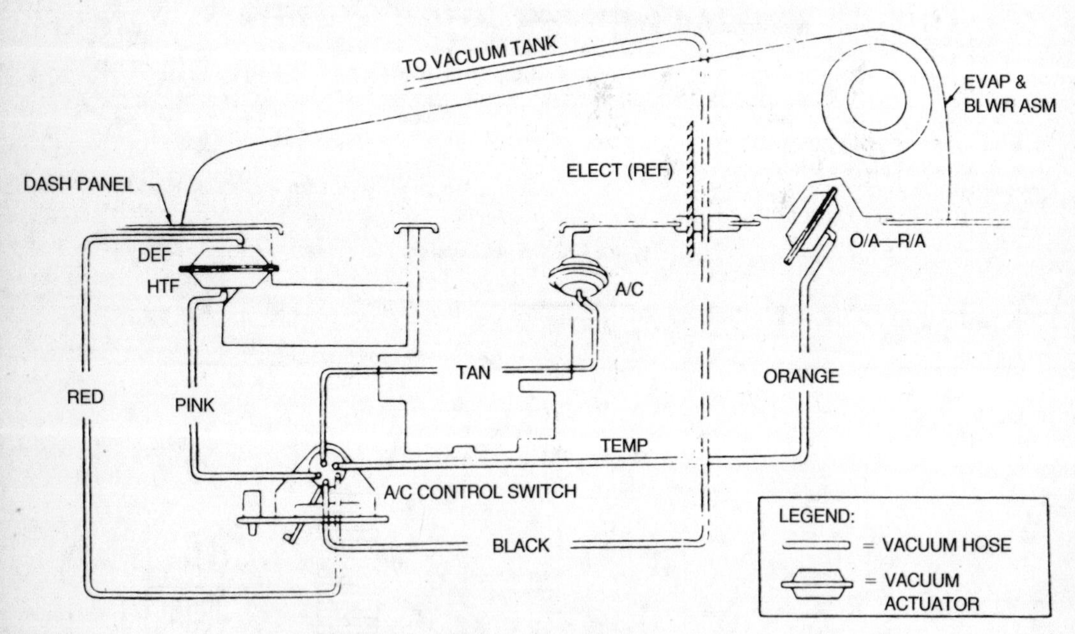

A/C vacuum schematic

1. Start the engine and allow to run at idle, with the cooling system at normal operating temperature.
2. Attach the center gauge hose to a single or multi-can dispenser.
3. With the multi-can dispenser inverted, allow one pound or the contents of one or two 14 oz. cans to enter the system through the low pressure side by opening the gauge low pressure control valve.
4. Close the low pressure gauge control valve and turn the air conditioning system on to engage the compressor. Place the blower motor in its high mode.
5. Open the low pressure gauge control valve and draw the remaining charge into the system. Refer to the capacity chart at the end of this section for the individual vehicle or system capacity.
6. Close the low pressure gauge control valve and the refrigerant source valve, on the multi-can dispenser. Remove the low pressure hose from the accumulator quickly to avoid loss of refrigerant through the Schrader valve.
7. Install the protective cap on the gauge port and check the system for leakage.
8. Test the system for proper operation.

Refrigerent Charge: 2.25 lbs

Windshield Wipers

For maximum effectiveness and longest element life, the windshield and wiper blades should be kept clean. Dirt, tree sap, road tar and so on will cause streaking, smearing and blade deterioration if left on the windshield. It is advisable to wash the windshield carefully with a commercial glass cleaner at least once a month. Wipe off the rubber blades with a wet rag afterwards. Do not attempt to move the

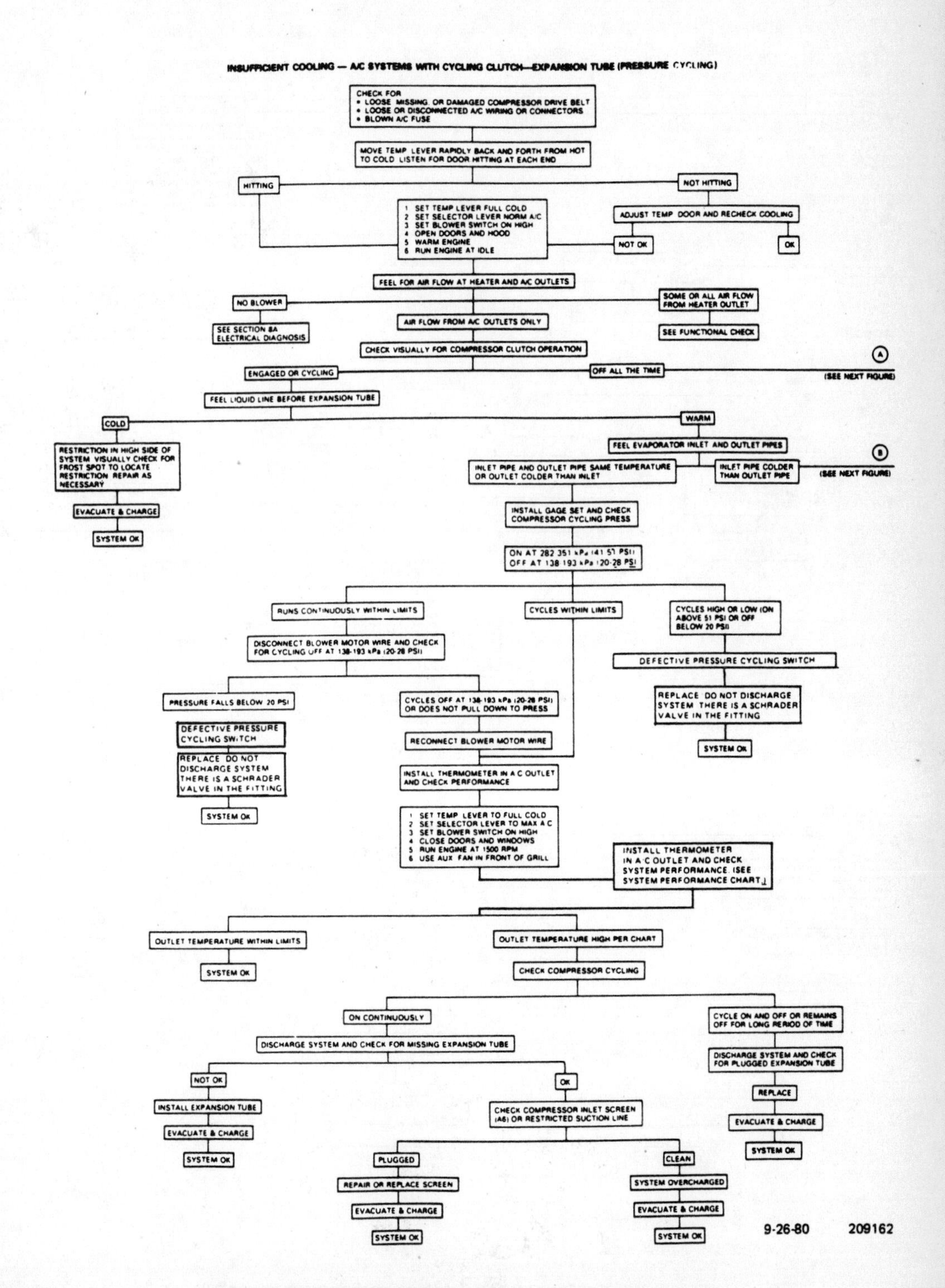

Troubleshooting the C.C.O.T. pressure cycling system—part 1

wipers back and forth by hand; damage to the motor and drive mechanism will result.

If the blades are found to be cracked, broken or torn they should be replaced immediately. Replacement intervals will vary with usage, although ozone deterioration usually limits blade lift to about one year. If the wiper pattern is smeared or streaked, or if the blade chatters across the glass, the blades should be replaced. It is easiest and most sensible to replace them in pairs.

There are basically three different types of

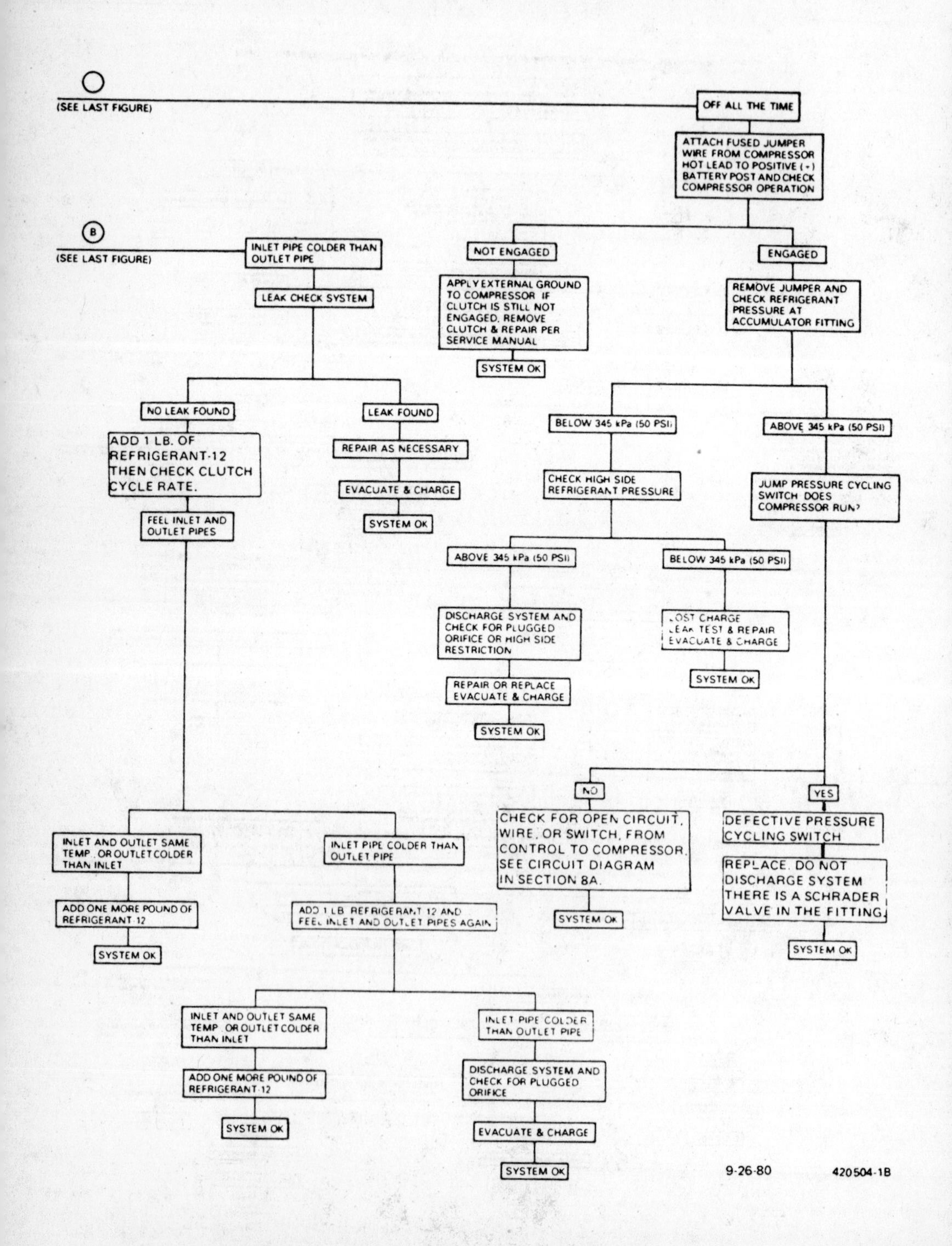

Troubleshooting the C.C.O.T. pressure cycling system—part 2

Troubleshooting Basic Air Conditioning Problems

Problem	Cause	Solution
There's little or no air coming from the vents (and you're sure it's on)	• The A/C fuse is blown • Broken or loose wires or connections • The on/off switch is defective	• Check and/or replace fuse • Check and/or repair connections • Replace switch
The air coming from the vents is not cool enough	• Windows and air vent wings open • The compressor belt is slipping • Heater is on • Condenser is clogged with debris • Refrigerant has escaped through a leak in the system • Receiver/drier is plugged	• Close windows and vent wings • Tighten or replace compressor belt • Shut heater off • Clean the condenser • Check system • Service system
The air has an odor	• Vacuum system is disrupted • Odor producing substances on the evaporator case • Condensation has collected in the bottom of the evaporator housing	• Have the system checked/repaired • Clean the evaporator case • Clean the evaporator housing drains
System is noisy or vibrating	• Compressor belt or mountings loose • Air in the system	• Tighten or replace belt; tighten mounting bolts • Have the system serviced
Sight glass condition Constant bubbles, foam or oil streaks Clear sight glass, but no cold air Clear sight glass, but air is cold Clouded with milky fluid	 • Undercharged system • No refrigerant at all • System is OK • Receiver drier is leaking dessicant	 • Charge the system • Check and charge the system • Have system checked
Large difference in temperature of lines	• System undercharged	• Charge and leak test the system
Compressor noise	• Broken valves • Overcharged • Incorrect oil level • Piston slap • Broken rings • Drive belt pulley bolts are loose	• Replace the valve plate • Discharge, evacuate and install the correct charge • Isolate the compressor and check the oil level. Correct as necessary. • Replace the compressor • Replace the compressor • Tighten with the correct torque specification
Excessive vibration	• Incorrect belt tension • Clutch loose • Overcharged • Pulley is misaligned	• Adjust the belt tension • Tighten the clutch • Discharge, evacuate and install the correct charge • Align the pulley
Condensation dripping in the passenger compartment	• Drain hose plugged or improperly positioned • Insulation removed or improperly installed	• Clean the drain hose and check for proper installation • Replace the insulation on the expansion valve and hoses
Frozen evaporator coil	• Faulty thermostat • Thermostat capillary tube improperly installed • Thermostat not adjusted properly	• Replace the thermostat • Install the capillary tube correctly • Adjust the thermostat
Low side low—high side low	• System refrigerant is low • Expansion valve is restricted	• Evacuate, leak test and charge the system • Replace the expansion valve
Low side high—high side low	• Internal leak in the compressor—worn	• Remove the compressor cylinder head and inspect the compressor. Replace the valve plate assembly if necessary. If the compressor pistons, rings or

Troubleshooting Basic Air Conditioning Problems (cont.)

Problem	Cause	Solution
Low side high—high side low (cont.)		cylinders are excessively worn or scored replace the compressor
	• Cylinder head gasket is leaking	• Install a replacement cylinder head gasket
	• Expansion valve is defective	• Replace the expansion valve
	• Drive belt slipping	• Adjust the belt tension
Low side high—high side high	• Condenser fins obstructed	• Clean the condenser fins
	• Air in the system	• Evacuate, leak test and charge the system
	• Expansion valve is defective	• Replace the expansion valve
	• Loose or worn fan belts	• Adjust or replace the belts as necessary
Low side low—high side high	• Expansion valve is defective	• Replace the expansion valve
	• Restriction in the refrigerant hose	• Check the hose for kinks—replace if necessary
	• Restriction in the receiver/drier	• Replace the receiver/drier
	• Restriction in the condenser	• Replace the condenser
Low side and high side normal (inadequate cooling)	• Air in the system	• Evacuate, leak test and charge the system
	• Moisture in the system	• Evacuate, leak test and charge the system

wiper blade refills, which differ in their method of replacement. One type has two release buttons, approximately ⅓ of the way up from the ends of the blade frame. Pushing the buttons down releases a lock and allows the rubber blade to be removed from the frame. The new blade slides back into the frame and locks in place.

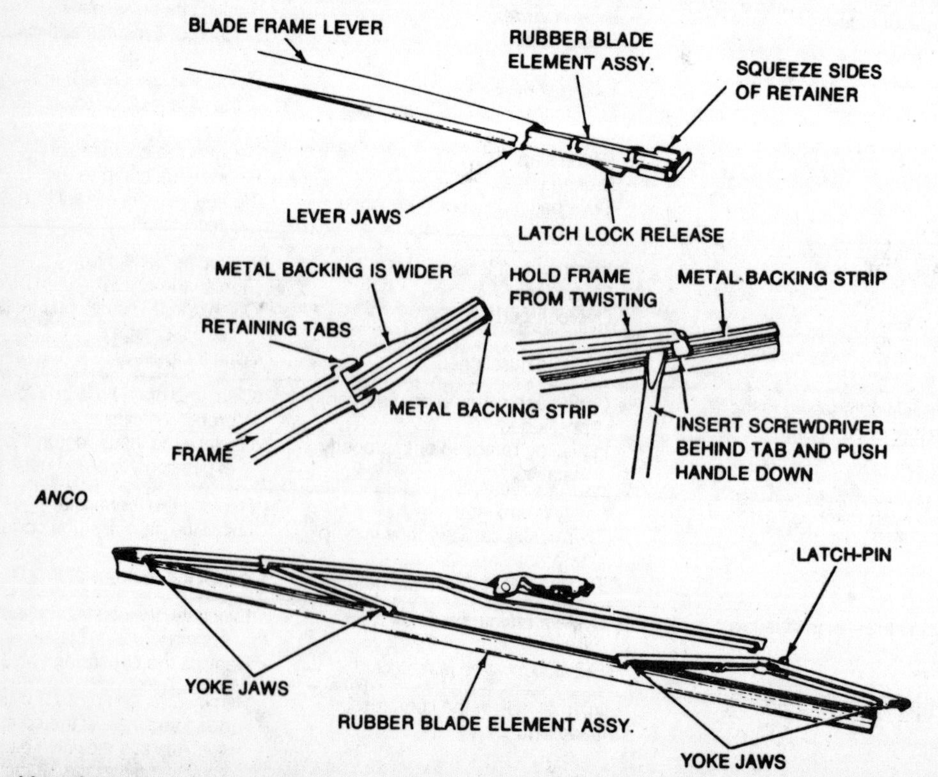

The rubber element can be changed without replacing the entire blade assembly; your car may have either one of these types of blades.

The second type of refill has two metal tabs which are unlocked by squeezing them together. The rubber blade can then be withdrawn from the frame jaws. A new one is installed by inserting it into the front frame jaws and sliding it rearward to engage the remaining frame jaws. There are usually four jaws; be certain when installing that the refill is engaged in all of them. At the end of its travel, the tabs will lock into place on the front jaws of the wiper blade frame.

The third type is a refill made from polycarbonate. The refill has a simple locking device at one end which flexes downward out of the groove into which the jaws of the holder fit, allowing easy release. By sliding the new refill through all the jaws and pushing through the slight resistance when it reaches the end of its travel, the refill will lock into position.

Regardless of the type of refill used, make sure that all of the frame jaws are engaged as the refill is pushed into place and locked. The metal blade holder and frame will scratch the glass if allowed to touch it.

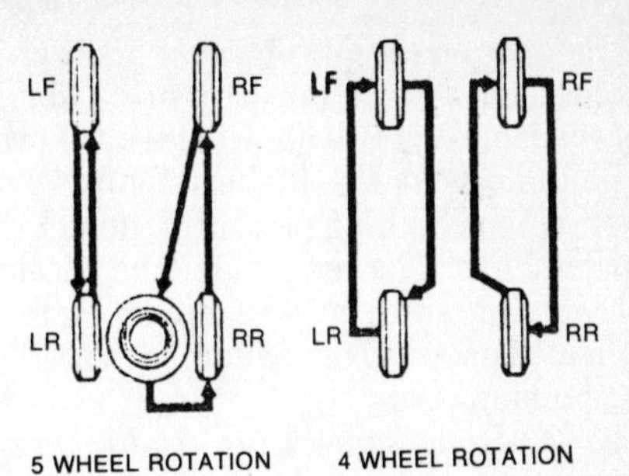

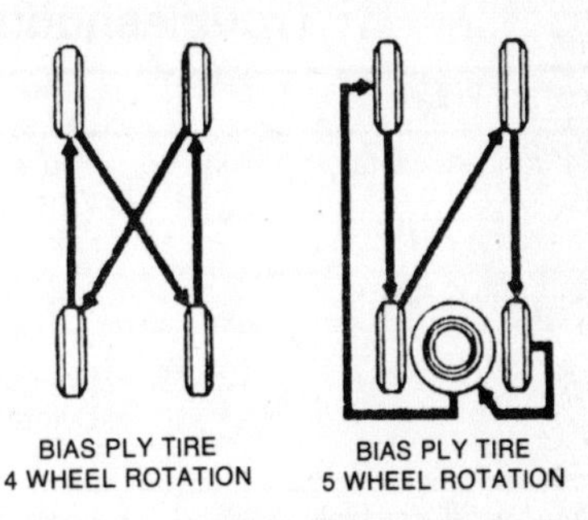

Correct rotation patterns for radial and bias/belted tires

Tires and Wheels

TIRE ROTATION

Tire rotation is recommended every 6,000 miles or so, to obtain maximum tire wear. The pattern you use depends on whether or not you have a usable spare. Radial tires should not be cross-switched (from one side of the car to the other); they last longer if their direction of rotation is not changed. Snow type tires sometimes have directional threads, indicted by arrows molded into the sidewalls; the arrow shows the direction of rotation. They will wear very rapidly if their direction of rotation is reversed.

NOTE: *Mark the wheel position or direction of rotation on radial tires or studded snow tires before removing them.*

CAUTION: *Avoid overtightening the lug nuts to prevent damage to the brake disc or drum. Alloy wheels can also be cracked by overtightening. Use of a torque wrench is highly recommended.*

TIRE DESIGN

1. All four tires should be of the same construction type. Radial, bias, or bias-belted tires should not be mixed.

2. The wheels must be the correct width for the tire. Tire dealers have charts of tire and rim compatibility. A mismatch can cause sloppy handling and rapid tire wear. The tread width should match the rim width (inside bead to inside bead) within an inch. For radial tires, the rim width should be 80% or less of the tire (not tread) width.

3. The height (mounted diameter) of the new tires can greatly change speedometer accuracy, engine speed at a given road speed, fuel mileage, acceleration, and ground clearance. Tire manufacturers furnish full measurement specifications.

NOTE: *Dimensions of tires marked the same size may vary significantly, even among tires from the same manufacturer.*

TIRE INFLATION

The tires should be checked frequently for proper air pressure. A chart in the glove com-

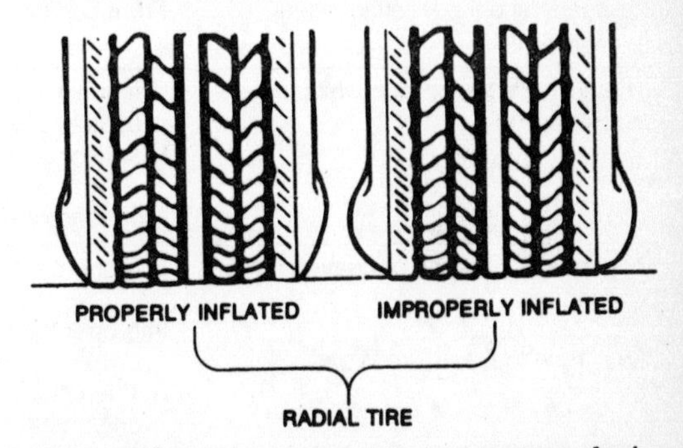

Don't judge a radial tire by its appearance. An improperly inflated radial tire looks similar to a properly inflated one.

partment or on the driver's door pillar gives the recommended inflation pressure. Maximum fuel economy and tire life will result if pressure is maintained at the highest figure given on chart. When checking pressures, do not neglect the spare tire. The tires should be checked before driving since pressure can increase as much as six pounds per square inch (psi) due to heat buildup.

NOTE: *Some spare tires require pressures considerably higher than those used in other tires.*

While you are the task of checking air pressure, inspect the tire treads for cuts, bruises and other damage. Check the air valves to be sure that they are tight. Replace any missing valve caps. There shouldn't be any body interference when loaded, on bumps, or in turning. It is a good idea to have your own accurate gauge, and to check pressures weekly. Not all

Troubleshooting Basic Wheel Problems

Problem	Cause	Solution
The car's front end vibrates at high speed	• The wheels are out of balance • Wheels are out of alignment	• Have wheels balanced • Have wheel alignment checked/adjusted
Car pulls to either side	• Wheels are out of alignment • Unequal tire pressure • Different size tires or wheels	• Have wheel alignment checked/adjusted • Check/adjust tire pressure • Change tires or wheels to same size
The car's wheel(s) wobbles	• Loose wheel lug nuts • Wheels out of balance • Damaged wheel • Wheels are out of alignment • Worn or damaged ball joint • Excessive play in the steering linkage (usually due to worn parts) • Defective shock absorber	• Tighten wheel lug nuts • Have tires balanced • Raise car and spin the wheel. If the wheel is bent, it should be replaced • Have wheel alignment checked/adjusted • Check ball joints • Check steering linkage • Check shock absorbers
Tires wear unevenly or prematurely	• Incorrect wheel size • Wheels are out of balance • Wheels are out of alignment	• Check if wheel and tire size are compatible • Have wheels balanced • Have wheel alignment checked/adjusted

Troubleshooting Basic Tire Problems

Problem	Cause	Solution
The car's front end vibrates at high speeds and the steering wheel shakes	• Wheels out of balance • Front end needs aligning	• Have wheels balanced • Have front end alignment checked
The car pulls to one side while cruising	• Unequal tire pressure (car will usually pull to the low side) • Mismatched tires • Front end needs aligning	• Check/adjust tire pressure • Be sure tires are of the same type and size • Have front end alignment checked
Abnormal, excessive or uneven tire wear See "How to Read Tire Wear"	• Infrequent tire rotation • Improper tire pressure • Sudden stops/starts or high speed on curves	• Rotate tires more frequently to equalize wear • Check/adjust pressure • Correct driving habits
Tire squeals	• Improper tire pressure • Front end needs aligning	• Check/adjust tire pressure • Have front end alignment checked

Tire Size Comparison Chart

"Letter" sizes			Inch Sizes	Metric-inch Sizes		
"60 Series"	"70 Series"	"78 Series"	1965–77	"60 Series"	"70 Series"	"80 Series"
			5.50-12, 5.60-12	165/60-12	165/70-12	155-12
		Y78-12	6.00-12			
		W78-13	5.20-13	165/60-13	145/70-13	135-13
		Y78-13	5.60-13	175/60-13	155/70-13	145-13
			6.15-13	185/60-13	165/70-13	155-13, P155/80-13
A60-13	A70-13	A78-13	6.40-13	195/60-13	175/70-13	165-13
B60-13	B70-13	B78-13	6.70-13	205/60-13	185/70-13	175-13
			6.90-13			
C60-13	C70-13	C78-13	7.00-13	215/60-13	195/70-13	185-13
D60-13	D70-13	D78-13	7.25-13			
E60-13	E70-13	E78-13	7.75-13			195-13
			5.20-14	165/60-14	145/70-14	135-14
			5.60-14	175/60-14	155/70-14	145-14
			5.90-14			
A60-14	A70-14	A78-14	6.15-14	185/60-14	165/70-14	155-14
	B70-14	B78-14	6.45-14	195/60-14	175/70-14	165-14
	C70-14	C78-14	6.95-14	205/60-14	185/70-14	175-14
D60-14	D70-14	D78-14				
E60-14	E70-14	E78-14	7.35-14	215/60-14	195/70-14	185-14
F60-14	F70-14	F78-14, F83-14	7.75-14	225/60-14	200/70-14	195-14
G60-14	G70-14	G77-14, G78-14	8.25-14	235/60-14	205/70-14	205-14
H60-14	H70-14	H78-14	8.55-14	245/60-14	215/70-14	215-14
J60-14	J70-14	J78-14	8.85-14	255/60-14	225/70-14	225-14
L60-14	L70-14		9.15-14	265/60-14	235/70-14	
	A70-15	A78-15	5.60-15	185/60-15	165/70-15	155-15
B60-15	B70-15	B78-15	6.35-15	195/60-15	175/70-15	165-15
C60-15	C70-15	C78-15	6.85-15	205/60-15	185/70-15	175-15
	D70-15	D78-15				
E60-15	E70-15	E78-15	7.35-15	215/60-15	195/70-15	185-15
F60-15	F70-15	F78-15	7.75-15	225/60-15	205/70-15	195-15
G60-15	G70-15	G78-15	8.15-15/8.25-15	235/60-15	215/70-15	205-15
H60-15	H70-15	H78-15	8.45-15/8.55-15	245/60-15	225/70-15	215-15
J60-15	J70-15	J78-15	8.85-15/8.90-15	255/60-15	235/70-15	225-15
	K70-15		9.00-15	265/60-15	245/70-15	230-15
L60-15	L70-15	L78-15, L84-15	9.15-15			235-15
	M70-15	M78-15				255-15
		N78-15				

Note: Every size tire is not listed and many size comparisons are approximate, based on load ratings. Wider tires than those supplied new with the vehicle, should always be checked for clearance.

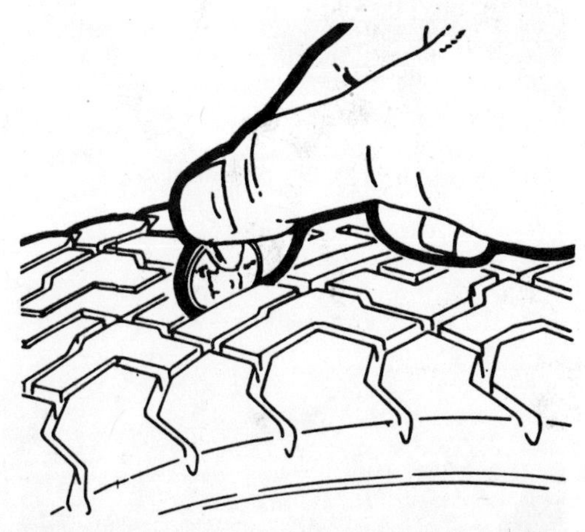

You can use a penny for tread wear checks; if the top of Lincoln's head is visible in two adjacent grooves, the tire should be replaced

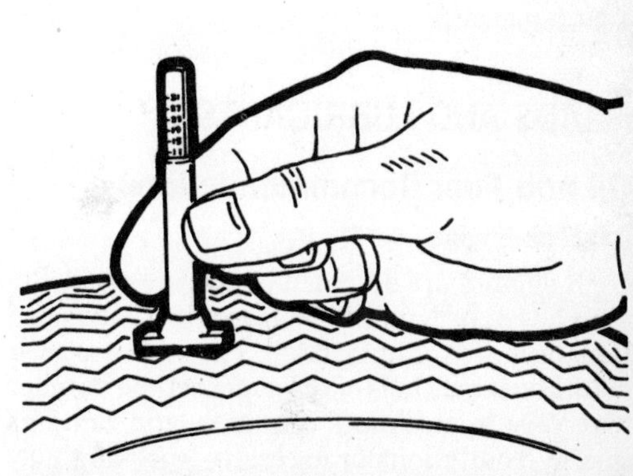

Inexpensive gauges are also available for measuring tread wear

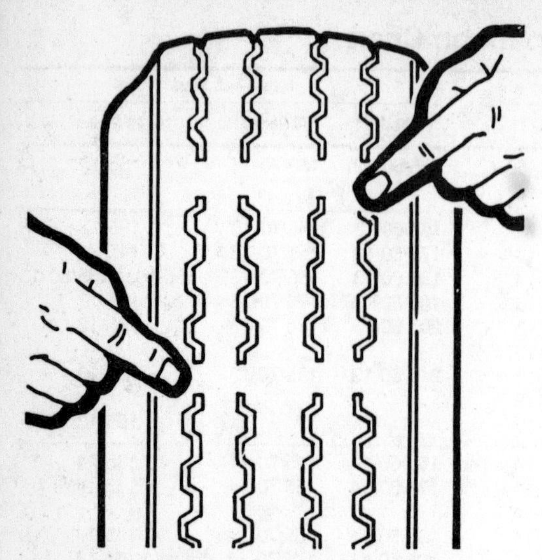

Tread wear indicators will appear as bands across the tread when the tire is due for replacement

gauges on service station air pumps can be trusted.

Inspect tires for uneven wear that might indicate the need for front end alignment or tire rotation. Tires should be replaced when a tread wear indicator appears as a solid band across the tread.

CARE OF SPECIAL WHEELS

Aluminum wheels should be cleaned and waxed regularly. Do not use abrasive cleaners,as they could damage the protective coating.

Valve Clearance Adjustment

On diesel engines the valve clearance should be checked and adjusted if necessary every 15,000 miles. This procedure is given in Chapter 2 under Tune-up Procedures. All gasoline engines are equipped with a hydraulic valve system which requires no adjustment or maintenance.

FLUIDS AND LUBRICANTS

Oil and Fuel Recommendations

Gasoline Engine

All engines are designed to operate on 91 Research Octane Number fuel (regular). Unleaded fuels only are recommended. The manufacturer points out that fuels of the same octane number may vary in antiknock qualities, and cautions that "...continuous or excessive knocking may result in engine damage and constitutes misuse of the engine for which Chevrolet Division is not responsible under the terms of the New Vehicle Waranty."

Only oils labeled SE or SF are approved under warranty. The manufacturer does not recommend the use of oil supplements on a regular basis, but does suggest that a Chevrolet dealer be consulted if a problem exists which can be solved by the temporary use of a specific additive. The accompanying illustration will be helpful in selecting the proper viscosity oil for gasoline engines.

Diesel Engine

The Chevette equipped with a diesel engine is designed to run only on diesel fuel. Number 2-D, which is usually the only diesel fuel avail-

On gasoline engines the oil dipstick is located on the passenger side as shown above. On diesel engines, it is located on the driver's side

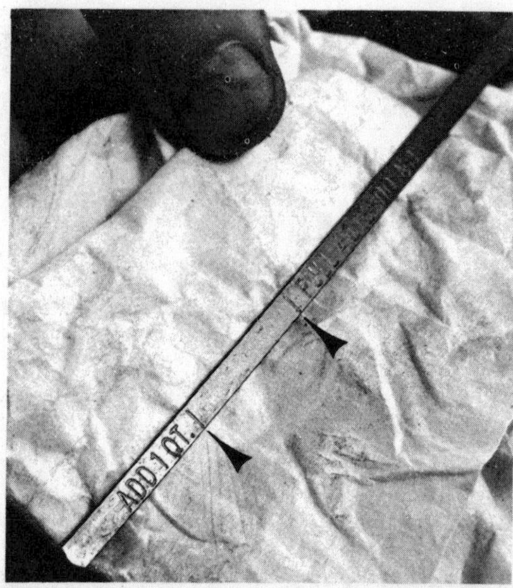

Add oil only when the level is even with or below the "Add 1 qt" mark

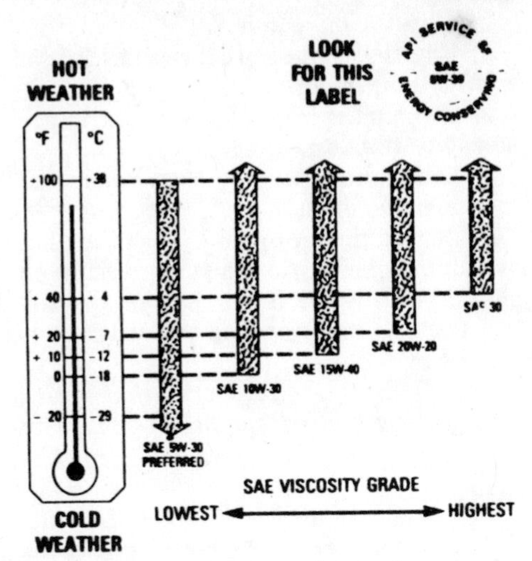

Engine oil viscosity chart-gasoline engine

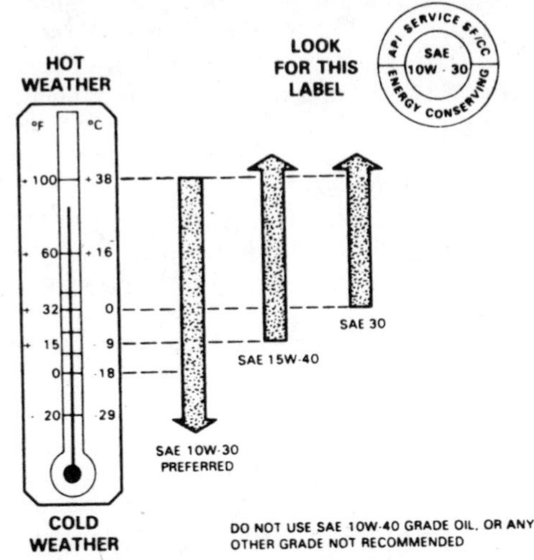

Engine oil viscosity chart-diesel engine

able, should be used if you expect the temperatures to be above −7°C (20°F). If temperatures are expected to be below −7°C (20°F) use number 1-D fuel if available. In some areas a winterized blend also called 2-D is available. Certain additives are also used during the winter months. Check with the service station operator to be sure you get the properly blended fuel.

NOTE: *Do not use number 2-D fuel at temperatures below −7°C (20°F), unless it is winterized either at the service station fuel pump or by the use of an additive.*

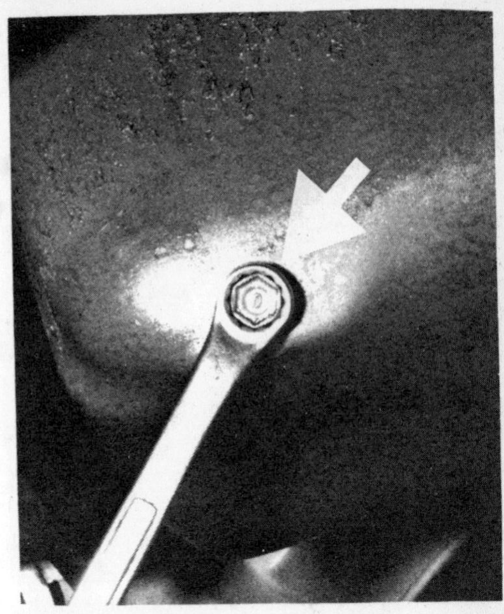

The oil drain plug on the gasoline engine is a 12mm hex head bolt

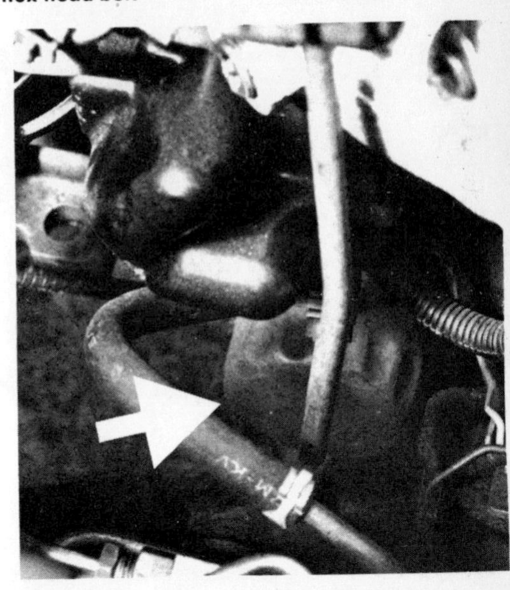

The oil filter on the gasoline engine is located on the driver's side of the engine as shown above. On the diesel engine, it is located on the passenger's side

Use only engine oils labeled SF/CC, SF/CD or SE/CC. It does not matter in what order these designations appear on the can as long as one is not missing. The use of engine oil additives is not recommended. Refer to the Engine Oil Viscocity Chart for diesel engines to help select the proper weight oil.

CHANGING OIL AND FILTER

GM recommends that the oil be changed every 6 months or 7500 miles, whichever comes

Bottom view of the oil filter on a gasoline engine. It will be easier to remove the filter from beneath the car

Lightly coat the filter gasket with fresh oil

first, for gasoline engines and every 3,750 miles or one year, whichever comes first, for diesel engines. However, this is only if the car is operated under normal conditions. Since many cars are operated beyond the normal conditions, the oil should be changed more frequently. It certainly won't do any harm. If your car is used under extreme conditions, such as dusty roads, trailer pulling, or short trips in cold climates, the oil should be changed at least every 3,000 miles or 3 months for gasoline engines and every 2,000 miles or 3 months for diesel engines.

It is also recommended that the oil filter be changed at every oil change. By leaving the old filter in, you are leaving almost a quart of worn oil in the engine which will cause the fresh oil to break down faster than normal.

Always drain the oil when the engine is at operating temperature as the oil will flow easier and more contaminants will be removed. You'll need a draining pan capable of holding at least 5 quarts.

Change the oil as follows:

1. Run the engine until it reaches normal operating temperature.
2. Jack up the front of the car and support it on safety stands.
3. Slide a drain pan of at least 5 quarts capacity under the oil pan.
4. Loosen the drain plug. Turn the plug out by hand. By keeping an inward pressure on the plug as you unscrew it, oil won't escape past the threads and you can remove without being burned by hot oil.

CAUTION: *The EPA warns that prolonged contact with used engine oil may cause a number of skin disorders, including cancer! You should make every effort to minimize your exposure to used engine oil. Protective gloves should be worn when changing the oil. Wash your hands and any other exposed skin areas as soon as possible after exposure to used engine oil. Soap and water, or waterless hand cleaner should be used.*

5. Allow the oil to drain completely and then install the drain plug. Don't overtighten the plug, or you'll be buying a new pan.
6. Using a strap wrench, remove the oil filter. Keep in mind that it's holding about one quart of dirty, hot oil.
7. Empty the old filter into the drain pan and dispose of the filter.
8. Using a clean rag, wipe off the filter adapter on the engine block. Be sure that the rag doesn't leave any lint which could clog an oil passage.
9. Coat the rubber gasket on the filter with fresh oil. Spin it into the engine by hand; when the gasket touches the adapter surface give it another ½-¾ turn. No more, or you'll squash the gasket and it will leak.
10. Refill the engine with 4 quarts of oil.
11. Start the car. If the oil pressure light does not turn off or the oil pressure gauge shows no pressure after a few seconds, shut off the engine and locate the problem.
12. If the oil pressure is OK and there are no leaks, shut the engine off and lower the car.

Transmission

FLUID RECOMMENDATION AND LEVEL CHECK

Manual

Check the level of the lubricant in the transmission at 7,500 mile intervals or every 6 months. The lubricant should be maintained at the level of the filler plug. To check the level, remove the square-headed plug from the side of the transmission case. A slight amount of fluid may run out (indicating the transmission is full) or you can use your finger to determine if the lubricant is at the filler plug. If not, top it up with SAE 80 or 80-90 gear oil in all 4-speed (70mm) transmissions. Cars operated in Canada and equipped with a 4-speed transmission should use the SAE 80 all year.

All Diesel engines equipped with 5-speed (69.5mm) transmissions use SAE 5W-30, type SF engine oil. All gasoline engines with 5-speed (77mm) transmissions use DEXRON®II automatic transmission fluid.

Automatic

Check the automatic transmission fluid level whenever you check the engine oil. It is even more important to check the fluid level when you are pulling a trailer or driving in a mountainous area. Automatic transmission fluid that smells burned or has a dark brown appearance is a signal of impending problems.

Check the fluid level with the car parked on a level spot, shift lever in Park, and with the engine running and warmed up.

1. Remove the dipstick, which is located in the engine compartment on the passenger's side.
2. Carefully touch the end of the dipstick to determine whether the fluid is cool, warm or hot.
3. Use a clean rag to wipe off the dipstick.
4. Fully reinsert the dipstick until the cap at the top if firmly seated.
5. Remove the dipstick and take your reading. If the fluid felt cool, the level should be about 3-10mm (1/8-3/8") below the **Add** mark. There are two raised dots below the **Add** mark to denote this range. If the fluid was warm, the fluid should be right around the **Add** mark. The level should be between the **Add** and **Full** marks if the fluid was hot to the touch.

NOTE: *One pint will raise the fluid level from* **Add** to **Full** when the transmission is hot. Be careful not to overfill the transmission, as this is just as bad as running with the fluid low.

If it is necessary to top up the transmission fluid use DEXRON®II automatic transmission fluid only.

DRAIN AND REFILL

Manual Transmission

4-SPEED AND 5-SPEED (GASOLINE ENGINE)

The manufacturer states that the transmission lubricant need never be changed. However, persons buying a used vehicle or those subjecting their cars to heavy-duty use may wish to change the lubricant. This may be done by re-

Manual transmission drain plug

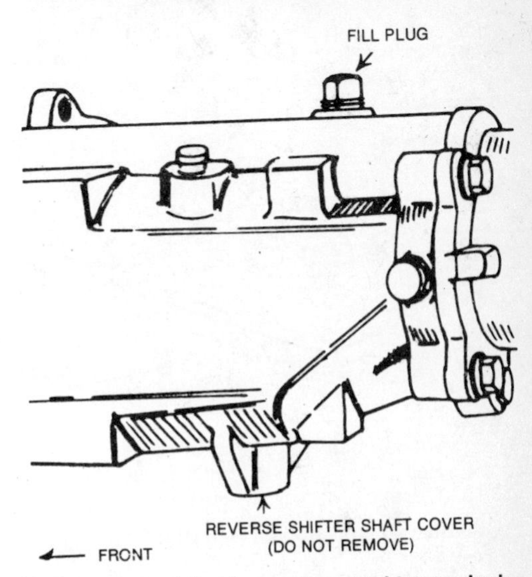

Bottom view of the 4-speed manual transmission. The fill plug is located on the driver's side of the transmission case

moving the drain plug and draining off the old lube. Dispose of this in the same manner as you would used oil. Reinstall the drain plug. Using a suction gun or squeeze bulb filler, fill the transmission to the level of the filler plug. Use SAE 80-90 or 90 GL-5 gear lubricant for the 4-speeed and DEXRON®II automatic transmission fluid for the 5-speed.

5-SPEED (DIESEL ENGINE)

The manufacturer recommends that the fluid be changed at the first 7,500 miles, then every 30,000 miles. The lubricant should be filled to the level of the filler plug hole. Use SAE 5W-30 SF engine oil.

Automatic Transmission

The manufacturer recommends that the automatic transmission oil pan should be drained, the screen cleaned, and fresh fluid added every

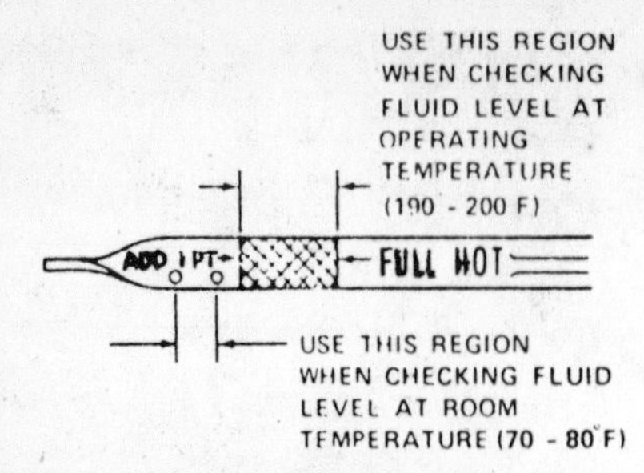

Automatic transmission dipstick markings

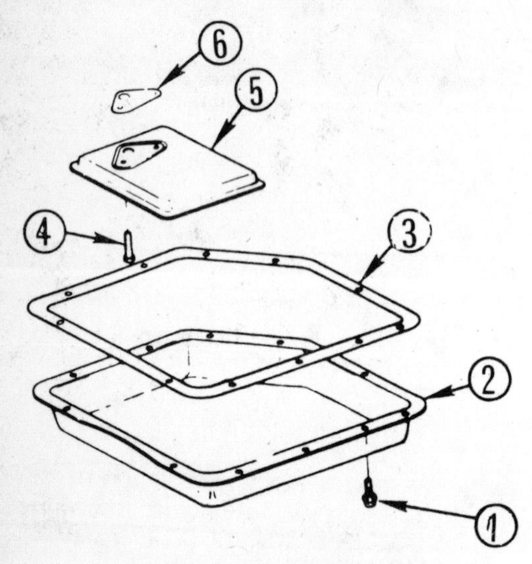

1. Oil pan bolt
2. Pan
3. Gasket
4. Filter screen bolt
5. Filter screen
6. Gasket

Automatic transmission oil pan and filter

60,000 miles (1976-78), 100,000 miles (1979-86 gasoline engines), 30,000 miles (1981-86 diesel engines). If you're frequently pulling a trailer, you should perform this service every 15,000 miles.

1. Jack up the front of the car and support the transmission with a jack at the vibration damper.
2. Place a drain pan under the transmission.
3. Remove the oil pan retaining bolts at the front and sides of the pan.
4. Loosen the rear pan retaining bolts about four turns.
5. Using a screwdriver, pry the transmission pan loose and let the fluid drain into the drain pan. Be careful not to gouge the pan mating surface on the transmission.
6. Remove the remaining bolts and remove the oil pan and its gasket. Throw the old gasket away.
7. Drain off all the fluid from the pan.
8. Clean the pan with solvent and let it dry.
9. Remove the two screen-to-valve body bolts, screen, and gasket. Throw the gasket away.
10. Give the screen a good cleaning in solvent and let it dry.
11. Install a new gasket on the screen and replace the two bolts. Tighten the two bolts to 6-10 ft. lbs. (8-14 Nm) 1976-77, 13-15 ft. lbs. 1978-86.
12. Install a new gasket on the oil pan and install the oil pan. Tighten the bolts to 10-13 ft. lbs. (14-18 Nm) 1976-77, 7-10 ft. lbs. 1978-86.
13. Lower the car and add the correct amount of DEXRON®II automatic transmission fluid through the filler tube. (See capacities chart). A long neck funnel is handy for this operation.
14. Place the selector in Park, apply the parking brake, start the engine and let it idle normally.
15. Shift the selector through each transmission range, place it in Park, and then check the fluid level.
16. Add fluid as necessary.

Differential (Drive Axle)

FLUID RECOMMENDATION AND LEVEL CHECK

It is recommended that the rear axle lubricant level be checked at each engine oil change interval. The proper lubricant is SAE 80 or 90 GL-5 gear lubricant. The filler plug is removed with a ⅜" drive ratchet and short extension. When the unit is cold, the level should be ½" below the filler plug hole; when it is hot, it should be even with the hole. Lubricant may be added by a suction gun.

Coolant

COOLANT RECOMMENDATION AND LEVEL CHECK

Once a month, the engine coolant level should be checked. This is quickly accomplished

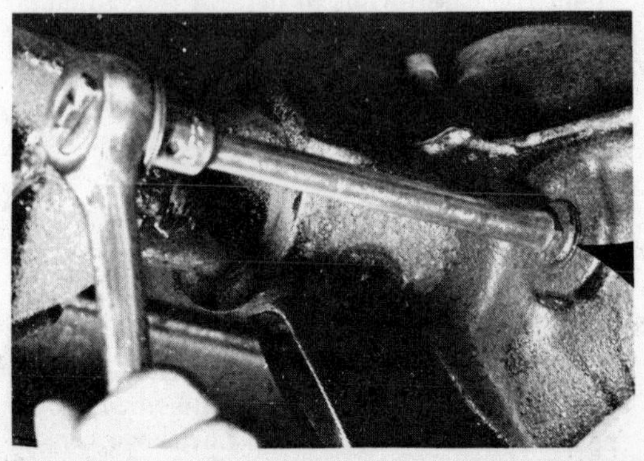

You'll need a ⅜ in. drive ratchet handle and an extension to remove the rear axle plug

by observing the level of coolant in the recovery tank, which is the translucent tank mounted to the right of the radiator, and connected to the radiator filler neck by a length of hose. As long as coolant is visible in the tank between the **Full Cold** and **Full Hot** marks, the coolant level is OK.

If coolant is needed, a 50/50 mix of ethylene glycol-based antifreeze and clear water should always be used for additions, both winter and summer. This is imperative on cars with air conditioning; without the antifreeze, the heater core could freeze when the air conditioning is used. Add coolant to the recovery tank through the capped opening; make additions only when the engine is cold.

The radiator hoses, clamps and radiator cap should be checked at the same time as the coolant level. Hoses which are brittle, cracked or swollen should be replaced. Clamps should be checked for tightness (screwdriver tight only-do not allow the clamp to cut into the hose or crush the fitting). The radiator cap gasket should be checked for any obvious tears, cracks or swelling, or any signs of incorrect seating in the radiator neck.

CAUTION: *To avoid injury when working with a hot engine, cover the radiator cap with a thick cloth. Wear a heavy glove to protect your hand. Turn the radiator cap slowly to the first stop, and allow all the pressure to vent (indicated when the hissing noise stops). When the pressure has been released, press down and remove the cap the rest of the way.*

DRAIN SYSTEM, FLUSH AND REFILL

The cooling system should be drained, flushed and refilled every two years or 30,000 miles, according to the manufacturer's recommendations. However, many mechanics prefer to change the coolant every year; it is cheap insurance against corrosion, overheating or freezing.

1. Remove the radiator cap when the engine is cool. See the preceding CAUTION about removing the cap.

CAUTION: *When draining the coolant, keep in mind that cats and dogs are attracted by the ethylene glycol antifreeze, and are quite likely to drink any that is left in an uncovered container or in puddles on the ground. This will prove fatal in sufficient quantity. Always drain the coolant into a sealable container. Coolant should be reused unless it is contaminated or several years old.*

2. With the radiator cap removed, run the engine until heat can be felt in the upper hose, indicating that the thermostat is open. The heater should be turned on to its maximum heat position, so that the core is flushed out.

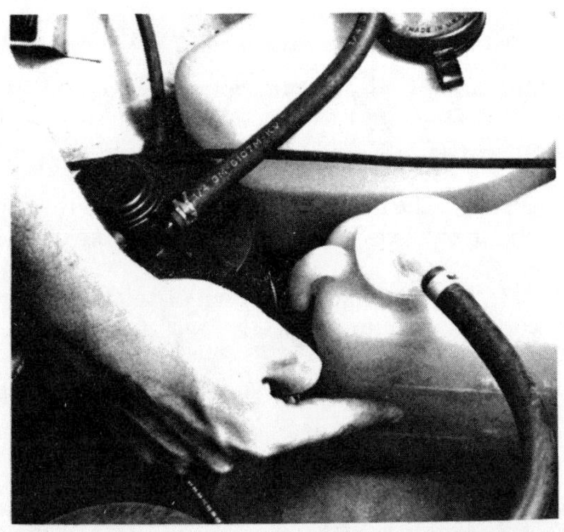

Coolant level should be at the lower mark when cold, higher mark when hot

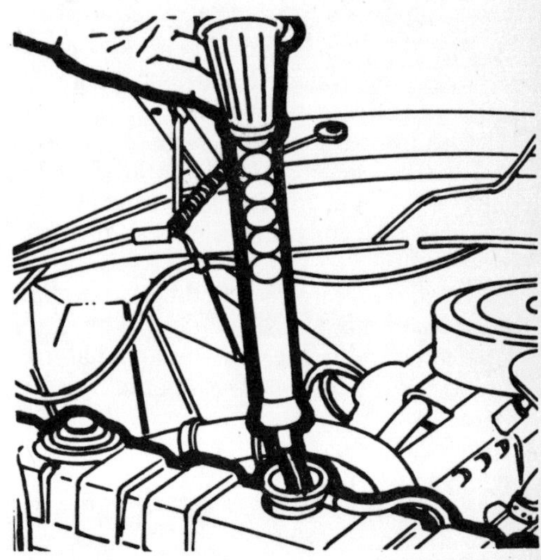

You can use an inexpensive tester to check anti-freeze protection

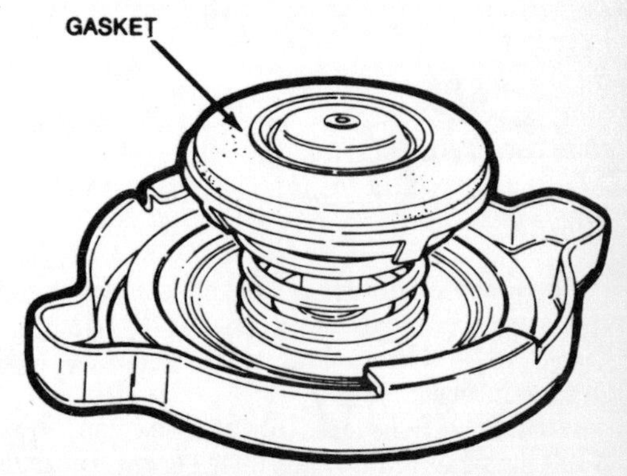

Check the condition of the radiator cap gasket

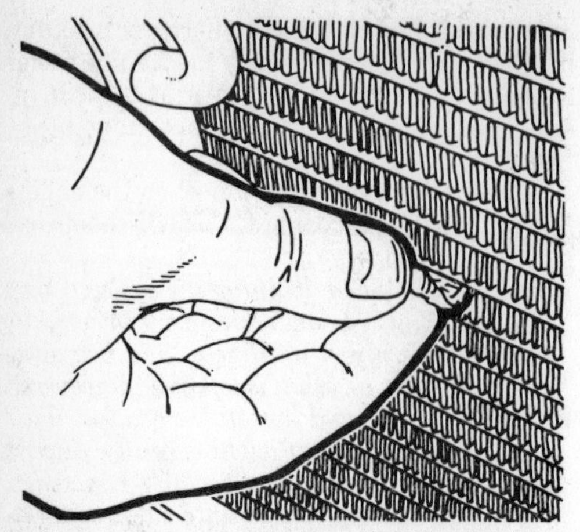

Clean the front of the radiator of any bugs, leaves or other debris at every yearly coolant change

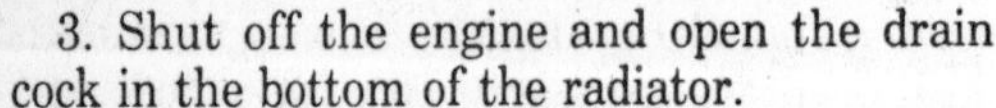

3. Shut off the engine and open the drain cock in the bottom of the radiator.
4. Close the drain cock and fill the cooling system with clear water. A cooling system flushing additive can be used, if desired.
5. Run the engine until it is hot again.
6. Drain the system, then flush with water until it runs clear.
7. Clean out the coolant recovery tank; remove the cap leaving the hoses in place. Remove the tank and drain it of any coolant. Clean it out with soap and water, empty it, and install it.
8. Close the drain cock and fill the radiator with a 50/50 mix of ethylene glycol base antifreeze and water to the base of the radiator filler neck. Fill the coolant recovery tank with the same solution to the **Full Hot** mark. Install the recovery tank cap.
9. Run the engine until the upper radiator hose is hot again (radiator cap still off). With the engine idling, add the 50/50 mix of antifreeze and water to the radiator until the level reaches the bottom of the filler neck. Shut off the engine and install the radiator cap, aligning the arrows with the overflow tube. Turn off the heater.

Master Cylinder

FLUID RECOMMENDATION AND LEVEL CHECK

The master cylinder is in the left rear side of the engine compartment, on the firewall. To check the fluid level as recommended at each oil change interval:

1. Clean off the area around the cap. Very small particles of dirt can cause serious difficulties in the brake system.

Master cylinder retaining clips (arrows)

After prying the retaining wires back, lift off the cover

2. Pry the two wire retaining clips off the cap and to one side with a screwdriver. Take off the cover.
3. The proper level in each of the two reservoirs is within ¼" of the top. Add fluid as necessary.
4. Replace the cover and snap the retaining wire back in place.

CAUTION: *Use only high-quality brake fluid specifically designated for disc brake systems. (DOT 3) Ordinary fluid will boil during heavy braking, causing complete loss of braking power.*

Power Steering Pump

LEVEL CHECK

The power steering hydraulic fluid level is checked with a dipstick inserted into the pump reservoir. The dipstick is attached to the reservoir cap. The level can be checked with the fluid either warm or cold; the car should be parked on a level surface. Check the fluid level every 12 months or 7,500 miles, whichever comes first.

1. With the engine off, unscrew the dipstick and check the level. If the engine is warm, the level should be between the **Hot** and **Cold** marks. If the engine is cold, the level should be between the **Add** and **Cold** marks.
2. If the level is low, add power steering fluid until correct. Be careful not to overfill, which will cause fluid loss and seal damage.

Steering Gear

There is no filler plug on the steering gear box. The unit is factory filled. It should be checked for leakage every 36,000 miles. An oily film is not evidence of leakage. Leakage is the actual loss of grease.

Chassis Greasing

The proper grease to be used is water-resistant EP chassis lubricant. A hand grease gun is satisfactory.

NOTE: *Ball joints must not be lubricated at temperatures below 10°F (–12°C).*

1. There are two steering linkage grease fittings, all reached from under the car. A grease gun with a flexible extension will allow you to reach all the fittings. Wipe off the fittings, install the gun, and pump in grease until it leaks out around the rubber seals. Wipe off the excess and the grease fitting.
2. There is a grease fitting above both upper ball joints and below both lower ball joints, four in all. Grease these as in Step 1.
3. Rub a little grease on the steering stops riveted to the lower control arms. Rub a little grease on the parking brake cable guides under the rear of the car.

Wheel Bearings

Clean and repack the front wheel bearings at each brake relining or 30,000 miles, whichever comes first. Please refer to Chapter 9 under Brake Disc removal and installation for this procedure.

Body Lubrication and Maintenance

Door, Hood and Trunk Hinges

Use a heavy grease or silicone lubricant on the hinges to avoid binding conditions. After the initial application, exercise the hinges a few times to assure proper lubrication

Door Locks

Apply graphite through the key slot. Insert the key and operate the lock several times to make sure the graphite has worked into the mechanism.

Windshield Washers

Fill the windshield washer tank with a cleaning solution. Do not use antifreeze as it may cause damage to the paint.

TRAILER TOWING

General Recommendations

Your car was primarily designed to carry passengers and cargo. It is important to remember that towing a trailer will place additional loads on your vehicle's engine, drive train, steering, braking and other systems. However, if you find it necessary to tow a trailer, using the proper equipment is a must.

Local laws may require specific equipment such as trailer brakes or fender mounted mirrors. Check your local laws.

Trailer Weight

The weight of the trailer is the most important factor. A good weight-to-horsepower ratio is about 35:1, 35 lbs. of GCW (Gross Combined Weight) for every horsepower your engine develops. Multiply the engine's rated horsepower by 35 and subtract the weight of the car passengers and luggage. The result is the approximate ideal maximum weight you should tow, although a a numerically higher axle ratio can help compensate for heavier weight.

Hitch Weight

Figure the hitch weight to select a proper hitch. Hitch weight is usually 9-11% of the trailer gross weight and should be measured with the trailer loaded. Hitches fall into three types: those that mount on the frame and rear bumper or the bolt-on or weld-on distribution type used for larger trailers. Axle mounted or clamp-on bumper hitches should never be used.

Check the gross weight rating of your trailer. Tongue weight is usually figured as 10% of gross trailer weight. Therefore, a trailer with a maximum gross weight of 2,000 lb. will have a maximum tongue weight of 200 lb. Class I trailers fall into this category. Class II trailers are those with a gross weight rating of 2,000-3,500 lb., while Class III trailers fall into the 3,500-6,000 lb. category. Class IV trailers are those over 6,000 lb. and are for use with fifth wheel trucks, only.

When you've determined the hitch that you'll need, follow the manufacturer's installation instructions, exactly, especially when it comes to fastener torques. The hitch will subjected to a lot of stress and good hitches come with hardened bolts. Never substitute an inferior bolt for a hardened bolt.

Cooling

ENGINE

One of the most common, if not THE most common, problems associated with trailer towing is engine overheating.

If you have a standard cooling system, without an expansion tank, you'll definitely need to get an aftermarket expansion tank kit, preferably one with at least a 2 quart capacity. These kits are easily installed on the radiator's overflow hose, and come with a pressure cap designed for expansion tanks.

Another helpful accessory is a Flex Fan. These fan are large diameter units are designed to provide more airflow at low speeds, with blades that have deeply cupped surfaces. The blades then flex, or flatten out, at high speed, when less cooling air is needed. These fans are far lighter in weight than stock fans, requiring less horsepower to drive them. Also, they are far quieter than stock fans.

If you do decide to replace your stock fan with a flex fan, note that if your car has a fan clutch, a spacer between the flex fan and water pump hub will be needed.

Aftermarket engine oil coolers are helpful for prolonging engine oil life and reducing overall engine temperatures. Both of these factors increase engine life.

While not absolutely necessary in towing Class I and some Class II trailers, they are recommended for heavier Class II and all Class III towing.

Engine oil cooler systems consist of an adapter, screwed on in place of the oil filter, a remote filter mounting and a multi-tube, finned heat exchanger, which is mounted in front of the radiator or air conditioning condenser.

TRANSMISSION

An automatic transmission is usually recommended for trailer towing. Modern automatics have proven reliable and, of course, easy to operate, in trailer towing.

The increased load of a trailer, however, causes an increase in the temperature of the automatic transmission fluid. Heat is the worst enemy of an automatic transmission. As the temperature of the fluid increases, the life of the fluid decreases.

It is essential, therefore, that you install an automatic transmission cooler.

The cooler, which consists of a multi-tube, finned heat exchanger, is usually installed in front of the radiator or air conditioning compressor, and hooked inline with the transmission cooler tank inlet line. Follow the cooler manufacturer's installation instructions.

Select a cooler of at least adequate capacity, based upon the combined gross weights of the car and trailer.

Cooler manufacturers recommend that you use an aftermarket cooler in addition to, and not instead of, the present cooling tank in your radiator. If you do want to use it in place of the radiator cooling tank, get a cooler at least two sizes larger than normally necessary.

NOTE: *A transmission cooler can, sometimes, cause slow or harsh shifting in the transmission during cold weather, until the fluid has a chance to come up to normal operating temperature. Some coolers can be purchased with or retrofitted with a temperature bypass valve which will allow fluid flow through the cooler only when the fluid has reached operating temperature, or above.*

Handling A Trailer

Towing a trailer with ease and safety requires a certain amount of experience. It's a good idea to learn the feel of a trailer by practicing turning, stopping and backing in an open area such as an empty parking lot.

PUSHING AND TOWING

WARNING: *Do not attempt to push start a Chevette or a Pontiac 1000, whether its equipped with an automatic or manual transmission. Under certain conditions this may damage the catalytic converter or other parts of the car.*

The car should not be towed to start, since there is a chance of the towed vehicle ramming the tow car. A Chevette or Pontiac 1000 may be towed with its rear wheels on the ground at speeds under 35 mph for distances up to 50 miles. If the car must be towed farther or faster, the driveshaft must be disconnected or the car must be towed on its front wheels.

Manual transmission models can be towed on all four wheels at freeway speeds for extensive distances, provided that the transmission is overfilled by about a quart of gear oil and a sturdy tow bar is used.

NOTE: *Whenever the car is towed with all*

four wheels on the ground, the steering column must not be locked.

JUMP STARTING

Jump starting is the only way to start a Chevette and Pontiac 1000 with a weak battery. The following method is recommended by the manufacturer.

CAUTION: *Do not attempt this procedure on a frozen battery. It will very likely explode. If your Chevette or 1000 is equipped with a Delco Freedom battery and the charge indicator is light, do not attempt to jump start the car.*

1. Turn off all electrical equipment. Place the automatic transmission in Park and the manual unit in neutral. Set the handbrake.
2. Make sure that the two vehicles are not contacting each other. It is a good idea to keep the engine running in the booster vehicle.
3. Remove all vent caps from both batteries and cover the openings with cloths. (On most maintenance free batteries this is not possible).
4. Attach one end of a jumper cable to the positive (+) terminal of the booster battery. The red cable is normally used. Attach the other end to the positive (+) terminal of the discharged battery.
5. Attach one end of the other cable (the black one) to the negative (-) terminal of the booster battery. Attach the other end to a heavy metal bracket (ground point) of the engine being started.

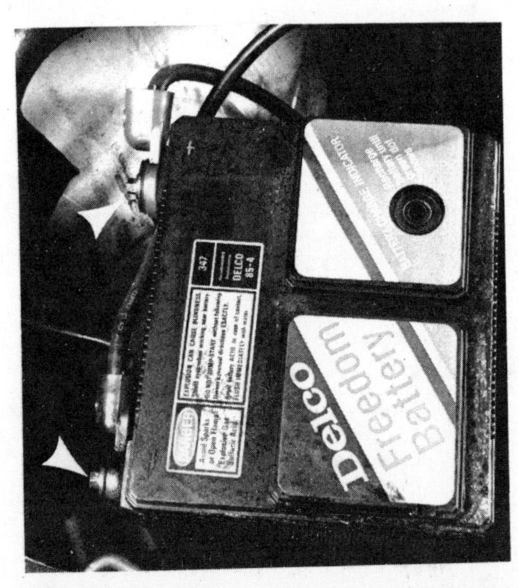

To jump start a side terminal battery, you'll need adapters (which are readily available) which attach under the retaining bolts (arrows)

CAUTION: *Do not use any part of the Delcotron (alternator) or mounting bracket as the final ground attachment.*

Be careful not to lean over the battery while making the last connections.

6. If the engine will not start, disconnect the batteries as soon as possible. If this is not done, the two batteries will soon reach a state of equilibrium, possibly with both of them too weak to start an engine. This should be no problem if the engine of the booster vehicle is left running fast enough to keep up the charge.
7. Reverse the procedure exactly to remove the jumper cables. Discard the rags, because they may have acid on them.

NOTE: *To jump start a Maintenance Free battery, you must first check the charge indicator on top of the battery. If the green dot is visible or the indicator is dark, you may jump the battery. If the indicator is light, under no circumstances should you jump the battery. The battery then must be replaced.*

JACKING AND HOISTING

The bumper jack supplied with the car should never be used for any service operation other than tire changing. NEVER get under the car while it is supported by a bumper jack. If the jack should slip or tip over, as bumper jacks often do, it would be exceedingly difficult to raise the car again while pinned underneath. Always block the wheels when changing tires.

The service operations in this book often require that one end or the other, or both, of the car can be raised and supported safely. The best arrangement is a grease pit or a vehicle hoist. The illustrations show the contact points for various types of lift equipment. A hydraulic floor jack is also referred to. It is realized that these items are not often found in the home ga-

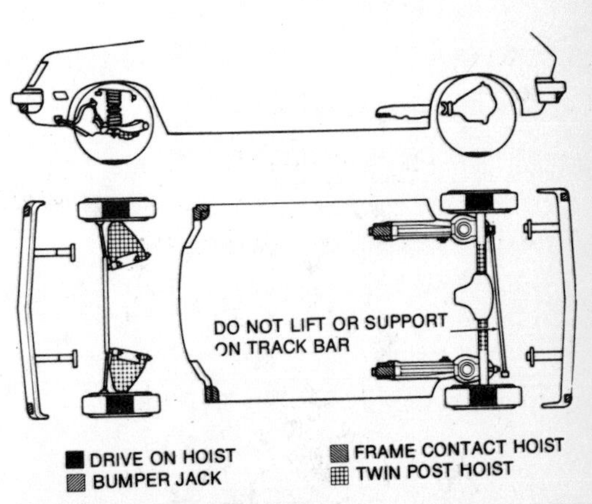

Jacking and hoisting points

rage, but there are reasonable and safe substitutes. Small hydraulic, screw or scissors jacks are satisfactory for raising the car. Heavy wooden blocks or adjustable jackstands should be used to support the car while it is being worked on.

Drive-on trestles, or ramps, are a handy and safe way to raise the car. These can be bought or constructed from suitable heavy timbers or steel.

In any case, it is always best to spend a little extra time to make sure that the car is lifted and supported safely.

CAUTION: *Concrete blocks are not recommended. They may break if the load is not evenly distributed.*

Capacities

Year	Engine No. Cyl Displacement Liters	Engine Crankcase Add ½ Qt For New Filter	Transmission Pts to Refill After Draining 4-Speed Manual	Transmission Pts to Refill After Draining 5-Speed Manual	Transmission Pts to Refill After Draining Automatic •	Drive Axle (pts)	Fuel Tank (gals)	Cooling System (qts) With Heater	Cooling System (qts) With A/C
1976–77	4-1.4	4	3	—	7	2.8	13	8.5	9
	4-1.6	4	3	—	7	2.8	13	8.5	9
1978	4-1.6	4	3	—	10	2	12.5	8.5	9
1979–86	4-1.6	4	3.5	4	6	1.75	12.5	9	9.25
1981–86	4-1.8 (diesel)	5 ②	—	3¼	6	1.75	12.5	9	①

① Not available
② 6 qts with new oil filter
• After refilling check fluid level and add as necessary. See text.

Vehicle Maintenance Schedule

Interval (Months or miles, whichever occurs first)	Services
SECTION A—Lubrication and General Maintenance	
Every 12 months or 3,750 miles (6,000 km)	Engine oil change (diesel engines) Oil filter change (diesel engines)
Every 12 months or 7,500 miles (12,000 km)	Chassis lubrication Fluid levels check Engine oil change (gasoline engines) Oil filter change (gasoline engines) Tire rotation Rear axle lube change Wheel bearing repack
Every 12 months or 15,000 miles (24,000 km)	Cooling system check
Every 30,000 miles (48,000 km)	Man. transmission fluid change (5 spd.) Auto. transmission fluid change (diesel) Manual steering gear check Clutch cross shaft lubrication
Every 60,000 miles (96,000 km)	Auto. transmission fluid change (1976–78)
Every 100,000 miles (160,000 km)	Auto. transmission fluid change (1979–87)
SECTION B—Safety Maintenance	
Every 12 months or 7,500 miles (12,000 km)	Owner safety checks Tire, wheel and disc brake check Exhaust system check Suspension and steering check Brake and power steering check
Every 12 months or 15,000 miles (24,000 km)	Drive belt check Drum brake and parking brake check Throttle linkage check Underbody flush and check Bumper check

Vehicle Maintenance Schedule (cont.)

Interval (Months or miles, whichever occurs first)	Services
SECTION C—Emission Control Maintenance Gasoline Engines	
At first 6 months or 7,500 miles (12,000 km) Then at 18 month/22,500 miles (36,000 km) Intervals	Thermo. controlled air cleaner check Carburetor choke check Engine idle speed adjustment Vacuum advance system, hoses check
Every 12 months or 15,000 miles (24,000 km)	Fuel filter replacement PCV system check PCV valve and filter replacement
Every 22,500 miles (36,000 km)	Spark plug wire check Idle stop solenoid and/or dashpot check Spark plug replacement Engine timing adjustment and distributor check Carburetor vacuum break adjustment
Every 24 months or 30,000 miles (48,000 km)	Evaporative control system (ECS) check Fuel cap, tank and lines check
Every 50,000 miles	Air cleaner replacement
Diesel Engines	
Every 15,000 miles (24,000 km)	Valve clearance check and adjust
Every 12 months or 15,000 miles (24,000 km)	Fuel cap, fuel lines and fuel tank inspect
Every 30,000 miles (48,000 km)	Adjust engine idle speed Replace air cleaner element Check and adjust fuel injection pump timing

Engine Performance and Tune-Up

2

TUNE-UP PROCEDURES

In order to extract the full measure of performance and economy from your engine it is essential that it is properly tuned at regular intervals. A regular tune-up will keep your cars engine running smoothly and well prevent the annoying breakdowns and poor performance associated with an untuned engine.

A complete tune-up should be performed at least every 15,000 miles (12,000 miles for early cars) or twelve months, whichever comes first.

NOTE: *1981 and later cars have increased their interval to 30,000 miles.*

This interval should be halved if the car is operated under severe conditions such as trailer towing, prolonged idling, start-and-stop driving, or if starting or running problems are noticed. It is assumed that the routine maintenance described in Chapter 1 has been kept up, as this will have a decided effect on the results of a tune-up. All of the applicable steps of a tune-up should be followed in order, as the result is a cummulative one.

If the specifications on the underhood tune-up sticker in the engine compartment of your car disagree with the Tune-Up Specifications chart in this chapter, the figures on the sticker must be used. The sticker often reflects changes made during the production run.

Spark Plugs

A typical spark plug consists of a metal shell surrounding a ceramic insulator. A metal electrode extends downward through the center of the insulator and protrudes a short distance.

Located at the end of the plug and attached these electrodes (measured in thousandths of an inch) is called spark plug gap. The spark plug in no way produces a spark but merely provides a gap across which the current can arc. The coil produces 20,000-25,000 Volts (the HEI transistorized ignition produces considerably more voltage than the standard type, approximately 50,000 volts), which travels to the distributor where it is distributed through the spark plug wires to the plugs. The current passes along the center electrode and jumps the gap to the side electrode and, in so doing, ignites the air/fuel mixture in the combustion chamber. All plugs specified for these cars have a resistor built into the center electrode to reduce interference to any nearby radio and television receivers. The resistor also cuts down on erosion of plug electrodes caused by excessively long sparking. Resistor spark plug wiring is original equipment on all cars.

Spark plug life and efficiency depend upon condition of the engine and the temperatures to which the plug is exposed. Combustion chamber temperatures are affected by many factors such as compression ratio of the engine, fuel/air mixtures, exhaust emission equipment, and the type of driving you do. Spark plug are designed and classified by number according to the heat range at which they will operate most efficiently. The amount of heat that the plug absorbs is determined by the length of the lower insulator. The longer the insulator (it extends farther into the engine), the hotter the plug will operate; the shorter it is, the cooler it will operate. A plug that has a short path for heat transfer and remains too cool will quickly accumulate deposits of oil and carbon since it is not hot enough to burn them off. This leads to plug fouling and consequently to misfiring. A plug that has a long path of heat transfer will have no deposits but, due to the excessive heat, the electrodes will burn away quickly and, in some instances, pre-ignition may result. Pre-ignition takes place when plug tips get so hot that they glow sufficiently to ignite the fuel/air mixture before the spark does. This early ignition will usually cause a pinging (sounding much like castanets) during low speeds and heavy loads. In severe cases, the heat may become enough to start the

Troubleshooting Engine Performance

Problem	Cause	Solution
Hard starting (engine cranks normally)	• Binding linkage, choke valve or choke piston • Restricted choke vacuum diaphragm • Improper fuel level • Dirty, worn or faulty needle valve and seat • Float sticking • Faulty fuel pump • Incorrect choke cover adjustment • Inadequate choke unloader adjustment • Faulty ignition coil • Improper spark plug gap • Incorrect ignition timing • Incorrect valve timing	• Repair as necessary • Clean passages • Adjust float level • Repair as necessary • Repair as necessary • Replace fuel pump • Adjust choke cover • Adjust choke unloader • Test and replace as necessary • Adjust gap • Adjust timing • Check valve timing; repair as necessary
Rough idle or stalling	• Incorrect curb or fast idle speed • Incorrect ignition timing • Improper feedback system operation • Improper fast idle cam adjustment • Faulty EGR valve operation • Faulty PCV valve air flow • Choke binding • Faulty TAC vacuum motor or valve • Air leak into manifold vacuum • Improper fuel level • Faulty distributor rotor or cap • Improperly seated valves • Incorrect ignition wiring • Faulty ignition coil • Restricted air vent or idle passages • Restricted air cleaner • Faulty choke vacuum diaphragm	• Adjust curb or fast idle speed • Adjust timing to specification • Refer to Chapter 4 • Adjust fast idle cam • Test EGR system and replace as necessary • Test PCV valve and replace as necessary • Locate and eliminate binding condition • Repair as necessary • Inspect manifold vacuum connections and repair as necessary • Adjust fuel level • Replace rotor or cap • Test cylinder compression, repair as necessary • Inspect wiring and correct as necessary • Test coil and replace as necessary • Clean passages • Clean or replace air cleaner filler element • Repair as necessary
Faulty low-speed operation	• Restricted idle transfer slots • Restricted idle air vents and passages • Restricted air cleaner • Improper fuel level • Faulty spark plugs • Dirty, corroded, or loose ignition secondary circuit wire connections • Improper feedback system operation • Faulty ignition coil high voltage wire • Faulty distributor cap	• Clean transfer slots • Clean air vents and passages • Clean or replace air cleaner filter element • Adjust fuel level • Clean or replace spark plugs • Clean or tighten secondary circuit wire connections • Refer to Chapter 4 • Replace ignition coil high voltage wire • Replace cap
Faulty acceleration	• Improper accelerator pump stroke • Incorrect ignition timing • Inoperative pump discharge check ball or needle • Worn or damaged pump diaphragm or piston	• Adjust accelerator pump stroke • Adjust timing • Clean or replace as necessary • Replace diaphragm or piston

Troubleshooting Engine Performance (cont.)

Problem	Cause	Solution
Faulty acceleration (cont.)	• Leaking carburetor main body cover gasket	• Replace gasket
	• Engine cold and choke set too lean	• Adjust choke cover
	• Improper metering rod adjustment (BBD Model carburetor)	• Adjust metering rod
	• Faulty spark plug(s)	• Clean or replace spark plug(s)
	• Improperly seated valves	• Test cylinder compression, repair as necessary
	• Faulty ignition coil	• Test coil and replace as necessary
	• Improper feedback system operation	• Refer to Chapter 4
Faulty high speed operation	• Incorrect ignition timing	• Adjust timing
	• Faulty distributor centrifugal advance mechanism	• Check centrifugal advance mechanism and repair as necessary
	• Faulty distributor vacuum advance mechanism	• Check vacuum advance mechanism and repair as necessary
	• Low fuel pump volume	• Replace fuel pump
	• Wrong spark plug air gap or wrong plug	• Adjust air gap or install correct plug
	• Faulty choke operation	• Adjust choke cover
	• Partially restricted exhaust manifold, exhaust pipe, catalytic converter, muffler, or tailpipe	• Eliminate restriction
	• Restricted vacuum passages	• Clean passages
	• Improper size or restricted main jet	• Clean or replace as necessary
	• Restricted air cleaner	• Clean or replace filter element as necessary
	• Faulty distributor rotor or cap	• Replace rotor or cap
	• Faulty ignition coil	• Test coil and replace as necessary
	• Improperly seated valve(s)	• Test cylinder compression, repair as necessary
	• Faulty valve spring(s)	• Inspect and test valve spring tension, replace as necessary
	• Incorrect valve timing	• Check valve timing and repair as necessary
	• Intake manifold restricted	• Remove restriction or replace manifold
	• Worn distributor shaft	• Replace shaft
	• Improper feedback system operation	• Refer to Chapter 4
Misfire at all speeds	• Faulty spark plug(s)	• Clean or replace spark plug(s)
	• Faulty spark plug wire(s)	• Replace as necessary
	• Faulty distributor cap or rotor	• Replace cap or rotor
	• Faulty ignition coil	• Test coil and replace as necessary
	• Primary ignition circuit shorted or open intermittently	• Troubleshoot primary circuit and repair as necessary
	• Improperly seated valve(s)	• Test cylinder compression, repair as necessary
	• Faulty hydraulic tappet(s)	• Clean or replace tappet(s)
	• Improper feedback system operation	• Refer to Chapter 4
	• Faulty valve spring(s)	• Inspect and test valve spring tension, repair as necessary
	• Worn camshaft lobes	• Replace camshaft
	• Air leak into manifold	• Check manifold vacuum and repair as necessary
	• Improper carburetor adjustment	• Adjust carburetor
	• Fuel pump volume or pressure low	• Replace fuel pump
	• Blown cylinder head gasket	• Replace gasket
	• Intake or exhaust manifold passage(s) restricted	• Pass chain through passage(s) and repair as necessary
	• Incorrect trigger wheel installed in distributor	• Install correct trigger wheel

Troubleshooting Engine Performance (cont.)

Problem	Cause	Solution
Power not up to normal	• Incorrect ignition timing • Faulty distributor rotor • Trigger wheel loose on shaft • Incorrect spark plug gap • Faulty fuel pump • Incorrect valve timing • Faulty ignition coil • Faulty ignition wires • Improperly seated valves • Blown cylinder head gasket • Leaking piston rings • Worn distributor shaft • Improper feedback system operation	• Adjust timing • Replace rotor • Reposition or replace trigger wheel • Adjust gap • Replace fuel pump • Check valve timing and repair as necessary • Test coil and replace as necessary • Test wires and replace as necessary • Test cylinder compression and repair as necessary • Replace gasket • Test compression and repair as necessary • Replace shaft • Refer to Chapter 4
Intake backfire	• Improper ignition timing • Faulty accelerator pump discharge • Defective EGR CTO valve • Defective TAC vacuum motor or valve • Lean air/fuel mixture	• Adjust timing • Repair as necessary • Replace EGR CTO valve • Repair as necessary • Check float level or manifold vacuum for air leak. Remove sediment from bowl
Exhaust backfire	• Air leak into manifold vacuum • Faulty air injection diverter valve • Exhaust leak	• Check manifold vacuum and repair as necessary • Test diverter valve and replace as necessary • Locate and eliminate leak
Ping or spark knock	• Incorrect ignition timing • Distributor centrifugal or vacuum advance malfunction • Excessive combustion chamber deposits • Air leak into manifold vacuum • Excessively high compression • Fuel octane rating excessively low • Sharp edges in combustion chamber • EGR valve not functioning properly	• Adjust timing • Inspect advance mechanism and repair as necessary • Remove with combustion chamber cleaner • Check manifold vacuum and repair as necessary • Test compression and repair as necessary • Try alternate fuel source • Grind smooth • Test EGR system and replace as necessary
Surging (at cruising to top speeds)	• Low carburetor fuel level • Low fuel pump pressure or volume • Metering rod(s) not adjusted properly (BBD Model Carburetor) • Improper PCV valve air flow • Air leak into manifold vacuum • Incorrect spark advance • Restricted main jet(s) • Undersize main jet(s) • Restricted air vents • Restricted fuel filter • Restricted air cleaner • EGR valve not functioning properly • Improper feedback system operation	• Adjust fuel level • Replace fuel pump • Adjust metering rod • Test PCV valve and replace as necessary • Check manifold vacuum and repair as necessary • Test and replace as necessary • Clean main jet(s) • Replace main jet(s) • Clean air vents • Replace fuel filter • Clean or replace air cleaner filter element • Test EGR system and replace as necessary • Refer to Chapter 4

Gasoline Engine Tune-Up Specifications

When analyzing compression test results, look for uniformity among cylinders rather than specific pressures.

	Engine			Spark Plugs		Distributor		Ignition Timing (deg)			Idle Speed (rpm)	
Year	Eng V.I.N. Code	No. Cyl Displace-ment liters	HP	Type	Gap (in.)	Point Dwell (deg)	Point Gap (in.)	Man. Trans	Auto Trans	Fuel Pump Pressure (psi)	Man. Trans	Auto Trans
1976–77	I	4-1.4	52 ①	R43TS	.035	Electronic		10B	10B	5–6.5	800(1000)	800(850)
	E	4-1.6	60 ②	R43TS	.035	Electronic		8B	10B	5–6.5	800(1000)	800(850)
1978	E	4-1.6	63 ③	R43TS	.035	Electronic		8B	8B	5–6.5	800(800)	800(800)
1979	E	4-1.6	70	R42TS	.035	Electronic		12B	18B(16B)	5–6.5	800(800)	750(750)
	O	4-1.6	74	R42TS	.035	Electronic		12B	18B(12B)	5–6.5	800(800)	750(750)
1980	9	4-1.6	70	R42TS	.035	Electronic		12B	18B	5–6.5	800	750(800)
	O	4-1.6	74	R42TS	.035	Electronic		12B	18B	5–6.5	800	750
1981	9	4-1.6	70	R42TS	.035	Electronic		18B	18B	5–6.5	800	700
1982	C	4-1.6	70	R42TS	.035	Electronic		8B	8B	5–6.5	800	700
1983–87	C	4-1.6	70	R42CTS	.035	Electronic		8B	8B	5–6.5	800	700

Figures in parenthesis are for California
B Before Top Dead Center
① 59 for 1977
② 62 for 1977
③ Optional H.O. engine rated at 68 bhp V.I.N. code J
NOTE: *The underhood specifications sticker occasionally reflects tune-up specification changes made in production. Sticker information must be followed if it disagrees with data supplied here.*
Part numbers in this chart are not recommendations by Chilton for any product by brand name.

Diesel Engine Tune-Up Specifications

Year	Engine No. Cyl. Displacement (liters)	Static Injection Timing	Fuel Injection Order	Compression (lbs)	Injection Nozzle Opening Pressure (psi)	Intake Valve Opens (deg)	Idle Speed▲	
							Man.	Auto.
'81–'82	4-(1.8)	18°B	1-3-4-2	441 ①	1707	32	625	725
'83–'84	4-(1.8)	11°B	1-3-4-2	441 ①	1707	32	620	720
'85–'86	4-(1.8)	18°B	1-3-4-2	441 ①	1707	32	625	—

NOTE: *The underhood specifications sticker often reflects changes made in production. Sticker figures must be used if they disagree with those in the above chart.*
▲ See underhood sticker for fast idle speed. ① At 200 rpm

fuel/air mixture burning throughout the combustion chamber rather than just to the front of the plug as in normal operation. At this time, the piston is rising in the cylinder making its compression stroke. The burning mass is compressed and an explosion results producing tremendous pressure. Something has to give, and it does; pistons are often damaged. Obviously, this detonation (explosion) is a destructive condition that can be avoided by installing a spark plug designed and specified for your particular engine.

A set of spark plugs usually requires replacement after 22,500 miles for all 1976-79 cars and 30,000 miles for all 1980 and later cars). The electrode on a new spark plug has a sharp edge but, with use, this edge becomes rounded by erosion causing the plug gap to increase. In normal operation, plug gap increases about 0.001" in every 1,000-2,000 miles. As the gap increases, the plug's voltage requirement also increases. It requires a greater voltage to jump the wider gap and about two to three times as much voltage to fire a plug a high speed and acceleration than at idle.

The higher voltage produced by the HEI ignition coil is one of the primary reasons for the prolonged replacement interval for spark plugs. A consistently hotter spark prevents the fouling of plugs for much longer than could normally be expected; this spark is also able to jump across a larger gap more efficiently than a spark from a conventional system. However, even plugs used with the HEI system wear after time in the engine.

Worn plugs become obvious during acceleration. Voltage requirement is greatest during acceleration and a plug with an enlarged gap may require more voltage than the coil is able to produce. As a result, the engine misses and sputters until acceleration is reduced. Reducing acceleration reduces the plug's voltage requirement and the engine runs smoother. Slow, city driving is hard on plugs. The long periods of idle experienced in traffic creates an overly rich gas mixture. The engine isn't running fast enough to completely burn the gas and, consequently, the plugs are fouled with gas deposits and engine idle becomes rough. In many cases, driving under the right conditions can effectively clean these fouled plugs.

NOTE: *There are several reasons why a spark plug will foul and you can usually learn which is at fault by just looking at the plug. A few of the most common reasons for plug fouling, and a description of the fouled plug's appearance, can be found in the color insert in this book.*

Accelerate your car to the speed where the engine begins to miss and then slow down to the point where the engine smooths out. Run at this speed for a few minutes and then accelerate again to the point of engine miss. With each repetition this engine miss should occur at increasingly higher speeds and then disappear altogether. Do not attempt to shortcut this procedure by hard acceleration. This approach will compound problems by fusing deposits into a hard permanent glaze. Dirty, fouled plugs may be cleaned by sandblasting. Many shops have a spark plug sandblaster. After sandblasting, the electrode should be filed to a sharp, square shape and then gapped to specifications. Gapping a plug too close will produce a rough idle while gapping it too wide will increase its voltage requirement and cause missing at high speed and during acceleration.

The type of driving you do may require a change in spark plug heat range. If the majority of you driving is done in the city and rarely at high speeds, plug fouling may necessitate changing to a plug with a heat range one number higher than that specified by the vehicle manufacturer.

Your car may specify an R44 plug. Frequent city driving may foul these plugs making engine operation rough. An R45 is the next hottest plug in the AC heat range (the higher the AC number, the hotter the plug) and its insulator is longer than the R44 so that it can absorb and retain more heat than the shorter R44. This hotter R45 burns off deposits even at low city speeds but would be too hot for prolonged turnpike driving. Using this plug at high speed would create dangerous pre-ignition. On the other hand, if the aforementioned Chevelle were used almost exclusively for long distance high speed driving, the specified R44 might be too hot resulting in rapid electrode wear and dangerous pre-ignition. In this case, it might be wise to change to a colder R43. If the car is used for abnormal driving (as in the examples above), or the engine has been modified for higher performance, then change to a plug of a different heat range may be necessary. For a modified car it is always wise to go to a colder plug as a protection against pre-ignition. It will require more frequent plug cleaning, but destructive detonation during acceleration will be avoided.

REMOVAL

When you're removing spark plugs, you should work on one at a time. Don't start by removing the plug wires all at once because unless you number them, they're going to get mixed up. On some cars though, it will be more convenient for you to remove all the wires before you start to work on the plugs. If this is necessary, take a minute before you begin and number the wires with tape before you take them off. The time you spend here will pay off later on.

1. Twist the spark plug boot and remove the boot from the plug. You may also use a plug wire removal tool designed especially for this purpose. Do not pull on the wire itself. When the wire has been removed, take a wire brush and clean the area around the plug. Make sure that all the grime is removed so that none will enter the cylinder after the plug has been removed.
2. Remove the plug using the proper size socket, extensions, and universals as necessary. The plugs require a 5/8" socket.
3. If removing the plug is difficult, drip some penetrating oil on the plug threads, allow it to work, then remove the plug. Also, be sure that the socket is straight on the plug, especially on those hard to reach plugs.

INSPECTION

Check the plugs for deposits and wear. If they are not going to be replaced, clean the plugs thoroughly. Remember that any kind of deposit will decrease the efficiency of the plug. Plugs can be cleaned on a spark plug cleaning machine, which can sometimes be found in service stations, or you can do an acceptable job of cleaning with a stiff brush. If the plugs are cleaned, the electrodes must be filed flat. use an ignition points file, not an emery board or the like, which will leave deposits. The electrodes must be filed perfectly flat with sharp edges; rounded edges reduce the spark plug voltage by as much as 50%.

Check spark plug gap before installation. The ground electrode (the L-shaped one connected to the body of the plug) must be parallel to the center electrode and the specified size wire gauge (see Tune-Up Specifications) should pass through the gap with a slight drag. Always check the gap on new plugs, too; they are not always set correctly at the factory. Do not use a flat feeler gauge when measuring the gap, because the reading will be inaccurate. Wire gapping tools usually have a bending tool attached. Use that to adjust the side electrode until the proper distance is obtained. Absolutely never bend the center electrode. Also, be careful not to bend the side electrode too far or too often; it may weaken and break off within the engine, requiring removal of the cylinder head to retrieve it.

INSTALLATION

1. Lubricate the threads of the spark plugs with a drop of oil. Install the plugs and tighten them hand-tight. Take care not to cross-thread them.
2. Tighten the spark plugs with a socket. Do not apply the same amount of force you would use for a bolt; just snug them in. If a torque wrench is available, tighten to 11-15 ft. lbs.
3. Install the wires on their respective plugs. Make sure the wires are firmly connected. You will be able to feel them click into place.

Carefully pull the spark plug boot off. Don't yank on the wire

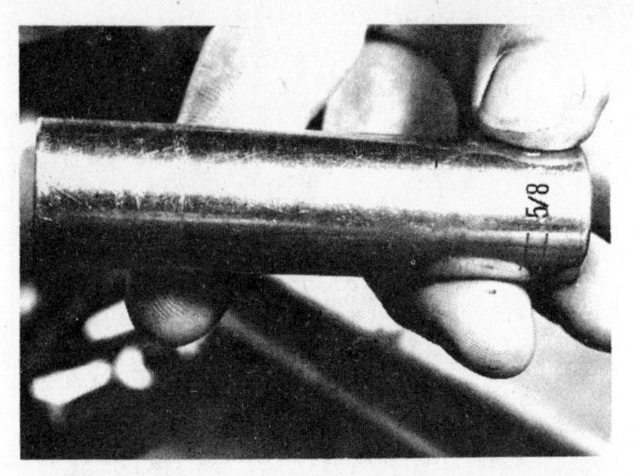

You'll need a ⅝ in. spark plug socket, not the more common $^{13}/_{16}$ in. variety

Turn the wrench counterclockwise to remove the spark plug

CHECKING AND REPLACING SPARK PLUG WIRES

Every 15,000 miles, inspect the spark plug wires for burns, cuts, or breaks in the insulation. Check the boots and the nipples on the distributor cap. Replace any damaged wiring.

Every 45,000 miles or so, the resistance of the wires should be checked with an ohmmeter. Wires with excessive resistance will cause misfiring, and may make the engine difficult to start in damp weather. Generally, the useful life of the cables is 45,000-60,000 miles.

To check resistance, remove the distributor cap, leaving the wires in place. Connect one lead of an ohmmeter to an electrode within the cap; connect the other lead to the corresponding spark plug terminal (remove it from the spark plug for this test). Replace any wire which shows a resistance over 30,000Ω. Generally speaking, resistance should not be over

The plug can usually be unscrewed by hand once it's loosened

Use a round wire gauge to check spark plug gap

25,000Ω, and 30,000Ω must be considered the outer limit of acceptability.

It should be remembered that resistance is also a function of length; the long the wire, the greater the resistance. Thus, if the wires on your car are longer than the factory originals, resistance will be higher, quite possibly outside these limits.

When installing new wires, replace them one at a time to avoid mixups. Start by replacing the longest one first. Install the boot firmly over the spark plug. Route the wire over the same path as the original. Insert the nipple firmly onto the tower on the distributor cap, then install the cap cover and latches to secure the wires.

NOTE: *For further information on spark plug wires, refer to the color insert on Spark Plug Analysis.*

Firing Order

To avoid confusion replace spark plug wires one at a time.

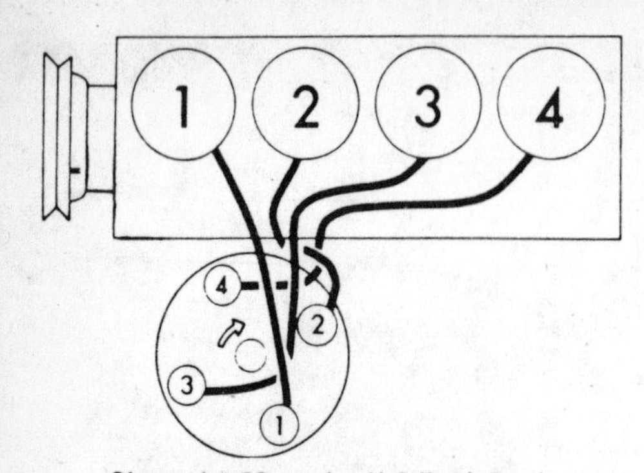

Chevrolet 98 cu. in. (1.6 liter) 4 cyl.
Engine firing order: 1-3-4-2
Distributor rotation: clockwise

Engine firing order

To remove the distributor cap, push down on the screw latches and release them by turning

Ignition System

Gasoline Engine

All gasoline engine Chevette and Pontiac 1000 models are equipped with High Energy Ignition (HEI). This is a pulse triggered, transistor-controlled, inductive discharge ignition system that uses no breaker points. The HEI distributor contains a pick-up assembly and an electronic module which perform the function of breaker points. Centrifugal and vacuum advance mechanisms are basically the same as those in breaker point distributors. 1981 and later models are equipped with EST (Electronic Spark Timing) distributors which have no mechanical or vacuum advance mechanisms. The ignition coil is mounted externally, on the left side of the engine, beneath the intake manifold, and is not visible on air conditioning equipped cars. The coil has a plastic cover.

The voltage delivered by this system is also far greater than the conventional system, enabling longer spark plug life as the hotter plug won't be as susceptible to fouling. There is no regular servicing of the distributor other than checking the distributor cap and rotor for burning and pitting.

No regular maintenance is necessary with HEI, but an occasional check of cap and rotor condition is a good idea. Look for pitting and burning

All of the HEI system components are housed in the distributor, except the coil

HEI SYSTEM PRECAUTIONS

Before going on to troubleshooting, it might be a good idea to take note of the following precautions:

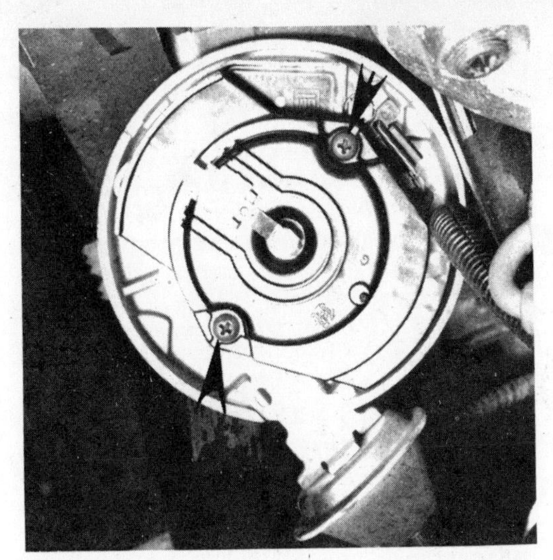

Unscrew the two phillips head screws (arrows) to remove the rotor

If the tip of the rotor is burned or pitted, replace it

Timing Light Use

Inductive pick-up timing lights are the best kind of use with HEI. Timing light which connect between the spark plug and the spark plug wire occasionally (not always) give false readings.

Spark Plug Wires

The plug wires used with HEI systems are of a different construction than conventional wires. When replacing them, make sure you get the correct wires, since conventional wires won't carry the voltage. Also, handle them carefully to avoid cracking or splitting them and never pierce them.

Tachometer Use

Not all tachometers will operate or indicate correctly when used on a HEI system. While some tachometers may give a reading, this does not necessarily mean the reading is correct. In addition, some tachometers hook up differently from others. If you can't figure out whether or not your tachometer will work on your car, check with the tachometer manufacturer. Dwell readings, or course, have no significance at all.

HEI System Testers

Instruments designed specifically for testing HEI systems are available from several tool manufacturers. Some of these will even test the module itself. However, the tests given in the following section will require only ohmmeter and a voltmeter.

TROUBLESHOOTING THE HEI SYSTEM

The symptoms of a defective component within the HEI system are exactly the same as those you would encounter in a conventional system. Some of these symptoms are:

- Hard or no Starting
- Rough Idle
- Poor Fuel Economy
- Engine misses under load or while accelerating

If you suspect a problem in your ignition system, there are certain preliminary checks which you should carry out before you begin to check the electronic portions of the system. First, it is extremely important to make sure the vehicle battery is in a good state of charge. A defective or poorly charged battery will cause the various components of the ignition system to read incorrectly when they are being tested. Second, Make sure all wiring connections are clean and tight, not only at the battery, but also at the distributor cap, ignition coil, and at the electronic control module.

Since the only change between electronic and conventional ignition systems is in the distributor component area, it is imperative to check the secondary ignition circuit first. If the secondary circuit checks out properly, then the engine condition is probably not the fault of the ignition system. To check the secondary ignition system, perform a simple spark test. Remove one of the plug wires and insert some sort of extension in the plug socket. An old spark plug with the ground electrode removed makes a good extension. Hold the wire and extension about ¼" away from the block and crank the engine. If a normal spark occurs, then the problem is most likely not in the ignition system. Check for fuel system problems, or fouled spark plugs.

If, however, there is no spark or a weak spark, then further ignition system testing will have to be done. Troubleshooting techniques fall into two categories, depending on the nature of the problem. The categories are (1) Engine cranks, but won't start or (2) Engine runs, but runs rough or cuts out. To begin with, let's consider the first case.

Engine Fails to Start

If the engine won't start, perform a spark test as described earlier. This will narrow the problem area down considerably. If no spark occurs, check for the presence of normal battery voltage of the battery (BAT) terminal in the distributor cap. The ignition switch must be in the ON position for this test. Either a voltmeter or a test light may be used for this test. Connect the test light wire to ground and probe end to the BAT terminal at the distributor. If the light comes on, you have voltage on the distributor. If the light fails to come on, this indicates an open circuit in the ignition primary wiring leading to the distributor. In this case, you will have to check wiring continuity back to the ignition switch using a test light. If there is battery voltage at the BAT terminal, but no spark at the plugs, then the problem lies within the distributor assembly. Go on to the distributor components test section.

Engine Runs, But Runs Roughly or Cuts Out

1. Make sure the plug wires are in good shape first. There should be no obvious cracks or breaks. You can check the plug wires with an ohmmeter, but do not pierce the wires with a probe. Check the chart for the correct plug wire resistance.

2. If the plug wires are OK, remove the cap assembly and check of moisture, cracks, ships, or carbon tracks, or any other high voltage leaks or failures. Replace the cap if any defects are found. Make sure the timer wheel rotates when the engine is cranked. If everything is all right so far, go on to the distributor components test section following.

DISTRIBUTOR COMPONENTS TESTING

If the trouble has been narrowed down to the units within the distributor, the following tests can help pinpoint the defective component. An ohmmeter with both high and low ranges should be used. These tests are made with the cap assembly removed and the battery wire disconnected. If a tachometer is connected to the TACH terminal, disconnect it before making these tests.

1. Connect an ohmmeter between the TACH and BAT terminals in the distributor cap. The primary coil resistance should be less than 1Ω.

2. To check the coil secondary resistance, connect an ohmmeter between the rotor button and BAT terminal. Note the reading. Connect the ohmmeter between the rotor button and the TACH terminal. Note the reading. The resistance in both cases should be between 6,000 and 30,000Ω. Be sure to test between the rotor button and both the BAT and TACH terminals.

3. Replace the coil only if the readings in Step 1 and Step 2 are infinite.

NOTE: *These resistance checks will not disclose shorted could windings. This condition can only be detected with scope analysis or a suitably designed coil tester. If these instruments are unavailable, replace the coil with a known good coil as a final coil test.*

4. To test the pick-up coil, first disconnect the white and green module leads. Set the ohmmeter on the high scale and connect it between a ground and either the white or green lead. Any resistance measurement less than infinity requires replacement of the pick-up coil.

5. Pick-up coil continuity is tested by connecting the ohmmeter (on low range) between the white and green leads. Normal resistance is between 650 and 850Ω, or 500 and 1500Ω on 1977 and later cars. Move the vacuum advance arm while performing this test. This will detect any break in coil continuity. Such a condition can cause intermittent misfiring. Replace the pick-up if the reading is outside the specified limits.

6. If no defects have been found at this time, you still have a problem, then the module will have to be checked. If you do not have access to a module tester, the only possible alternative is a substitution test. If the module fails the substitution test, replace it.

HEI SYSTEM MAINTENANCE

Except for periodic checks of the spark plug wires, and an occasional check of the distributor cap for cracks (see Steps 1 and 2 under Engine Runs, But Runs Rough or Cuts Out for details), no maintenance is required on the HEI System. No periodic lubrication is necessary; engine oil lubricates the lower bushing, and an oil-filled reservoir lubricates the upper bushing.

COMPONENT REPLACEMENT

Integral Ignition Coil

1. Disconnect the negative battery cable. Disconnect the feed and module wire terminal connectors from the distributor cap.

2. Remove the ignition set retainer, if equipped.

3. Remove the 4 coil cover-to-distributor cap screws.

5. Using a blunt drift, press the coil wire spade terminals up out of the distributor cap.

6. Lift the coil up out of the distributor cap.

7. Remove and clean the coil spring, rubber seal washer and coil cavity of the distributor cap.

8. Coat the rubber seal with a dielectric lubricant furnished in the replacement ignition coil package.
9. Install the coil asssembly in the distributor cap, along with the coil spring.
10. Connect the coil wire spade terminals to their respective places in the distributor housing.
11. Install the coil cap and retaining screws. Install the ignition set retainer, if equipped.
12. Connect the distributor cap electrical connections. Connect the negative battery cable.

Distributor Cap

1. Disconnect the negative battery cable. Remove the feed and module wire terminal connectors from the distributor cap.
2. Remove the retainer and spark plug wires from the cap.
3. Depress and release the 4 distributor cap-to-housing retainers and lift off the cap assembly.
4. Remove the 4 coil cover screws and cover.
5. Using a finger or a blunt drift, push the spade terminals up out of the distributor cap.
6. Remove all 4 coil screws and lift the coil, coil spring and rubber seal washer out of the cap coil cavity.
7. Using a new distributor cap, reverse the above procedure to assemble being sure to clean and lubricate the rubber seal washer with dielectric lubricant.

Rotor

1. Disconnect the negative battery cable. Disconnect the feed and module wire connector from the distributor.
2. Depress and release the 4 distributor cap-to-housing retainers and lift off the cap assembly.
3. Remove the two rotor attaching screws and rotor.
4. Reverse the above procedure to install.

Vacuum Advance (1976-80)

1. Disconnect the negative battery cable. Remove the distributor cap and rotor as previously described.
2. Disconnect the vacuum hose from the vacuum advance unit.
3. Remove the two vacuum advance retaining screws, pull the advance unit outward, rotate and disengage the operating rod from its tang.
4. Reverse the above procedure to install.

Module

1. Disconnect the negative battery cable. Remove the distributor cap and rotor as previously described.
2. Disconnect the harness connector and pick-up coil spade connectors from the module. Be careful not to damage the wires when removing the connector.
3. Remove the two screws and module from the distributor housing.
4. Coat the bottom of the new module with dielectric lubricant supplied with the new module. Reverse the above procedure to install.

HEI SYSTEM TACHOMETER HOOKUP

Connect the positive tachometer lead to the coil terminal that is connected to the distributor. Connect the negative lead to a good ground. Please note, however, that some tachometers must connect to the coil terminal and the battery positive terminal. Check the tachometer manufacturer's instructions to make sure it is compatable with the HEI system..

WARNING: *Never ground the tach terminal as the HEI electronic module could be damaged.*

Diesel Engine

A conventional ignition system is not needed on the diesel engine, because it uses compression hear rather than a manufactured spark to ignite its air/fuel mixture. An electrically operated glow plug system is used on the diesel engine to pre-heat the combustion chambers for easy cold startup.

Ignition Timing

Models Without EST Distributor

NOTE: *Follow all the instructions on the Vehicle Emissions Control Information label located on the radiator support panel.*

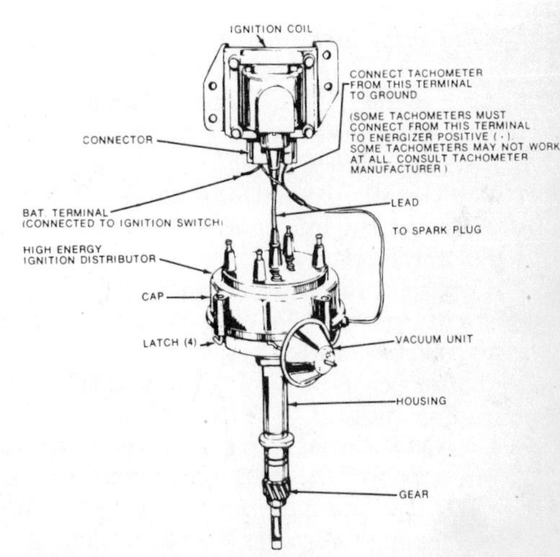

HEI system—This illustration is a representative schematic and does not depict actual component location

1. Bring the engine to a normal operating temperature. Stop the engine and connect a tachometer. Disconnect and plug the PCV hose at the vapor canister and the vacuum hose at the distributor vacuum advance unit (on models so equipped). Start the engine and check curb idle speed. Adjust as necessary.

2. Stop the engine, clean the timing marks and mark them with chalk to make them more visible.

3. Connect the pick-up lead of the timing light to the number one spark plug. Use a jumper lead or adapter between the wire and plug, better yet use a timing light with an inductive type pick-up.

WARNING: *Do not pierce the wire or attempt to insert a wire between the boot and the wire. Connect the timing light power leads according to the manufacturer's instructions.*

4. Start the engine and aim the timing light at the timing marks. If the marks align, stop the engine, reconnect the PCV and vacuum hoses, and remove the timing light.

5. If adjustment is necessary, loosen the distributor clamp and rotate the distributor clamp and rotate the distributor to align the marks. Tighten the clamp and recheck the timing.

NOTE: *Air conditioned models require removal of the compressor, bracket, and belt to reach the distributor clamp.*

CAUTION: *Do not disconnect air conditioner refrigerant lines. Move compressor and bracket to one side.*

6. Reset the curb idle speed if necessary, stop the engine, and remove the tachometer and timing light. Reconnect the PCV and vacuum hoses.

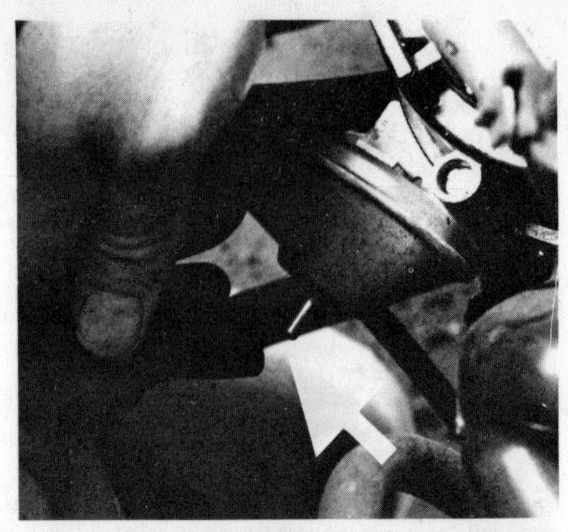

Disconnect and plug the distributor vacuum line

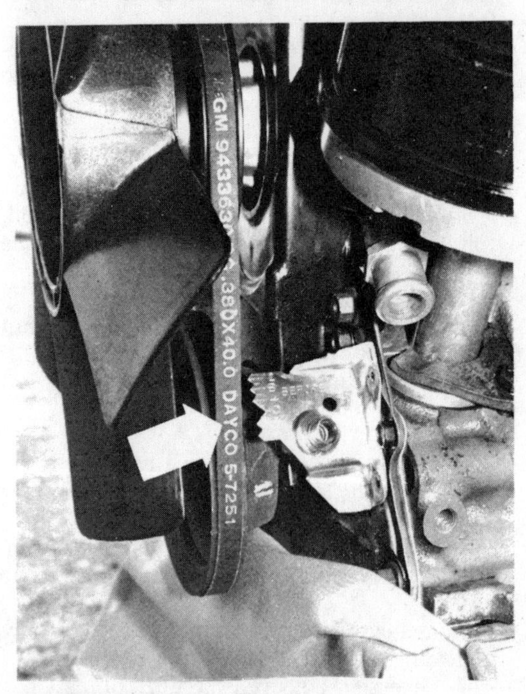

The arrow indicates the timing scale

Models with EST Distributor

NOTE: *Engines with Electronic Timing (EST) can be identified by the absence of a vacuum and a mechanical spark advance on the distributor. EST allows continuous spark timing adjustments to be made by the ECM (Electronic Control Module).*

1. Follow all instructions on the Vehicle Emissions Control information label located on the radiator support panel.

2. Connect the pick-up lead of the timing light to the number one spark plug. Use a jumper lead or adapter between the wire and plug, better yet use a timing light with an inductive type pick-up.

WARNING: *Do not pierce the wire or attempt to insert a wire between the boot and the wire. Connect the timing light power leads according to the manufacturer's instructions.*

3. Start the engine and make sure it is operating at normal operating temperature.

4. Increase idle and disconnect the four (4) terminal EST connectors at the distributor. This will cause the engine to operate in the bypass timing mode.

NOTE: *Steps 3-4 are important, because if the engine is at idle and not warm enough, when the EST terminal is disconnected, the oxygen sensor could cool off, putting the system into an open loop operation resulting in the engine shutting off.*

5. With the engine running, aim the timing light at the timing mark.

6. If a change is necessary, loosen the distributor hold-down clamp bolt at the base of the distributor. While observing the mark with the

The flash of the timing light will "stop" the timing marks which allows you to see if they align. Be careful that the timing light wires don't dangle into the fan or its belt

timing, slightly rotate the distributor until the correct timing is indicated. Tighten the hold-down bolt, and recheck the timing.

7. Turn off the engine and reconnect all wires.

NOTE: *Models with air conditioning require removal of the compressor since it is mounted directly above the distributor.*

CAUTION: *Do not disconnect the refrigerant lines. Move the compressor and bracket to one side.*

Valve Lash

Gasoline Engine

All gasoline engines are equipped with a hydraulic valve system which requires no adjustment or maintenance.

Diesel Engine

NOTE: *The rocker arm shaft bracket bolts and nuts should be tightened to 20 ft. lbs. before adjusting the valves.*

1. Unscrew the retaining bolts and remove the cylinder head cover.
2. Rotate the crankshaft until the No. 1 or No. 4 piston is t TDC of the compression stroke.
3. Start with the intake valve on the No. 1 cylinder and insert a feeler gauge of the correct thickness (intake: 0.010", exhaust: 0.014") into the gap between the valve stem cap and the rocker arm. If adjustment is required, loosen the lock nut on top of the rocker arm and turn the adjusting screw clockwise to decrease the gap and counterclockwise to increase it. When the proper clearance is reached, tighten the lock nut and then recheck the gap. Adjust the remaining three valves in this step (see illustration) in the same manner.
4. Rotate the crankshaft one complete revolution and then adjust the remaining valves accordingly.

Carburetor

IDLE SPEED ADJUSTMENT

1976-78

Two idle speeds are controlled by a solenoid on models without both automatic transmission and air conditioning. One is normal curb idle speed (solenoid energized). The other is base idle speed (solenoid de-energized), which is 200 rpm lower than curb idle speed and prevents dieseling when the ignition is turned off. On cars with air conditioning the solenoid is energized when the air conditioning is on to maintain curb idle speed.

1. With the engine at normal operating temperature, air cleaner on, choke open, and the air conditioner off, attach a tachometer to the engine following the manufacturer's instructions. Apply the parking brake, block the rear wheels, disconnect and plug the PCV hose at the vapor canister and the vacuum advance hose at the distributor.
2. For cars without automatic transmission and air conditioning, turn the idle solenoid in or out to obtain the curb idle speed stated in the tune-up specification chart, then disconnect the wire from the solenoid.
3. With the automatic transmission in Drive or the manual transmission in Neutral, set the base idle speed to 200 rpm lower than the curb idle speed by turning the ⅛" hex screw located in the end of the solenoid. Reconnect the wire to the solenoid.
4. Cars with both automatic transmission and air conditioning must have a green wire with double white stripe connected to the idle solenoid, NOT a brown wire. Correct this if necessary.
5. With the air conditioning off and the automatic transmission in Drive turn the ⅛" hex screw in the end of the solenoid until fully bottomed.
6. Turn the entire solenoid assembly to obtain 950 rpm.

The adjustment screw is at the center of the solenoid

7. Adjust the curb idle speed by turning the hex screw out to obtain the correct rpm. (See tune-up specifications chart.).

8. Check the ignition timing and adjust if necessary. Readjust the solenoid assembly and curb idle speed if necessary.

9. Stop the engine, remove the tachometer, and connect the PCV and vacuum hoses.

1979-82

Refer to the Vehicle Emission Control Information sticker on the vehicle for the latest specification information and idle speed adjustment procedure.

1983 and Later

On these models, the carburetor mixture and idle speed are adjusted by the Computer Command Control (CCC) System. However, it is possible to adjust the basic idle speed as follows:

1. Set the parking brake and block the drive wheels.
2. Verify ignition timing.
3. Disconnect the EGR vacuum source at the carburetor and cap the port.
4. Disconnect and plug the vacuum hoses for the canister purge and purge control at the canister.
5. Attach a tachometer to the engine following the manufacturer's instructions
6. With the engine running, adjust the idle speed screw to the rpm specified on the vehicle emission control information label.
7. Unplug and reconnect the vacuum hoses.

NOTE: *See Chapter Four for an explanation of the (CCC) System.*

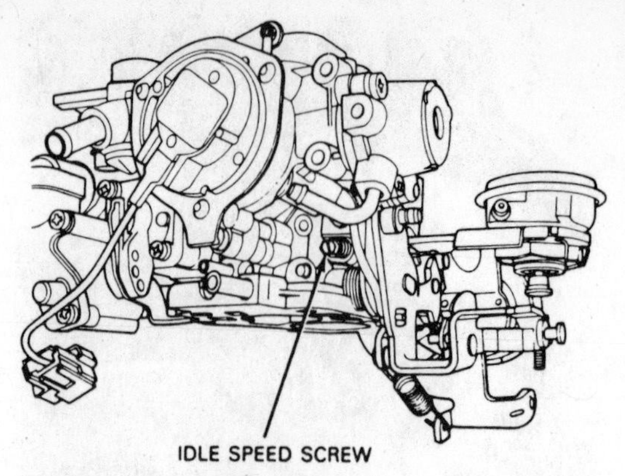

Idle adjustment screw, 1983–87

IDLE MIXTURE ADJUSTMENT

Carburetor idle mixture is preset at the factory and a plastic limiter cap is mounted on the idle mixture screw. The cap limits the mixture screw to approximately one turn leaner (clockwise) without breaking the cap. Idle mixture should be adjusted at major carburetor overhaul. Before suspecting the carburetor as the cause of poor performance or rough idle, check the ignition system thoroughly, including the distributor, timing, spark plugs and wires. Also be sure to check the air cleaner, evaporative emission system, PCV system, EGR valve and engine compression. Check the intake manifold, vacuum hoses and other connections for leaks and cracks.

NOTE: *On 1978-80 models, a change was made on some General Motors carburetors to limit the range of idle mixture adjustment on the rich side. In other words, backing out the*

The arrow points to the idle mixture screw

Cut the tab and remove the limiter cap

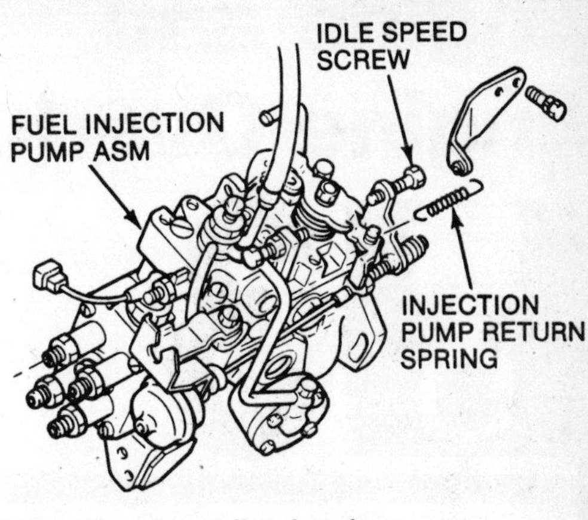

Base idle screw—diesel engine

adjustment screw will not make an appreciable difference. The new procedure requires the use of artificial enrichment through the addition of propane. Since it is not feasible to buy a tank of propane for one or two carburetor adjustments, the procedure for cars from 1978-80 are not covered here. On 1981 and later models, the idle mixture is adjusted by the CCC system and requires no manual adjustment.

1976-77

1. With the engine at normal operating temperature, air cleaner on, choke open, and air conditioning off, attach a tachometer to the engine. Apply parking brake, block the rear wheels, and disconnect and plug the PCV hose at vapor canister and vacuum advance hose at the distributor.
2. Start the engine and check ignition timing. Adjust the timing as necessary. Replace vacuum advance hose.
3. Place automatic transmission in Drive or manual transmission in Neutral.

NOTE: *If the mixture screw is removed from the carburetor, gently seat it, then back it out 3 turns. Continue with step 4.*

4. Remove the air cleaner, cut the tab off the limiter cap and remove the cap from the screw. Replace the air cleaner. Obtain the maximum idle speed by turning the mixture screw clockwise (leaner) or counterclockwise (richer).
5. Turn the idle speed solenoid in or out to obtain the higher idle speed stated on the underhood tune-up specifications sticker.
6. While turning the idle mixture screw clockwise (leaner), watch the tachometer to obtain the lower idle speed stated on the underhood specifications sticker.
7. Stop engine, remove the tachometer, and replace the PCV and vacuum advance hoses.

Diesel Engine Idle Speed Adjustment

1. Set the parking brake and block the wheels.
2. Place the transmission in Neutral. Connect a tachometer as per the manufacturer's instructions.
3. Start the engine and allow it to reach normal operating temperature.
4. Loosen the lock nut on the idle speed adjusting screw and turn the screw to obtain the correct idle speed (see underhood specifications sticker).
5. Tighten the lock nut, turn the engine off and disconnect the tachometer.

Engine and Engine Overhaul

3

ENGINE ELECTRICAL

HEI Distributor

All Chevette and Pontiac 1000 models are equipped with High Energy Ignition (HEI). This is a pulse triggered, transistor controlled, inductive discharge ignition system that uses no breaker points. The HEI distributor contains a pick-up assembly and an electronic module which perform the function normally done by breaker points. The unit automatically controls the dwell period, stretching it with the increased speed of the engine. No dwell adjustment is necessary. On models through 1980, centrifugal and vacuum advance mechanisms are basically the same as those in breaker point distributors. 1981 and later models are equipped with EST (Electronic Spark Timing) distributors which have no mechanical or vacuum advance mechanism. The capacitor in the distributor only serves to reduce radio noise. The ignition coil is mounted externally of the distributor.

Distributor mounting is at the front of the engine on the left side.

REMOVAL AND INSTALLATION

1. If the car is air conditioned: disconnect the electrical lead at the air conditioning compressor, remove the compressor mounting through bolt and two adjusting bolts. Remove the two bolts and remove the upper compressor mounting bracket. Raise the car and remove the two bolts securing the lower compressor mounting bracket. Pull the bracket outward for clearance and lower the car.
2. Remove the air cleaner.
3. Remove the distributor cap and place it out of the way.
4. Remove the ignition coil cover by prying on the flat located on the front edge of the cover.
5. Remove the coil mounting bracket bolts.
6. Disconnect the electrical connector with red and brown wires that go from the coil to the distributor.
7. Remove the fuel pump, gasket, and push rod, making a note of which direction the push rod is installed. It's important that the push rod be installed in exactly the same direction as removed.
8. Scribe a mark on the engine in line with the rotor. Note the approximate position of the distributor housing in relation to the engine.
9. Remove the distributor hold down bolt and clamp.
10. Remove the distributor.
11. Install the distributor in reverse order of removal, making sure that the distributor is fully seated.

INSTALLATION ENGINE DISTURBED

1. Remove the No. 1 spark plug and place a finger over the spark plug hole. Turn the engine until compression is felt in the No. 1 cylinder.
2. Install the distributor with the distributor body scribe mark aligned with the mark on the engine and with the rotor pointing toward the distributor cap No. 1 spark plug tower.
3. Install the holddown clamp and nut, but do not tighten them securely.
4. Install the distributor cap by aligning the tab in the cap with the notch in the housing and securing the four latches.
5. Connect the wiring harness connector to the terminals on the side of the cap. The connector will attach one way only. Reconnect the vacuum advance line.
6. Check and adjust the ignition timing. Securely tighten the distributor holddown clamp.

Alternator

A Delcotron 10-S1 series alternator is used. This unit also contains a solid state, integrated circuit voltage regulator. The alternator is non-

HEI connections are difficult to reach on the Chevette/1000. The distributor is fairly accessible (except on models with A/C) but the ignition coil is hidden under the intake manifold

The arrow points to the distributor hold-down bolt

adjustable and requires no periodic maintenance.

The diesel Chevette is fitted with an Hitachi alternator, which is equipped with an IC regulator and drives a vacuum pump mounted at its rear.

ALTERNATOR PRECAUTIONS

The following are a few precautions to observe in servicing the Delcotron (AC) generator and the regulator.

1. When installing a battery, be certain that the ground polarity of the battery and the ground polarity of the generator and regulator are the same.
2. When connecting a booster battery, be sure to connect the correct battery terminals together.
3. When hooking up a charger, connect the correct leads to the battery terminals.
4. Never operate the car on an open circuit. Be sure all battery, alternator and generator connections are tight.
5. Do not short across or ground any of the terminals on the generator or regulator.
6. Never polarize an AC system.
7. Do not use test lamps of more than 12 volts for checking diode continuity.
8. Avoid long soldering times when replacing diodes or transistors, as prolonged heat will damage them. Always use a heat sink.
9. Always disconnect the battery ground terminal when servicing any AC system. This will prevent accidentally reversing polarity.
10. Always disconnect the battery and AC generator if electric welding equipment is being used on the car.
11. Never jump a battery for starting purposes with more than 12 volts.

REMOVAL AND INSTALLATION

1. Disconnect the negative battery cable.
2. Disconnect the alternator wiring. On the Chevette diesel, remove the fan shroud and fresh air duct, then disconnect the oil and vacuum lines at the vacuum pump.
3. Remove the brace bolt and the drive belt.
4. Support the alternator, remove the mounting bolt, and remove the alternator.

   NOTE: *On the diesel, the mount bolts are removed from below the car.*
5. Installation is the reverse of removal. Adjust drive belt deflection to ½″ under moderate thumb pressure.

Regulator

The regulator is a micro circuit unit built in to the alternator. The unit requires no voltage adjustment.

Starter

Engine cranking is accomplished by a solenoid actuated starter motor powered by the ve-

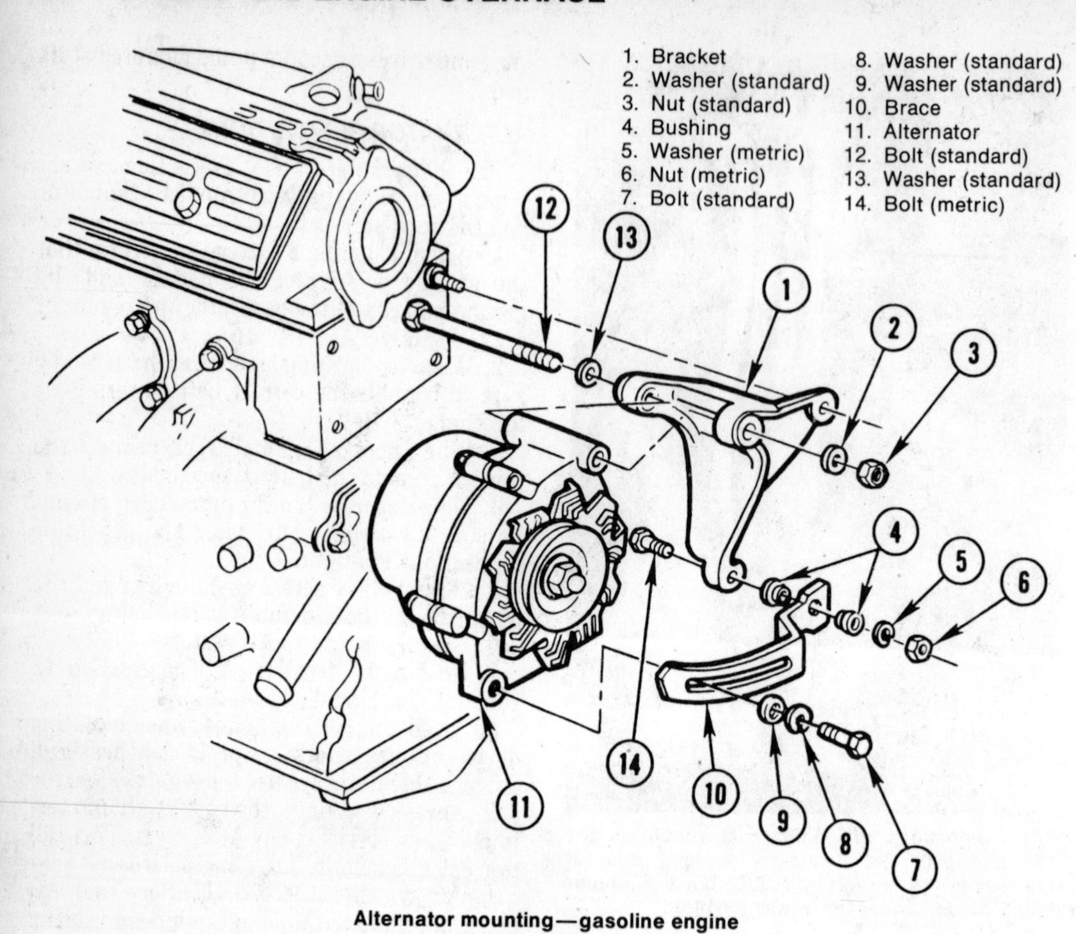

Alternator mounting—gasoline engine

Troubleshooting Basic Charging System Problems

Problem	Cause	Solution
Noisy alternator	• Loose mountings • Loose drive pulley • Worn bearings • Brush noise • Internal circuits shorted (High pitched whine)	• Tighten mounting bolts • Tighten pulley • Replace alternator • Replace alternator • Replace alternator
Squeal when starting engine or accelerating	• Glazed or loose belt	• Replace or adjust belt
Indicator light remains on or ammeter indicates discharge (engine running)	• Broken fan belt • Broken or disconnected wires • Internal alternator problems • Defective voltage regulator	• Install belt • Repair or connect wiring • Replace alternator • Replace voltage regulator
Car light bulbs continually burn out—battery needs water continually	• Alternator/regulator overcharging	• Replace voltage regulator/alternator
Car lights flare on acceleration	• Battery low • Internal alternator/regulator problems	• Charge or replace battery • Replace alternator/regulator
Low voltage output (alternator light flickers continually or ammeter needle wanders)	• Loose or worn belt • Dirty or corroded connections • Internal alternator/regulator problems	• Replace or adjust belt • Clean or replace connections • Replace alternator or regulator

Alternator and Regulator Specifications

	Alternator		Regulator		
Year	Manufacturer	Output (amps)	Manufacturer	Type	Volts @ 85°
1976–80	Delco Remy	32	Delco Remy	Integral	13.8–14.8
1981–87	Delco Remy	42 ②	Delco Remy	Integral	—
1981–86	Hitachi	55 ①	Hitachi	Integral	—

① 1983–86—50
② Optional alternators: 66, 78 amps

hicle battery. The motor on the gasoline engine is a Delco-Remy unit similar to previous Chevrolet starters. No periodic lubrication of the motor or solenoid is necessary.

The Chevette diesel is equipped with an Hitachi reduction gear starter motor which is solenoid activated.

REMOVAL AND INSTALLATION

Gasoline Engine

1976-79 CARS WITHOUT POWER BRAKES

1. Disconnect the negative battery cable and remove the air cleaner.
2. Disconnect the electrical connector from the oil pressure sending unit and remove the sending unit.

NOTE: *The oil pressure sending unit has a harness lock. To disconnect the electrical connector, lift the tab on the collar of the lock and remove the lock assembly.*

3. Disconnect the wires from the starter solenoid.
4. Remove the brace screw from the bottom of the starter housing.
5. Remove the two starter-to-flywheel housing mounting screws.
6. Hold the starter with both hands and tip it past the engine mount bracket, then upward between the intake manifold and wheel arch.
7. Installation is the reverse of removal.

1980-87 CARS WITHOUT POWER BRAKES

1. Disconnect the battery ground cable.
2. Remove the air cleaner.
3. Disconnect the gas line at the carburetor and move to one side.
4. Disconnect the vacuum hoses at the carburetor.
5. Remove the splash shield from the distributor coil and move to one side.
6. Using a 6″ and 12″ extension with a universal socket, remove the upper starter bolt.
7. Remove the lower starting bolt and move the starter as necessary to disconnect the starter wiring.

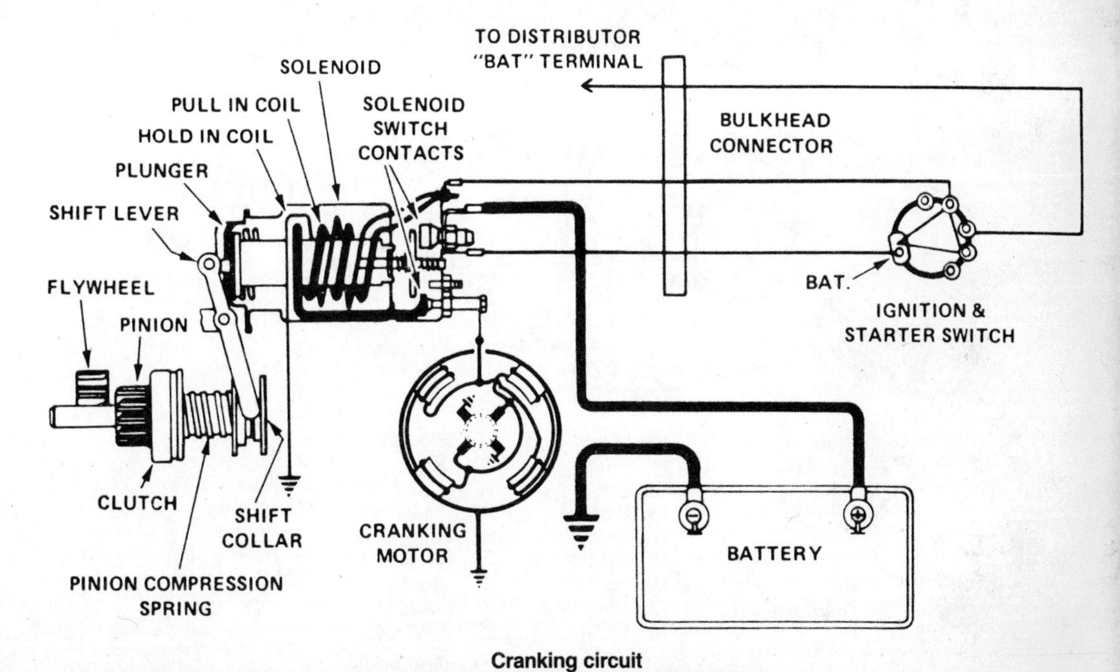

Cranking circuit

8. Remove the master cylinder mounting nuts to gain access for removing the starter.
9. Installation is the reverse of removal.

1976-79 CARS WITH POWER BRAKES WITHOUT AIR CONDITIONING

1. Disconnect the battery negative cable and remove the air cleaner.
2. Remove the distributor cap and place it aside.
3. Remove the fuel line from the fuel pump to the carburetor.
4. Disconnect the electrical connector from the ignition coil. Remove the three coil bracket retaining screws and remove the coil with bracket.

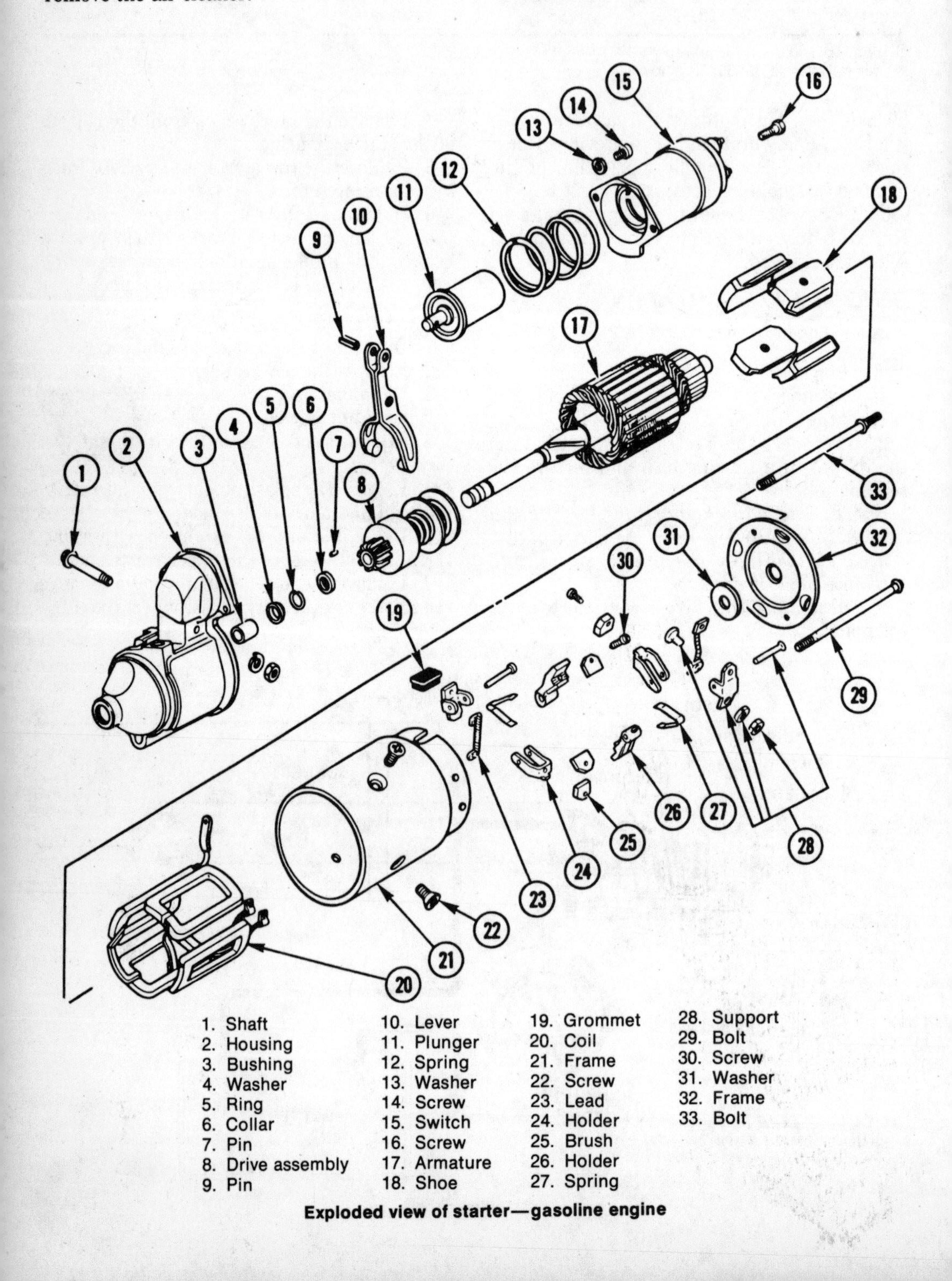

Exploded view of starter—gasoline engine

5. Disconnect the vacuum hose to the distributor vacuum advance unit.
6. Disconnect the electrical connector from the oil pressure sending unit and remove the sending unit. See the preceding Note concerning the oil pressure sender harness lock.
7. Disconnect the wires from the starter solenoid.
8. Remove the brace screw from the bottom of the starter housing.
9. Remove the two starter-to-flywheel housing mounting screws.
10. Hold the starter with both hands and remove it by sliding it toward the front of the car.
11. Installation is the reverse of removal.

1976-79 CARS WITH POWER BRAKES AND AIR CONDITIONING

1. Disconnect the negative battery cable and remove the air cleaner.
2. Remove the upper starter-to-flywheel housing mounting screw.
3. Remove the two steering column lever cover screws.
4. Remove the mast jacket lower bracket screw.
5. Remove the upper steering column mounting bracket.
6. Disconnect the four electrical connectors from the steering column.
7. Raise the car.

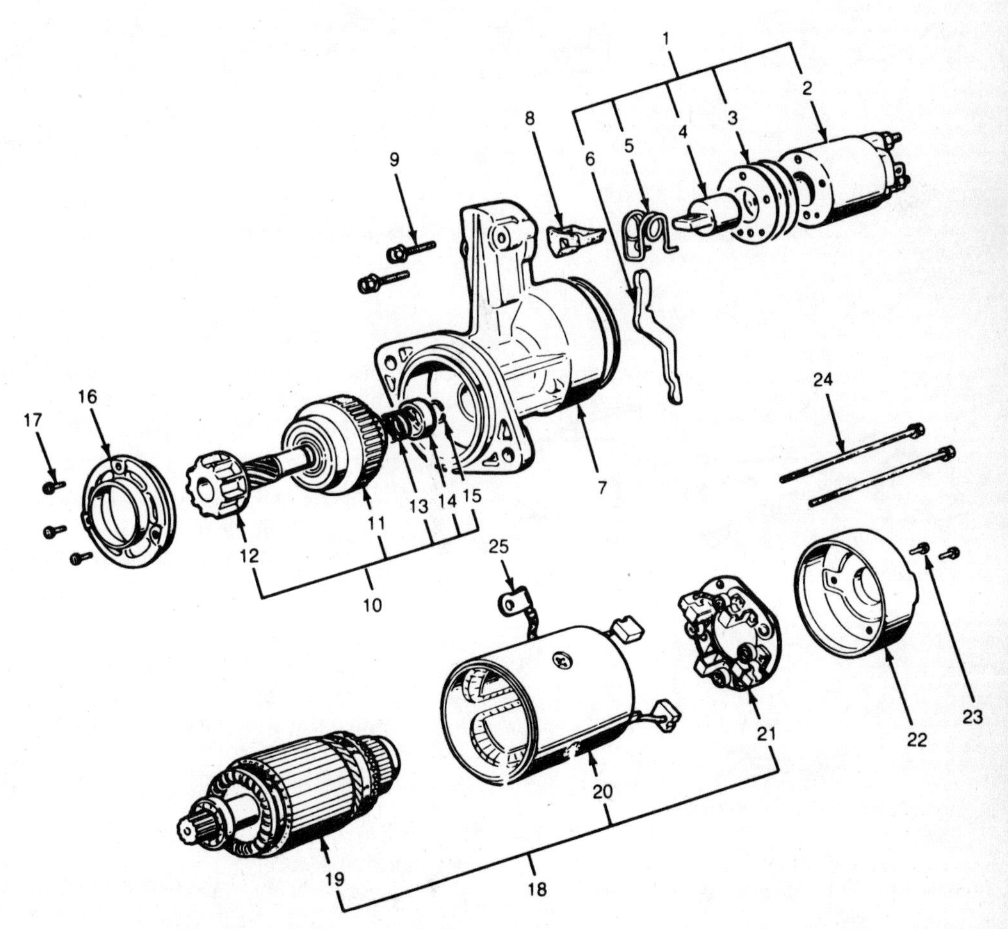

1. Solenoid assembly
2. Solenoid
3. Adjusting plate
4. Plunger
5. Torsion spring
6. Shift lever
7. Gear case
8. Dust cover
9. Bolt
10. Pinion assembly
11. Clutch
12. Pinion shaft
13. Return spring
14. Pinion stop retainer
15. Pinion stop retainer clip
16. Bearing retainer
17. Screw
18. Motor assembly
19. Armature
20. Frame
21. Brush holder
22. Rear cover
23. Screw
24. Through bolt
25. Lead wire

Exploded view of starter—diesel engine

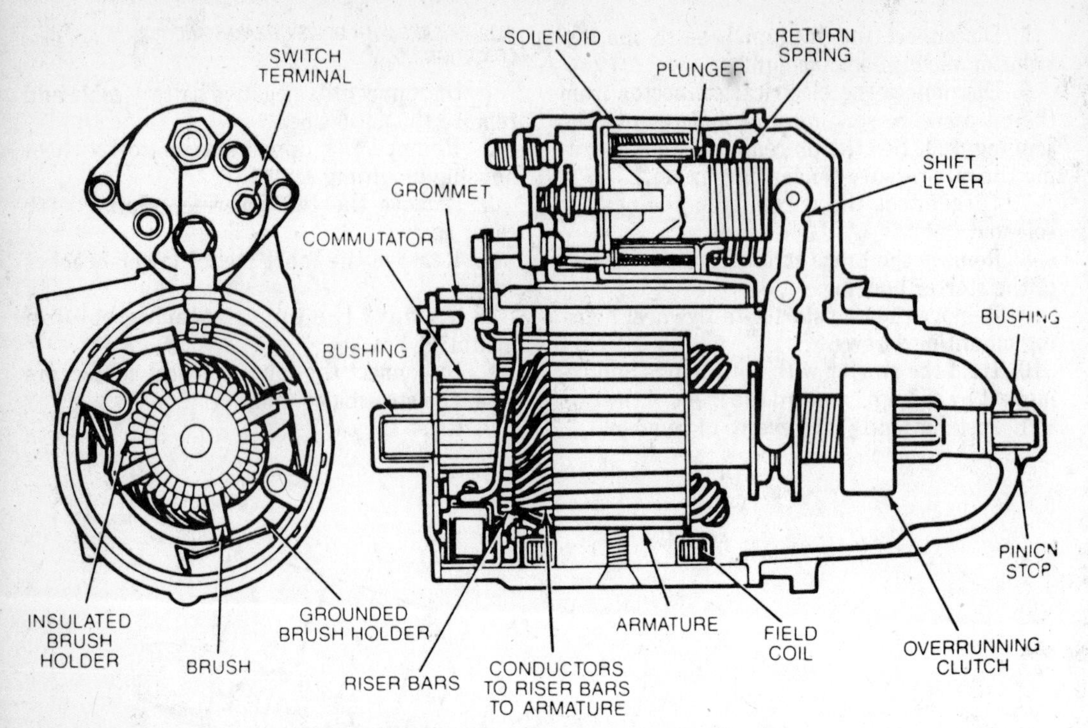

Cross section view of the starter motor-gasoline engine

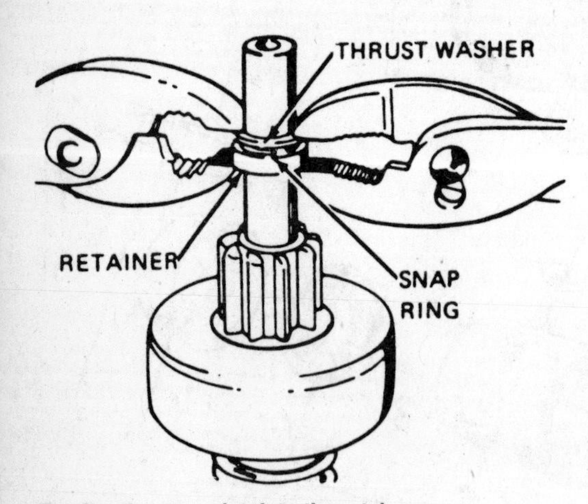

Forcing the snap-ring into the retainer

8. Disconnect the flexible coupling (rag joint) and push it aside.
9. Disconnect the wires from the starter solenoid.
10. Remove the brace screw from the bottom of the starter housing.
11. Remove the lower starter-to-flywheel housing mounting screw.
12. To gain clearance, raise the engine ½″ with a jack placed under the left side of the engine.
13. Remove the starter by lowering it through the opening at the bottom of the engine.
14. Installation is the reverse of removal.

1980-87 CARS WITH POWER BRAKES

1. Disconnect the battery ground cable.
2. Remove the air cleaner.
3. Disconnect the gas line at the carburetor and move it to one side.
4. Remove the splash shield from the distributor coil and move to one side.
5. Using a 6″ and 12″ extension with a universal socket, remove the upper starter bolt.
6. Remove the steering column cover screws and remove the cover.
7. Remove the steering column upper nuts and toe pan screw.
8. Raise the front of the car and make sure it is supported securely.
9. Remove the steering shaft from the steering coupling. Lower the vehicle and move the steering column from inside of the car to gain access to the starter.
10. Installation is the reverse of removal.

Diesel Engine

1. Disconnect the negative battery cable.
2. Disconnect the starter wiring after labeling. The starter is located at the right rear of the engine.

3. Remove the upper mounting nut and the lower mounting bolt, then remove the starter.
4. Installation is the reverse of removal.

Starter Drive

REMOVAL AND INSTALLATION

Gasoline Engine

1. Disconnect the field coil connector(s) from the starter solenoid terminal and remove the starter through-bolts.
2. Remove the commutator end frame, field frame assembly, and the armature from the drive housing.
3. Remove the starter drive by sliding the two-piece thrust collar off the armature shaft. Install a ½" pipe coupling or other suitable cylinder onto the shaft to butt against the edge of the retainer. Using a hammer, tap the coupling to force the retainer toward the armature end of the snapring.
4. Use pliers to remove the snapring from the groove in the shaft. If the snapring becomes distorted, use a new one upon assembly. Remove the retainer and starter drive from the armature.

Inspect all parts, replacing where necessary. Do not use grease dissolving solvent when cleaning starter parts, the drive mechanism and internal electrical insulation will be damaged.

To install:

5. Apply silicone lubricant to the drive end of the armature and slide the drive assembly onto the armature with the pinion outward. Install the retainer on the armature with its cupped surface facing away from the pinion.
6. Install the snapring on the shaft by standing the armature on a wood surface (commutator end down), placing the snapring on the end of the shaft held in position with a wood block, and tapping the wood block with a hammer. Slide the snapring into its groove on the shaft. Place the thrust collar on the shaft with its shoulder against the snapring.
7. With the armature on a flat surface, place the retainer and thrust collar next to the snapring. Using pliers on both sides of the shaft at the same time, grip the retainer and thrust collar and squeeze until the snapring is forced into the retainer.
8. Apply silicone lubricant to the drive housing bushing. With the thrust collar in place against the snapring and retainer, slide the armature and starter drive assembly into the drive housing. Engage the solenoid shift lever with the drive assembly.
9. Place the field frame over the armature and apply sealing compound between the frame and solenoid case. Using care to avoid damage to the brushes, position the field frame against the drive housing.

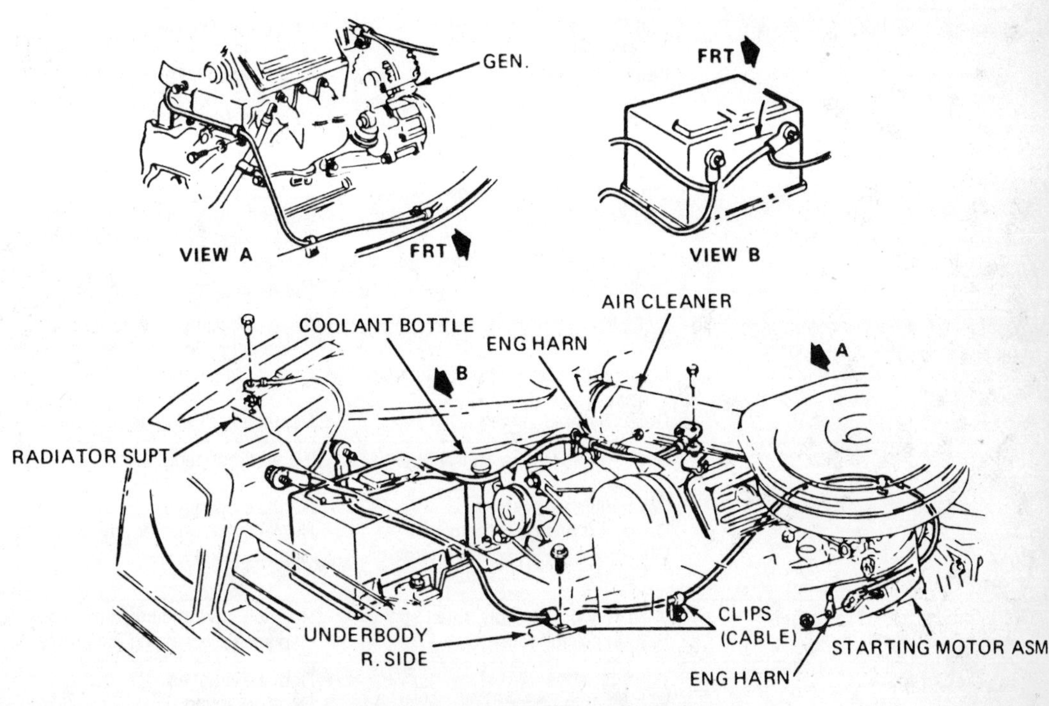

Battery hold down and cable routing

10. Use silicone lubricant to lubricate the commutator end frame bushing. Install the leather washer onto the armature shaft and slide the commutator end frame onto the armature shaft.

11. Install the through-bolts and reconnect the field coil connector(s) to the starter solenoid terminal.

Battery

REMOVAL AND INSTALLATION

To remove the battery simply remove the hold down bolts and loosen and remove the cable ends at the battery.

Make sure the carrier is in sound condition and is capable of holding the battery firmly and keeping it level. To prevent the battery from shaking in its carrier, the holddown bolts should be relatively tight, not tight enough, however, to place a sever strain on the battery case or cover.

Be sure to replace the battery terminals on the proper posts.

ENGINE MECHANICAL

Design

All gasoline engine models are powered by a 1.4 or 1.6 liter, in line four cylinder, overhead camshaft engine. These engines are either 85 or 98 cu. in., respectively.

The cylinder block is made of cast iron. Each cylinder has individual intake and exhaust ports. The valve lifters are mounted in the head, next to their respective valves and are operated by lobes on the camshaft.

Troubleshooting Basic Starting System Problems

Problem	Cause	Solution
Starter motor rotates engine slowly	• Battery charge low or battery defective	• Charge or replace battery
	• Defective circuit between battery and starter motor	• Clean and tighten, or replace cables
	• Low load current	• Bench-test starter motor. Inspect for worn brushes and weak brush springs.
	• High load current	• Bench-test starter motor. Check engine for friction, drag or coolant in cylinders. Check ring gear-to-pinion gear clearance.
Starter motor will not rotate engine	• Battery charge low or battery defective	• Charge or replace battery
	• Faulty solenoid	• Check solenoid ground. Repair or replace as necessary.
	• Damage drive pinion gear or ring gear	• Replace damaged gear(s)
	• Starter motor engagement weak	• Bench-test starter motor
	• Starter motor rotates slowly with high load current	• Inspect drive yoke pull-down and point gap, check for worn end bushings, check ring gear clearance
	• Engine seized	• Repair engine
Starter motor drive will not engage (solenoid known to be good)	• Defective contact point assembly	• Repair or replace contact point assembly
	• Inadequate contact point assembly ground	• Repair connection at ground screw
	• Defective hold-in coil	• Replace field winding assembly
Starter motor drive will not disengage	• Starter motor loose on flywheel housing	• Tighten mounting bolts
	• Worn drive end busing	• Replace bushing
	• Damaged ring gear teeth	• Replace ring gear or driveplate
	• Drive yoke return spring broken or missing	• Replace spring
Starter motor drive disengages prematurely	• Weak drive assembly thrust spring	• Replace drive mechanism
	• Hold-in coil defective	• Replace field winding assembly
Low load current	• Worn brushes	• Replace brushes
	• Weak brush springs	• Replace springs

The camshaft is belt driven and housed on the top of the cylinder head. It is supported by five bearings in a cam carrier. Bearing inserts are not used.

The crankshaft is also supported by five main bearings. It is lubricated through oil holed which lead from the main oil supply on the left side of the block. Number five bearing is the end thrust bearing.

The pistons are made of a cast aluminum alloy and incorporate the use of two compression rings and one oil control ring.

The crankshaft also drives, by way of a gear, the distributor and the oil pump. A cam on the shaft of the distributor drives the fuel pump.

Beginning in 1981, the Chevette offers an optional diesel engine. This is a 1.8 liter inline 4-cylinder overhead camshaft engine on which the belt-driven camshaft rides in five bearings. The valves are operated by direct acting rocker arms, while adjustment is manually obtained through lash adjusters on the opposite end of each rocker arm. The cast iron, cross-flow cylinder head incorporates a precombustion chamber which adds to smooth performance and easy startup characteristics.

The injection pump and the oil pump are also driven off of a cog belt by means of the crankshaft. The crankshaft is supported in the cast iron cylinder block by five main bearings with the thrust being taken on the center bearing.

Understanding the Engine

The basic piston engine is a metal block containing a series of chambers. The upper engine block is usually an iron or aluminum alloy casting, consisting of outer walls, which form hollow jackets around the cylinder walls. The lower block provides a number of rigid mounting points for the bearings which hold the crankshaft in place, and is known as the crankcase. The hollow jackets of the upper block add to the rigidity of the engine and contain the liquid coolant which carries the heat away from the cylinders and other engine parts. The block of an air cooled engine consists of a crankcase which provides for the rigid mounting of the crankshaft and for studs which hold the cylinders in place. In a water cooled engine, only the cylinder head is bolted to the top of the block. The water pump is mounted directly to the block.

The crankshaft is a long, iron or steel shaft mounted rigidly in the bottom of the crankcase, at a number of points (usually 4-7). The crankshaft is free to turn and contains a number of counterweighted crankpins (one for each cylinder) that are offset several inches from the center of the crankshaft and turn in a circle as the crankshaft turns. The crankpins are centered under each cylinder. Pistons with circular rings to seal the small space between the pistons and wall of the cylinders are connected to the crankpins by steel connecting rods. The rods connect the pistons at their upper ends with the crankpins at their lower ends.

When the crankshaft spins, the pistons move up and down in the cylinders, varying the volume of each cylinder, depending on the position of the piston. Two openings in each cylinder head (above the cylinders) allow the intake of the air/fuel mixture and the exhaust of burned gases. The volume of the combustion chamber must be variable for the engine to compress the fuel charge before combustion, to make use of the expansion of the burning gasses and to exhaust the burned gasses and take in a fresh fuel mixture. As the pistons are forced downward by the expansion of burning fuel, the connection rods convert the reciprocating (up and down) motion of the pistons into rotary (turning) motion of the crankshaft. A round flywheel at the rear of the crankshaft provides a large, stable mass to smooth out the rotation.

The cylinder heads form tight covers for the tops of the cylinders and contain machined chambers into which the fuel mixture is forced as it is compressed by the pistons reaching the upper limit of their travel. Each combustion chamber contains one intake valve, one exhaust valve and one spark plug per cylinder. The spark plugs are screwed into holes in the cylinder head so that the tips protrude into the combustion chambers. The valve in each opening in the cylinder head is opened and closed by the action of the camshaft. The camshaft is driven by the crankshaft through a chain or belt at ½ crankshaft speed (the camshaft gear is twice the size of the crankshaft gear). The valves are operated either through rocker arms and pushrods (overhead valve engine) or directly by the camshaft (overhead cam engine).

Lubrication oil is stored in a pan at the bottom of the engine and is forced fed to all parts of the engine by a gear type pump, driven from the crankshaft. The oil lubricates the entire engine and also seals the piston rings, giving good compression.

Engine Overhaul

Most engine overhaul procedures are fairly standard. In addition to specific parts replacement procedures and complete specifications for your individual engine, this chapter also is a guide to accepted rebuilding procedures. Examples of standard rebuilding practice are shown and should be used along with specific details concerning your particular engine.

Competent and accurate machine shop services will ensure maximum performance, reliability and engine life. Procedures marked with the symbol shown above should be performed by a competent machine shop, and are provided so that you will be familiar with the procedures necessary to a successful overhaul.

In most instances it is more profitable for the do-it-yourself mechanic to remove, clean and inspect the component, buy the necessary parts and deliver these to a shop for actual machine work.

On the other hand, much of the rebuilding work (crankshaft, block, bearings, pistons, rods, and other components) is well within the scope of the do-it-yourself mechanic.

TOOLS

The tools required for an engine overhaul or parts replacement will depend on the depth of your involvement. With a few exceptions, they will be tools found in a mechanic's tool kit (see Chapter 1). More in-depth work will require any or all of the following:

- a dial indicator (reading in thousandths) mounted on a universal base.
- micrometers and telescope gauges.
- jaw and screw-type pullers
- scraper
- valve spring compressor
- ring groove cleaner
- piston ring expander and compressor
- ridge reamer
- cylinder hone or glaze breaker
- Plastigage®
- engine stand

Use of most of these tools is illustrated in this chapter. Many can be rented for a one-time use from a local parts jobber or tool supply house specializing in automotive work.

Occasionally, the use of special tools is called for. See the information on Special Tools and the Safety Notice in the front of this book before substituting another tool.

INSPECTION TECHNIQUES

Procedures and specifications are given in this chapter for inspecting, cleaning and assessing the wear limits of most major components. Other procedures such as Magnaflux and Zyglo can be used to locate material flaws and stress cracks. Magnaflux is a magnetic process applicable only to ferrous materials. The Zyglo process coats the material with a flourescent dye penetrant and can be used on any material. Check for suspected surface cracks can be more readily made using spot check dye. The dye is sprayed onto the suspected area, wiped off and the area sprayed with a developer. Cracks will show up brightly.

OVERHAUL TIPS

Aluminum has become extremely popular for use is engines, due to its low weight. Observe the following precautions when handling aluminum parts:

Never hot tank aluminum parts (the caustic hot-tank solution will eat the aluminum).

Remove all aluminum parts (identification tag, etc.) from engine parts prior to hot-tanking.

Always coat threads lightly with engine oil or antiseize compounds before installation, to prevent seizure.

Never overtorque bolts or spark plugs, especially in aluminum threads.

Stripped threads in any component can be repaired using any of several commercial repair kits (Heli-Coil®, Microdot®, Keenserts®, etc.).

When assembling the engine, any parts that will be in frictional contact must be prelubed to provide lubrication at initial start-up. Any product specifically formulated for this purpose can be used, but the engine oil is not recommended as a pre-lube.

When semi-permanent (locked, but removable) installation bolts or nuts is desired, threads should be cleaned and coated with Loctite or other similar, commercial non-hardening sealant.

REPAIRING DAMAGED THREADS

Several methods of repairing damaged threads are available. Heli-Coil®, Keenserts®, and Microdot® are among the most widely used. All involve basically the same principle - drilling out stripped threads, tapping the hole and installing a prewound insert - making welding, plugging and oversize fasteners unnecessary.

Two types of thread repair inserts are usually supplied: a standard type for most Inch Coarse, Inch Fine, Metric Course and Metric Fine thread sizes and a spark plug type to fit most spark plug port sizes. Consult the individual manufacturer's catalog to determine exact applications. Typical thread repair kits will contain a selection of prewound threaded inserts, a tap (corresponding to the outside diameter threads of the insert) and an installation tool. Spark plug inserts usually differ because they

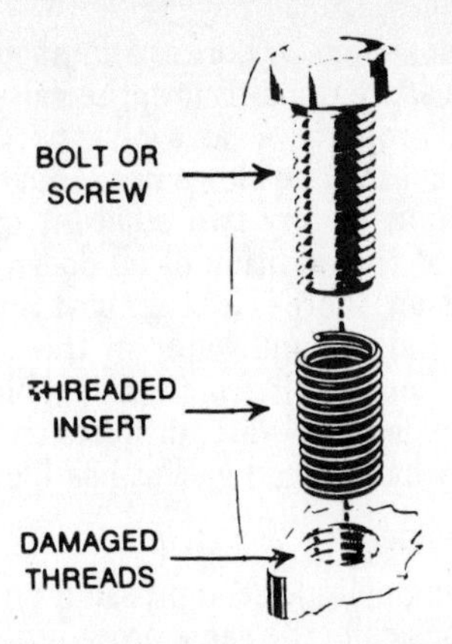

Damaged bolt holes can be repaired with thread repair inserts

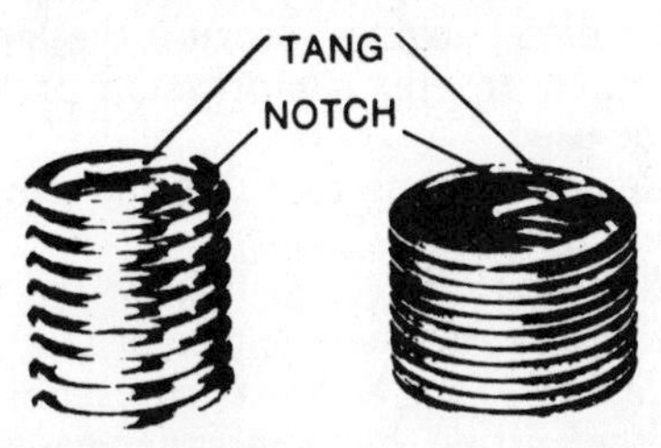

Standard thread repair insert (left) and spark plug thread insert (right)

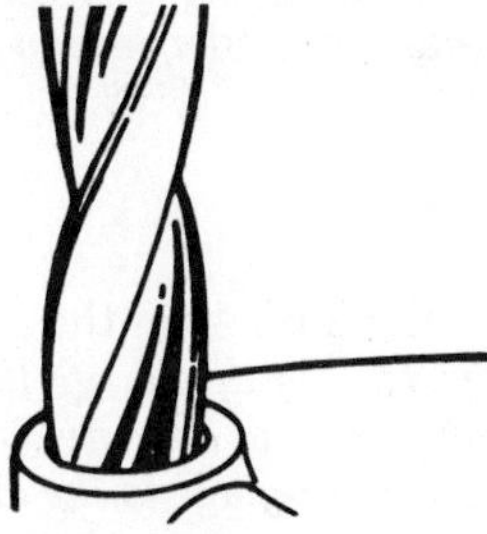

Drill out the damaged threads with specified drill. Drill completely through the hole or to the bottom of a blind hole.

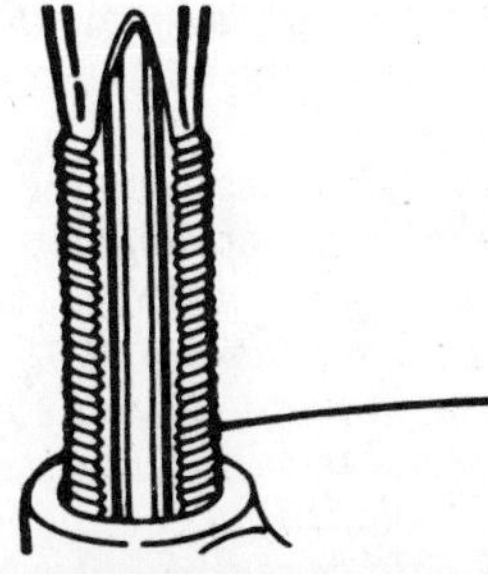

With the tap supplied, tap the hole to receive the thread insert. Keep the tap well oiled and back it out frequently to avoid clogging the threads

require a tap equipped with pilot threads and a combined reamer/tap section. Most manufacturers also supply blister-packed thread repair inserts separately in addition to a master kit

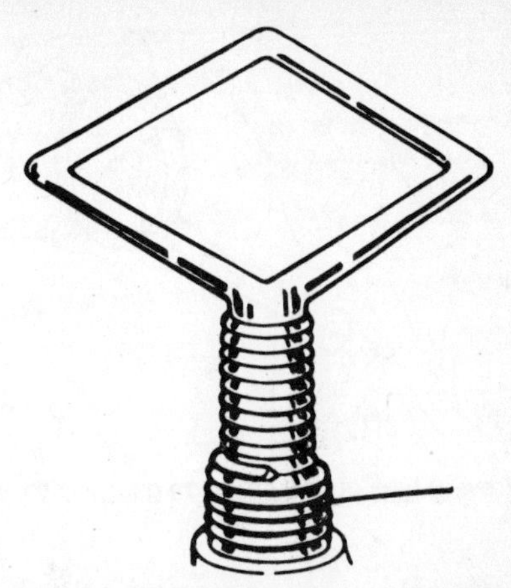

Screw the threaded insert onto the installation tool until the tang engages the slot. Screw the insert into the tapped hole until it is a ¼–½ turn below the top surface, after installation break off the tang with a hammer and punch

containing a variety of taps and inserts plus installation tools.

Before effecting a repair to a threaded hole, remove any snapped, broken or damaged bolts or studs. Penetrating oil can be used to free frozen threads; the offending item can be removed with locking pliers or with a screw or stud extractor. After the hole is clear, the thread can be repaired, as follows:

CHECKING ENGINE COMPRESSION

A noticeable lack of engine power, excessive oil consumption and/or poor fuel mileage measured over and extended period are all indicators of internal engine wear. Worn piston rings, scored or worn cylinder bores, blown head gaskets, sticking or burnt valves and worn valve seats are all possible culprits here. A check of each cylinder's compression will help you locate the problems.

As mentioned in the Tools and Equipment section of Chapter 1, a screw-in type of compression gauge is more accurate than the type you simply hold against the spark plug hole, although it takes slightly longer to use. It's worth it to obtain a more accurate reading. Follow the procedures below for gasoline and diesel engine cars.

Gasoline Engines

1. Warm up the engine to normal operating temperature.
2. Remove all spark plugs.
3. Disconnect the high tension lead from the ignition coil.
4. On carbureted cars, fully open the throttle either by operating the carburetor throttle linkage by hand or by having an assistant floor the accelerator pedal. On fuel injected cars, discon-

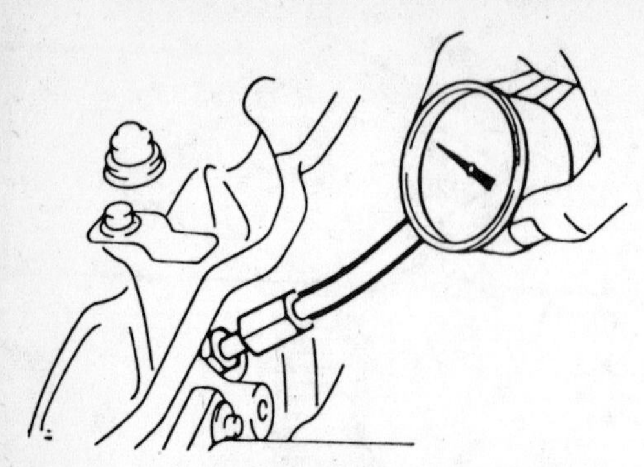

The screw-in type of compression gauge is more accurate

nect the cold start valve and all injector connections.

5. Screw the compression gauge into the No. 1 spark plug hole until the fitting is snug.

WARNING: *Be careful not to crossthread the plug hole. On aluminum cylinder heads use extra care, as the threads in these heads are easily ruined.*

6. Ask an assistant to depress the accelerator pedal fully on both carbureted and fuel injected cars. Then, while you read the compression gauge, ask the assistant to crank the engine two or three times in short bursts using the ignition switch.

7. Read the compression gauge at the end of each series of cranks, and record the highest of these readings. Repeat this procedure for each of the engine's cylinders. Compare the highest reading of each cylinder to the compression pressure specifications in the Tune-Up Specifications chart in Chapter 2. The specs in this chart are at maximum values. A cylinder's compression pressure is usually acceptable if it is not less than 80% of maximum. The difference between each cylinder should be no more than 12-14 pounds.

8. If a cylinder is unusually low, pour a tablespoon of clean engine oil into the cylinder through the spark plug hole and repeat the compression test. If the compression comes up after adding the oil, it appears that the cylinder's piston rings or bore are damaged or worn. If the pressure remains low, the valves may not be seated properly (a valve job is needed), or the head gasket may be blown near that cylinder. If compression in any two adjacent cylinders is low, and if the addition of oil doesn't help the compression, there is leakage past the head gasket. Oil and coolant water in the combustion chamber can result from this problem. There may be evidence of water droplets on the engine dipstick when a head gasket has blown.

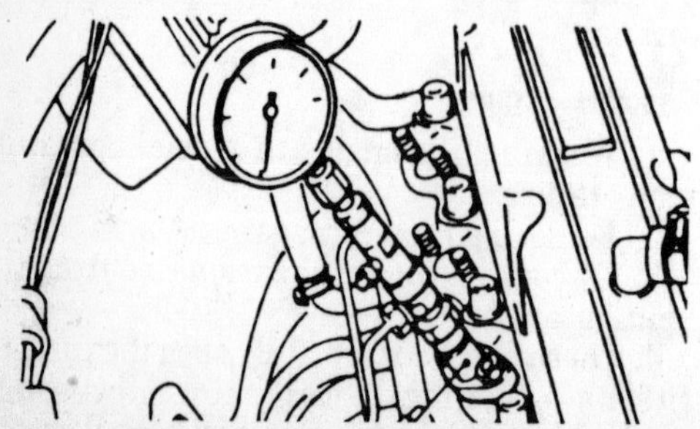

Diesel engines require a special compression gauge adapter

Diesel Engines

Checking cylinder compression on diesel engines is basically the same procedure as on gasoline engines except for the following:

1. A special compression gauge adaptor suitable for diesel engines (because these engines have much greater compression pressures) must be used.

2. Remove the injector tubes and remove the injectors from each cylinder.

NOTE: *Don't forget to remove the washer underneath each injector; otherwise, it may get lost when the engine is cranked.*

3. When fitting the compression gauge adaptor to the cylinder head, make sure the bleeder of the gauge (if equipped) is closed.

4. When installing the injector assemblies, install new washers underneath each injector.

Engine

REMOVAL

1. Remove the hood from the car.

CAUTION: *Do not discharge the air conditioning compressor or disconnect any air conditioning lines. Damage to the air conditioning system or personal injury could result.*

2. Disconnect the battery cables.

3. Remove the battery cable clips from the frame rail.

4. Drain the cooling system. Disconnect the radiator hoses from the engine and heater hoses at the heater.

CAUTION: *When draining the coolant, keep in mind that cats and dogs are attracted by the ethylene glycol antifreeze, and are quite likely to drink any that is left in an uncovered container or in puddles on the ground. This will prove fatal in sufficient quantity. Always drain the coolant into a sealable container. Coolant should be reused unless it is contaminated or several years old.*

5. Tag and disconnect any wires leading from the engine.

6. Remove the radiator upper support and remove the radiator and engine fan. On the diesel, you must remove the oil cooler.

7. Remove the air cleaner assembly.

Standard Torque Specifications and Fastener Markings

In the absence of specific torques, the following chart can be used as a guide to the maximum safe torque of a particular size/grade of fastener.

- There is no torque difference for fine or coarse threads.
- Torque values are based on clean, dry threads. Reduce the value by 10% if threads are oiled prior to assembly.
- The torque required for aluminum components or fasteners is considerably less.

U.S. Bolts

SAE Grade Number	1 or 2			5			6 or 7		
Number of lines always 2 less than the grade number.									
Bolt Size (Inches)—(Thread)	Maximum Torque			Maximum Torque			Maximum Torque		
	Ft./Lbs.	Kgm	Nm	Ft./Lbs.	Kgm	Nm	Ft./Lbs.	Kgm	Nm
¼—20	5	0.7	6.8	8	1.1	10.8	10	1.4	13.5
—28	6	0.8	8.1	10	1.4	13.6			
5/16—18	11	1.5	14.9	17	2.3	23.0	19	2.6	25.8
—24	13	1.8	17.6	19	2.6	25.7			
⅜—16	18	2.5	24.4	31	4.3	42.0	34	4.7	46.0
—24	20	2.75	27.1	35	4.8	47.5			
7/16—14	28	3.8	37.0	49	6.8	66.4	55	7.6	74.5
—20	30	4.2	40.7	55	7.6	74.5			
½—13	39	5.4	52.8	75	10.4	101.7	85	11.75	115.2
—20	41	5.7	55.6	85	11.7	115.2			
9/16—12	51	7.0	69.2	110	15.2	149.1	120	16.6	162.7
—18	55	7.6	74.5	120	16.6	162.7			
⅝—11	83	11.5	112.5	150	20.7	203.3	167	23.0	226.5
—18	95	13.1	128.8	170	23.5	230.5			
¾—10	105	14.5	142.3	270	37.3	366.0	280	38.7	379.6
—16	115	15.9	155.9	295	40.8	400.0			
⅞— 9	160	22.1	216.9	395	54.6	535.5	440	60.9	596.5
—14	175	24.2	237.2	435	60.1	589.7			
1— 8	236	32.5	318.6	590	81.6	799.9	660	91.3	894.8
—14	250	34.6	338.9	660	91.3	849.8			

Metric Bolts

Relative Strength Marking	4.6, 4.8			8.8		
Bolt Markings						
Bolt Size Thread Size x Pitch (mm)	Maximum Torque			Maximum Torque		
	Ft./Lbs.	Kgm	Nm	Ft./Lbs.	Kgm	Nm
6 x 1.0	2–3	.2–.4	3–4	3–6	.4–.8	5–8
8 x 1.25	6–8	.8–1	8–12	9–14	1.2–1.9	13–19
10 x 1.25	12–17	1.5–2.3	16–23	20–29	2.7–4.0	27–39
12 x 1.25	21–32	2.9–4.4	29–43	35–53	4.8–7.3	47–72
14 x 1.5	35–52	4.8–7.1	48–70	57–85	7.8–11.7	77–110
16 x 1.5	51–77	7.0–10.6	67–100	90–120	12.4–16.5	130–160
18 x 1.5	74–110	10.2–15.1	100–150	130–170	17.9–23.4	180–230
20 x 1.5	110–140	15.1–19.3	150–190	190–240	26.2–46.9	160–320
22 x 1.5	150–190	22.0–26.2	200–260	250–320	34.5–44.1	340–430
24 x 1.5	190–240	26.2–46.9	260–320	310–410	42.7–56.5	420–550

Troubleshooting Engine Mechanical Problems

Problem	Cause	Solution
External oil leaks	• Fuel pump gasket broken or improperly seated	• Replace gasket
	• Cylinder head cover RTV sealant broken or improperly seated	• Replace sealant; inspect cylinder head cover sealant flange and cylinder head sealant surface for distortion and cracks
	• Oil filler cap leaking or missing	• Replace cap
	• Oil filter gasket broken or improperly seated	• Replace oil filter
	• Oil pan side gasket broken, improperly seated or opening in RTV sealant	• Replace gasket or repair opening in sealant; inspect oil pan gasket flange for distortion
	• Oil pan front oil seal broken or improperly seated	• Replace seal; inspect timing case cover and oil pan seal flange for distortion
	• Oil pan rear oil seal broken or improperly seated	• Replace seal; inspect oil pan rear oil seal flange; inspect rear main bearing cap for cracks, plugged oil return channels, or distortion in seal groove
	• Timing case cover oil seal broken or improperly seated	• Replace seal
	• Excess oil pressure because of restricted PCV valve	• Replace PCV valve
	• Oil pan drain plug loose or has stripped threads	• Repair as necessary and tighten
	• Rear oil gallery plug loose	• Use appropriate sealant on gallery plug and tighten
	• Rear camshaft plug loose or improperly seated	• Seat camshaft plug or replace and seal, as necessary
	• Distributor base gasket damaged	• Replace gasket
Excessive oil consumption	• Oil level too high	• Drain oil to specified level
	• Oil with wrong viscosity being used	• Replace with specified oil
	• PCV valve stuck closed	• Replace PCV valve
	• Valve stem oil deflectors (or seals) are damaged, missing, or incorrect type	• Replace valve stem oil deflectors
	• Valve stems or valve guides worn	• Measure stem-to-guide clearance and repair as necessary
	• Poorly fitted or missing valve cover baffles	• Replace valve cover
	• Piston rings broken or missing	• Replace broken or missing rings
	• Scuffed piston	• Replace piston
	• Incorrect piston ring gap	• Measure ring gap, repair as necessary
	• Piston rings sticking or excessively loose in grooves	• Measure ring side clearance, repair as necessary
	• Compression rings installed upside down	• Repair as necessary
	• Cylinder walls worn, scored, or glazed	• Repair as necessary
	• Piston ring gaps not properly staggered	• Repair as necessary
	• Excessive main or connecting rod bearing clearance	• Measure bearing clearance, repair as necessary
No oil pressure	• Low oil level	• Add oil to correct level
	• Oil pressure gauge, warning lamp or sending unit inaccurate	• Replace oil pressure gauge or warning lamp
	• Oil pump malfunction	• Replace oil pump
	• Oil pressure relief valve sticking	• Remove and inspect oil pressure relief valve assembly
	• Oil passages on pressure side of pump obstructed	• Inspect oil passages for obstruction

Troubleshooting Engine Mechanical Problems (cont.)

Problem	Cause	Solution
No oil pressure (cont.)	• Oil pickup screen or tube obstructed • Loose oil inlet tube	• Inspect oil pickup for obstruction • Tighten or seal inlet tube
Low oil pressure	• Low oil level • Inaccurate gauge, warning lamp or sending unit • Oil excessively thin because of dilution, poor quality, or improper grade • Excessive oil temperature • Oil pressure relief spring weak or sticking • Oil inlet tube and screen assembly has restriction or air leak • Excessive oil pump clearance • Excessive main, rod, or camshaft bearing clearance	• Add oil to correct level • Replace oil pressure gauge or warning lamp • Drain and refill crankcase with recommended oil • Correct cause of overheating engine • Remove and inspect oil pressure relief valve assembly • Remove and inspect oil inlet tube and screen assembly. (Fill inlet tube with lacquer thinner to locate leaks.) • Measure clearances • Measure bearing clearances, repair as necessary
High oil pressure	• Improper oil viscosity • Oil pressure gauge or sending unit inaccurate • Oil pressure relief valve sticking closed	• Drain and refill crankcase with correct viscosity oil • Replace oil pressure gauge • Remove and inspect oil pressure relief valve assembly
Main bearing noise	• Insufficient oil supply • Main bearing clearance excessive • Bearing insert missing • Crankshaft end play excessive • Improperly tightened main bearing cap bolts • Loose flywheel or drive plate • Loose or damaged vibration damper	• Inspect for low oil level and low oil pressure • Measure main bearing clearance, repair as necessary • Replace missing insert • Measure end play, repair as necessary • Tighten bolts with specified torque • Tighten flywheel or drive plate attaching bolts • Repair as necessary
Connecting rod bearing noise	• Insufficient oil supply • Carbon build-up on piston • Bearing clearance excessive or bearing missing • Crankshaft connecting rod journal out-of-round • Misaligned connecting rod or cap • Connecting rod bolts tightened improperly	• Inspect for low oil level and low oil pressure • Remove carbon from piston crown • Measure clearance, repair as necessary • Measure journal dimensions, repair or replace as necessary • Repair as necessary • Tighten bolts with specified torque
Piston noise	• Piston-to-cylinder wall clearance excessive (scuffed piston) • Cylinder walls excessively tapered or out-of-round • Piston ring broken • Loose or seized piston pin • Connecting rods misaligned • Piston ring side clearance excessively loose or tight • Carbon build-up on piston is excessive	• Measure clearance and examine piston • Measure cylinder wall dimensions, rebore cylinder • Replace all rings on piston • Measure piston-to-pin clearance, repair as necessary • Measure rod alignment, straighten or replace • Measure ring side clearance, repair as necessary • Remove carbon from piston

Troubleshooting Engine Mechanical Problems (cont.)

Problem	Cause	Solution
Valve actuating component noise	• Insufficient oil supply	• Check for: (a) Low oil level (b) Low oil pressure (c) Plugged push rods (d) Wrong hydraulic tappets (e) Restricted oil gallery (f) Excessive tappet to bore clearance
	• Push rods worn or bent	• Replace worn or bent push rods
	• Rocker arms or pivots worn	• Replace worn rocker arms or pivots
	• Foreign objects or chips in hydraulic tappets	• Clean tappets
	• Excessive tappet leak-down	• Replace valve tappet
	• Tappet face worn	• Replace tappet; inspect corresponding cam lobe for wear
	• Broken or cocked valve springs	• Properly seat cocked springs; replace broken springs
	• Stem-to-guide clearance excessive	• Measure stem-to-guide clearance, repair as required
	• Valve bent	• Replace valve
	• Loose rocker arms	• Tighten bolts with specified torque
	• Valve seat runout excessive	• Regrind valve seat/valves
	• Missing valve lock	• Install valve lock
	• Push rod rubbing or contacting cylinder head	• Remove cylinder head and remove obstruction in head
	• Excessive engine oil (four-cylinder engine)	• Correct oil level

Troubleshooting the Cooling System

Problem	Cause	Solution
High temperature gauge indication—overheating	• Coolant level low	• Replenish coolant
	• Fan belt loose	• Adjust fan belt tension
	• Radiator hose(s) collapsed	• Replace hose(s)
	• Radiator airflow blocked	• Remove restriction (bug screen, fog lamps, etc.)
	• Faulty radiator cap	• Replace radiator cap
	• Ignition timing incorrect	• Adjust ignition timing
	• Idle speed low	• Adjust idle speed
	• Air trapped in cooling system	• Purge air
	• Heavy traffic driving	• Operate at fast idle in neutral intermittently to cool engine
	• Incorrect cooling system component(s) installed	• Install proper component(s)
	• Faulty thermostat	• Replace thermostat
	• Water pump shaft broken or impeller loose	• Replace water pump
	• Radiator tubes clogged	• Flush radiator
	• Cooling system clogged	• Flush system
	• Casting flash in cooling passages	• Repair or replace as necessary. Flash may be visible by removing cooling system components or removing core plugs.
	• Brakes dragging	• Repair brakes
	• Excessive engine friction	• Repair engine
	• Antifreeze concentration over 68%	• Lower antifreeze concentration percentage
	• Missing air seals	• Replace air seals
	• Faulty gauge or sending unit	• Repair or replace faulty component

Troubleshooting the Cooling System (cont.)

Problem	Cause	Solution
High temperature gauge indication—overheating (cont.)	• Loss of coolant flow caused by leakage or foaming • Viscous fan drive failed	• Repair or replace leaking component, replace coolant • Replace unit
Low temperature indication—undercooling	• Thermostat stuck open • Faulty gauge or sending unit	• Replace thermostat • Repair or replace faulty component
Coolant loss—boilover	• Overfilled cooling system • Quick shutdown after hard (hot) run • Air in system resulting in occasional "burping" of coolant • Insufficient antifreeze allowing coolant boiling point to be too low • Antifreeze deteriorated because of age or contamination • Leaks due to loose hose clamps, loose nuts, bolts, drain plugs, faulty hoses, or defective radiator • Faulty head gasket • Cracked head, manifold, or block • Faulty radiator cap	• Reduce coolant level to proper specification • Allow engine to run at fast idle prior to shutdown • Purge system • Add antifreeze to raise boiling point • Replace coolant • Pressure test system to locate source of leak(s) then repair as necessary • Replace head gasket • Replace as necessary • Replace cap
Coolant entry into crankcase or cylinder(s)	• Faulty head gasket • Crack in head, manifold or block	• Replace head gasket • Replace as necessary
Coolant recovery system inoperative	• Coolant level low • Leak in system • Pressure cap not tight or seal missing, or leaking • Pressure cap defective • Overflow tube clogged or leaking • Recovery bottle vent restricted	• Replenish coolant to FULL mark • Pressure test to isolate leak and repair as necessary • Repair as necessary • Replace cap • Repair as necessary • Remove restriction
Noise	• Fan contacting shroud • Loose water pump impeller • Glazed fan belt • Loose fan belt • Rough surface on drive pulley • Water pump bearing worn • Belt alignment	• Reposition shroud and inspect engine mounts • Replace pump • Apply silicone or replace belt • Adjust fan belt tension • Replace pulley • Remove belt to isolate. Replace pump. • Check pulley alignment. Repair as necessary.
No coolant flow through heater core	• Restricted return inlet in water pump • Heater hose collapsed or restricted • Restricted heater core • Restricted outlet in thermostat housing • Intake manifold bypass hole in cylinder head restricted • Faulty heater control valve • Intake manifold coolant passage restricted	• Remove restriction • Remove restriction or replace hose • Remove restriction or replace core • Remove flash or restriction • Remove restriction • Replace valve • Remove restriction or replace intake manifold

NOTE: *Immediately after shutdown, the engine enters a condition known as heat soak. This is caused by the cooling system being inoperative while engine temperature is still high. If coolant temperature rises above boiling point, expansion and pressure may push some coolant out of the radiator overflow tube. If this does not occur frequently it is considered normal.*

Troubleshooting the Serpentine Drive Belt

Problem	Cause	Solution
Tension sheeting fabric failure (woven fabric on outside circumference of belt has cracked or separated from body of belt)	• Grooved or backside idler pulley diameters are less than minimum recommended • Tension sheeting contacting (rubbing) stationary object • Excessive heat causing woven fabric to age • Tension sheeting splice has fractured	• Replace pulley(s) not conforming to specification • Correct rubbing condition • Replace belt • Replace belt
Noise (objectional squeal, squeak, or rumble is heard or felt while drive belt is in operation)	• Belt slippage • Bearing noise • Belt misalignment • Belt-to-pulley mismatch • Driven component inducing vibration • System resonant frequency inducing vibration	• Adjust belt • Locate and repair • Align belt/pulley(s) • Install correct belt • Locate defective driven component and repair • Vary belt tension within specifications. Replace belt.
Rib chunking (one or more ribs has separated from belt body)	• Foreign objects imbedded in pulley grooves • Installation damage • Drive loads in excess of design specifications • Insufficient internal belt adhesion	• Remove foreign objects from pulley grooves • Replace belt • Adjust belt tension • Replace belt
Rib or belt wear (belt ribs contact bottom of pulley grooves)	• Pulley(s) misaligned • Mismatch of belt and pulley groove widths • Abrasive environment • Rusted pulley(s) • Sharp or jagged pulley groove tips • Rubber deteriorated	• Align pulley(s) • Replace belt • Replace belt • Clean rust from pulley(s) • Replace pulley • Replace belt
Longitudinal belt cracking (cracks between two ribs)	• Belt has mistracked from pulley groove • Pulley groove tip has worn away rubber-to-tensile member	• Replace belt • Replace belt
Belt slips	• Belt slipping because of insufficient tension • Belt or pulley subjected to substance (belt dressing, oil, ethylene glycol) that has reduced friction • Driven component bearing failure • Belt glazed and hardened from heat and excessive slippage	• Adjust tension • Replace belt and clean pulleys • Replace faulty component bearing • Replace belt
"Groove jumping" (belt does not maintain correct position on pulley, or turns over and/or runs off pulleys)	• Insufficient belt tension • Pulley(s) not within design tolerance • Foreign object(s) in grooves • Excessive belt speed • Pulley misalignment • Belt-to-pulley profile mismatched • Belt cordline is distorted	• Adjust belt tension • Replace pulley(s) • Remove foreign objects from grooves • Avoid excessive engine acceleration • Align pulley(s) • Install correct belt • Replace belt
Belt broken (Note: identify and correct problem before replacement belt is installed)	• Excessive tension • Tensile members damaged during belt installation • Belt turnover • Severe pulley misalignment • Bracket, pulley, or bearing failure	• Replace belt and adjust tension to specification • Replace belt • Replace belt • Align pulley(s) • Replace defective component and belt

Troubleshooting the Serpentine Drive Belt (cont.)

Problem	Cause	Solution
Cord edge failure (tensile member exposed at edges of belt or separated from belt body)	• Excessive tension • Drive pulley misalignment • Belt contacting stationary object • Pulley irregularities • Improper pulley construction • Insufficient adhesion between tensile member and rubber matrix	• Adjust belt tension • Align pulley • Correct as necessary • Replace pulley • Replace pulley • Replace belt and adjust tension to specifications
Sporadic rib cracking (multiple cracks in belt ribs at random intervals)	• Ribbed pulley(s) diameter less than minimum specification • Backside bend flat pulley(s) diameter less than minimum • Excessive heat condition causing rubber to harden • Excessive belt thickness • Belt overcured • Excessive tension	• Replace pulley(s) • Replace pulley(s) • Correct heat condition as necessary • Replace belt • Replace belt • Adjust belt tension

General Engine Specifications

Year	Engine No. Cyl Displacement (cu in.) liters	Carburetor Type	Horsepower @ rpm	Torque @ rpm (ft. lbs.)	Compression Ratio	Oil Pressure @ 2000 rpm
1976–77	4-1.4 (85)	1 bbl	52 ① @ 5300	67 @ 3400	8.5:1	39–46
	4-1.6 (98)	1 bbl	60 ② @ 5300	77 @ 3200	8.5:1	39–46
1978	4-1.6 (98)	1 bbl	63 @ 4800	82 @ 3200	8.6:1	34–42
	4-1.6 HO (98)	1 bbl	68 @ 5000	84 @ 3200	8.6:1	34–42
1979–80	4-1.6 (98)	2 bbl	70 @ 5200	82 @ 2400	8.6:1	55
	4-1.6 HO (98)	2 bbl	74 @ 5200	88 @ 2800	8.6:1	55
1981	4-1.6 (98)	2 bbl	70 @ 5200	88 @ 2400	8.5:1	55
1982–87	4-1.6 (98)	2 bbl	65 @ 5200	80 @ 3200	9.4:1	57 ③
1981–86	4-1.8 (111) Diesel	Fuel Injection	51 @ 5000	72 @ 2000	22.0:1	64 ④

① 57 for 1977
② 63 for 1977
③ @ 1200 rpm
④ @ 5000 rpm

N.A. Not Available
Bore and stroke for all 1.4 engines is 82 x 66.2 mm
Bore and stroke for all 1.6 engines is 82 x 75.7 mm

8. Disconnect the following items:

a. Fuel line at the rubber hose along the frame rail. On the diesel, disconnect and plug the fuel lines at the injector pump and position them out of the way.

b. Automatic transmission throttle valve linkage.

c. Accelerator cable.

9. On air conditioned cars, remove the compressor from its mount and lay it aside. If equipped with power steering, remove the power steering pump and bracket and lay it aside.

10. Raise the car and support it with jackstands.

11. Remove the engine strut (shock type) on the diesel.

12. Disconnect the exhaust pipe at the exhaust manifold.

13. Remove the flywheel dust cover on manual transmission cars or the torque converter underpan on automatic transmission cars.

14. On automatic transmission cars, remove the torque converter-to-flywheel bolts.

15. Remove the converter housing or flywheel housing-to-engine retaining bolts and lower the car.

16. Position a floor jack or other suitable support under the transmission.

Valve Specifications

Year	Engine No. Cyl Displace-ment liters	Seat Angle (deg)	Face Angle (deg)	Spring Test Pressure Nm @ mm (lbs. @ in.)	Spring Installed Height (mm)	Stem to Guide Clearance mm (in.)		Stem Diameter (in.)	
						Intake	Exhaust	Intake	Exhaust
1976–87 (gas)	4-1.4	46	45	284 @ 32 (68 @ 1.26)	32 (1.26 in.)	.015–.045 ① (.0006–.0017 in.)	.035–.065 ② (.0014–.0025 in.)	7.97 (.3138 in.)	7.95 (.3130 in.)
	4-1.6	45 ③	46 ③	284 @ 32 (68 @ 1.26)	32 (1.26 in.)	.015–.045 ① (.0006–.0017 in.)	.035–.065 ② (.0014–.0025 in.)	7.97 (.3138 in.)	7.95 (.3130 in.)
1981–86 (diesel)	4-1.8	45	45	④	40.9 (1.61)	.0038–.0711 (.0015–.0028)	.0457–.0762 (.0018–.0030)	7.94–7.96 (.3128–.3134)	7.94–7.95 (.3126–.3132)

① 1976—.0018–.0021
② 1976—.0026–.0029
③ 1976–77—Seat angle 46, Face angle 45
④ OUTER Spring: 143–165 @ 41 (32–37 @ 1.614)
INNER Spring: 83–96 @ 38.5 (19–22 @ 1.516)

Crankshaft and Connecting Rod Specifications

All measurements are given in inches

Year	Engine No. Cyl Displacement liters	Crankshaft				Connecting Rod		
		Main Brg Journal Dia	Main Brg Oil Clearance	Shaft End-Play	Thrust on No.	Journal Diameter	Oil Clearance	Side Clearance
1976	4-1.4	2.0075–2.0085	.0009–.0025	.004–.008	4	1.809–1.810	.0014–.0030	.004–.012
	4-1.6	2.0075–2.0085	.0009–.0025	.004–.008	4	1.809–1.810	.0014–.0030	.004–.012
1977	4-1.4	2.0078–2.0088	.0009–.0026	.004–.008	4	1.809–1.810	.0014–.0031	.004–.012
1977–87	4-1.6	2.0078–2.0088	①	.004–.008	4	1.809–1.810	.0014–.0031	.004–.012
1981–86	4-1.8 Diesel	2.201–2.202	.0015–.0027	.0024–.0094	3	1.927–1.928	.0016–.0032 ②	N.A.

① 1976–78—All .0009–.0026
1979–86—#1 thru 4—.0005–.0018
#5—.0009–.0026

② .0016–.0027—1983 and later

Ring Side Clearance

All measurements are given in mm except engine displacement, inches are given in parentheses

Year	Engine No. Cyl Displacement liters	Top Compression	Bottom Compression	Oil Control
1976–77	4-1.4	.305–.686 (.0012–.0027 in.)	.305–.813 (.0012–.0032 in.)	.000–.127 (.0000–.0050 in.)
1977–83	4-1.6	.305–.686 (.0012–.0027 in.)	.305–.813 (.0012–.0032 in.)	.000–.127 (.0000–.0050 in.)
1984–87	4-1.6	.030–.068 (.0012–.0027)	.030–.082 (.0012–.0032)	.009–.216 (.0003–.0086)
1981–82	4-1.8 Diesel	.089–.125 (.0035–.0049)	.036–.051 (.0014–.0020)	.031–.071 (.0012–.0028)
1983–86	4-1.8 Diesel	.089–.125 (.0035–.0049)	.05–.085 (.0019–.0033)	.031–.071 (.0012–.0028)

Ring Gap

All measurements are given in mm except engine displacement, inches are given in parentheses

Year	Engine No. Cyl Displacement liters	Top Compression	Bottom Compression	Oil Control
1976–83	4-1.4, 1.6	.229–.483 (.009–.019 in.)	.203–.452 (.008–.018 in.)	.381–1.397 (.015–.055 in.)
1984–87	4-1.6	.250–.460 (.0010–.018)	.203–.452 (.008–.018)	.250–1.270 (.0010–.050)
1981–86	4-1.8 Diesel	.198–.399 (.0078–.0157)	.198–.399 (.0078–.0157)	.198–.399 (.0078–.0157)

Torque Specifications

All readings in Nm, ft. lbs. given in parentheses

Year	Engine No. Cyl Displace-ment liters	Cylinder Head Bolts	Rod Bearing Bolts	Main Bearing Bolts	Crankshaft Pulley or Damper Bolt	Flywheel to Crankshaft Bolts	Manifold	
							Intake	Exhaust
1976–77	4-1.4, 1.6	95–100 (70–80)	46–54 (34–40)	54–75 (40–52)	90–115 (65–85)	54–75 (40–52)	18–24 (13–18)	①
1978–87	4-1.6	100 (75)	54 (40)	68 (50)	100 (75)	68 (50)	20 (15) ④	①·②
1981–86	4-1.8 Diesel	③	84.5 (65)	88.4 (68)	150 (110)	N/A	39 (30)	N/A

① Center bolts—18–24 (13–18); end bolts—26–34 (19–25)
② 1983–86, all bolts—18 (25)
③ First tighten to 21–36 ft. lbs. then retighten to 83–98 (new bolt), 90–105 (reused bolt)
④ 1983–86: 24 (18)

17. Remove the safety straps from the front engine mounts and remove the mount nuts.
18. Remove the oil filter on the diesel.
19. Install the engine lifting apparatus.
20. Remove the engine by pulling forward to clear the transmission while lifting slowly. Check to make sure that all necessary disconnections have been made and that proper clearance exists with surrounding components. Remove the lifting apparatus.

Piston Clearance

All measurements are in mm except engine displacement, inches are given in parenthesis

Year	Engine No. Cyl Displacement liters	Piston to Bore Clearance (mm)
1976–77	4-1.4	.020–.040 (.0008–.0016 in.) ①
1977–83	4-1.6	.020–.040 (.0008–.0016 in.) ①
1984–87	4-1.6	.043–.069 (.0017–.0028)
1981–82	4-1.8 Diesel	.0152–.0356 (.006–.0014)
1983–86	4-1.8 Diesel	.005–.050 (.0002–.0017)

① Measured 48 mm (1½ in.) from top of piston

INSTALLATION

1. Install the engine lifting apparatus and install guide pins in the engine block.
2. Install the engine in the car by aligning the engine with the transmission housing.
3. Install the front engine mount nuts and safety straps.
4. Raise the car and support it with jackstands.
5. Install the engine-to-transmission housing bolts. Tighten to 25 ft. lbs.
6. On automatic transmission cars, install the torque converter to the flywheel. Torque the bolts to 35 ft. lbs.
7. Install the flywheel dust cover or torque converter underpan as applicable.
8. Install the engine strut on the diesel.
9. Install the exhaust pipe to the exhaust manifold and lower the car.
10. Install the air conditioning compressor or the power steering pump if necessary, and adjust drive belt tension.
11. Connect the following items:
    a. Fuel lines.
    b. Automatic transmission throttle valve linkage.
    c. Accelerator cable.
12. Install the air cleaner.
13. Install the engine fan, radiator, and radiator upper support. Install the oil cooler if so equipped.
14. Connect all wires previously disconnected.
15. Connect the radiator and heater hoses and fill the cooling system.

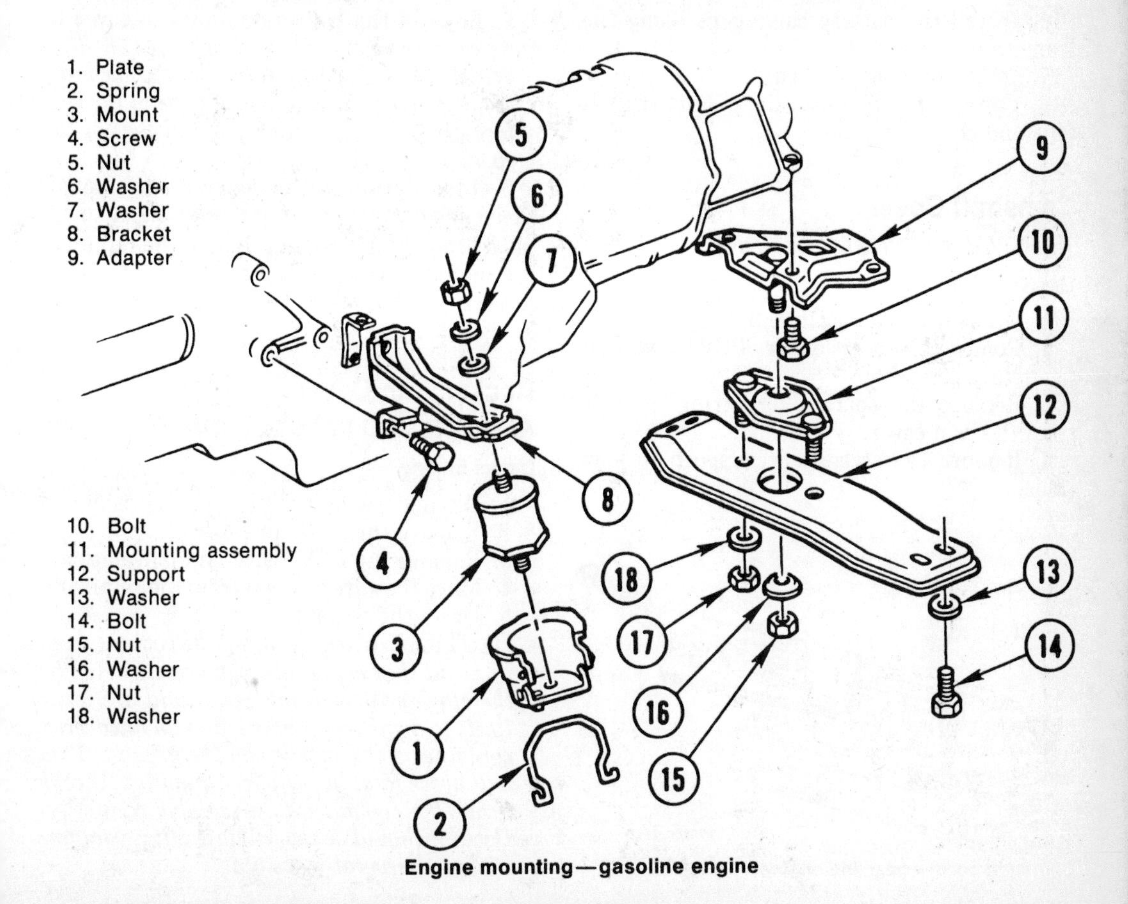

Engine mounting—gasoline engine

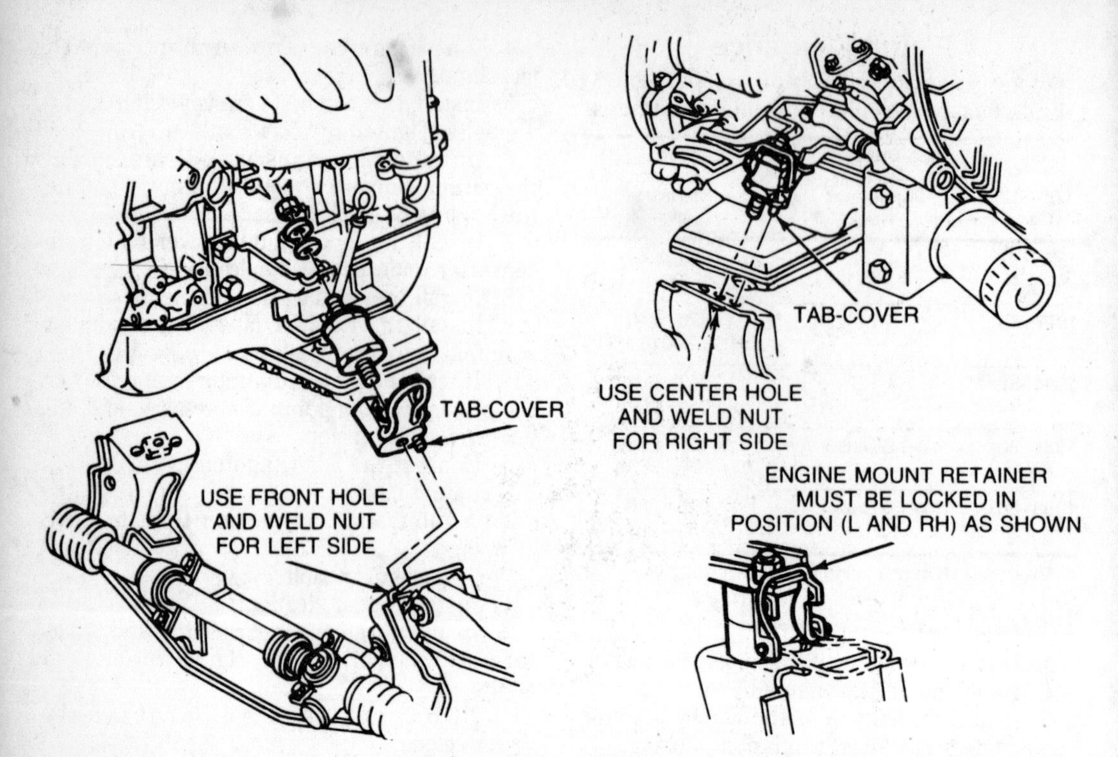

Engine mounting—diesel engine

16. Install the battery cable clips along the frame rail.
17. Install the engine hood.
18. Connect the battery cables, start the engine and check for leaks.

Camshaft Cover

REMOVAL AND INSTALLATION

Gasoline Engine

1. Disconnect the negative battery cable.
2. Remove the air cleaner, PCV valve and heat stove assembly.
3. Remove the spark plug wiring harness from the cam cover.
4. Remove the accelerator support and lay aside.

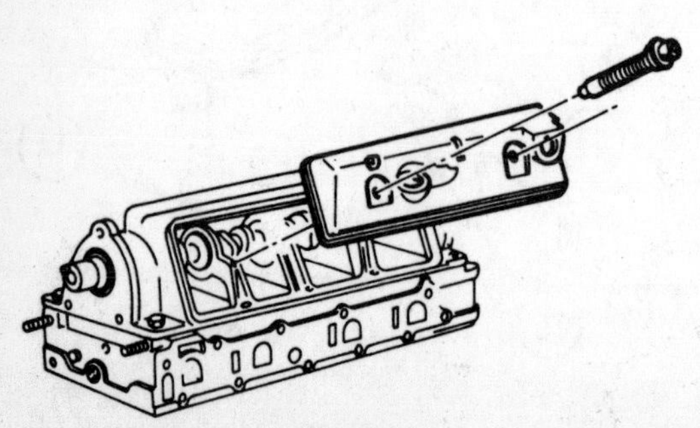

Camshaft cover—gasoline engine

5. Remove the bolts retaining the cover to the cam carrier.

WARNING: *The original sealer may be hard to break loose. Be careful not to bend the seal face of the cover or nick the seal face of the carrier.*

6. Installation is the reverse of removal. Clean and degrease the mating surfaces and apply a bead of RTV sealant. Install the retaining nut and gasket assemblies and torque to 15 in. lbs.

Rocker Arm Cover

REMOVAL AND INSTALLATION

Diesel Engine

1. Disconnect the negative battery cable.
2. Remove the fresh air hose.
3. Remove the PCV Valve and move aside.
4. Move the wire harness from the retainers.
5. Drain the coolant.

CAUTION: *When draining the coolant, keep in mind that cats and dogs are attracted by the ethylene glycol antifreeze, and are quite likely to drink any that is left in an uncovered container or in puddles on the ground. This will prove fatal in sufficient quantity. Always drain the coolant into a sealable container. Coolant should be reused unless it is contaminated or several years old.*

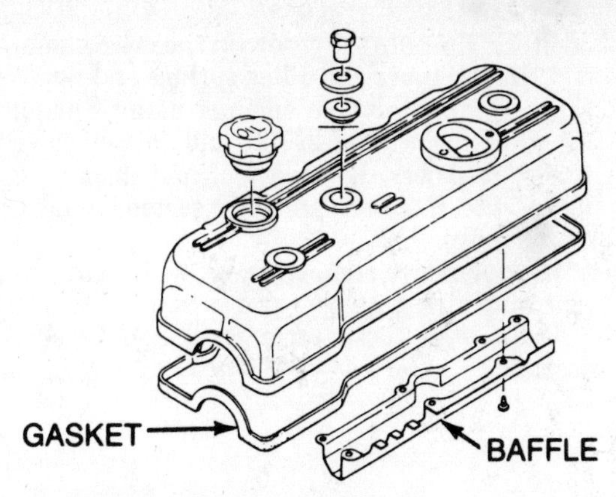

Rocker arm cover—diesel engine

6. Remove the heater hose at the left hand insulator.
7. Disconnect the wire at the defogger relay, if so equipped.
8. Remove the rocker arm cover nuts and remove the cover.
9. Installation is the reverse of removal. Refill the cooling system and torque the cover nuts to 7 ft. lbs.

Valve Stem Oil Seal and Valve Spring

REMOVAL AND INSTALLATION

Gasoline Engine

NOTE: *A special valve spring compressor is necessary for this procedure. (Tool No. J-25477)*

1. Remove the rocker arm from the valve to be serviced.
2. Remove the spark plug from the cylinder to be serviced.
3. Install an air hose adapter in the spark plug hole and apply air pressure to hold the valve in place.
4. Using the spring compressor, compress the valve spring, remove the rocker arm guide, valve locks, caps and valve spring.
5. Remove the valve stem oil seal.
6. Install the new valve stem oil seal.
7. Compress the valve spring and cap and install the valve locks and rocker arm guide.
8. Release the compressor while making sure that the locks seat correctly in the upper groove of the valve stem. Grease can be used to hold the locks while releasing the compressor.
9. Remove the air hose adapter, install the spark plug, and install the rocker arm.

Diesel Engine

REMOVAL

1. Remove rocker arm cover as previously outlined.
2. Remove rocker arm shaft and bracket assembly as outlined under Rocker Arm removal and Installation.
3. Rotate engine to T.D.C. for cylinder being serviced.
4. Remove valve stem end caps.

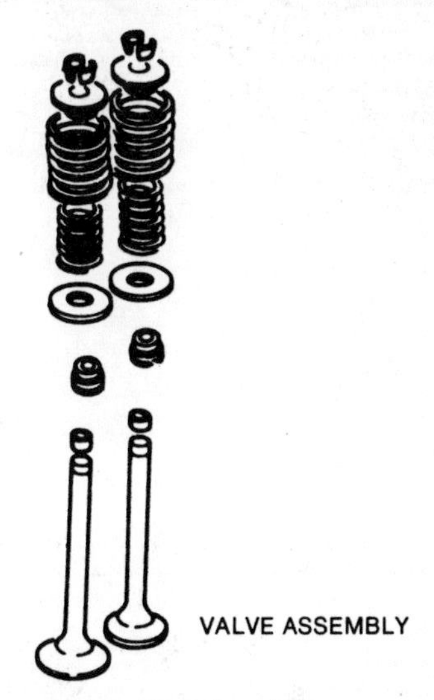

Valve assembly—diesel engine

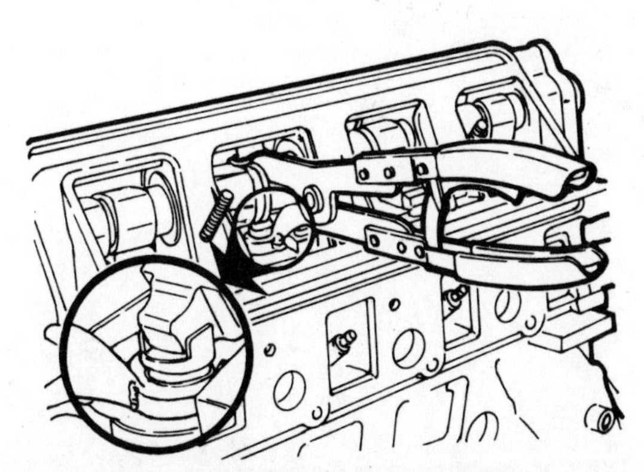

Valve spring compressing tool—gasoline engine

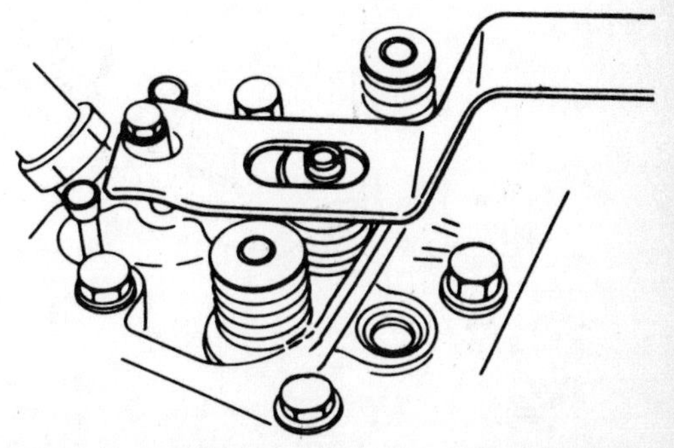

Valve spring compressing tool—diesel engine

5. Compress valve spring using tool J-29760. Remove valve collets and remove valve spring upper seat and valve springs.
6. Remove valve stem oil seal.
7. Remove valve spring lower seat.

INSTALLATION

1. Lubricate valve stem and valve spring lower seat with clean engine oil.
2. Install new seal over valve stem and onto valve guide. Check that projection on inner face of oil seal fits onto the groove in the valve guide.
3. Install inner and outer springs and upper seat. Compress valve springs using Spring Compressing Tool J-29760 and install valve spring retainers. Remove tool and inspect to make sure retainers are fully seated in valve stem groove.
4. Apply valve stem end caps with clean engine oil and install stem and caps.
5. Reinstall rocker arm shaft and bracket assembly.

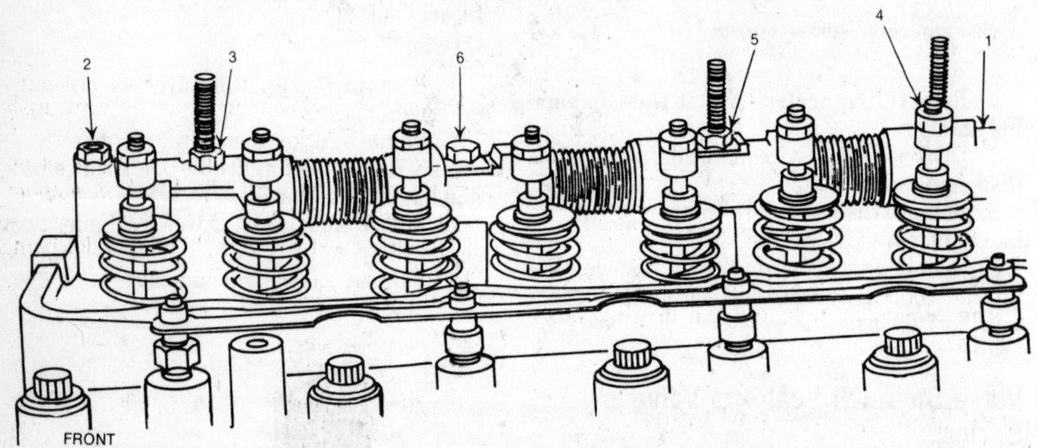

Rocker arm shaft bracket bolt and nut loosening and tightening sequence—diesel engine

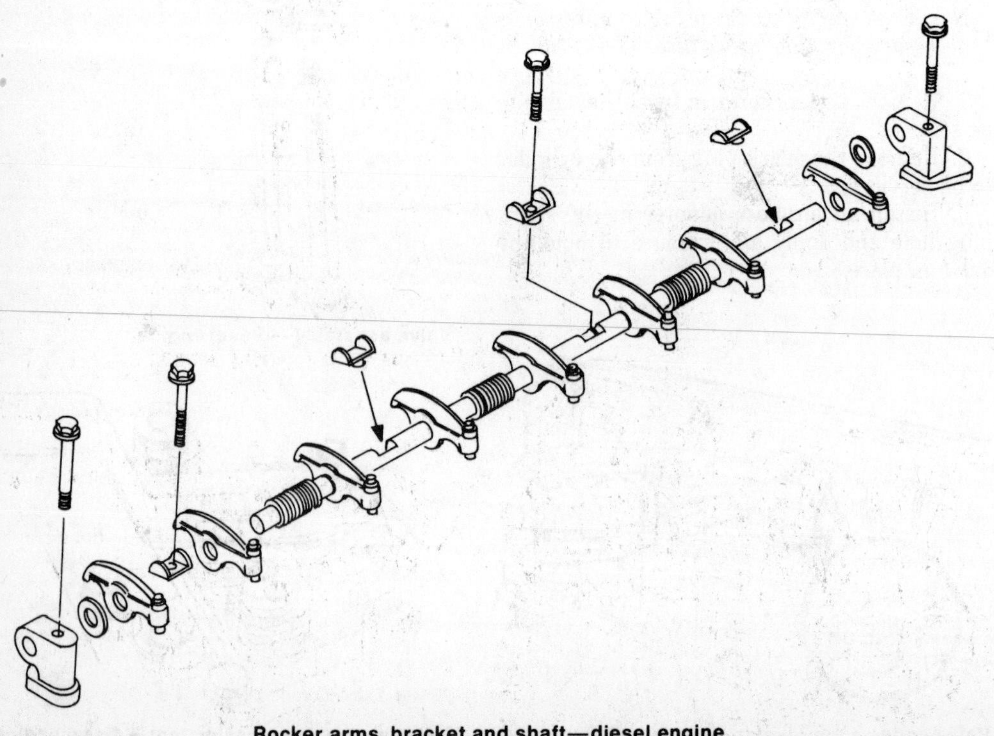
Rocker arms, bracket and shaft—diesel engine

Rocker Arm

REMOVAL AND INSTALLATION

Gasoline Engine

NOTE: *A special valve spring compressor is necessary for this procedure. Also prelubricate new rocker arms with Molykote or its equivalent.*

1. Remove the camshaft cover.
2. Using the special valve spring compressor, compress the valve springs and remove the rocker arms. Keep the rocker arms and guides in order so that they can be installed in their original locations.
3. To install the rocker arms, compress the valve springs and install the rocker arm guides.
4. Position the rocker arms in the guides and on the valve lash adjusters.
5. Install the camshaft cover.

Diesel Engine

1. Disconnect the negative battery cable.
2. Remove the cylinder head cover.
3. Remove the rocker arm shaft bracket bolts and nuts in sequence. Loosen them in this order: 6-1-2-5-4-3. remove the rocker arm shaft bracket and the rocker arm assembly.
4. Remove the rocker arms.
5. Apply a generous amount of clean engine oil to the rocker arm shaft, rocker arms and the valve stem end caps.
6. Install the rocker arm shaft assembly and then tighten the bolts to 20 ft. lbs. in the sequence given in Step 3.
7. Adjust the valves as previously detailed and reinstall the cylinder head cover.

Valve Adjustment

Gasoline Engine

Adjustment of the hydraulic valve lash adjusters is not possible.

Cleanliness should be exercised when handling the valve lash adjusters. Before installation of lash adjusters, fill them with oil and check the lash adjuster oil hole in the cylinder head to make sure that it is free of foreign matter.

Diesel Engine

NOTE: *The rocker arm shaft bracket bolts and nuts should be tightened to 20 ft. lbs. before adjusting the valves.*

1. Unscrew the retaining bolts and remove the cylinder head cover.
2. Rotate the crankshaft until the NO. 1 cylinder or NO. 4 piston is at TDC of the compression stroke.
3. Start with the intake valve on the NO. 1 cylinder and insert a feeler gauge of the correct thickness (intake: 0.25mm, exhaust: 0.35mm) into the gap between the valve step cap and the rocker arm. If adjustment is required, loosen the lock nut on top of the rocker arm and turn the adjusting screw clockwise to decrease the gap and counterclockwise to increase it. When the proper clearance is reached, tighten the lock nut and then recheck the gap. Adjust the remaining three valves in this step in the same manner.
4. Rotate the crankshaft one complete revolution and then adjust the remaining valves accordingly.

CYLINDER NO.	1		2		3		4	
VALVES	I	E	I	E	I	E	I	E
STEP. 1	○	○	○			○		
STEP. 2				◎	◎		◎	◎

I : INTAKE VALVE
E: EXHAUST VALVE

Valve adjustment torque sequence—diesel engine

Thermostat

REMOVAL AND INSTALLATION

1. Drain the radiator.

CAUTION: *When draining the coolant, keep in mind that cats and dogs are attracted by the ethylene glycol antifreeze, and are quite likely to drink any that is left in an uncovered container or in puddles on the ground. This will prove fatal in sufficient quantity. Always drain the coolant into a sealable container. Coolant should be reused unless it is contaminated or several years old.*

2. Remove the thermostat housing bolts and remove the housing with upper hose attached, gasket and thermostat.

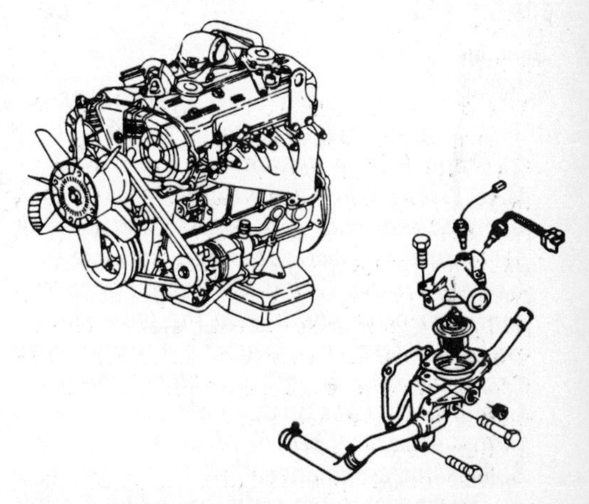

Thermostat housing assembly—diesel engine

Install the new thermostat with the spring down

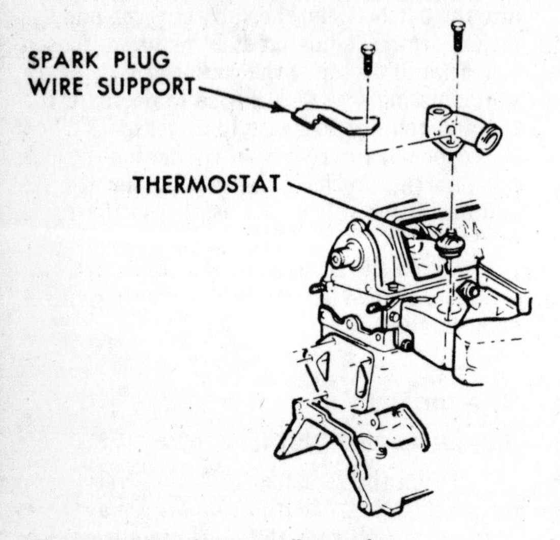

Thermostat housing—gasoline engine

3. Install the thermostat. Use a new gasket on the thermostat housing and install the thermostat housing bolts.
4. Install the upper radiator hose at the water outlet.
5. Fill the cooling system.

Intake Manifold

Gasoline Engine

REMOVAL

1. Disconnect negative battery cable.
2. Drain cooling system.

CAUTION: *When draining the coolant, keep in mind that cats and dogs are attracted by the ethylene glycol antifreeze, and are quite likely to drink any that is left in an uncovered container or in puddles on the ground. This will prove fatal in sufficient quantity. Always drain the coolant into a sealable container. Coolant should be reused unless it is contaminated or several years old.*

3. Remove air cleaner.
4. Disconnect upper radiator and heater hoses at intake manifold.
5. Remove the EGR valve, located on the intake manifold.
6. Disconnect all electrical wiring vacuum hoses and the accelerator linkage from the carburetor. Remove the fuel line from the carburetor.
7. If vehicle is equipped with air conditioning, perform the following operations before continuing.
   a. Remove radiator upper support.
   b. Remove the generator and air conditioning drive belts, including the two air conditioning adjusting bolts.
   c. Remove fan blade and pulley.
   d. Remove the timing belt cover.
   e. Move the compressor so it is out of the way. CAUTION: Do not disconnect any of the tubing in the air conditioning system as personal injury may result.
   f. Raise the vehicle and remove the lower air conditioning compressor bracket.
   g. Lower the vehicle and remove the upper air conditioning compressor bracket.
8. Remove the coil and set aside.
9. Remove the intake manifold bolts and remove manifold.

INSTALLATION

NOTE: *If a new intake manifold is being installed, transfer the following parts from the old one.*

- Thermostat and housing
- Carburetor
- Vacuum fittings and plugs

1. With the new gasket, and gasket surface well cleaned, install the new manifold.
2. Install manifold bolts and torque to 20 Nm (15 ft. lbs.).
3. Remount the coil.
4. For vehicles equipped with air conditioning, the following steps must be completed before continuing.
   a. Install the upper air conditioning compressor bracket.

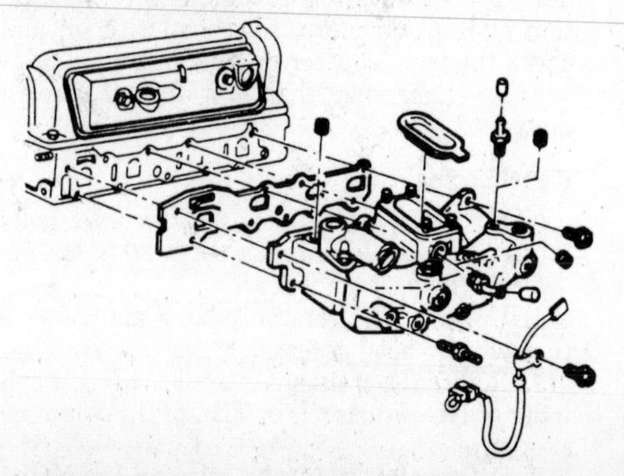

Intake manifold—gasoline engine

b. Raise the vehicle and install the lower air conditioning compressor bracket.
c. Lower the vehicle and install the air conditioning compressor.
d. Install the timing bolt cover.
e. Install the pulley and fan blades.
f. Install the air conditioning drive belt, two adjusting bolts and adjust as necessary.
g. Install the generator drive belt and adjust as necessary.
h. Install the radiator upper support.
5. Connect all electrical wiring, vacuum hoses and accelerator linkage to the carburetor. Install the fuel line to the carburetor.
6. Install the EGR valve. Torque to 13-18 ft. lbs.
7. Connect the upper radiator and heater hoses to intake manifold.
8. Refill the cooling system.
9. Install the air cleaner.
10. Connect the battery cable, start the engine and check for leaks.

Diesel Engine

REMOVAL AND INSTALLATION

1. Disconnect the negative battery cable.
2. Disconnect the fresh air hose and the vent hose. Remove the fuel separator.
3. Tag and disconnect all electrical connectors, the accelerator linkage and the glow plug wires.
4. Disconnect the injector lines at the injection pump and at the injector nozzles. Remove the injector lines and the holddown clamps.
5. Remove the glow plug line at the cylinder head.
6. If equipped with power steering, remove the drive belt, the idler pulley and the bracket.
7. Remove the upper half of the front cover and the bracket.
8. Unscrew the mounting bolts and remove the intake manifold.
9. Place a new gasket over the mounting studs on the cylinder head and install the manifold. Tighten the bolts to 30 ft. lbs.
10. Installation of the remaining components is in the reverse order of removal.

Exhaust Manifold

Gasoline Engine

REMOVAL

1. Remove the negative battery cable.
2. Raise the vehicle and disconnect the exhaust pipe from the manifold.
3. Lower the vehicle and remove the carburetor heat tube.
4. On California models, remove the pulse air injection tubing.
5. Remove the exhaust manifold bolts and manifold.

INSTALLATION

1. Install the manifold and manifold bolts. Install the inner upper bolts first as these are guidebolts.

NOTE: *Exhaust manifold center bolts must be torqued to 20 Nm (15 ft. lbs.). The end legs must be torqued to 30 Nm (22 ft. lbs.).*

2. On California models, install the pulse air injection tubing.
3. Install the carburetor heat tube.
4. Raise the vehicle and connect the exhaust pipe to the manifold.
5. Lower the vehicle and connect the battery cable. Start the engine and check for leaks.

Diesel Engine

REMOVAL

1. Disconnect the negative battery cable.
2. Raise the vehicle and support it safely.
3. Disconnect the exhaust pipe from the exhaust manifold.

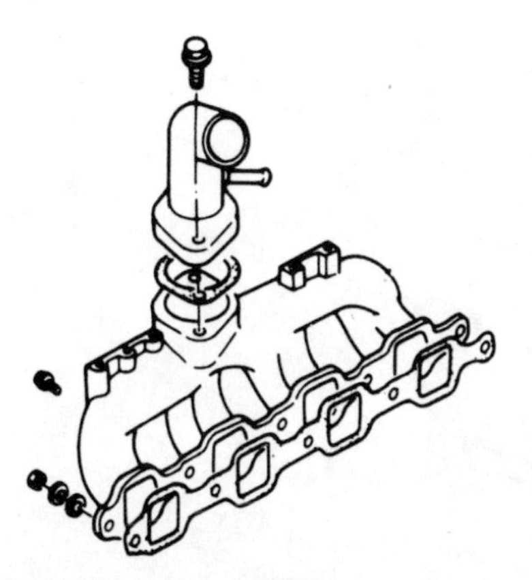

Intake manifold—diesel engine

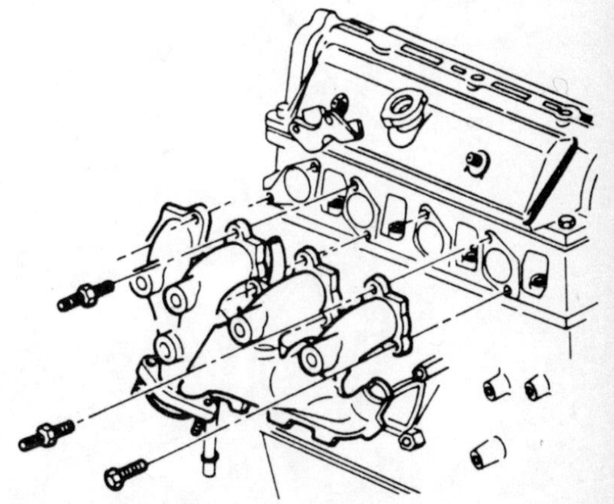

Exhaust manifold—gasoline engine

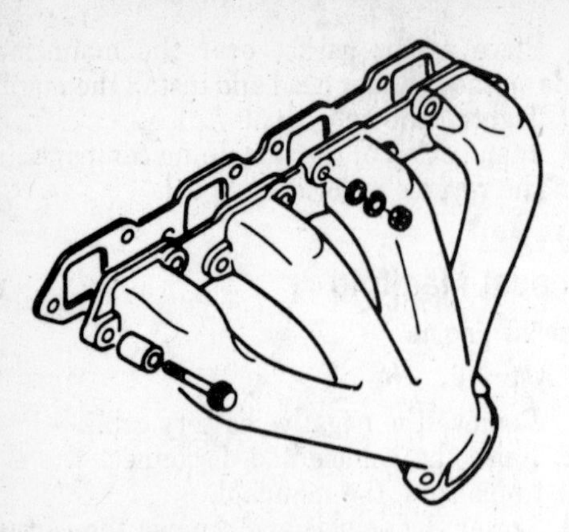

Exhaust manifold—diesel engine

4. Remove the power steering belt, flex hose and pump.
5. Remove the exhaust manifold bolts and remove the manifold.

INSTALLATION

1. Installation is the reverse of removal.
2. Clean all mating surfaces and install a new gasket.
3. Tighten the bolts a little at a time starting with the inner bolts and working outward.

Air Conditioning Compressor

REMOVAL AND INSTALLATION

1. Disconnect the negative battery cable.
2. Discharge the air conditioning system, as outlined in Chapter One.
3. Remove the coupled fitting block bolt at the compressor.
4. Remove the mounting bracket bolt.
5. Remove the drive belt and disconnect the electrical connections.
6. Remove the compressor.
7. Installation is the reverse of removal.
8. Check drive belt tension as outlined in Chapter One.
9. Evacuate and recharge the system as outlined in Chapter One.

Radiator

REMOVAL AND INSTALLATION

CAUTION: *Do not remove the radiator cap while the engine is still hot as the hot steam may cause personal injury.*

1. Drain the radiator.

CAUTION: *When draining the coolant, keep in mind that cats and dogs are attracted by the ethylene glycol antifreeze, and are quite*

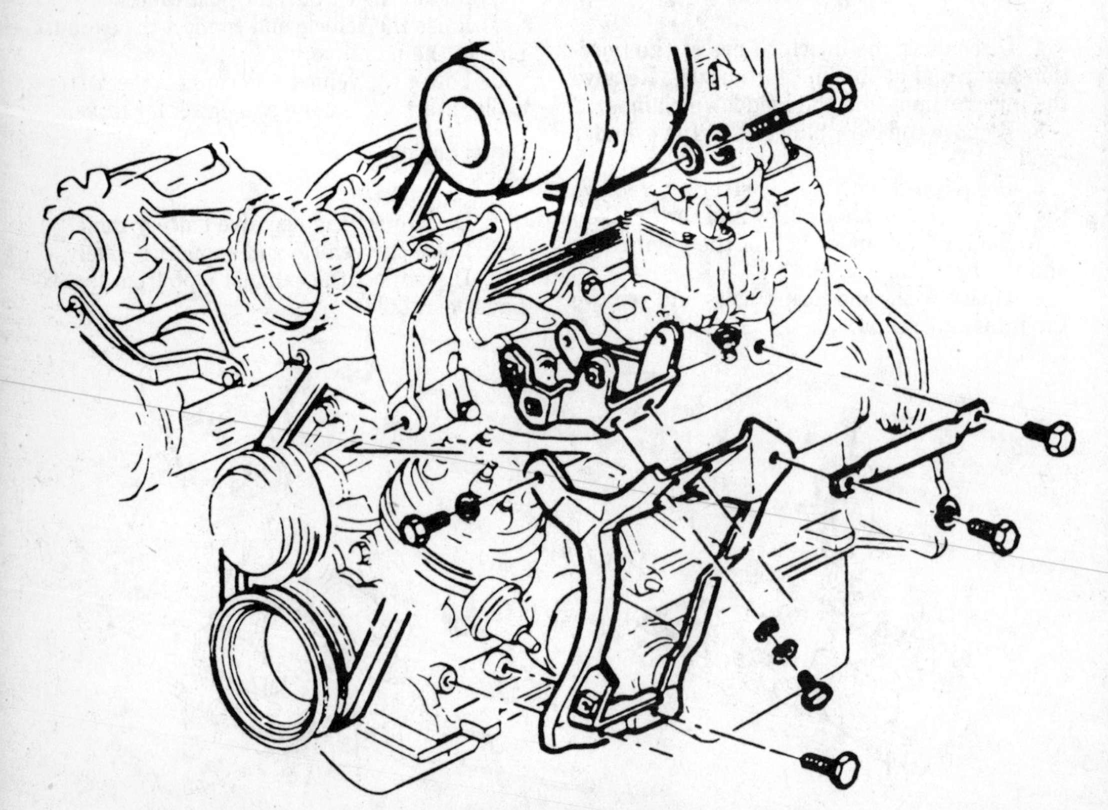

Compressor mounting

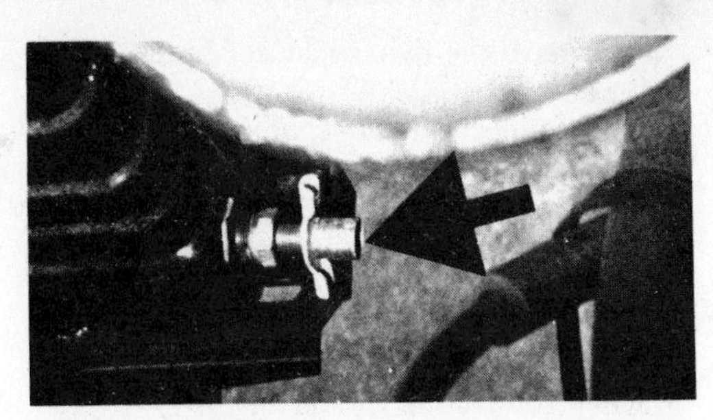

Radiator petcock

Radiator hoses are retained by screw clamps

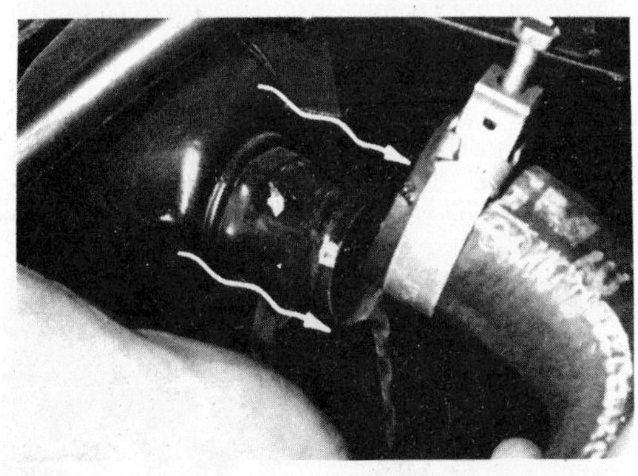

Remove the hoses by twisting and pulling simultaneously

likely to drink any that is left in an uncovered container or in puddles on the ground. This will prove fatal in sufficient quantity. Always drain the coolant into a sealable container. Coolant should be reused unless it is contaminated or several years old.

2. Disconnect the upper and lower radiator hoses and the coolant recovery reservoir hose.
3. Remove the radiator baffle or shroud. Remove the baffle by removing the four baffle-to-radiator support screws. Remove the shroud by removing the two upper screws and the two middle screws. Remove the upper radiator shroud. Remove the lower shroud from its mounting clips.
4. Disconnect and plug the transmission cooler lines if necessary.
5. Remove the radiator upper mounting panel or brackets and lift the radiator out of the lower brackets.
6. To install, reverse the removal procedure.

Condenser

REMOVAL AND INSTALLATION

CAUTION: *Do not remove the radiator cap while the engine is still hot as the hot steam may cause personal injury.*

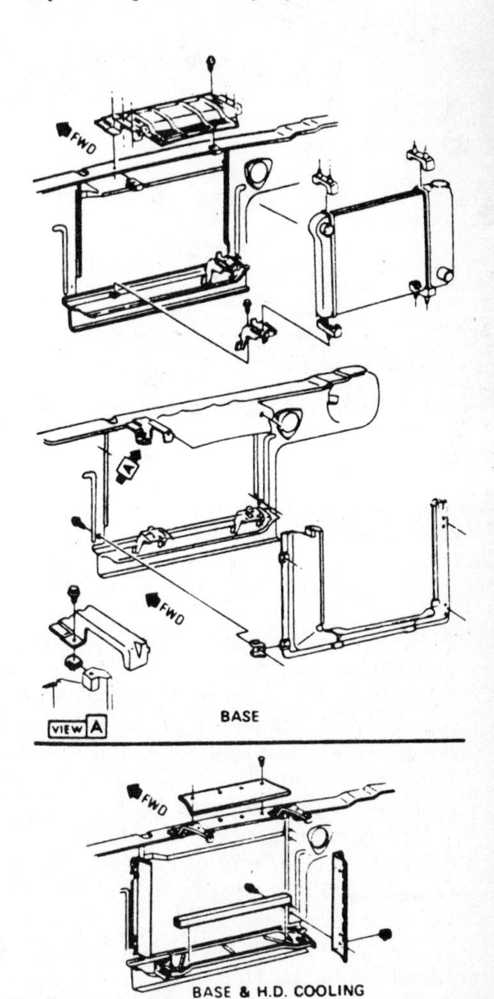

Radiator mounting—without A/C

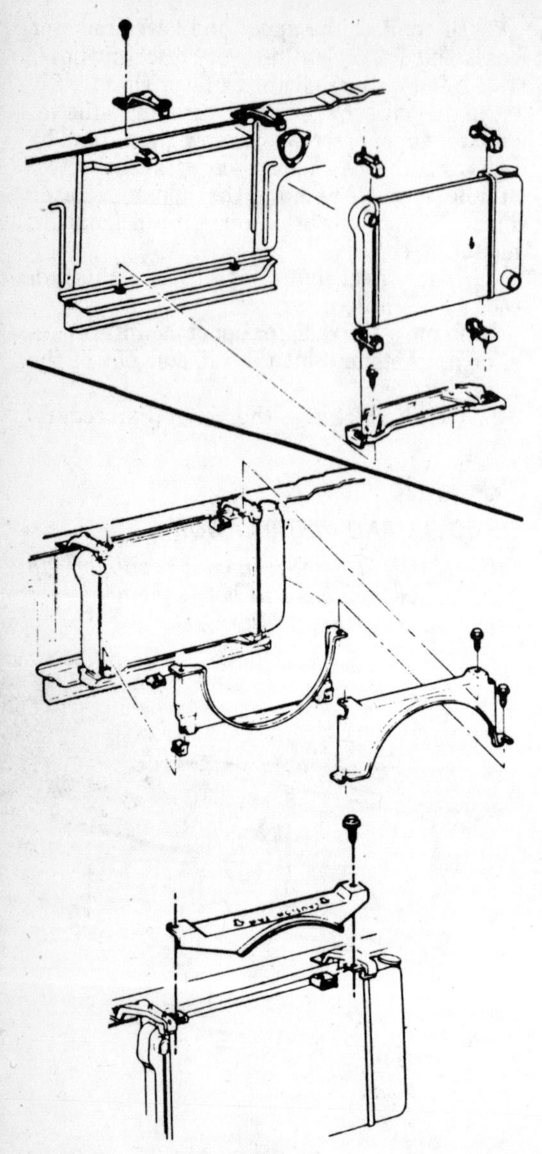

Radiator mounting—with A/C

1. Disconnect the negative battery cable.
2. Drain the radiator.

CAUTION: *When draining the coolant, keep in mind that cats and dogs are attracted by the ethylene glycol antifreeze, and are quite likely to drink any that is left in an uncovered container or in puddles on the ground. This will prove fatal in sufficient quantity. Always drain the coolant into a sealable container. Coolant should be reused unless it is contaminated or several years old.*

3. Discharge the air conditioning system, as outlined in Chapter One.
4. Remove the upper radiator support brackets.
5. Remove the two condenser bracket to radiator support nuts.
6. Disconnect the air conditioning hoses at the condenser.
7. Move the radiator rearward and lift out the condenser.
8. Reverse the above steps to install and add 2 oz. of clean refrigerant oil to a new condenser. Use new O-rings coated with clean refrigerant oil when connecting the refrigerant lines.
9. Evacuate, charge and check the system as outlined in Chapter One.

Water Pump

REMOVAL AND INSTALLATION

Gasoline Engine

1. Disconnect the battery negative cable and remove engine drive belt(s).
2. Remove the engine fan, spacer (air conditioned models) and the pulley.

WARNING: *A bent or damaged fan assembly should always be replaced. Do not attempt repairs as fan balance is critical. If unbalanced, the fan could fail and break apart while in use.*

3. Remove the timing belt front cover by removing the two upper bolts, center bolt and two lower nuts.
4. Drain the coolant from the engine.

CAUTION: *When draining the coolant, keep in mind that cats and dogs are attracted by the ethylene glycol antifreeze, and are quite likely to drink any that is left in an uncovered container or in puddles on the ground. This will prove fatal in sufficient quantity. Always drain the coolant into a sealable container. Coolant should be reused unless it is contaminated or several years old.*

5. Remove the lower radiator hose and the heater hose at the water pump.
6. Turn the crankshaft pulley so that the mark on the pulley is aligned with the 0 mark

The thermostat housing is retained by two bolts (arrows)

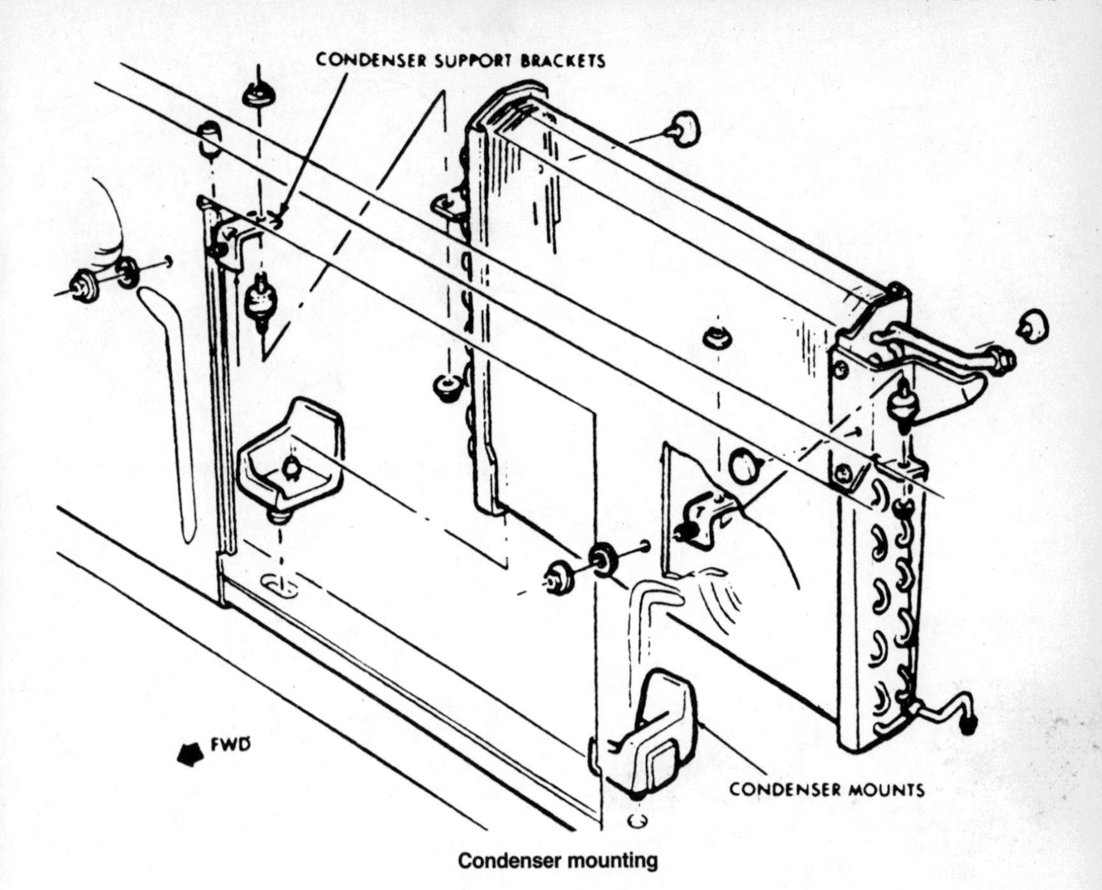

Condenser mounting

on the timing scale and that a 1/8" drill bit can be inserted through the timing belt upper cover and cam gear.

7. Remove the idler pulley and pull the timing belt off the gear. Don't disturb crankshaft position.

8. Remove the water pump retaining bolts and remove the pump and gasket from the engine.

9. Clean all the old gasket material from the cylinder case.

10. With a new gasket in place on the water pump, position the water pump in place on the cylinder case and install the water pump retaining bolts.

11. Install the timing belt onto the cam gear.

12. Apply sealer to the idler pulley attaching bolt and install the bolt and the idler pulley. Turn the idler pulley counterclockwise on its mounting bolt to remove the slack in the timing belt.

13. Use a tension gauge to adjust timing belt tension. Check belt tension midway between the tenisoner and the cam sprocket on the idler

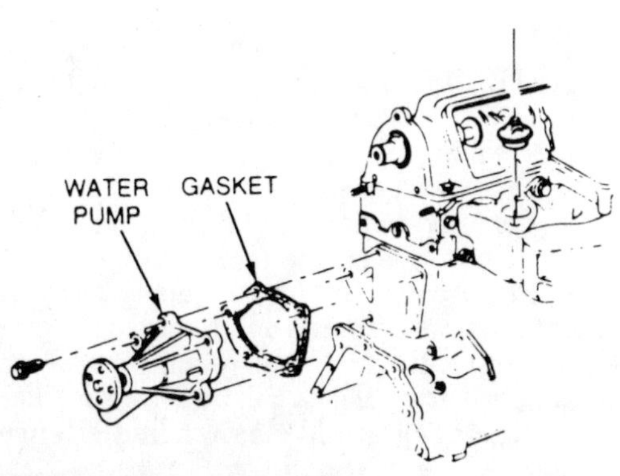

Water pump—gasoline engine

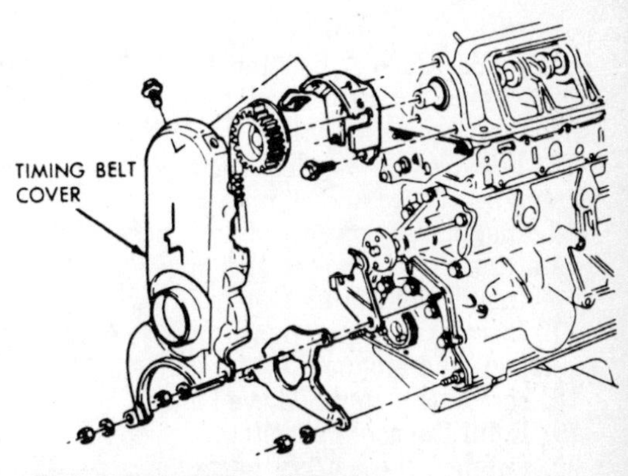

Timing belt front cover fasteners

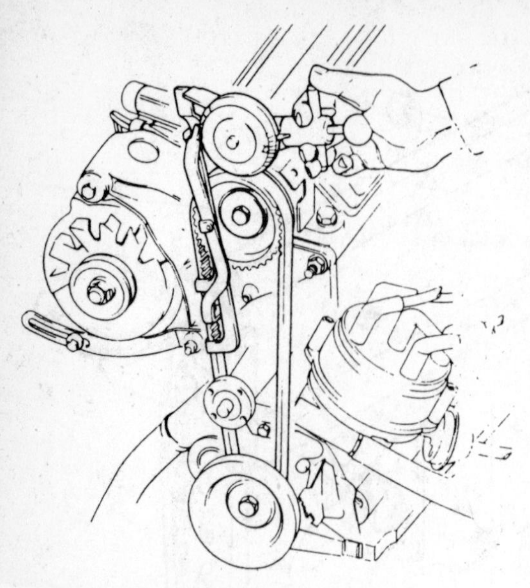

Checking timing belt tension

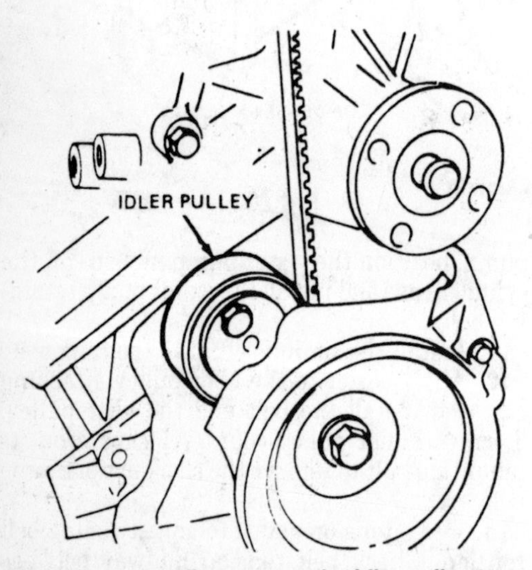

It's necessary to first remove the idler pulley to remove the water pump

pulley side. Correct belt tension is 55 lbs. for 1976, 70 lbs. for 1977 and later. Torque the idler pulley mounting bolt to 13-18 ft. lbs.

14. Remove the ⅛" drill bit from the upper timing belt cover and cam gear.
15. Install the lower radiator hose and the heater hose to the water pump.
16. Install the timing belt front cover.
17. Install the water pump pulley, spacer (if equipped) and engine fan.
18. Install the engine drive belt(s).
19. Refill the cooling system.
20. Connect the battery negative cable.
21. Start the engine and check for leaks.

Water pump attaching bolts—diesel engine

Diesel Engine

1. Disconnect the negative battery cable and drain the cooling system.

   CAUTION: *When draining the coolant, keep in mind that cats and dogs are attracted by the ethylene glycol antifreeze, and are quite likely to drink any that is left in an uncovered container or in puddles on the ground. This will prove fatal in sufficient quantity. Always drain the coolant into a sealable container. Coolant should be reused unless it is contaminated or several years old.*
2. Remove the fan shroud, fan assembly and the accessory drive belts.
3. Unscrew the retaining bolts and remove the damper pulley.
4. Remove the upper and lower halves of the front cover and then remove the bypass hose at the pump.
5. Unscrew the pump retaining bolts and remove the pump assembly.
6. Installation is in the reverse order of removal.

Cylinder Head

Gasoline Engine

REMOVAL

NOTE: *In order to complete the rocker arm removal a special tool (#J-25477) is necessary.*

1. Disconnect the battery negative cable.
2. Remove the accessory drive belts.
3. Remove the engine fan.
4. Remove the timing belt upper cover retaining screws and nuts and remove the cover.
5. Loosen the idler pulley and remove the timing belt from the camshaft drive sprocket.
6. Remove the air cleaner and silencer assembly.
7. Drain the cooling system. Disconnect the

upper radiator hose at the thermostat and the heater hose at the intake manifold.

CAUTION: *When draining the coolant, keep in mind that cats and dogs are attracted by the ethylene glycol antifreeze, and are quite likely to drink any that is left in an uncovered container or in puddles on the ground. This will prove fatal in sufficient quantity. Always drain the coolant into a sealable container. Coolant should be reused unless it is contaminated or several years old.*

8. Remove the accelerator cable support bracket.
9. Remove the spark plug wires from the cam cover.
10. Disconnect the electrical connections at:
   a. Idle solenoid
   b. Choke
   c. Temperature sending unit
   d. Alternator
11. Raise the car and disconnect the exhaust pipe at the manifold.
12. Lower the car and remove the bolt holding the dipstick tube bracket to the exhaust manifold.
13. Disconnect the fuel line at the carburetor.
14. Remove the coil cover and disconnect the secondary voltage wire from the coil.
15. Remove the coil bracket fasteners and lay the coil aside.
16. Remove the cam cover as follows:
   a. Remove the PCV valve.
   b. Remove the heat stove assembly.
   c. Remove the spark plug wiring harness from cam cover.
17. Remove the rocker arms by depressing the valve spring with tool #J-25477. Place the rocker arms and guides in a rack so they may be installed in the same location.
18. Remove the nut and gasket assemblies from the studs in the camashaft carrier. Remove the studs and cam carrier. It may be necessary to use a sharp wedge to separate the carrier from the cylinder head. Be careful not to damage the mating surfaces.
19. Remove the cylinder head and manifold assembly.

INSTALLATION

1. Intall the cylinder head gasket over the dowel pins with the note "This Side Up" facing up.
2. Replace the cylinder head and manifold.
3. Replace the cam carrier. Apply a thin, continuous coat of Loctite #75 (or equivalent) to both surfaces (head and cam carrier). Wipe the excess sealer from the cylinder head. Coat the threads of the cylinder head bolts with sealing compound and install bolts finger tight. Tight-

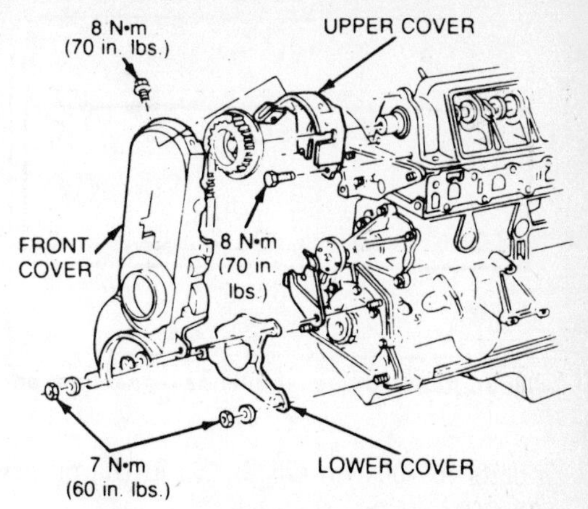

Timing belt cover retaining screws-gasoline engine

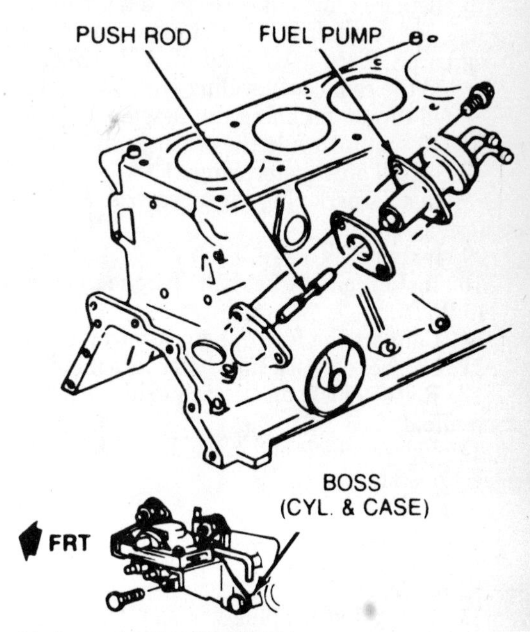

Fuel pump and coil fasteners

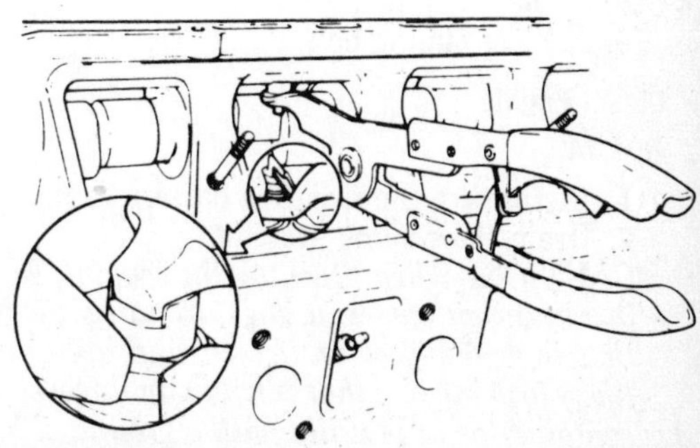

Depressing the valve spring for rocker arm removal-gasoline engine

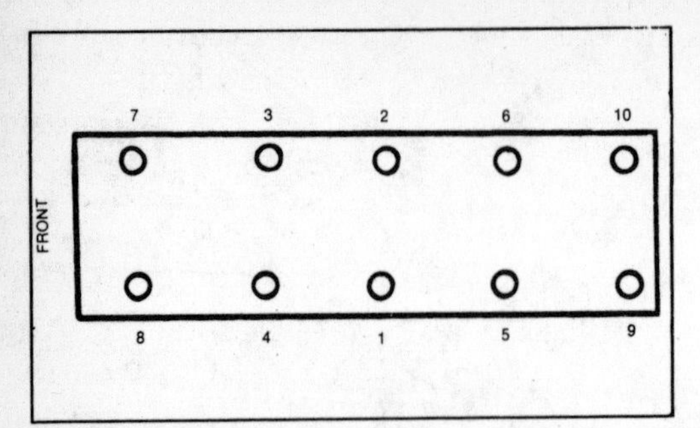

Cylinder head torque sequence—gasoline engine

en bolts to 100 Nm (75 lb. ft.) in the proper sequence.

4. Install cam cover attaching studs.
5. Install rocker arms and apply Molycoat or equivalent.
6. Replace camshaft cover gasket. Clean surfaces on camshaft cover and cam carrier with degreaser. Place a 1/8" bead of RTV sealer all around the cam cover sealing area. Install covers and torque retaining nut assemblies to 1.6 Nm (15 in. lbs.) while the sealer is still wet.
7. Install accelerator support.
8. Install spark plug wiring harness and heat stove assembly.
9. Install PCV valve.
10. Install coil bracket bolt. Torque to 20 Nm (15 lb. ft.).
11. Connect the fuel line to carburetor.
12. Replace dipstick tube bracket to manifold.
13. Raise vehicle and attach exhaust pipe to manifold.
14. Lower vehicle and make the electrical connections at:
    a. Idle solenoid
    b. Choke
    c. Temperature sending switch
    d. Generator
15. Connect spark plug wires.
16. Connect air cleaner and silencer assembly.
17. Connect upper radiator hose and heater hose at the inlet manifold.
18. Replace engine coolant.
19. Replace timing belt.

Diesel Engine

REMOVAL

1. Disconnect the negative battery cable.
2. Drain the cooling system.

CAUTION: *When draining the coolant, keep in mind that cats and dogs are attracted by the ethylene glycol antifreeze, and are quite likely to drink any that is left in an uncovered container or in puddles on the ground. This will prove fatal in sufficient quantity. Always drain the coolant into a sealable container. Coolant should be reused unless it is contaminated or several years old.*

3. Remove the cylinder head cover.
4. Disconnect the bypass hose. Remove the upper half of the front cover.
5. Loosen the tension pulley bolts and slide the timing belt off of the two upper gears.
6. Unscrew the bearing cap bolts and then remove the camshaft as detailed later in this section.
7. Tag and disconnect the glow plug resistor wire.
8. Disconnect the injector lines at the injector pump and at the injector nozzles and then remove the injector lines. Disconnect and plug the fuel leak-off hose.
9. Disconnect the exhaust pipe at the manifold.
10. Remove the oil feed pipe from the rear of the cylinder head.
11. Disconnect the upper radiator hose and position it out of the way.
12. Remove the head bolts in the sequence shown and then remove the cylinder head with the intake and exhaust manifolds installed.

INSTALLATION

NOTE: *The gasket surfaces on both the head and the block must be clean of any foreign matter and free of nicks or heavy scratches. Cylinder bolt threads in the block and on the bolt must also be clean.*

13. Place a new gasket over the dowel pins with the word **TOP** facing up.
14. Apply engine oil to the threads and the seating face of the cylinder head bolts, install them and then tighten them in the proper sequence.
15. Install the camshaft and rocker arm assemble. Loosen the adjusting screws so that the entire rocker arm assembly is held in a free state.
16. Reinstall the timing belt as outlined later in this section.
17. Connect the upper radiator hose and the oil feed pipe.
18. Connect the exhaust pipe to the manifold.
19. Install the fuel leek-off hose. Connect the injector lines.

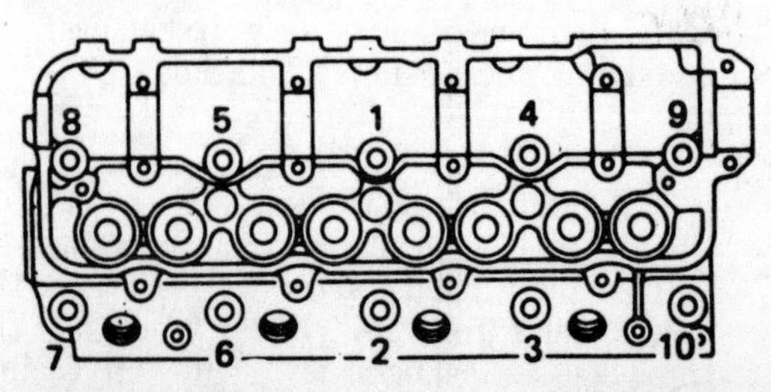

Cylinder head torque sequence—diesel engine

20. Connect the glow plug resistor wire.

21. Adjust the valve clearance as previously detailed. Install the cylinder head cover.

Cylinder Head Overhaul

Gasoline Engine

DISASSEMBLY

NOTE: *For ease in servicing cylinder head, remove generator mounting bracket, exhaust manifold and intake manifold before continuing.*

1. Using tool J-8062 or equivalent, compress valve spring and remove valve locks.
2. Release compressor tool and remove spring cap, spring and valve stem seal.
3. Remove valves from cylinder head, placing them in a rack so they may be returned to their original position.

CLEANING AND INSPECTION

1. Clean all carbon from combustion chambers and valve ports using tool J-8089 or equivalent.
2. Thoroughly clean valve guides using tool J-8101.
3. Clean valve stems and heads on a buffing wheel.
4. Clean carbon deposits from head gasket mating surface.
5. Inspect the cylinder head for cracks in the exhaust ports, combustion chambers, or external cracks to the water chamber.
6. Inspect the valves for burned heads, cracked faces or damaged stems.

WARNING: *Excessive valve stem to bore clearance will cause excessive oil consumption and may cause valve breakage. Insufficient clearance will result in noisy and sticky functioning of the valve and disturb engine smoothness.*

7. Measure valve stem clearance as follows: Clamp a dial indicator on one side of the cylinder head locating the indicator so that movement of the valve stem from side to side (crosswise to the head) will cause a direct movement of the indicator stem. The indicator stem must contact the side of the valve stem just above the the valve guide. With the valve head dropped about 2.0mm off the valve seat; move the stem of the valve from side to side using light pressure to obtain a clearance reading. If clearance exceeds specifications it will be necessary to ream valve guides for oversize valves as outlined. Oversize valves are available in: 0.075mm, 0.150mm, and 0.300mm.
8. Check valve spring tension with tool J-8056 spring tester. Springs should be compressed to the specified height and checked against the specifications chart. Springs should be replaced if not within 10 lbs. (44N) of the specified load.

ASSEMBLY

1. Insert valve in proper port.
2. Check installed height of valve. If necessary, grind the tip of the valve to obtain a dimension of 18mm above the head. This is required to assure correct operation of the valve lash adjusters.

WARNING: *Do not grind more than 0.75mm from any valve tip, otherwise interference between the rocker arm and valve cap may occur.*

3. Install valve stem oil seal.

NOTE: *Two valve stem oil seals are used. The intake is identified by the letters IN on the seal. The exhaust is identified by EX and a color coded retainer. DO NOT MIX SEALS ON INSTALLATION.*

4. Place valve spring and cap over valve stem and compress with tool J-8062.
5. Install valve locks and release compressor tool. Make sure that the locks seat properly in the groove on the valve stem. Grease may be used to hold the locks in place while releasing the compressor tool.
6. Install remaining valves in the same manner.
7. Check the installed height of the valve springs. Measure from the top of the spring seat, or shim, to the top of the spring. If out of specification, add shim(s) to correct.

Diesel Engine

DISASSEMBLY AND ASSEMBLY

NOTE: *See Rocker Arm Removal and Installation procedure previously outlined.*

VALVE GUIDE

REMOVAL AND INSTALLATION

Gasoline Engine

Valves with oversize stems are available. Remove the cylinder head and remove the camshaft from the cylinder head. Remove the valves and ram the valve guides with an appropriate oversize reamer.

Diesel Engine

Check the amount of wear in valve guide to determine the clearance between valves.

1. Drive out the valve guide with tool J-26512 fitted against the valve guide from lower face of the cylinder head.
2. Apply engine oil to the outer circumference of the valve guide. Set the installer (J-26512) to the valve guide, then drive the guide

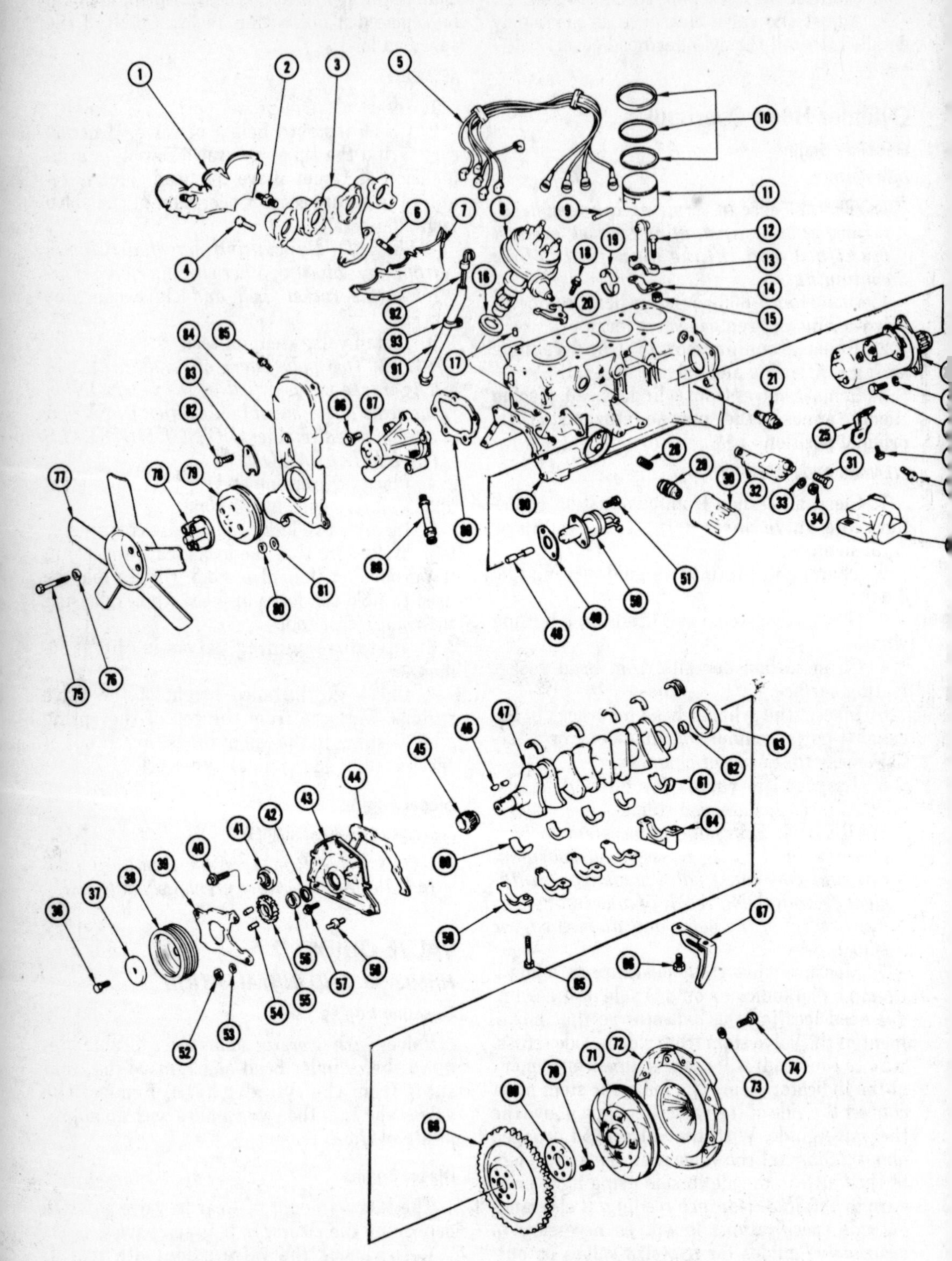

Exploded view of the cylinder block and related parts—gasoline engine

into position from the upper face of the cylinder head using a hammer. The valve guide should always be replaced together with the valve as a set.

Hot Plug

REMOVAL AND INSTALLATION

Diesel Engine

1. Remove the hot plug in the following manner. Insert a suitable round bar sizing 3-5mm in diameter into nozzle holder fitting hold to touch the hot plug, then drive out the hot plugs using a hammer.
2. Install lock ball into groove in hot plug. Drive the hot plug into cylinder head by aligning lock ball in hot plug with groove in cylinder head.
3. Press the hot plug into position by applying 4500 to 5000 kg (9922.5 to 11025 lbs.) pressure using a bench press with a piece of metal fitted against the hot plug face for protection. After installation, grind the face of hot plug flush with the face of the cylinder head.

Valve Seat Insert

REMOVAL AND INSTALLATION

Diesel Engine

1. Check valve seat contact width, condition of seat contact, scores, dents, etc.
2. Check the amount of valve seat depression (from lower face of cylinder head to valve face) using a depth gauge with a valve fitted into cylinder head.
3. Arc-weld excess metal around inner face of the valve seat insert and allow to cool off a few minutes, then pry off the valve seat insert with screw drivers.
4. Press a new valve insert into the bore using a bench press. After installation of the valve seat insert, grind finish the seating face with a seat grinder carefully noting the seating angle, contact width and depression. Lap the valve and seat as the final step.

Oil Pan

REMOVAL AND INSTALLATION

Gasoline Engine

TURBO HYDRA-MATIC 180 AUTOMATIC AND MANUAL TRANSMISSION

NOTE: *A special lifting tool is necessary for this procedure. This tool can be fabricated from channel iron; pattern it after the tool shown in the illustration.*

1. Remove the heater housing assembly from the firewall and rest it on top of the engine.
2. Drain the cooling system.

CAUTION: *When draining the coolant, keep in mind that cats and dogs are attracted by*

1. Stove
2. Stud
3. Manifold
4. Bolt
5. Wires
6. Stud
7. Stove
8. Distributor
9. Piston pin
10. Piston ring
11. Piston
12. Bolt
13. Rod
14. Cap
15. Nut
16. Gasket
17. Pin
18. Bolt
19. Connecting rod bearing
20. Clamp
21. Switch
22. Motor and switch
23. Washer
24. Bolt
25. Brace
26. Bolt
27. Bolt
28. Valve
29. Connector
30. Element
31. Bolt
32. Coil
33. Washer
34. Nut
35. Shield
36. Bolt
37. Washer
38. Pulley
39. Cover
40. Bolt
41. Pulley
42. Seal
43. Cover
44. Gasket
45. Gear
46. Key
47. Crankshaft
48. Fuel pump pushrod
49. Gasket
50. Fuel pump
51. Bolt
52. Nut
53. Washer
54. Pin
55. Sprocket
56. Spacer
57. Bolt
58. Stud
59. Cap
60. Bearing
61. Bearing
62. Bearing
63. Seal
64. Cap
65. Bolt
66. Bolt
67. Deflector
68. Flywheel
69. Retainer
70. Bolt
71. Plate
72. Clutch cover and pressure plate
73. Lockwasher
74. Bolt
75. Bolt
76. Lockwasher
77. Fan
78. Spacer
79. Pulley
80. Nut
81. Washer
82. Bolt
83. Cover
84. Cover
85. Bolt
86. Bolt
87. Water pump
88. Nipple
89. Gasket
90. Engine Cylinder Block
91. Tube
92. Gauge
93. Clamp

Exploded view of the cylinder block and related parts—gasoline engine

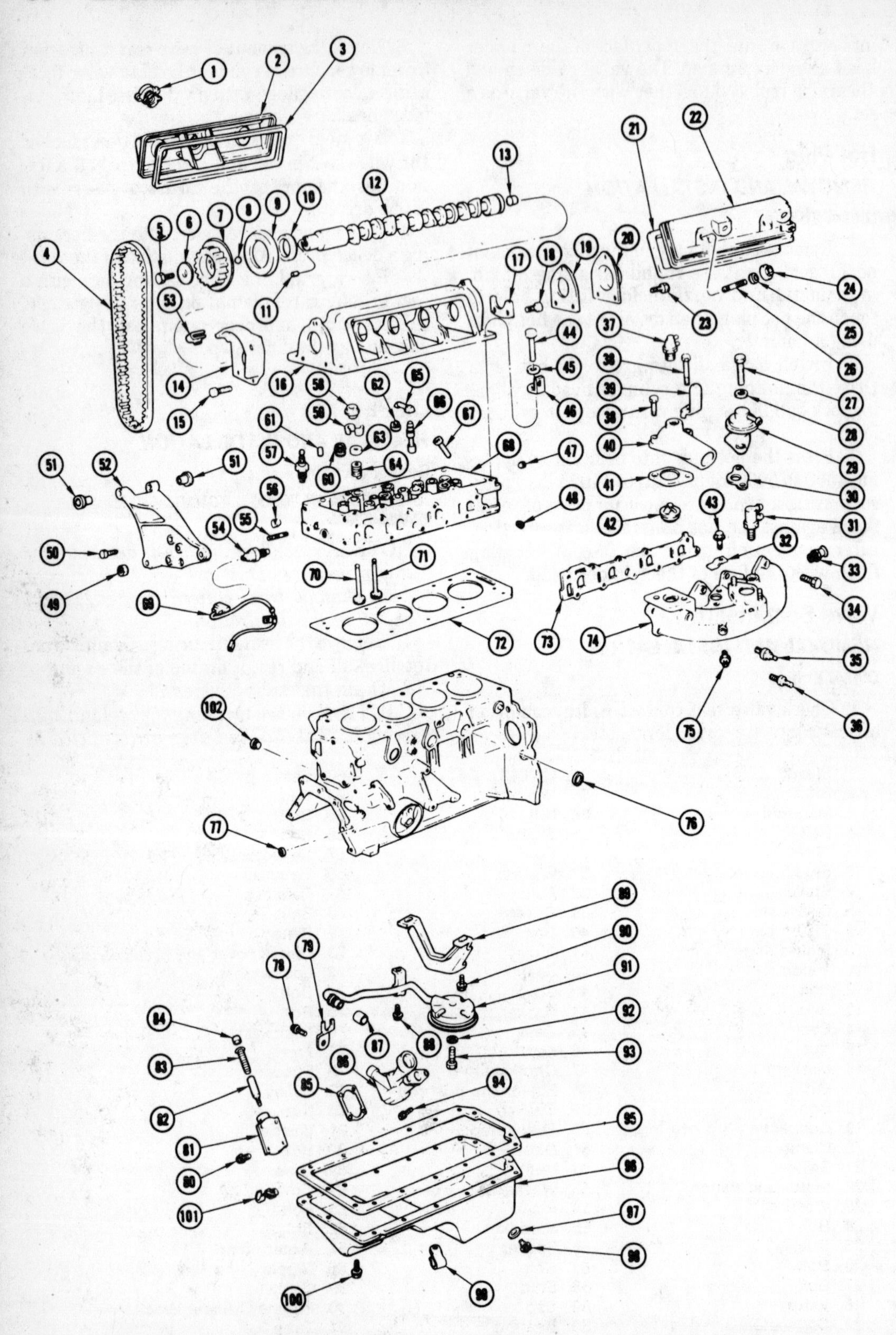

Exploded view of the cylinder head, oil pan and related parts—gasoline engine

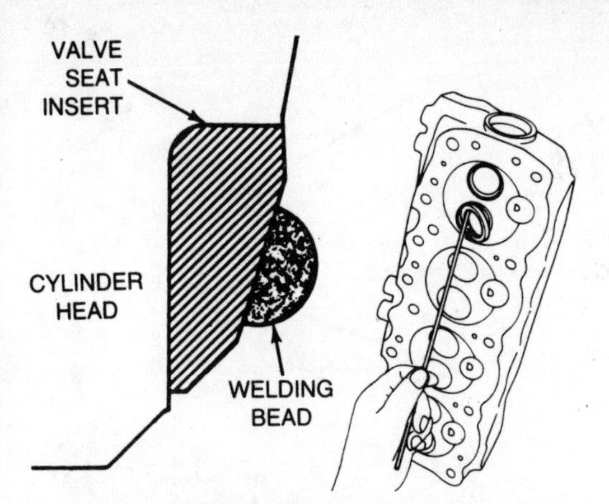

Valve seat insert replacement—diesel engine

the ethylene glycol antifreeze, and are quite likely to drink any that is left in an uncovered container or in puddles on the ground. This will prove fatal in sufficient quantity. Always drain the coolant into a sealable container. Coolant should be reused unless it is contaminated or several years old.

3. Remove upper radiator support. On air conditioning equipped vehicles, remove the upper half of the fan shroud.
4. Remove radiator hoses and radiator.

NOTE: *If equipped with automatic transmission, disconnect the cooler lines from the radiator.*

5. If equipped with air conditioning, remove the condenser to radiator support attaching nuts and remove condenser from support. Lay it on top of the engine.
6. Remove the engine mount retaining nuts and clips.
7. Disconnect the fuel line from the charcoal canister.
8. Raise the vehicle and drain the engine oil.

CAUTION: *The EPA warns that prolonged contact with used engine oil may cause a number of skin disorders, including cancer! You should make every effort to minimize your exposure to used engine oil. Protective gloves should be worn when changing the oil. Wash your hands and any other exposed skin areas as soon as possible after exposure to used engine oil. Soap and water, or waterless hand cleaner should be used.*

9. Remove the exhaust pipe bolts at the manifold.
10. Remove the body to cross member braces.
11. On manual transmission equipped vehicles, remove the rack and pinion-to-front crossmember attaching bolts. Pull the unit down and out of the way.

1. Cap
2. Cover
3. Gasket
4. Bolt
5. Bolt
6. Washer
7. Sprocket
8. Ball
9. Guide
10. Seal
11. Pin
12. Camshaft
13. Plug
14. Cover
15. Bolt
16. Housing
17. Retainer
18. Bolt
19. Gasket
20. Cover
21. Gasket
22. Cover
23. Bolt
24. Nut
25. Gasket
26. Stud
27. Bolt
28. Lockwasher
29. Valve
30. Gasket
31. Fitting
32. Support
33. Nipple
34. Bolt
35. Gauge
36. Stud
37. Switch
38. Bolt
39. Support
40. Outlet
41. Gasket
42. Thermostat
43. Bolt
44. Bolt
45. Washer
46. Bracket
47. Plug
48. Plug
49. Nut
50. Bolt
51. Bushing
52. Bracket
53. Nut
54. Switch
55. Stud
56. Plug
57. Plug
58. Cap
59. Key
60. Seal
61. Pin
62. Guide
63. Seal
64. Spring
65. Arm
66. Adjuster
67. Extension
68. Head
69. Wire
70. Valve
71. Valve
72. Cylinder head gasket
73. Intake manifold gasket
74. Intake manifold
75. Fitting
76. Plug
77. Plug
78. Screw
79. Clamp
80. Screw
81. Cover
82. Valve
83. Spring
84. Plug
85. Gasket
86. Oil pump
87. Seal
88. Bolt
89. Support
90. Screw
91. Pipe
92. Washer
93. Bolt
94. Bolt
95. Gasket
96. Pan
97. Gasket
98. Screw
99. Clip
100. Screw
101. Clip
102. Plug

Exploded view of the cylinder head, oil pan and related parts—gasoline engine

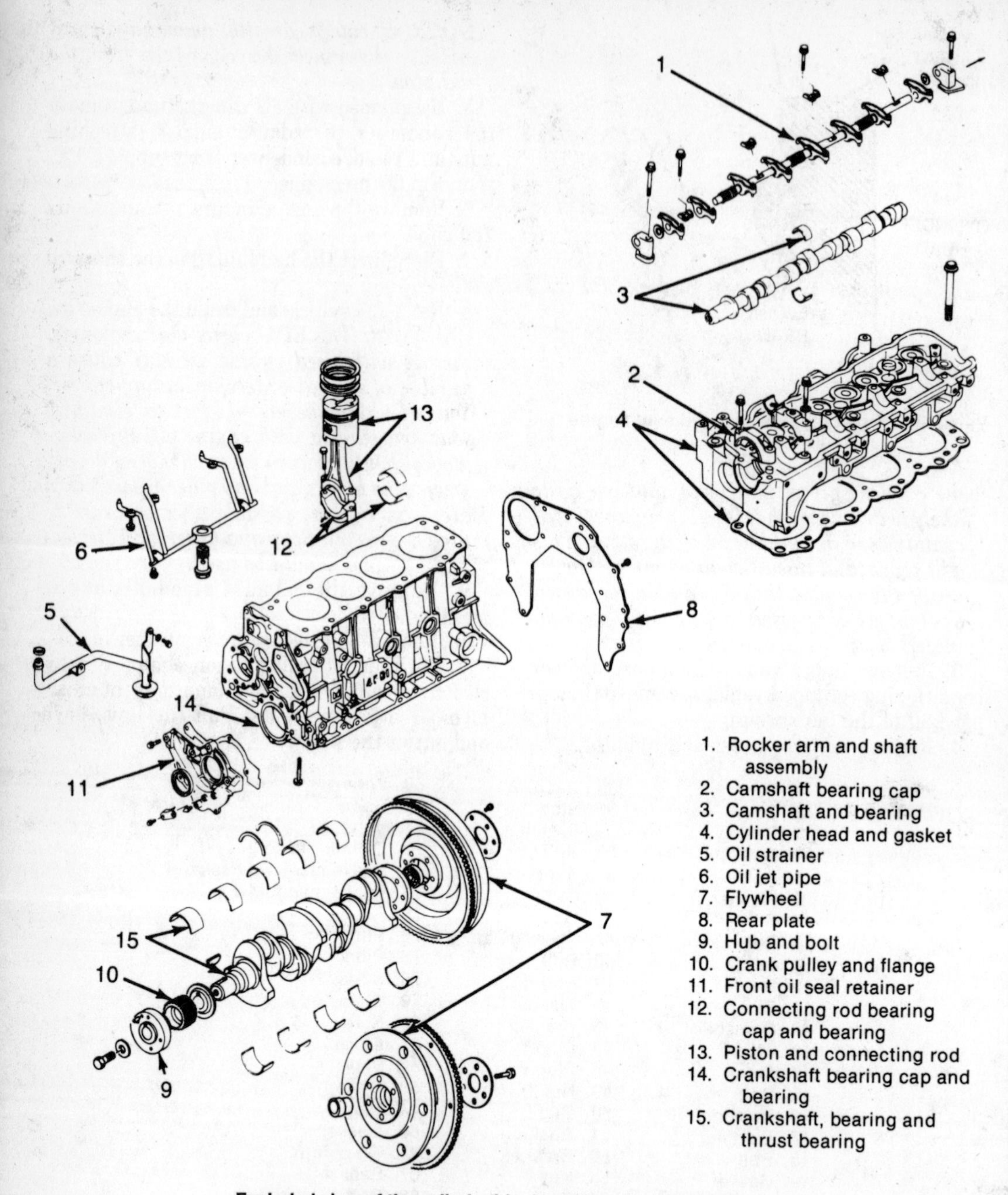

Exploded view of the cylinder block and head—diesel engine

12. Remove the stabilizer from the body.
13. Install tool J-26436 and raise the engine.
14. Remove the oil pan bolts.
15. With the oil pan lowered down from the block, remove the oil pump suction pipe. On 1976-77 models remove the screen. On newer models, the screen is attached to the pick-up tube.
16. Remove the oil pan through the front of the car. On vehicles equipped with manual transmission, lower the oil pan about 1 inch, rotate the front of the pan to the right and the rear to the left. Tilt the pan 45 degrees and remove it.

NOTE: *Most 1978 and later engines have RTV sealer in between the block and the oil pan. These can be identified by a smooth sealing surface on the oil pan rather than having a raised bead. These units MUST be reassembled using RTV sealer. The use of a gasket may allow an oil leak to develop.*

Conversely, if the oil pan has a raised bead, a

gasket MUST be used for reinstallation. The use of RTV sealer in this case could cause an oil leak to develop.

Before installing an oil pan using RTV, it is necessary to remove all old RTV sealer which is loose or will interfere with the installation. All old RTV need not be removed. The new sealer may be placed on top of the remaining RTV.

17. Install a new oil pump suction pipe and screen seal in the oil pump.
18. Lay the suction pipe and screen in the oil pan.
19. Clean the mating surfaces of the block and oil pan as necessary. Apply RTV or a gasket to the oil pan.
20. Tilt the pan and install it under the block.
21. Attach the oil pan bolts. Torque to 6 Nm (55 in. lbs.). On oil pans using RTV sealer, the bolts must be attached while the sealer is still wet.
22. Replace the rack and pinion-to-front crossmember bolts.
23. Attach the exhaust pipe to the manifold.
24. Lower the engine on to the engine mounts and remove the lifting tool. Attach the mounting nuts and clips.
25. Install the heater core housing.
26. Connect the fuel line to the charcoal canister.
27. If equipped with air conditioning, install the condenser assembly and attach the radiator support.
28. Install the radiator and attach the hoses.
29. If equipped with automatic transmission, connect the cooler lines to the radiator.
30. Install the upper radiator support.
31. On air conditioning equipped models, install the upper half of the fan shroud.
32. Refill the cooling system.
33. Refill the crankcase with oil.
34. Start the engine and check for leaks.

TURBO HYDRA-MATIC 200 AUTOMATIC TRANSMISSION

1. Disconnect the negative battery cable.
2. Remove the air cleaner.
3. Remove the heater housing assembly from the front of the dash and rest on top of the engine.
4. Pull back the motor mount wire restraints and remove the motor mount pins.
5. Remove the radiator upper support or fan shroud, as necessary.
6. Raise the vehicle and drain the crankcase.

CAUTION: *When draining the coolant, keep in mind that cats and dogs are attracted by the ethylene glycol antifreeze, and are quite likely to drink any that is left in an uncovered container or in puddles on the ground. This will prove fatal in sufficient quantity. Always drain the coolant into a sealable container. Coolant should be reused unless it is contaminated or several years old.*

7. Remove the flywheel splash shield.
8. Remove the rack and pinion assembly.
9. Loosen the converter to rear exhaust pipe clamp bolts.
10. Install tool J-26436 and raise the engine.
11. Remove the oil pan bolts and remove the oil pan.

NOTE: *Most 1978 and later engines have RTV sealer in between the block and the oil pan. These can be identified by a smooth sealing surface on the oil pan rather than having a raised bead. These units MUST be reassembled using RTV sealer. The use of a gasket may allow an oil leak to develop.*

Conversely, if the oil pan has a raised bead, a gasket MUST be used for reinstallation. The use of RTV sealer in this case could cause an oil leak to develop.

Before installing an oil pan using RTV, it is necessary to remove all old RTV sealer which is loose or will interfere with the installation. All old RTV need not be removed. The new sealer may be placed on top of the remaining RTV.

12. Place a bead of RTV sealant on the oil pan and while still wet position up against the block. Install the attaching bolts and torque to 6 Nm (55 in. lbs.).
13. Lower the engine onto the mounts and remove tool J-26436.
14. Tighten the converter to rear exhaust pipe clamp bolts to 23 ft. lbs.
15. Install the rack and pinion to the front crossmember. Torque the bolts to 14 ft. lbs.
16. Install the flywheel and lower the vehicle.
17. Install the radiator upper support or fan shroud.
18. Install the engine mount nuts. Torque the nuts to 48 ft. lbs., then position the wire restraints.
19. Install the heater assembly to the front of the dash.
20. Fill the crankcase with oil.
21. Install the air cleaner and the negative battery cable. Start the engine and check for leaks.

Diesel Engine

1. Remove the engine as detailed earlier in this section.
2. Support the engine on a stand.
3. Unscrew the nuts and bolts attaching the oil pan to the crankcase and then remove the pan.
4. Clean the mating surfaces of the oil pan and the block. Apply a suitable liquid gasket to the front and rear mating surfaces and then install a new gasket.

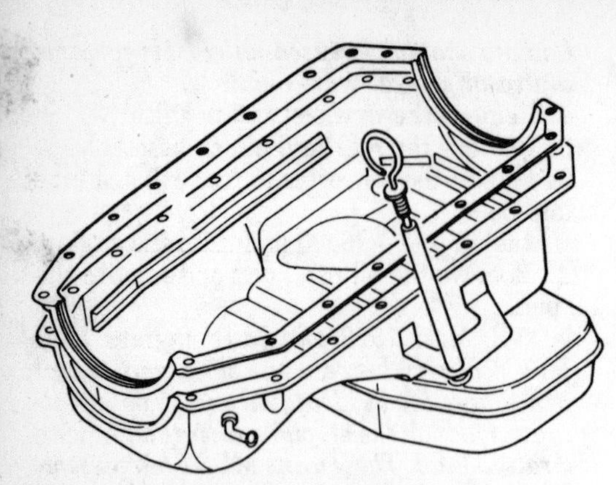

Oil pan assembly—diesel engine

5. Install the oil pan retaining bolts and tighten them to 5 ft. lbs.
6. Reinstall the engine.

Oil Pump

REMOVAL AND INSTALLATION

Gasoline Engine

1976-77

1. Remove the ignition coil attaching bolts and lay the coil aside.
2. Raise the car and remove the fuel pump, pushrod and gasket.
3. Lower the car and remove the distributor. On air conditioned cars, remove the compressor mounting bolts and lay it aside. Do not disconnect any refrigerant lines.
4. Raise the car and remove the oil pan.
5. Remove the oil pump pipe and screen assembly clamp and remove the bolts attaching the pipe and screen assembly to the cylinder and case.
6. Remove the pipe and screen assembly from the oil pump.
7. Remove the pick-up tube seal from the oil pump.
8. Remove the oil pump attaching bolts and remove the oil pump.

To install:

9. Install the oil pump. Torque the oil pump bolts to 45-60 in. lbs.

NOTE: *Make certain that the pilot on the oil pump engages the case.*

10. Install the pick-up tube seal in the oil pump.
11. Install the pick-up pipe and screen assembly in the oil pump and install the pick-up pipe and screen clamp. Torque the clamp bolt to 70-95 in. lbs. Torque the pick-up tube and screen mounting bolt to 19-25 ft. lbs.
12. Install the oil pan.
13. Lower the car and install the distributor.
14. Raise the car and install the fuel pump with gasket and pushrod.
15. Lower the car and install the ignition coil. Torque the coil bracket attaching bolts to 13-18 ft. lbs.

1978-87

REMOVAL

1. Remove the coil attaching bracket bolts and set the coil aside.
2. Raise the car and remove the fuel pump, pushrod and gasket.
3. Lower the car and remove the distributor.
4. On air conditioned cars, remove the compressor mounting bolts and lay it aside. Do not disconnect any refrigerant lines.
5. Raise the car and remove the oil pan.
6. If equipped with a 200 automatic transmission, remove the oil pump screen and pick-up tube assembly.
7. Remove the oil pump.
8. Remove the oil pump cover bolts.
9. Remove the cover and gasket.
10. Remove the pump and gear assembly.
11. Remove the pressure regulator valve and connecting parts.
12. If necessary, remove the pick-up tube from the pump and replace it with a new tube and O-ring seal. Do not separate the screen from the tube as they are one unit.

Clean the parts of the pump with solvent and allow to dry. Inspect the body of the pump for cracks and inspect the gears of the pump for damage or excessive wear. Also check the inside of the pump for any wear that would permit oil

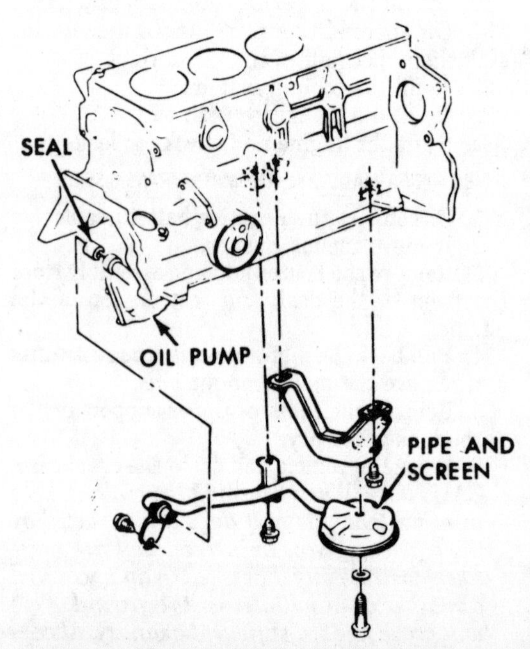

Oil pump installation-gasoline engine

to leak past the ends of the gears. Check the pick-up tube and screen for any damage. If the gears or body of the pump are damaged, replace the entire oil pump assembly.

INSTALLATION

1. Install the pressure regulator valve and connecting parts.
2. Install the pump gear assemblies.
3. Replace the cover and torque the bolts to 9 Nm (85 in. lbs.).
4. Install the oil pump and attaching screws.
5. Install the oil pan.
6. Replace the distributor.
7. Raise the vehicle and install the fuel pump gasket, fuel pump and pushrod assembly.
8. Lower the vehicle and install the coil attaching bracket bolts. Torque to 20 Nm (15 ft. lbs.).

Diesel Engine

1. Remove the timing belt as previously detailed.
2. Unscrew the four allen bolts attaching the oil pump to the front plate and remove the pump complete with the pulley.
3. Coat the vane with clean engine oil and then install it with the taper side toward the cylinder body.
4. Install a new O-ring, coated with engine oil, into the pump housing.
5. Position the rotor in the vane and then install the pump body together with the pulley. Tighten the allen bolts to 15 ft. lbs.
6. Install the timing belt as previously detailed.

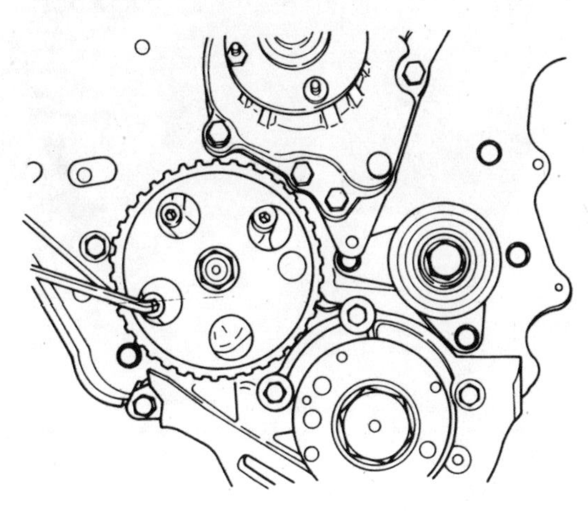

Removing the four allen head bolts retaining the oil pump—diesel engine

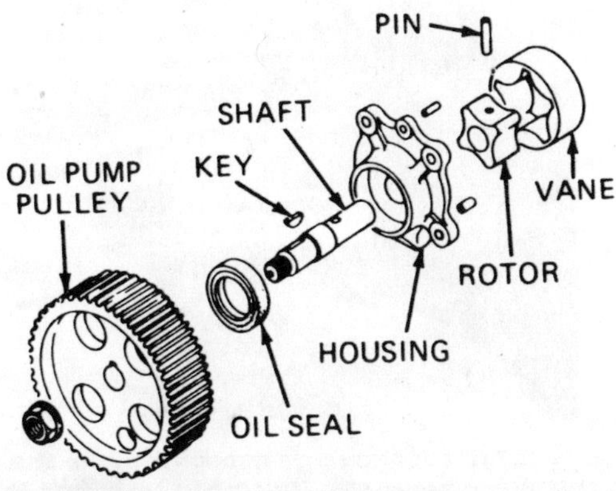

Oil pump assembly-diesel engine

Timing Belt Cover

REMOVAL AND INSTALLATION

Upper Front Cover

ALL ENGINES

1. Disconnect the negative battery cable. Remove the radiator upper mounting panel or fan shroud.
2. Remove the engine accessory drive belts on the gasoline engine. Remove the bypass hose on the diesel engine.
3. Remove the engine fan.
4. Remove the cover retaining screws and nuts and remove the cover.

To install:

5. Align the screw slots on the upper and lower parts of the cover.
6. Install the cover retaining screws and nuts.
7. Install the engine fan.
8. Install the engine accessory drive belts or the bypass hose.
9. Connect the negative battery cable.

Lower Front Cover

ALL ENGINES

1. Disconnect the negative battery cable.
2. Loosen the alternator and the air conditioning compressor bolts, if so equipped. Remove the drive belt.
3. Remove the damper pulley-to-crankshaft bolt and washer and remove the pulley.
4. Remove the upper front timing belt cover as outlined previously.
5. Remove the lower cover retaining nut (gasoline) or bolts (diesel). Remove the lower cover.

To install:

6. Align the cover with the studs on the engine block.
7. Install the lower front cover retaining nut or bolts.
8. Install the upper front timing belt cover.
9. Install the crankshaft damper pulley. Torque the retaining bolt to the specified torque.

10. Install the drive belt and tighten the alternator and compressor mounting bolts.
11. Connect the negative battery cable.

Upper Rear Cover

ALL EXCEPT DIESEL ENGINE

1. Disconnect the negative battery cable.
2. Remove the upper and lower front cover, the timing belt, and the camshaft timing sprocket.
3. Remove the three screws retaining the camshaft sprocket cover to the camshaft carrier.
4. Inspect the condition of the cam seal.
5. Position and align a new gasket over the end of the camshaft and against the camshaft carrier.
6. Install the three camshaft sprocket cover retaining screws.
7. Install the camshaft sprocket, timing belt, and upper and lower front covers.
8. Connect the negative battery cable.

Timing Belt and Sprockets

REMOVAL AND INSTALLATION

Gasoline Engine

CAUTION: *Do not discharge the air conditioner compressor or disconnect any air conditioning lines. Damage to the air conditioning system or personal injury could result.*

NOTE: *A belt tension gauge is necessary for the completion of this procedure.*

1. Rotate the engine so the timing mark on the camshaft pulley is at 0 degrees, #1 cylinder is at Top Dead Center. With #1 cylinder at TDC, a ⅛" drill rod may be inserted through a hole in the timing belt upper rear cover into a hole in the camshaft drive sprocket. This is provided to verify camshaft timing and to facilitate installation of the belt.
2. Remove the timing belt lower cover.
3. Loosen the idler pulley retaining bolt and allow the idler to rotate clockwise.
4. Remove the timing belt from the camshaft and crankshaft sprockets.
5. Remove the distributor cap and mark the location of the rotor at #1 cylinder firing position. For vehicles equipped with air conditioning, remove the air conditioning compressor and the lower compressor bracket. DO NOT disconnect any lines!
6. Remove the timing belt sprocket bolt and washer.
7. Remove camshaft sprocket.
8. Remove crankshaft sprocket.

To install:

9. Place crankshaft sprocket on end of crankshaft. Be sure that the locating tabs face outward.
10. Align the dowel in the camshaft sprocket with the locating hole in the end of the camshaft.
11. Apply Locktite® sealer or equivalent to the threads of the bolt and install bolt and washer. Torque to 100 Nm (75 ft. lbs.).
12. Install belt on camshaft and crankshaft sprockets.
13. Using a ¼" allen wrench, rotate the idler pulley counterclockwise on its attaching bolt until all slack is taken out of the belt. Tighten the bolt.
14. To facilitate the installation of the timing belt, #1 cylinder should be at TDC. If necessary, rotate the crankshaft clockwise a mini-

Mark the location of the rotor in No. 1 spark plug firing position on the distributor housing—gasoline engine

A ½ in. drill rod should go through the hole in the rear of the upper rear timing belt cover and the hole in the camshaft sprocket—gasoline engine

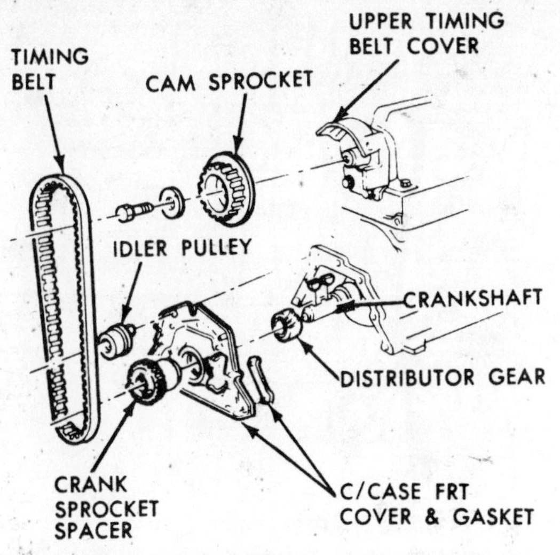

Timing belt and related parts—gasoline engine

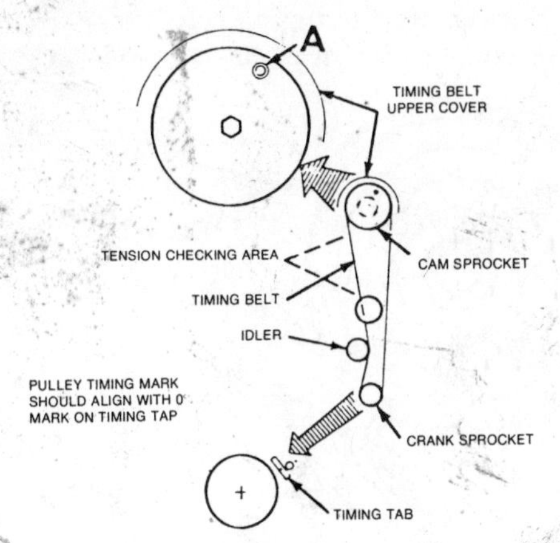

Camshaft alignment and timing belt tension check—gasoline engine.

BELT SIZE	ACCEPTABLE OPERATING RANGE	ADJUSTMENT SPECIFICATION
19mm	222 - 356N (50–80 LB.)	311±31N (70±7 LB.)

Timing belt adjustment specifications

mum of one revolution. Stop when #1 cylinder reaches TDC. DO NOT reverse direction.

15. Install a belt tension gauge between the camshaft sprocket and the idler pulley on the slack side (see illustration).

16. Adjust to the proper tension by loosening the idler attaching bolt. Using the ¼" allen wrench, rotate the idler pulley until the proper tension is attained. Torque the attaching bolt to 20 Nm (15 ft. lbs.).

17. Install the timing belt lower cover and front cover.

18. Replace the distributor cap.

19. For vehicles with air conditioning, replace the lower compressor bracket and the air conditioning compressor.

20. Attach the negative battery cable.

Diesel Engine

NOTE: *In order to complete this procedure you will need three special tools. A gear puller (J-22888), a fixing plate (J-29761), and a belt tension gauge (J-26486).*

1. Disconnect the negative battery cable.
2. Drain the cooling system.

CAUTION: *When draining the coolant, keep in mind that cats and dogs are attracted by the ethylene glycol antifreeze, and are quite likely to drink any that is left in an uncovered container or in puddles on the ground. This will prove fatal in sufficient quantity. Always drain the coolant into a sealable container. Coolant should be reused unless it is contaminated or several years old.*

3. Remove the fan shroud, cooling fan and the pulley.
4. Disconnect the bypass hose and then remove the upper half of the front cover.
5. With the No. 1 piston at TDC of the compression stroke, make sure that the notch mark

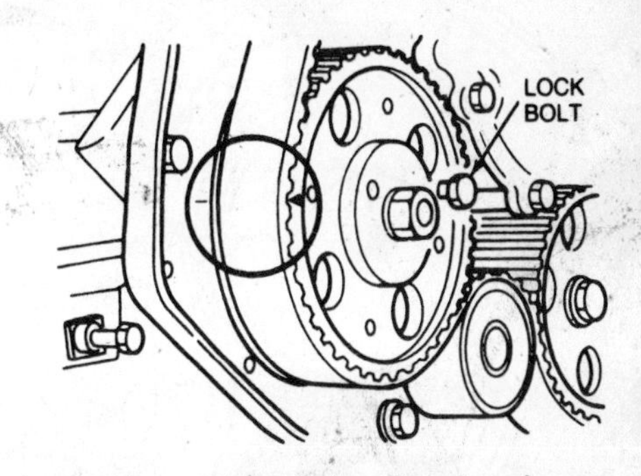

Injector gear setting mark—diesel engine

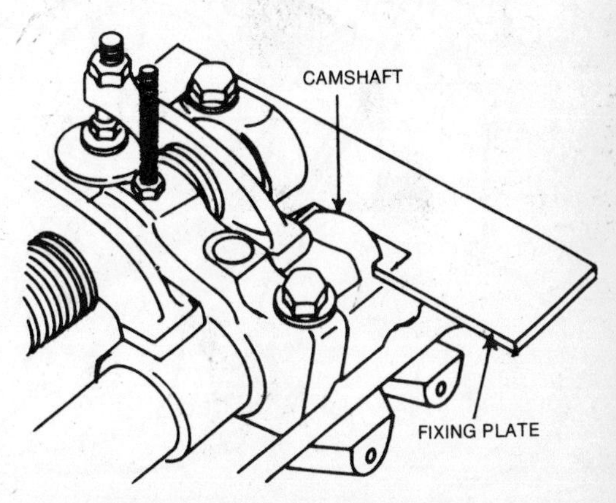

Camshaft fixing plate—diesel engine

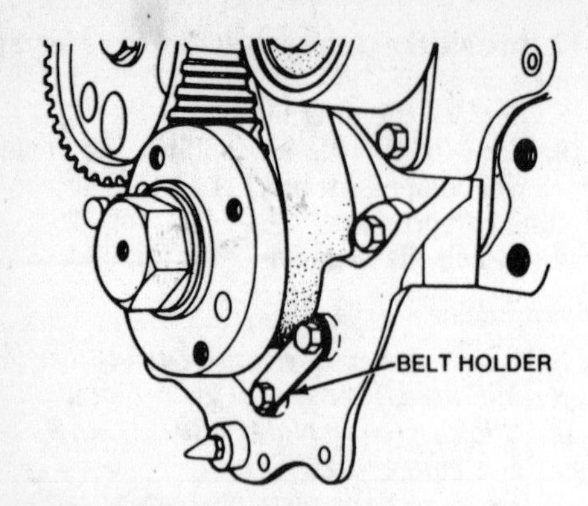

Timing belt holder—diesel engine

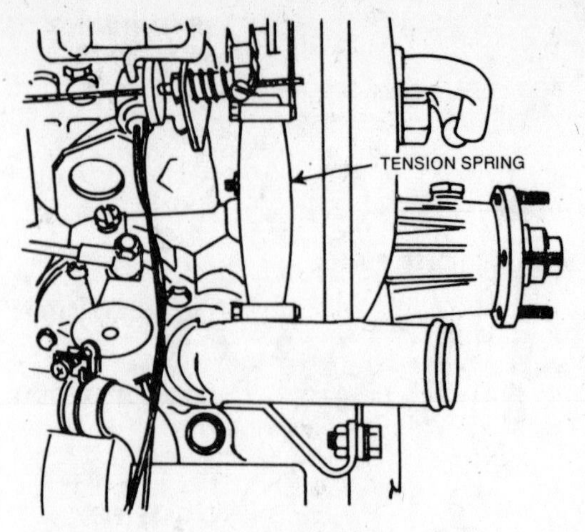

Tension spring—diesel engine

on the injection pump gear is aligned with the index marks on the front plate. If so, thread a lock bolt (8mm x 1.25) through the gear and into the front plate.

6. Remove the cylinder head cover and install a fixing plate (J-29761) in the slot at the rear of the cam. This will prevent the cam from rotating during the procedure.

7. Remove the crankshaft damper pulley and check to make sure that the No. 1 piston is still at TDC.

8. Remove the lower half of the front cover and then remove the timing belt holder from the bottom of the front plate.

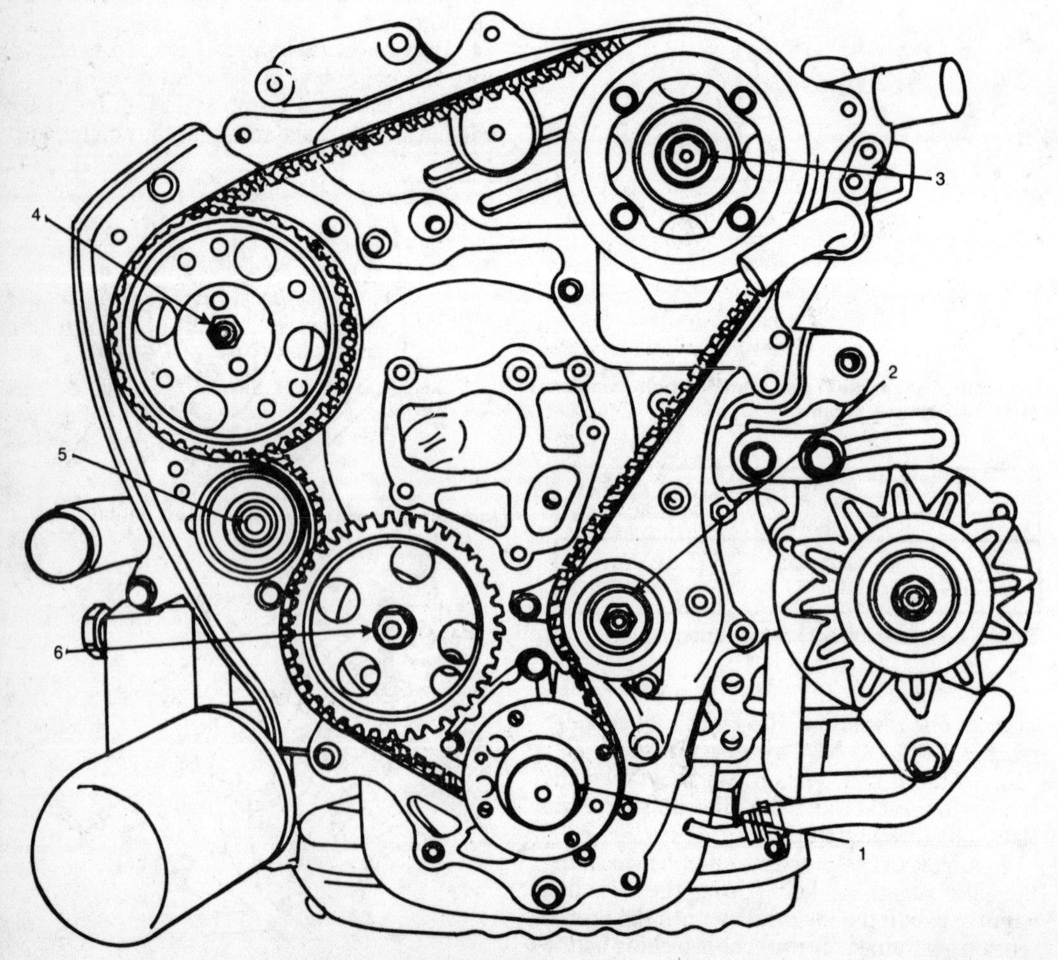

Timing belt installation sequence—diesel engine

9. Remove the tension spring behind the front plate, next to the injection pump.

10. Loosen the tension pulley and slide the timing belt off the pulleys.

11. Remove the camshaft gear retaining bolt, install a gear puller and remove the gear.

To install:

12. Reinstall the cam gear loosely so that it can be turned smoothly by hand.

13. Slide the timing belt back over the gears and note the following: the belt should be properly tensioned between the pulleys, the cogs and the belt and the gears should be properly engaged, the crankshaft should not be turned and the belt slack should be concentrated at the two tension pulleys. Push the tension pulley in with your finger and install the tension spring.

14. Partially tighten the tension pulley bolts in sequence (top first, bottom second) so as to prevent any movement of the pulley.

15. Tighten the camshaft gear retaining bolt to 45 ft. lbs. Remove the injection pump gear lock bolt.

16. Remove the fixing plate from the end of the cam.

Tightening the tension pulley bolts in sequence—top first, bottom second

Final tightening sequence of the tension pulley and plate bolts—diesel engine

17. Install the crankshaft damper pulley and then check that the No. 1 piston is still at TDC. Do not try to adjust it by moving the crankshaft.

18. Check that the marks on the injection pump gear and the front plate are still aligned and that the fixing plate still fits properly into the slot on the camshaft.

19. Loosen the tensioner pulley and plate bolts, concentrate the looseness of the timing belt around the tensioner and then tighten the bolts.

20. Belt tension should be 46-63 lbs. checked at a point midway between the upper two pulleys.

21. Remove the damper pulley again and install the belt holder in position away from the timing belt.

22. Installation of the remaining components is in the reverse order of removal.

Crankcase Front Cover

REMOVAL AND INSTALLATION

Gasoline Engines

NOTE: *A special oil seal alignment tool is required for this procedure.*

1. Disconnect the negative battery cable.

2. Remove the upper and lower front timing belt covers, crankshaft pulley, idler pulley, timing belt, and the crankshaft timing sprocket.

3. Remove the three oil pan bolts and the cover attaching bolts.

4. Remove the old cover, gasket and the front portion of the oil pan gasket.

5. Inspect the crankshaft front oil seal and replace it if necessary.

To Install:

6. Replace the crankcase cover gasket, cut the front portion of the oil pan gasket, and apply RTV sealer or its equivalent to the cut-off portion of the oil pan gasket.

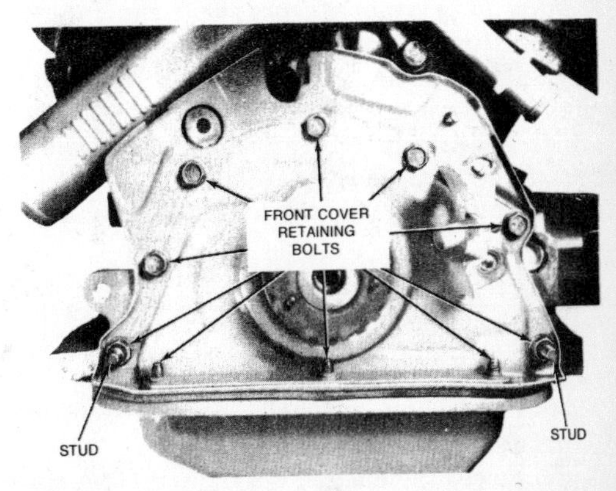

Crankcase front cover retaining bolts—gasoline engines

7. Using the special oil seal alignment tool, install the front cover. Torque the cover bolts to 75-110 in. lbs.

8. Install the crankshaft timing sprocket, timing belt, idler and crankshaft pulleys. Adjust timing belt tension using all parts of Step 19 in Timing Belt and Sprockets Removal and Installation. Install the upper and lower front timing belt covers.

9. Connect the negative battery cable.

Camshaft

REMOVAL AND INSTALLATION

NOTE: *The camshaft is supported on five bearings surfaces in the cam carrier, located on top of the cylinder head. Bearing inserts are not used.*

Gasoline Engine

NOTE: *A special valve spring compressor is necessary for this procedure. Also, if replacing camshaft or rocker arms, prelube new parts with Molykote or its equivalent.*

1. Disconnect the negative battery cable.
2. Remove engine accessory drive belts.
3. Remove the engine fan and pulley.
4. Remove the upper and lower front timing belt covers.
5. Loosen the idler pulley and remove the timing belt from the camshaft sprocket.
6. Remove the camshaft sprocket attaching bolt and washer and remove the camshaft sprocket.
7. Remove the camshaft covers. Using the special valve spring compressor, remove the valve rocker arms and guides. Keep the rocker arms and guides in order so that they can be installed in their original locations.
8. Remove any components necessary to gain working clearance.

NOTE: *The heater assembly will probably have to be removed from the firewall to gain working clearance.*

9. Remove the camshaft carrier rear cover.
10. Remove the camshaft thrust plate bolts. Slide the camshaft slightly to the rear and remove the thrust plate.
11. Remove the engine mount nuts and wire retainers.
12. Using a floor jack, raise the engine.
13. Remove the camshaft from the camshaft carrier.

To install:

14. Install the camshaft into the camshaft carrier.
15. Lower the engine.
16. Install the engine mount nuts and attach the retaining wires.
17. Slide the camshaft to the rear and install thrust plate. Slide the camshaft forward.
18. Position and align a new gasket over the end of the camshaft, against the camshaft carrier. Using RTV sealer, install the camshaft carrier rear cover.
19. Position and align a new gasket over the end of the camshaft, against the camshaft carrier, and install the upper rear timing belt cover.
20. Install any components which were removed to gain working clearance.
21. Install the valve rocker arms and guides in their original locations using the special valve spring compressor. Install the camshaft covers.
22. Align the dowel in the camshaft sprocket with the hole in the end of the camshaft and install the sprocket.
23. Apply Locktite® sealer or its equivalent to the sprocket retaining bolt threads and install the bolt and washer. Torque the sprocket retaining bolt to 65-85 ft. lbs.
24. Turn the crankshaft counterclockwise to bring the #1 cylinder to top dead center. Check to make sure the distributor rotor is in firing position from #1 cylinder. Place a 1⁄8" drill rod through the cam sprocket quick check hole into the hole in the upper timing belt cover. If the holes do not line up, loosen the timing belt and rotate the camshaft until it is properly aligned.
25. Adjust timing belt tension as outlined in Timing Belt and Sprocket Removal and Installation.
26. Install the upper and lower front timing belt covers.
27. Install the engine fan and pulley.
28. Install the engine accessory drive belts.
29. Connect the negative battery cable.

Diesel Engine

NOTE: *In order to complete this procedure you will need a gear puller (J-22888) and a fixing plate (J-29761).*

1. Remove the cylinder head cover.
2. Remove the timing belt as previously detailed. Remove the plug.
3. Install the fixing plate into the slot at the rear of the camshaft.
4. Remove the camshaft gear retaining bolt and then use a puller to remove the cam gear.
5. Remove the rocker arms and shaft as previously detailed.
6. Unscrew the bolts attaching the front head plate and then remove the plate.
7. Unscrew the camshaft bearing cap retaining bolts and remove the bearing caps with the cap side bearings.
8. Lift out the camshaft oil seal and then remove the camshaft.

9. Coat the cam and cylinder head journals with clean engine oil.
10. Position the camshaft back in the cylinder head with a new oil seal.
11. Apply a suitable liquid gasket to the cylinder head face of the No. 1 camshaft bearing cap.
12. Install the remaining bearing caps. Install the rocker arm shaft assembly leaving the adjusting screws loose.
13. Install the front head plate.
14. Install the timing belt as previously detailed.
15. Adjust the valve clearance to specifications and then install the cylinder head cover.

Pistons and Connecting Rods (Gasoline Engine)

REMOVAL

1. Remove the oil pan, oil pump and cylinder head as previously outlined.
2. For the cylinder being serviced, turn crankshaft until piston is at bottom of the stroke. Place a cloth on top of the piston.
3. Use a ridge reamer to remove any ridge and/or deposits from the upper end of the cylinder bore.
4. Turn the crankshaft until the piston is at top of stroke and remove cloth and cuttings.
5. Remove the connecting rod cap and cover the studs with plastic tubing or other similar devices. Remove assembly.

DISASSEMBLY

1. Remove connecting rod bearings from connecting rods and caps. If bearings are being reused, place them in a rack so they may be reinstalled in their original position.
2. Remove piston rings by expanding and sliding them off the pistons. Tool J-25220 is available for this purpose.
3. Place connecting rod and piston assembly on Tool J-24086-20. Using an arbor press and piston pin remover, J-24086-8, press the piston pin out of connecting rod and piston.

NOTE: *The above special tools or their equivalents may be used.*

CLEANING AND INSPECTION

Connecting Rods

1. Wash connecting rods in cleaning solvent and dry with compressed air.
2. Check for twisted or bent rods and inspect for nicks or cracks. Replace connecting rods that are damaged.

Pistons

1. Clean varnish from piston skirts and pins with a cleaning solvent. Clean the ring grooves with a groove cleaner and make sure oil ring holes and slots are clean.

WARNING: *Do not wire brush any part of the piston.*

2. Inspect the piston for cracked ring lands, skirts or pin bosses, wavy or worn ring lands, scuffed or damaged skirts, eroded areas at top of the piston. Replace pistons that are damaged or show signs of excessive wear. Inspect the grooves for nicks or burrs that might cause the rings to hang up.

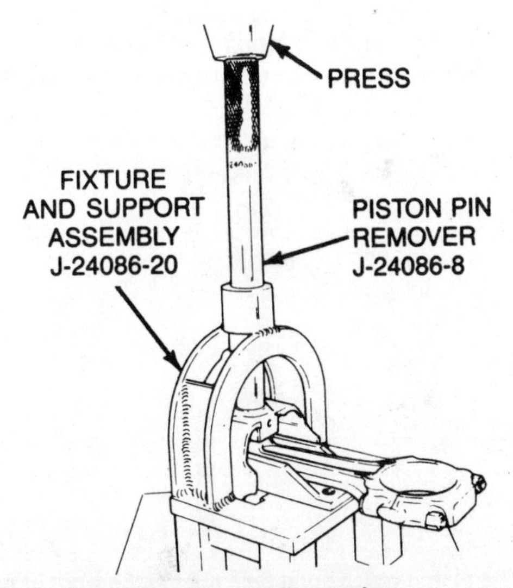

Removing piston pin—gasoline engine

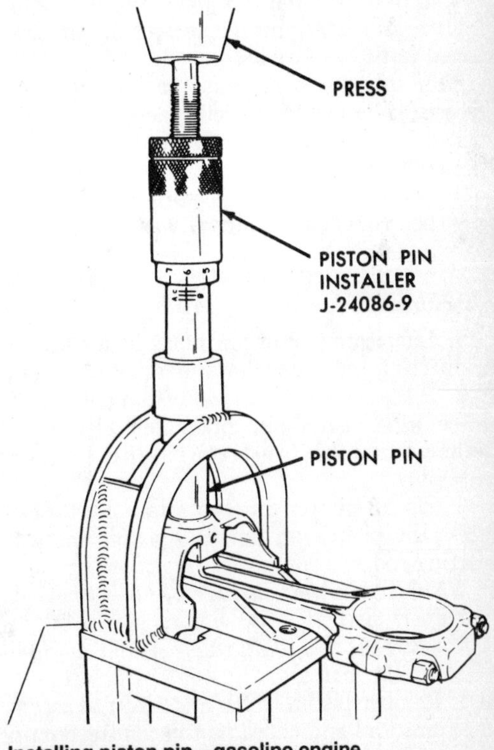

Installing piston pin—gasoline engine

Piston Pins

The piston pin clearance is designed to maintain adequate clearance under all engine operating conditions. Because of this, the piston and piston pin are a matched set and not serviced separately.

Inspect piston pin bores and piston pins for wear. Piston pin bores and piston pins must be free of varnish or scuffing when being measured. The piston pin should be measured with a micrometer and the piston pin bore should be measured with a dial bore gauge or an inside micrometer. If clearance is in excess of the 0.026mm wear limit, the piston and piston pin assembly should be replaced.

Piston Selection

1. Check used piston to cylinder bore clearance as follows:
   a. Measure the cylinder bore diameter with a telescopic gauge.
   b. Measure the piston diameter (at skirt across centerline of piston pin).
   c. Subtract piston diameter from cylinder bore diameter to determine piston-to-bore clearance.
   d. Compare piston-to-bore clearance obtained with those clearances recommended in specifications section, and determine if piston-to-bore clearance is in acceptable range.
2. If used piston is not acceptable, check piston size and determine if a new piston can be selected to fit cylinder bore.
3. If cylinder bore must be reconditioned, measure new piston diameter (across centerline of piston pin) then hone cylinder bore to obtain preferable clearance.
4. Select new piston and mark piston to identify the cylinder for which it was fitted.

ASSEMBLY

1. Lubricate piston pin holes in piston and connecting rod to facilitate installation of pin.
2. Place connecting rod in piston and hold in place with piston pin guide and piston pin. Place assembly on fixture and support assembly.
3. Using piston pin installer, J-24086-9, press the piston pin into the piston and connecting rod.

   WARNING: *After installer hub bottoms on support assembly, do not exceed 5000 psi pressure, as this could cause structural damage to the tool.*
4. Remove piston and connecting rod assembly from tool and check piston for freedom of movement on piston pin.

Piston Rings

All compression rings are marked on the upper side of the ring. When installing compression rings, make sure the marked side is toward the top of the piston. The top ring is treated with molybdenum for maximum life.

The oil control rings are of the three piece type, consisting of two segments (rails) and a spacer.

1. Select rings comparable in size to the piston being used.
2. Slip the compression ring in the cylinder bore; then press the ring down into the cylinder bore about 6mm (above ring travel). Be sure ring is square with cylinder wall.
3. Measure the space or gap between the ends of the ring with a feeler gauge.
4. If the gap between the ends of the ring is below specifications, remove the ring and try another for fit.
5. Fit each compression ring to the cylinder in which it is going to be used.
6. If the pistons have not been cleaned and inspected as outlined, do so.
7. Slip the outer surface of the top and second compression ring into the respective piston ring groove and roll the ring entirely around the groove to make sure that the ring is free. If binding occurs at any point the cause should be determined, and if caused by ring groove, remove by dressing with a fine cut file. If the binding is caused by a distorted ring, check a new ring.
8. Install piston rings as follows:
   a. Install oil ring spacer in groove.
   b. Hold spacer ends butted and install lower steel oil ring rail with gap properly located.
   c. Install upper steel oil ring rail with gap properly located.
   d. Flex the oil ring assembly to make sure the ring is free. If binding occurs at any point the cause should be determined, and if caused

The piston notch must face toward the front of the engine—gasoline engine

by ring groove, remove by dressing groove with a fine cut file. If binding is caused by a distorted ring, check a new ring.

e. Install second compression ring with gaps properly located.

f. Install top compression ring with gap properly located.

9. Proper clearance of the piston ring in its piston ring groove is very important to provide proper ring action and reduce wear. Therefore, when fitting new rings, the clearances between the surfaces of the ring and groove should be measured.

INSTALLATION

Cylinder bores must be clean before piston installation. This may be accomplished with a hot water and detergent wash. After cleaning, the bores should be swabbed several times with light engine oil and a clean dry cloth.

1. Lubricate connecting rod bearings and install in rods and rod caps.
2. Lightly coat pistons, rings and cylinder walls with light engine oil.
3. With bearing caps removed, cover the connecting rod bolts with plastic tubing or other similar device.
4. Install each connecting rod and piston assembly in its respective bore. Install with notch on piston facing front of engine. Use tool J-26468 to compress the rings. Guide the connecting rod into place on the crankshaft journal. Use a hammer handle and light blows to install the piston into the bore. Hold the ring compressor firmly against the cylinder block until all piston rings have entered the cylinder bore.
5. Remove the plastic tubing from the connecting rod bolts.
6. Install the bearing caps and torque retaining nuts to specification. Be sure to install new pistons in the same cylinders for which they were fitted, and used pistons in the same cylinder from which they were removed. Each connecting rod and bearing cap should be marked, beginning at the front of the engine. The numbers on the connecting rod and bearing cap must be on the same side when installed in the cylinder bore. If a connecting rod is ever transposed from one block or cylinder to another, new bearings should be fitted and the connecting rod should be numbered to correspond with the new cylinder number.

ROD BEARING INSPECTION AND REPLACEMENT

Connecting rod bearings are of the precision insert type and do not utilize shims for adjustment. If clearances are found to be excessive, a new bearing will be required. Service bearings are available in standard, 0.026mm U.S. and 0.050mm U.S. for use with new and used standard crankshafts, and in 0.250mm U.S. and 0.500mm U.S. for reconditioned crankshafts.

1. Remove the connecting rod cap and bearing.
2. Inspect the bearing for evidence of wear or damage. Bearings showing the above should not be reinstalled.
3. Wipe both upper and lower bearing shells and crankpin clean of oil.
4. Measure the crankpin for out-of-round or taper with a micrometer. If not within specifications, replace or recondition the crankshaft. If within specifications and a new bearing is to be installed, measure the maximum diameter of the crankpin to determine new bearing size required.
5. If within specifications, measure new or used bearing clearances with Plastigage® or its equivalent. If a bearing is being fitted to an out-of-round crankpin, be sure to fit the maximum diameter of the crankpin. If the bearing is fitted to the minimum diameter and the crankpin is out-ot-round 0.025mm, interference between the bearing and crankpin will result in rapid bearing failure.

   a. Place a piece of gauging plastic the full width of the crankpin, parallel to the crankshaft.

   b. Install the bearing in the connecting rod and cap.

   c. Install the bearing cap and evenly torque the nuts to specifications. Do not turn the crankshaft with the gauging plastic installed.

   d. Remove the bearing cap and using the scale on the gauging plastic envelope, measure the gauging plastic width at its widest point.

6. If the clearance exceeds specifications select a new, correct size bearing and remeasure the clearance. Be sure to check what size bearing is being removed in order to determine proper replacement size bearing.

   NOTE: *If the clearance cannot be brought to within specifications, the crankpin will have to be machined to the closest undersize. If the crankpin is already at maximum undersize, replace the crankshaft.*

7. Coat the bearing surface with oil, install the rod cap and torque the nuts to specifications.
8. When all connecting rod bearings have been installed, tap each rod lightly (parallel to the crankpin) to make sure they have clearance.
9. Measure all connecting rod side clearances (see specifications), between the connecting rod cap and side of crankpin.

Pistons and Connecting Rods (Diesel Engine)

REMOVAL

1. Remove the engine assembly as outlined earlier in this chapter.
2. Remove the timing belt.
3. Remove the cam cover.
4. Remove the rocker arm assembly.
5. Remove the camshaft.
6. Remove the cylinder head assembly.
7. Remove the oil pan.
8. Remove the carbon deposits from the upper part of the cylinder wall (cylinders to be serviced) with a scraper.
9. Remove the connecting rod cap nuts and remove the bearing and cap.
10. Remove the piston and connecting rod by pushing on the edge of the connecting rod with a hammer handle or piece of wood.

NOTE: *Refer to the piston disassembly illustration for removal of the piston pin and rings.*

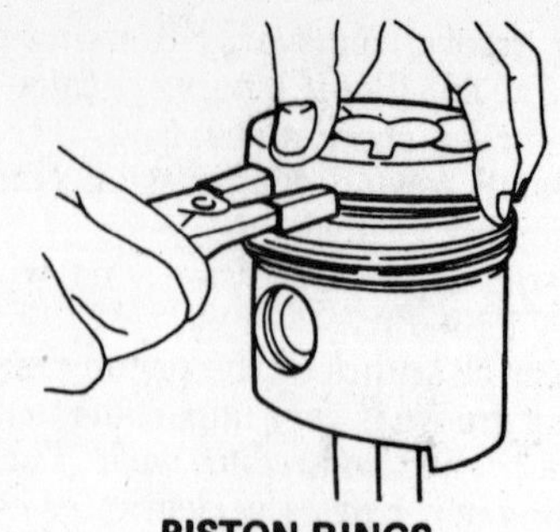

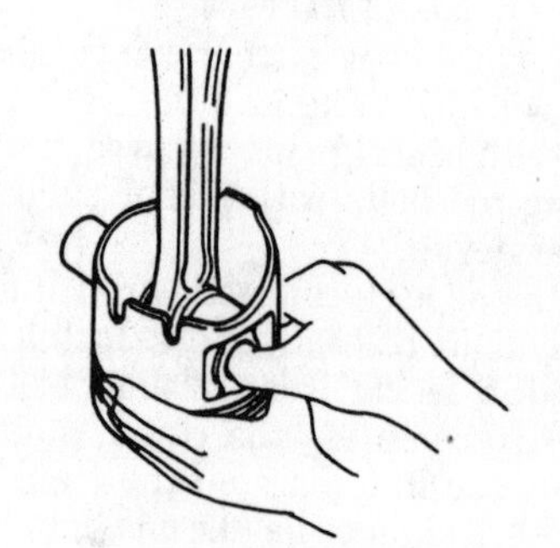

Piston disassembly—diesel engine

INSPECTION

Pistons

1. Check the pistons for scuffs, cracking or wear. Replace the pistons with new ones if found to be defective.
2. Measure the clearance between the pistons and cylinder walls as follows:
   a. With an outside micrometer, measure the diameter of the piston at a point below the piston head (grading position) in direction at a right angle to the piston pin. Standard is 63.7mm.
   b. With a cylinder bore indicator, measure the cylinder bore diameter at the lower section where the amount of wear is smallest. Compare the value obtained with the cylinder bore diameter to determine the clearance. If the amount of clearance deviates from 0.005-0.045mm, replace the pistons with new ones.

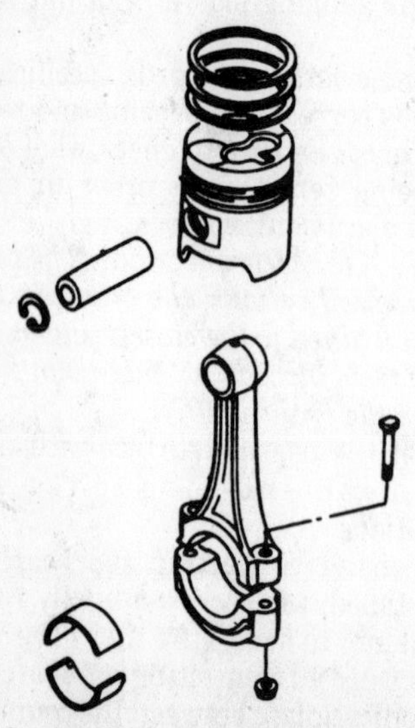

Piston and connecting rod—diesel engine

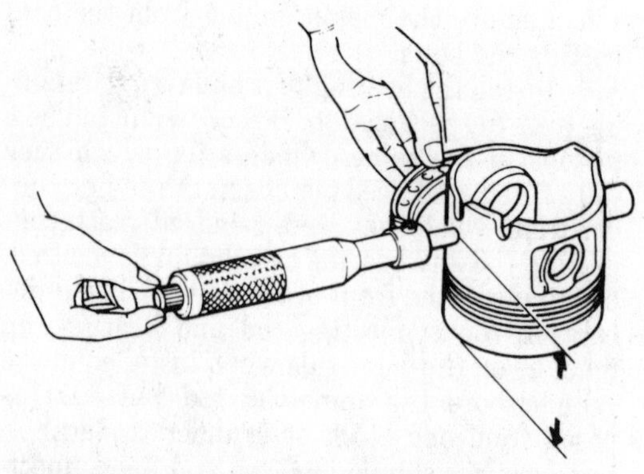

Measuring piston diameter—diesel engine

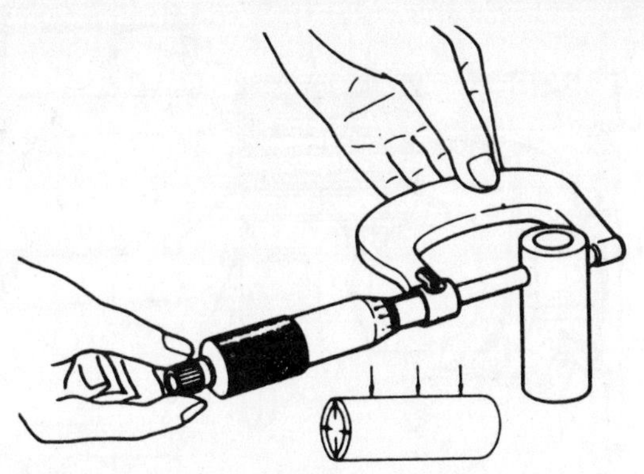

Measuring piston pin outside diameter—diesel engine

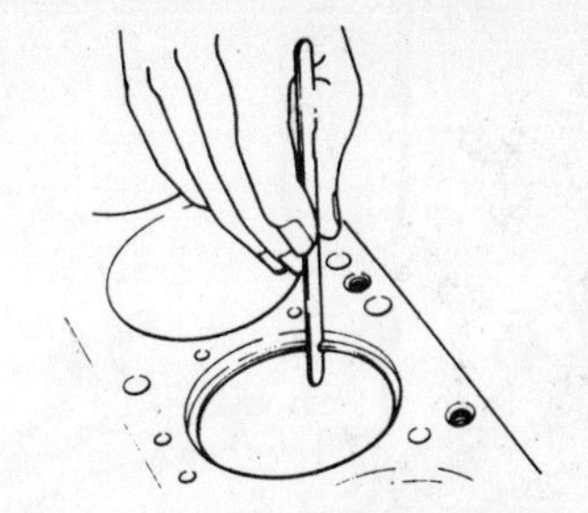

Measuring piston ring gap—diesel engine

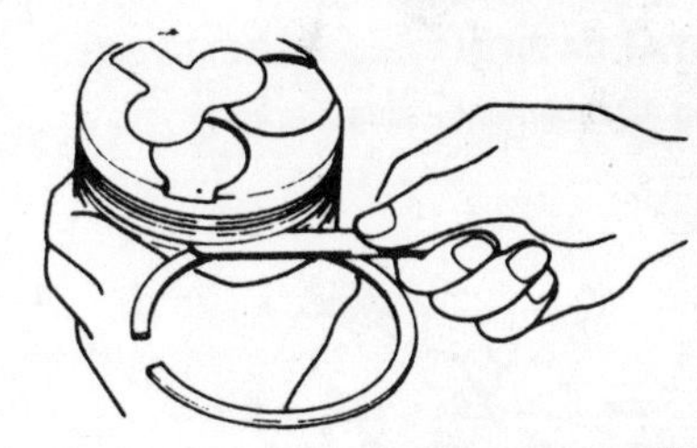

Measuring piston ring and ring groove—diesel engine

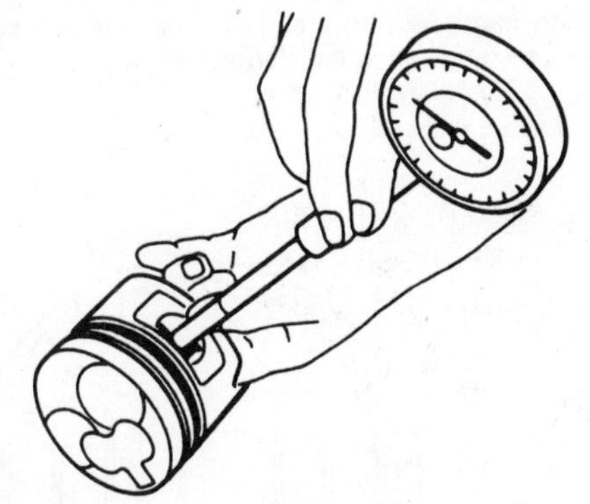

Measuring clearance between piston pin and hole—diesel engine

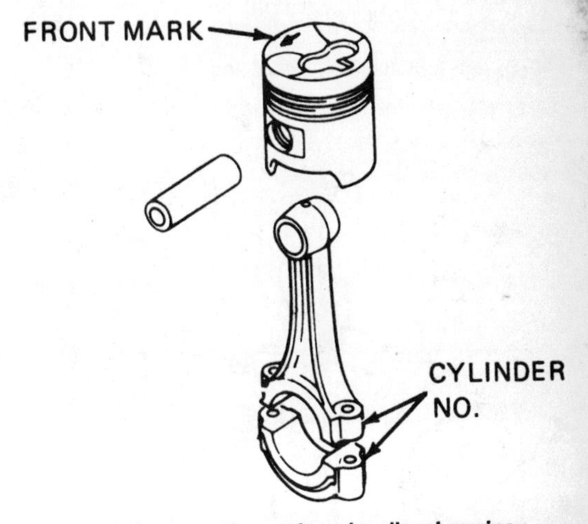

Piston and connecting rod mark—diesel engine

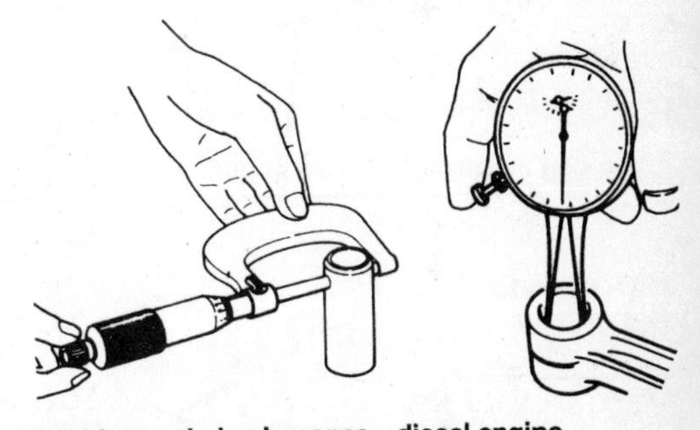

Bushing and pin clearance—diesel engine

Piston Pins

Visually inspect for damage, wear or other abnormal conditions. Measure the diameter at several points around the circumference, then check the clearance between the piston pin and piston pin hole.

Pin outside diameter:

- Standard - 25.0mm
- Limit - 24.97mm

Piston pin and hole:

- •Standard - 0.002-0.012mm
- •Limit - 0.05mm

Piston Rings

The piston rings should be replaced with new ones whenever the engine is overhauled or if found to be worn or damaged.

1. Insert the piston rings into the cylinder bore and push them down to the skirt (portion where bore diameter is smallest) using the piston head. This will position piston rings at a right angle to the cylinder wall. Measure the ring gap with a feeler gauge. Replace the piston rings with new ones if the measured value is beyond the limit shown in the chart.
2. With a feeler gauge, measure the clearance between the piston ring and ring grooves in the piston at several points around the circumference of the piston. Replace the piston rings together with the piston if the measured value is greater than 0.15mm or if abnormal

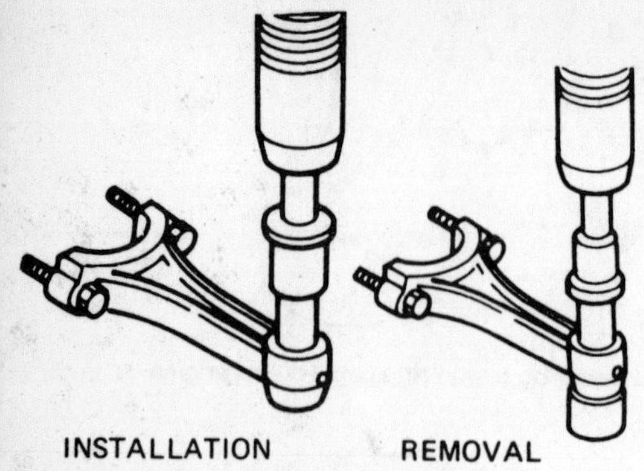

Bushing replacement—diesel engine

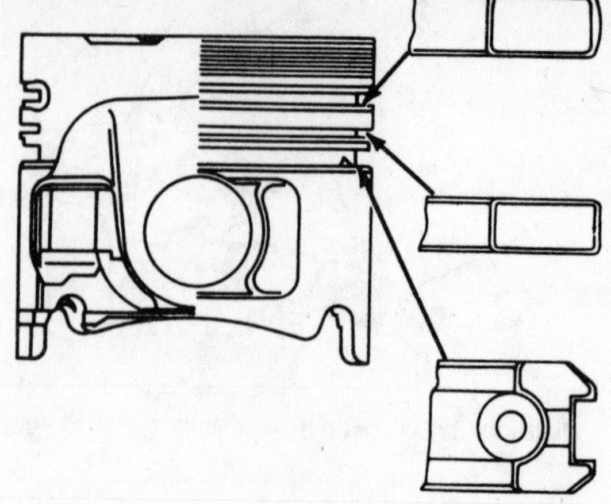
Oil ring installation, the ends of the coil expander should be opposed to the oil ring gap—diesel engine

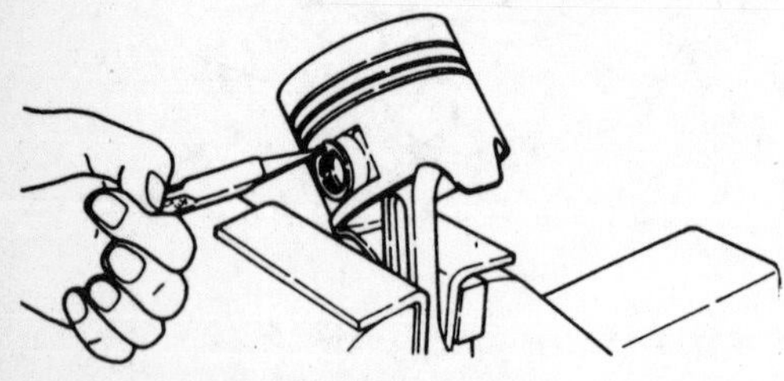
Snap ring installation—diesel engine

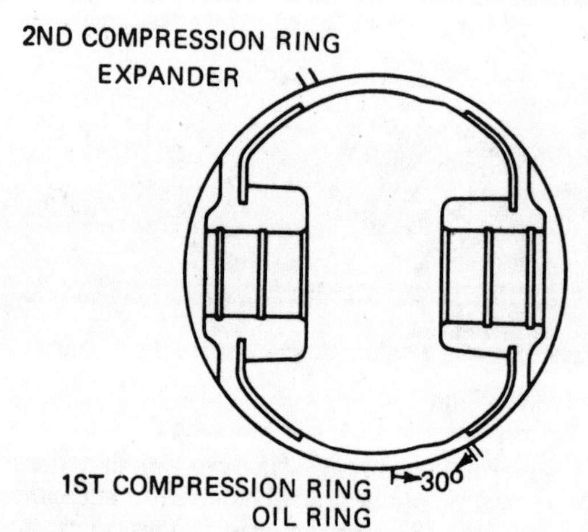

Ring gap location—diesel engine

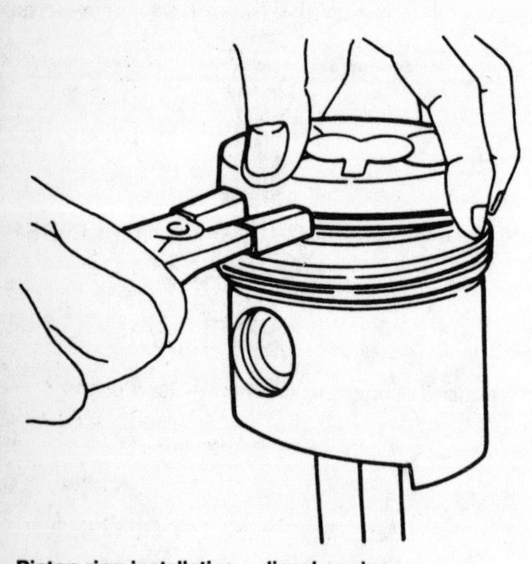
Piston ring installation—diesel engine

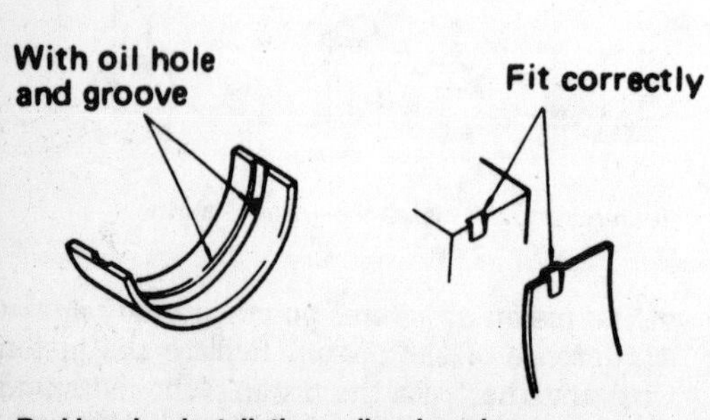

Rod bearing installation—diesel engine

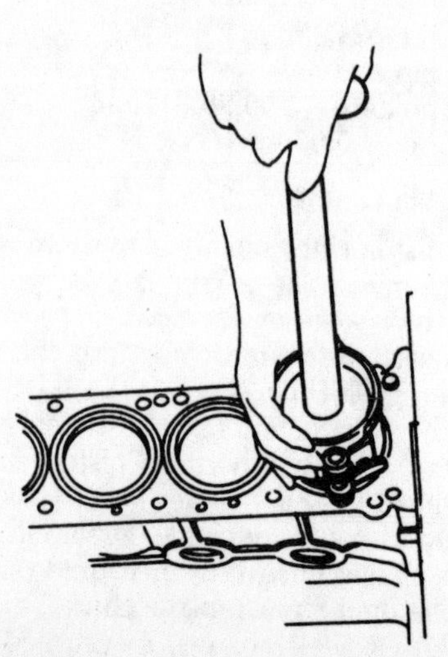
Piston installation—diesel engine

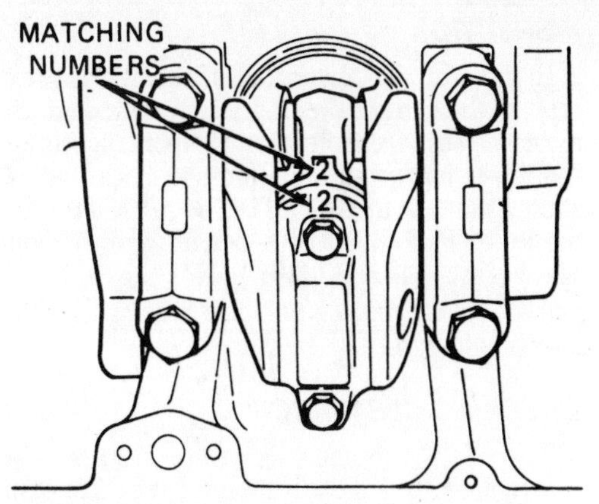

Installation of bearing cap—diesel engine

contact is noticeable on the upper or lower face of the piston rings.

NOTE: *Refer to the Piston and Ring Specifications Chart at the beginning of this chapter.*

Connecting Rods

If distortion of connecting rod is suspicious, remove piston from the connecting rod and check for parallelism. Check the connecting rods for distortion and bending by installing on a connecting rod alignment tool. Correct or replace the connecting rod if the amount of distortion is greater than 0.2mm or bending is greater than 0.15mm per 100mm of length.

Bushing Replacement

Measure the inside diameter of the connecting rod, small end bushing and outside diameter of the piston pin clearance between bushing and piston pin 0.05mm

1. Remove and install bushing using remover/installer J-29765 as shown. Align the bushing hole with the connecting rod oil hole.
2. After installing a new bushing, finish the bushing bore with a pin hole grinder.

REASSEMBLY

1. Install the piston on the connecting rod, so that combustion chamber on piston head is on the same side with the cylinder number mark side (side with bearing stopper) of the connecting rod big end. Mark on the connecting rod should be on the same side of the front mark on the piston.
2. Apply engine oil to the piston pin and install it into the piston pin hole in the piston using finger pressure.
3. Install the snap rings into slots in piston pin hole properly.
4. Install the piston rings in sequence of coil expander, oil ring, 2nd compression ring and 1st compression ring.
5. Install the 1st and 2nd compression rings and oil ring with the **N** mark facing upward. The ends of the coil expander should be opposed to the oil ring gap.

NOTE: *After installation of piston rings, apply engine oil to the circumference of the rings and check that each ring rotates smoothly.*

INSTALLATION

1. Apply clean engine oil to bearing surfaces, outer edge of piston and rings. Be sure rod bearing projected portions are fitted to the recess in the rod and cap.
2. The position ring gaps should be set in piston is 180 degrees apart.
3. Using a piston installer, push piston (with its notched mark to front of engine) into the cylinder until the connecting rod is brought into contact with the crank pin. Use a piece of wood or hammer handle to push piston into bore (Piston Installer J-8037).
4. Install the connecting rod bearing cap by aligning it with the cylinder number mark on the connecting rod.
5. Apply engine oil to the threads and seating face of the nuts, then install and tighten the nuts to 88 Nm (65 ft. lbs.).
6. Check that crankshaft turns smoothly.
7. The remainder of the installation is the reverse of removal.

Crankshaft (Gasoline Engine)

REMOVAL

The crankshaft can be removed with the engine is disassembled for overhaul or without complete disassembly as outlined below.

1. With the engine removed from the vehicle, remove the following:
   a. Drive belts and pulleys
   b. Timing belt front upper and lower covers
   c. Timing belt and idler pulley
   d. Coil
   e. Fuel pump and pushrod
   f. Distributor
   g. Crankcase front cover
   h. Oil pan
   i. Oil pump and pickup tube
   j. Spark plugs
2. Check the connecting rod caps for cylinder number identification. If necessary, mark caps with corresponding cylinder number.
3. Remove the connecting rod caps and push the pistons to the top of the bores.
4. Remove the main bearing caps, rear main oil seal and lift crankshaft out of cylinder block.

CLEANING AND INSPECTION

1. Wash crankshaft in solvent and dry with compressed air.
2. Measure dimensions of main bearing journals and crankpins with a micrometer for out-of-round, taper or undersize (see specifications).
3. Check crankshaft for runout by supporting at the front and rear main bearings journals in V-blocks and check at the front and rear intermediate journals with a dial indicator (see specifications).
4. Replace or recondition the crankshaft if out of specifications.

Main Bearings (Gasoline Engine)

Main bearings are of the precision insert type and do not utilize shims for adjustment. If clearances are found to be excessive, a new bearing, both upper and lower halves, will be repaired. Service bearings are available in standard, 0.026mm, 0.050mm, 0.250mm and 0.500mm undersizes.

Selective fitting of main bearing inserts is necessary in production in order to obtain close tolerances. For this reason you may find one half of a standard insert with one half of a 0.026mm undersize insert which will decrease the clearance 0.013mm from using a full standard bearing.

When a production crankshaft cannot be precision fitted by this method, it is then ground 0.250mm undersize ON ONLY THOSE MAIN JOURNALS THAT CANNOT BE PROPERLY FITTED, ALL JOURNALS WILL NOT NECESSARILY BE GROUND. A 0.250mm undersize bearing will then be used for precision fitting in the same manner as previously described.

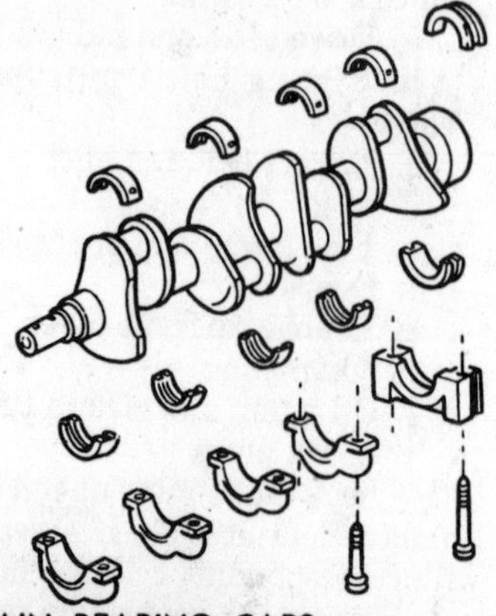

Main bearings—gasoline engine

INSPECTION

In general, the lower half of the bearing, except #1 bearing shows a greater wear and the most distress from fatigue. If upon inspection the lower half is suitable for use, it can be assumed that the upper half is also satisfactory. If the lower half shows evidence of wear or damage, both upper and lower halves should be replaced. Never replace one half without replacing the other half.

CHECKING CLEARANCE

To obtain the most accurate results with Plastigage® (or its equivalent), a wax-like plastic material which will compress evenly without damaging either surface, certain precautions should be observed.

If the engine is out of the vehicle and upside down, the crankshaft will rest on the upper bearings and the total clearance can be measured between the lower bearing and journal. If the engine is to remain in the vehicle, the crankshaft should be supported both front and rear to remove the clearance from the upper bearing. The total clearance can then be measured between the lower bearing and journal.

To assure the proper seating of the crankshaft, all bearing cap bolts should be at their specified torque. In addition, preparatory to checking fit of bearings, the surface of the crankshaft journal and bearing should be wiped clean of oil.

1. Starting with the rear main bearing, remove bearing cap and wipe oil from journal and bearing cap.
2. Place a piece of gauging plastic the full width of the bearing (parallel to the crankshaft) on the journal. Do not rotate the crankshaft while the gauging plastic is between the bearing and the journal.
3. Install the bearing cap and evenly torque the retaining bolts to specifications. Bearing cap MUST be torqued to specifications in order to assure proper reading. Variations in torque affect the compression of the plastic gauge.
4. Remove the bearing cap. The flattened gauging plastic will be found adhering to either the bearing shell or journal.
5. On the edge of gauging plastic envelope there is a graduated scale which is correlated in thousandths of a millimeter. Without removing the gauging plastic, measure its compressed width (at the widest point) with the graduations on the gauging plastic envelope.

Normally, main bearing journals wear evenly and are not out-of-round. However, if a bearing is being fitted to an out-of-round journal 0.025mm max, be sure to fir to the maximum diameter of the journal: If the bearing is fitted to the minimum diameter and the journal is out-of-round 0.025mm, interference between the bearing and journal will result in rapid bearing failure.

If the flattened gauging plastic tapers toward the middle or ends, there is a difference in clearance indicating taper, low spot or other irregularity of the bearing or journal. Be sure to measure the journal with a micrometer if the flattened gauging plastic indicates more than 0.025mm difference.

6. If the bearing clearance is within specifications, the bearing insert is satisfactory. If the clearance is not within specifications, replace the insert. Always replace both upper and lower insert as a unit. If a new bearing cap is being installed and clearance is less than 0.025mm, inspect for burrs or nicks, if none are found then install shims as required.

7. A standard 0.025mm or 0.050mm undersize bearing may produce the proper clearance. If not, it will be necessary to regrind the crankshaft journal for use with the next undersize bearing. After selecting new bearing, recheck clearance.

8. Proceed to the next bearing. After all bearings have been checked, rotate the crankshaft to see that there is no excessive drag. When checking #1 main bearing, loosen accessory drive belts and timing belt so as to prevent tapered reading with plastic gauge.

9. Measure crankshaft end play (see specifications) by forcing the crankshaft to the extreme front position. Measure at the front end of the #5 bearing with a feeler gauge.

10. Install a new rear main bearing oil seal.

REPLACEMENT

Main bearings may be replaced with or without removing the crankshaft.

With Crankshaft Removal

1. Remove and inspect the crankshaft.
2. Remove the main bearings from the cylinder block and main bearing caps.
3. Coat bearing surfaces of new, correct size main bearings with oil and install in the cylinder block and main bearing caps.
4. Install crankshaft.

Without Crankshaft Removal

1. With oil pan, oil pump and spark plugs removed, remove cap on main bearing requiring replacement and remove bearing from cap.
2. Install a main bearing removing and installing tool in oil hole in crankshaft journal. If such a tool is not available, a cotter pin may be bent as required to do the job.
3. Rotate the crankshaft clockwise as viewed from the front of the engine. This will roll the upper bearing out of the block.
4. Oil new selected size upper bearing and insert plain (unnotched) end between crankshaft and indented, or notched, side of block. Rotate the bearing into place and remove the tool from oil hole in crankshaft journal.
5. Oil new lower bearing and install in bearing cap.
6. Install main bearing cap with arrows pointing toward front of engine.
7. Torque all main bearing caps, EXCEPT THE REAR MAIN CAP, to specifications. Torque rear main bearing cap to 14-16 Nm (10-12 ft. lbs.) then tap end of crankshaft, first rearward, then forward with a lead hammer. This will line up rear main bearing and crankshaft thrust surfaces. Retorque all main bearing caps to specification.

Crankshaft and Main Bearings (Diesel Engine)

REMOVAL

1. Remove the engine as previously outlined in this chapter.
2. Remove the fan and pulley.
3. Remove the upper dust cover.
4. Remove the lower cover.
5. Remove the timing belt cover.
6. Remove the cam cover.
7. Rotate the crankshaft and install a camshaft holding tool No. J-29761, or equivalent, then install an injection pump lock bolt. Refer to Injection Pump removal and installation in Chapter 4.
8. Remove the adjusting spring.
9. Remove the cam gear.
10. Remove the crankshaft hub and gear.
11. Remove the front cover bolts.
12. Rotate the engine on the stand.

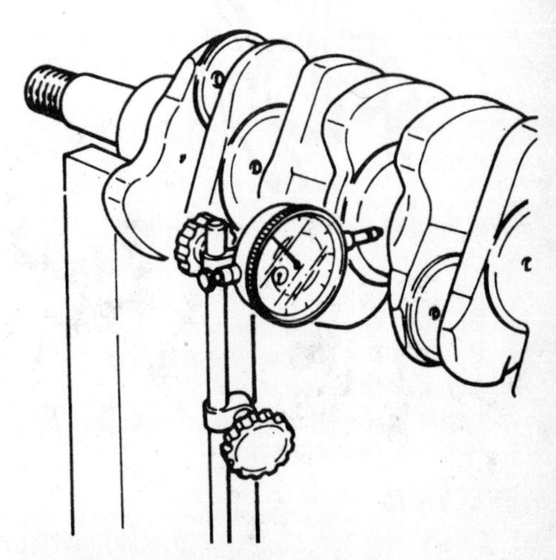

Crankshaft runout—diesel engine

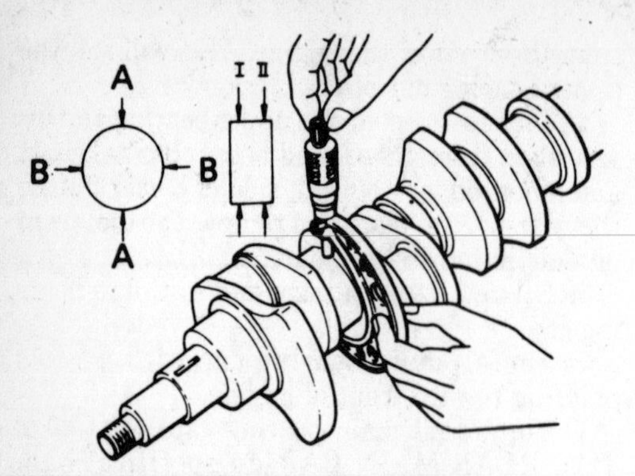

Journal and pin diameter—diesel engine

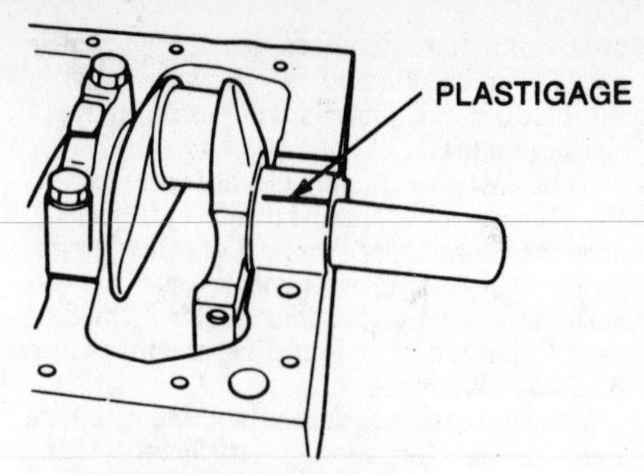

Install plastigage—diesel engine

Bearing and journal clearance—diesel engine

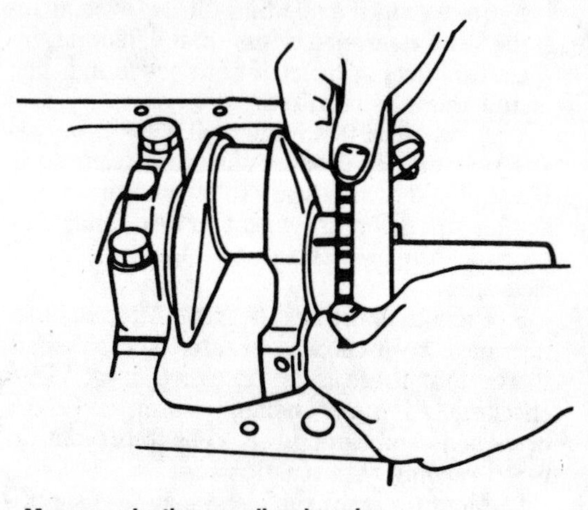
Measure plastigage—diesel engine

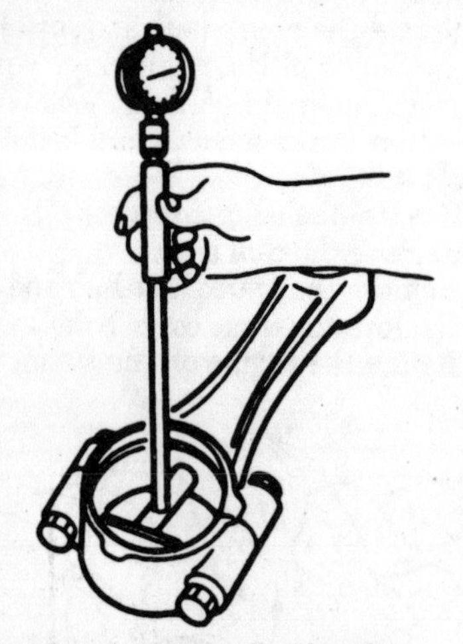
Pin and bearing clearance—diesel engine

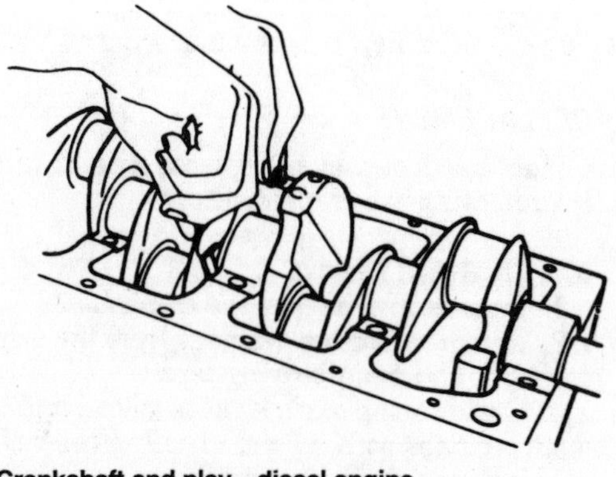
Crankshaft end play—diesel engine

13. Remove the oil pan front cover.
14. Remove the oil strainer.
15. Remove the connecting rod caps.
16. Remove the rear main caps.
17. Remove the flywheel or flexplate.
18. Remove the crankshaft.

INSPECTION

1. Check the faces of the crankshaft journals, crankpin and oil seal fitting faces for wear and damage, and oil port restrictions. No attempt should be made to grind finish the faces of the crankshaft journals and crankpins.

2. Support the crankshaft on aligner or V-blocks at #1 and #5 journals and check for runout by turning the crankshaft carefully in one direction with the probe of a dial indicator resting on #3 journal. Take the highest reading. If the amount of runout is greater than 0.06mm, correct or replace the crankshaft.

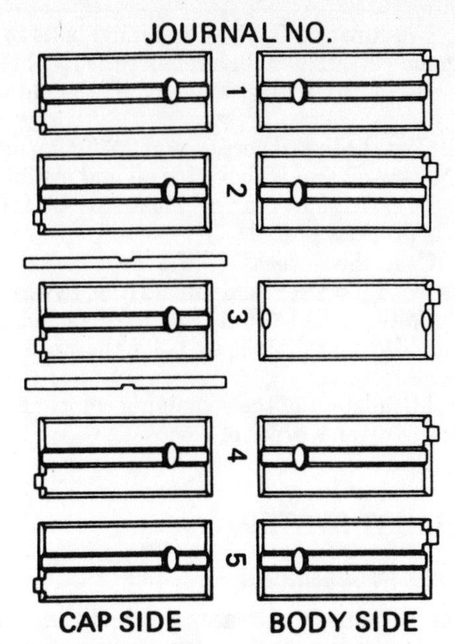

Main bearing installation—diesel engine

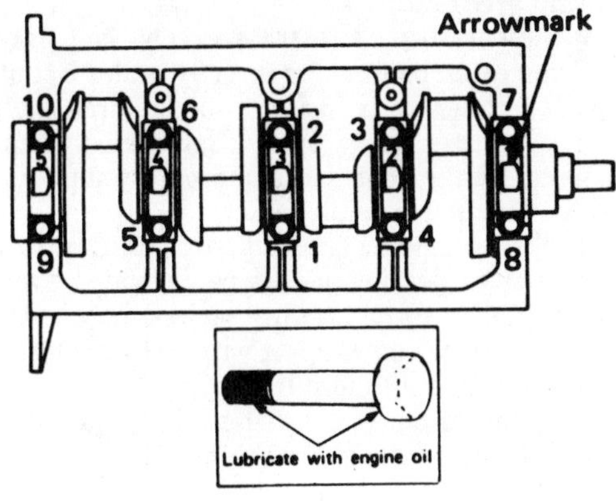

Bearing cap bolt torque sequence—diesel engine

3. Measure the diameters of the crankshaft journals and crankpins at the front and rear (I and II) in directions of A and B, to determine the amount of wear and taper wear.

Standard Journal Diameter:

- 55.92-55.935mm

Standard Pin Diameter:

- 48.925-48.94mm

Inspect and measure bearing inside diameter as follows:

a. Check the inner face of the bearings for pin holes, separation or sculling. Replace the entire set of bearing if any of them are found to be defective.

b. Install crankshaft bearings into position on the cylinder blocks. Then install the bearing caps and bolts. Tighten the bearing cap bolts to 100 Nm (75 ft. lbs.) and measure the inside diameter with an inside micrometer or a cylinder bore indicator. Standard bearing and journal clearance is 0.039-0.08mm.

c. Install the connecting rod bearing on the rod big end with the bearing cap. Install and torque the bearing cap bolts to 80 Nm (60 ft. lbs.), then measure the inside diameter of the bearing with an inside micrometer or a cylinder bore indicator.

Pin and bearing clearance:

- Standard - 0.04-0.07mm
- Limit - 0.12mm

Measurement of clearance with gauging plastic.

a. Wipe the crankshaft journals and crankpins to remove oil.

b. Install the bearings on the cylinder block and mount the crankshaft in position carefully; then turn the crankshaft about thirty degrees to ensure a good contact between the crankshaft and bearings.

c. Position gauging plastic over the crankshaft journal in direction in line with the axis of the crankshaft, so that it covers the entire width of the bearing.

d. Install the bearing cap and tighten the bearing cap bolts to 95 Nm (70 ft. lbs.). Do not turn the crankshaft with gauging plastic installed.

e. Remove the bearing cap and check the width of the gauging plastic against the scale printed on the packet.

e. Follow the same steps to measure the oil clearance between the crankpins and bearings.

Check crankshaft end play as follows:

a. Install the bearings on the cylinder block and position the crankshaft over the bearings.

b. Install the thrust bearing in position on both sides of the #3 journal.

c. Move the crankshaft fully endwise and check the clearance between the crankshaft and thrust bearing using a feeler gauge. If the clearance is greater than 0.3mm, replace the thrust bearings with new ones; standard value is 0.06-0.24mm.

INSTALLATION

1. Install the bearings properly and apply generous amounts of engine oil to the inner face of the bearings. Position the crankshaft over the bearings carefully, then install the thrust bearing. The bearings should be installed correctly in their respective position. Install the thrust bearing with the oil grooved side turned outward.

2. Apply a coat of silicone gasket evenly to the joining faces fo the No. 5 bearing caps and cylinder body. The No. 1 and No. 5 bearing caps

should be installed flush with the face of the cylinder body.

3. Apply engine oil to the threads and seating face of the bolts. Install the bearing caps in sequence of cylinder numbers with the arrow mark pointing toward the front of the engine and semitighten the bolts. Then retighten the bolts to 88-99 Nm (65-72 ft. lbs.).

Rear Main Oil Seal

REPLACEMENT

Gasoline Engine

1. Remove the engine from the car and place it on a stand.
2. Remove the oil pan.
3. Remove the rear main bearing cap.
4. Clean the bearing cap and case.
5. Check the crankshaft seal for excessive wear, etc.
6. Install a new crankshaft seal. Make sure that it is properly seated against the rear main bearing seal bulkhead.
7. Apply RTV sealer or its equivalent to the bearing cap horizontal split line.
8. With the sealer still wet, install the rear main bearing cap. On 1976-77 models, tighten the cap bolts to 40-52 ft. lbs. On 1978 and later models, tighten the cap bolts to 10-12 ft. lbs., then tap the crankshaft first rearward the forward and tighten the bolts to 50 ft. lbs.
9. Apply RTV sealer or its equivalent in the vertical grooves of the rear main bearing cap.
10. Remove any excess sealer and install the oil pan. Torque the oil pan bolts to 45-60 in. lbs.
11. Install the engine in the car.

Diesel Engine

1. Remove the transmission as detailed later in this section. If equipped with a manual transmission remove the clutch.

WITH CRANKSHAFT INSTALLED MINUS REAR BEARING CAP, SLIDE REAR SEAL OVER CRANK END UNTIL IT SEATS AGAINST CASE. THEN INSTALL REAR BEARING CAP.

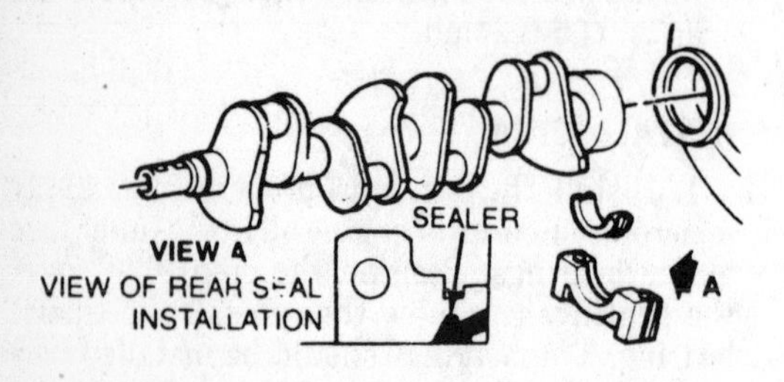

COMPLETELY FILL BEARING CAP GROOVE WITH SEALING COMPOUND UNTIL SEALING COMPOUND COMES OUT AT SPLIT LINE OF CASE AND BEARING CAP. GAP MUST NOT EXIST ALLOWING OIL LEAK.

Rear main oil seal

2. Unscrew the flywheel retaining bolts in a diagonal pattern and then remove the flywheel.
3. Use a screwdriver and pry off the old oil seal.
4. Coat the lipped portion and the fitting face of the new oil seal with engine oil and install it into the crankshaft bearing. Make sure that the seal is properly seated.
5. Coat the threads of the new mounting bolts with Loctite® and install the flywheel. Tighten the bolts to 40 ft. lbs. in a diagonal sequence. Do not reuse the old bolts, they must be new.
6. Installation of the remaining components is in the reverse order of removal.

EXHAUST SYSTEM

Safety Precautions

For a number of reasons, exhaust system work can be the most dangerous type of work you can do on your car. Always observe the following precautions:

- Support the car extra securely. Not only will you often be working directly under it, but you'll frequently be using a lot of force, say, heavy hammer blows, to dislodge rusted parts. This can cause a car that's improperly supported to shift and possibly fall.
- Wear goggles. Exhaust system parts are always rusty. Metal chips can be dislodged, even when you're only turning rusted bolts. Attempting to pry pipes apart with a chisel makes the chips fly even more frequently.
- If you're using a cutting torch, keep it a great distance from either the fuel tank or lines. Stop what you're doing and feel the temperature of the fuel bearing pipes on the tank frequently. Even slight heat can expand and/or vaporize fuel, resulting in accumulated vapor, or even a liquid leak, near your torch.
- Watch where your hammer blows fall and make sure you hit squarely. You could easily tap a brake or fuel line when you hit an exhaust system part with a glancing blow. Inspect all lines and hoses in the area where you've been working.

CAUTION: *Be very careful when working on or near the catalytic converter. External temperatures can reach 1,500°F (816°C) and more, causing severe burns. Removal or installation should be performed only on a cold exhaust system.*

Special Tools

A number of special exhaust system tools can be rented from auto supply houses or local stores that rent special equipment. A common one is a tail pipe expander, designed to enable you to join pipes of identical diameter.

It may also be quite helpful to use solvents designed to loosen rusted bolts or flanges. Soaking rusted parts the night before you do the job can speed the work of freeing rusted parts considerably. Remember that these solvents are often flammable. Apply only to parts after they are cool!

COMPONENT REPLACEMENT

System components may be welded or clamped together. The system consists of a head pipe, catalytic converter, intermediate pipe, muffler and tail pipe, in that order from the engine to the back of the car.

The head pipe is bolted to the exhaust manifold. Various hangers suspend the system from the floor pan. When assembling exhaust system parts, the relative clearances around all system parts is extremely critical. See the accompanying illustration and observe all clearances during assembly. In the event that the system is welded, the various parts will have to be cut apart for removal. In these cases, the cut parts may not be reused. To cut the parts, a hacksaw is the best choice. An oxy-acetylene cutting torch may be faster but the sparks are DANGEROUS near the fuel tank, and, at the very least, accidents could happen, resulting in damage to other under-car parts, not to mention yourself!

The following replacement steps relate to clamped parts:

1. Raise and support the car on jackstands. It's much easier on you if you can get the car up on 4 stands. Some pipes need lots of clearance for removal and installation. If the system has been in the car for a long time, spray the clamped joints with a rust dissolving solutions such as WD-40® or Liquid Wrench®, and let it set according to the instructions on the can.

2. Remove the nuts from the U-bolts; don't be surprised if the U-bolts break while removing the nuts. Age and rust account for this. Besides, you shouldn't reuse old U-bolts. When

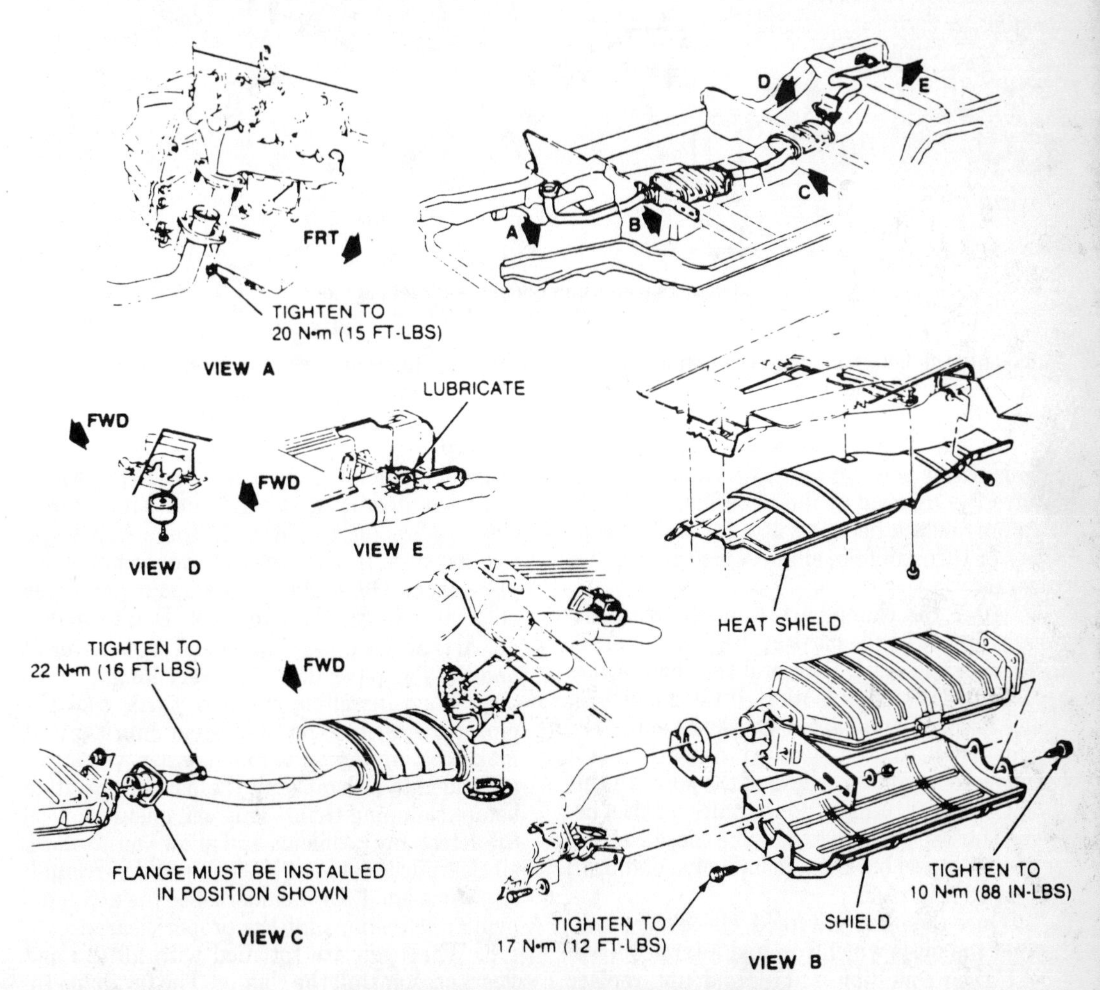

Exhaust system components—gasoline engine

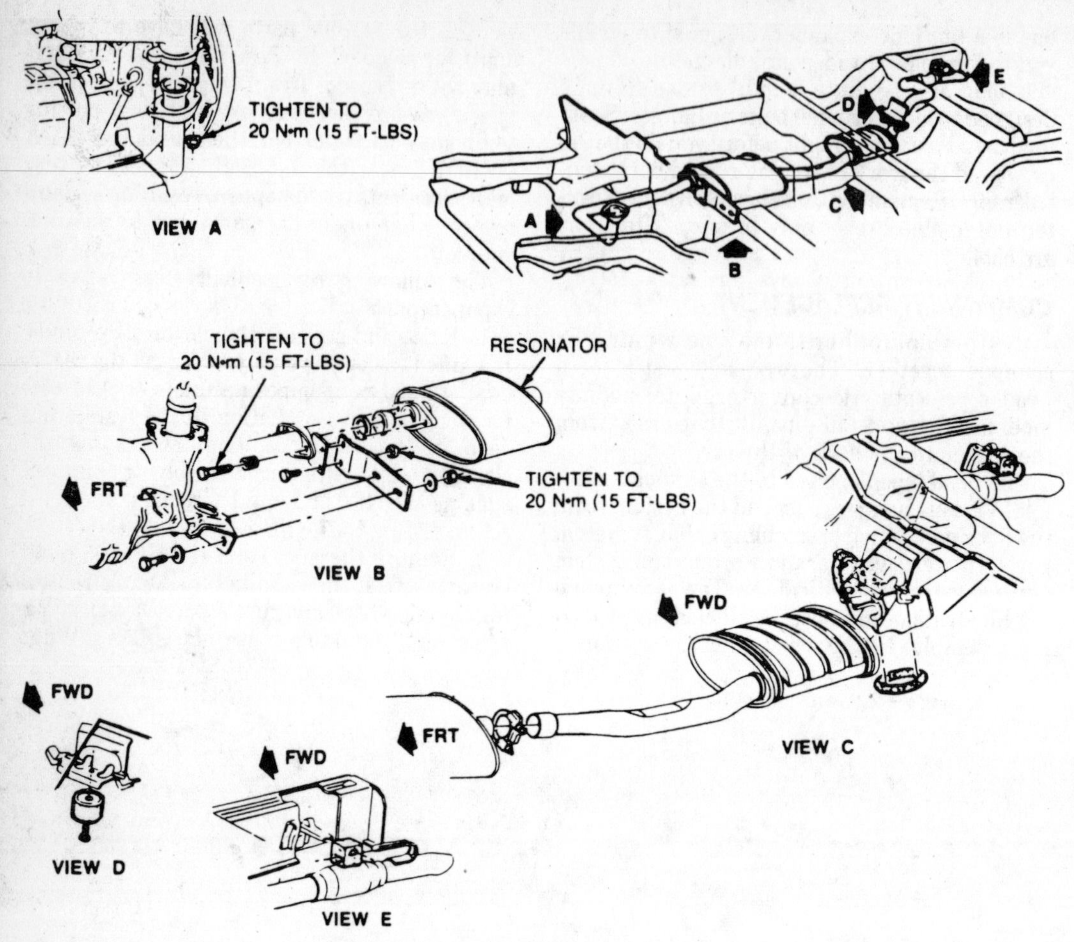

Exhaust system components—diesel engine

unbolting the headpipe from the exhaust manifold, make sure that the bolts are free before trying to remove them. If you snap a stud in the exhaust manifold, the stud will have to be removed with a bolt extractor, which often necessitates the removal of the manifold itself. The headpipe uses a necked collar for sealing purposes at the manifold, eliminating the need for a gasket.

3. After the clamps are removed from the joints, first twist the parts at the joints to break loose rust and scale, then pull the components apart with a twisting motion. If the parts twist freely but won't pull apart, check the joint. The clamp may have been installed so tightly that it has caused a slight crushing of the joint. In this event, the best thing to do is secure a chisel designed for the purpose and, using the chisel and a hammer, peel back the female pipe end until the parts are freed.

4. Once the parts are freed, check the condition of the pipes which you had intended keeping. If their condition is at all in doubt, replace them too. You went to a lot of work to get one or more components out. You don't want to have to go through that again in the near future. If you are retaining a pipe, check the pipe end. If it was crushed by a clamp, it can be restored to its original diameter using a pipe expander, which can be rented at most good auto parts stores. Check, also, the condition of the exhaust system hangers. If ANY deterioration is noted, replace them. Oh, and one note about parts: use only parts designed for your car. Don't use fits-all parts or flex pipes. The fits-all parts never fit and the flex pipes don't last very long.

5. When installing the new parts, coat the pipe ends with exhaust system lubricant. It makes fitting the parts much easier. It's also a good idea to assemble all the parts in position before clamping them. This will ensure a good fit, detect any problems and allow you to check all clearances between the parts and surrounding frame and floor members. See the accompanying illustrations for the proper clearances.

6. When you are satisfied with all fits and clearances, install the clamps. The headpipe-to-manifold nuts should be torqued to 20 ft. lbs. If

the studs were rusty, wire-brush them clean and spray them with WD-40® or Liquid Wrench®. This will ensure a proper torque reading. Position the clamps on the slip points as illustrated. The slits in the female pipe ends should be under the U-bolts, not under the clamp end. Tighten the U-bolt nuts securely, without crushing the pipe. The pipe fit should be tight, so that you can't swivel the pipe by hand. Don't forget: always use new clamps. When the system is tight, recheck all clearances. Start the engine and check the joints for leaks. A leak can be felt by hand. MAKE CERTAIN THAT THE CAR IS SECURE ON THE JACKSTANDS BEFORE GETTING UNDER IT WITH THE ENGINE RUNNING!! If any leaks are detected, tighten the clamp until the leak stops. If the pipe starts to deform before the leak stops, reposition the clamp and tighten it. If that still doesn't stop the leak, it may be that you don't have enough overlap on the pipe fit. Shut off the engine and try pushing the pipe together further. Be careful; the pipe gets hot quickly.

7. When everything is tight and secure, lower the car and take it for a road test. Make sure there are no unusual sounds or vibration. Most new pipes are coated with a preservative, so the system will be pretty smelly for a day or two while the coating burns off.

Emission Controls

4

GASOLINE ENGINE EMISSION CONTROLS

Positive Crankcase Ventilation

Positive Crankcase Ventilation (PCV) is a system which returns combustible gases which have leaked past the piston rings into the crankcase, back through the intake manifold for reburning. This leakage is the normal result of the necessary working clearance of the piston rings. If these gases were to remain in the crankcase they would react with the oil to form sludge. Since there is also a certain amount of unburned fuel in the gases, dilution of the oil would occur. Both sludge and diluted oil will accelerate the wear of the engine.

Along with gases returning to the intake manifold, the PCV valve also returns a certain amount of additional air. The carburetor used with this system has been calibrated to compensate for the additional air intake.

The system consists of a hose connecting the air cleaner to the cam cover and another hose connecting the PCV valve mounted in a grommet in the cam cover and the intake manifold.

The PCV valve regulates the flow of combustion gases through the system. During engine idle and deceleration when intake manifold vacuum is high, the PCV valve restricts vapor flow to the intake manifold. When the engine is accelerated or is at constant speed, intake manifold vacuum is low and the PCV valve allows crankcase gases to flow into the intake manifold. Should the engine backfire, the plunger inside the valve is forced against its seat preventing the backfire from traveling through the PCV valve and into the engine crankcase.

The PCV valve is checked for proper operation simply by removing it from the grommet in the cam cover and shaking. If the plunger in the valve rattles, the valve is good and can be replaced. At the required mileage intervals, install a new PCV valve and use compressed air to blow out the PCV valve hose to eleminate any restrictions.

PCV valve removal and istallation are covered in Chapter One.

Exhaust Gas Recirculation

Exhaust Gas Recirculation (EGR), is used to reduce oxides of nitrogen (NOx) exhaust emissions. NOx formation occurs at very high combustion temperatures so that the EGR system reduces combustion temperature slightly by introducing small amounts of inert exhaust gas into the intake manifold. The result is reduced formation of NOx.

The EGR valve is mounted on the intake manifold and contains a vacuum diaphragm. The unit is operated by intake manifold vacuum and controls the flow of exhaust gases.

A vacuum signal supply port is located in the throttle body of the carburetor above the throttle plate. Vacuum is supplied to the EGR valve 9causing recirculation), at part-throttle conditions. EGR does not occur at idle or at wide open throttle.

Some models also use a thermal vacuum switch (TSV), mounted in the outlet water housing to block vacuum to the EGR valve until engine coolant temperature is approximately 100°F (38°C).

An engine that idles roughly may be caused by a bad EGR valve. Push on the diaphragm plate to check for freedom of movement. If it sticks, replace the valve. Hook up a vacuum gauge between the signal tube and the vacuum hose. With the engine running and warmed up, increase the engine speed to obtain 5 in.Hg of vacuum. Remove the vacuum hose downward. This should be accompanied by increased engine speed. REplace the vacuum hose and check to see that the the plate moves upward. The engine speed should drop. If the diaphragm is not

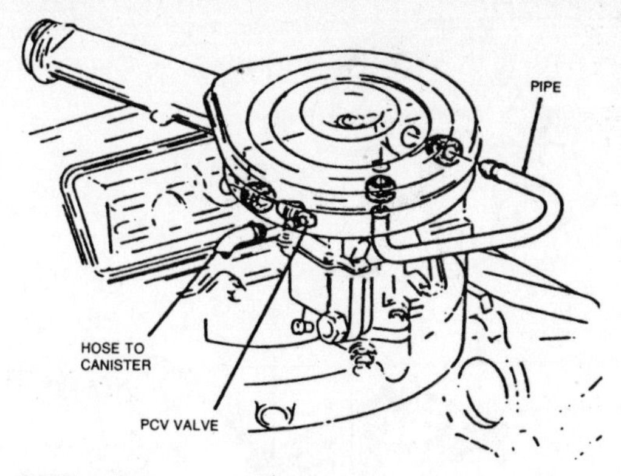

PCV system

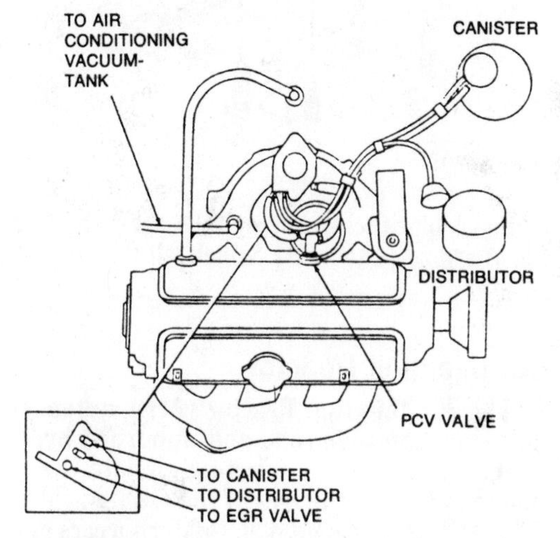

Emission hose routing without air injection (non-California)

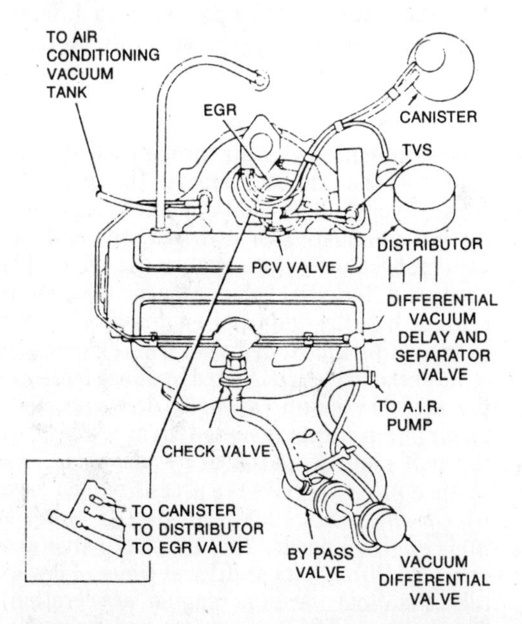

Emission hose routing with air injection (California)

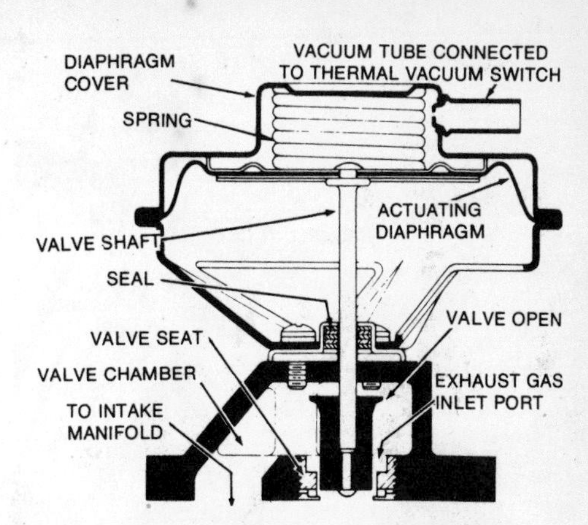

Cross-section of an EGR valve (typical)

moving check for vacuum at the EGR hose. If there is none, check for leaking, plugged, or misplaced hoses. If the diaphragm moves but there is no change in rpm, check for blocked EGR manifold passages.

EGR VALVE REMOVAL AND INSTALLATION

1. Disconnect the vacuum line at the EGR valve.
2. Remove the bolt securing the EGR valve and remove the valve from the intake manifold.
3. Use a new gasket and install the EGR valve on the intake manifold. Torque the mounting bolt to 13-18 ft. lbs.
4. Connect the vacuum line to the valve.

THERMAL VACUUM SWITCH CHECK

NOTE: *This test must be performed with the engine at normal operating temperatures, permitting the vacuum signal to reach the EGR valve.*

1. Remove the EGR valve vacuum hose at EGR valve and attach the hose to a vacuum gauge.
2. Start the engine and open the throttle partially. Do not race the engine. As the trhottle is opened, the vacuum gauge should respond proportionately.
3. If the vacuum gauge responds correctly, remove it and replace the hose to the EGR valve.
4. If the gauge does not react correctly, remove the carburetor to switch hose at the switch and attach the vacuum gauge to it. Repeat Step 2. If the gauge responds to the opening of the throttle, the switch is defective and must be replaced.
5. If the gauge does not respond to the opening throttle, suspect a plugged hose or a defective carburetor.

Location of EGR thermal vacuum switch

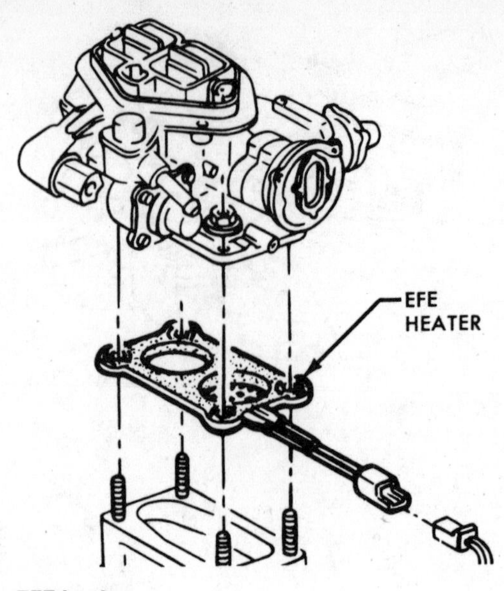

EFE heater

THERMAL VACUUM SWITCH REMOVAL AND INSTALLATION

1. Disconnect the vacuum lines.
2. Remove the switch from the thermostat housing.
3. Use sealer on the threads of the switch, install the switch and torque to 15 ft. lbs.
4. Turn the switch head if necessary toalign forhose routing and connect vacuum hoses.

Early Fuel Evaporation System (EFE)

The electric EFE system utilizes a ceramic heater grid located underneath the primary bore of the carburetor as part of the carburetor insulator gasket. It heads the incoming fuel-air charge for improved vaporization and driveability on cold drive-way.

On 1980 models when the ignition switch is turned on, voltage is applied to a snap action bimetal switch. If engine coolant temperature is below calibrated value, a circuit is completed to the heater and current begins to flow. The heater, incorporating a positive temperature coefficient (PTC) semiconductor element, increases in temperature and then self-regulates at a calibrated temperature, except at high engine speeds when the fuel-air flow will reduce the temperature below the regulated value. When coolant temperature reaches the calibrated value, the snap action switch breaks the circuit and shuts off the heater.

On 1981 and later models when the ignition switch is turned on and engine coolant temperature is low, voltage is applied to the EFE relay through the ECM. With the EFE relay energized, voltage is applied to the EFE heater. When coolant temperature increased, the ECM de-energizes the relay which shuts off EFE heater.

Air Injection Reactor

The Air Injection Reactor (AIR) system reduces carbon monoxide and unburned hydrocarbon emissions by injecting air into the exhaust system at the rear of the exhaust valves. The AIR system is used on California cars only. The system consists of an air pump, air injection tubes (one for each cylinder), a vacuum differential valve, an air by-pass valve, a differential vacuum delay and separator valve, a check valve, and the required hoses to connect the components.

The air pump (with an integral filter), compresses and injects the air through the air manifolds into the exhaust system to the rear of the exhaust valves. The additional air brings about further combustion of hydrocarbons and carbon monoxide in the exhaust manifold. The vacuum differential valve stops air injection to prevent backfiring during engine deceleration by activating the air by-pass valve. The vacuum differential valve is triggered by sharp increases in manifold vacuum. On engine dedeleration total air pump output is vented to the atmosphere through a muffler in the air by-pass valve. Also in the air by-pass valve is a pressure relief valve which vents excess air from the air pump at high engine speeds. The by-pass valve also vents air through its muffler at times of low intake manifold vacuum (engine acceleration). This low manifold vacuum venting is controlled by the differential vacuum delay and separator

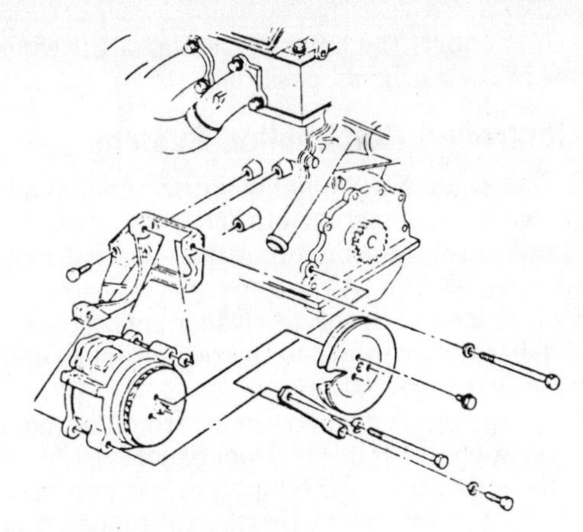

Air pump mounting details

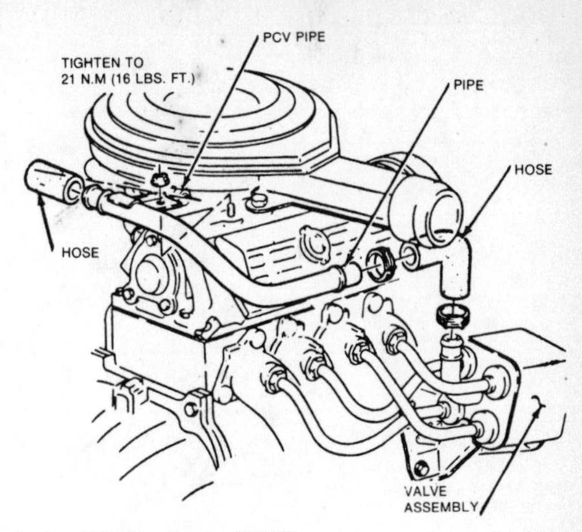

Pulse Air System—PAIR

valve which blocks this venting during very short periods of 20 seconds or less to prevent possible overheating of the catalytic converter. The check valve prevents exhaust gases from entering the air pump.

When properly installed and maintained the AIR system will effectively reduce contaminating exhausts. However, if any AIR component or any engine component that operates in conjunction with the AIR system malfunctions, the pollutant level will be increased. Whenever the AIR system seems to be malfunctioning, the engine tune-up should be checked, particularly the PCV system, carburetor, and other systems which directly affect the fuel-air ratio.

AIR PUMP REMOVAL AND INSTALLATION

WARNING: *Do not pry on the pump housing or clamp the pump in a vise; the housing is soft and may become distorted.*

1. Disconnect the air output hose at the pump.
2. Hold the pump pulley from rotating and loosen the pulley bolts. Remove the drive belt and pump pulley.
3. Remove the air pump mounting bolts and remove the air pump.
4. Install the air pump by reversing the removal procedure.

Air Management System-Pulse Air System-PAIR

The PAIR system is used only on California cars. It consists of a pulse air valve which has four check valves. The firing ofthe engine creates a pulsating flow of exhaust gases which are either positive or negative, depending whether the xhaust valve is seated or not.

If the pressure is positive the check valve is forced closed and no exhaust gas will be able to fow past the valve and into the fresh air supply.

If there is negative pressure, a vacuum, in the exhaust system, the check valve will open and allow fresh air to be drawn in and mixed with the exhaust gases. During high engine rpm the check valve will remain closed.

If one or more ofthe check valves has failed the engine may surge or perform poorly. A short hissing noise may also indicate a defective pulse air valve. Inspect the valve.

When exhaust gases are allowed to pass through the pulse air valve, excessive heat will be transferred to the valve body. This will be indicated by burned off paint or deteriorated rubber hoses. Replace the air valve as necessary.

To inspect the pulse air valve create a vacuum at the hose end of the valve to 5kPa (15 in.Hg). The vacuum is permitted to drop to 17 kPa (5 in.Hg) in tow seconds. If the vacuum drops in less than two seconds, replace the valve.

PULSE AIR VALVE REMOVAL AND INSTALLATION

1. Remove the air cleaner and disconnect the rubber hose from the pulse air valve.
2. Disconnect the support bracket and remove the attaching bolts.
3. Remove the pulse air valve.
4. Install the new pulse air valve and tighten attaching bolts to 14-18 Mn (10-13 ft. lbs.).
5. Connect the support bracket.
6. Connect the rubber hose to the pulse air valve and install the air cleaner.

NOTE: *In some cases the support bracket is not present in the vehicle. If so, simply omit this step.*

Evaporative Emission Control

The Evaporative Control System (ECS) limits gasoline vapor escape into the atmosphere. A domed fuel tank and pressure-vacuum filler cap

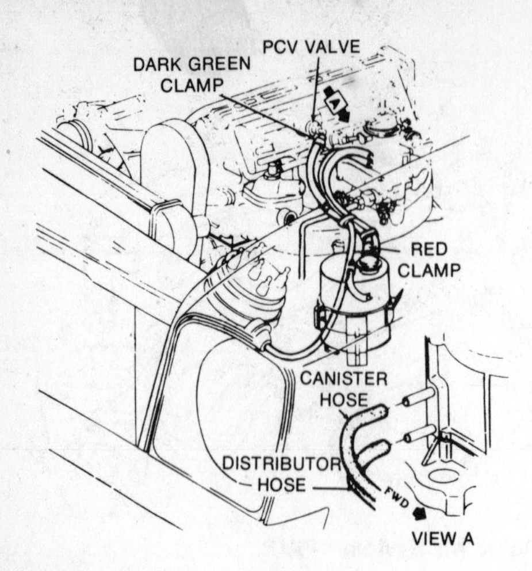

Evaporative emission control system

is used with a plastic, charcoal-filled storage canister.

Fuel vapors travel from the fuel tank vent pipe (located above fuel level in the dome of the fuel tank), by way of steel tubing and fuel-resistant rubber hose to the plastic vapor storage canister in the engine compartment. Fuel vapors are routed into the PCV system for burning when ported carburetor vacuum operates a valve in the canister. As fuel is pumped from the tank, a relief valve in the tank cap opens to allow air to enter the fuel tank.

CHARCOAL CANISTER REMOVAL AND INSTALLATION

1. Carefully note the installed position of the hose connected to the canister, then disconnect the hoses.
2. Loosen the mounting clamps and remove the canister. To replace the canister filter, remove the filter from the bottom of the canister with your fingers.

Check to ensure that the hose connection openings are clear and check the purge valve by applying vacuum to it. If OK, it will hold vacuum. Check the condition of the hoses and replace as necessary. When replacing ECS hoses, use only fuel-resistant hose marked EVAP.

If the purge valve is defective, disconnect the lines at the valve and snap off the valve cap. Turn the cap slowly as the diaphragm is under spring tension. Remove the diaphragm, spring retainer, and spring. Check all orifices and replace parts as necessary. Install the spring, spring retainer, diaphragm and cap. Connect the lines to the valve.

3. Install a new filter in the bottom of the charcoal canister.
4. Install the canister and tighten its mounting clamp bolts.
5. Connect the hoses to the top of the canister in their original positions.

Controlled Combustion System

The Controlled Combustion System (CCS) increases combustion efficiency by means of leaner carburetor mixtures and revised distributor calibration. Also, a thermostatically-controlled damper in the air cleaner snorkel maintains warm air intake to the carburetor to optimize fuel vaporization.

An air intake duct routes air from the radiator support to the air cleaner snorkel, then to the air cleaner. Air temperature is automatically controlled by a thermostatic damper inside the air cleaner snorkel. The damper selects warm air from the exhaust manifold heat stove when air temperature is below 50°F (10°C). When air temperature is above 110°F (43°C), the damper selects outside air from the air intake duct.

When replacing the air cleaner, remove the air cleaner from the air intake snorkel and the carburetor and throw it away. Check the carburetor air horn gasket and replace it if damaged or cracked, and install a new air cleaner.

Catalytic Converter

All models are equipped with an underfloor cayalytic converter. The converter contains pellets coated with the cayalyst material containing platinum and palladium. The converter reduces hydrocarbon and carbon monoxide emissions by transforming them into carbon dioxide and water through a chemical reaction which takes place at great heat.

Unleaded fuel only must be used with converter equipped cars because lead in leaded fuel is not consumed in the combustion process and will enter the converter and coat the pellets, eventually rendering the catalytic converter useless for emission control. To ensure the use of unleaded fuel only, all models have a small diameter fuel inlet filler which will accept only the smaller unleaded fuel nozzle.

Oxygen Sensor

An oxygen sensor is used on all models. The sensor protrudes into the exhaust stream and monitors the oxygen content of the exhaust gases. The difference between the oxygen content of the exhaust gases and that of the outside air generates a voltage signal to the ECM. The ECM monitors this voltage and, depending upon the value of the signal received, issues a command to adjust for a rich or a lean condition.

No attempt should ever be made to measure the voltage output of the sensor. The current

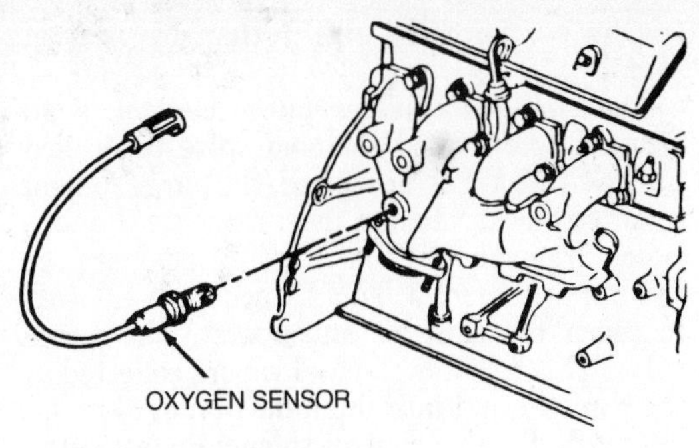

Exhaust oxygen sensor

drain of any conventional voltmeter would be such that it would permanently damage the sensor. No jumpers, test leads or any other electrical connections should ever be made to the sensor. Use these tools ONLY on the ECM side of the wiring harness connector AFTER disconnecting it from the sensor.

REMOVAL AND INSTALLATION

The oxygen sensor must be replaced every 30,000 miles (48,000 km.). The sensor may be difficult to remove when the engine temperature is below 120°F (49°C). Excessive removal force may damage the threads in the exhaust manifold or pipe; follow the removal procedure carefully.

1. Disconnect the negative battery cable.
1. Locate the oxygen sensor. It protrudes from the center of the exhaust manifold at the front of the engine compartment (it looks somewhat like a spark plug). If necessary raise the car for access.
2. Disconnect the electrical connector from the oxygen sensor.

WARNING: *The oxygen sensor uses a permanently attached pigtail and connector. Do not remove the pigtail from the oxygen.*

3. The oxygen sensor may be difficult to remove when the engine temperature is below 120°F. Spray a commercial heat riser solvent onto the sensor threads and allow it to soak in for at least five minutes.

WARNING: *Excessive force may damage the threads in the exhaust manifold. Also care so the that the in-line electrical connector and the louvered end are free of grease, dirt and other contaminants.*

4. Carefully unscrew and remove the sensor.
5. To install, first coat the new sensor's threads with G.M. anti-seize compound No. 5613695 or the equivalent. This is not a conventional anti-seize paste. The use of a regular compound may electrically insulate the sensor, rendering it inoperative. You must coat the threads with an electrically conductive anti-seize compound.
6. Installation torque is 30 ft. lbs. (42 Nm.). Do not overtighten.
7. Reconnect the electrical connector. Be careful not to damage the electrical pigtail. Check the sensor boot for proper fit and installation.

Computer Controlled Catalytic Converter (C-4) System

The GM designed Computer Controlled Catalytic Converter System (C-4 System), was introduced in 1979 and used on California Chevettes in 1980. The C-4 System primarily maintains the ideal air/fuel ratio at which the catalytic converter is most effective. Some versions of the system also control ignition timing of the distributor.

Major components of the system include an Electronic Control Module (ECM), an oxygen sensor, and electronically controlled variable-mixture carburetor, and a three-way oxidation-reduction catalytic converter.

The oxygen sensor generates a voltage which varies with exhaust gas oxygen content. Lean mixtures (more oxygen) reduce voltage; rich mixtures (less oxygen) increase voltage. Voltage output is sent to the ECM.

An engine temperature sensor installed in the engine coolant outlet monitors coolant temperatures. Vacuum controlled switches and throttle position sensors also monitor engine conditions and supply signals to the ECM.

The Electronic Control Module (ECM) monitors the voltage input of the oxygen sensor along with information from other input signals. It processes these signals and generates a control signal sent to the carburetor. The control signal cycles between ON (lean command) and OFF (rich command). The amount of ON and OFF times (called a duty cycle) is a function of the input voltage sent to the ECM by the oxygen sensor. The ECM has a calibration unit called a PROM (Programmable Read-Only Memory) which contains the specific instructions for a given engine application. In other words, the PROM unit is specifically programmed or tailor made for the system in which it is installed. The PROM assembly is a replaceable component which plugs into a socket on the ECM and requires a special tool for removal and installation.

To maintain good idle and driveability under all conditions, other input signals are used to modify the ECM output signal. Besides the sensors and switches already mentioned, these input signals include the manifold absolute pressure (MAP) or vacuum sensors and the barometric pressure (BARO) sensor. The MAP or vacuum sensors sense changes in manifold vacuum, while the BARO sensor senses changes in barometric (ambient atmospheric) pressure. On important function of the BARO sensor is the maintenance of good engine performance at various altitudes.

Computer Command Control (CCC) System

The CCC system is used on all 1981 and later carbureted engines. The CCC has many components in common with the C-4 System (although they should never be interchanged between systems). These include the Electtronic Control Module (ECM), which is capable of monitoring and adjusting more sensors and components than the ECM used on the C-4 System, an oxygen sensor, an electronically controlled variable-mixture carburetor, a three-way catalytic converter, throttle position and coolant sensors, a barometric pressure (BARO) sensor, a manifold absolute pressure (MAP) sensor, a check engine light for the instrument cluster.

Components used almost exclusively by the CCC system include the Air Injection Reaction (AIR) Management System, charcoal canister purge solenoid, EGR valve control, vehicle speed sensor (located in the instrument cluster), transmission torque converter clutch solenoid (automatic transmission models only), idle speed control, and early fuel evaporative (EFE) system.

See the operation descriptions under C-4 System for those components (except the ECM) the CCC System shares with the C-4 System.

The CCC System ECM, in addition to monitoring sensors and sending a control signal to the carburetor, also control the following components or sub-systems; charcoal canister purge, AIR Management System, idle speed control, automatic transmission converter lock-up, distributor ignition timing, EGR valve control, EFE control and the air conditioner compressor clutch operation. The CCC ECM is equipped with a PROM assembly similar to the one used in the C-4 ECM. See above for description.

The AIR Management System is an emission control which provides additional oxygen either to the catalyst or cylinder head ports (in some cases exhaust manifold). An AIR Management System, composed of an air switching valve and/or an air control valve, controls the air pump flow and is itself controlled by the ECM. A complete description of the AIR System is given elsewhere in this unit repair section. The major difference between the CCC AIR System and the systems used on other cars is that the flow of air from the air pump is controlled electrically by the ECM, rather than by vacuum signal.

The charcoal canister purge control is an electrically operated solenoid valve controlled by the ECM. When energized, the purge control solenoid blocks vacuum from reaching the canister purge valve. When the ECM de-energizes the purge control solenoid, vacuum is allowed to reach the canister and operate the purge valve. This releases the fuel vapors collected in the canister and into the induction system.

The EGR valve control solenoid is activated by the ECM in similar fashion to the canister purge solenoid. When the engine is cold, the ECM energizes the solenoid, which blocks the vacuum signal to the EGR valve. When the engine is warm, the ECM de-energizes the solenoid and the vacuum signal is allowed to reach and activate the EGR valve.

The Early Fuel Evaporative (EFE) System is used on some engines to provide rapid heat to the engine induction system to promote smooth start-up and operation. There are two types of systems; vacuum servo and electrically heated. They use different means to achieve the same end, which is to pre-heat the incoming air/fuel mixture. They are controlled by the ECM.

The Transmission Converter Clutch (TCC) lock is controlled by the ECM through an electrical solenoid in the automatic transmission. When the vehicle speed sensor in the instrument panel signals the ECM that the vehicle has reached the correct road speed, the ECM energizes the solenoid which allows the torque converter to mechanically couple the engine to the transmission. When the brake pedal is pushed or during deceleration, passing, etc., the ECM returns the transmission to fluid drive.

The idle speed control adjusts the idle speed to load conditions, and will lower the idle speed under no-load or low-load conditions to conserve gasoline.

C-4 AND CCC SYSTEM-BASIC TROUBLESHOOTING

NOTE: *The following explains how to activate the Trouble Code signal light in the instrument cluster and gives an explanation of what each code means. This is not a full C-4 or CCC System troubleshooting and isolation procedure.*

Before suspecting the C-4 or CCC System or any of its components as faulty, check the ignition system including distributor, timing, spark plugs and wires. Check the engine compression, air cleaner, and emission control components not controlled by the ECM. Also check the intake manifold, vacuum hoses, and hose connections for leaks and the carburetor bolts for tightness.

The following symptoms could indicate a possible problem with the C-4 or CCC System.

1. Detonation
2. Stalls or rough idle-cold
3. Stalls or rough idle-hot
4. Missing
5. Hesitation
6. Surges
7. Poor gasoline mileage
8. Sluggish or spongy performance
9. Hard starting-cold
10. Hard starting-hot
11. Objectionable exhaust odors
12. Cuts out

As a bulb and system check, the Check Engine light will come on when the ignition switch is turned to the ON position but the engine is not started.

The Check Engine light will also produce the trouble code of codes by a series of flashes which translates as follows. When the diagnostic test lead (C-4) or terminal (CCC) under the dash is grounded, with the ignition in the ON position and the engine not running, the Check Engine light will flash once, pause, then flash twice in rapid succession. This is a code 12, which indicates that the diagnostic system is working. After a longer pause, the code 12 will repeat itself two more times. The cycle will then repeat itself until the engine is started or the ignition is turned OFF.

When the engine is started, the Check Engine light will remain on for a few seconds, then turn off. If the Check Engine light remains on, the self-diagnostic system has detected a problem. If the test lead (C-4) or test terminal (CCC) is then grounded, the trouble code will flash three times. If more than one problem is found, each trouble code will flash three times. Trouble codes will flash in numerical order (lowest code number to highest). The trouble codes series will repeat as long as the test lead or terminal is grounded.

A trouble code indicates a problem with a given circuit. For example, trouble code 14 indicates a problem in the cooling sensor circuit. This includes the coolant sensor, its electrical harness, and the Electronic Control Module (ECM).

Since the self-diagnostic system cannot diagnose every possible fault in the system, the absence of a trouble code does not mean the system is trouble-free. To determine problems withing the system which do not activate a trouble code, a system performance check must be made. This job should be left to a qualified technician.

In the case of an intermittent fault in the system, the Check Engine light will go out when the fault goes away, but the trouble code will remain in the memory of the ECM. Therefore, if a trouble code can be obtained even though the Check Engine light is not on, the trouble code must be evaluated. It must be determined if the fault is intermittant or if the engine must be at certain operating conditions (under load, etc.) before the Check Engine light will come on. Some trouble codes will not be recorded in the ECM until the engine has been operated at part throttle for about 5 to 18 minutes.

On the C-4 System, the ECM erases all trouble codes every time the ignition is turned off. In the case of intermittant faults, a long term memory is desirable. This can be produced by connecting the orange connector/lead from terminal **S** of the ECM directly to the battery (or to a hot fuse panel terminal). This terminal must be disconnected after diagnosis is complete or it will drain the battery.

On the CCC System, a trouble code will be stored until terminal **R** of the ECM has been disconnected from the battery for 10 seconds.

An easy way to erase the computer memory on the CCC system is to disconnect the battery terminals from the battery. If this method is used, don't forget to reset clocks and electronic preprogrammable radios. Another method is to remove the fuse marked ECM in the fuse panel. Not all models have such a fuse.

ACTIVATING THE TROUBLE CODE

On the C-4 System, activate the trouble code by grounding the trouble code test lead under the instrument panel (usually a white and black wire or a wire with a green connector). Run a jumper wire from the lead to ground.

On the CCC System, locate the test terminal under the instrument panel. Ground the test lead. On many systems, the test lead is situated side by side with a ground terminal. In addition, on some models, the partition between the test terminal and the ground terminal has a cut out section so that a spade terminal can be used to connect the two terminals.

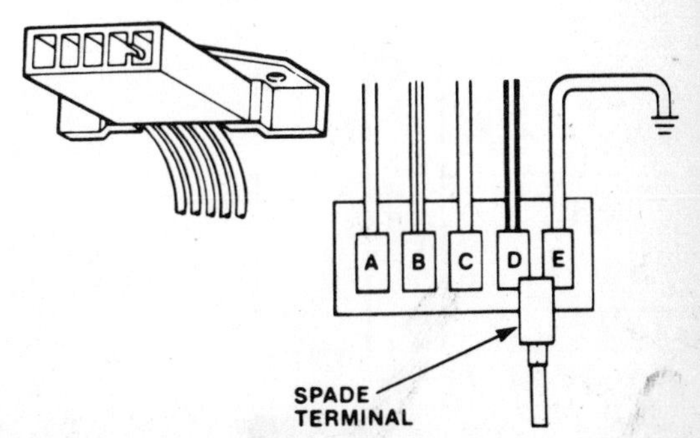

CCC system test terminal ground location found under the instrument panel

Explanation of Trouble Codes GM C—4 and CCC Systems

Ground test lead or terminal AFTER engine is running.

Trouble Code	Applicable System	Notes	Possible Problem Area
12	C-4, CCC		No tachometer or reference signal to computer (ECM). This code will only be present while a fault exists, and will not be stored if the problem is intermittent.
13	C-4, CCC		Oxygen sensor circuit. The engine must run for about five minutes at part throttle (and under road load—CCC equipped cars) before this code will show.
13 & 14 (at same time)	C-4		See code 43.
13 & 43 (at same time)	C-4		See code 43.
14	C-4, CCC		Shorted coolant sensor circuit. The engine has to run 2 minutes before this code will show.
15	C-4, CCC		Open coolant sensor circuit. The engine has to operate for about five minutes at part throttle before this code will show.
21	C-4 C-4, CCC		Shorted wide open throttle switch and/or open closed-throttle switch circuit (when used). Throttle position sensor circuit. The engine must be run up to 10 seconds (25 seconds—CCC System) below 800 rpm before this code will show.
23	C-4, CCC		Open or grounded carburetor mixture control (M/C) solenoid circuit.
24	CCC		Vehicle speed sensor (VSS) circuit. The car must operate up to five minutes at road speed before this code will show.
32	C-4, CCC		Barometric pressure sensor (BARO) circuit output low.
32 & 55 (at same time)	C-4		Grounded +8V terminal or V(REF) terminal for barometric pressure sensor (BARO), or faulty ECM computer.
34	C-4		Manifold absolute pressure (MAP) sensor output high (after ten seconds and below 800 rpm).

34	CCC		Manifold absolute pressure (MAP) sensor circuit or vacuum sensor circuit. The engine must run up to five minutes below 800 RPM before this code will set.
35	CCC		Idle speed control (ISC) switch circuit shorted (over ½ throttle for over two seconds).
41	CCC		No distributor reference pulses to the ECM at specified engine vacuum. This code will store in memory.
42	CCC		Electronic spark timing (EST) bypass circuit grounded.
43	C-4		Throttle position sensor adjustment (on some models, engine must run at part throttle up to ten seconds before this code will set).
44	C-4, CCC		Lean oxygen sensor indication. The engine must run up to five minutes in closed loop (oxygen sensor adjusting carburetor mixture), at part throttle and under road load (drive car) before this code will set.
44 & 55 (at same time)	C-4, CCC		Faulty oxygen sensor circuit.
45	C-4, CCC	Restricted air cleaner can cause code 45	Rich oxygen sensor system indication. The engine must run up to five minutes in closed loop (oxygen sensor adjusting carburetor mixture), at part throttle under road load before this code will set.
51	C-4, CCC		Faulty calibration unit (PROM) or improper PROM installation in electronic control module (ECM). It takes up to thirty seconds for this code to set.
52 & 53	C-4		"Check Engine" light off: Intermittent ECM computer problem. "Check Engine" light on: Faulty ECM computer (replace.)
52	C-4, CCC		Faulty ECM computer.
53	CCC		Faulty ECM computer.
54	C-4, CCC		Faulty mixture control solenoid circuit and/or faulty ECM computer.
55	C-4		Faulty oxygen sensor, open manifold absolute pressure sensor. Faulty throttle position sensor or ECM computer.
55	CCC		Grounded +8 volt supply (terminal 19 of ECM computer connector), grounded 5 volt reference (terminal 21 of ECM computer connector), faulty oxygen sensor circuit or faulty ECM computer.

NOTE: *Ground the test lead or terminal according to the instructions given in Basic Troubleshooting above.*

DIESEL ENGINE EMISSION CONTROLS

The Exhaust Gas Recirculation System (EGR) and the Positive Crankcase Ventilation System (PCV) are the only emission control systems that the diesel engine requires. Although the Diesel PCV system differs in appearance and construction, it still performs the same function; to reroute combustion blow-by from the crankcase to the intake manifold for reburning.

This system is of a closed type, consisting of: a baffle plate inside the cam cover for separating oil particles from blow-by gas, a PCV valve on the cam cover that is opened at a specified differential pressure between the cam cover and intake manifold for controlling pressure in the cam cover, and a hose connecting the PCV valve and inlet pipe.

PCV valve removal and installation procedures are covered in Chapter One.

Beginning on 1984 models the EGR system is used to reduce combustion temperature in the combustion chamber, thereby reducing oxides of nitrogen emissions.

Recirculation gas is drawn into the intake pipe on the intake manifold through a stainless steel pipe and an EGR valve from an exhaust manifold. The EGR valve is an ON/OFF device with no control over the quantity of EGR gas flow.

Auxiliary devices of the EGR system are a vacuum switching valve, an EGR controller, a thermoswitch which senses coolant temperature, an engine speed sensor which senses engine speed, and a control lever position sensor which senses an injection pump control lever angle. Injection pump control lever angle is transformed into voltage output by control lever position sensor.

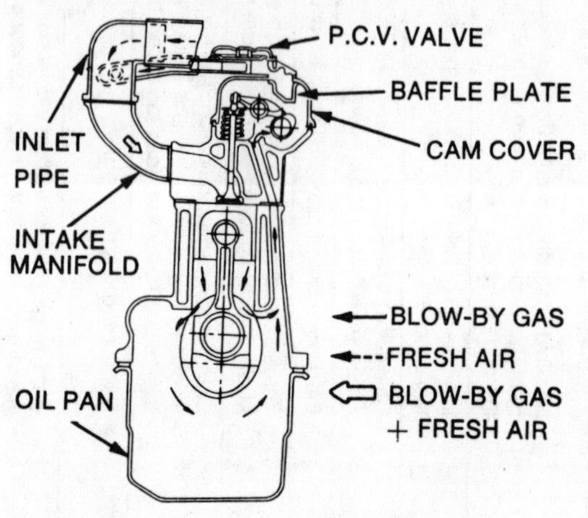

Crankcase ventilation system—diesel engine

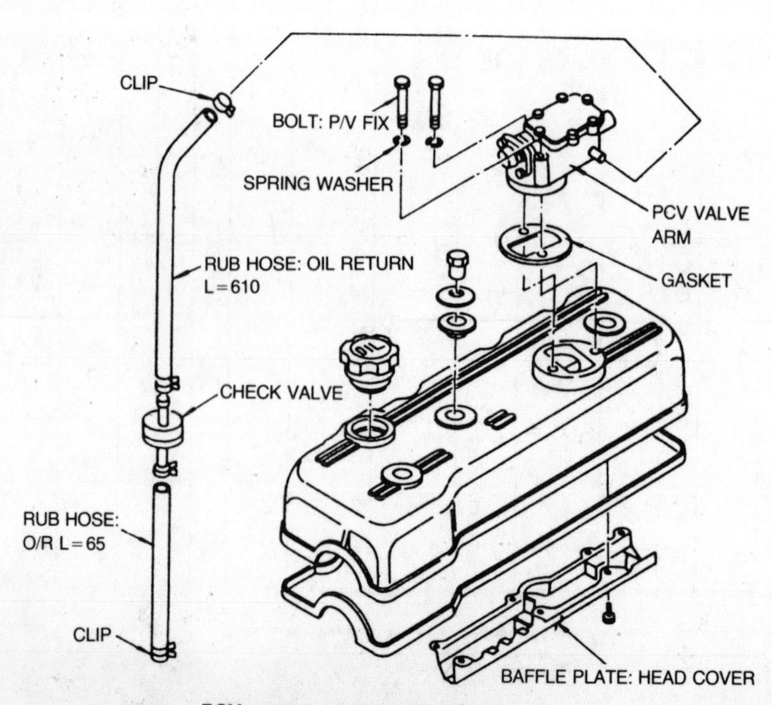

PCV system components-diesel engine

EGR SYSTEM INSPECTION AND ADJUSTMENT

EGR Valve

Check vacuum diaphragm function by applying an outside vacuum source to the vacuum supply tube at the top of the vacuum diaphragm. The diaphragm should not leak down and should move to the fully up position at about 350 mmHg (13.8 in.Hg) vacuum.

Thermoswitch

Submerge the end of the thermoswitch in water and raise the temperature of the water gradually and make a continuity test across the terminal body using a circuit tester.

Vacuum Switching Valve

Proper operation of the vacuum switching valve can be checked by carefully listening for noise that is accompanied with electrical operation of plunger. The plunger can be operated electrically by connecting the connector terminals directly to the battery with suitable cables.

EGR Controller

Connect a voltmeter to the Light Green/Black and Black/Yellow color coded wire terminals at the vacuum switching valve wiring connector. The Light Green/Black wire is positive and the Black/Yellow wire is negative. The EGR controller is normal if the voltage is about 12 volts when the engine speed is over 1200 rpm.

Control Lever Position Sensor

Connect a voltmeter to the Blue/Yellow and Blue/Red color coded terminals without disconnecting the control lever position sensor connector. The Blue/Yellow wire is positive and the Blue/Red wire is negative. Then move the control lever so as to set the clearance between the control lever and the idle stopper bolt is 7mm. Control lever position sensor is normal if the voltage is in the range of 3.3-4.4 volt, after starting the engine.

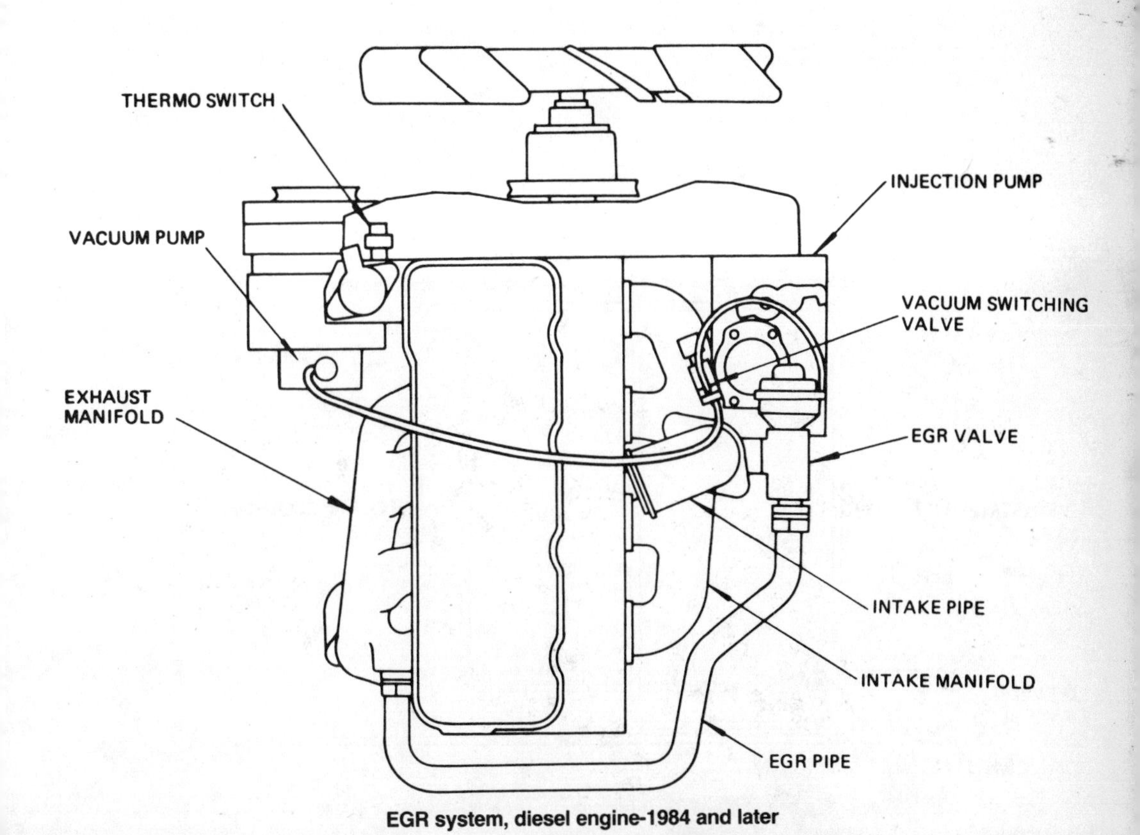

EGR system, diesel engine-1984 and later

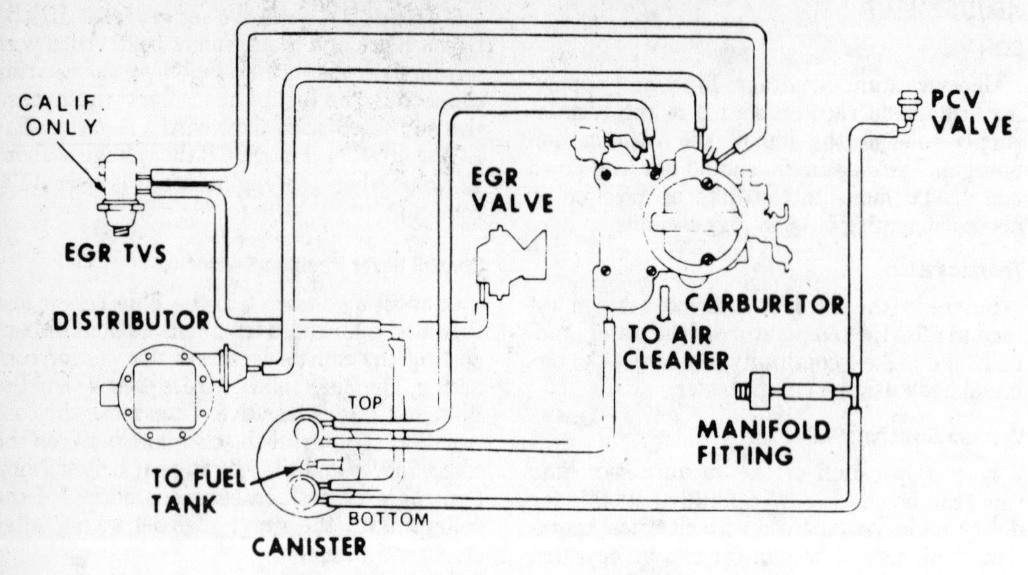

Vacuum circuit—1976–78, Calif. & high altitude

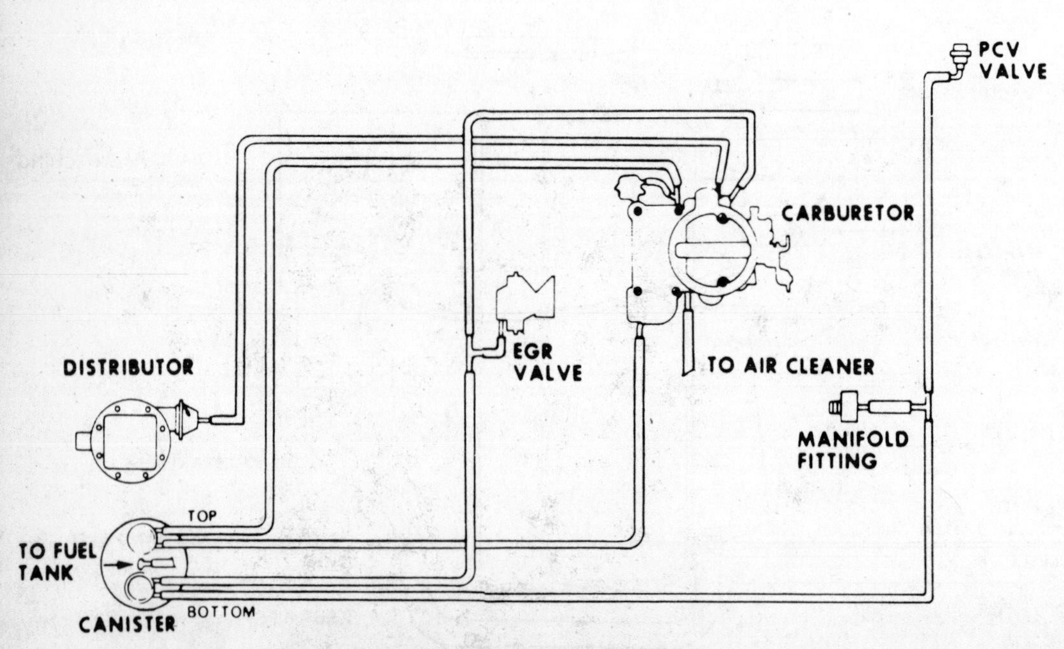

Vacuum circuit—1976–78, low altitude

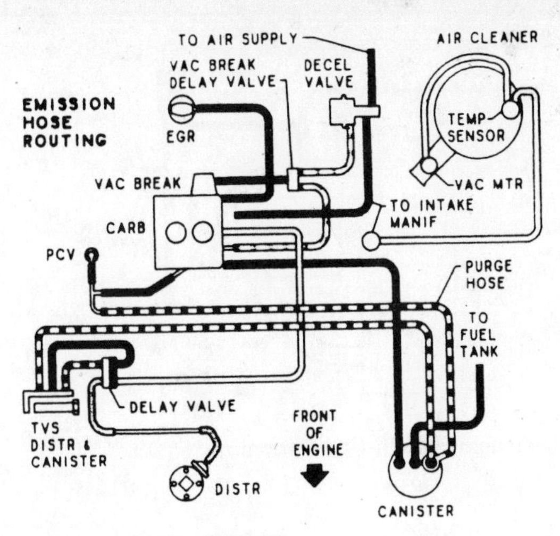

Vacuum circuit—1979–80

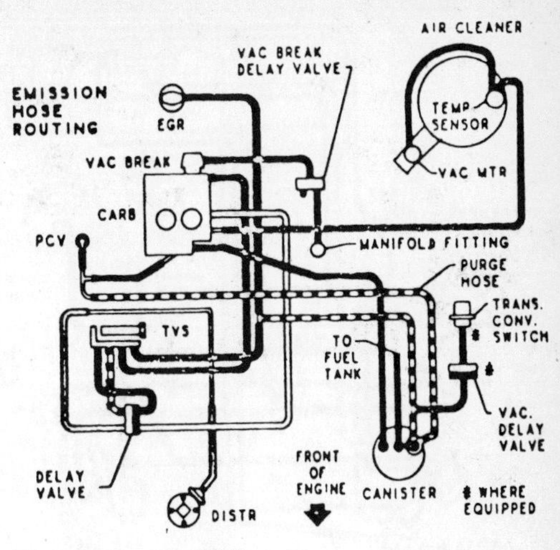

Vacuum circuit—1982

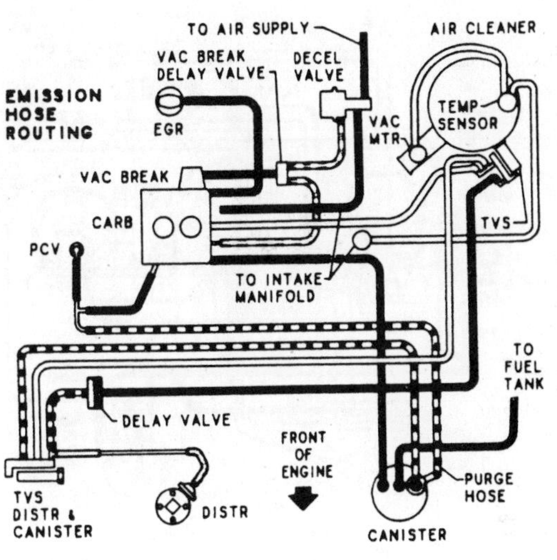

Vacuum circuit—1979–80

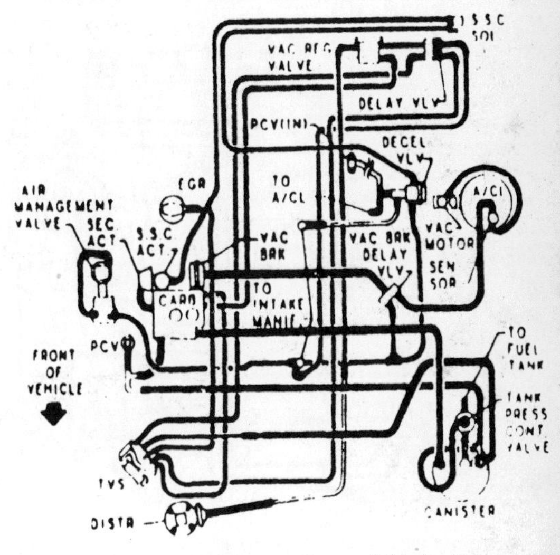

Vacuum circuit—1983, man. trans. & high alt.

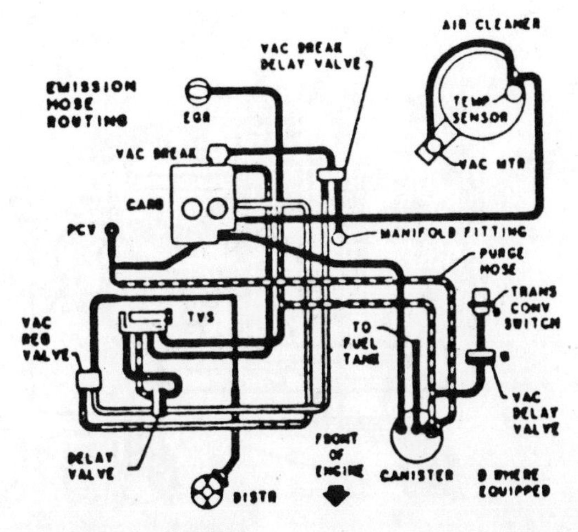

Vacuum circuit—1981

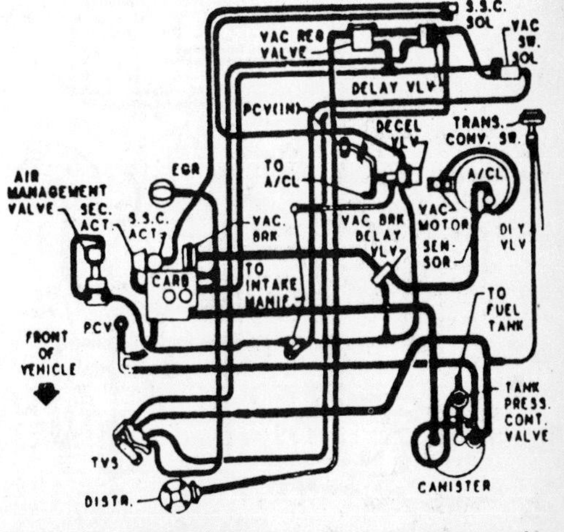

Vacuum circuit—1983, auto. trans. & power steering

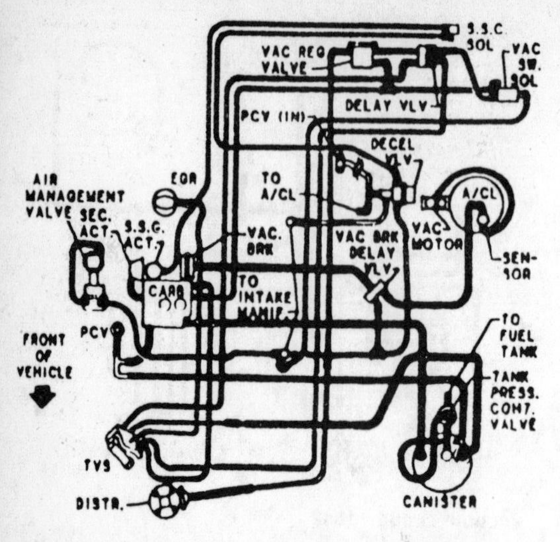

Vacuum circuit—1983, man. trans. A/C & high alt.

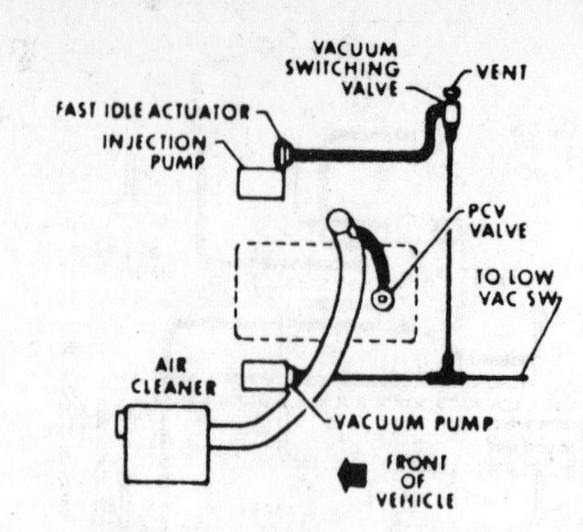

Vacuum circuit—1983—diesel

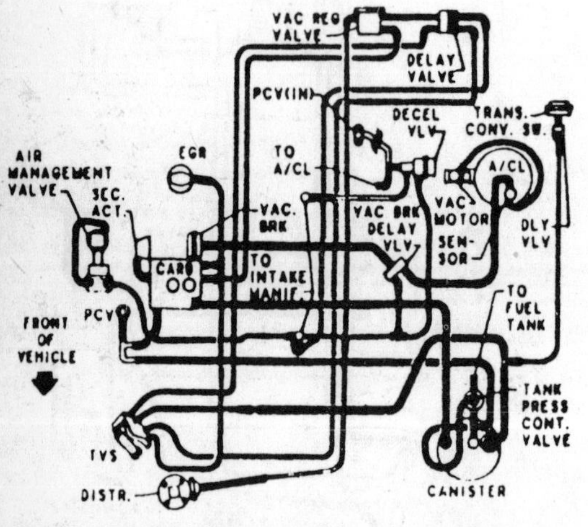

Vacuum circuit—1983, auto. trans. without power steering

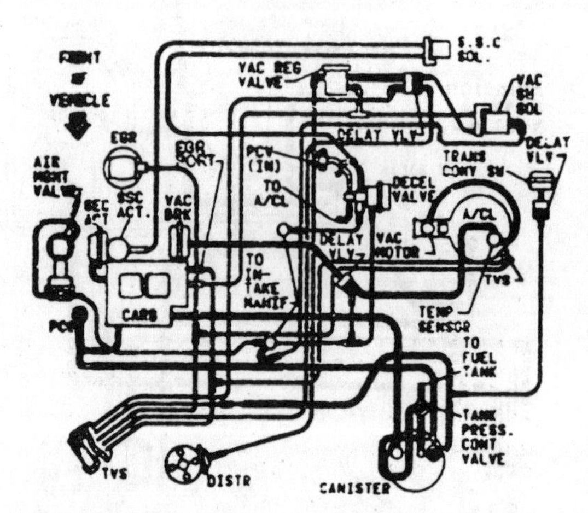

Vacuum circuit—1984, auto. trans. federal

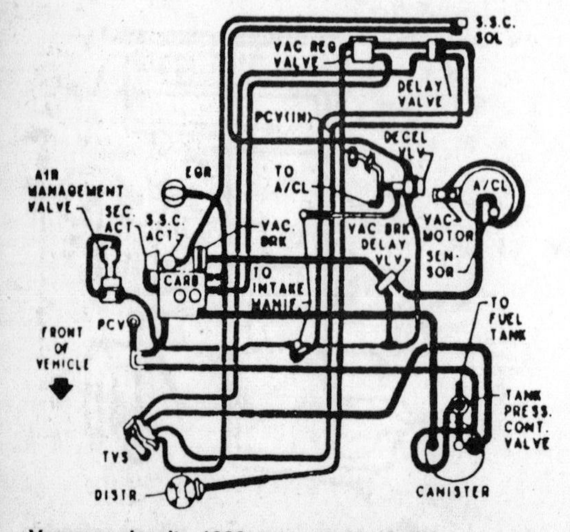

Vacuum circuit—1983, man. trans. (Calif.)

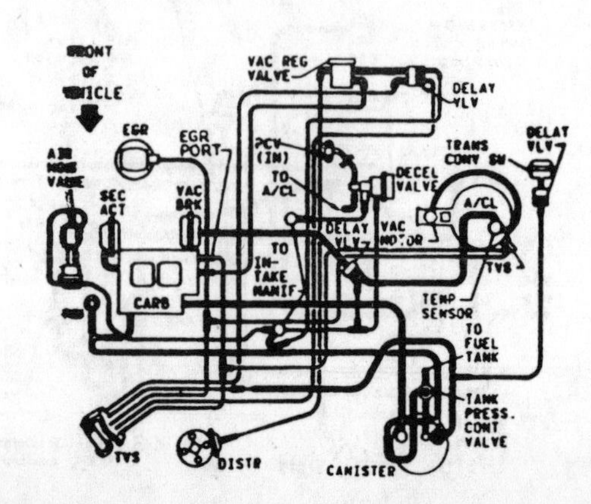

Vacuum circuit—1984, auto. trans. federal

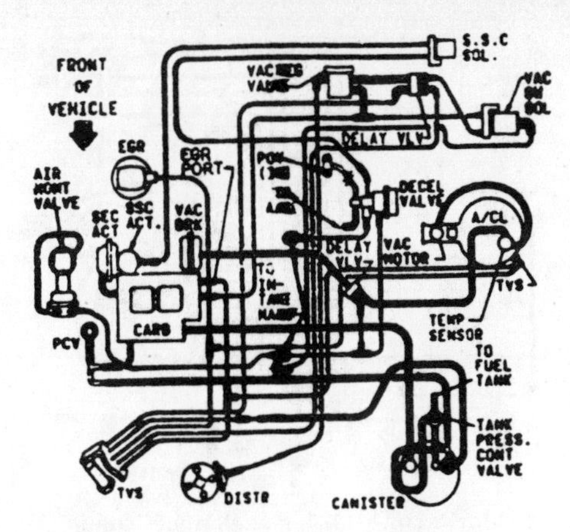

Vacuum circuit—1984, man. trans. federal

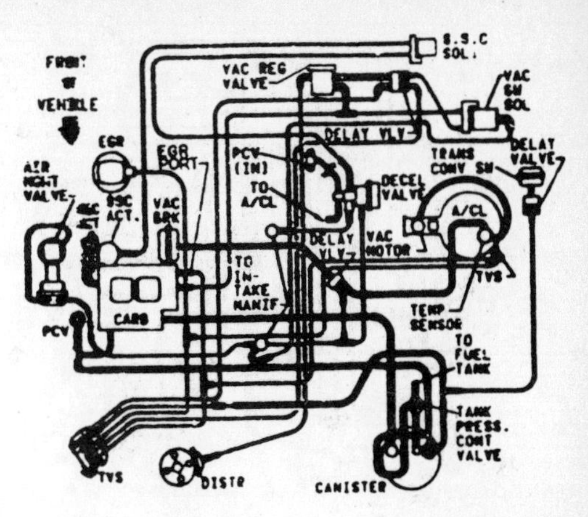

Vacuum circuit—1984, auto. trans., low alt. & Calif.

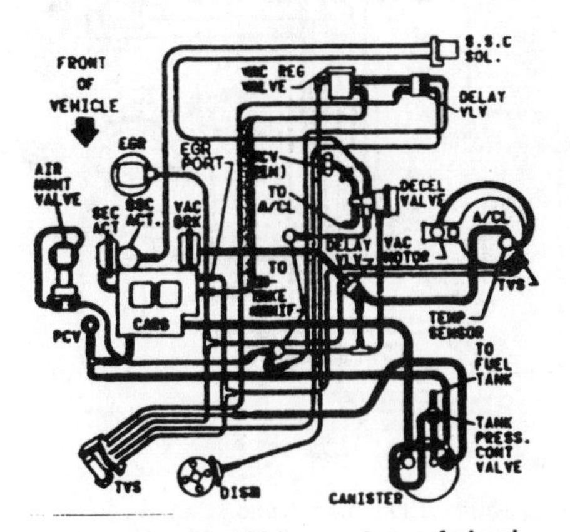

Vacuum circuit—1984, man. trans. federal

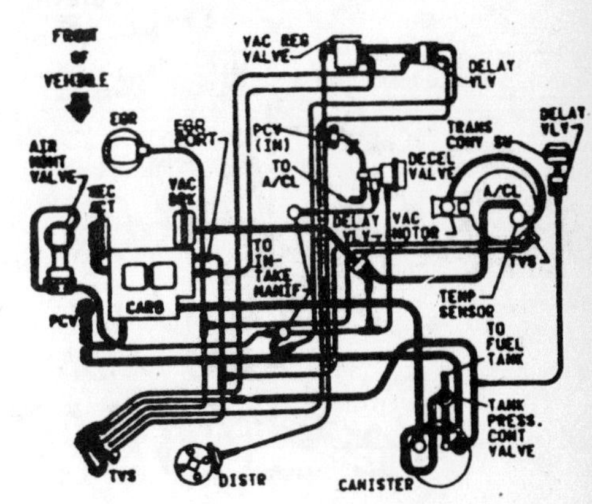

Vacuum circuit—1984, auto. trans., low alt. & Calif.

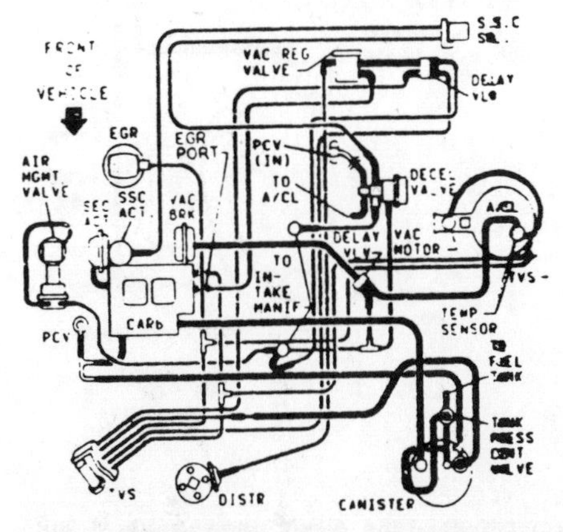

Vacuum circuit—1984, man. trans. federal

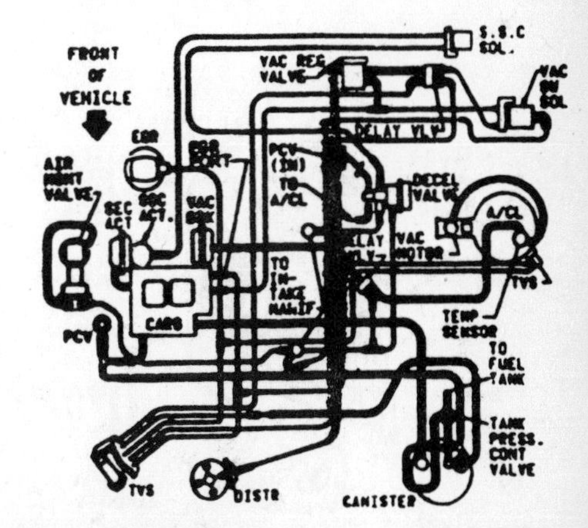

Vacuum circuit—1984, man. trans., low alt. & Calif.

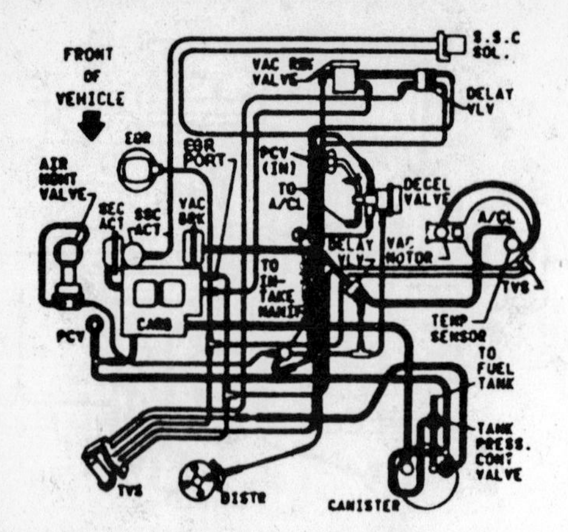

Vacuum circuit—1984, man. trans., Calif.

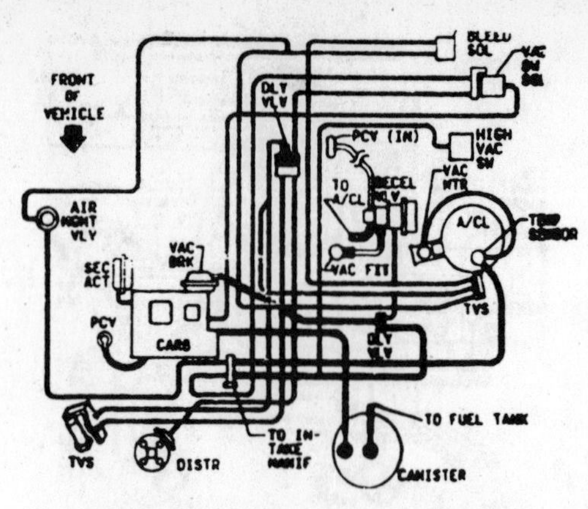

Vacuum circuit—1984, man. trans., Canada

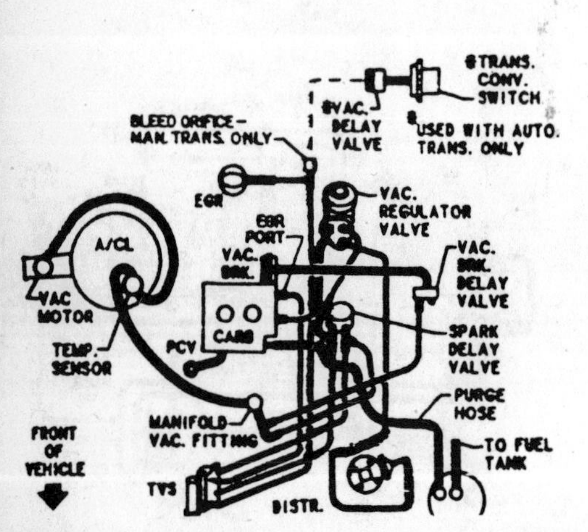

Vacuum circuit—1984, man. trans. & auto. trans., Canada

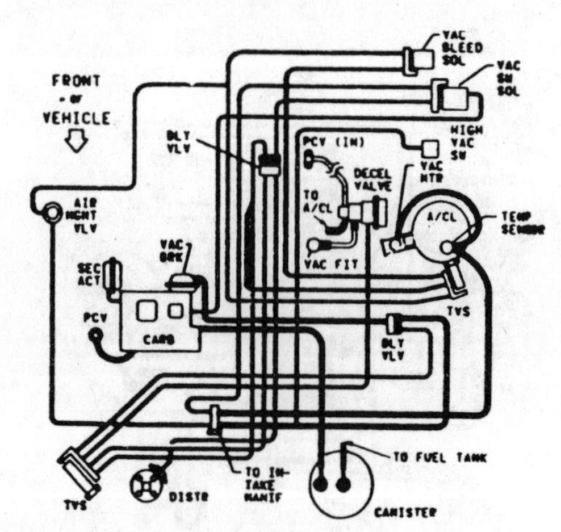

Vacuum circuit—1984, man. trans., Canada

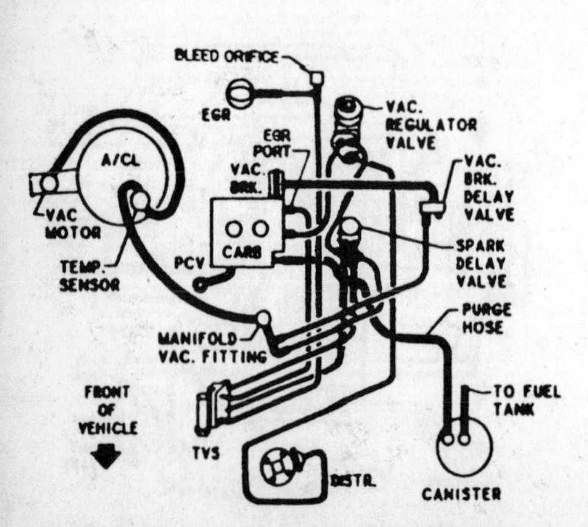

Vacuum circuit—1984, man. trans., Canada

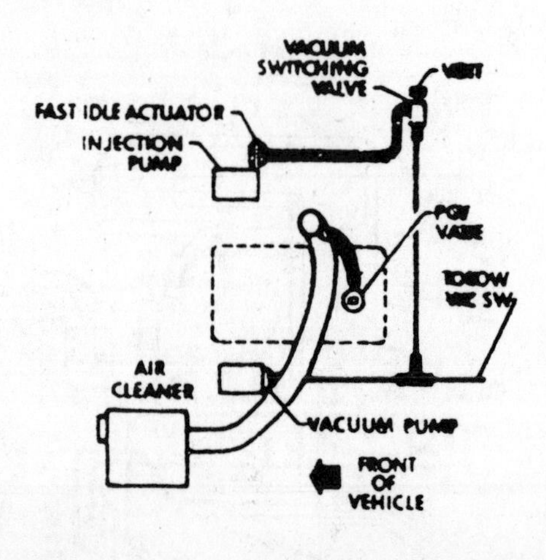

Vacuum circuit—1984 diesel, man. trans. & auto. trans., federal

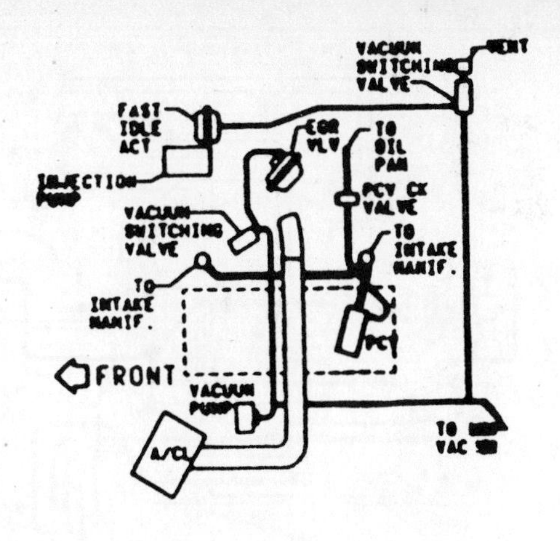

Vacuum circuit—1984 diesel, man. trans., Calif.

Vacuum circuit—1985—federal

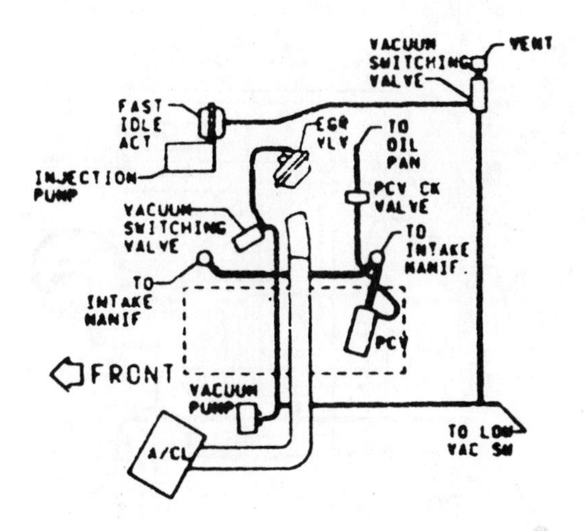

Vacuum circuit—1984 diesel, man. trans., Calif.

Vacuum circuit—1985—federal

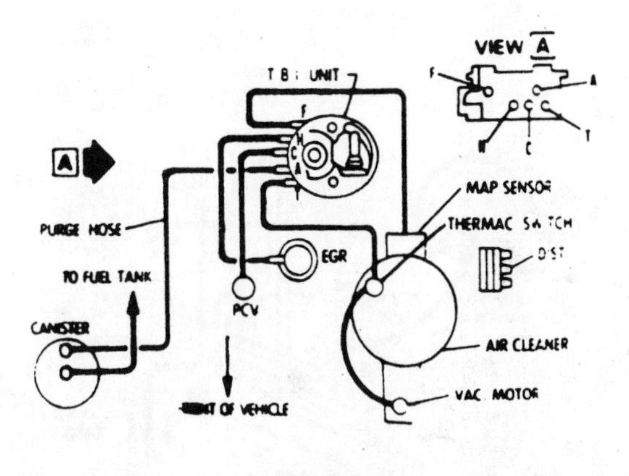

Vacuum circuit—1984 diesel, man. trans. & auto. trans., federal

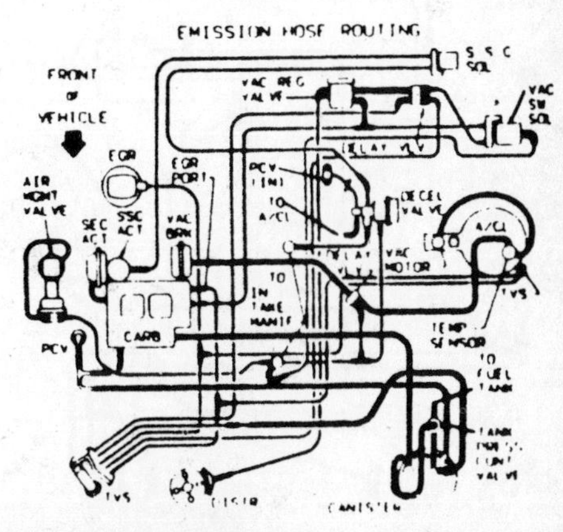

Vacuum circuit—1985—federal

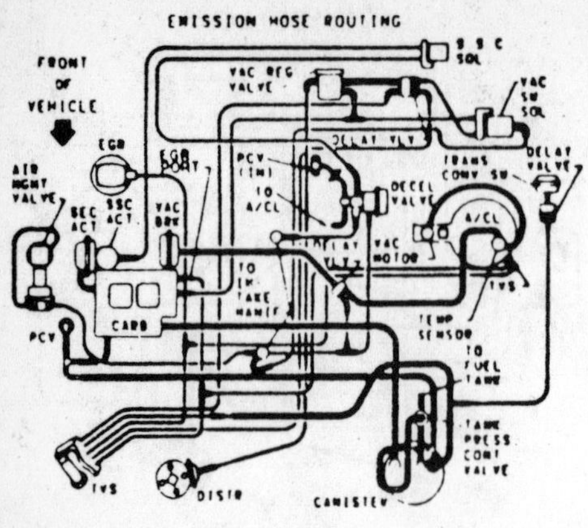

Vacuum circuit—1985—federal

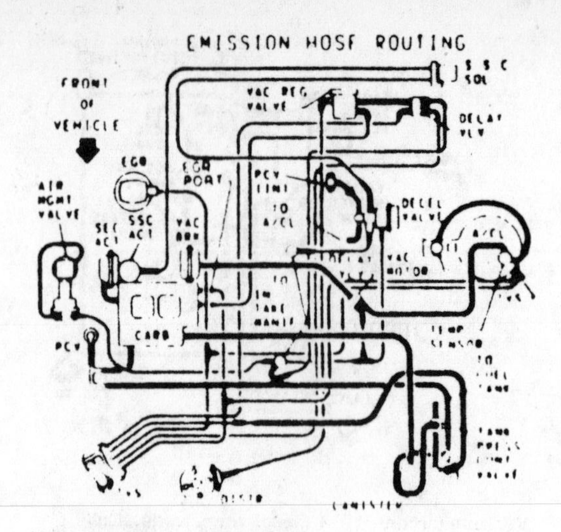

Vaccum circuit—1985—Calif.

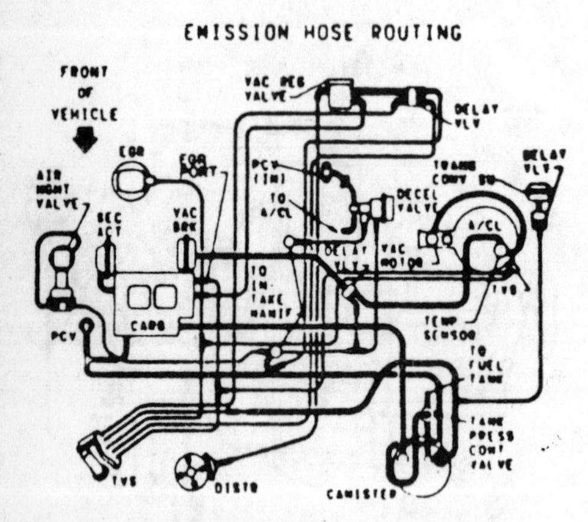

Vacuum circuit—1985—Calif.

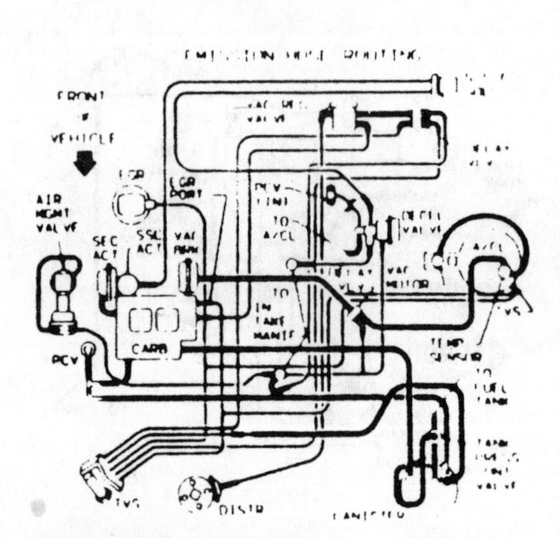

Vacuum circuit—1985—Calif.

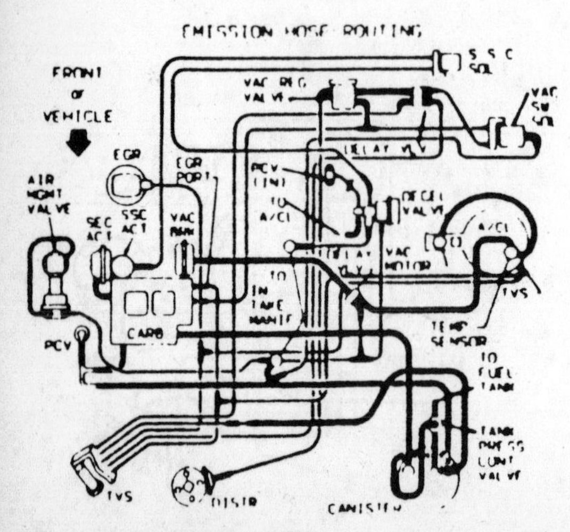

Vacuum circuit—1985—Calif.

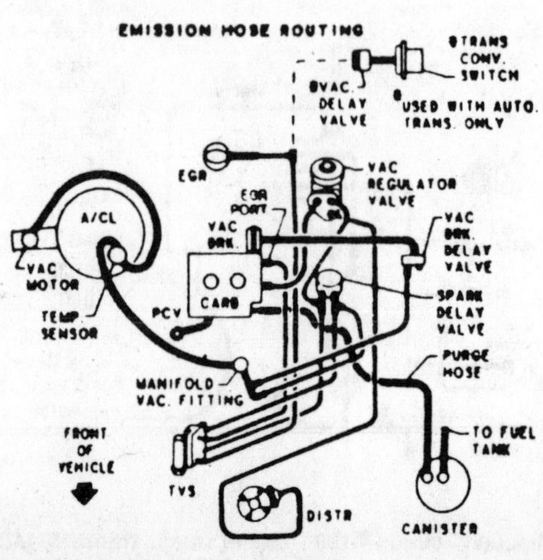

Vacuum circuit—1985—Canada.

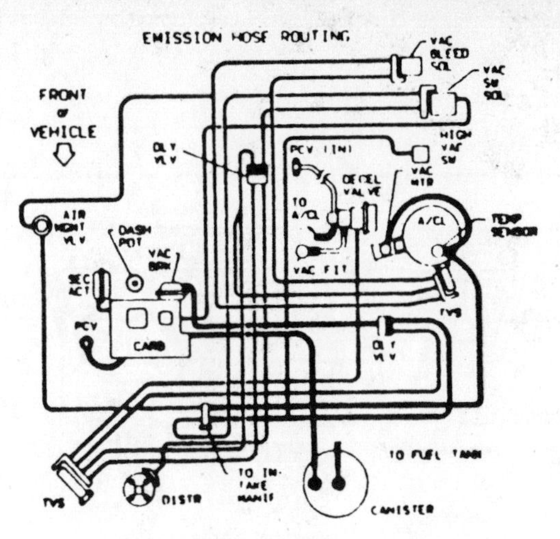

Vacuum circuit—1985—Canada.

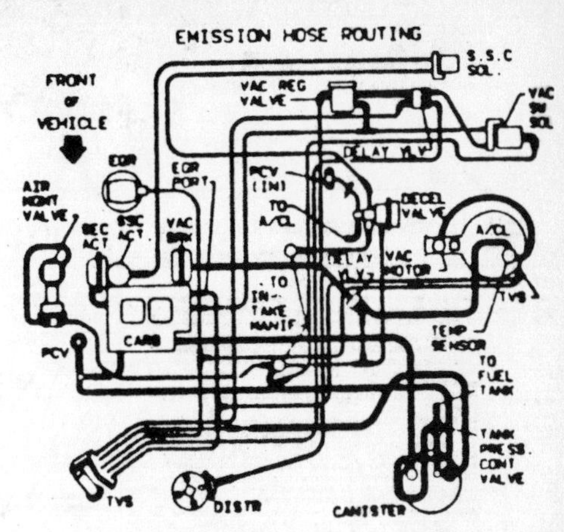

Vacuum circuit—1986, auto. trans. without A/C, federal

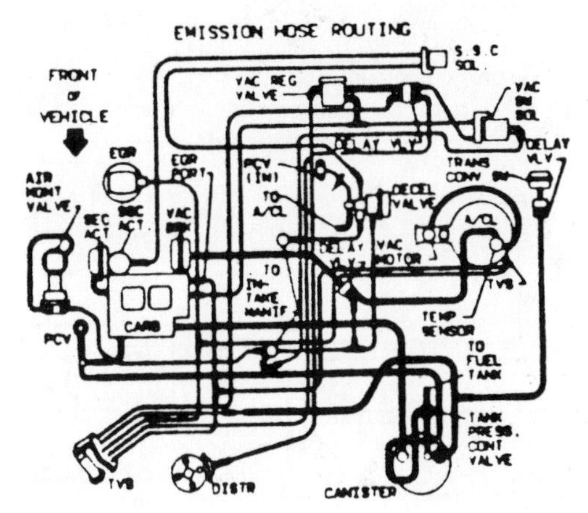

Vacuum circuit—1986, auto. trans. & power steering, federal

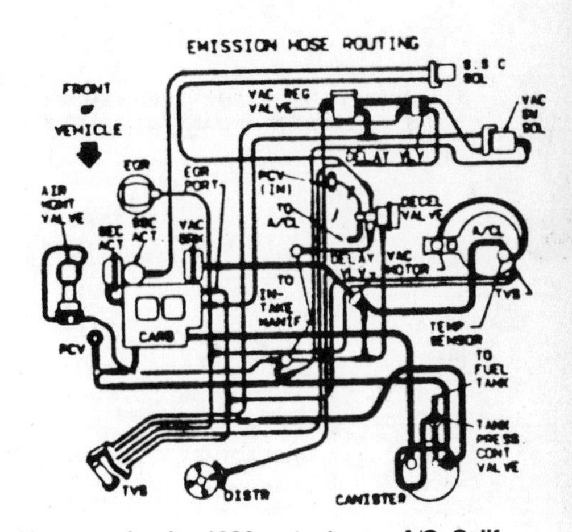

Vacuum circuit—1986, auto. trans., A/C, Calif.

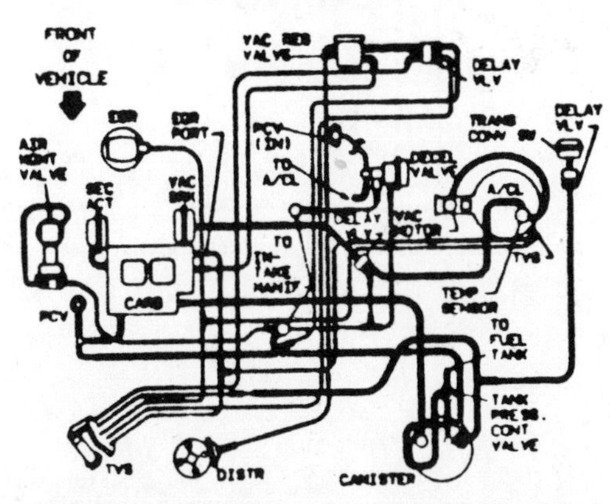

Vacuum circuit—1986, auto. trans. without power steering, federal

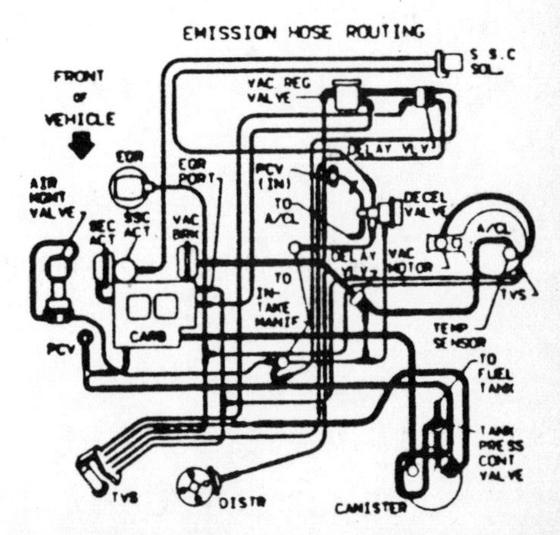

Vacuum circuit—1986, auto. trans., without A/C, Calif.

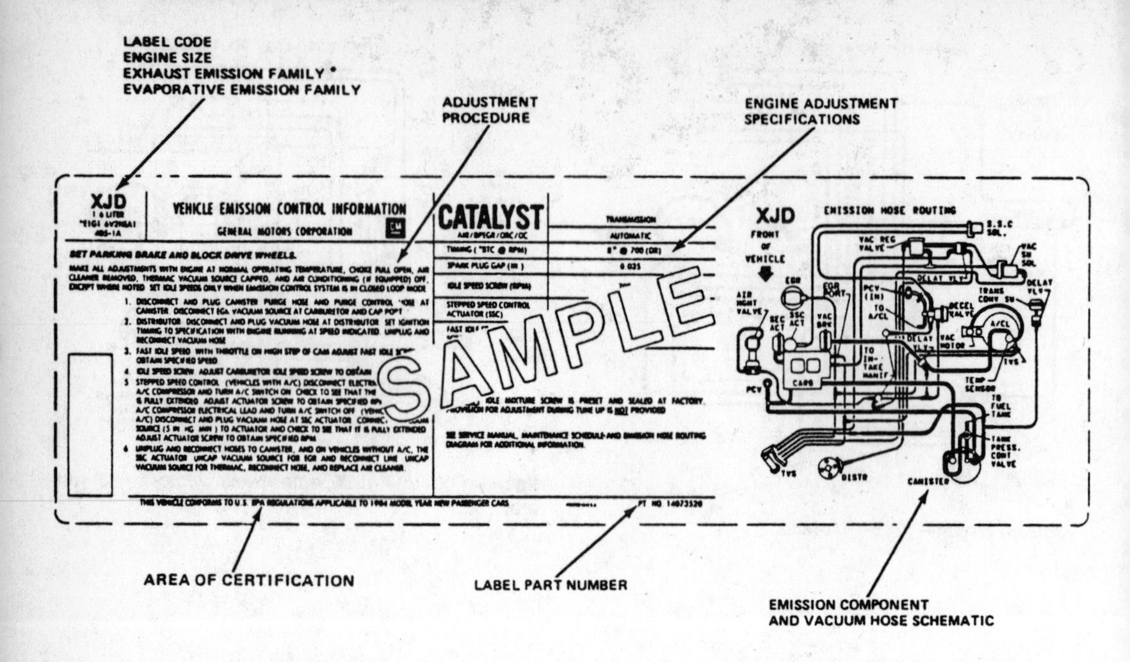

"ALWAYS REFER TO THE VEHICLE EMISSION CONTROL INFORMATION LABEL FOR THE CORRECT AND MOST CURRENT SPECIFICATIONS".

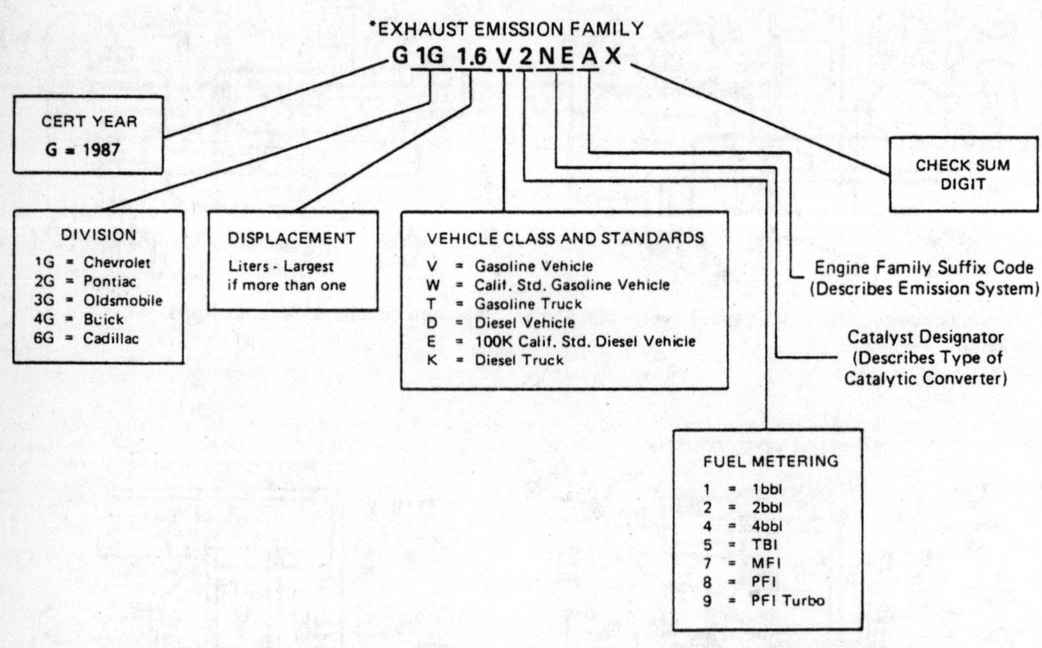

Sample and explanation of an underhood Vehicle Emission Control Label, 1987 shown

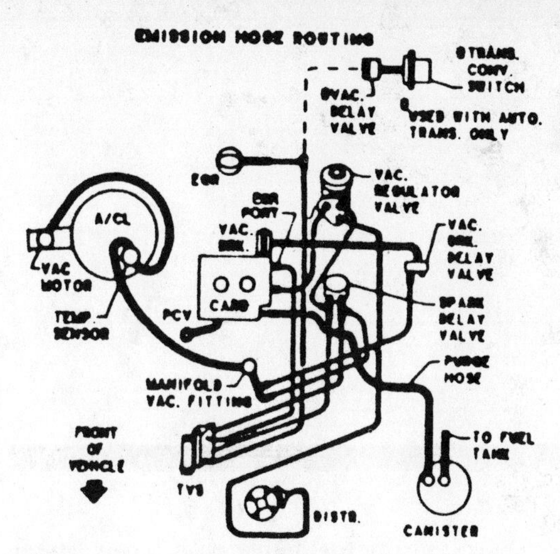

Vacuum circuit—1986, w/NM5, Canada

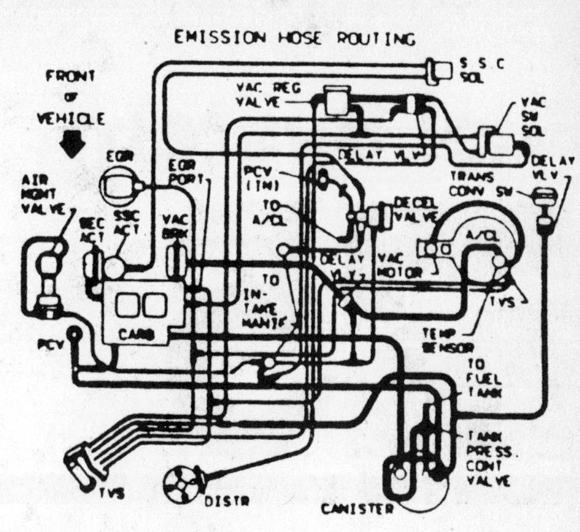

Vacuum circuit—1986, auto. trans. & power steering exc. A/C, Calif.

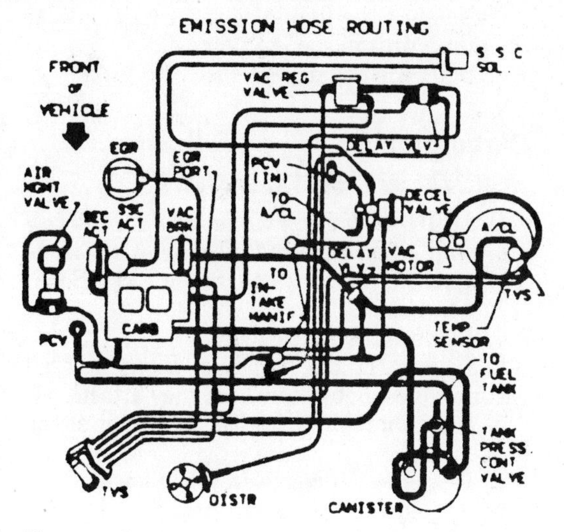

Vacuum circuit—1986, auto. trans. without A/C, federal

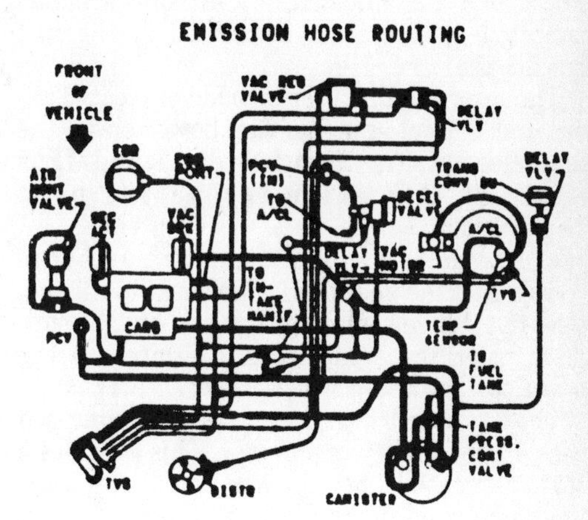

Vacuum circuit—1986, auto. trans. exc. power steering & A/C, Calif.

Fuel System

GASOLINE ENGINE FUEL SYSTEM

All 1976-78 Chevettes use a Rochester 1ME carburetor. The unit incorporates an automatic choke with an electronically heated choke coil. The choke coil is heated in a housing which is mounted on a bracket connected to the fuel bowl.

The internal fuel filter is made of pleated paper and is located in the fuel bowl behind the fuel inlet nut. The throttle body of the 1ME is made of aluminum for better heat dispersement.

The carburetor identification number is stamped on the float bowl, right next to the fuel inlet nut. When replacing the fuel bowl, be sure to transfer the identification number to the new float bowl.

The 1979 and later Chevettes are equipped with a 2-bbl Holley carburetor. This provides a slight increase in horsepower and at the same time, improves the fuel economy.

Fuel Pump

CAUTION: *Never smoke when working around gasoline! Avoid all sources of sparks or ignition. Gasoline vapors are EXTREMELY volatile!*

REMOVAL AND INSTALLATION

NOTE: *Air conditioned cars require removal of the rear compressor bracket to gain working room.*

1. Working from under the car, remove the ignition coil.
2. On some later models, it may be necessary to remove the air cleaner assembly and the distributor cap.
3. Disconnect the fuel inlet and outlet lines at the pump and plug the inlet line.
4. Remove the two pump mounting bolts and lockwashers and remove the fuel pump and gasket.
5. Install the fuel pump with a new gasket coated with sealer. Tighten the two mounting bolts.
6. Connect the fuel inlet and outlet lines at the pump. Install the ignition coil.
7. Start the engine and check for leaks.

Carburetor

REMOVAL AND INSTALLATION

CAUTION: *Never smoke when working around gasoline! Avoid all sources of sparks or ignition. Gasoline vapors are EXTREMELY volatile!*

1. Remove the air cleaner.
2. Disconnect the fuel line. Disconnect all vacuum lines, but note where they attach.
3. Disconnect the electrical connector at the choke.
4. Disconnect the accelerator linkage.
5. Disconnect the solenoid electrical connector.
6. On cars with an automatic transmission, disconnect the detent cable.
7. Remove the carburetor retaining nuts and remove the carburetor/solenoid assembly.
8. On 1980 and later models remove the electric EFE insulator gasket.
9. Installation is the reverse of removal. Start the engine and check for leaks.

FLOAT LEVEL ADJUSTMENT

1. Remove the top of the carburetor.

CAUTION: *Never smoke when working around gasoline! Avoid all sources of sparks or ignition. Gasoline vapors are EXTREMELY volatile!*

2. Hold the float retaining pin in place and push down on the float arm at the outer end against the top of the float needle valve.
3. Measure the distance from the bump on the top of the float at the end to the bowl gasket surface, without the gasket.

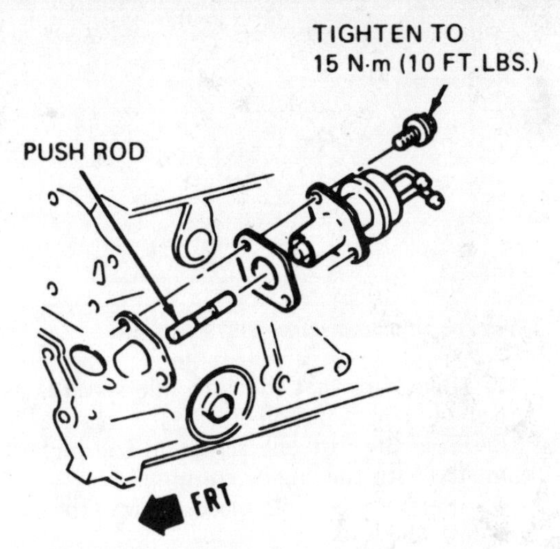

Fuel pump installation

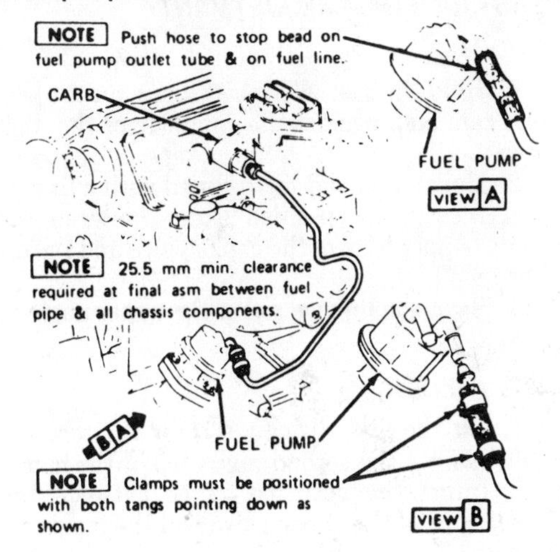

Fuel pump hoses

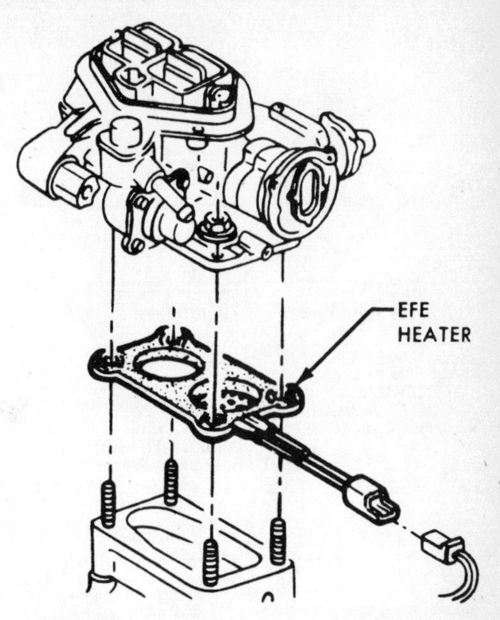

Carburetor mounting-1979 and later (1979 models are not equipped with EFE heater)

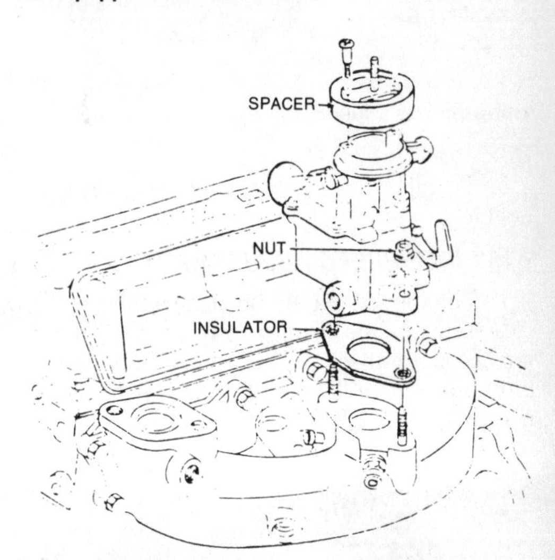

Carburetor mounting details—through 1978

4. To adjust, bend the float arm at the point where it joins the float.

METERING ROD ADJUSTMENT

Through 1978

1. Remove the top of the carburetor.

CAUTION: *Never smoke when working around gasoline! Avoid all sources of sparks or ignition. Gasoline vapors are EXTREMELY volatile!*

2. Back out the idle stop solenoid and rotate the fast idle cam so that the fast idle screw does not contact the cam.

3. With the throttle valve completely closed, make sure that the power piston is all the way up.

4. Insert the specified size gauge between the bowl gasket surface with no gasket and the lower surface of the metering rod holder, next to the metering rod.

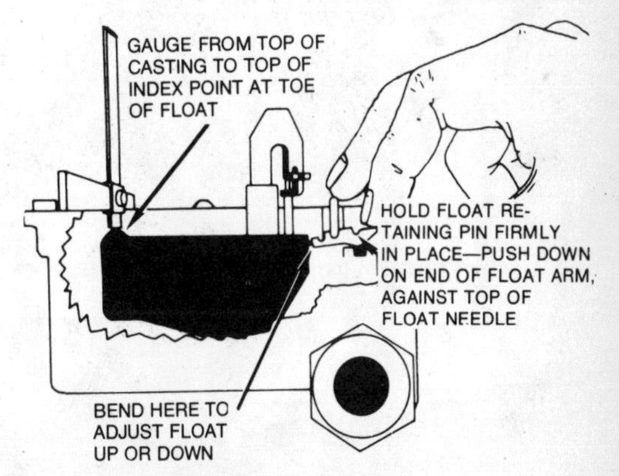

Float level adjustment—1976–78

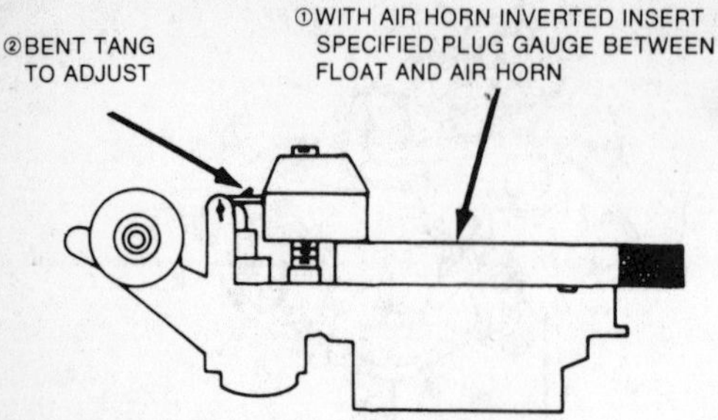

Float level adjustment—1979 and later

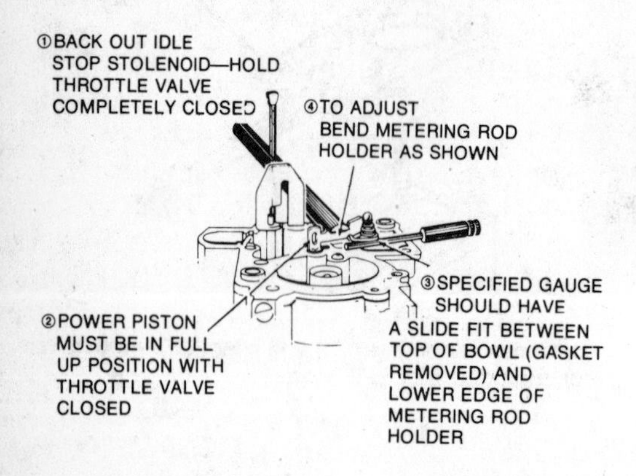

Metering rod adjustment

5. To adjust, carefully bend the metering rod holder.

FAST IDLE SPEED ADJUSTMENT

1. The engine should be at normal temperature with the air cleaner in place. On 1976-78 models, disconnect and plug the EGR valve vacuum line. On 1979 and later models disconnect and plug the EGR port at the carburetor.

Fast idle adjusting screw—1976-78

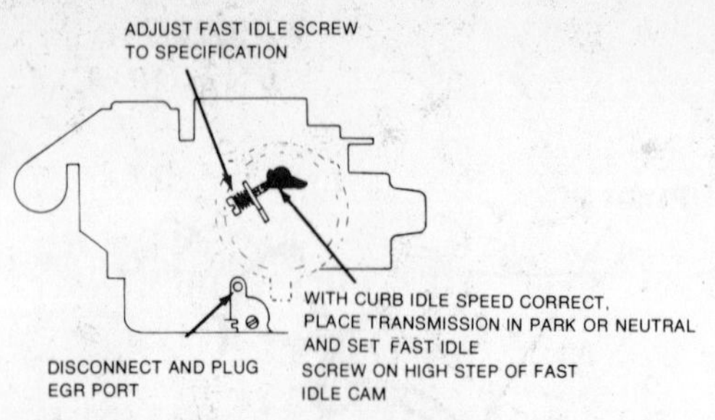

Fast idle adjusting screw—1979 and later

2. Make sure that the curb idle speed is as specified using a tachometer.
3. Place the fast idle screw on the highest cam step with the engine running.
4. Adjust the fast idle speed screw to the correct fast idle speed.

FAST IDLE CAM ADJUSTMENT

1976-78

1. Hold the fast idle speed screw on the second cam step against the shoulder of the high step.
2. Hold the choke valve closed with a finger.
3. Insert the specified gauge between the center upper edge of the choke valve and the air horn wall.
4. Bend the linkage rod at the upper angle to adjust.

1979 and Later

1. Set the fast idle cam so that the screw is held against the second high step of the cam.
2. Insert the specified gauge between the lower edge of the choke valve and the inside air horn wall.
3. Bend the tang to adjust.

VACUUM BREAK ADJUSTMENT

1976-78

1. Place the fast idle speed screw on the highest cam step.

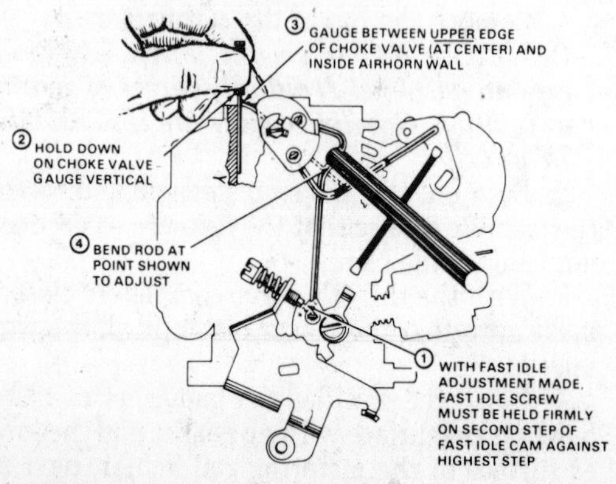

Fast idle cam adjustment—1976-78

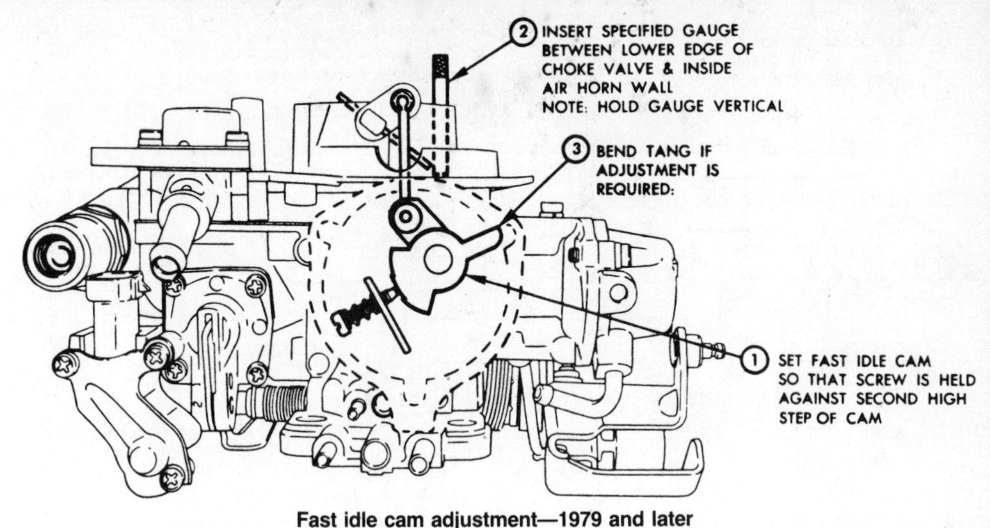

Fast idle cam adjustment—1979 and later

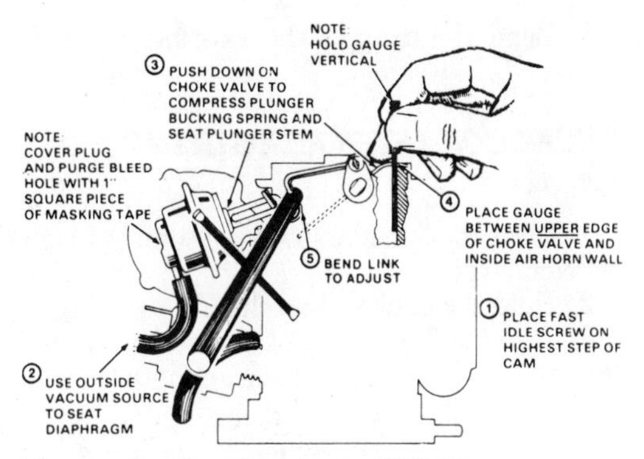

Vacuum break adjustment—1976–78

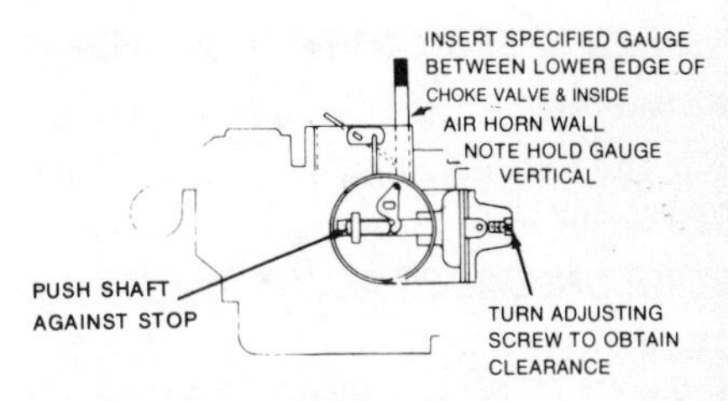

Vacuum break adjustment—1979

2. Tape over the bleed hole in the diaphragm unit. Apply suction by mouth to seat the diaphragm.

3. Push down on the choke valve with a finger.

4. Insert the gauge between the upper edge of the choke valve and the air horn wall.

5. Bend the link to adjust.

1979

1. Position the fast idle cam by opening throttle ⅓ open, manually closing choke plate, then closing throttle. Check to see that fast idle screw rests on top step.

2. Note position of choke index. Remove the three screws and ring retaining the choke assembly. Unplug wire from choke housing and remove entire choke assembly as a unit (bimetal assembly, grounding ring, nylon eye, and plastic housing).

3. With a screwdriver or suitable tool, push diaphragm shaft against stop.

4. Take slack out of linkage by holding the choke housing shaft tang (the tang that mates with the bimetal eye) in the direction of the choke plate closing.

5. Insert a specified gauge between lower edge of choke and air horn wall (with no weight on the choke plates).

6. Turn adjusting screw in or out with an Allen wrench to obtain specified clearance.

7. After adjustment, reassemble in the following sequence: plastic core housing, grounding ring, nylon eye, bimetal assembly, retaining ring, 3 attaching screws. Rotate the bimetal cover making sure choke valves operate in both directions without interference of binding. Return index on bimetal cover to original position and tighten screws to 7 in. lbs. Plug wire back onto choke housing.

1980 and Later

1. Apply an external vacuum source and seat the vacuum break diaphragm.

2. Push the fast idle cam lever down (clockwise) to close the choke valve.

3. Take the slack out of the linkage in the open choke direction.

4. Insert the specified gauge between the lower edge of the choke valve and the inside air horn wall. Hold the gauge vertical.

5. Turn the adjusting screw to obtain the clearance.

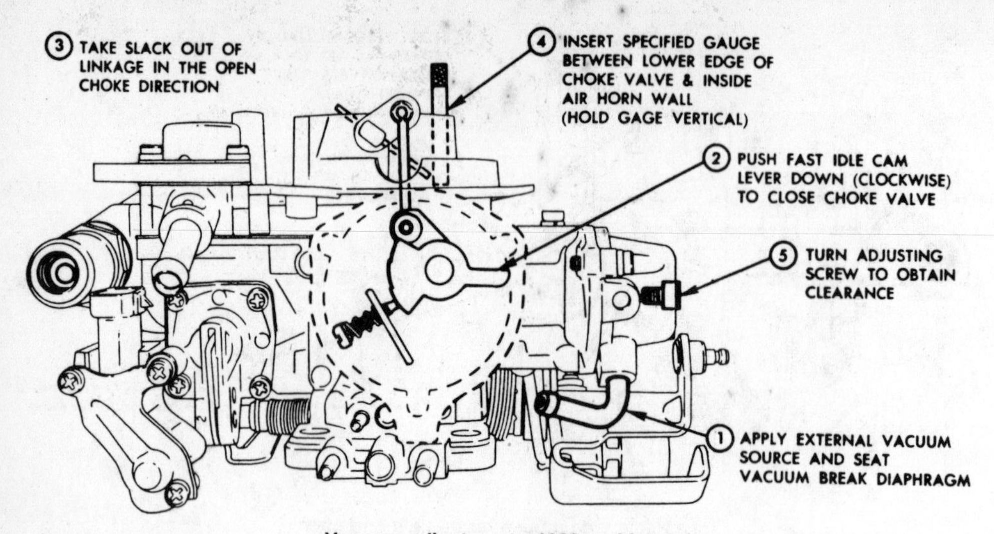

Vacuum adjustment—1980 and later

STEPPED SPEED CONTROL SYSTEM (SSC)

1983 and Later

For the SSC adjustment, please refer to the illustrations.

CHOKE UNLOADER ADJUSTMENT

1976-78

1. Hold the throttle valve wide open.
2. Hold down the choke valve with a finger and insert the specified gauge between the upper edge of the choke valve and the inside air horn wall.
3. Bend the linkage tang to adjust.

1979 and Later

1. Position the throttle lever to wide-open.
2. Insert the specified gauge between the lower edge of the choke valve and the inside air horn wall. Hold the gauge vertical.
3. Bend the tang at the existing radius to adjust.

CHOKE COIL LEVER ADJUSTMENT

1976-78

1. Place the fast idle speed screw on the highest cam step.
2. Hold the choke valve closed.
3. Insert a 3mm gauge through the hole in the arm on the choke housing and into the hole in the casting.
4. Bend the link to adjust.

ELECTRIC CHOKE ADJUSTMENT

1976-78

1. Place the fast idle cam follower on the high step.
2. Loosen the three retaining screws and ro-

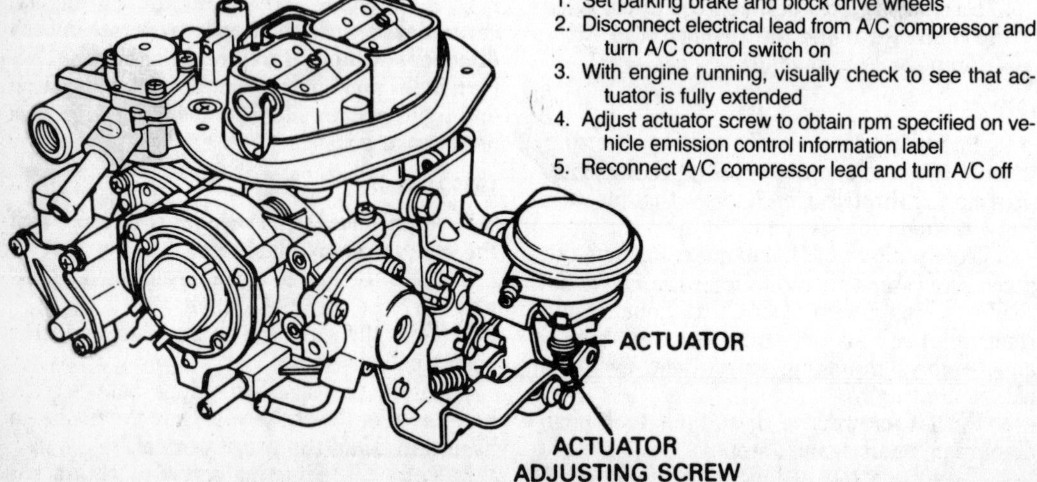

Stepped speed control adjustment—1983 and later with A/C

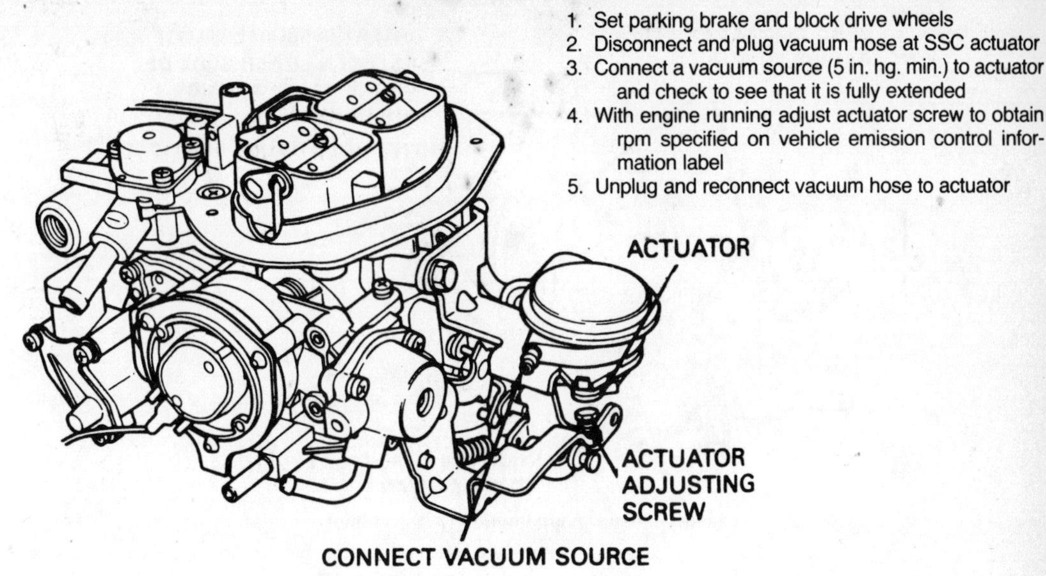

Stepped speed control adjustment-1983 and later without A/C

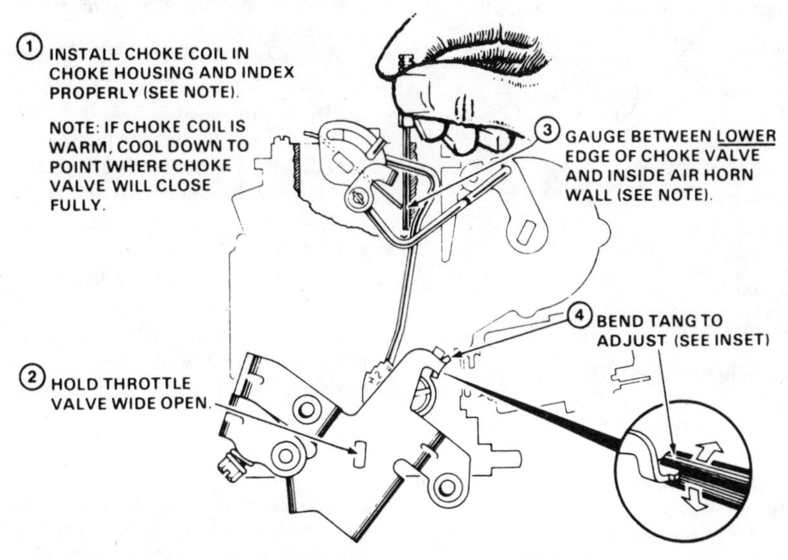

Choke unloader adjustment—1976–78

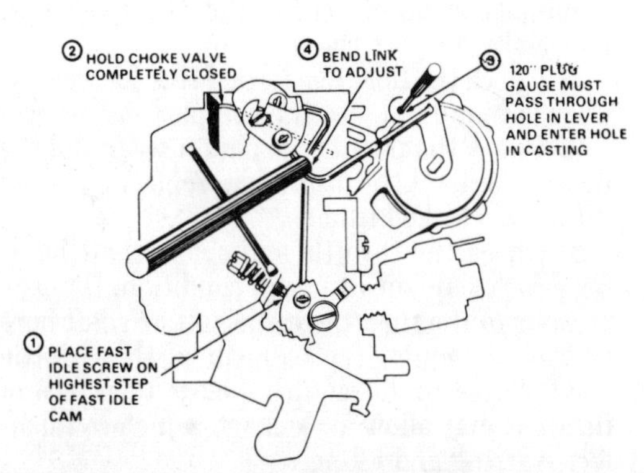

Choke coil cover adjustment—1976–78

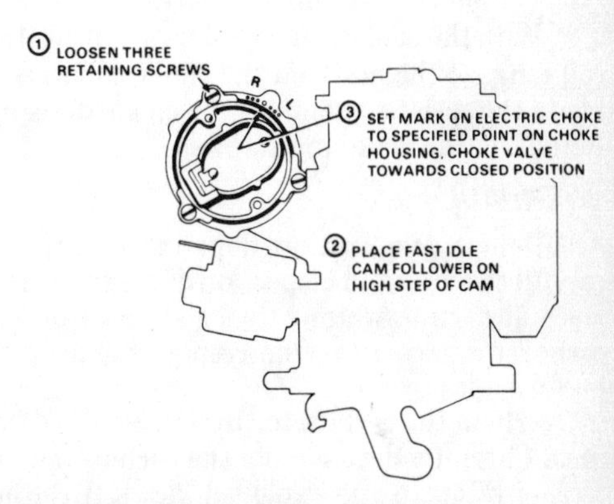

Electric choke adjustment—1976–78

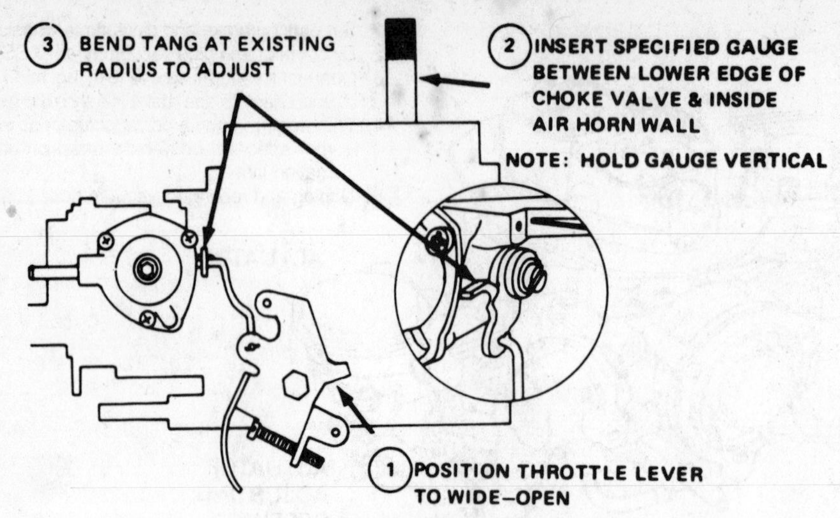

Choke unloader adjustment—1979 and later

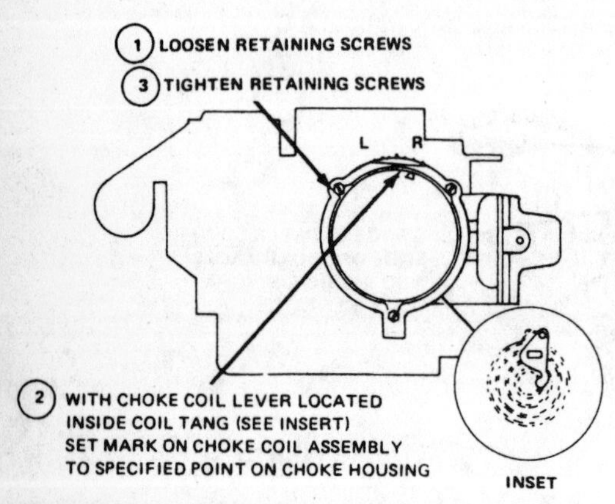

Electric choke adjustment—1979

tate the cover counterclockwise until the choke valve just closes.

3. Align the index mark on the cover with the specified housing mark.
4. Tighten the three screws.

1979

1. Loosen the retaining screws.
2. With the choke coil lever located inside the coil tang set the mark on the choke coil assembly to the specified point on the choke housing. Retighten the retaining screws.

OVERHAUL

Efficient carburetion depends greatly on careful cleaning and inspection during overhaul since dirt, gum, water or varnish in or on the carburetor parts are often responsible for poor performance.

Overhaul the carburetor in a clean, dust free area. Carefully disassembly the carburetor, referring often to the exploded views. Keep all similar and look-alike parts segregated during disassembly and cleaning to avoid accidental interchange during assembly. Make a note of all jet sizes.

When the carburetor is disassembled, wash all parts (except diaphragms, electric choke units, pump plunger and any other plastic, leather, fiber, or rubber parts) in clean carburetor solvent. Do not leave the parts in the solvent any longer than is necessary to sufficiently loosen the dirt and deposits. Excessive cleaning may remove the special finish from the float bowl and choke valve bodies, leaving these parts unfit for service. Rinse all parts in clean solvent and blow them dry with compressed air or allow them to air dry, while resting on clean, lintless paper. Wipe clean all cork, plastic, leather and fiber parts with clean, lint free cloth.

Blow out all passages and jets with compressed air and be sure that there are no restrictions or blockages. Never use wire or similar tools to clean jets, fuel passages or air bleeds. Clean all jets and valves separately to avoid accidental interchange.

Examine all parts for wear or damage. If wear or damage is found, replace the defective parts. Especially, inspect the following:

1. Check the float needle and seat for wear. If wear is found, replace the complete assembly.
2. Check the float hinge pin for wear and the float(s) for dents or distortion. replace the float if fuel has leaked into it.
3. Check the throttle and choke shaft bores for wear or an out-of-round condition. Damage or wear to the throttle arm, shaft or shaft bore will often require replacement of the throttle body. These parts require a close tolerance of fit; wear may allow air leakage, which could affect starting and idling.

NOTE: *Throttle shaft and bushings are not*

normally included in overhaul kits. They can be purchased separately.

4. Inspect the idle mixture adjusting needles for burrs and grooves. Any such condition requires replacement of the needle, since you will not be able to obtain a satisfactory idle.

5. Test the accelerator pump check valves. They should pass air one way, but not the other. Test for proper seating by blowing and sucking on the valve. Replace the valve as necessary. If the valve is satisfactory, wash the valve again to remove moisture.

6. Check the bowl cover for warped surfaces with a straightedge.

7. Closely inspect the valves and seats for wear and damage, replacing as necessary.

8. After the carburetor is assembled, check the choke valve for freedom of operation.

Carburetor overhaul kits are recommended for each overhaul. these kits contain all gaskets and new parts to replace those which deteriorate most rapidly. Failure to replace all of the parts supplied with the kit (especially gaskets) can result in poor performance later.

Carburetor Specifications

Year	Carburetor Identification Number ①	Float Level (in.)	Metering Rod (in.)	Fast Idle Speed (rpm)	Fast Idle Cam (in.)	Vacuum Break (in.)	Choke Unloader (in.)	Choke Setting (notches)
1976–77	17056030	5/32	0.072	2000 ②	0.065	0.070	0.165	3 Rich
	17056036							
	17056031							
	17056037							
	17056032	5/32	0.073	2000 ③	0.045	0.070	0.200	3 Rich
	17056034							
	17056033							
	17056035							
	17056330	5/32	0.072	2000	0.065	0.070	0.165	3 Rich
	1705631							
	17056332	5/32	0.073	2000	0.045	0.070	0.200	2 Rich
	17056333							
	17056334							
	17056335	5/32	0.073	2000	0.045	0.120	0.200	3 Rich
1978	17058031	5/32	0.080	2400	0.105	0.150	0.500	2 Rich
	17058032	5/32	0.080	2400	0.080	0.130	0.500	3 Rich
	17058034							
	17058036							
	17058038							
	17058033	5/32	0.080	2400	0.080	0.130	0.500	2 Rich
	17058037							
	17058042	5/32	0.080	2400	0.080	0.130 ④	0.500	2 Rich
	17058044							
	17058332							
	17058334							
	17058035	5/32	0.080	2300	0.080	0.130	0.500	3 Rich
	17058045	5/32	0.080	2300 ⑤	0.080	0.130 ④	0.500	2 Rich
	17058035							
1979	466361	0.50	NA	2500	0.110	0.245	0.350	2 Rich
	466363							

Carburetor Specifications (cont.)

Year	Carburetor Identification Number ①	Float Level (in.)	Metering Rod (in.)	Fast Idle Speed (rpm)	Fast Idle Cam (in.)	Vacuum Break (in.)	Choke Unloader (in.)	Choke Setting (notches)
1979	466369							
	466371							
	466362	0.50	NA	2500	0.110	0.250	0.350	2 Rich
	466364							
	466370							
	466372							
	466365	0.50	NA	2500	0.130	0.300	0.350	1 Rich
	466366							
	466367							
	466368							
	466373							
	466374							
	466375	0.50	NA	2500	0.130	0.300	0.350	1 Rich
	466376							
1980	14004461	0.50	NA	2500	0.110	0.120	0.350	Fixed
	14004462	0.50	NA	2500	0.110	0.120	0.350	Fixed
	14004463	0.50	NA	2500	0.110	0.120	0.350	Fixed
	14004464	0.50	NA	2500	0.110	0.120	0.350	Fixed
	14004465	0.50	NA	2500	0.110	0.120	0.350	Fixed
	14004466	0.50	NA	2500	0.110	0.120	0.350	Fixed
	14004467	0.50	NA	2500	0.110	0.120	0.350	Fixed
	14004468	0.50	NA	2500	0.110	0.120	0.350	Fixed
	14004469	0.50	NA	2500	0.130	0.300	0.350	Fixed
	14004470	0.50	NA	2500	0.130	0.300	0.350	Fixed
	14004471	0.50	NA	2600	0.130	0.275	0.350	Fixed
	14004472	0.50	NA	2600	0.130	0.275	0.350	Fixed
1981	All	0.50	NA	2500	0.130	0.300	0.350	Fixed
1982	All	0.50	NA	⑥	0.080	0.080	0.270	Fixed
1983	14048827	0.50	NA	⑥	0.080	0.080	0.270	Fixed
	14048828	0.50	NA	⑥	0.080	0.080	0.300	Fixed
	14048829	0.50	NA	⑥	0.080	0.080	0.270	Fixed
1984–87	14068690	0.50	NA	⑥	0.080	0.270	0.350	Fixed
	14068691	0.50	NA	⑥	0.080	0.270	0.350	Fixed
	14068692	0.50	NA	⑥	0.080	0.300	0.350	Fixed
	14076363	0.50	NA	⑥	0.080	0.300	0.350	Fixed

① Stamped on float bowl, next to fuel inlet nut
② 2200 rpm for the first two numbers
③ 2200 rpm for the last two numbers
④ .160 above 30,000 miles
⑤ Non-adjustable by design
⑥ See underhood decal
NA—Not applicable

Most carburetor manufacturers supply overhaul kits of three basic types: minor repair; major repair; and gasket kits. Basically, they contain the following:

Minor Repair Kits:

- All gaskets
- Float needle valve
- All diagrams
- Spring for the pump diaphragm

Major Repair Kits:

- All jets and gaskets
- All diaphragms
- Float needle valve
- Pump ball valve
- Float
- Complete intermediate rod
- Intermediate pump lever
- Some cover holddown screws and washers

Gasket kits:

- All gaskets

After cleaning and checking all components, reassemble the carburetor, using new parts and referring to the exploded view. When reassembling, make sure that all screws and jets are right in their seat, but do not overtighten, as the tip will be distorted. Tighten all screws gradually, in rotation. Do not tighten needle valves into their seats; uneven jetting will result. Always use new gaskets. Be sure to adjust the float level.

NOTE: *Most carburetor rebuilding kits contain a sheet of specific instructions pertaining to the carburetor the kit is for.*

DIESEL ENGINE FUEL SYSTEM

The Chevette diesel fuel system consists of a high pressure fuel injection pump driven by the camshaft timing belt, four pressure activated fuel injectors installed in the cylinder head and connected by fuel lines to the pump, a fuel filter with built in water separator, drain and hand primer, a fuel tank and connecting fuel feed and return lines. The injection pump is equipped with an electrically operated fuel cut-off solenoid which halts fuel flow (and the engine) whenever the ignition key is turned to the OFF position.

Idle Speed

ADJUSTMENT

1. Set the parking brake and block the wheels.
2. Place the transmission in Neutral. Connect a tachometer as per the manufacturers instructions.
3. Start the engine and allow it to reach normal operating temperature.
4. Loosen the lock nut on the idle speed adjusting screw and turn the screw to obtain the correct idle speed (see underhood specifications sticker).
5. Tighten the lock nut, turn the engine off and disconnect the tachometer.

Fast Idle Speed

ADJUSTMENT

1. Set the parking brake and block the wheels.
2. Place the transmission in neutral.
3. Connect a tachometer.
4. Start the engine and allow it to run until it reaches normal operating temperature.
5. Apply vacuum to the fast idle actuator.
6. Loosen the lock nut on the fast idle adjusting screw and adjust the knurled nut to obtain the fast idle speed specified on the emission label. After adjusting, retighten the lock nut.

Injection Pump

REMOVAL AND INSTALLATION

NOTE: *This procedure will require the use of two special tools: a gear puller (J-22888) and a fixing plate (J-29761). It is a long and complicated procedure and must be performed in conjunction with the following injection timing procedure. We do not suggest that the average amateur mechanic perform these procedures.*

1. Disconnect the negative battery cable.
2. Drain the cooling system. Remove the fan shroud, radiator and coolant recovery tank.

CAUTION: *When draining the coolant, keep in mind that cats and dogs are attracted by the ethylene glycol antifreeze, and are quite likely to drink any that is left in an uncovered container or in puddles on the ground. This will prove fatal in sufficient quantity. Always drain the coolant into a sealable container. Coolant should be reused unless it is contaminated or several years old.*

3. Disconnect the bypass hose leading from the front cover and then remove the upper half of the front cover.

NOTE: *Fan removal may facilitate better access to certain front cover retaining bolts.*

4. Loosen the timing belt tension pulley and plate bolts. Slide the tensioner over.
5. Unscrew the two retaining bolts and remove tension spring from behind the front plate, by the injection pump.
6. Remove the injection pump gear retaining nut and then remove the gear with a gear puller.
7. Tag and disconnect any wires, hoses or cables leading from the pump. Disconnect and plug the fuel feed lines.

8. Remove the fuel filter. Disconnect the injector lines at the pump and at the injector nozzles and remove the lines.
9. Unscrew the four retaining bolts and remove the pump rear bracket.
10. Unscrew the nuts attaching the pump flange to the front plate and then remove the pump complete with the fast idle device and return spring. To install:
11. Place the pump in position and tighten the flange bolts. Position the rear bracket and tighten the bracket-to-pump bolts. There should be no clearance between the rear bracket and pump bracket.
12. Reconnect all wires, hoses and cable.
13. Slide the pump gear onto its shaft, making sure that it is aligned with the key groove. Turn the gear until the notch mark aligns with the index mark on the front plate. Thread a lock bolt (8mm x 1.25) through the gear and into the front plate and then tighten the retaining nut to 45 ft. lbs.
14. Remove the cylinder head cover. Position the No. 1 piston at TDC of the compression stroke and install the fixing plate into the slot in the rear of the camshaft to prevent it from rotating.
15. Unscrew the cam gear retaining bolt and, using a puller, remove the gear. Reinstall the gear loosely so that it can be turned smoothly by hand.
16. Grasp the timing belt on each side near the lower half of the front cover; move it back and forth until the cogs on the belt engage with those on the lower gears. Slide the belt over the pump gear and then over the cam gear (you may need to turn the cam gear slightly to facilitate proper engagement of the cogs).
17. Make sure that any slack in the belt is

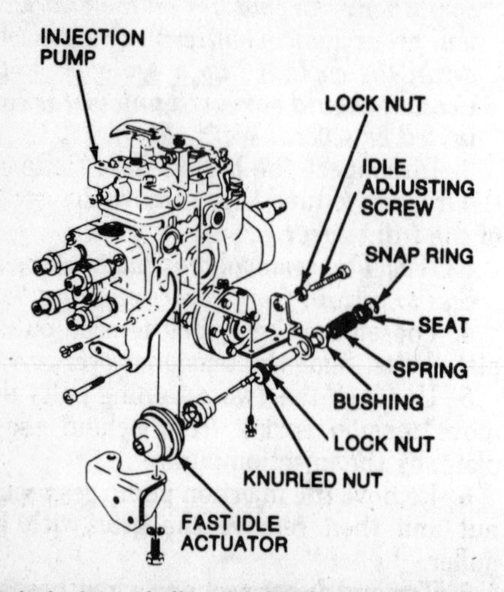

Exploded view of diesel injection pump linkage showing the idle adjusting screw and the fast idle adjuster (knurled nut)

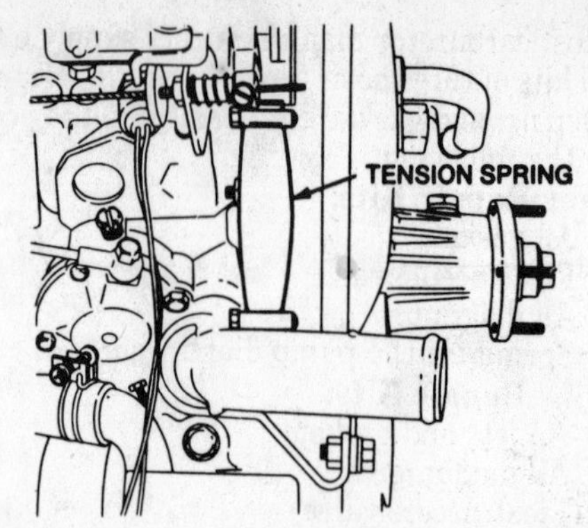

Tension spring, located behind the front plate beside the injection pump on diesel engine

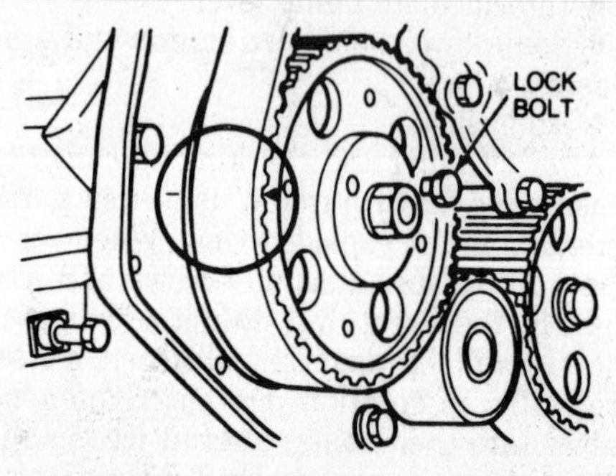

Use a lockbolt to ensure that the index marks on the injection pump gear and the front plate stay in alignment—diesel engine

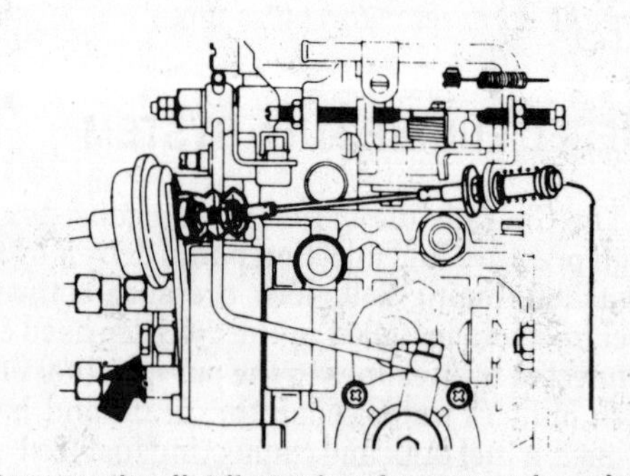

Remove the distributor head screw and washer

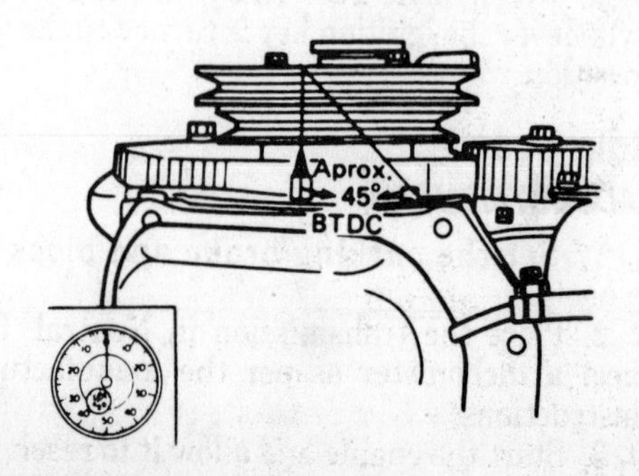

Zeroing the dial indicator

concentrated around the tension pulley and NOT around or between the two upper gears. Depress the tension pulley with your finger and then install the tension spring.

18. Partially tighten the tension pulley bolts; first the upper, then the lower. Tighten the cam gear retaining bolt to 45 ft. lbs.

19. Remove the pump gear lock bolt. Remove the fixing plate from the end of the camshaft.

20. Check that the No. 1 piston is still at TDC. Check that the marks on the front plate and the pump gear are still aligned. Check that the fixing plate still fits properly into the rear of the camshaft.

WARNING: *If these three steps do not check out correctly, repeat the entire procedure. DO NOT attempt to compensate by moving the camshaft, pump gear or crankshaft.*

21. Loosen the tension pulley and plate bolts. Make sure the belt slack is concentrated around the pulley and then tighten the bolts in the same manner as before. Belt tension should be checked at a point between the cam gear and the pump gear.

22. Installation of the remaining components is in the reverse order of removal.

23. Check the injection timing.

Injection Timing

1. Check that the No. 1 piston is at TDC of the compression stroke. Make sure that the timing belt is properly tensioned and the timing marks are aligned.

2. Remove the cylinder head cover and check that the fixing plate used in the previous section will still fit smoothly into the slot at the rear of the camshaft.

3. Remove the injection lines as detailed earlier and then remove the distributor head screw and washer.

4. Position a Static Timing Gauge (J-29763) and a dial indicator in the distributor head hole. Set the lift approximately 1mm from the end of the plunger.

5. Turn the crankshaft until the No. 1 piston is 45-60° BTDC and then zero the dial indicator.

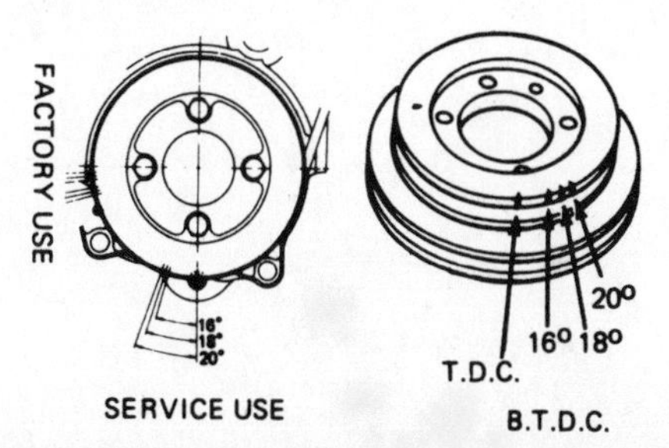

Staic timing notches on the damper pulley

NOTE: *The damper pulley is notched with eleven lines; four in one position, seven in another. The group of four are to be used for static timing.*

6. Turn the crankshaft until the 18 degrees notch on the damper pulley is aligned with the timing pointer.

7. The dial indicator should read 0.5mm. If it does not, hole the crankshaft in the 18 degrees position, loosen the two nuts on the injection pump flange and move the pump until the proper reading is achieved. Swivel the pump up to retard the timing and down to advance the timing. When adjustment is correct, retighten the pump flange nuts.

8. Remove the dial indicator and install the distributor head screw and washer.

9. Install the cylinder head cover, injection lines and fuel filter.

10. Reconnect all necessary wires and hoses. Installation of the remaining components is in the reverse order of removal.

Fuel Injection Nozzle

REMOVAL AND INSTALLATION

CAUTION: *The primary function of an injection nozzle is to distribute fuel in the combustion chamber. Do not, under any circumstances, crank the engine while an injection line or injector is disconnected.*

1. Disconnect the negative battery cable.

2. Remove the fresh air duct and disconnect the PCV hose.

3. Disconnect the injection line at the injection nozzle and then loosen it at the injection pump. Carefully move it out of the way.

4. Remove the fuel return line.

5. Unscrew and remove the injector.

6. Installation is in the reverse order of removal.

FUEL TANK

REMOVAL AND INSTALLATION

All Models

1. Disconnect the battery.

2. Drain the fuel tank.

CAUTION: *Never smoke when working around gasoline! Avoid all sources of sparks or ignition. Gasoline vapors are EXTREMELY volatile!*

3. Raise the rear of the car and support it safely on jackstands.

4. Disconnect the meter wire at the rear harness connector and the ground strap at the fuel tank reinforcement.

Troubleshooting Basic Fuel System Problems

Problem	Cause	Solution
Engine cranks, but won't start (or is hard to start) when cold	• Empty fuel tank • Incorrect starting procedure • Defective fuel pump • No fuel in carburetor • Clogged fuel filter • Engine flooded • Defective choke	• Check for fuel in tank • Follow correct procedure • Check pump output • Check for fuel in the carburetor • Replace fuel filter • Wait 15 minutes; try again • Check choke plate
Engine cranks, but is hard to start (or does not start) when hot—(presence of fuel is assumed)	• Defective choke	• Check choke plate
Rough idle or engine runs rough	• Dirt or moisture in fuel • Clogged air filter • Faulty fuel pump	• Replace fuel filter • Replace air filter • Check fuel pump output
Engine stalls or hesitates on acceleration	• Dirt or moisture in the fuel • Dirty carburetor • Defective fuel pump • Incorrect float level, defective accelerator pump	• Replace fuel filter • Clean the carburetor • Check fuel pump output • Check carburetor
Poor gas mileage	• Clogged air filter • Dirty carburetor • Defective choke, faulty carburetor adjustment	• Replace air filter • Clean carburetor • Check carburetor
Engine is flooded (won't start accompanied by smell of raw fuel)	• Improperly adjusted choke or carburetor	• Wait 15 minutes and try again, without pumping gas pedal • If it won't start, check carburetor

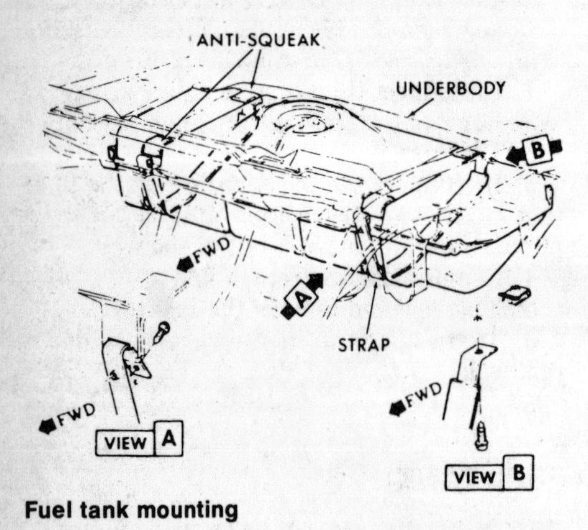

Fuel tank mounting

5. Disconnect the fuel filler neck hose and the vent hose.
6. Disconnect the fuel feed line and the vapor line at the hose connections.
7. Remove the fuel tank strap rear support bolts and lower and remove the fuel tank.
8. To install the tank, reverse the above steps.

CHILTON'S FUEL ECONOMY & TUNE-UP TIPS

55 WAYS TO IMPROVE FUEL ECONOMY

Tune-up • Spark Plug Diagnosis • Emission Controls

Fuel System • Cooling System • Tires and Wheels

General Maintenance

CHILTON'S FUEL ECONOMY & TUNE-UP TIPS

Fuel economy is important to everyone, no matter what kind of vehicle you drive. The maintenance-minded motorist can save both money and fuel using these tips and the periodic maintenance and tune-up procedures in this Repair and Tune-Up Guide.

There are more than 130,000,000 cars and trucks registered for private use in the United States. Each travels an average of 10-12,000 miles per year, and, and in total they consume close to 70 billion gallons of fuel each year. This represents nearly ⅔ of the oil imported by the United States each year. The Federal government's goal is to reduce consumption 10% by 1985. A variety of methods are either already in use or under serious consideration, and they all affect you driving and the cars you will drive. In addition to "down-sizing", the auto industry is using or investigating the use of electronic fuel delivery, electronic engine controls and alternative engines for use in smaller and lighter vehicles, among other alternatives to meet the federally mandated Corporate Average Fuel Economy (CAFE) of 27.5 mpg by 1985. The government, for its part, is considering rationing, mandatory driving curtailments and tax increases on motor vehicle fuel in an effort to reduce consumption. The government's goal of a 10% reduction could be realized — and further government regulation avoided — if every private vehicle could use just 1 less gallon of fuel per week.

How Much Can You Save?

Tests have proven that almost anyone can make at least a 10% reduction in fuel consumption through regular maintenance and tune-ups. When a major manufacturer of spark plugs sur-

TUNE-UP

1. Check the cylinder compression to be sure the engine will really benefit from a tune-up and that it is capable of producing good fuel economy. A tune-up will be wasted on an engine in poor mechanical condition.
2. Replace spark plugs regularly. New spark plugs alone can increase fuel economy 3%.
3. Be sure the spark plugs are the correct type (heat range) for your vehicle. See the Tune-Up Specifications.

Heat range refers to the spark plug's ability to conduct heat away from the firing end. It must conduct the heat away in an even pattern to avoid becoming a source of pre-ignition, yet it must also operate hot enough to burn off conductive deposits that could cause misfiring.

The heat range is usually indicated by a number on the spark plug, part of the manufacturer's designation for each individual spark plug. The numbers in bold-face indicate the heat range in each manufacturer's identification system.

Manufacturer	**Typical Designation**
AC	R **45** TS
Bosch (old)	WA **145** T30
Bosch (new)	HR **8** Y
Champion	RBL **15** Y
Fram/Autolite	41**5**
Mopar	P-**62** PR
Motorcraft	BRF-**42**
NGK	BP **5** ES-15
Nippondenso	W **16** EP
Prestolite	14GR **5** 2A

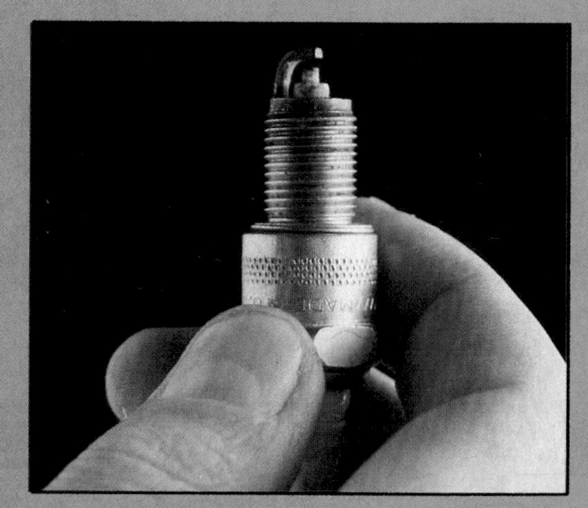

Periodically, check the spark plugs to be sure they are firing efficiently. They are excellent indicators of the internal condition of your engine.

On AC, Bosch (new), Champion, Fram/Autolite, Mopar, Motorcraft and Prestolite, a higher number indicates a hotter plug. On Bosch (old), NGK and Nippondenso, a higher number indicates a colder plug.

4. Make sure the spark plugs are properly gapped. See the Tune-Up Specifications in this book.
5. Be sure the spark plugs are firing efficiently. The illustrations on the next 2 pages show you how to "read" the firing end of the spark plug.
6. Check the ignition timing and set it to specifications. Tests show that almost all cars have incorrect ignition timing by more than 2°.

veyed over 6,000 cars nationwide, they found that a tune-up, on cars that needed one, increased fuel economy over 11%. Replacing worn plugs alone, accounted for a 3% increase. The same test also revealed that 8 out of every 10 vehicles will have some maintenance deficiency that will directly affect fuel economy, emissions or performance. Most of this mileage-robbing neglect could be prevented with regular maintenance.

Modern engines require that all of the functioning systems operate properly for maximum efficiency. A malfunction anywhere wastes fuel. You can keep your vehicle running as efficiently and economically as possible, by being aware of your vehicle's operating and performance characteristics. If your vehicle suddenly develops performance or fuel economy problems it could be due to one or more of the following:

PROBLEM	POSSIBLE CAUSE
Engine Idles Rough	Ignition timing, idle mixture, vacuum leak or something amiss in the emission control system.
Hesitates on Acceleration	Dirty carburetor or fuel filter, improper accelerator pump setting, ignition timing or fouled spark plugs.
Starts Hard or Fails to Start	Worn spark plugs, improperly set automatic choke, ice (or water) in fuel system.
Stalls Frequently	Automatic choke improperly adjusted and possible dirty air filter or fuel filter.
Performs Sluggishly	Worn spark plugs, dirty fuel or air filter, ignition timing or automatic choke out of adjustment.

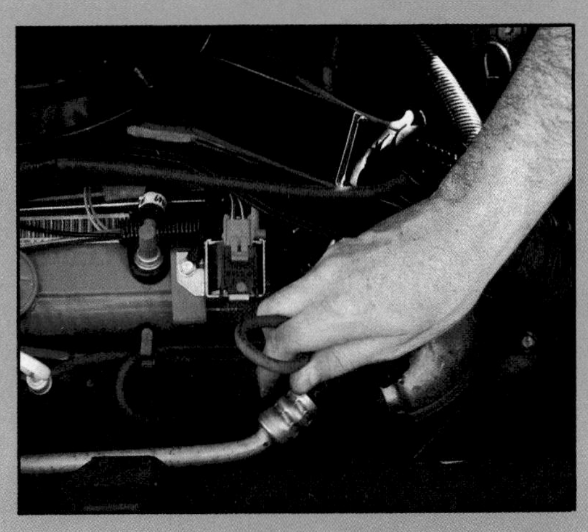

Check spark plug wires on conventional point type ignition for cracks by bending them in a loop around your finger.

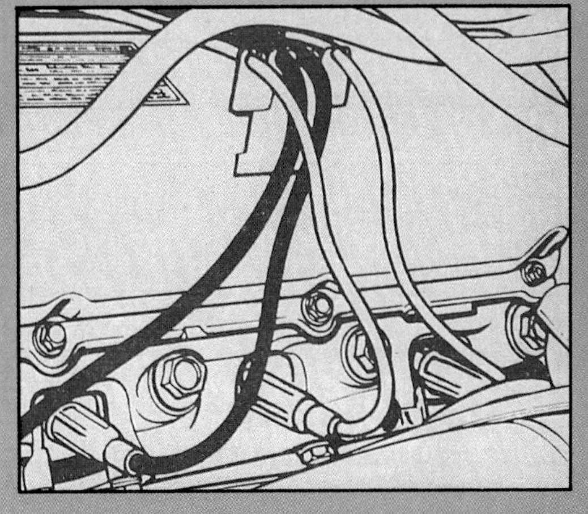

Be sure that spark plug wires leading to adjacent cylinders do not run too close together. (Photo courtesy Champion Spark Plug Co.)

7. If your vehicle does not have electronic ignition, check the points, rotor and cap as specified.

8. Check the spark plug wires (used with conventional point-type ignitions) for cracks and burned or broken insulation by bending them in a loop around your finger. Cracked wires decrease fuel efficiency by failing to deliver full voltage to the spark plugs. One misfiring spark plug can cost you as much as 2 mpg.

9. Check the routing of the plug wires. Misfiring can be the result of spark plug leads to adjacent cylinders running parallel to each other and too close together. One wire tends to pick up voltage from the other causing it to fire "out of time".

10. Check all electrical and ignition circuits for voltage drop and resistance.

11. Check the distributor mechanical and/or vacuum advance mechanisms for proper functioning. The vacuum advance can be checked by twisting the distributor plate in the opposite direction of rotation. It should spring back when released.

12. Check and adjust the valve clearance on engines with mechanical lifters. The clearance should be slightly loose rather than too tight.

SPARK PLUG DIAGNOSIS

Normal

APPEARANCE: This plug is typical of one operating normally. The insulator nose varies from a light tan to grayish color with slight electrode wear. The presence of slight deposits is normal on used plugs and will have no adverse effect on engine performance. The spark plug heat range is correct for the engine and the engine is running normally.
CAUSE: Properly running engine.
RECOMMENDATION: Before reinstalling this plug, the electrodes should be cleaned and filed square. Set the gap to specifications. If the plug has been in service for more than 10-12,000 miles, the entire set should probably be replaced with a fresh set of the same heat range.

Oil Deposits

APPEARANCE: The firing end of the plug is covered with a wet, oily coating.
CAUSE: The problem is poor oil control. On high mileage engines, oil is leaking past the rings or valve guides into the combustion chamber. A common cause is also a plugged PCV valve, and a ruptured fuel pump diaphragm can also cause this condition. Oil fouled plugs such as these are often found in new or recently overhauled engines, before normal oil control is achieved, and can be cleaned and reinstalled.
RECOMMENDATION: A hotter spark plug may temporarily relieve the problem, but the engine is probably in need of work.

Incorrect Heat Range

APPEARANCE: The effects of high temperature on a spark plug are indicated by clean white, often blistered insulator. This can also be accompanied by excessive wear of the electrode, and the absence of deposits.
CAUSE: Check for the correct spark plug heat range. A plug which is too hot for the engine can result in overheating. A car operated mostly at high speeds can require a colder plug. Also check ignition timing, cooling system level, fuel mixture and leaking intake manifold.
RECOMMENDATION: If all ignition and engine adjustments are known to be correct, and no other malfunction exists, install spark plugs one heat range colder.

Photos Courtesy Fram Corporation

Carbon Deposits

APPEARANCE: Carbon fouling is easily identified by the presence of dry, soft, black, sooty deposits.
CAUSE: Changing the heat range can often lead to carbon fouling, as can prolonged slow, stop-and-start driving. If the heat range is correct, carbon fouling can be attributed to a rich fuel mixture, sticking choke, clogged air cleaner, worn breaker points, retarded timing or low compression. If only one or two plugs are carbon fouled, check for corroded or cracked wires on the affected plugs. Also look for cracks in the distributor cap between the towers of affected cylinders.
RECOMMENDATION: After the problem is corrected, these plugs can be cleaned and reinstalled if not worn severely.

MMT Fouled

APPEARANCE: Spark plugs fouled by MMT (Methycyclopentadienyl Maganese Tricarbonyl) have reddish, rusty appearance on the insulator and side electrode.
CAUSE: MMT is an anti-knock additive in gasoline used to replace lead. During the combustion process, the MMT leaves a reddish deposit on the insulator and side electrode.
RECOMMENDATION: No engine malfunction is indicated and the deposits will not affect plug performance any more than lead deposits (see Ash Deposits). MMT fouled plugs can be cleaned, regapped and reinstalled.

Ash (Lead) Deposits

APPEARANCE: Ash deposits are characterized by light brown or white colored deposits crusted on the side or center electrodes. In some cases it may give the plug a rusty appearance.
CAUSE: Ash deposits are normally derived from oil or fuel additives burned during normal combustion. Normally they are harmless, though excessive amounts can cause misfiring. If deposits are excessive in short mileage, the valve guides may be worn.
RECOMMENDATION: Ash-fouled plugs can be cleaned, gapped and reinstalled.

High Speed Glazing

APPEARANCE: Glazing appears as shiny coating on the plug, either yellow or tan in color.
CAUSE: During hard, fast acceleration, plug temperatures rise suddenly. Deposits from normal combustion have no chance to fluff-off; instead, they melt on the insulator forming an electrically conductive coating which causes misfiring.
RECOMMENDATION: Glazed plugs are not easily cleaned. They should be replaced with a fresh set of plugs of the correct heat range. If the condition recurs, using plugs with a heat range one step colder may cure the problem.

Detonation

APPEARANCE: Detonation is usually characterized by a broken plug insulator.
CAUSE: A portion of the fuel charge will begin to burn spontaneously, from the increased heat following ignition. The explosion that results applies extreme pressure to engine components, frequently damaging spark plugs and pistons.

Detonation can result by over-advanced ignition timing, inferior gasoline (low octane) lean air/fuel mixture, poor carburetion, engine lugging or an increase in compression ratio due to combustion chamber deposits or engine modification.
RECOMMENDATION: Replace the plugs after correcting the problem.

Photos Courtesy Champion Spark Plug Co.

EMISSION CONTROLS

13. Be aware of the general condition of the emission control system. It contributes to reduced pollution and should be serviced regularly to maintain efficient engine operation.

14. Check all vacuum lines for dried, cracked or brittle conditions. Something as simple as a leaking vacuum hose can cause poor performance and loss of economy.

15. Avoid tampering with the emission control system. Attempting to improve fuel econ-

FUEL SYSTEM

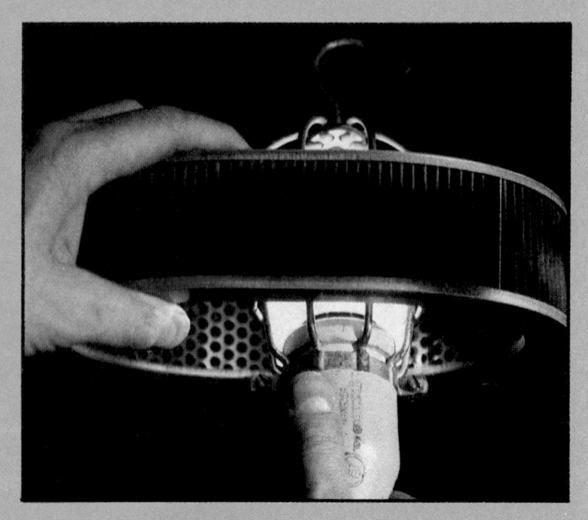

Check the air filter with a light behind it. If you can see light through the filter it can be reused.

Extremely clogged filters should be discarded and replaced with a new one.

18. Replace the air filter regularly. A dirty air filter richens the air/fuel mixture and can increase fuel consumption as much as 10%. Tests show that ⅓ of all vehicles have air filters in need of replacement.

19. Replace the fuel filter at least as often as recommended.

20. Set the idle speed and carburetor mixture to specifications.

21. Check the automatic choke. A sticking or malfunctioning choke wastes gas.

22. During the summer months, adjust the automatic choke for a leaner mixture which will produce faster engine warm-ups.

COOLING SYSTEM

29. Be sure all accessory drive belts are in good condition. Check for cracks or wear.

30. Adjust all accessory drive belts to proper tension.

31. Check all hoses for swollen areas, worn spots, or loose clamps.

32. Check coolant level in the radiator or expansion tank.

33. Be sure the thermostat is operating properly. A stuck thermostat delays engine warm-up and a cold engine uses nearly twice as much fuel as a warm engine.

34. Drain and replace the engine coolant at least as often as recommended. Rust and scale

TIRES & WHEELS

38. Check the tire pressure often with a pencil type gauge. Tests by a major tire manufacturer show that 90% of all vehicles have at least 1 tire improperly inflated. Better mileage can be achieved by over-inflating tires, but never exceed the maximum inflation pressure on the side of the tire.

39. If possible, install radial tires. Radial tires deliver as much as ½ mpg more than bias belted tires.

40. Avoid installing super-wide tires. They only create extra rolling resistance and decrease fuel mileage. Stick to the manufacturer's recommendations.

41. Have the wheels properly balanced.

omy by tampering with emission controls is more likely to worsen fuel economy than improve it. Emission control changes on modern engines are not readily reversible.

16. Clean (or replace) the EGR valve and lines as recommended.

17. Be sure that all vacuum lines and hoses are reconnected properly after working under the hood. An unconnected or misrouted vacuum line can wreak havoc with engine performance.

---

23. Check for fuel leaks at the carburetor, fuel pump, fuel lines and fuel tank. Be sure all lines and connections are tight.

24. Periodically check the tightness of the carburetor and intake manifold attaching nuts and bolts. These are a common place for vacuum leaks to occur.

25. Clean the carburetor periodically and lubricate the linkage.

26. The condition of the tailpipe can be an excellent indicator of proper engine combustion. After a long drive at highway speeds, the inside of the tailpipe should be a light grey in color. Black or soot on the insides indicates an overly rich mixture.

27. Check the fuel pump pressure. The fuel pump may be supplying more fuel than the engine needs.

28. Use the proper grade of gasoline for your engine. Don't try to compensate for knocking or "pinging" by advancing the ignition timing. This practice will only increase plug temperature and the chances of detonation or pre-ignition with relatively little performance gain.

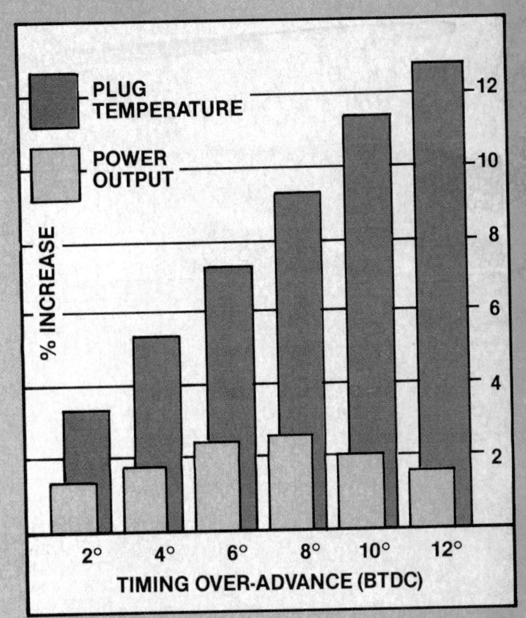

Increasing ignition timing past the specified setting results in a drastic increase in spark plug temperature with increased chance of detonation or preignition. Performance increase is considerably less. (Photo courtesy Champion Spark Plug Co.)

---

that form in the engine should be flushed out to allow the engine to operate at peak efficiency.

35. Clean the radiator of debris that can decrease cooling efficiency.

36. Install a flex-type or electric cooling fan, if you don't have a clutch type fan. Flex fans use curved plastic blades to push more air at low speeds when more cooling is needed; at high speeds the blades flatten out for less resistance. Electric fans only run when the engine temperature reaches a predetermined level.

37. Check the radiator cap for a worn or cracked gasket. If the cap does not seal properly, the cooling system will not function properly.

---

42. Be sure the front end is correctly aligned. A misaligned front end actually has wheels going in differed directions. The increased drag can reduce fuel economy by .3 mpg.

43. Correctly adjust the wheel bearings. Wheel bearings that are adjusted too tight increase rolling resistance.

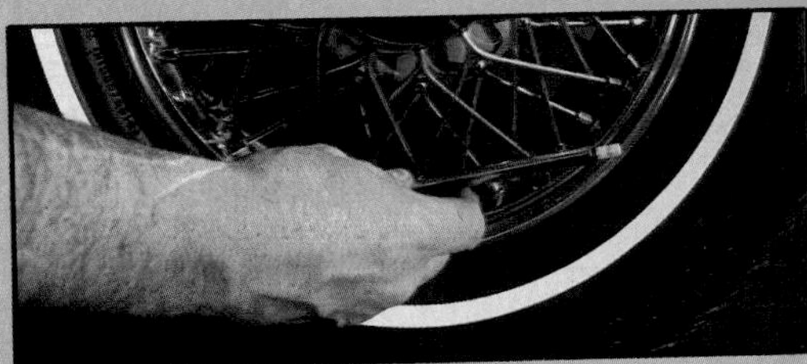

Check tire pressures regularly with a reliable pocket type gauge. Be sure to check the pressure on a cold tire.

GENERAL MAINTENANCE

Check the fluid levels (particularly engine oil) on a regular basis. Be sure to check the oil for grit, water or other contamination.

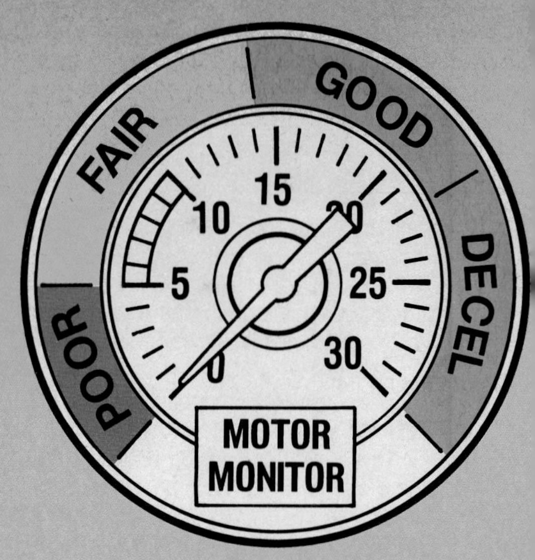

A vacuum gauge is another excellent indicator of internal engine condition and can also be installed in the dash as a mileage indicator.

44. Periodically check the fluid levels in the engine, power steering pump, master cylinder, automatic transmission and drive axle.

45. Change the oil at the recommended interval and change the filter at every oil change. Dirty oil is thick and causes extra friction between moving parts, cutting efficiency and increasing wear. A worn engine requires more frequent tune-ups and gets progressively worse fuel economy. In general, use the lightest viscosity oil for the driving conditions you will encounter.

46. Use the recommended viscosity fluids in the transmission and axle.

47. Be sure the battery is fully charged for fast starts. A slow starting engine wastes fuel.

48. Be sure battery terminals are clean and tight.

49. Check the battery electrolyte level and add distilled water if necessary.

50. Check the exhaust system for crushed pipes, blockages and leaks.

51. Adjust the brakes. Dragging brakes or brakes that are not releasing create increased drag on the engine.

52. Install a vacuum gauge or miles-per-gallon gauge. These gauges visually indicate engine vacuum in the intake manifold. High vacuum = good mileage and low vacuum = poorer mileage. The gauge can also be an excellent indicator of internal engine conditions.

53. Be sure the clutch is properly adjusted. A slipping clutch wastes fuel.

54. Check and periodically lubricate the heat control valve in the exhaust manifold. A sticking or inoperative valve prevents engine warm-up and wastes gas.

55. Keep accurate records to check fuel economy over a period of time. A sudden drop in fuel economy may signal a need for tune-up or other maintenance.

Chassis Electrical

6

UNDERSTANDING AND TROUBLESHOOTING ELECTRICAL SYSTEMS

With the rate at which both import and domestic manufacturers are incorporating electronic control systems into their production lines, it won't be long before every new vehicle is equipped with one or more on-board computer. These electronic components (with no moving parts) should theoretically last the life of the vehicle, provided nothing external happens to damage the circuits or memory chips.

While it is true that electronic components should never wear out, in the real world malfunctions do occur. It is also true that any computer-based system is extremely sensitive to electrical voltages and cannot tolerate careless or haphazard testing or service procedures. An inexperienced individual can literally do major damage looking for a minor problem by using the wrong kind of test equipment or connecting test leads or connectors with the ignition switch ON. When selecting test equipment, make sure the manufacturers instructions state that the tester is compatible with whatever type of electronic control system is being serviced. Read all instructions carefully and double check all test points before installing probes or making any test connections.

The following section outlines basic diagnosis techniques for dealing with computerized automotive control systems. Along with a general explanation of the various types of test equipment available to aid in servicing modern electronic automotive systems, basic repair techniques for wiring harnesses and connectors is given. Read the basic information before attempting any repairs or testing on any computerized system, to provide the background of information necessary to avoid the most common and obvious mistakes that can cost both time and money. Although the replacement and testing procedures are simple in themselves, the systems are not, and unless one has a thorough understanding of all components and their function within a particular computerized control system, the logical test sequence these systems demand cannot be followed. Minor malfunctions can make a big difference, so it is important to know how each component affects the operation of the overall electronic system to find the ultimate cause of a problem without replacing good components unnecessarily. It is not enough to use the correct test equipment; the test equipment must be used correctly.

Safety Precautions

CAUTION: *Whenever working on or around any computer based microprocessor control system, always observe these general precautions to prevent the possibility of personal injury or damage to electronic components.*

- Never install or remove battery cables with the key ON or the engine running. Jumper cables should be connected with the key OFF to avoid power surges that can damage electronic control units. Engines equipped with computer controlled systems should avoid both giving and getting jump starts due to the possibility of serious damage to components from arcing in the engine compartment when connections are made with the ignition ON.
- Always remove the battery cables before charging the battery. Never use a high output charger on an installed battery or attempt to use any type of "hot shot" (24 volt) starting aid.
- Exercise care when inserting test probes into connectors to insure good connections without damaging the connector or spreading the pins. Always probe connectors from the rear (wire) side, NOT the pin side, to avoid accidental shorting of terminals during test procedures.

• Never remove or attach wiring harness connectors with the ignition switch ON, especially to an electronic control unit.

• Do not drop any components during service procedures and never apply 12 volts directly to any component (like a solenoid or relay) unless instructed specifically to do so. Some component electrical windings are designed to safely handle only 4 or 5 volts and can be destroyed in seconds if 12 volts are applied directly to the connector.

• Remove the electronic control unit if the vehicle is to be placed in an environment where temperatures exceed approximately 176°F (80°C), such as a paint spray booth or when arc or gas welding near the control unit location in the car.

ORGANIZED TROUBLESHOOTING

When diagnosing a specific problem, organized troubleshooting is a must. The complexity of a modern automobile demands that you approach any problem in a logical, organized manner. There are certain troubleshooting techniques that are standard:

1. Establish when the problem occurs. Does the problem appear only under certain conditions? Were there any noises, odors, or other unusual symptoms?
2. Isolate the problem area. To do this, make some simple tests and observations; then eliminate the systems that are working properly. Check for obvious problems such as broken wires, dirty connections or split or disconnected vacuum hoses. Always check the obvious before assuming something complicated is the cause.
3. Test for problems systematically to determine the cause once the problem area is isolated. Are all the components functioning properly? Is there power going to electrical switches and motors? Is there vacuum at vacuum switches and/or actuators? Is there a mechanical problem such as bent linkage or loose mounting screws? Doing careful, systematic checks will often turn up most causes on the first inspection without wasting time checking components that have little or no relationship to the problem.
4. Test all repairs after the work is done to make sure that the problem is fixed. Some causes can be traced to more than one component, so a careful verification of repair work is important to pick up additional malfunctions that may cause a problem to reappear or a different problem to arise. A blown fuse, for example, is a simple problem that may require more than another fuse to repair. If you don't look for a problem that caused a fuse to blow, for example, a shorted wire may go undetected.

Experience has shown that most problems tend to be the result of a fairly simple and obvious cause, such as loose or corroded connectors or air leaks in the intake system; making careful inspection of components during testing essential to quick and accurate troubleshooting. Special, hand held computerized testers designed specifically for diagnosing the system are available from a variety of aftermarket sources, as well as from the vehicle manufacturer, but care should be taken that any test equipment being used is designed to diagnose that particular computer controlled system accurately without damaging the control unit (ECU) or components being tested.

NOTE: *Pinpointing the exact cause of trouble in an electrical system can sometimes only be accomplished by the use of special test equipment. The following describes commonly used test equipment and explains how to put it to best use in diagnosis. In addition to the information covered below, the manufacturer's instructions booklet provided with the tester should be read and clearly understood before attempting any test procedures.*

TEST EQUIPMENT

Jumper Wires

Jumper wires are simple, yet extremely valuable, pieces of test equipment. Jumper wires are merely wires that are used to bypass sections of a circuit. The simplest type of jumper wire is merely a length of multistrand wire with an alligator clip at each end. Jumper wires are usually fabricated from lengths of standard automotive wire and whatever type of connector (alligator clip, spade connector or pin connector) that is required for the particular vehicle being tested. The well equipped tool box will have several different styles of jumper wires in several different lengths. Some jumper wires are made with three or more terminals coming from a common splice for special purpose testing. In cramped, hard-to-reach areas it is advisable to have insulated boots over the jumper wire terminals in order to prevent accidental grounding, sparks, and possible fire, especially when testing fuel system components.

Jumper wires are used primarily to locate open electrical circuits, on either the ground (-) side of the circuit or on the hot (+) side. If an electrical component fails to operate, connect the jumper wire between the component and a good ground. If the component operates only with the jumper installed, the ground circuit is open. If the ground circuit is good, but the component does not operate, the circuit between the power feed and component is open. You can sometimes connect the jumper wire directly from the battery to the hot terminal of the com ponent, but first make sure the component uses 12 volts in operation. Some electrical components, such as fuel injectors, are designed to operate on about 4 volts and running 12 volts directly to the injector terminals can burn out the wiring. By inserting an inline fuseholder between a set of test leads, a fused jumper wire can be used for bypassing open circuits. Use a 5 amp fuse to provide protection against voltage spikes. When in doubt, use a voltmeter to check the voltage input to the component and measure how much voltage is being applied normally. By moving the jumper wire successively back from the lamp toward the power source, you can isolate the area of the circuit where the open is located. When the component stops functioning, or the power is cut off, the open is in the segment of wire between the jumper and the point previously tested.

CAUTION: *Never use jumpers made from wire that is of lighter gauge than used in the circuit under test. If the jumper wire is of too small gauge, it may overheat and possibly melt. Never use jumpers to bypass high resistance loads (such as motors) in a circuit. Bypassing resistances, in effect, creates a short circuit which may, in turn, cause damage and fire. Never use a jumper for anything other than temporary bypassing of components in a circuit.*

12 Volt Test Light

The 12 volt test light is used to check circuits and components while electrical current is flowing through them. It is used for voltage and ground tests. Twelve volt test lights come in different styles but all have three main parts; a ground clip, a probe, and a light. The most commonly used 12 volt test lights have pick-type probes. To use a 12 volt test light, connect the ground clip to a good ground and probe wherever necessary with the pick. The pick should be sharp so that it can penetrate wire insulation to make contact with the wire, without making a large hole in the insulation. The wrap-around light is handy in hard to reach areas or where it is difficult to support a wire to push a probe pick into it. To use the wrap around light, hook the wire to probed with the hook and pull the trigger. A small pick will be forced through the wire insulation into the wire core.

CAUTION: *Do not use a test light to probe electronic ignition spark plug or coil wires. Never use a pick-type test light to probe wiring on computer controlled systems unless specifically instructed to do so. Any wire insulation that is pierced by the test light probe should be taped and sealed with silicone after testing.*

Like the jumper wire, the 12 volt test light is used to isolate opens in circuits. But, whereas the jumper wire is used to bypass the open to operate the load, the 12 volt test light is used to locate the presence of voltage in a circuit. If the test light glows, you know that there is power up to that point; if the 12 volt test light does not glow when its probe is inserted into the wire or connector, you know that there is an open circuit (no power). Move the test light in successive steps back toward the power source until the light in the handle does glow. When it does glow, the open is between the probe and point previously probed.

NOTE: *The test light does not detect that 12 volts (or any particular amount of voltage) is present; it only detects that some voltage is present. It is advisable before using the test light to touch its terminals across the battery posts to make sure the light is operating properly.*

Self-Powered Test Light

The self-powered test light usually contains a 1.5 volt penlight battery. One type of self-powered test light is similar in design to the 12 volt test light. This type has both the battery and the light in the handle and pick-type probe tip. The second type has the light toward the open tip, so that the light illuminates the contact point. The self-powered test light is dual purpose piece of test equipment. It can be used to test for either open or short circuits when power is isolated from the circuit (continuity test). A powered test light should not be used on any computer controlled system or component unless specifically instructed to do so. Many engine sensors can be destroyed by even this small amount of voltage applied directly to the terminals.

Open Circuit Testing

To use the self-powered test light to check for open circuits, first isolate the circuit from the vehicle's 12 volt power source by disconnecting the battery or wiring harness connector. Connect the test light ground clip to a good ground and probe sections of the circuit sequentially with the test light. (start from either end of the circuit). If the light is out, the open is between the probe and the circuit ground. If the light is on, the open is between the probe and end of the circuit toward the power source.

Short Circuit Testing

By isolating the circuit both from power and from ground, and using a self-powered test light, you can check for shorts to ground in the circuit. Isolate the circuit from power and ground. Connect the test light ground clip to a good ground and probe any easy-to-reach test point in the circuit. If the light comes on, there is a short somewhere in the circuit. To isolate the short, probe a test point at either end of the isolated circuit (the light should be on). Leave the test light probe connected and open connectors, switches, remove parts, etc., sequentially, until the light goes out. When the light goes out, the short is between the last circuit component opened and the previous circuit opened.

NOTE: *The 1.5 volt battery in the test light does not provide much current. A weak battery may not provide enough power to illuminate the test light even when a complete circuit is made (especially if there are high resistances in the circuit). Always make sure that the test battery is strong. To check the battery, briefly touch the ground clip to the probe; if the light glows brightly the battery is strong enough for testing. Never use a self-powered test light to perform checks for opens or shorts when power is applied to the electrical system under test. The 12 volt vehicle power will quickly burn out the 1.5 volt light bulb in the test light.*

Voltmeter

A voltmeter is used to measure voltage at any point in a circuit, or to measure the voltage drop across any part of a circuit. It can also be used to check continuity in a wire or circuit by indicating current flow from one end to the other. Voltmeters usually have various scales on the meter dial and a selector switch to allow the selection of different voltages. The voltmeter has a positive and a negative lead. To avoid damage to the meter, always connect the negative lead to the negative (-) side of circuit (to ground or nearest the ground side of the circuit) and connect the positive lead to the positive (+) side of the circuit (to the power source or the nearest power source). Note that the negative voltmeter lead will always be black and that the positive voltmeter will always be some color other than black (usually red). Depending on how the voltmeter is connected into the circuit, it has several uses.

A voltmeter can be connected either in parallel or in series with a circuit and it has a very high resistance to current flow. When connected in parallel, only a small amount of current will flow through the voltmeter current path; the rest will flow through the normal circuit current path and the circuit will work normally. When the voltmeter is connected in series with a circuit, only a small amount of current can flow through the circuit. The circuit will not work properly, but the voltmeter reading will show if the circuit is complete or not.

Available Voltage Measurement

Set the voltmeter selector switch to the 20V position and connect the meter negative lead to the negative post of the battery. Connect the positive meter lead to the positive post of the battery and turn the ignition switch ON to provide a load. Read the voltage on the meter or digital display. A well charged battery should register over 12 volts. If the meter reads below 11.5 volts, the battery power may be insufficient to operate the electrical system properly. This test determines voltage available from the battery and should be the first step in any electrical trouble diagnosis procedure. Many electrical problems, especially on computer controlled systems, can be caused by a low state of charge in the battery. Excessive corrosion at the battery cable terminals can cause a poor contact that will prevent proper charging and full battery current flow.

Normal battery voltage is 12 volts when fully charged. When the battery is supplying current to one or more circuits it is said to be "under load". When everything is off the electrical system is under a "no-load" condition. A fully charged battery may show about 12.5 volts at no load; will drop to 12 volts under medium load; and will drop even lower under heavy load. If the battery is partially discharged the voltage decrease under heavy load may be excessive, even though the battery shows 12 volts or more at no load. When allowed to discharge further, the battery's available voltage under load will decrease more severely. For this reason, it is important that the battery be fully charged during all testing procedures to avoid errors in diagnosis and incorrect test results.

Voltage Drop

When current flows through a resistance, the voltage beyond the resistance is reduced (the larger the current, the greater the reduction in voltage). When no current is flowing, there is no voltage drop because there is no current flow. All points in the circuit which are connected to the power source are at the same voltage as the power source. The total voltage drop always equals the total source voltage. In a long circuit with many connectors, a series of small, unwanted voltage drops due to corrosion at the connectors can add up to a total loss of voltage which impairs the operation of the normal loads in the circuit.

INDIRECT COMPUTATION OF VOLTAGE DROPS

1. Set the voltmeter selector switch to the 20 volt position.
2. Connect the meter negative lead to a good ground.

3. Probe all resistances in the circuit with the positive meter lead.

4. Operate the circuit in all modes and observe the voltage readings.

DIRECT MEASUREMENT OF VOLTAGE DROPS

1. Set the voltmeter switch to the 20 volt position.

2. Connect the voltmeter negative lead to the ground side of the resistance load to be measured.

3. Connect the positive lead to the positive side of the resistance or load to be measured.

4. Read the voltage drop directly on the 20 volt scale.

Too high a voltage indicates too high a resistance. If, for example, a blower motor runs too slowly, you can determine if there is too high a resistance in the resistor pack. By taking voltage drop readings in all parts of the circuit, you can isolate the problem. Too low a voltage drop indicates too low a resistance. If, for example, a blower motor runs too fast in the MED and/or LOW position, the problem can be isolated in the resistor pack by taking voltage drop readings in all parts of the circuit to locate a possibly shorted resistor. The maximum allowable voltage drop under load is critical, especially if there is more than one high resistance problem in a circuit because all voltage drops are cumulative. A small drop is normal due to the resistance of the conductors.

HIGH RESISTANCE TESTING

1. Set the voltmeter selector switch to the 4 volt position.

2. Connect the voltmeter positive lead to the positive post of the battery.

3. Turn on the headlights and heater blower to provide a load.

4. Probe various points in the circuit with the negative voltmeter lead.

5. Read the voltage drop on the 4 volt scale. Some average maximum allowable voltage drops are:

FUSE PANEL – 7 volts
IGNITION SWITCH – 5volts
HEADLIGHT SWITCH – 7 volts
IGNITION COIL (+) – 5 volts
ANY OTHER LOAD – 1.3 volts

NOTE: *Voltage drops are all measured while a load is operating; without current flow, there will be no voltage drop.*

Ohmmeter

The ohmmeter is designed to read resistance (ohms) in a circuit or component. Although there are several different styles of ohmmeters, all will usually have a selector switch which permits the measurement of different ranges of resistance (usually the selector switch allows the multiplication of the meter reading by 10, 100, 1000, and 10,000). A calibration knob allows the meter to be set at zero for accurate measurement. Since all ohmmeters are powered by an internal battery (usually 9 volts), the ohmmeter can be used as a self-powered test light. When the ohmmeter is connected, current from the ohmmeter flows through the circuit or component being tested. Since the ohmmeter's internal resistance and voltage are known values, the amount of current flow through the meter depends on the resistance of the circuit or component being tested.

The ohmmeter can be used to perform continuity test for opens or shorts (either by observation of the meter needle or as a self-powered test light), and to read actual resistance in a circuit. It should be noted that the ohmmeter is used to check the resistance of a component or wire while there is no voltage applied to the circuit. Current flow from an outside voltage source (such as the vehicle battery) can damage the ohmmeter, so the circuit or component should be isolated from the vehicle electrical system before any testing is done. Since the ohmmeter uses its own voltage source, either lead can be connected to any test point.

NOTE: *When checking diodes or other solid state components, the ohmmeter leads can only be connected one way in order to measure current flow in a single direction. Make sure the positive (+) and negative (-) terminal connections are as described in the test procedures to verify the one-way diode operation.*

In using the meter for making continuity checks, do not be concerned with the actual resistance readings. Zero resistance, or any resistance readings, indicate continuity in the circuit. Infinite resistance indicates an open in the circuit. A high resistance reading where there should be none indicates a problem in the circuit. Checks for short circuits are made in the same manner as checks for open circuits except that the circuit must be isolated from both power and normal ground. Infinite resistance indicates no continuity to ground, while zero resistance indicates a dead short to ground.

RESISTANCE MEASUREMENT

The batteries in an ohmmeter will weaken with age and temperature, so the ohmmeter must be calibrated or "zeroed" before taking measurements. To zero the meter, place the selector switch in its lowest range and touch the two ohmmeter leads together. Turn the calibration knob until the meter needle is exactly on zero.

NOTE: *All analog (needle) type ohmmeters must be zeroed before use, but some digital ohmmeter models are automatically calibrated when the switch is turned on. Self-calibrating digital ohmmeters do not have an adjusting knob, but its a good idea to check for a zero readout before use by touching the leads together. All computer controlled systems require the use of a digital ohmmeter with at least 10 meagohms impedance for testing. Before any test procedures are attempted, make sure the ohmmeter used is compatible with the electrical system or damage to the on-board computer could result.*

To measure resistance, first isolate the circuit from the vehicle power source by disconnecting the battery cables or the harness connector. Make sure the key is OFF when disconnecting any components or the battery. Where necessary, also isolate at least one side of the circuit to be checked to avoid reading parallel resistances. Parallel circuit resistances will always give a lower reading than the actual resistance of either of the branches. When measuring the resistance of parallel circuits, the total resistance will always be lower than the smallest resistance in the circuit. Connect the meter leads to both sides of the circuit (wire or component) and read the actual measured ohms on the meter scale. Make sure the selector switch is set to the proper ohm scale for the circuit being tested to avoid misreading the ohmmeter test value.

CAUTION: *Never use an ohmmeter with power applied to the circuit. Like the self-powered test light, the ohmmeter is designed to operate on its own power supply. The normal 12 volt automotive electrical system current could damage the meter.*

Ammeters

An ammeter measures the amount of current flowing through a circuit in units called amperes or amps. Amperes are units of electron flow which indicate how fast the electrons are flowing through the circuit. Since Ohms Law dictates that current flow in a circuit is equal to the circuit voltage divided by the total circuit resistance, increasing voltage also increases the current level (amps). Likewise, any decrease in resistance will increase the amount of amps in a circuit. At normal operating voltage, most circuits have a characteristic amount of amperes, called "current draw" which can be measured using an ammeter. By referring to a specified current draw rating, measuring the amperes, and comparing the two values, one can determine what is happening within the circuit to aid in diagnosis. An open circuit, for example, will not allow any current to flow so the ammeter reading will be zero. More current flows through a heavily loaded circuit or when the charging system is operating.

An ammeter is always connected in series with the circuit being tested. All of the current that normally flows through the circuit must also flow through the ammeter; if there is any other path for the current to follow, the ammeter reading will not be accurate. The ammeter itself has very little resistance to current flow and therefore will not affect the circuit, but it will measure current draw only when the circuit is closed and electricity is flowing. Excessive current draw can blow fuses and drain the battery, while a reduced current draw can cause motors to run slowly, lights to dim and other components to not operate properly. The ammeter can help diagnose these conditions by locating the cause of the high or low reading.

Multimeters

Different combinations of test meters can be built into a single unit designed for specific tests. Some of the more common combination test devices are known as Volt/Amp testers, Tach/Dwell meters, or Digital Multimeters. The Volt/Amp tester is used for charging system, starting system or battery tests and consists of a voltmeter, an ammeter and a variable resistance carbon pile. The voltmeter will usually have at least two ranges for use with 6, 12 and 24 volt systems. The ammeter also has more than one range for testing various levels of battery loads and starter current draw and the carbon pile can be adjusted to offer different amounts of resistance. The Volt/Amp tester has heavy leads to carry large amounts of current and many later models have an inductive ammeter pickup that clamps around the wire to simplify test connections. On some models, the ammeter also has a zero-center scale to allow testing of charging and starting systems without switching leads or polarity. A digital multimeter is a voltmeter, ammeter and ohmmeter combined in an instrument which gives a digital readout. These are often used when testing solid state circuits because of their high input impedance (usually 10 megohms or more).

The tach/dwell meter combines a tachometer and a dwell (cam angle) meter and is a specialized kind of voltmeter. The tachometer scale is marked to show engine speed in rpm and the dwell scale is marked to show degrees of distributor shaft rotation. In most electronic ignition systems, dwell is determined by the control unit, but the dwell meter can also be used to check the duty cycle (operation) of some electronic engine control systems. Some tach/dwell meters are powered by an internal battery, while others take their power from the car battery in use. The battery powered testers usually require calibration much like an ohmmeter before testing.

Special Test Equipment

A variety of diagnostic tools are available to help troubleshoot and repair computerized engine control systems. The most sophisticated of these devices are the console type engine analyzers that usually occupy a garage service bay, but there are several types of aftermarket electronic testers available that will allow quick circuit tests of the engine control system by plugging directly into a special connector located in the engine compartment or under the dashboard. Several tool and equipment manufacturers offer simple, hand held testers that measure various circuit voltage levels on command to check all system components for proper operation. Although these testers usually cost about $300-$500, consider that the average computer control unit (or ECM) can cost just as much and the money saved by not replacing perfectly good sensors or components in an attempt to correct a problem could justify the purchase price of a special diagnostic tester the first time it's used.

These computerized testers can allow quick and easy test measurements while the engine is operating or while the car is being driven. In addition, the on-board computer memory can be read to access any stored trouble codes; in effect allowing the computer to tell you where it hurts and aid trouble diagnosis by pinpointing exactly which circuit or component is malfunctioning. In the same manner, repairs can be tested to make sure the problem has been corrected. The biggest advantage these special testers have is their relatively easy hookups that minimize or eliminate the chances of making the wrong connections and getting false voltage readings or damaging the computer accidentally.

NOTE: *It should be remembered that these testers check voltage levels in circuits; they don't detect mechanical problems or failed components if the circuit voltage falls within the preprogrammed limits stored in the tester PROM unit. Also, most of the hand held testers are designed to work only on one or two systems made by a specific manufacturer.*

A variety of aftermarket testers are available to help diagnose different computerized control systems. Owatonna Tool Company (OTC), for example, markets a device called the OTC Monitor which plugs directly into the assembly line diagnostic link (ALDL). The OTC tester makes diagnosis a simple matter of pressing the correct buttons and, by changing the internal PROM or inserting a different diagnosis cartridge, it will work on any model from full size to subcompact, over a wide range of years. An adapter is supplied with the tester to allow connection to all types of ALDL links, regardless of the number of pin terminals used. By inserting an updated PROM into the OTC tester, it can be easily updated to diagnose any new modifications of computerized control systems.

Wiring Harnesses

The average automobile contains about ½ mile of wiring, with hundreds of individual connections. To protect the many wires from damage and to keep them from becoming a confusing tangle, they are organized into bundles, enclosed in plastic or taped together and called wire harnesses. Different wiring harnesses serve different parts of the vehicle. Individual wires are color coded to help trace them through a harness where sections are hidden from view.

A loose or corroded connection or a replacement wire that is too small for the circuit will add extra resistance and an additional voltage drop to the circuit. A ten percent voltage drop can result in slow or erratic motor operation, for example, even though the circuit is complete. Automotive wiring or circuit conductors can be in any one of three forms:

1. Single strand wire
2. Multistrand wire
3. Printed circuitry

Single strand wire has a solid metal core and is usually used inside such components as alternators, motors, relays and other devices. Multistrand wire has a core made of many small strands of wire twisted together into a single conductor. Most of the wiring in an automotive electrical system is made up of multistrand wire, either as a single conductor or grouped together in a harness. All wiring is color coded on the insulator, either as a solid color or as a colored wire with an identification stripe. A printed circuit is a thin film of copper or other conductor that is printed on an insulator backing. Occasionally, a printed circuit is sandwiched between two sheets of plastic for more protection and flexibility. A complete printed circuit, consisting of conductors, insulating material and connectors for lamps or other components is called a printed circuit board. Printed circuitry is used in place of individual wires or harnesses in places where space is limited, such as behind instrument panels.

Wire Gauge

Since computer controlled automotive electrical systems are very sensitive to changes in resistance, the selection of properly sized wires is critical when systems are repaired. The wire gauge number is an expression of the cross section area of the conductor. The most common system for expressing wire size is the American Wire Gauge (AWG) system.

Wire cross section area is measured in circular mils. A mil is 1/1000" (0.001"); a circular mil is the area of a circle one mil in diameter. For example, a conductor 1/4" in diameter is 0.250 in. or 250 mils. The circular mil cross section area of the wire is 250 squared (250^2)or 62,500 circular mils. Imported car models usually use metric wire gauge designations, which is simply the cross section area of the conductor in square millimeters (mm^2).

Gauge numbers are assigned to conductors of various cross section areas. As gauge number increases, area decreases and the conductor becomes smaller. A 5 gauge conductor is smaller than a 1 gauge conductor and a 10 gauge is smaller than a 5 gauge. As the cross section area of a conductor decreases, resistance increases and so does the gauge number. A conductor with a higher gauge number will carry less current than a conductor with a lower gauge number.

NOTE: *Gauge wire size refers to the size of the conductor, not the size of the complete wire. It is possible to have two wires of the same gauge with different diameters because one may have thicker insulation than the other.*

12 volt automotive electrical systems generally use 10, 12, 14, 16 and 18 gauge wire. Main power distribution circuits and larger accessories usually use 10 and 12 gauge wire. Battery cables are usually 4 or 6 gauge, although 1 and 2 gauge wires are occasionally used. Wire length must also be considered when making repairs to a circuit. As conductor length increases, so does resistance. An 18 gauge wire, for example, can carry a 10 amp load for 10 feet without excessive voltage drop; however if a 15 foot wire is required for the same 10 amp load, it must be a 16 gauge wire.

An electrical schematic shows the electrical current paths when a circuit is operating properly. It is essential to understand how a circuit works before trying to figure out why it doesn't. Schematics break the entire electrical system down into individual circuits and show only one particular circuit. In a schematic, no attempt is made to represent wiring and components as they physically appear on the vehicle; switches and other components are shown as simply as possible. Face views of harness connectors show the cavity or terminal locations in all multi-pin connectors to help locate test points.

If you need to backprobe a connector while it is on the component, the order of the terminals must be mentally reversed. The wire color code can help in this situation, as well as a keyway, lock tab or other reference mark.

NOTE: *Wiring diagrams are not included in this book. As trucks have become more complex and available with longer option lists, wiring diagrams have grown in size and complexity. It has become almost impossible to provide a readable reproduction of a wiring diagram in a book this size. Information on ordering wiring diagrams from the vehicle manufacturer can be found in the owner's manual.*

WIRING REPAIR

Soldering is a quick, efficient method of joining metals permanently. Everyone who has the occasion to make wiring repairs should know how to solder. Electrical connections that are soldered are far less likely to come apart and will conduct electricity much better than connections that are only "pig-tailed" together. The most popular (and preferred) method of soldering is with an electrical soldering gun. Soldering irons are available in many sizes and wattage ratings. Irons with higher wattage ratings deliver higher temperatures and recover lost heat faster. A small soldering iron rated for no more than 50 watts is recommended, especially on electrical systems where excess heat can damage the components being soldered.

There are three ingredients necessary for successful soldering; proper flux, good solder and sufficient heat. A soldering flux is necessary to clean the metal of tarnish, prepare it for soldering and to enable the solder to spread into tiny crevices. When soldering, always use a resin flux or resin core solder which is non-corrosive and will not attract moisture once the job is finished. Other types of flux (acid core) will leave a residue that will attract moisture and cause the wires to corrode. Tin is a unique metal with a low melting point. In a molten state, it dissolves and alloys easily with many metals. Solder is made by mixing tin with lead. The most common proportions are 40/60, 50/50 and 60/40, with the percentage of tin listed first. Low priced solders usually contain less tin, making them very difficult for a beginner to use because more heat is required to melt the solder. A common solder is 40/60 which is well suited for all-around general use, but 60/40 melts easier, has more tin for a better joint and is preferred for electrical work.

Soldering Techniques

Successful soldering requires that the metals to be joined be heated to a temperature that will melt the solder—usually 360-460°F (182-238°C). Contrary to popular belief, the purpose of the soldering iron is not to melt the solder itself, but to heat the parts being soldered to a temperature high enough to melt the solder when it is touched to the work. Melting flux-cored solder on the soldering iron will usually destroy the effectiveness of the flux.

NOTE: *Soldering tips are made of copper for good heat conductivity, but must be "tinned" regularly for quick transference of heat to the project and to prevent the solder from sticking to the iron. To "tin" the iron, simply heat it and touch the flux-cored solder to the tip; the solder will flow over the hot tip. Wipe the excess off with a clean rag, but be careful as the iron will be hot.*

After some use, the tip may become pitted. If so, simply dress the tip smooth with a smooth file and "tin" the tip again. An old saying holds that "metals well cleaned are half soldered." Flux-cored solder will remove oxides but rust, bits of insulation and oil or grease must be removed with a wire brush or emery cloth. For maximum strength in soldered parts, the joint must start off clean and tight. Weak joints will result in gaps too wide for the solder to bridge.

If a separate soldering flux is used, it should be brushed or swabbed on only those areas that are to be soldered. Most solders contain a core of flux and separate fluxing is unnecessary. Hold the work to be soldered firmly. It is best to solder on a wooden board, because a metal vise will only rob the piece to be soldered of heat and make it difficult to melt the solder. Hold the soldering tip with the broadest face against the work to be soldered. Apply solder under the tip close to the work, using enough solder to give a heavy film between the iron and the piece being soldered, while moving slowly and making sure the solder melts properly. Keep the work level or the solder will run to the lowest part and favor the thicker parts, because these require more heat to melt the solder. If the soldering tip overheats (the solder coating on the face of the tip burns up), it should be retinned. Once the soldering is completed, let the soldered joint stand until cool. Tape and seal all soldered wire splices after the repair has cooled.

Wire Harness and Connectors

The on-board computer (ECM) wire harness electrically connects the control unit to the various solenoids, switches and sensors used by the control system. Most connectors in the engine compartment or otherwise exposed to the elements are protected against moisture and dirt which could create oxidation and deposits on the terminals. This protection is important because of the very low voltage and current levels used by the computer and sensors. All connectors have a lock which secures the male and female terminals together, with a secondary lock holding the seal and terminal into the connector. Both terminal locks must be released when disconnecting ECM connectors.

These special connectors are weather-proof and all repairs require the use of a special terminal and the tool required to service it. This tool is used to remove the pin and sleeve terminals. If removal is attempted with an ordinary pick, there is a good chance that the terminal will be bent or deformed. Unlike standard blade type terminals, these terminals cannot be straightened once they are bent. Make certain that the connectors are properly seated and all of the sealing rings in place when connecting leads. On some models, a hinge-type flap provides a backup or secondary locking feature for the terminals. Most secondary locks are used to improve the connector reliability by retaining the terminals if the small terminal lock tangs are not positioned properly.

Molded-on connectors require complete replacement of the connection. This means splicing a new connector assembly into the harness. All splices in on-board computer systems should be soldered to insure proper contact. Use care when probing the connections or replacing terminals in them as it is possible to short between opposite terminals. If this happens to the wrong terminal pair, it is possible to damage certain components. Always use jumper wires between connectors for circuit checking and never probe through weatherproof seals.

Open circuits are often difficult to locate by sight because corrosion or terminal misalignment are hidden by the connectors. Merely wiggling a connector on a sensor or in the wiring harness may correct the open circuit condition. This should always be considered when an open circuit or a failed sensor is indicated. Intermittent problems may also be caused by oxidized or loose connections. When using a circuit tester for diagnosis, always probe connections from the wire side. Be careful not to damage sealed connectors with test probes.

All wiring harnesses should be replaced with identical parts, using the same gauge wire and connectors. When signal wires are spliced into a harness, use wire with high temperature insulation only. With the low voltage and current levels found in the system, it is important that the best possible connection at all wire splices be made by soldering the splices together. It is seldom necessary to replace a complete harness. If replacement is necessary, pay close attention to insure proper harness routing. Secure the harness with suitable plastic wire clamps to prevent vibrations from causing the harness to wear in spots or contact any hot components.

NOTE: *Weatherproof connectors cannot be replaced with standard connectors. Instruc-*

tions are provided with replacement connector and terminal packages. Some wire harnesses have mounting indicators (usually pieces of colored tape) to mark where the harness is to be secured.

In making wiring repairs, it's important that you always replace damaged wires with wires that are the same gauge as the wire being replaced. The heavier the wire, the smaller the gauge number. Wires are color-coded to aid in identification and whenever possible the same color coded wire should be used for replacement. A wire stripping and crimping tool is necessary to install solderless terminal connectors. Test all crimps by pulling on the wires; it should not be possible to pull the wires out of a good crimp.

Wires which are open, exposed or otherwise damaged are repaired by simple splicing. Where possible, if the wiring harness is accessible and the damaged place in the wire can be located, it is best to open the harness and check for all possible damage. In an inaccessible harness, the wire must be bypassed with a new insert, usually taped to the outside of the old harness.

When replacing fusible links, be sure to use fusible link wire, NOT ordinary automotive wire. Make sure the fusible segment is of the same gauge and construction as the one being replaced and double the stripped end when crimping the terminal connector for a good contact. The melted (open) fusible link segment of the wiring harness should be cut off as close to the harness as possible, then a new segment spliced in as described. In the case of a damaged fusible link that feeds two harness wires, the harness connections should be replaced with two fusible link wires so that each circuit will have its own separate protection.

NOTE: *Most of the problems caused in the wiring harness are due to bad ground connections. Always check all vehicle ground connections for corrosion or looseness before performing any power feed checks to eliminate the chance of a bad ground affecting the circuit.*

Repairing Hard Shell Connectors

Unlike molded connectors, the terminal contacts in hard shell connectors can be replaced. Weatherproof hard-shell connectors with the leads molded into the shell have non-replaceable terminal ends. Replacement usually involves the use of a special terminal removal tool that depress the locking tangs (barbs) on the connector terminal and allow the connector to be removed from the rear of the shell. The connector shell should be replaced if it shows any evidence of burning, melting, cracks, or breaks. Replace individual terminals that are burnt, corroded, distorted or loose.

NOTE: *The insulation crimp must be tight to prevent the insulation from sliding back on the wire when the wire is pulled. The insulation must be visibly compressed under the crimp tabs, and the ends of the crimp should be turned in for a firm grip on the insulation.*

The wire crimp must be made with all wire strands inside the crimp. The terminal must be fully compressed on the wire strands with the ends of the crimp tabs turned in to make a firm grip on the wire. Check all connections with an ohmmeter to insure a good contact. There should be no measurable resistance between the wire and the terminal when connected.

Mechanical Test Equipment

Vacuum Gauge

Most gauges are graduated in inches of mercury (in.Hg), although a device called a manometer reads vacuum in inches of water (in. H_2O). The normal vacuum reading usually varies between 18 and 22 in.Hg at sea level. To test engine vacuum, the vacuum gauge must be connected to a source of manifold vacuum. Many engines have a plug in the intake manifold which can be removed and replaced with an adapter fitting. Connect the vacuum gauge to the fitting with a suitable rubber hose or, if no manifold plug is available, connect the vacuum gauge to any device using manifold vacuum, such as EGR valves, etc. The vacuum gauge can be used to determine if enough vacuum is reaching a component to allow its actuation.

Hand Vacuum Pump

Small, hand-held vacuum pumps come in a variety of designs. Most have a built-in vacuum gauge and allow the component to be tested without removing it from the vehicle. Operate the pump lever or plunger to apply the correct amount of vacuum required for the test specified in the diagnosis routines. The level of vacuum in inches of Mercury (in.Hg) is indicated on the pump gauge. For some testing, an additional vacuum gauge may be necessary.

Intake manifold vacuum is used to operate various systems and devices on late-model vehicles. To correctly diagnose and solve problems in vacuum control systems, a vacuum source is necessary for testing. In some cases, vacuum can be taken from the intake manifold when the engine is running, but vacuum is normally provided by a hand vacuum pump. These hand vacuum pumps have a built-in vacuum gauge that allow testing while the device is still attached to the component. For some tests, an additional vacuum gauge may be necessary.

HEATER AND AIR CONDITIONER

Blower

REMOVAL AND INSTALLATION

1. Disconnect the negative battery cable.
2. Disconnect the electrical lead from the blower motor.
3. Scribe a mark to reference the blower motor flange-to-case position.
4. Remove the blower motor-to-case attaching screws and remove the blower motor and wheel as an assembly. Pry the flange gently if the sealer acts as an adhesive.
5. Remove the blower wheel retaining nut and separate the blower and wheel.
6. Reverse Steps 1-5 to install. Be sure to align the scribe marks made during removal.

NOTE: *Assemble the blower wheel to the motor with the open end of the wheel away from the motor. If necessary, replace the sealer at the motor flange.*

The heater blower is located on the passenger side of the firewall

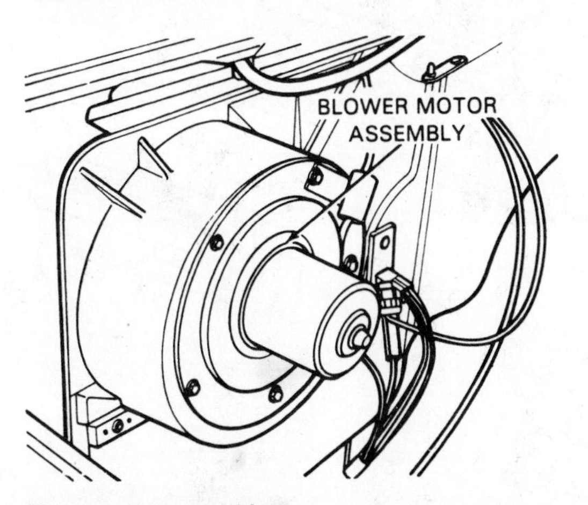

Blower motor assembly

Heater Core

REMOVAL AND INSTALLATION

Without Air Conditioning

1. Disconnect the negative battery cable.
2. Drain the radiator.

CAUTION: *When draining the coolant, keep in mind that cats and dogs are attracted by the ethylene glycol antifreeze, and are quite likely to drink any that is left in an uncovered container or in puddles on the ground. This will prove fatal in sufficient quantity. Always drain the coolant into a sealable container. Coolant should be reused unless it is contaminated or several years old.*

3. Disconnect the heater hoses at the heater core tube connections. Use care when detaching the hoses as the core tube attachments can easily be damaged if too much force is used on them. If the hoses will not come off, cut the hose just forward of the core tube connection. Remove the remaining piece by splitting it lengthwise. When the hoses are removed, install plugs in the core tubes to prevent coolant spilling out when the core is removed.

NOTE: *The larger diameter hose goes to the water pump; the smaller diameter hose goes to the thermostat housing.*

4. Remove the screws around the perimeter of the heater core cover on the engine side of the dash panel.
5. Pull the heater core cover from its mounting in the dash panel.
6. Remove the core from the distributor assembly.
7. Reverse the removal procedure to install. Be sure that the core-to-case sealer is intact before replacing the core; use new sealer if necessary. When installation is complete, check for coolant leaks.

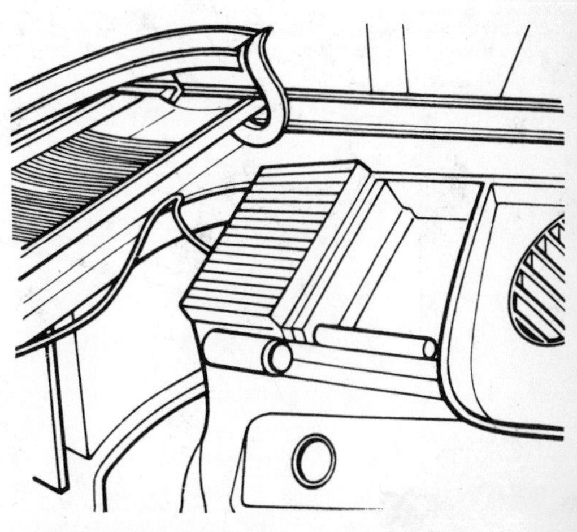

Heater core replacement

With Air Conditioning

1. Disconnect the negative battery cable.
2. Disconnect the heater hoses at the core with a drain pan under the car. Plug the hoses to prevent spillage.

CAUTION: *When draining the coolant, keep in mind that cats and dogs are attracted by the ethylene glycol antifreeze, and are quite likely to drink any that is left in an uncovered container or in puddles on the ground. This will prove fatal in sufficient quantity. Always drain the coolant into a sealable container. Coolant should be reused unless it is contaminated or several years old.*

3. Remove the air conditioning hose bracket.
4. Remove the heater core case cover and remove the core from the case.
5. Reverse to install.

Control Head Assembly

REMOVAL AND INSTALLATION

1. Disconnect the negative battery cable.
2. Remove the four instrument panel bezel attaching screws located above and below the air conditioning control head assembly.
3. Remove the knob and related hardware from the radio controls, if so equipped.
4. Remove the instrument panel bezel.
5. Remove the three heater/air conditioning control to instrument panel attaching screws.
6. Slide the control out from the dash opening, being careful not to kink the bowden cables or damage the vacuum hoses or connectors.
7. Disconnect the vacuum and electrical connectors and bowden cables and remove the control head.
8. Installation is the reverse of removal.

Evaporator Core

REMOVAL AND INSTALLATION

1. Disconnect the negative battery cable.
2. Discharge the air conditioning system as outlined in Chapter One.
3. Remove the heater core case to distributor assembly attaching screws (do not disconnect

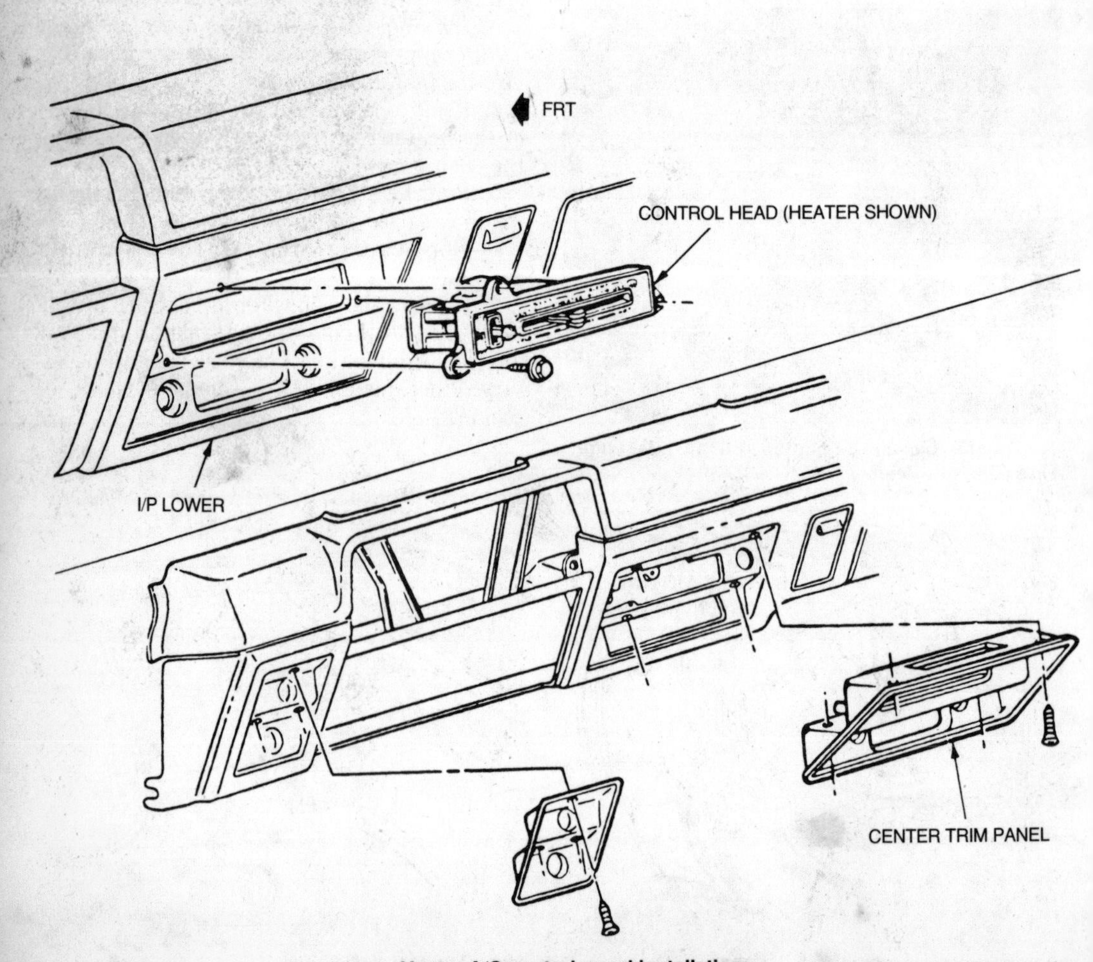

Heater A/C control panel installation

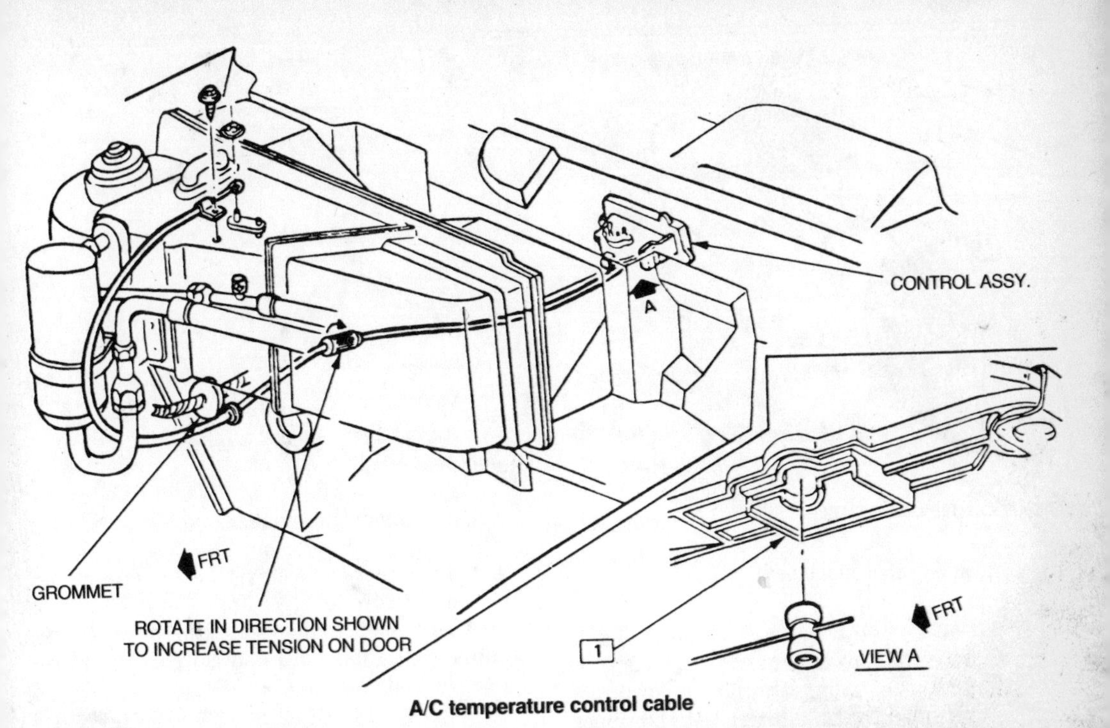

A/C temperature control cable

the heater hoses). Roll the assembly forward away from the distributor case.

4. Remove the accumulator and brackets. Plug the open lines at once.

5. Remove the temperature door cable and temperature door access cover. Position the control door arm so as not to interfere with removal of the upper evaporator case cover.

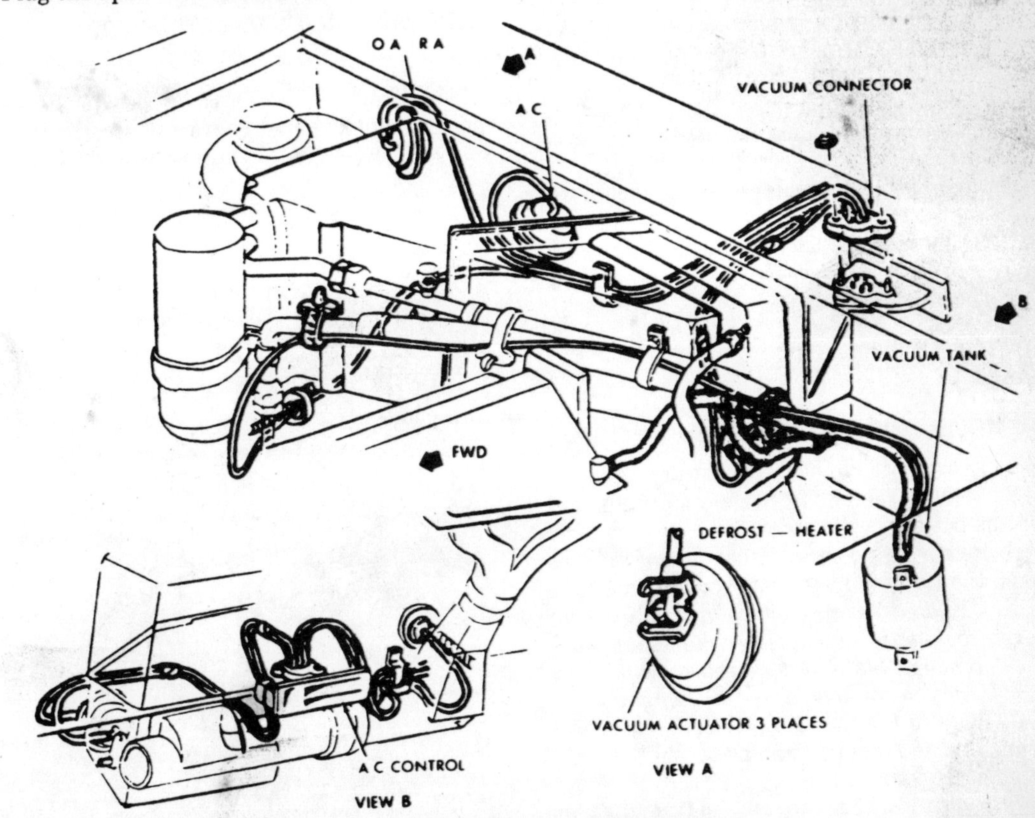

A/C vacuum hose routing

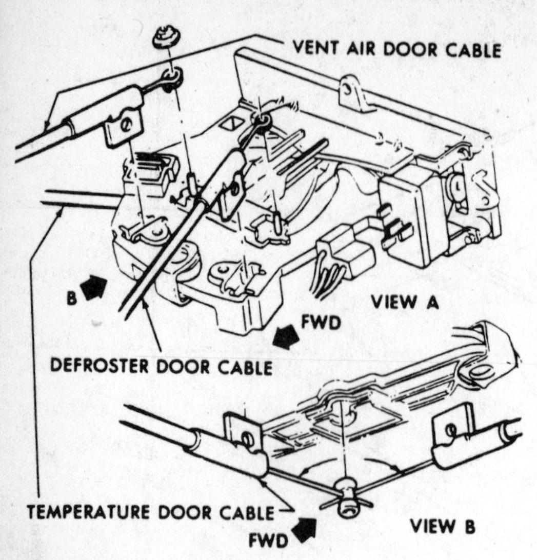

Heater bowden cable attachment

6. Remove the blower motor.
7. Remove the sealer around the exposed portion of the outlet tube located at the upper surface of the evaporator case.
8. Remove the evaporator core.
9. Install the sealer around the exposed portion of the outlet tube located at the upper surface of the evaporator case.
10. Install the blower motor.
11. Install the temperature door cable and access cover.
12. Install the accumulator. When connecting the inlet and outlet lines use new O-ring seals coated with clean refrigerant oil.
13. Reposition the heater core and install the attaching screws.
14. Reconnect the battery cable.
15. Evacuate, charge and check the system. Refer to Chapter One.

RADIO

REMOVAL AND INSTALLATION

1. Disconnect the negative battery cable.
2. Remove the nut from the mounting stud on the bottom of the radio.
3. Remove all control knobs and/or spacers from the right and left radio control shafts.
NOTE: *The volume control knob and tuning control knob will fit on either shaft but are not interchangeable. The tone control knob and balance control knob are interchangeable.*
4. Remove the four screws from the center trim plate and pull the trim plate and the radio forward slightly.
5. Disconnect the antenna lead from the rear of the radio.

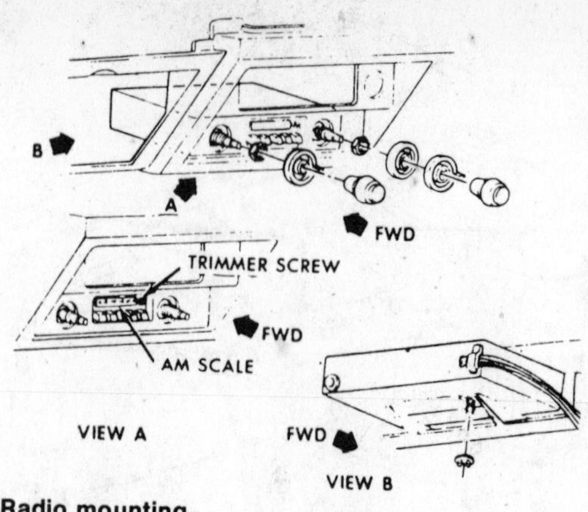

Radio mounting

6. Disconnect the speaker and electrical connectors from the radio harness.
7. Disconnect the electrical connectors from the rear window defogger and cigarette lighter.
8. Use a deep well socket to remove the retaining nuts from both control shafts and remove the radio.
9. To install, reverse the removal procedure.

WINDSHIELD WIPERS

Motor

REMOVAL AND INSTALLATION

Front

1. Working inside the car, reach up under the instrument panel above the steering column and loosen, but do not remove, the trans-

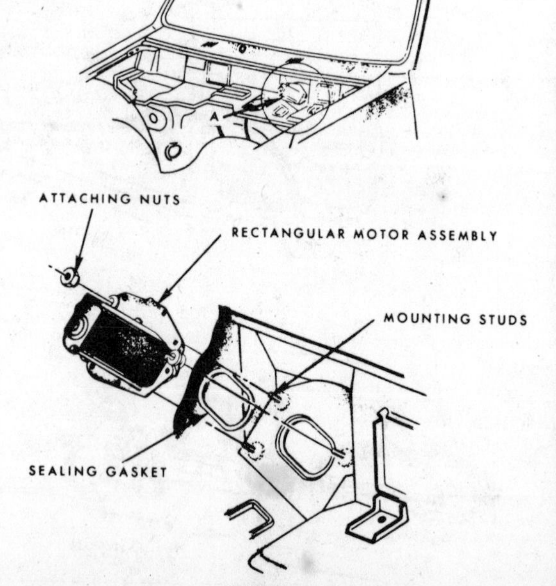

Wiper motor mounting

mission drive link-to-motor crank arm attaching nuts.

2. Disconnect the transmission drive link from the motor crank arm.

3. Raise the hood and disconnect the motor wiring.

4. Remove the three motor attaching bolts.

5. Remove the motor while guiding the crank arm through the hole.

6. To install, align the sealing gasket to the base of the motor and reverse the rest of the removal procedure. Tighten the motor attaching bolts to 30-40 in. lbs. Tighten the transmission drive link-to-motor crank arm attaching nuts to 25-35 in. lbs.

NOTE: *If the wiper motor-to-dash panel sealing gasket is damaged during removal, it should be replaced with a new gasket to prevent possible water leaks.*

Rear

1. Disconnect the negative battery cable.

2. Remove the wiper arm and blade assembly.

3. Remove the wiper motor cover retaining screws.

4. Remove the mounting bracket attaching screws and bolts.

5. Disconnect the electrical connector and remove the wiper motor and transmission assembly.

6. Instalation is the reverse of removal.

Wiper Blade

REMOVAL AND INSTALLATION

1. To replace the wiper blade, lift up on the spring release tab on the wiper arm connector and work the blade assembly off.

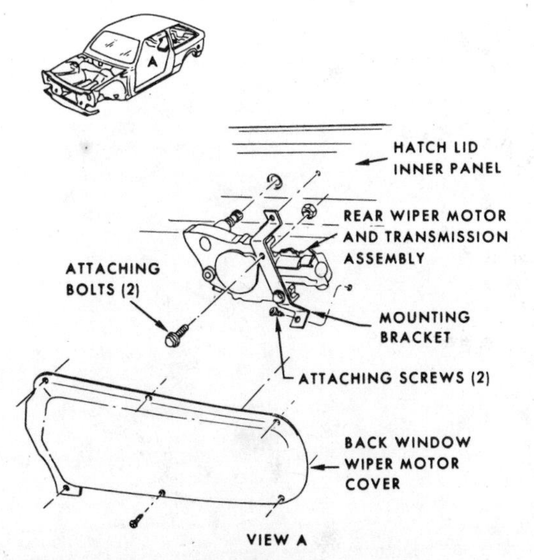

Rear wiper motor removal and installation

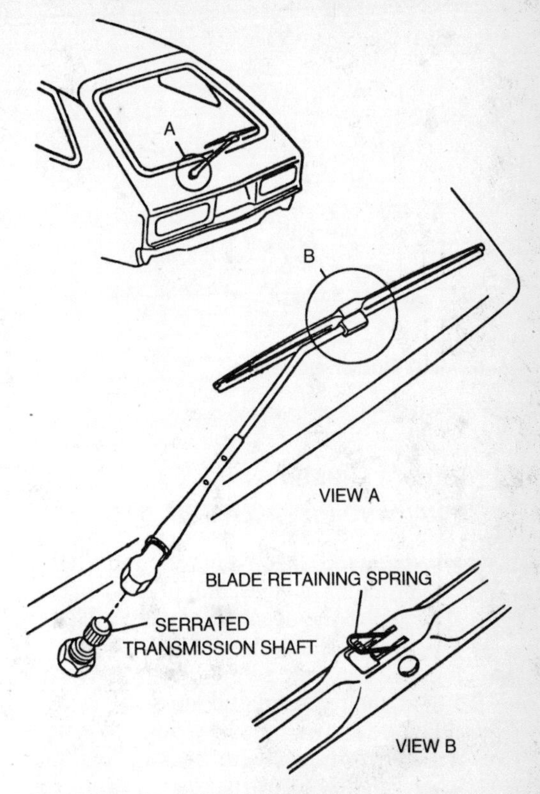

Rear wiper blade and arm removal and installation

2. Snap the new blade assembly into place.

NOTE: *For the rubber insert replacement refer to Chapter one.*

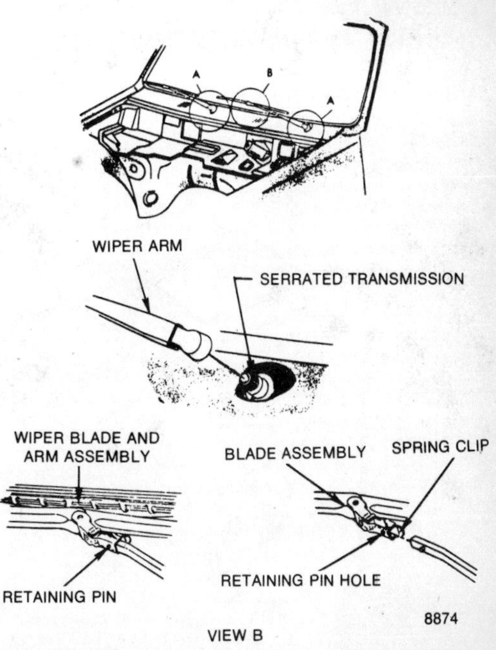

Front wiper blade and arm removal and installation

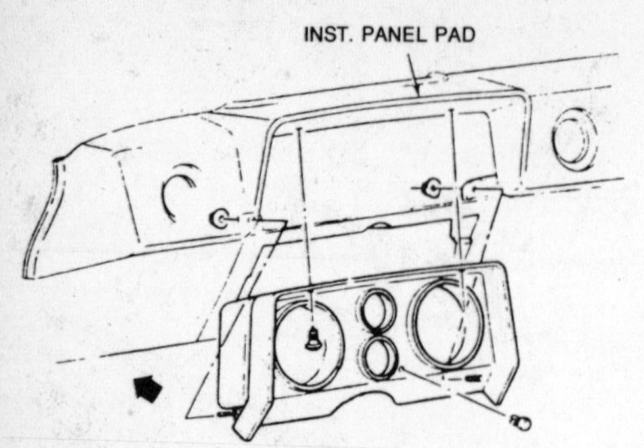

Instrument cluster mounting

Instrument Cluster

REMOVAL AND INSTALLATION

The instrument cluster must be removed to replace light bulbs, gauges, and printed circuit.

1. Disconnect the negative battery cable.
2. Remove the clock stem knob.
3. Remove the four screws and remove the instrument cluster bezel and lens.
4. Remove the two nuts securing the instrument cluster to the instrument panel and pull the cluster slightly forward.
5. Disconnect the electrical connector and speedometer cable from the cluster and remove it.
6. Installation is the reverse of removal.

Console

REMOVAL AND INSTALLATION

Refer to the accompanying illustration.

Windshield Wiper Switch

REMOVAL AND INSTALLATION

The wiper switch is controlled by the combination switch and is located in the steering column. Please refer to Wiper/Washer Removal and Installation in the Steering section in Chapter 8.

Headlight Switch

REMOVAL AND INSTALLATION

1. Disconnect the negative battery cable.
2. Pull the headlight switch control knob to the **On** position.
3. Reach up under the instrument panel and depress the switch shaft retainer button while pulling on the switch control shaft knob.

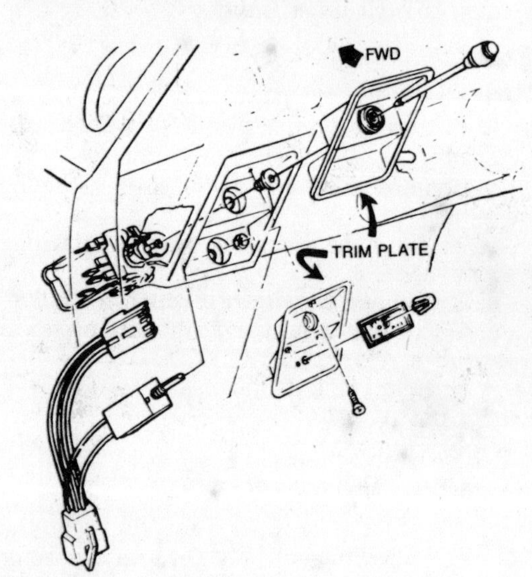

Headlight switch mounting

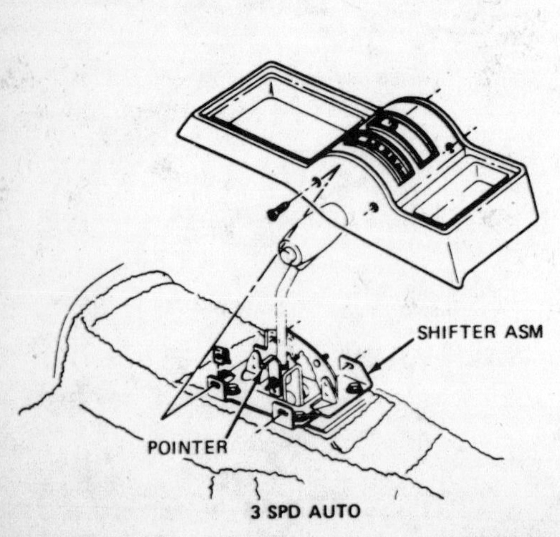

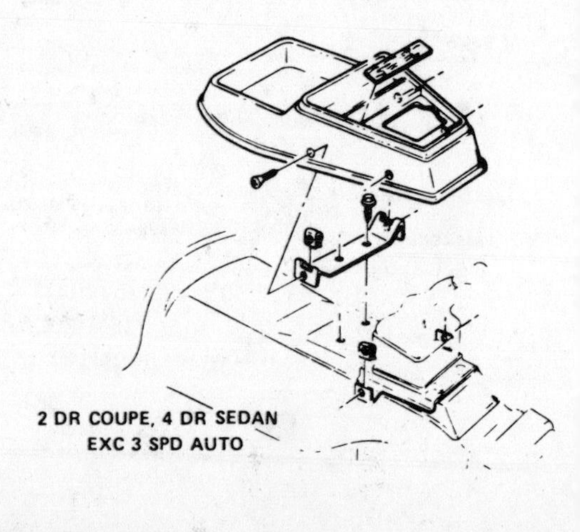

Console mounting

4. Remove the three screws and remove the headlight switch trim plate.
5. Use a large bladed screwdriver to remove the light switch ferrule nut from the front of the instrument panel.
6. Disconnect the multi-contact connector from the bottom of the headlight switch. (A small screwdriver will aid removal).
7. Installation is the reverse of removal.

Clock

REMOVAL AND INSTALLATION

1. Disconnect the negative battery cable.
2. Remove the instrument cluster as outlined earlier and disconnect the clock retaining nuts and wiring connector.
3. Installation is the reverse of removal.

Back-up Light Switch

REMOVAL AND INSTALLATION

The back-up light switch is combined with the neutral start on automatic transmissions. On both manual and automatic transmissions the switch is mounted on the transmission and is outlined in Chapter 7.

Speedometer Cable

One end of the speedometer cable and casing assembly is connected to the back of the speedometer behind the instrument cluster and the other end to a speedometer gear in the transmission case. The inside cable may be removed by disconnecting the cable assembly behind the cluster assembly and pulling the inside cable out of the casing. Feed the new cable in the casing from the top and make sure it is fully seated in the transmission gear at the bottom.

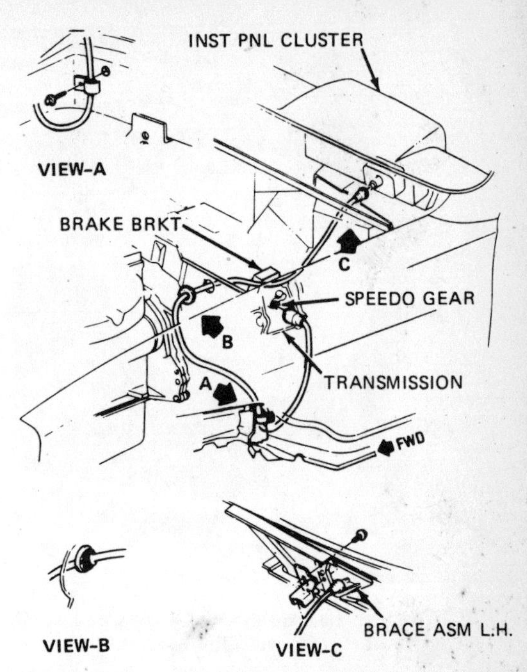

Speedometer cable and casing installation

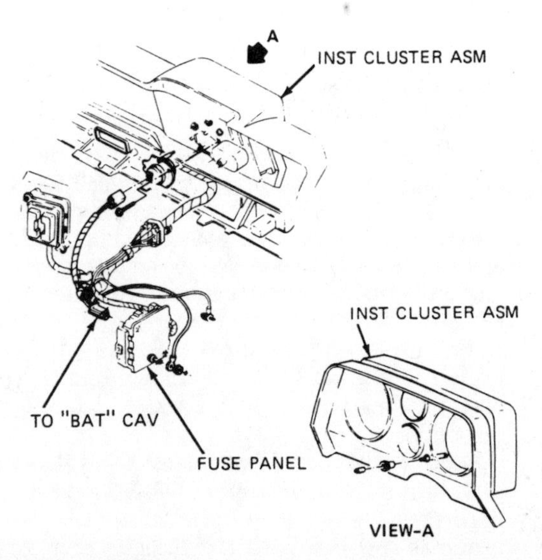

Clock installation

LIGHTING

Headlights

REMOVAL AND INSTALLATION

1. Remove the four phillips screws that retain the headlight bezel. With a hooked tool pull the retaining spring to one side to release the headlamp.

Arrows point out the headlight bezel retaining screw

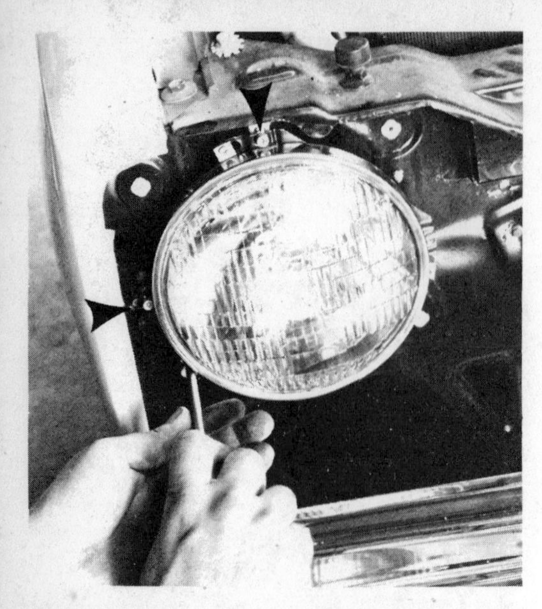

These are the headlight aiming screws, don't touch them when removing the headlight

Unsnap the connector from the headlight

2. Rotate the right head lamp clockwise to release it from the aiming pins. Rotate the left headlamp counterclockwise to release it.
3. Pull out the headlight and detach the electrical connector.
4. Remove the retaining ring.
5. Install the new headlight in the reverse order of removal.

Front Parking Lights, Turn Signals and Side Marker Lights

REMOVAL AND INSTALLATION

The bulb socket for these lights is reached from under the front bumper or under the front wheel well.

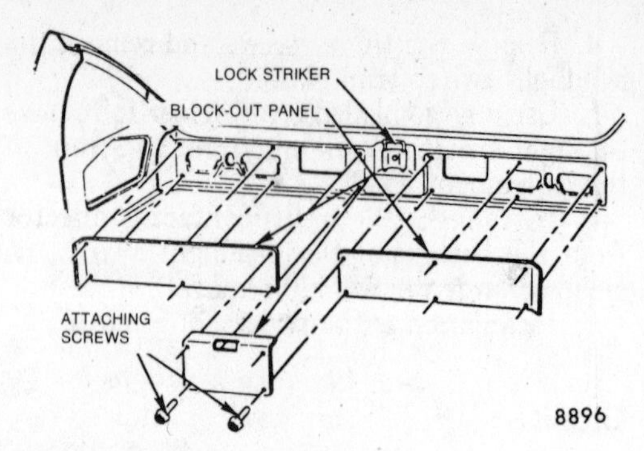

Block-out panel

1. Turn the bulb socket counterclockwise 90° and lift out.
2. Pull the bulb out of the socket and replace it with a new bulb. Test the operation of the bulb.
3. Replace the bulb socket in the housing and turn it clockwise 90° to lock it in place.

Rear Parking Lights and Turn Signals

REMOVAL AND INSTALLATION

1. On the inside of the car, remove the blockout panel.
2. Remove the bulb from the socket and replace as necessary.
3. To install, reverse the procedure.

Rear Side Marker Lamp

1. Remove the lens attaching screws and lens.
2. Remove the bulb from the socket and replace it with a new bulb.
3. Install the lens with the attaching screws.

TRAILER WIRING

Wiring the car for towing is fairly easy. There are a number of good wiring kits available and these should be used, rather than trying to design your own. All trailers will need brake lights and turn signals as well as tail lights and side marker lights. Most states require extra marker lights for overly wide trailers. Also, most states have recently required back-up lights for trailers, and most trailer manufacturers have been building trailers with back-up lights for several years.

Additionally, some Class I, most Class II and just about all Class III trailers will have electric brakes.

Add to this number an accessories wire, to operate trailer internal equipment or to charge the trailer's battery, and you can have as many as seven wires in the harness.

Determine the equipment on your trailer and buy the wiring kit necessary. The kit will contain all the wires needed, plus a plug adapter set which included the female plug, mounted on the bumper or hitch, and the male plug, wired into, or plugged into the trailer harness.

When installing the kit, follow the manufacturer's instructions. The color coding of the wires is standard throughout the industry.

One point to note, some domestic vehicles, and most imported vehicles, have separate turn signals. On most domestic vehicles, the brake lights and rear turn signals operate with the same bulb. For those vehicles with separate turn signals, you can purchase an isolation unit so that the brake lights won't blink whenever the turn signals are operated, or, you can go to your local electronics supply house and buy four diodes to wire in series with the brake and turn signal bulbs. Diodes will isolate the brake and turn signals. The choice is yours. The isolation units are simple and quick to install, but far more expensive than the diodes. The diodes, however, require more work to install properly, since they require the cutting of each bulb's wire and soldering in place of the diode.

One final point, the best kits are those with a spring loaded cover on the vehicle mounted socket. This cover prevents dirt and moisture from corroding the terminals. Never let the vehicle socket hang loosely. Always mount it securely to the bumper or hitch.

NOTE: *For more information on towing a trailer please refer to Chapter 1.*

CIRCUIT PROTECTION

Fuses And Flashers

The fuse panel is located under the instrument panel on the left hand side. The headlight circuit is protected by a circuit breaker in the light switch. An electrical overload will cause

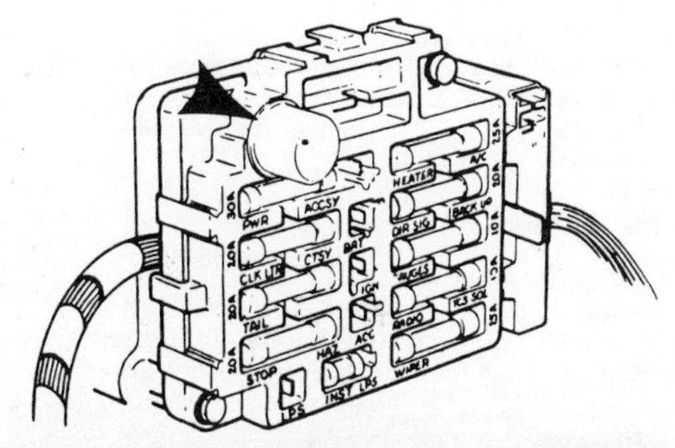

1976–80 fuse box—flasher is indicated by arrow

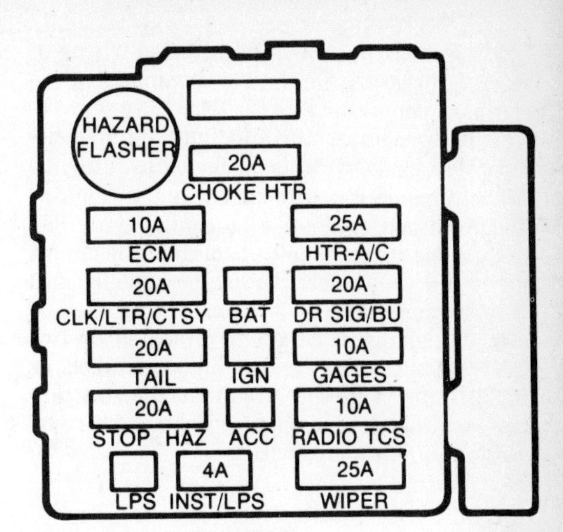

Fuse panel—1981 and later

the lights to go on and off, or in some cases to stay off. If this condition develops, check the wiring circuits immediately.

An Air Conditioning high blower speed fuse, 30 amp, is located in an inline fuse holder running from the junction block to the Air Conditioning relay.

Fusible Link

In addition to circuit breakers and fuses, the wiring harness incorporates fusible links to protect the wiring. Links are used rather than a fuse in wiring circuits that are not normally fused, such as the ignition circuit. Fusible links are color coded red in the charging and load circuits to match color coding of the circuit they protect. Each link is four gauge sizes smaller than the cable it is designed to protect and are marked on the insulation with wire gauge size because the heavy insulation makes the link appear a heavier gauge than it actually is.

Engine compartment wiring harnesses incorporate several fusible links. The same size wire with special hypalon insulation must be used when replacing fusible link.

The links are:

1. A molded splice at the starter solenoid "Bat" terminal, 14 gauge red wire. Servicing requires splicing in a new link.
2. A 16 gauge red fusible link is located at

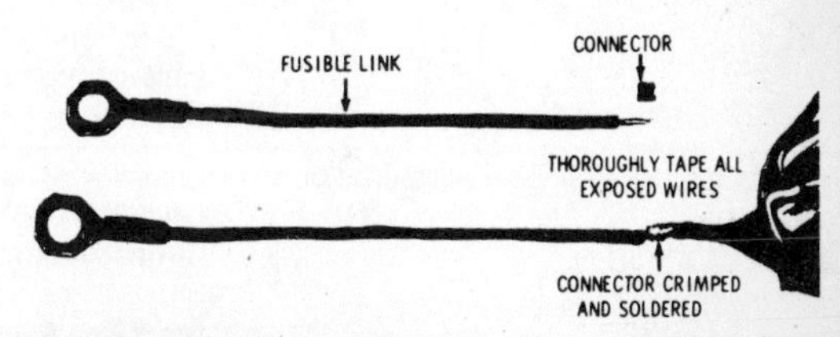

Fusible link replacement

junction block to protect all unfused wiring of 12 gauge or larger. The link is terminated at the bulkhead connector.

3. The generator warning light and field circuitry (16 gauge wire) is protected by a fusible link (20 gauge red wire) used in the "battery feed to voltage regulator #3 terminal" wire. The link is installed as a molded splice in the circuit at the junction block. Service by splicing in a new 20 gauge wire.

4. The ammeter circuit is protected by two red 20 gauge wire fusible links installed as molded splices in the circuit at the junction block and battery to starter circuit. Service by splicing in new gauge wires.

REPLACEMENT

1. Disconnect the battery ground cable.
2. Disconnect the fusible link from the junction block or starter solenoid.
3. Cut the harness directly behind the connector to remove the damaged fusible link.
4. Strip the harness wire approximately ½".
5. Connect the new fusible link to the harness wire using a crimp on connector. Solder the connection using rosin core solder.
6. Tape all exposed wires with plastic electrical tape.
7. Connect the fusible link to the junction block or starter solenoid and reconnect the battery ground cable.

Troubleshooting Basic Windshield Wiper Problems

Problem	Cause	Solution
Electric Wipers		
Wipers do not operate— Wiper motor heats up or hums	• Internal motor defect • Bent or damaged linkage • Arms improperly installed on linking pivots	• Replace motor • Repair or replace linkage • Position linkage in park and reinstall wiper arms
Wipers do not operate— No current to motor	• Fuse or circuit breaker blown • Loose, open or broken wiring • Defective switch • Defective or corroded terminals • No ground circuit for motor or switch	• Replace fuse or circuit breaker • Repair wiring and connections • Replace switch • Replace or clean terminals • Repair ground circuits
Wipers do not operate— Motor runs	• Linkage disconnected or broken	• Connect wiper linkage or replace broken linkage
Vacuum Wipers		
Wipers do not operate	• Control switch or cable inoperative • Loss of engine vacuum to wiper motor (broken hoses, low engine vacuum, defective vacuum/fuel pump) • Linkage broken or disconnected • Defective wiper motor	• Repair or replace switch or cable • Check vacuum lines, engine vacuum and fuel pump • Repair linkage • Replace wiper motor
Wipers stop on engine acceleration	• Leaking vacuum hoses • Dry windshield • Oversize wiper blades • Defective vacuum/fuel pump	• Repair or replace hoses • Wet windshield with washers • Replace with proper size wiper blades • Replace pump

Troubleshooting Basic Turn Signal and Flasher Problems

Most problems in the turn signals or flasher system can be reduced to defective flashers or bulbs, which are easily replaced. Occasionally, problems in the turn signals are traced to the switch in the steering column, which will require professional service.
F = Front R = Rear • = Lights off ○ = Lights on

Problem	Solution
Turn signals light, but do not flash	• Replace the flasher
No turn signals light on either side	• Check the fuse. Replace if defective. • Check the flasher by substitution • Check for open circuit, short circuit or poor ground
Both turn signals on one side don't work	• Check for bad bulbs • Check for bad ground in both housings
One turn signal light on one side doesn't work	• Check and/or replace bulb • Check for corrosion in socket. Clean contacts. • Check for poor ground at socket
Turn signal flashes too fast or too slow	• Check any bulb on the side flashing too fast. A heavy-duty bulb is probably installed in place of a regular bulb. • Check the bulb flashing too slow. A standard bulb was probably installed in place of a heavy-duty bulb. • Check for loose connections or corrosion at the bulb socket
Indicator lights don't work in either direction	• Check if the turn signals are working • Check the dash indicator lights • Check the flasher by substitution
One indicator light doesn't light	• On systems with 1 dash indicator: See if the lights work on the same side. Often the filaments have been reversed in systems combining stoplights with taillights and turn signals. Check the flasher by substitution • On systems with 2 indicators: Check the bulbs on the same side Check the indicator light bulb Check the flasher by substitution

Troubleshooting Basic Dash Gauge Problems

Problem	Cause	Solution
Coolant Temperature Gauge		
Gauge reads erratically or not at all	• Loose or dirty connections • Defective sending unit	• Clean/tighten connections • Bi-metal gauge: remove the wire from the sending unit. Ground the wire for an instant. If the gauge registers, replace the sending unit.
	• Defective gauge	• Magnetic gauge: disconnect the wire at the sending unit. With ignition ON gauge should register COLD. Ground the wire; gauge should register HOT.
Ammeter Gauge—Turn Headlights ON (do not start engine). Note reaction		
Ammeter shows charge	• Connections reversed on gauge	• Reinstall connections
Ammeter shows discharge	• Ammeter is OK	• Nothing
Ammeter does not move	• Loose connections or faulty wiring • Defective gauge	• Check/correct wiring • Replace gauge
Oil Pressure Gauge		
Gauge does not register or is inaccurate	• On mechanical gauge, Bourdon tube may be bent or kinked	• Check tube for kinks or bends preventing oil from reaching the gauge
	• Low oil pressure	• Remove sending unit. Idle the engine briefly. If no oil flows from sending unit hole, problem is in engine.
	• Defective gauge	• Remove the wire from the sending unit and ground it for an instant with the ignition ON. A good gauge will go to the top of the scale.
	• Defective wiring	• Check the wiring to the gauge. If it's OK and the gauge doesn't register when grounded, replace the gauge.
	• Defective sending unit	• If the wiring is OK and the gauge functions when grounded, replace the sending unit
All Gauges		
All gauges do not operate	• Blown fuse • Defective instrument regulator	• Replace fuse • Replace instrument voltage regulator
All gauges read low or erratically	• Defective or dirty instrument voltage regulator	• Clean contacts or replace
All gauges pegged	• Loss of ground between instrument voltage regulator and car • Defective instrument regulator	• Check ground • Replace regulator
Warning Lights		
Light(s) do not come on when ignition is ON, but engine is not started	• Defective bulb • Defective wire	• Replace bulb • Check wire from light to sending unit
	• Defective sending unit	• Disconnect the wire from the sending unit and ground it. Replace the sending unit if the light comes on with the ignition ON.
Light comes on with engine running	• Problem in individual system • Defective sending unit	• Check system • Check sending unit (see above)

Troubleshooting Basic Lighting Problems

Problem	Cause	Solution
Lights		
One or more lights don't work, but others do	• Defective bulb(s) • Blown fuse(s) • Dirty fuse clips or light sockets • Poor ground circuit	• Replace bulb(s) • Replace fuse(s) • Clean connections • Run ground wire from light socket housing to car frame
Lights burn out quickly	• Incorrect voltage regulator setting or defective regulator • Poor battery/alternator connections	• Replace voltage regulator • Check battery/alternator connections
Lights go dim	• Low/discharged battery • Alternator not charging • Corroded sockets or connections • Low voltage output	• Check battery • Check drive belt tension; repair or replace alternator • Clean bulb and socket contacts and connections • Replace voltage regulator
Lights flicker	• Loose connection • Poor ground • Circuit breaker operating (short circuit)	• Tighten all connections • Run ground wire from light housing to car frame • Check connections and look for bare wires
Lights "flare"—Some flare is normal on acceleration—if excessive, see "Lights Burn Out Quickly"	• High voltage setting	• Replace voltage regulator
Lights glare—approaching drivers are blinded	• Lights adjusted too high • Rear springs or shocks sagging • Rear tires soft	• Have headlights aimed • Check rear springs/shocks • Check/correct rear tire pressure
Turn Signals		
Turn signals don't work in either direction	• Blown fuse • Defective flasher • Loose connection	• Replace fuse • Replace flasher • Check/tighten all connections
Right (or left) turn signal only won't work	• Bulb burned out • Right (or left) indicator bulb burned out • Short circuit	• Replace bulb • Check/replace indicator bulb • Check/repair wiring
Flasher rate too slow or too fast	• Incorrect wattage bulb • Incorrect flasher	• Flasher bulb • Replace flasher (use a variable load flasher if you pull a trailer)
Indicator lights do not flash (burn steadily)	• Burned out bulb • Defective flasher	• Replace bulb • Replace flasher
Indicator lights do not light at all	• Burned out indicator bulb • Defective flasher	• Replace indicator bulb • Replace flasher

Troubleshooting the Heater

Problem	Cause	Solution
Blower motor will not turn at any speed	• Blown fuse • Loose connection • Defective ground • Faulty switch • Faulty motor • Faulty resistor	• Replace fuse • Inspect and tighten • Clean and tighten • Replace switch • Replace motor • Replace resistor
Blower motor turns at one speed only	• Faulty switch • Faulty resistor	• Replace switch • Replace resistor
Blower motor turns but does not circulate air	• Intake blocked • Fan not secured to the motor shaft	• Clean intake • Tighten security
Heater will not heat	• Coolant does not reach proper temperature • Heater core blocked internally • Heater core air-bound • Blend-air door not in proper position	• Check and replace thermostat if necessary • Flush or replace core if necessary • Purge air from core • Adjust cable
Heater will not defrost	• Control cable adjustment incorrect • Defroster hose damaged	• Adjust control cable • Replace defroster hose

Drive Train 7

UNDERSTANDING THE MANUAL TRANSMISSION

Because of the way an internal combustion engine breathes, it can produce torque, or twisting force, only within a narrow speed range. Most modern, overhead valve engines must turn at about 2,500 rpm to produce their peak torque. By 4,500 rpm they are producing so little torque that continued increases in engine speed produce no power increases.

The torque peak on overhead camshaft engines is, generally, much higher, but much narrower.

The manual transmission and clutch are employed to vary the relationship between engine speed and the speed of the wheels so that adequate engine power can be produced under all circumstances. The clutch allows engine torque to be applied to the transmission input shaft gradually, due to mechanical slippage. The car can, consequently, be started smoothly from a full stop.

The transmission changes the ratio between the rotating speeds of the engine and the wheels by the use of gears. 4-speed or 5-speed transmissions are most common. The lower gears allow full engine power to be applied to the rear wheels during acceleration at low speeds.

The clutch drive plate is a thin disc, the center of which is splined to the transmission input shaft. Both sides of the disc are covered with a layer of material which is similar to brake lining and which is capable of allowing slippage without roughness or excessive noise.

The clutch cover is bolted to the engine flywheel and incorporates a diaphragm spring which provides the pressure to engage the clutch. The cover also houses the pressure plate. The driven disc is sandwiched between the pressure plate and the smooth surface of the flywheel when the clutch pedal is released, thus forcing it to turn at the same speed as the engine crankshaft.

The transmission contains a mainshaft which passes all the way through the transmission, from the clutch to the driveshaft. This shaft is separated at one point, so that front and rear portions can turn at different speeds.

Power is transmitted by a countershaft in the lower gears and reverse. The gears of the countershaft mesh with gears on the mainshaft, allowing power to be carried from one to the other. All the countershaft gears are integral with that shaft, while several of the mainshaft gears can either rotate independently of the shaft or be locked to it. Shifting from one gear to the next causes one of the gears to be freed from rotating with the shaft and locks another to it. Gears are locked and unlocked by internal dog clutches which slide between the center of the gear and the shaft. The forward gears usually employ synchronizers; friction members which smoothly bring gear and shaft to the same speed before the toothed dog clutches are engaged.

The clutch is operating properly if:

1. It will stall the engine when released with the vehicle held stationary.
2. The shift lever can be moved freely between 1st and reverse gears when the vehicle is stationary and the clutch disengaged.

A clutch pedal free-play adjustment is incorporated in the linkage. Inadequate free-play wears all parts of the clutch releasing mechanisms and may cause slippage. Excessive free-play may cause inadequate release and hard shifting of gears.

Some clutches use a hydraulic system in place of mechanical linkage. If the clutch fails to release, fill the clutch master cylinder with fluid to the proper level and pump the clutch pedal to fill the system with fluid. Bleed the system in the same way as a brake system. If leaks are located, tighten loose connections or overhaul the master or slave cylinder as necessary.

The Chevette and Pontiac 1000 were available with a 4-speed (70mm) fully synchronized transmission through 1981. On 1982 and later gasoline models, an optional 5-speed (77mm) was also available. All diesel models were eqiuipped with a 5-speed (69.5mm) transmission. Gear shifting is accomplished by an internal shifter shaft. No adjustment of the mechanism is possible.

Back-Up Light Switch

REMOVAL AND INSTALLATION

1. Set the brake and raise and support the vehicle safely.
2. Pull the electrical connector from the switch. The switch is located horizontally at the rear of the transmission on either the right or left side.
3. Using a box end wrench, remove the switch from the rear of the transmission case.
4. Install the switch using a new gasket. check the operation of the switch by placing the transmission in the reverse detent.

Transmission

REMOVAL AND INSTALLATION

Gasoline Engine

1. Remove the shift lever as outlined in this chapter.
2. Raise the car on a hoise and drain the lubricant from the transmission.
3. Remove the driveshaft as described in the next chapter.
4. Disconnect the speedometer cable and back-up light switch.
5. Disconnect the return spring and clutch cable at the clutch release fork.
6. Remove the crossmember-to-transmission mount bolts.
7. Remove the exhaust manifold nuts and converter-to-tailpipe bolts and nuts. Remove

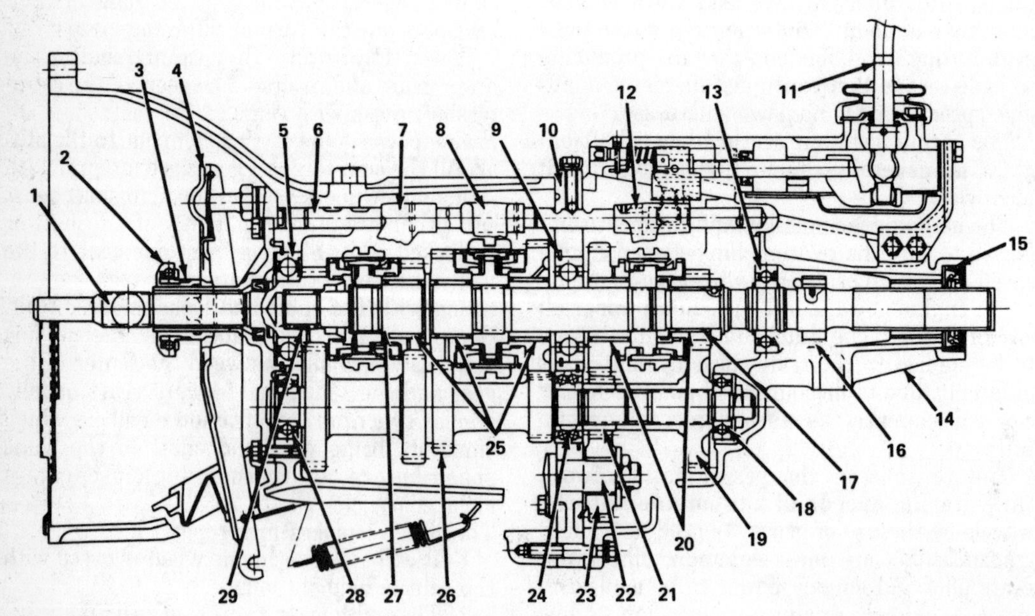

1. Drive gear
2. Release bearing
3. Drive gear bearing retainer
4. Shift fork
5. Drive gear bearing
6. Shifter shaft
7. 3rd & 4th shift fork
8. 1st & 2nd shift fork
9. Mainshaft bearing
10. Center support
11. Shift lever
12. 5th & reverse shift fork
13. Mainshaft rear bearing
14. Extension housing
15. Rear seal
16. Speedometer drive gear
17. 5th gear assy
18. Counter gear rear bearing
19. 5th counter gear
20. Needle bearing
21. Reverse counter gear
22. Reverse idler shaft
23. Reverse idler gear
24. Counter gear bearing
25. Needle bearing
26. Counter gear
27. Mainshaft
28. Counter gear front bearing
29. Needle gearing

Cross section of the 5-speed manual transmission (diesel)

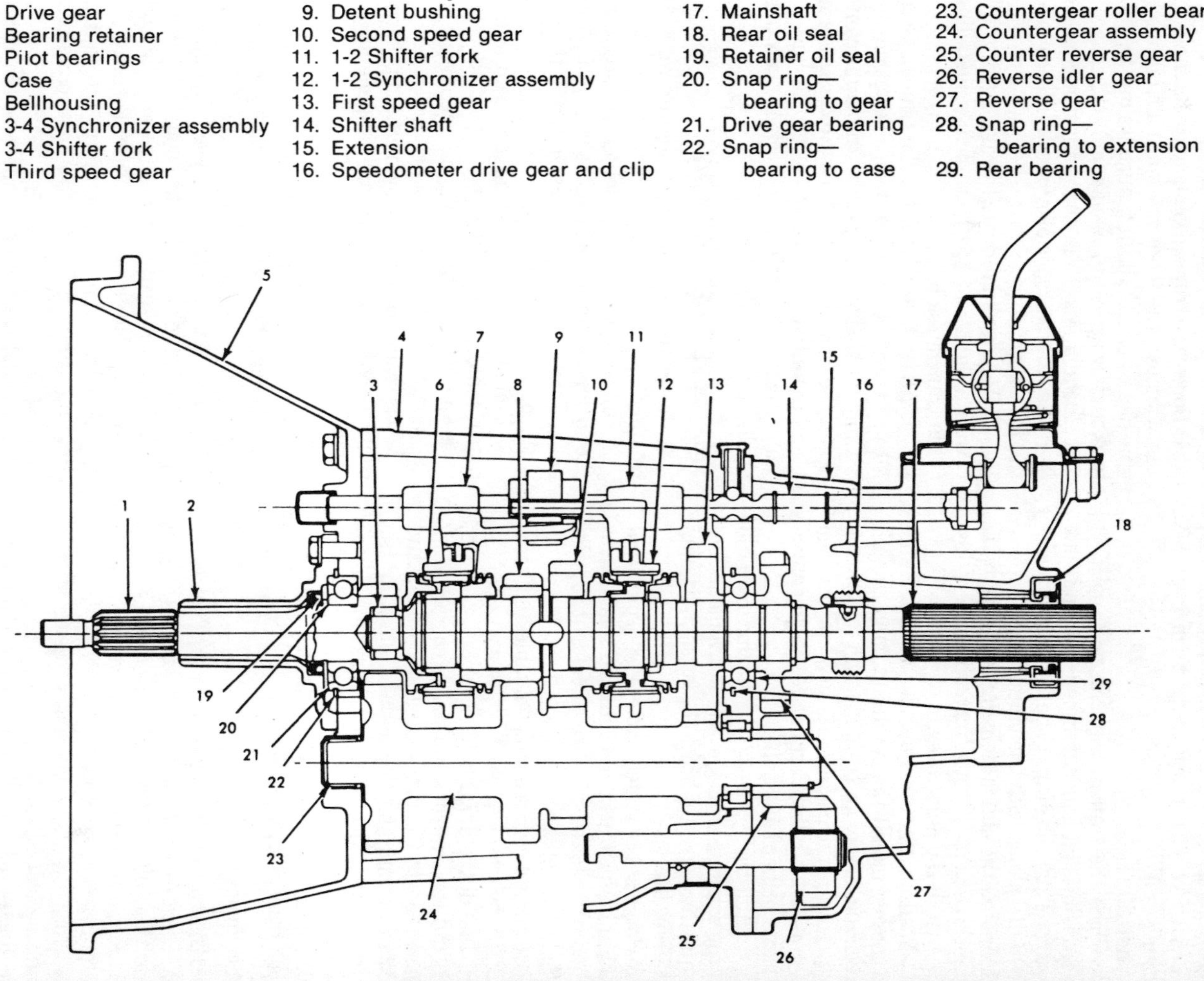

Cross section of the 4-speed transmission

the converter-to-transmission bracket bolts and remove the converter.

8. Remove the crossmember-to-frame bolts and remove the crossmember.

9. Remove the dust cover.

10. Remove the clutch housing-to-engine retaining bolts, slide the transmission and clutch housing to the rear, and remove the transmission.

To install:

11. Place the transmission in gear, position the transmission and clutch housing, and slide forward. Turn the output shaft to align the input shaft splines with the clutch hub.

12. Install the clutch housing retaining bolts and lockwashers. Torque the bolts to 25 ft. lbs.

13. Install the dust cover.

14. Position the crossmember to the frame and loosely install the retaining bolts. Install the crossmember-to-transmission mounting bolts. Torque the center nuts to 33 ft. lbs.; the end nuts to 21 ft. lbs. Torque the crossmember-to-frame bolts to 40 ft. lbs.

15. Install the exhaust pipe to the manifold and the converter bracker on the transmission. Torque the converter bracket rear support nuts to 150 in. lbs.

16. Connect the clutch cable. Perform Initial Ball Stud Adjustment and Clutch Cable Attachment and Adjustment. Also, adjust clutch pedal free-play, if necessary.

17. Connect the speedometer cable and back-up light switch.

18. Install the driveshaft.

19. Fill the transmission to the correct level. Please refer to Chapter One under Fluids And Lubricants and the Capacities Chart for the correct type and quanity of lubricant. Lower the car.

20. Install the shift lever and check operation of the transmission.

Diesel Engine

1. Disconnect the negative battery cable.

2. Unscrew the retaining screws and then remove the shift lever console.

3. Remove the mounting screws and remove the shift lever assembly.

4. Unscrew and remove the upper starter mounting bolts.

5. Raise the front of the car and drain the lubricant from the transmission.

6. Remove the driveshaft as detailed in Chapter 7.

7. Disconnect the speedometer and the back-up light switch wires.

8. Disconnect the return spring and clutch cable at the clutch release fork.

9. Remove the starter lower bolt and support the starter.

10. Unscrew the retaining bolts and disconnect the exhaust pipe from the manifold.

11. Remove the flywheel inspection cover.

12. Unscrew the rear transmission support mounting bolt. Support the transmission underneath the case and then remove the rear support from the frame.

13. Lower the transmission approximately 4".

14. Remove the transmission housing-to-engine block bolts. Pull the transmission straight back and away from the engine.

15. Installation of the remaining components is in the reverse order of removal. Please note the following:

a. Be sure to lubricate the drive gear shaft with a light coat of grease before installing the transmission.

b. After installation, fill the transmission to the level of the filler hole. Please refer to Chapter One under Fluids And Lubricants and the Capacities Chart for the correct type and quanity of lubricant. Lower the car.

20. Install the shift lever and check operation of the transmission.

SHIFT LEVER REPLACEMENT

1. Remove the floor console and/or boot retainer.

2. Raise the shift lever boot to gain access to the locknut on the lever. Loosen the locknut and unscrew the upper portion of the shift lever with the knob attached.

3. Remove the foam insulator to gain access to the control assembly bolts.

4. Remove the three bolts on the extension and remove the control assembly.

5. Use caution when removing the clip on the control housing as the internal components are under spring pressure.

6. Remove the locknut, boot retainer, and seat from the threaded end of the shift lever.

7. Remove the spring and guide from the forked end of the shift lever.

8. To assemble the shift lever, install the spring and guide on the forked end of the lever.

9. Install the seat, boot retainer and the locknut over the threaded end of the lever.

10. Assemble the components in the control housing and install the clip on the control housing.

11. Install the control assembly on the extension making sure that the fork at the lower end of the lever engages the shifter shaft lever arm pin. Torque the shift lever retaining bolts to 35 in. lbs.

12. Install the foam insulator, boot, retainer, and/or floor console.

13. Slide the boot below the threaded portion of the shift lever and install the upper shift lever. Tighten the locknut.

4-Speed (70mm) TRANSMISSION OVERHAUL

Transmission Case

DISASSEMBLY

1. Place the transmission so that it is resting on the bell housing.
2. Drive the spring pin from the shifter shaft arm assembly and the shifter shaft, then remove the shifter shaft arm assembly.
3. Remove the 5 extension housing-to-case bolts and the extension housing.
4. Press down on the speedometer gear retainer, then remove the gear and the retainer from the mainshaft.
5. Remove the snaprings from the shifter shaft, then the Reverse shifter shaft cover, the shifter shaft detent cap, the spring, the ball and the interlock lock pin.
6. Pull the Reverse lever shaft outward to disengage the Reverse idler, then remove the idler shaft with the gear attached.
7. Remove the Reverse gear ssnapring, the Reverse countershaft gear and the gears.
8. Turn the case on its side and remove the clutch gear bearing retainer bolts, the retainer and the gasket.
9. Remove the clutch gear ball bearing-to-bell housing snapring, then the bell housing-to-case bolts.
10. Turn the case so that it rests on the bell housing, then expand the mainshaft bearing snapring and remove the case by lifting it off the mainshaft.

NOTE: *Make sure that the mainshaft assembly, the countergear and shifter shaft assembly stay with the bell housing.*

11. Lift the entire mainshaft assembly complete with shifter forks and countergear from the bell housing.

ASSEMBLY

1. Using a press, install the shielded ball bearing to the clutch gear shaft with the snapring groove up.

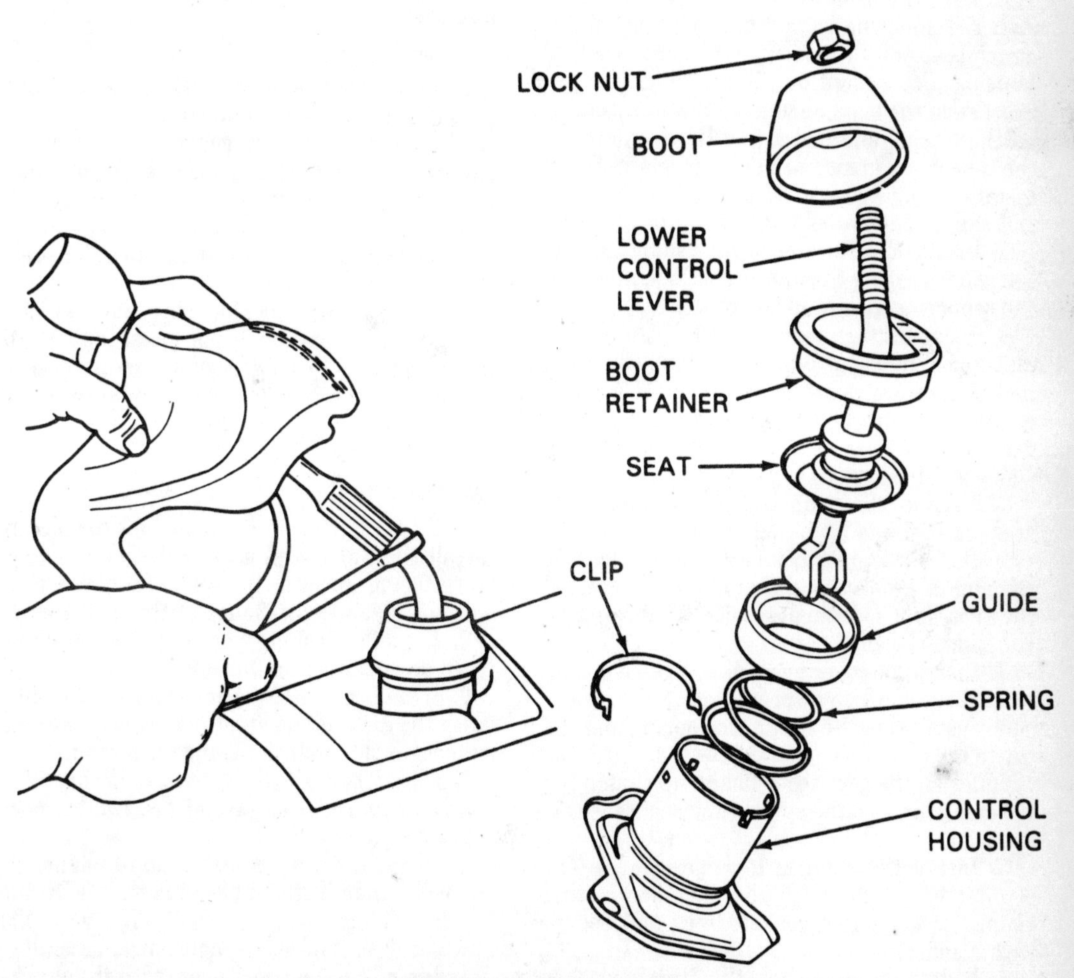

Shift lever removal—4 speed

2. Install the snapring on the clutch gear shaft. Place the pilot bearings into the clutch gear cavity, using heavy grease to hold them in place.

3. Assemble the clutch gear to the mainshaft and the detent lever to the shift shaft with the roll pin.

4. Position the 1st/2nd gear shifter so that it engages the detent lever.

5. Assemble the 3rd/4th gear shifter fork to the detent bushing and slide the assembly on the shift shaft to place it below the 1st/2nd shifter fork arm.

6. Install the shifter assembly to the synchronizer sleeve grooves on the mainshaft.

5. With the front of the bell housing resting on wooden blocks, place a thrust washer over the hole for the countergear shaft. The thrust washer must be placed in the holes in the bellhousing.

6. Mesh the countershaft gears to the mainshaft gears and install this assembly into the bellhousing.

7. Turn the bellhousing on its side, then install the snapring to the ball bearing on the clutch gear and the bearing retainer to the bell housing. Use sealant on the 4 retaining bolts.

8. Turn the bell housing (so that it is resting on the blocks) and install the Reverse lever to the case using grease to hold it in place. When installing the Reverse lever, the screwdriver slot should be parallel to the front of the case.

9. Install the Reverse lever ssnapring and the roller bearing-to-countergear opening with the ssnapring groove inside of the case.

10. Using rubber cement, install the gasket on the bell housing. Before installing the case, make sure the synchronizers are in the Neutral position, the detent bushing slot is facing outward and the Reverse lever is flush with the inside wall of the case.

11. Expand the snapring in the mainshaft case opening and let it slide over the bearing.

12. Install the interlock lock pin with locking compound to hold the shifter shaft in place and the idler shaft so it engages with the Reverse lever inside the shaft.

13. Install the cover over the screwdriver arm to hold the Reverse lever in place.

14. Install the detent ball, the spring and the cap in the case, then the Reverse gear (with the chamfer on the gear teeth facing up). Push the Reverse gear onto the splines and secure with a snapring.

15. Install the smaller Reverse gear on the countergear shaft (with the shoulder resting against the countergear bearing) and secure with a snapring.

16. Install the snapring, the thrust washer and the Reverse idler gear (with the gear teeth chamfer facing down) to the idler shaft, then secure with the thrust washer and the ssnapring.

17. Install the shifter shaft snap rings and engage the speedometer gear retainer in the hole in the mainshaft (with the retainer loop toward the front), then slide the speedometer gear over the mainshaft and into position.

NOTE: *Before installation, heat the gear to 175°F; use an oven or heat lamp, not a torch.*

18. Place the extension housing and the gasket on the case, then loosely install the two pilot bolts (one in the top right hand corner and the other in the bottom left hand corner) and the other three bolts. The pilot bolts must be installed in the right holes to prevent splitting the case.

19. Assemble the shifter shaft arm over the shifter shaft, align with the drilled hole near the end of the shaft, then drive the spring pin into the shifter shaft arm and shaft.

20. Turn the case on its side and loosely install the two pilot bolts through the bell housing and then the 4 retaining bolts.

Mainshaft

DISASSEMBLY

1. Separate the shift shaft assembly and countergear from the mainshaft.

2. Remove the clutch gear and the blocking ring from the mainshaft; make sure you don't lose any of the clutch gear roller bearings.

3. Remove the 3rd/4th gear synchronizer hub snapring and the hub, using an arbor press (if necessary).

4. Remove the blocking ring and the 3rd speed gear. Using an arbor press and press plates, remove the ball bearing from the rear of the mainshaft. Remove the remaining parts from the mainshaft keeping them in order for later reassembly.

ASSEMBLY

1. With the rear of the mainshaft turned up, install the 2nd speed gear with the clutching teeth facing upward; the rear face of the gear will butt against the flange of the mainshaft.

2. Install a blocking ring (with the clutching teeth down) over the 2nd speed gear.

3. Install the 1st/2nd synchronizer assembly (with the fork slot down), then press it onto the splines on the mainshaft until it bottoms.

NOTE: *Make sure the notches of the blocking ring align with the keys of the synchronizer assembly.*

4. Install the synchronizer hub-to-mainshaft snapring, then install a blocking ring (with the notches facing down) so they align with the keys of the 1st/2nd gear synchronizer assembly.

5. Install the 1st speed gear (with the clutching teeth down), then the rear ball bearing

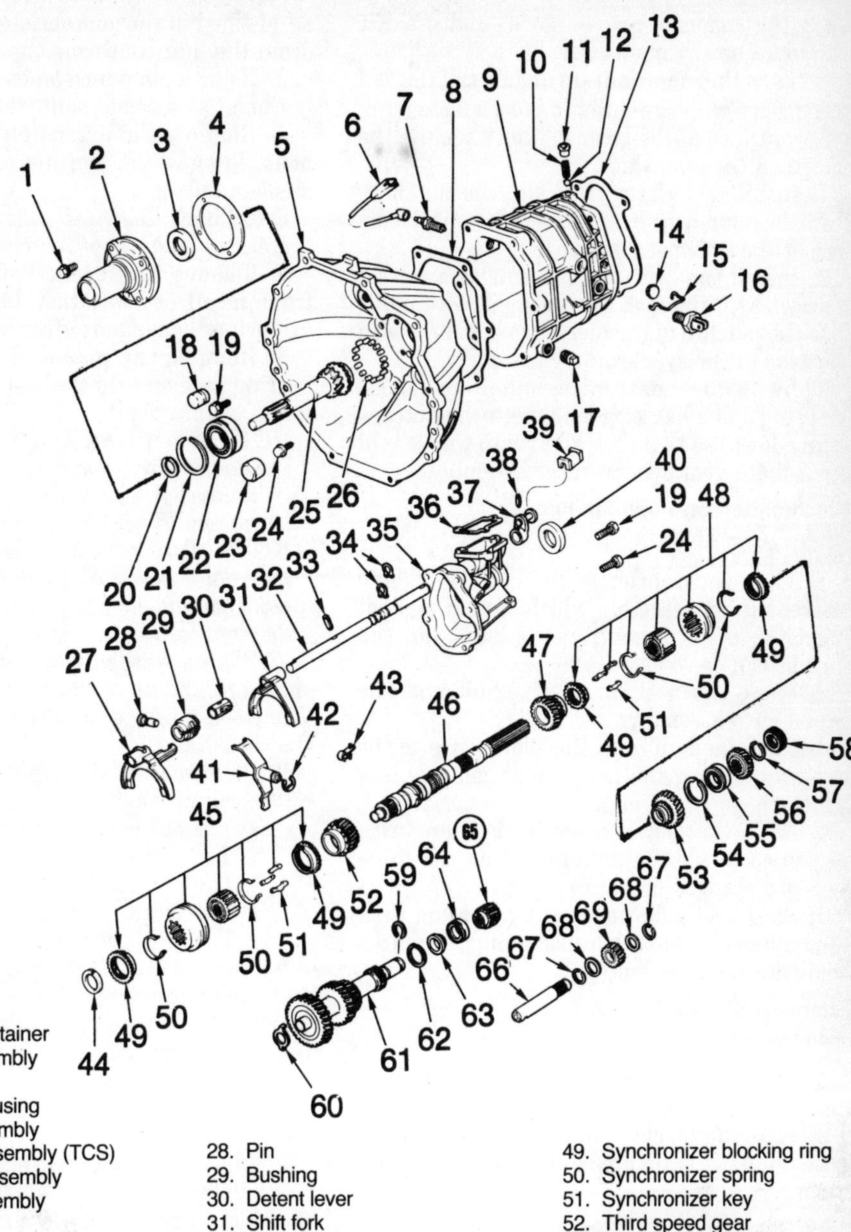

1. Bolt
2. Bearing retainer
3. Seal assembly
4. Gasket
5. Clutch housing
6. Wire assembly
7. Switch assembly (TCS)
8. Gasket assembly
9. Case assembly
10. Spring
11. Cap
12. Ball
13. Gasket
14. Cap
15. Retainer
16. Back-up light switch
17. Plug
18. Cap
19. Bolt
20. Retaining ring
21. Locating ring
22. Bearing assembly
23. Bearing assembly
24. Bolt
25. Main drive gear
26. Bearing rollers
27. Shift fork
28. Pin
29. Bushing
30. Detent lever
31. Shift fork
32. Shift shaft
33. Pin
34. Lock ring
35. Extension assembly
36. Gasket
37. Arm assembly
38. Pin
39. Bushing
40. Seal
41. Reverse shaft and lever
42. Lock ring
43. Clip
44. Retaining ring
45. Synchronizer assembly
46. Mainshaft
47. Second speed gear
48. Synchronizer assembly
49. Synchronizer blocking ring
50. Synchronizer spring
51. Synchronizer key
52. Third speed gear
53. First speed gear
54. Locating ring
55. Mainshaft rear bearing
56. Reverse gear
57. Retaining ring
58. Speedometer drive gear
59. Retainer ring
60. Thrust washer
61. Countershaft gear
62. Locating ring
63. Bearing race
64. Bearing assembly
65. Countershaft reverse gear
66. Reverse idler shaft
67. Retainer ring
68. Thrust washer
69. Reverse idler gear

Exploded view of the 70mm Four speed transmission

(with the snapring groove down) and press it into place on the mainshaft.

6. Turn the mainshaft up and install the 3rd speed gear (with the clutching teeth facing up); the front face of the gear will butt against the flange on the mainshaft.

7. Install a blocking ring (with the clutching teeth facing down) over the synchronizer surface of the 3rd speed gear.

8. Install the 3rd/4th gear synchronizer assembly (with the fork slot facing down); make sure the notches of the blocking ring align with the keys of the synchronizer assembly.

9. Install the synchronizer hub-to-mainshaft snapring and a blocking ring (with the notches facing down) so that they align with the keys of the 3rd/4th gear synchronizer assembly.

Synchronizer Keys And Springs

REPLACEMENT

1. The synchronizer hubs and the sliding sleeves are an assembly which should be kept together as an assembly; the keys and the springs can be replaced.

2. Mark the position of the hub and the sleeve for reassembly.

3. Push the hub from the sliding sleeve; the keys will fall out and the springs can be easily removed.

4. Place the new springs in position (with one on each side of the hub) so that the three keys are engaged by both springs.

5. Place and hold the keys in position, then slide the sleeve into the hub aligning the marks made during disassembly.

Extension Oil Seal

REPLACEMENT

1. Pry the oil seal and drive the bushing from rear of the extension housing.

2. Coat the inside diameter of the seal and bushing with transmission fluid and install them.

Drive Gear Bearing Oil Seal

REPLACEMENT

Pry out the old seal and install a new one making sure that it bottoms properly in its bore.

5-SPEED (77MM) TRANSMISSION OVERHAUL

Transmission Case

DISASSEMBLY

NOTE: *Many special tools and an arbor press are required to properly disassemble and assemble this transmission. Read the entire procedure carefully before starting the job.*

1. Remove the transmission from the vehicle as outlined in the appropriate car section, then drain the lubricant from the transmission.

2. Using a pin punch and a hammer, carefully the offset lever-to-shift rail roll pin.

3. Remove the extension housing-to-case bolts. Remove the housing and offset lever as an assembly.

CAUTION: *DO NOT attempt to remove the housing with the offset lever in place.*

4. Remove the detent ball and the spring from the offset lever, then the roll pin from the extension housing or offset lever.

5. Remove the plastic funnel, the thrust bearing race and thrust bearing from the rear of the countershaft.

NOTE: *The funnel and race may be found inside the extension.*

6. Remove the cover-to-case bolts and lift the cover assembly off of the case.

NOTE: *Two of the cover bolts are alignment type dowel bolts. Mark the location of these bolts so that they may be reinstalled in their original locations.*

7. Place a wooden block under the 5th gear shift fork and drive the roll pin from the fork. The wood must be used to prevent damage to the shift rail.

8. Remove the following items from the rear of the countershaft.

a. The 5th gear synchronizer snapring.
b. The shift fork.
c. The 5th gear synchronizer sleeve.
d. The blocking ring.
e. The 5th speed drive gear.

9. Remove the 5th gear synchronizer springs and the inserts from the sleeve and the hub. Mark the sleeve and the hub so that they may be properly reassembled.

10. Remove the snapring from the 5th speed driven gear. Using the Kent-Moore puller tool No. J-25215, remove the driven gear.

11. Mark the front bearing cap and the case, so that the cap may be reinstalled in its proper position, then remove the front bearing cap.

12. Remove the front bearing race and the end play shim(s) from the bearing cap. Using a small pry bar, carefully pry the oil seal from the cap.

13. Rotate the clutch shaft until the flat surface on the main drive gear faces the countershaft, then remove the clutch shaft and the main gear unit from the case.

NOTE: *The clutch shaft bearing is pressed on; an arbor press must be used to replace the bearing if the bearing is rough.*

14. Remove the mainshaft rear bearing race and tilt the shaft upward, then remove the output shaft assembly from the case.

15. Unhook the overcenter spring from the front of the case.

16. Remove the Reverse lever C-clip and the pivot bolt.

17. Rotate the 5th/Reverse shift rail clockwise, to disengage it from the Reverse lever, then remove the rail from the rear of the case.

18. Drive the roll pin from the forward end of the Reverse idler shaft, then remove the Reverse idler shaft, the rubber O-ring and the gear from the case.

19. Remove the gear countershaft snapring and the spacer.

20. Insert a brass drift through the main drive gear opening in the front of the case, so that it contacts the countershaft gear assembly. Using an arbor press (positioned at the other end of the drift), carefully press the countershaft gear rearward (just enough) to remove the countershaft rear bearing.

NOTE: *During the assembly, note that the bearing identification numbers should face outward.*

21. Move the countershaft assembly rearward, tilt it upward, then remove the assembly from the case. Mark the position of the front countershaft thrust washer (so that it may be reinstalled properly), then remove the washer from the case.

22. Remove the countershaft rear bearing spacer.

23. Drive the roll pin from the front of the Reverse idler shaft, then remove the shaft and the gear from the case.

NOTE: *Mark the position of the gear, so that it may be reinstalled properly.*

24. Using an arbor press, remove the countershaft front bearing from the case.

25. Remove the clutch shaft front bearing.

27. Using a flat drift and a hammer, carefully tap out the rear extension and the adapter housing seal.

ASSEMBLY

NOTE: *If a replacement fastener is used, be sure that it matches the original EXACTLY. Many metric fasteners are used in this transmission.*

1. Apply a coat of Loctite® 601 to the outer cage of the front countershaft bearing, then press the bearing into its bore until it is flush with the case.

2. Apply a coat of petroleum jelly to the tabbed countershaft thrust washer, then install the washer so that its tab engages the corresponding depression in the case.

3. Tip the case on end and install the countershaft into the front bearing bore.

4. Install the countershaft rear bearing spacer and coat the rear countershaft bearing with petroleum jelly. Using the Kent-Moore installer tool No. J-29895 and the sleeve protector tool No. J-33032, install the rear countershaft bearing.

NOTE: *When properly installed, the rear bearing will extend 3mm beyond the case surface.*

5. Position the Reverse idler gear into the case (with the shift lever groove facing rearward) and install the Reverse idler shaft from the rear of the case.

6. Install the shaft retaining pin.

7. Install the mainshaft assembly and the rear mainshaft bearing race into the case.

8. Using an arbor press, install the clutch shaft/main gear bearing (if removed).

9. Coat the main drive gear roller bearings with petroleum jelly and install them into the rear of the clutch shaft/main gear unit.

10. Install the thrust bearing and the race into the rear of the clutch shaft/main gear unit.

11. Install the 4th gear blocking ring onto the mainshaft.

12. Install the clutch shaft/main gear unit into the case, engaging the 3rd/4th synchronizer blocking ring.

13. Evenly and carefully tap a new front bearing cap seal into place.

14. Install the front bearing race into the front bearing cap; do not install the front bearing cap shims.

15. Temporarily install the front bearing cap, without sealant.

16. Install the following:

a. The 5th/Reverse lever.

b. The pivot bolt.

c. The C-clip retainer.

NOTE: *Coat the pivot bolt threads with nonhardening sealant (RTV is preferred). Also, be sure to engage the Reverse lever fork in the Reverse idler gear.*

17. Install the countershaft rear bearing spacer and the snapring.

18. Install the 5th speed gear onto the mainshaft.

19. Install the 5th/Reverse rail through the rear case opening and into the 5th/Reverse lever, then rotate the rail to engage it with the lever.

20. Position the 5th speed synchronizer assembly on the 5th speed shift fork, then slide the assembly onto the countershaft and the 5th/Reverse rail.

NOTE: *The 5th/Reverse rail roll pin hole must be aligned with the hole of the 5th speed shift fork.*

21. Support the 5th speed shift fork rail and the fork with a block of wood, then drive the roll pin into place.

22. Install the:

a. Thrust race against the 5th speed synchronizer hub, then retain with the snapring.

b. Needle type thrust bearing against the thrust race on the countershaft (coat the bearing and the race with petroleum jelly).

c. Lipped thrust race over the needle type thrust bearing.

d. Plastic funnel into the hole in the end of the countershaft gear.

23. Temporarily install the extension/adapter housing and the bolts.

24. Turn the case on end. Mount a dial indicator on the extension/adapter housing, so that the indicator needle contacts the end of the mainshaft, then zero the indicator needle.

25. Pull upward on the mainshaft to remove the end play, then read the indicator and record the reading.

26. Select a shim pack which measures 0.025-0.130mm thicker than the end play reading obtained during Step 26.

27. Position the case horizontally. Remove the front bearing cap and the bearing race, then install the shim pack. Reinstall the bearing race.

28. Apply a ⅛" bead of RTV sealer on the front bearing cap-to-case mating surface. Align the case and the cap matchmarks. Install the bearing cap and torque the bolts to 15 ft. lbs.

29. Recheck the end play; no play should be evident.

30. Remove the extension and adapter housing, then carefully drive a new housing seal into place.

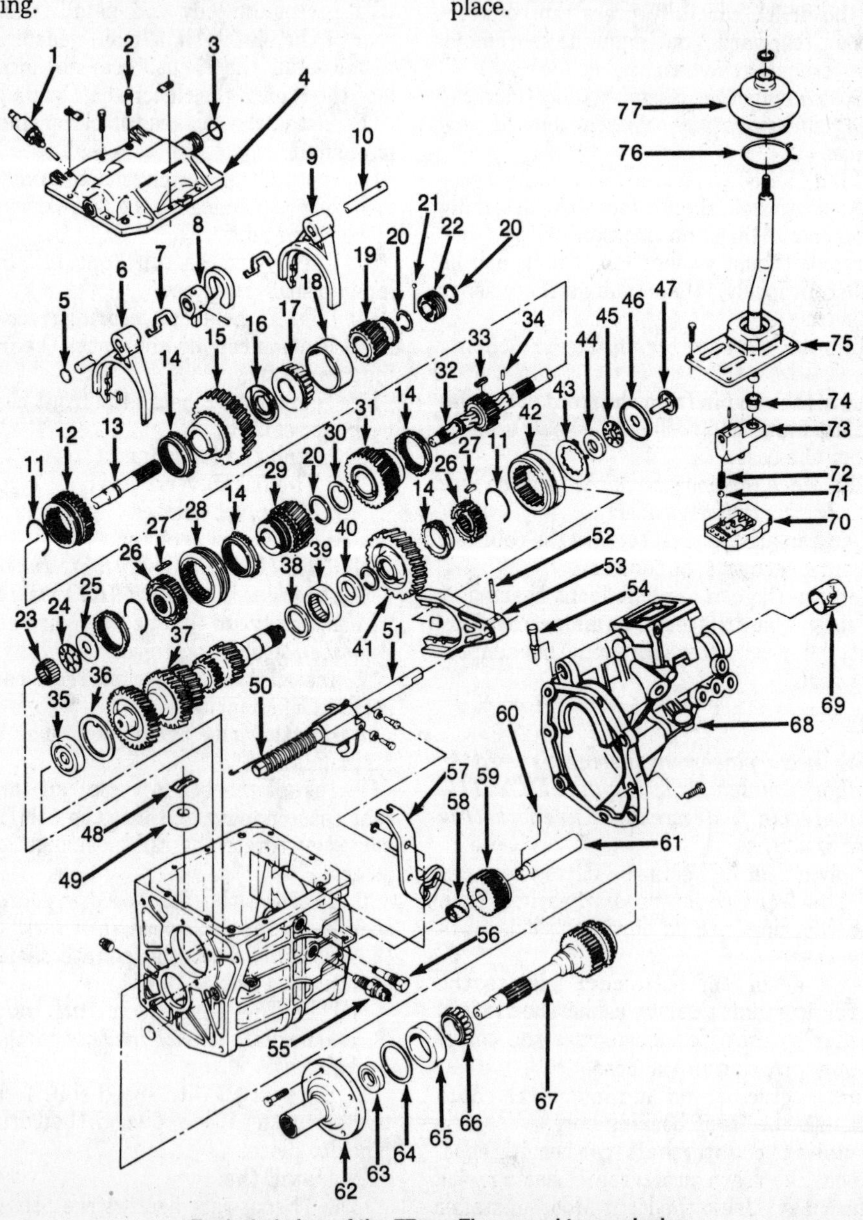

Exploded view of the 77mm Five speed transmission

31. Move the shift forks of the cover and the synchronizer sleeves to their Neutral positions.

32. Apply a 1/8" bead of RTV sealer to the cover-to-case mating surface. While aligning the shift forks with the synchronizer sleeves, carefully lower the cover assembly into case.

33. Center the cover and to engage the Reverse relay lever, then install the alignment type (dowel) cover attaching bolts. Install the remaining cover bolts and torque to 10 ft. lbs.

NOTE: *The offset lever-to-shift rail roll pin hole must be positioned vertically; if not, repeat Steps 32, 33 and 34.*

34. Apply a 1/8" bead of RTV sealer to the extension/adapter housing-to-case mating surface and install the housing over the mainshaft.

NOTE: *The shift rail must be positioned so that it just enters the shift cover opening.*

35. Install the detent spring into the offset lever and place the steel ball into the Neutral guide plate detent. Apply pressure on the steel ball with the detent spring and the offset lever, then slide the offset lever on the shift rail and seat the extension/adapter against the case.

36. Install the extension/adapter housing bolts and torque to 25 ft. lbs.

37. Install the roll pin into the offset lever and the shift rail.

38. Install the damper sleeve in the offset lever. Coat the back up lamp switch threads with RTV sealant, then install the switch into the case and torque to 15 ft. lbs.

Mainshaft

DISASSEMBLY

1. Remove the thrust bearing and the washer from the front of the mainshaft.

2. Scribe matchmarks on the 3rd/4th synchronizer hub and the sleeve to indicate their relationship for proper reassembly.

3. Remove the 3rd/4th synchronizer blocking ring, the sleeve and hub from the mainshaft as an assembly. Mark the positions of these items, so that they may be properly reassembled.

4. Remove the snapring, the tabbed thrust washer and the 2nd gear from the mainshaft.

5. Using an arbor press and the puller tool, remove the 5th speed gear from the mainshaft.

6. Slide the rear mainshaft bearing off of the mainshaft.

7. Remove the 1st gear thrust washer, the roll pin, the 1st speed gear and the blocking ring.

8. Scribe matchmarks on the 1st/2nd synchronizer hub and the sleeve for reassembly purposes.

9. Remove the insert spring and the inserts from the 1st/Reverse sliding gear, then the gear from the mainshaft.

CAUTION: *Do not attempt to remove the 1st/2nd/Reverse hub from the mainshaft as these parts are machined as a matched set from the factory.*

1. Switch
2. Alignment (dowel) bolt
3. O-ring
4. Transmission cover
5. Plug
6. 3rd–4th shift fork
7. Selector plate
8. Selector arm and interlock plate
9. 1st–2nd shift fork
10. Shift rail
11. Synchronizer insert spring
12. Reverse sliding gear
13. Mainshaft
14. Blocking ring
15. 1st speed gear
16. Thrust washer
17. Rear bearing
18. Bearing cup
19. 5th speed driven gear
20. Snap-ring
21. Ball
22. Speedometer drive gear
23. Clutch shaft needle bearing
24. Needle thrust bearing
25. Thrust bearing race
26. 3rd–4th synchronizer hub
27. Synchronizer insert
28. 3rd–4th synchronizer sleeve
29. 3rd speed gear
30. Thrust washer
31. 2nd speed gear
32. Mainshaft
33. Insert
34. Roll pin
35. Front countershaft thrust bearing
36. Thrust washer
37. Countergear unit
38. Bearing spacer
39. Rear countershaft bearing
40. Spacer
41. 5th speed gear
42. 5th synchronizer sleeve
43. Thrust washer
44. Bearing race
45. Needle thrust bearing
46. Thrust race
47. Plastic funnel
48. Retainer
49. Magnet
50. Overcenter spring
51. 5th-reverse shift rail
52. Roll pin
53. 5th-reverse shift fork
54. Breather
55. Back-up lamp switch
56. Reverse lever pivot bolt
57. Reverse lever
58. Reverse idler gear bushing
59. Reverse idler gear
60. Roll pin
61. Reverse idler shaft
62. Front bearing cap
63. Oil seal
64. Shim
65. Front bearing cup
66. Front bearing
67. Main drive gear and shaft unit
68. Extension housing
69. Bushing
70. Detent plate
71. Detent ball
72. Spring
73. Offset lever
74. Bushing
75. Lever assembly
76. Retainer
77. Boot

Exploded view of the 77mm Five speed transmission

ASSEMBLY

1. Lubricate the mainshaft and the gear bores with a liberal coating of transmission lubricant.

2. Align and install the 1st/2nd synchronizer sleeve on the mainshaft, using the matchmarks made during disassembly.

3. If removed, install the synchronizer inserts and the springs into the 1st/2nd synchronizer sleeve.

NOTE: *The tanged end of each spring should be positioned on the same insert but that the open face of each spring should be opposite the other.*

4. Install the blocking ring and the 2nd speed gear onto the mainshaft.

5. Install the tabbed thrust washer and the 2nd speed gear snapring onto the mainshaft.

NOTE: *Be sure that the washer tab is fully seated into the mainshaft notch.*

6. Install the blocking ring and the 1st speed gear onto the mainshaft.

7. Carefully drive the 1st gear roll pin into place, then install the 1st gear thrust washer.

8. Slide the mainshaft rear bearing onto the mainshaft.

9. Using an arbor press and the special tools, press the 5th speed gear onto the mainshaft.

10. Install the 3rd speed gear, the 3rd/4th synchronizer assembly and the thrust bearing onto the mainshaft; the synchronizer hub offset must face forward.

Cover

DISASSEMBLY

1. Place the selector arm plates and the shift rail in the Neutral position (centered).

2. Rotate the shift rail counterclockwise until the selector arm disengages from the selector arm plates. The selector arm roll pin will now be accessible.

3. Using a $^{3}/_{16}$" pin punch and a hammer, carefully drive out the selector arm roll pin, then remove the shift rail.

4. Remove the shift forks, the selector arm plates, the selector arm, the roll pin and the interlock plate.

5. Remove the nylon inserts and the selector arm plates from the shift forks. Mark the positions of the inserts and the plates so they may be properly reinstalled.

ASSEMBLY

1. Attach the nylon inserts to the shift forks and install the selector arm plates into the shift forks.

2. If removed, apply sealer to the edges of the shift rail plug, then carefully tap the plug into place.

3. Coat the shift rail and the rail bores with petroleum jelly, then slide the rail into the cover until the end is flush with the inside edge of the cover.

4. With the offset of the 1st/2nd shift fork facing the rear of the cover, install the fork into the cover and push the shift rail through the fork.

NOTE: *The the 1st/2nd fork is the larger of the two forks.*

5. Place the selector arm and the C-shaped interlock plate into the cover, then insert the shift rail through the arm.

NOTE: *The widest part of the interlock plate must face away from the cover and the selector arm roll pin hole must face downward, toward the rear of the cover.*

6. With the offset of the 3rd/4th shift fork facing the rear of the cover, install the fork into the cover. The 3rd/4th shift fork selector arm plate must be positioned under the 1st/2nd arm plate. Push the shift rail completely forward, through the 3rd/4th fork and into the cover bore.

7. Rotate the shift rail so that the forward selector arm plate faces away from but parallel to the cover.

8. After aligning the holes, install the selector arm-to-shift rail roll pin.

NOTE: *To prevent the roll pin from contacting the selector arm plates when shifting, the roll pin must be installed flush with the surface of the selector arm.*

9. Install the O-ring into the groove of the shift rail oil seal.

10. Installation of the shift rail oil seal should be performed as follows:

a. Install the Kent-Moore tool No. J-26628-2 over the threaded end of the shift rail.

b. Lubricate the lip of the oil seal with petroleum jelly.

c. Slide the seal over the protector tool and onto the shift rail.

d. Using the Kent-Moore seal installer tool No. J-26628-1, seat the seal in the cover.

CLEANING AND INSPECTION

The parts (except the nylon or plastic) should be thoroughly cleaned in cleaning solvent. The nylon or plastic parts, which are to be reused should just be wiped clean with a cloth. The assembled roller bearings should be dried with compressed air.

CAUTION: *Do not spin the bearings with the compressed air as they could shatter and cause personal injury. The individual bearing rollers, washers and thrust bearings should be allowed to air dry after cleaning, though they may be wiped with a clean cloth.*

Inspect the parts for excessive wear and/or damage such as scoring, cracks, nicks or rough edges; replace the defective parts. To check the condition of the assembled bearings, first clean and dry them, then coat the bearings with light engine oil. Slowly spin the bearings by hand and check for any signs of roughness. If the bearing does not feel perfectly smooth, it should be replaced.

5-Speed (69.5mm) Transmission Overhaul

Transmission Case

DISASSEMBLY

NOTE: *The use of an arbor press is required to properly disassemble and assemble this transmission. Read the entire procedure carefully before starting the job.*

1. Remove the drain plug and allow the lubricant to drain from the case.
2. Remove the throwout bearing and the fork from the transmission as outlined in the appropriate car section.
3. Remove the drive gear bearing retainer. If damaged, remove the ball stud.
4. Remove the Belleville spring from the front of the drive gear bearing.
5. Remove the bolt, the retainer and the speedometer driven gear from the side of the case.
6. Remove the shift lever quadrant from the extension housing.
7. Remove the back up light switch.
8. Remove the extension housing bolts and the housing.
9. Remove the snaprings, the speedometer drive gear, the spacer and the bearing from the mainshaft.
10. Remove the snapring, then the thrust washer and the lock ball from the driveshaft.
11. Remove the large snapring from the main drive gear bearing.
12. Remove the following components from the case as an assembly:
    a. The center support
    b. The mainshaft
    c. The countergear
    d. The drive gear
13. Using a drift punch and a hammer, carefully drive the roll pins from the 1st/2nd, the 3rd/4th and the 5th/Reverse shift forks. Support the shaft ends with a bar or a block of wood to prevent damage to these components.
14. Remove the detent spring plate mounting bolts, the detent spring plate, the 3 springs and the balls from the center support.
15. Remove the shifter shafts from the center support, the shift forks from the shafts and the interlock pins from the center support.
16. Move the 1st/2nd synchronizer sleeve to the 1st gear position and the 3rd/4th synchronizer sleeve into the 3rd gear position.
17. Using the Kent-Moore holdling fixture tool No. J-29768, install it on the end of the drive gear shaft and countergear. Remove the countergear retaining nut and the washer.
18. Using a puller, remove the ball bearing and the 5th speed gear from the countershaft.
19. Remove the 5th gear, the blocking ring and the needle bearing from the mainshaft.
20. Remove the self locking nut from the Reverse idler gear shaft.
21. Remove the thrust washers and the Reverse idler gear from the Reverse idler gear shaft.
22. Bend the locking retainer of the mainshaft nut away from the nut, then remove the mainshaft nut.
23. Remove the 5th/Reverse synchronizer locking retainer, the 4th/Reverse synchronizer assembly, the Reverse gear, the needle bearing, the collar and the thrust washer from the mainshaft.
24. Remove the Reverse gear from the countergear and the holding fixture (installed during Step 17).
25. Move the synchronizer sleeves back to their Neutral positions.
26. Expand the countergear bearing snapring (using snapring pliers) and gently tap on the front of the center support. Expand the mainshaft bearing snapring and move the mainshaft inward then remove the countergear and the mainshaft.
27. Remove the drive gear, the needle bearing and the blocking ring from the end of the mainshaft.

ASSEMBLY

1. If removed, install the countergear and the mainshaft ssnaprings into the center support. Also, install the Reverse idler shaft into the center support.
2. Install the drive gear onto the front of the mainshaft and engage it with the countergear.
3. Install the holding fixture in the same manner as the disassembly, in Step 17.
4. With the mainshaft and the countergears meshed, slide the center support onto the mainshaft. Expand the mainshaft snapring and continue to push the center support on until the mainshaft bearing groove aligns with the snapring. Release the mainshaft snapring to lock the mainshaft bearing into place. Repeat the same procedure to seat the countergear snap ring.
5. Move the synchronizer sleeves to engage both the 1st and the 3rd gear tangs in order to lock the gears.

6. Install the Reverse gear onto the countergear.

7. Install the thrust washer on the mainshaft (with the oil groove facing the rear), then install the collar, the needle bearing and the Reverse gear onto the mainshaft.

8. Install the 5th/Reverse synchronizer (with the face of the higher clutch hub boss facing the Reverse gears).

9. Install the locking retainer and the mainshaft nut onto the mainshaft, then torque the nut to 94 ft. lbs. and then bend the locking retainer tabs to lock the nut.

10. Install the thrust washers and the Reverse idler gear on the Reverse idler gear shaft. Thread a new self locking nut onto the Reverse idler shaft and torque the nut to 80 ft. lbs.

NOTE: *The flange of the plate side thrust washer must be fitted to the center support.*

11. Install the synchronizer blocking ring and the 5th speed gear (with the needle bearings) onto the mainshaft.

12. Install the 5th speed gear (of the countergear), the ball bearing, the washer and a new self locking nut onto the rear of the countergear, then torque the nut to 80 ft. lbs.

13. Remove the holding fixture and move the synchronizer sleeves back to their Neutral positions.

14. Grease the interlock pins and install them into the center support.

15. Place the shift forks into position on the synchronizer sleeves. Install the shifter shafts through their respective forks from the rear of the center support, except the 5th/Reverse shaft, which is installed from the front of the support.

16. Install the three detent balls, the springs, the detent plate gasket and the detent plate, then torque the detent plate bolts to 14 ft. lbs.

17. Using a drift punch and a hammer, carefully install the retaining pins into the shift forks. Remember to support the shafts with a bar or a block of wood to prevent damage.

18. If removed, lubricate the countergear needle bearing and install it into the front of the case. The bearing should be driven into place while a socket is positioned on the outer bearing race.

19. Install a new center support-to-case gasket on the case and the center support/mainshaft/countergear/drive gear assembly into the case.

20. Install the large snapring onto the shaft of the drive gear bearing.

21. Install the lock ball, the thrust washer and the snapring onto the mainshaft.

22. Using a feeler gauge, check the clearance between the 5th speed gear (of the mainshaft) and its thrust washer. The clearance should be 0.25-0.40mm. If necessary, adjust the clearance by purchasing a thrust washer of the correct thickness which will replace the existing washer. The thrust washers are available in thickness ranging from 7.8-8.3mm in 0.08mm increments.

NOTE: *Use care when removing and installing the snapring; it must be replaced if it becomes distorted.*

23. Install these parts on the mainshaft behind the 5th gear ssnapring, in this order:

a. The ball bearing.
b. The snapring.
c. The speedometer gear clip.
d. The speedometer drive gear.

24. Using a new gasket, attach the extension housing to the center support and torque the bolts to 27 ft. lbs.

25. Using a new gasket, install the shift lever quadrant onto the extension housing and torque the bolts to 14 ft. lbs.

26. Install the speedometer driven gear and torque the bolt to 14 ft. lbs.

27. Install the back up light switch into the extension housing.

28. Install the belleville washer in the front of the drive gear bearing.

NOTE: *The dished side of the washer should face the bearing.*

29. Using a new gasket, install the drive gear bearing retainer. Before installing the three lower bearing retainer bolts, coat the threads with Permatex® No. 2 sealer (or its equivalent). Torque the bearing retainer bolts to 14 ft. lbs.

30. Install the throw out bearing and the fork.

31. Install the transmission according to the procedure in the Chevette car section.

Mainshaft

DISASSEMBLY

1. Using an arbor press and the Kent-Moore tool No. J-22912-01, remove the mainshaft rear bearing.

2. Remove the thrust washer, the 1st speed gear, the needle bearings and the spacer.

3. Remove the 1st/2nd synchronizer assembly, the 2nd speed gear and the needle bearings.

4. Remove the snapring from in front of the 3rd/4th synchronizer and slide the synchronizer off the mainshaft.

Drive Gear Bearing

REMOVAL AND INSTALLATION

1. Remove the snapring from the drive gear shaft.

2. Using an arbor press and the Kent-Moore tool No. J-22912-01, press the drive gear shaft through the bearing.

3. To install, reverse the removal procedures.

Countergear Bearing

REMOVAL AND INSTALLATION

The bearing is removed in the same manner as the drive gear bearing, using the same special tool and an arbor press. Note that the groove on the bearing is installed towards the rear of the transmission.

Extension Housing Or Drive Gear Retainer Seals

REMOVAL AND INSTALLATION

Using a small pry bar, pry the seals from the housing. Install the new seals by carefully tapping them into place.

Mainshaft

ASSEMBLY

1. Install the 3rd speed gear (with the needle bearings) onto the front of the mainshaft.

NOTE: *The coned side of the gear is installed toward the front of the mainshaft.*

2. Install the 3rd/4th synchronizer assembly onto the mainshaft, with the large chamfered end facing the front of the case; retain the synchronizer with the snapring.

3. Install the 2nd speed gear (with the needle bearings) onto the rear of the mainshaft.

NOTE: *The coned side of the gear is installed facing the rear of the mainshaft.*

4. Install the 1st/2nd synchronizer assembly onto the mainshaft, with the large chamfered end facing the rear of the case.

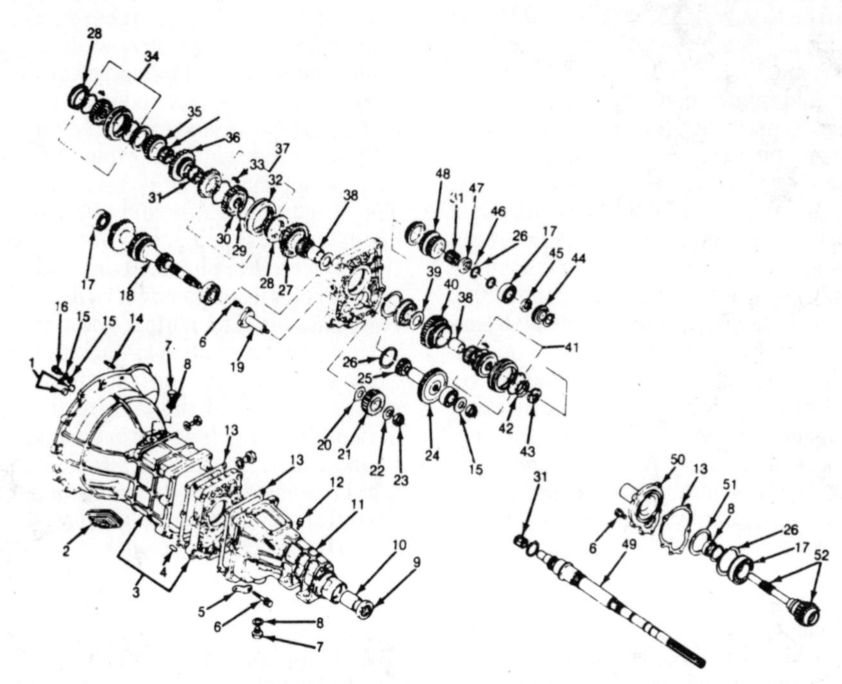

1. Shift rod plug
2. Dust cover
3. Case with center support
4. Pin
5. Return spring bracket
6. Bolt
7. Plug
8. Seal
9. Seal
10. Bushing
11. Extension
12. Ventilator
13. Gasket
14. Starter locating stud
15. Washer
16. Shift fork support
17. Ball bearing assembly
18. Countergear
19. Reverse idler shaft
20. Reverse idler front thrust washer
21. Reverse idler gear
22. Reverse idler rear thrust washer
23. Self-locking nut
24. 5th speed gear
25. Reverse gear
26. Snap-ring
27. 1st speed gear assembly
28. Blocking ring
29. Synchronizer insert spring
30. Synchronizer hub
31. Needle bearing
32. Synchronizer sleeve
33. Synchronizer insert (key)
34. 3rd–4th synchronizer assembly
35. 3rd gear assembly
36. 2nd gear assembly
37. 1st–2nd synchronizer assembly
38. Collar
39. Thrust washer
40. Reverse gear (mainshaft)
41. 5th-reverse synchronizer assembly
42. Mainshaft lockwasher
43.. Mainshaft nut
44. Speedometer drive gear
45. Spacer
46. Ball
47. Selective thrust washer
48. 5th speed gear (mainshaft)
49. Mainshaft
50. Drive gear bearing retainer
51. Belleville spring
52. Main drive gear and shaft assembly

Exploded view of the 69.5mm Five speed transmission

5. Install the 1st speed gear (with the spacer and the needle bearings), with the coned end facing the front of the case.

6. Install the 1st gear thrust washer, with the slots of the washer facing the gear.

7. Press the rear bearing onto the mainshaft according to the previous procedure under "Removal and Installation".

CLUTCH

The purpose of the clutch is to disconnect and connect engine power at the transmission. A car at rest requires a lot of engine torque to get all that weight moving. An internal combustion engine does not develop a high starting torque (unlike steam engines), so it must be allowed to operate without any load until it builds up enough torque to move the car. Torque increases with engine rpm. The clutch allows the engine to build up torque by physically disconnecting the engine from the transmission, relieving the engine of any load or resistance. The transfer of engine power to the transmission (the load) must be smooth and gradual; if it weren't, drive line components would wear out or break quickly. This gradual power transfer is made possible by gradually releasing the clutch pedal. The clutch disc and pressure plate are the connecting link between the engine and transmission. When the clutch pedal is released, the disc and plate contact each other (clutch engagement), physically joining the engine and transmission. When the pedal is pushed in, the disc and plate separate (the clutch is disengaged), disconnecting the engine from the transmission.

The clutch assembly consists of the flywheel, the clutch disc, the clutch pressure plate, the throwout bearing and fork, the actuating linkage and the pedal. The flywheel and clutch pressure plate (driving members) are connected to the engine crankshaft and rotate with it. The clutch disc is located between the flywheel and pressure plate, and splined to the transmission shaft. A driving member is one that is attached to the engine and transfers engine power to a driven member (clutch disc) on the transmission shaft. A driving member (pressure plate) rotates (drives) a driven member (clutch disc) on contact and, in so doing, turns the transmission shaft. There is a circular diaphragm spring within the pressure plate cover (transmission side). In a relaxed state (when the clutch pedal is fully released), this spring is convex; that is, it is dished outward toward the transmission. Pushing in the clutch pedal actuates an attached linkage rod. Connected to the other end of this rod is the throwout bearing fork. The throwout bearing is attached to the fork. When the clutch pedal is depressed, the clutch linkage pushes the fork and bearing forward to contact the diaphragm spring of the pressure plate. The outer edges of the spring are secured to the pressure plate and are pivoted on rings so that when the center of the spring is compressed by the throwout bearing, the outer edges bow outward and, by so doing, pull the pressure plate in the same direction: away from the clutch disc. This action separates the disc from the plate, disengaging the clutch and allowing the transmission to be shifted into another gear. A coil type clutch return spring attached to the clutch pedal arm permits full release of the pedal. Releasing the pedal pulls the throwout bearing away from the diaphragm spring resulting in a reversal of spring position. As bearing pressure is gradually released from the spring center, the outer edges of the spring bow outward, pushing the pressure plate into closer contact with the clutch disc. As the disc and plate move closer together, friction between the two increases and slippage is reduced until, when full spring pressure is applied (by fully releasing the pedal), The speed of the disc and plate are the same. This stops all slipping, creating a direct connection between the plate and disc which results in the transfer of power from the engine to the transmission. The clutch disc is now rotating with the pressure plate at engine speed and, because it is splined to the transmission shaft, the shaft now turns at the same engine speed. Understanding clutch operation can be rather difficult at first; if you're still confused after reading this, consider the following analogy. The action of the diaphragm spring can be compared to that of an oil can bottom. The bottom of an oil can is shaped very much like the clutch diaphragm spring and pushing in on the can bottom and then releasing it produces a similar effect. As mentioned earlier, the clutch pedal return spring permits full release of the pedal and reduces linkage slack due to wear. As the linkage wears, clutch free-pedal travel will increase and free-travel will decrease as the clutch wears. Free-travel is actually throwout bearing lash.

The diaphragm spring type clutches used are available in two different designs: flat diaphragm springs or bent spring. The bent fingers are bent back to create a centrifugal boost ensuring quick re-engagement at higher engine speeds. This design enables pressure plate load to increase as the clutch disc wears and makes low pedal effort possible even with a heavy duty clutch. The throwout bearing used with the bent finger design is 1¼" long and is shorter than the bearing used with the flat finger design. These bearings are not interchangeable. If the longer bearing is used with the bent finger clutch, free-pedal travel will not exist. This results in clutch slippage and rapid wear.

The transmission varies the gear ratio between the engine and rear wheels. It can be shifted to change engine speed as driving conditions and loads change. The transmission allows disengaging and reversing power from the engine to the wheels.

Chevette and Pontiac 1000 manual transmission models use a cable operated, diaphragm spring type clutch. The clutch cable is attached to the clutch pedal at its upper end and is threaded at its lower end where it attaches to the clutch fork. The clutch release fork pivots on a ball stud located opposite the clutch cable attaching point. The pressure plate, clutch disc, and throwout bearing are of conventional design.

When the clutch pedal is depressed, the clutch release fork pivots on the ball stud and pushes the thowout bearing forward. The thowout bearing presses against the inner ends of the pressure plate diaphragm spring fingers to release pressure on the clutch disc, disengaging the clutch. The return spring preloads the clutch release mechanism to remove any looseness. Slutch pedal free-play will increase with release mechanism wear and will decrease with clutch disc wear.

Clutch Disc and Pressure Plate

REMOVAL AND INSTALLATION

Gasoline Engine

1. Raise the car.
2. Remove the transmission.
3. Remove the throwout bearing from the clutch fork by sliding the fork off the ball stud against spring tension. If the ball stud is to be replaced, remove the locknut and stud from the bellhousing.
4. If the balance marks on the pressure plate and the flywheel are not easily seen, remark them with paint or centerpunch.
5. Alternately loosen the pressure plate-to-flywheel attaching bolts one turn at a time until spring tension is released.
6. Support the pressure plate and cover assembly, then remove the bolts and the clutch assembly.

WARNING: *Do not disassemble the clutch cover and pressure plate for repair. If defective, replace the assembly.*

7. Align the balance marks on the clutch assembly and flywheel. Place the clutch disc on the pressure plate with the long end of the splined hub facing forward and the damper springs inside the pressure plate. Insert a used or dummy shaft through the cover and clutch disc.

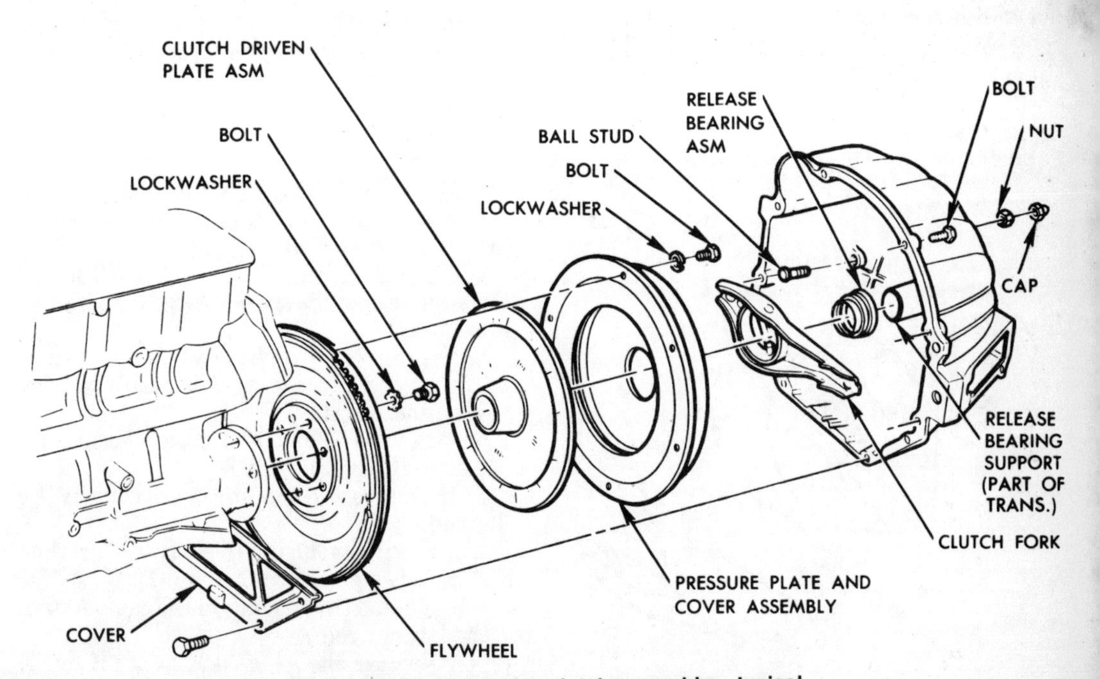

Four speed transmission clutch assembly—typical

8. Position the assembly against the flywheel and insert the dummy shaft into the pilot bearing in the crankshaft.

9. Align the balance marks and install the pressure plate-to-flywheel bolts finger tight.

WARNING: *Tighten all bolts evenly and gradually until tight to avoid possible clutch distortion. Torque the bolts to 18 ft. lbs. and remove the dummy shaft.*

10. Pack the groove on the inside of the throwout bearing with graphite grease. Coat the fork groove wnd ball stud depression with the lubricant.

11. Install the throwout bearing and release fork assembly in the bellhousing with the fork spring hooked under the ball stud and the fork spring fingers inside the bearing groove.

12. Position the transmission and clutch housing and install the clutch housing attaching bolts and lockwashers. Torque the bolts to 25 ft. lbs. (33 Nm).

13. Complete the transmission installation.

NOTE: *Check position of the engine in the front mounts and realign as necessary.*

A special gauge (part no. J-28449 or its equivalent) is necessary to adjust the ball position.

14. Perform Initial Ball Stud Adjustment and Clutch Cable Attachment and Adjustment. Adjust clutch pedal free-play if necessary.

15. Lower the car and check operation of the clutch and transmission.

Diesel Engine

1. Remove the transmission as described later in this chapter.

2. Mark the clutch assembly to flywheel so that it can be installed in the original position.

3. Install aligning Tool J-24547 or an appropriate dummy shaft through the pressure plate and disc.

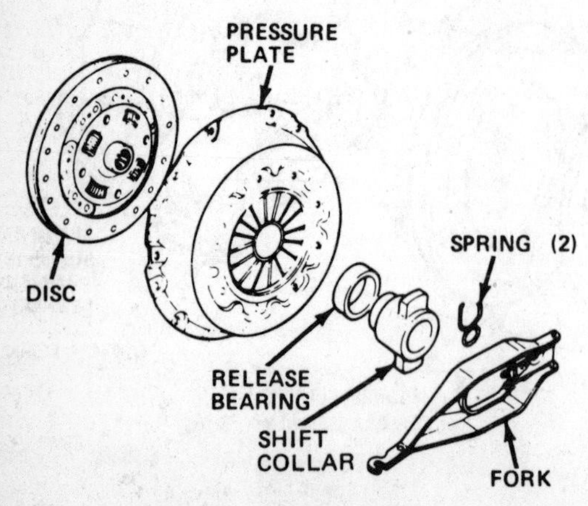

Clutch assembly—diesel engine

4. Remove the release bearing to fork retaining springs and remove the release bearing with the support.

5. Remove the shift fork from the transmission ball stud.

6. Installation is the reverse of removal. Install the clutch assembly in the original position while aligning with Tool J-24547 or equivalent. Tighten the bolts evenly to 14 ft. lbs.

INITIAL BALL STUD ADJUSTMENT

4- and 5-Speed Gas Engine

1. Install throwout bearing assembly, release fork, and ball stud to the transmission.

2. Install and secure the transmission to the engine.

3. Cycle the clutch once.

4. Place the special gauge (Part No. J-28449) so that the flat end is against the front face of the clutch housing and the hooked end is located at the bottom depression in the clutch fork.

5. Turn the ball stud inward by hand until the throwout bearing makes contact with the clutch spring.

6. Install the locknut and tighten it to 25 ft. lbs. (33 Nm), being careful not to change the ball stud adjustment.

7. Remove the gauge by pulling outward at the housing end.

CLUTCH CABLE ATTACHMENT AND ADJUSTMENT

1976-77

These adjustments are made before the return spring is installed and with the clutch cable attached to the clutch pedal at its upper end.

1. Place the clutch cable through the hole in the clutch fork.

2. Pull the clutch cable until the clutch pedal is firmly against the pedal bumper and hold it in position.

3. Push the release fork forward until the throwout bearing contacts the clutch spring fingers and hold it in position.

4. Thread the nut or the cable until it bottoms out against the spherical surface of the release fork.

5. Depress the clutch pedal to the floor a minimum of 4 times to establish cable position at clearance points.

6. To obtain the correct clutch pedal lash, use either Step 7 or Step 8.

7. See View **A** of the assompanying illustration.

a. Place a 4.35mm thick gauge or shim stock against surface **D** of nut **B**.

b. Thread the locknut on the cable **A** until the locknut contacts the gauge.

c. Remove the gauge and back off nut **B** until it contacts the locknut.

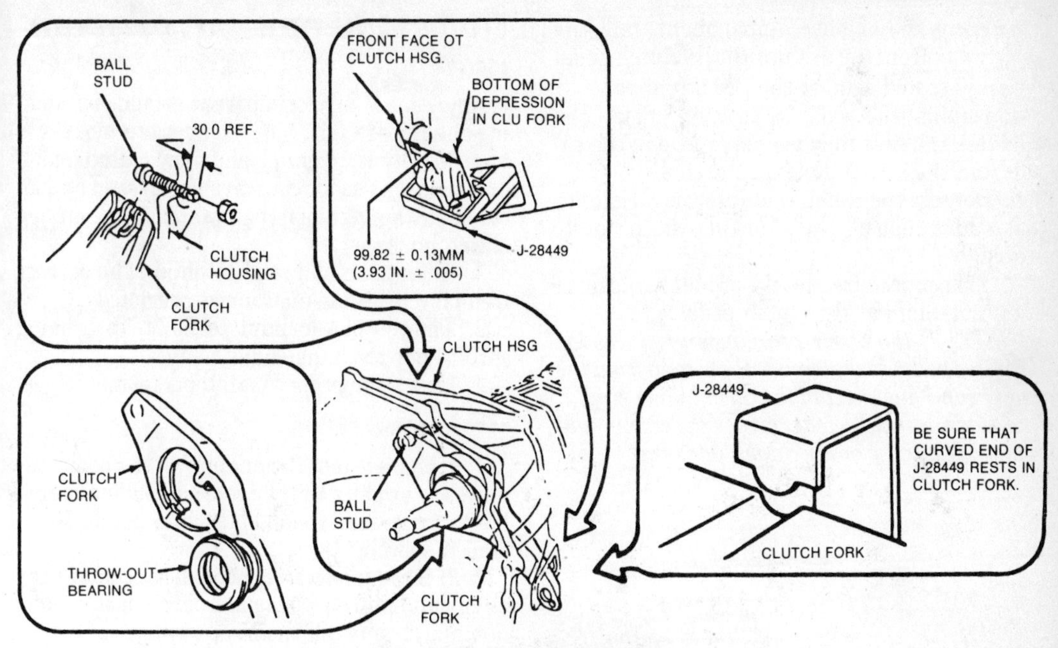

Ball stud adjustment

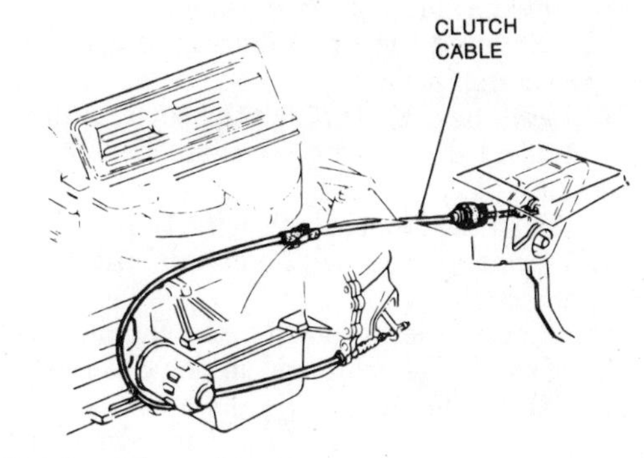

Clutch cable positioning

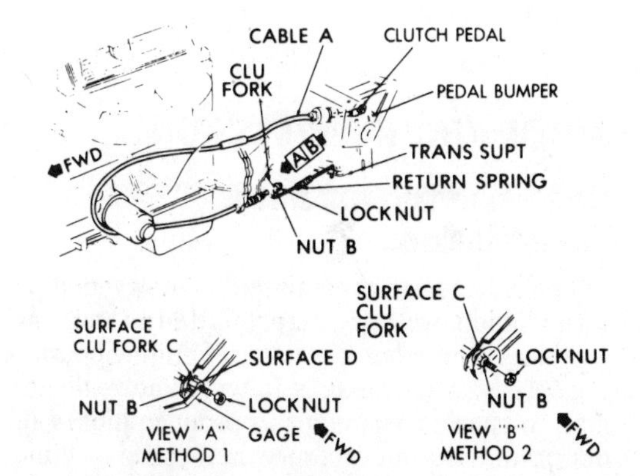

Clutch cable adjustment 1976–77

d. Tighten the locknut to 4 ft. lbs.

8. See View **B** of the accompanying illustration.

a. Turn nut **B** 4 turns counterclockwise.

The clutch fork locknut is a 10 mm nut

b. Thread the locknut on the cable **A** until the locknut contacts nut **B**.

c. Tighten the locknut to 4 ft. lbs.

9. Attach the return spring.

10. This procedure should yield 21mm ± 6mm lash at the clutch pedal.

1978 and Later

The following adjustments are to be made with the cable and loose parts assembled to the front of the dash and the cable attached to the clutch pedal.

1. Place the cable through the hole in the clutch fork and properly seat it.
2. Install the return spring.

3. From the engine compartment, pull the cable away from the dash until the clutch pedal is firmly seated against the pedal bumper.

4. Holding the pedal in position, install the circlip in the first fully visible groove in the cable from the sleeve. Release the cable.

5. Depress the clutch cable at least 4 times to make sure that all the elements are properly seated.

6. This procedure should produce a lash of 21mm ± 6mm at the clutch pedal.

NOTE: *If the above procedure produces excessive pedal lash, remove the circlip from the cable and move it into the dash by one ring. If the lash is insufficient remove the circlip and move it away from the dash one ring.*

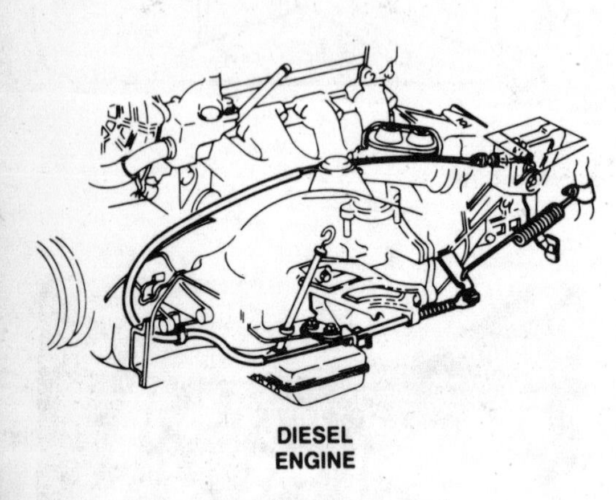

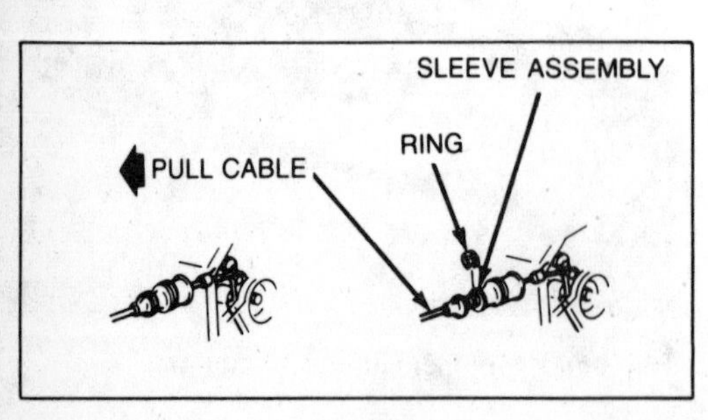

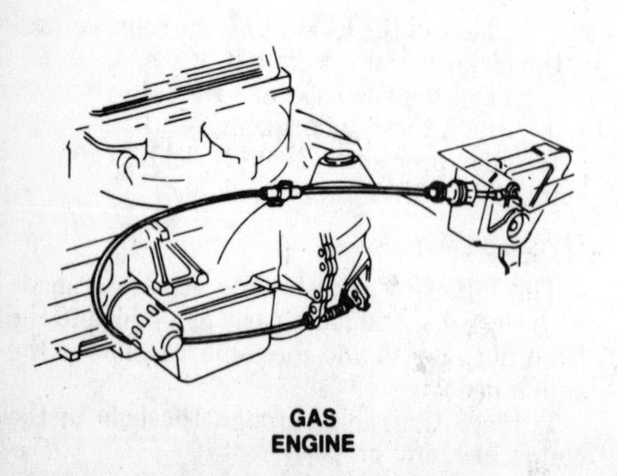

Clutch cable adjustment—1978 and later

CLUTCH PEDAL FREE-PLAY ADJUSTMENT

1976-77

Adjustment for normal wear is made by turning the release fork ball stud counterclockwise to give 21mm ± 6mm lash at the clutch pedal.

1. Loosen the locknut on the ball stud end located to the right of the transmission on the clutch housing.

2. Adjust the ball stud to obtain the correct free-play (lash) as mentioned previously.

3. Tighten the locknut to 25 ft. lbs., being careful not to change adjustment.

4. Check for proper clutch operation.

1978 and Later

1. If there is insufficient play in the pedal, remove the circlip from the cable and allow the cable to move into the dash by one notch. Reinstall the circlip.

2. If there is excessive pedal lash, remove the circlip and pull the cable out of the dash by one notch and reinstall the circlip ring.

CLUTCH CABLE REPLACEMT

1. Disconnect the return spring and clutch cable at the clutch release fork.

2. Disconnect the cable form the upper end of the clutch pedal.

3. Pull the cable through the body reinforcement and disconnect it from the fender retainer.

4. Push the new cable through the body reinforcement and attach the cable end to the clutch pedal.

5. Route the cable down to the clutch release fork. Install the cable end in the release fork and install the nuts.

6. Perform Initial Ball Stud Adjustment and Clutch Cable Attachment and Adjustment. Also, adjust clutch pedal free-play if necessary.

AUTOMATIC TRANSMISSION

Understanding Automatic Transmissions

The automatic transmission allows engine torque and power to be transmitted to the rear wheels within a narrow range of engine operating speeds. The transmission will allow the engine to turn fast enough to produce plenty of power and torque at very low speeds, while keeping it at a sensible rpm at high vehicle speeds. The transmission performs this job entirely without driver assistance. The transmission uses a light fluid as the medium for the transmission of power. This fluid also works in the operation of various hydraulic control cir-

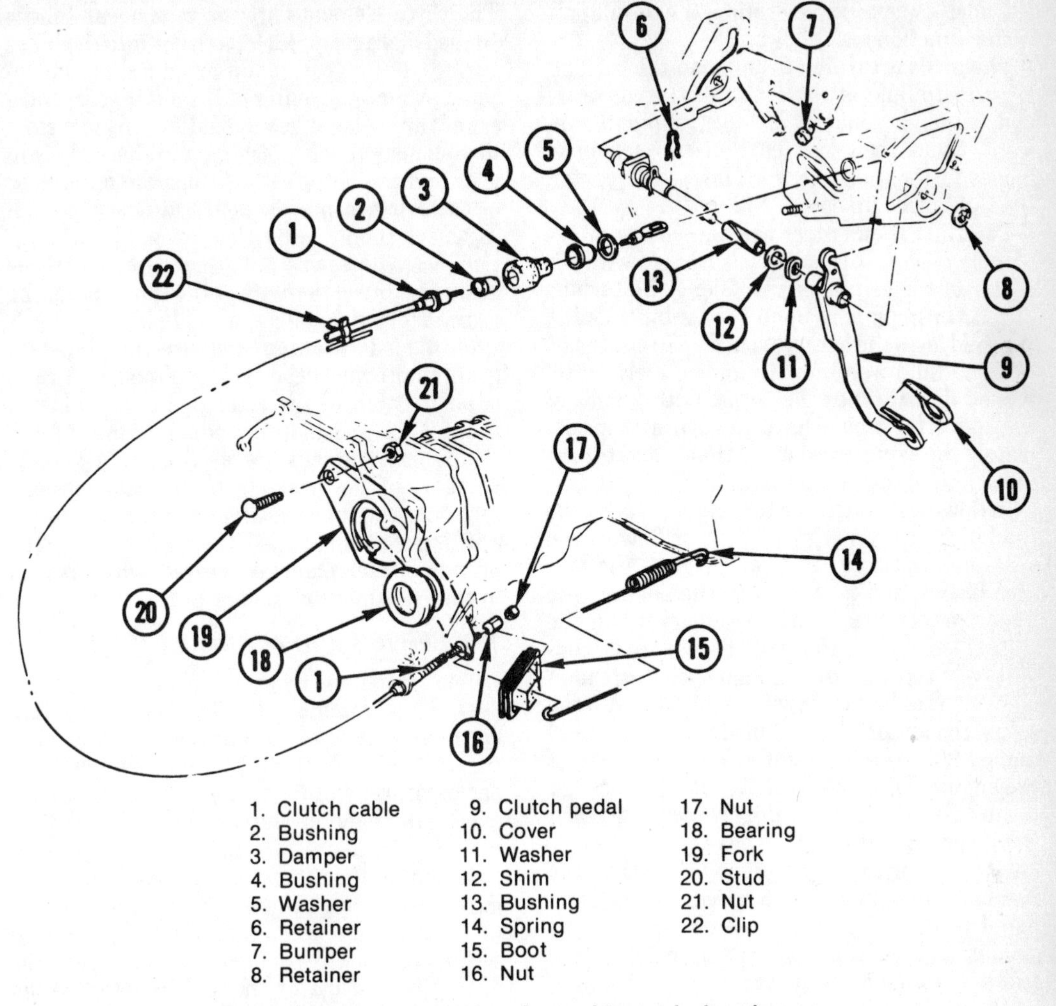

Clutch linkage components—4-speed transmission shown

cuits and as a lubricant. Because the transmission fluid performs all of these three functions, trouble within the unit can easily travel from one part to another. For this reason, and because of the complexity and unusual operating principles of the transmission, a very sound understanding of the basic principles of operation will simplify troubleshooting.

THE TORQUE CONVERTER

The torque converter replaces the conventional clutch. It has three functions:

1. It allows the engine to idle with the vehicle at a standstill, even with the transmission in gear.

2. It allows the transmission to shift from range to range smoothly, without requiring that the driver close the throttle during the shift.

3. It multiplies engine torque to an increasing extent as vehicle speed drops and throttle opening is increased. This has the effect of making the transmission more responsive and reduces the amount of shifting required.

The torque converter is a metal case which is shaped like a sphere that has been flattened on opposite sides. It is bolted to the rear end of the engine's crankshaft. Generally, the entire metal case rotates at engine speed and serves as the engine's flywheel.

The case contains three sets of blades. One set is attached directly to the case. This set forms the torus or pump. Another set is directly connected to the output shaft, and forms the turbine. The third set is mounted on a hub which, in turn, is mounted on a stationary shaft through a one-way clutch. This third set is known as the stator.

A pump, which is driven by the converter hub at engine speed, keeps the torque converter full of transmission fluid at all times. Fluid flows continuously through the unit to provide cooling.

Under low speed acceleration, the torque converter functions as follows:

The torus is turning faster than the turbine. It picks up fluid at the center of the converter and, through centrifugal force, slings it outward. Since the outer edge of the converter moves faster than the portions at the center, the fluid picks up speed.

The fluid then enters the outer edge of the turbine blades. It then travels back toward the center of the converter case along the turbine blades. In impinging upon the turbine blades, the fluid loses the energy picked up in the torus.

If the fluid were now to immediately be returned directly into the torus, both halves of the converter would have to turn at approximately the same speed at all times, and torque input and output would both be the same.

In flowing through the torus and turbine, the fluid picks up two types of flow, or flow in two separate directions. It flows through the turbine blades, and it spins with the engine. The stator, whose blades are stationary when the vehicle is being accelerated at low speeds, converts one type of flow into another. Instead of allowing the fluid to flow straight back into the torus, the stator's curved blades turn the fluid almost 90° toward the direction of rotation of the engine. Thus the fluid does not flow as fast toward the torus, but is already spinning when the torus picks it up. This has the effect of allowing the torus to turn much faster than the turbine. This difference in speed may be compared to the difference in speed between the smaller and larger gears in any gear train. The result is that engine power output is higher, and engine torque is multiplied.

As the speed of the turbine increases, the fluid spins faster and faster in the direction of engine rotation. As a result, the ability of the stator to redirect the fluid flow is reduced. Under cruising conditions, the stator is eventually forced to rotate on its one-way clutch in the direction of engine rotation. Under these conditions, the torque converter begins to behave almost like a solid shaft, with the torus and turbine speeds being almost equal.

THE PLANETARY GEARBOX

The ability of the torque converter to multiply engine torque is limited. Also, the unit tends to be more efficient when the turbine is rotating at relatively high speeds. Therefore, a planetary gearbox is used to carry the power output of the turbine to the driveshaft.

Planetary gears function very similarly to conventional transmission gears. However, their construction is different in that three elements make up one gear system, and, in that all three elements are different from one another. The three elements are: an outer gear that is shaped like a hoop, with teeth cut into the inner surface; a sun gear, mounted on a shaft and located at the very center of the outer gear; and a set of three planet gears, held by pins in a ring-like planet carrier, meshing with both the sun gear and the outer gear. Either the outer gear or the sun gear may be held stationary, providing more than one possible torque multiplication factor for each set of gears. Also, if all three gears are forced to rotate at the same speed, the gearset forms, in effect, a solid shaft.

Most modern automatics use the planetary gears to provide either a single reduction ratio of about 1.8:1, or two reduction gears: a low of about 2.5:1, and an intermediate of about 1.5:1. Bands and clutches are used to hold various portions of the gearsets to the transmission case or to the shaft on which they are mounted. Shifting is accomplished, then, by changing the portion of each planetary gearset which is held to the transmission case or to the shaft.

THE SERVOS AND ACCUMULATORS

The servos are hydraulic pistons and cylinders. They resemble the hydraulic actuators used on many familiar machines, such as bulldozers. Hydraulic fluid enters the cylinder, under pressure, and forces the piston to move to engage the band or clutches.

The accumulators are used to cushion the engagement of the servos. The transmission fluid must pass through the accumulator on the way to the servo. The accumulator housing contains a thin piston which is sprung away from the discharge passage of the accumulator. When fluid passes through the accumulator on the way to the servo, it must move the piston against spring pressure, and this action smooths out the action of the servo.

THE HYDRAULIC CONTROL SYSTEM

The hydraulic pressure used to operate the servos comes from the main transmission oil pump. This fluid is channeled to the various servos through the shift valves. There is generally a manual shift valve which is operated by the transmission selector lever and an automatic shift valve for each automatic upshift the transmission provides: i.e., 2-speed automatics have a low/high shift valve, while 3-speeds have a 1-2 valve, and a 2-3 valve.

There are two pressures which effect the operation of these valves. One is the governor pressure which is affected by vehicle speed. The other is the modulator pressure which is affected by intake manifold vacuum or throttle position. Governor pressure rises with an increase in vehicle speed, and modulator pressure rises as the throttle is opened wider. By responding

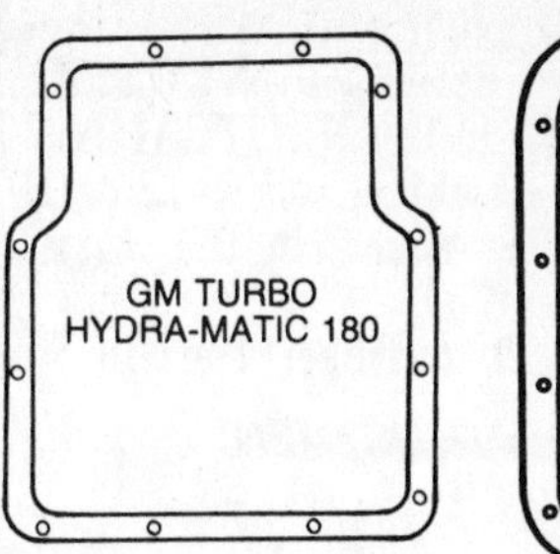

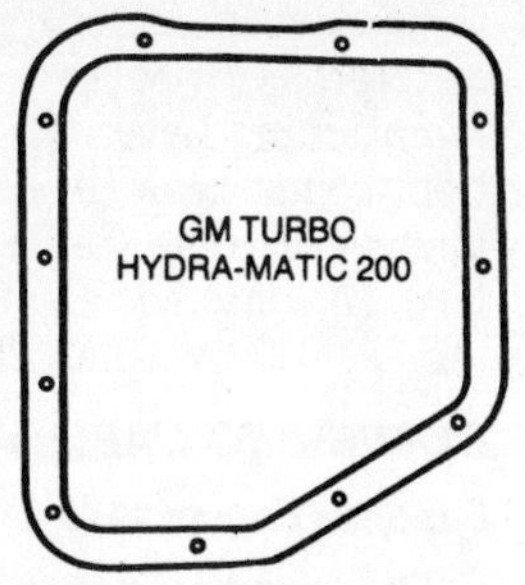

The transmissions can be identified by the shape of the pan

to these two pressures, the shift valves cause the upshift points to be delayed with increased throttle opening to make the best use of the engine's power output.

Most transmissions also make use of an auxiliary circuit for downshifting. This circuit may be actuated by the throttle linkage or the vacuum line which actuates the modulator, or by a cable or solenoid. It applies pressure to a special downshift surface on the shift valve or valves.

The transmission modulator also governs the line pressure, used to actuate the servos. In this way, the clutches and bands will be actuated with a force matching the torque output of the engine.

Application

Chevettes and Pontiac 1000s equipped with automatic transmission use either the Turbo Hydra-Matic 200 or 180 automatic transmission. Both units are fully automatic and provide three forward speeds and reverse.

Neutral Saftey/Back-Up Switch

REMOVAL AND INSTALLATION

1. Remove the floor console cover.
2. Disconnect the electrical connectors on the back-up, seat belt warning, and neutral starter contacts on the switch.
3. Place the shift lever in Neutral.
4. Remove the two switch attaching screws and remove the switch.
5. Make sure that the shift lever is in the Neutral position before installing the switch assembly.
6. Place the neutral start switch assembly in position on the shift lever making sure that the pin on the lever is in the slot of the switch.

NOTE: *When installing the same switch, align the contact support slot with the service adjustment hole in the switch and insert a $^3/_{32}$" drill bit to hold the switch in Neutral. Remove the drill bit after the switch is fastened to the shift lever mounting bracket.*

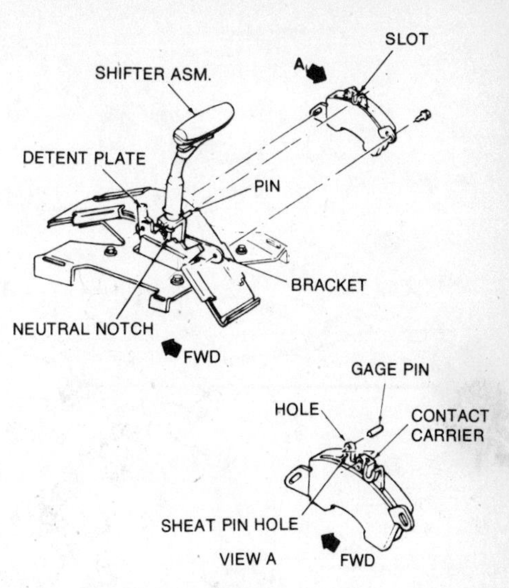

Neutral switch replacement

7. Install the two switch attaching screws.
8. Move the shift lever out of Neutral to shear the plastic pin.
9. Connect the electrical connectors to the switch contacts. Apply the parking brake and start the engine. Check to make sure that the engine starts only in Park or Neutral. Make sure that the backup lights work only in Reverse. Check that the seat belt warning system operates.
10. Stop the engine and install the floor console cover.

SHIFT LINKAGE ADJUSTMENT

1976-81

1. Place the shift lever in the Neutral position of the detent plate.
2. Disconnect the rod from the lower end of the shift lever. Place the transmission lever in the Neutral position. Do this by moving the lever clockwise to the maximum detent (Park), then moving the lever clockwise two (2) detent positions (Neutral).
3. Adjust the rod until the hole in the rod aligns with the pin on the lower end of the shift lever. Install the rod on the pin and secure it by adding the washer and spring clip.

WARNING: *Any inaccuracies in the adjustment may result in premature failure of the transmission due to operation without the controls in full detent. Such operation results in a loss of fluid pressure and in turn, only a partial engagement of the clutches with sufficient pressure to cause apparently normal operation of the vehicle will result in the failure of clutches or various other internal parts after only a few miles of operation.*

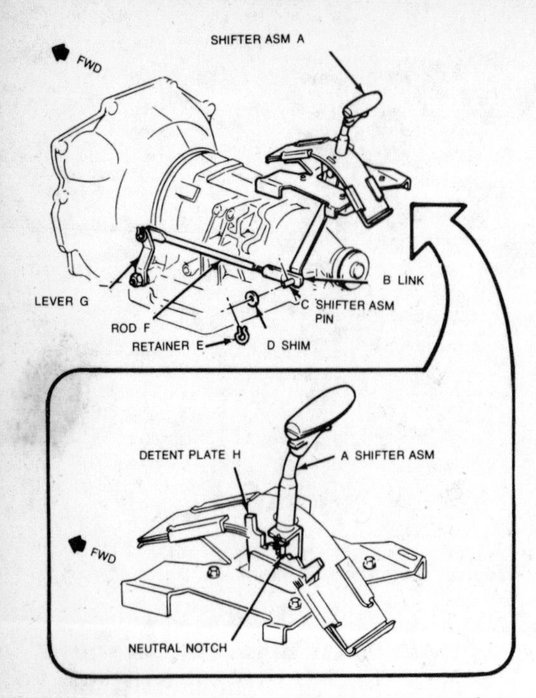

Shift linkage adjustment—1976–81

1982 and Later

1. Position the Shifter Assembly (A) in the NEUTRAL notch of Detent Plate (H).

2. With Link (B) loosely assembled to Rod (F) and Rod (F) attched to Lever (G), put Lever (G) into the NEUTRAL position. Obtain NEUTRAL position by moving Lever (G) clockwise to maximum detent position (PARK), then counterclockwise two detents to NEUTRAL. Maintaining Lever (G) in the NEUTRAL position, adjust Link (B) until the hole in Link (B) aligns with the Shifter Asm Pin (C); install Link (B) onto the Pin (C).

3. Add the washer (D) and insert the clip (E).

DOWNSHIFT CABLE ADJUSTMENT

Gasoline Engine 1976-81

The transmission has a cable between the carburetor linkage and the transmission which provides transmission downshifting.

1. Remove the air cleaner.
2. Disengage the snap lock by pushing up on the bottom. Release the lock and cable.
3. Disconnect the snap lock assembly from the bracket by compressing the locking tabs.
4. Disconnect the cable from the carburetor.
5. Remove the clamp around the oil filler tube. Remove the screw and the washer that secure the cable to the transmission and disconnect the cable.
6. Install a new seal on the cable and lubricate it with transmission fluid.
7. Connect the transmission end of the cable and attach it to the transmission with the screw and washer.
8. Feed the cable in front of the oil filler tube and attach it to the tube with the clamp.
9. Feed the cable through the mounting bracket and snap lock assembly and attach it to the carburetor lever.

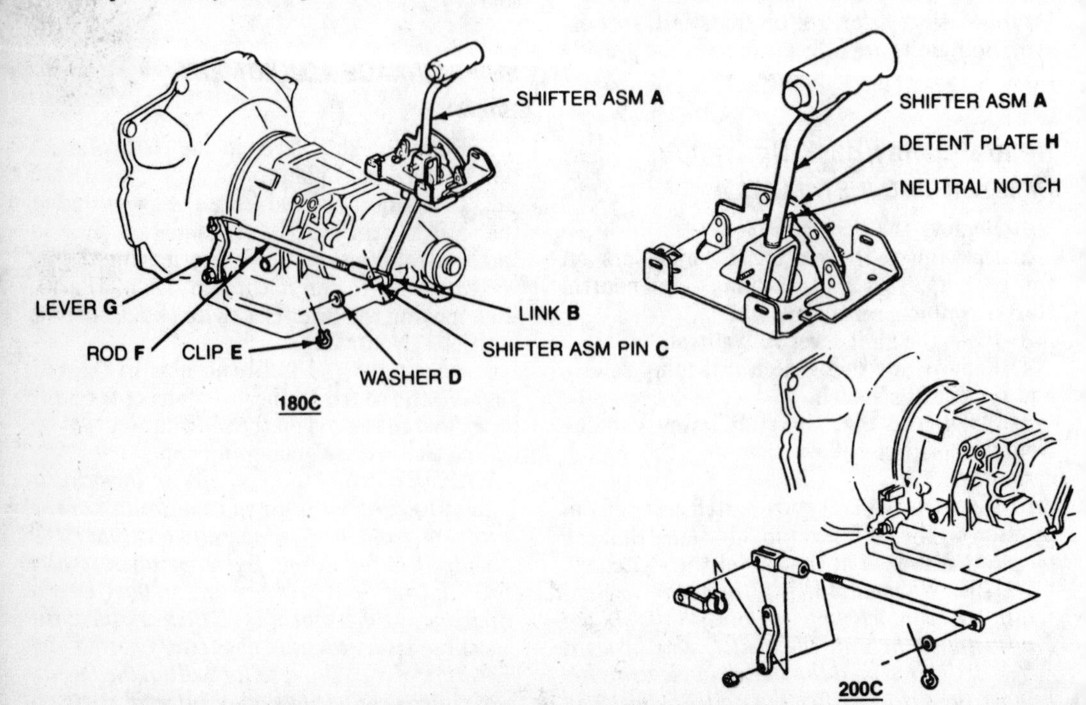

Shift linkage adjustment—1982 and later

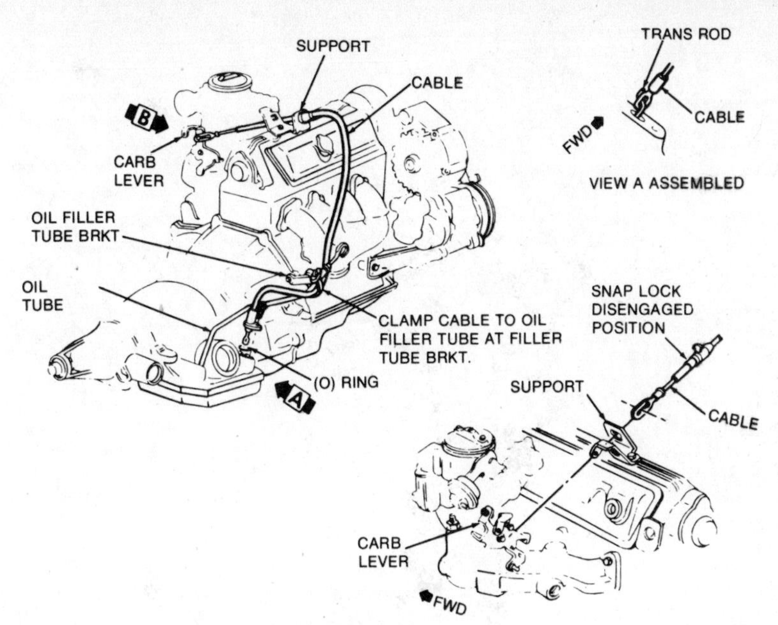

Downshift cable adjustment—1976–81

10. With the cable attached to both the transmission and the carburetor lever, move the carburetor lever to the wide open throttle position. Push the snap lock flush and return carburetor lever to normal position.
11. Install the air cleaner.

1982-87 Gasoline Engine

1. After installation of the cable to the transmission, engine bracket, and throttle lever, check to assure that the cable slider is in the zero or fully re-adjusted position. (if not refer to the readjustment procedure which follows).
2. Rotate the throttle lever to the Full Travel Stop position.

RE-ADJUSTMENT

NOTE: *In case readjustment is necessary because of inadvertent adustment before or during assembly, or for repair, perform the following:*

1. Depress and hold the metal re-adjust tab.
2. Move the slider back through the fitting in direction away from the throttle lever until the slider stops against the fitting.
3. Release the metal re-adjust tab.
4. Repeat Step 2 of the preceding adjustment procedure.

Diesel Engine

1. After installation into the transmission, install the cable fitting into the engine bracket.

NOTE: *The slider must not ratchet through the fitting before or during assembly into the bracket. If this condition exist use the readjustment procedure which follows.*

2. Install the cable terminal to the fuel injection pump lever.
3. Open the injection pump lever to the Full Throttle Stop position to automatically adjust the slider on the cable to the correct setting.

NOTE: *The lock tab must not be depressed during this operation.*

4. Release the injection pump lever.

RE-ADJUSTMENT

NOTE: *In case re-adjustment is necessary because of inadvertent adjustment during assembly, or for repair, perform the following:*

1. Depress and hold the metal lock tab.
2. Move the slider back through the fitting in the direction away from the throttle lever until the slider stops against the fitting.
3. Release the metal lock tab.
4. Repeat steps 2, 3 and 4 of the preceding adjustment procedure.

PAN REMOVAL AND INSTALLATION, FLUID AND FILTER CHANGE

Transmission fluid should be drained while at normal operating temperature.

WARNING: *Transmission fluid temperature can exceed 350°F.*

1. Raise the car and support the transmission with a suitable jack at the transmission vibration damper.
2. Place a receptacle of at least three quarts capacity under the transmission oil pan. Remove the oil pan attaching bolts from the front and side of the pan.
3. Loosen the rear pan attaching bolts approximately 4 turns.

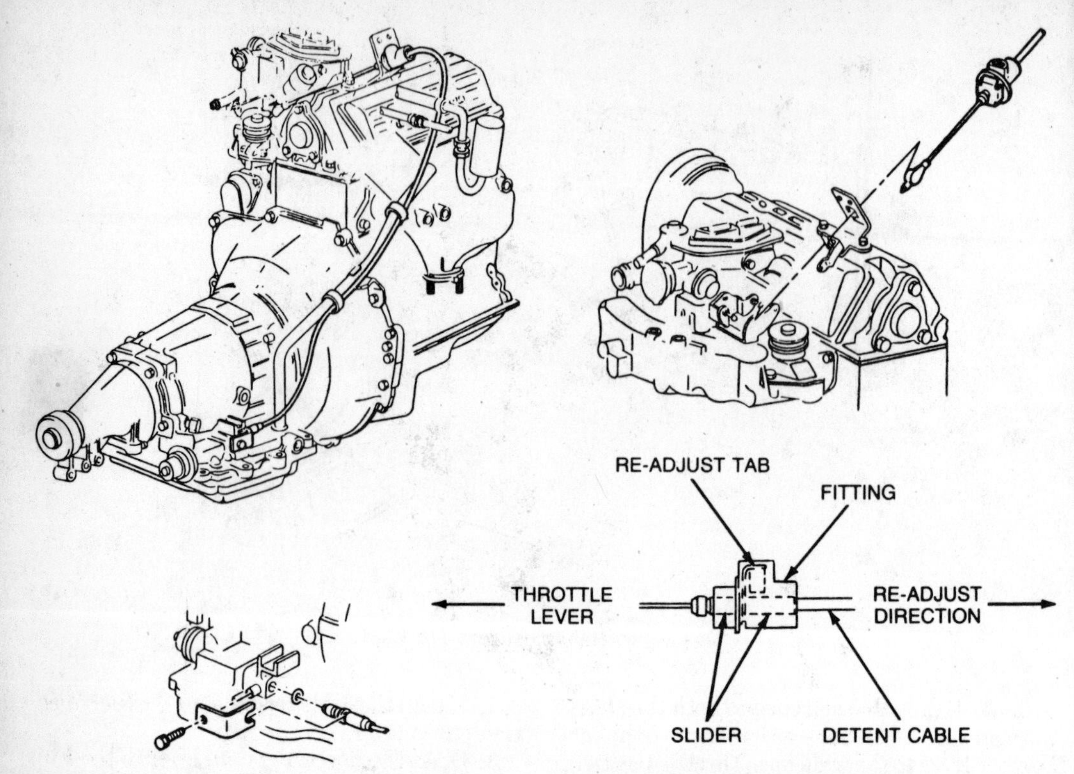

Downshift cable adjustment—1982 and later gasoline engine

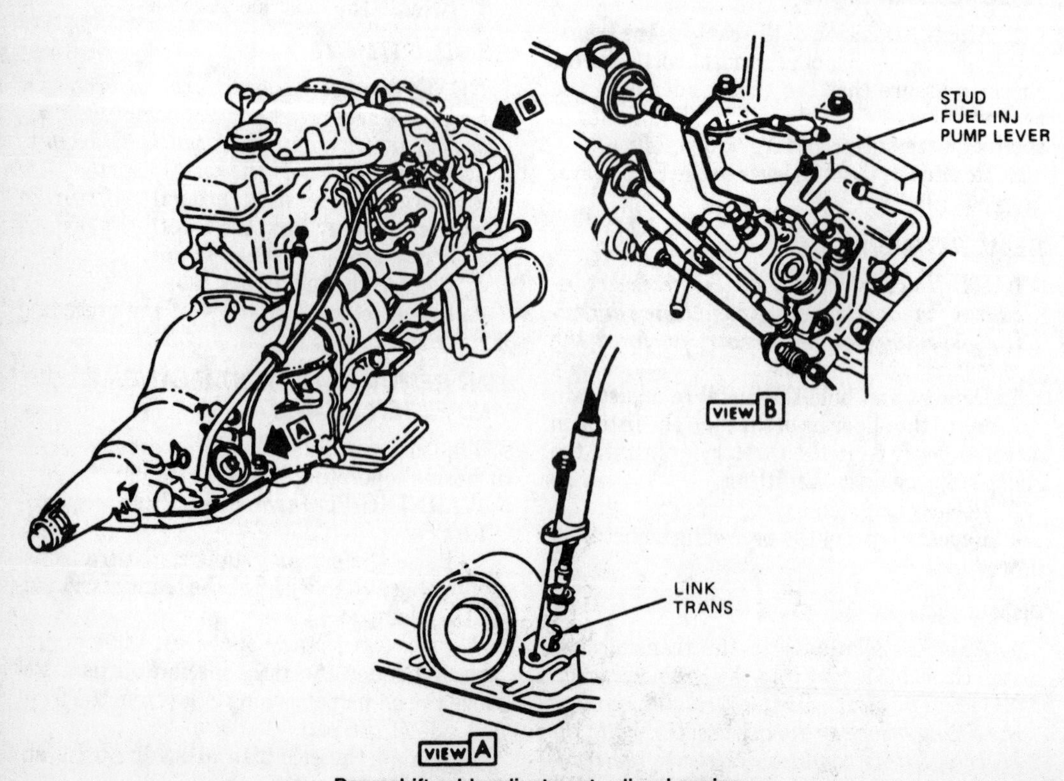

Downshift cable adjustment—diesel engine

4. Drain the fluid by carefully prying the oil pan loose with a screwdriver.

5. After the fluid has drained, remove the remaining oil pan attaching bolts. Remove the oil pan and gasket. Throw the old gasket away.

6. Drain the remaining fluid from the pan. Thoroughly clean the pan with solvent and dry with compressed air.

7. Remove the two screen-to-valve body bolts and remove the screen and gasket. Discard the gasket.

8. Thoroughly clean the screen in solvent and dry with compressed air.

9. Install the new gasket on the screen and install the bolts. Torque the bolts to 14 ft. lbs. for the Model 180 transmission and 11 ft. lbs. for the Model 200.

10. Install a new gasket on the oil pan and install the oil pan. Tighten the bolts to 8 ft. lbs. for the Model 180 transmission and 12 ft. lbs. for the 200 transmission.

11. Lower the car and add about 6 pints of Dexron® II automatic transmission fluid through the filler tube. If the transmission has been overhauled add about 4.9 quarts of fluid.

12. With the transmission in Park, apply the parking brake, start the engine and let it idle (not fast idle). Do not race the engine.

13. Move the gear selector lever slowly through all positions, return the lever to Park, and check the transmission fluid level.

14. Add fluid as necessary to raise the level between the dimples on the dipstick. Be careful not to overfill the transmission; approximately one pint of fluid will raise the level to the correct amount.

DRIVELINE

Driveshaft and U-Joints

A one-piece driveshaft is mounted to the companion flange with a conventional universal joint at the rear. The driveshaft is connected to the transmission output shaft with a splined slip yoke. The slip yoke contains a thrust spring which seats against the end of the transmission output shaft. The thrust spring MUST be installed for proper operation.

The universal joints are of the long-life design and do not require periodic inspection or lubrication. When the joints are disassembled, repack the bearings and lubricate the reservoirs at the end of the trunnions with chassis grease and replace the dust seals.

Driveshaft

REMOVAL AND INSTALLATION

1. Raise the car. Scribe matchmarks on the driveshaft and the companion flange and disconnect the rear universal joint by removing the trunnion bearing straps.

2. Move the driveshaft to the rear under the axle to remove the slip yoke from the transmission. Watch for oil leakage from the transmission output shaft housing.

3. Install the driveshaft in the reverse order of removal. Tighten the trunnion strap bolts to 16 ft. lbs.

Universal Joint

REMOVAL AND INSTALLATION

1. Remove the driveshaft.

2. For reassembly purposes, scribe a line on the transmission end of the driveshaft and on the slip yoke. Remove the snaprings from the trunnion yoke.

3. Support the trunnion yoke on a piece of 1¼" ID pipe on an arbor press or bench vise. Use a suitable socket or rod to press on the trunnion until the bearing cup is almost out. Grasp the cup in the vise and work the cup out of the yoke. Press the trunnion in the opposite direction to remove the other cup.

4. Clean and inspect the dust seals, bearing rollers, and trunnions. Lubricate the bearings. Make sure that the lubricant reservoir at the

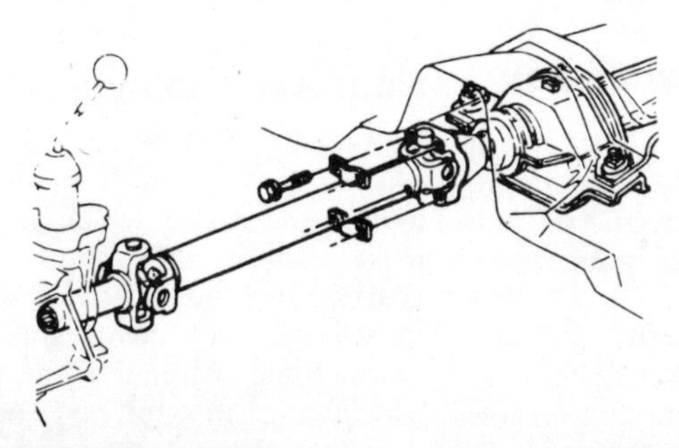

Driveshaft mounting

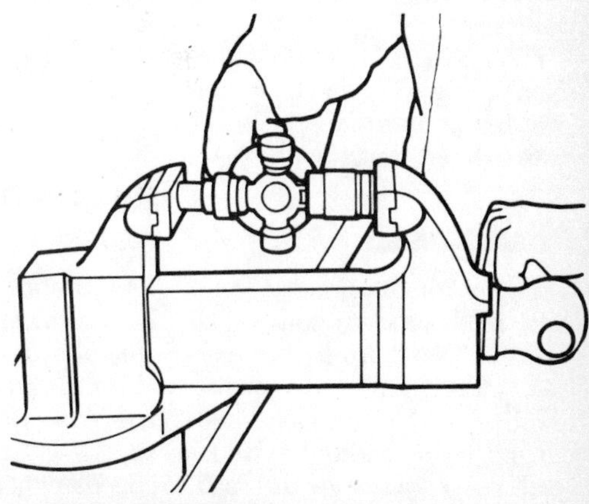

Removing the U-joint from the driveshaft

end of each trunnion is completely filled with lubricant. A squeeze bottle is recommended to fill the reservoirs from the bottom to prevent air pockets.

5. When installing a U-joint rebuilding kit, place the dust seals on the trunnions with the cavities of the seals toward the end of the trunnions. Use caution when pressing the seals onto the trunnions to prevent seal distortion and to assure proper seal seating.

NOTE: *Install the transmission yoke on the front of the driveshaft as marked in Step 2. If this is not done, driveline vibration may result.*

6. To assemble, position the trunnion into the yoke. Partially install one bearing cup into

Troubleshooting Basic Driveshaft and Rear Axle Problems

When abnormal vibrations or noises are detected in the driveshaft area, this chart can be used to help diagnose possible causes. Remember that other components such as wheels, tires, rear axle and suspension can also produce similar conditions.

BASIC DRIVESHAFT PROBLEMS

Problem	Cause	Solution
Shudder as car accelerates from stop or low speed	• Loose U-joint • Defective center bearing	• Replace U-joint • Replace center bearing
Loud clunk in driveshaft when shifting gears	• Worn U-joints	• Replace U-joints
Roughness or vibration at any speed	• Out-of-balance, bent or dented driveshaft • Worn U-joints • U-joint clamp bolts loose	• Balance or replace driveshaft • Replace U-joints • Tighten U-joint clamp bolts
Squeaking noise at low speeds	• Lack of U-joint lubrication	• Lubricate U-joint; if problem persists, replace U-joint
Knock or clicking noise	• U-joint or driveshaft hitting frame tunnel • Worn CV joint	• Correct overloaded condition • Replace CV joint

BASIC REAR AXLE PROBLEMS

First, determine when the noise is most noticeable.

Drive Noise: Produced under vehicle acceleration.

Coast Noise: Produced while the car coasts with a closed throttle.

Float Noise: Occurs while maintaining constant car speed (just enough to keep speed constant) on a level road.

Road Noise

Brick or rough surfaced concrete roads produce noises that seem to come from the rear axle. Road noise is usually identical in Drive or Coast and driving on a different type of road will tell whether the road is the problem.

Tire Noise

Tire noises are often mistaken for rear axle problems. Snow treads or unevenly worn tires produce vibrations seeming to originate elsewhere. **Temporarily** inflating the tires to 40 lbs will significantly alter tire noise, but will have no effect on rear axle noises (which normally cease below about 30 mph).

Engine/Transmission Noise

Determine at what speed the noise is most pronounced, then stop the car in a quiet place. With the transmission in Neutral, run the engine through speeds corresponding to road speeds where the noise was noticed. Noises produced with the car standing still are coming from the engine or transmission.

Front Wheel Bearings

While holding the car speed steady, lightly apply the footbrake; this will often decease bearing noise, as some of the load is taken from the bearing.

Rear Axle Noises

Eliminating other possible sources can narrow the cause to the rear axle, which normally produces noise from worn gears or bearings. Gear noises tend to peak in a narrow speed range, while bearing noises will usually vary in pitch with engine speeds.

NOISE DIAGNOSIS

The Noise Is	Most Probably Produced By
• Identical under Drive or Coast	• Road surface, tires or front wheel bearings
• Different depending on road surface	• Road surface or tires
• Lower as the car speed is lowered	• Tires
• Similar with car standing or moving	• Engine or transmission
• A vibration	• Unbalanced tires, rear wheel bearing, unbalanced driveshaft or worn U-joint
• A knock or click about every 2 tire revolutions	• Rear wheel bearing
• Most pronounced on turns	• Damaged differential gears
• A steady low-pitched whirring or scraping, starting at low speeds	• Damaged or worn pinion bearing
• A chattering vibration on turns	• Wrong differential lubricant or worn clutch plates (limited slip rear axle)
• Noticed only in Drive, Coast or Float conditions	• Worn ring gear and/or pinion gear

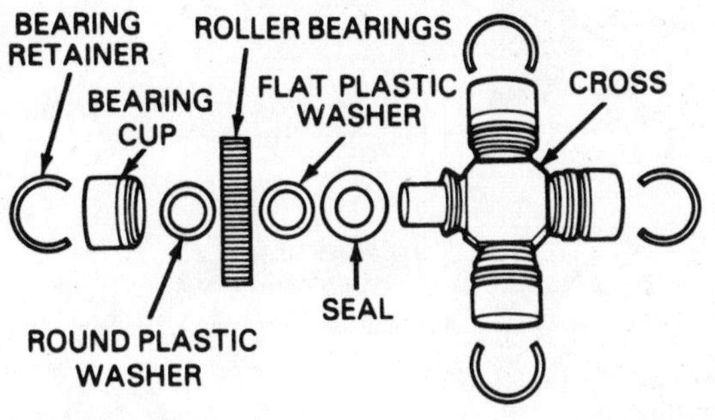

U-joint rebuilding kit

the yoke and start the trunnion into the bearing cup. Partially install the other cup, align the trunnion into the cup, and press the cups into the yoke.

7. Install the snaprings.
8. Install the driveshaft.

REAR AXLE

Axle Shaft, Bearing, and Seal

REMOVAL AND INSTALLATION

1. Raise the car. Remove the wheel and tire assembly and the brake drum.
2. Clean the area around the differential carrier cover.
3. Remove the differential carrier cover to drain the rear axle lubricant.
4. Use a metric allen wrench to unscrew the differential pinion shaft. It may be necessary to shorten the allen wrench to do this.
5. Push the flanged end of the axle shaft toward the center of the car and remove the C-lock from the bottom end of the shaft.
6. Remove the axle shaft from the housing making sure not to damage the oil seal.
7. If replacing the seal only, remove the oil

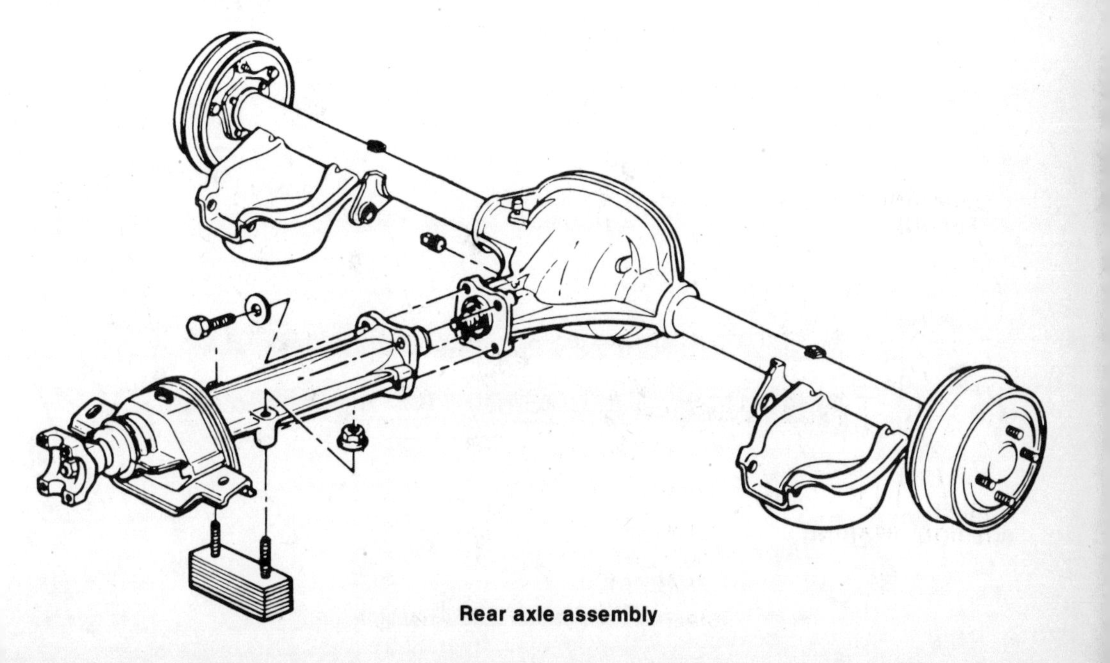
Rear axle assembly

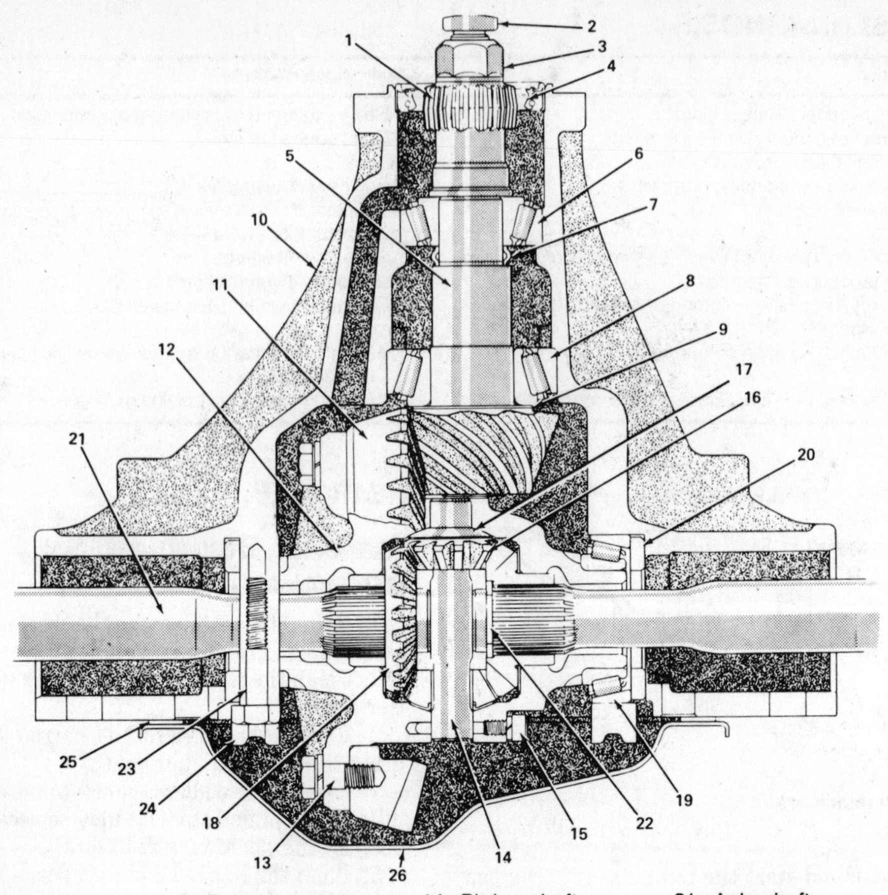

1. Drive coupling
2. Thrust washer
3. Lock nut
4. Oil seal
5. Drive pinion
6. Pinion front bearing
7. Preload spacer
8. Pinion rear bearing
9. Pinion depth shim
10. Differential carrier
11. Ring gear
12. Differential case
13. Ring gear bolt
14. Pinion shaft
15. Lock screw
16. Pinion gear
17. Thrust washer
18. Side gear
19. Differential bearing
20. Shim/spacer
21. Axle shaft
22. Axle shaft 'C' lock
23. Bearing cap bolt
24. Bearing cap
25. Differential cover gasket
26. Differential cover

Cross-section of the differential

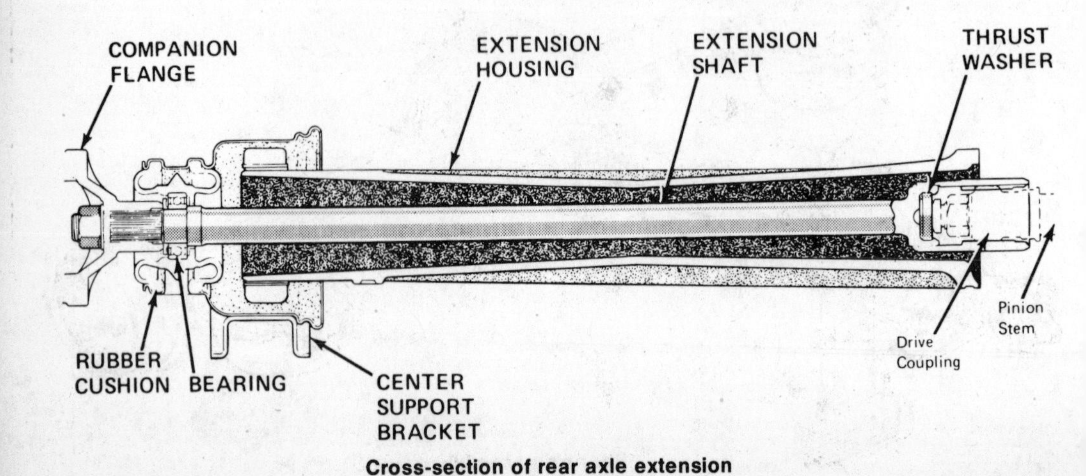

Cross-section of rear axle extension

seal by using the button end of the axle shaft. Insert the button end of the shaft behind the steel case of the oil seal and carefully pry the seal out of the bore.

8. To remove the bearings, insert a bearing and seal remover into the bore so the the tool head grasps behind the bearing. Slide the washer against the seal or bearing and turn the nut against the washer. Attach a slide hammer and remove the bearing.

9. Lubricate a new bearing with hypoid lubricant and install it into the housing with a bearing installer tool. Make sure that the tool contacts the end of the axle tube to make sure that the bearing is at the proper depth.

10. Lubricate the cavity between the seal lips with a high melting point wheel bearing grease. Place a new oil seal on the seal installation tool and position the seal in the axle housing bore. Tap the seal into the bore flush with the end of the housing.

11. To install the axle shaft, slide the axle shaft into place making sure that the splines on the end of the shaft do not damage the oil seal and that they engage the splines of the differential side gear. Install the C-lock on the button end of the axle shaft and push the shaft outward so that the shaft lock seats in the counterbore of the differential side gear.

12. Position the differential pinion shaft through the case and pinions, aligning the hole in the shaft with the lockscrew hole. Install the lockscrew.

13. Clean the gasket mounting surfaces on the differential carrier and carrier cover. Install the carrier cover using a new gasket and tighten the cover bolts in a crosswise pattern to 22 ft. lbs.

14. Fill the rear axle with lubricant to the bottom of the filler hole.

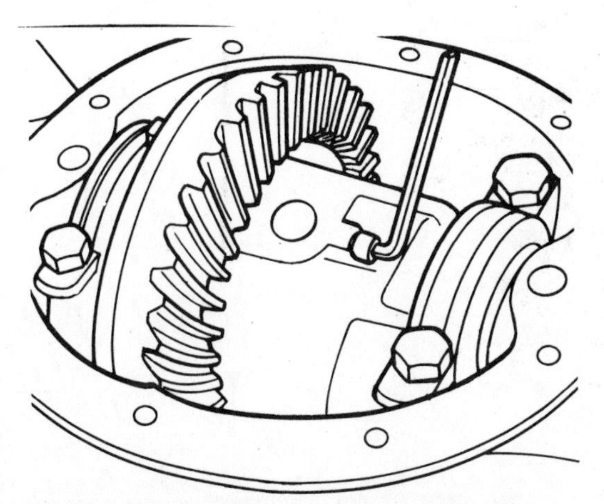

Remove the lock screw with a metric allen wrench. It may be necessary to shorten the wrench

15. Install the brake drum and the wheel and tire assembly.

16. Lower the car.

Axle Extension

REMOVAL AND INSTALLATION

1. Raise the car and support it safely.

2. Disconnect the propeller shaft from the companion flange, then remove from the transmission.

3. Place a jackstand under the front of the rear axle carrier housing.

CAUTION: *The extension must be supported safely to avoid possible injury when it is disconnected.*

4. Disconnect the center support bracket from the underbody.

5. Disconnect the extension housing flange from the axle housing and remove it carefully.

NOTE: *It may be necessary to pry the extension housing from the axle housing.*

6. To install position ther extension assembly to the axle carrier. Support the front end of the carrier with a jackstand and attach the flange to axle carrier bolts.

7. Connect the center support bracket to the underbody.

8. Reconnect the propeller shaft. Make sure that the thrust spring is in place.

9. Lower the vehicle to the floor.

Axle Assembly

REMOVAL AND INSTALLATION

1. Raise the car and support it safely.

2. Place an adjustable lifting device under the axle.

3. Disconnect the shock absorbers from the axle.

4. remove the propeller shaft.

5. Disconnect the stabilizer bar, tie rod and rear axle extension bracket.

CAUTION: *Support the axle extension so that it does not swing down rapidly when disconnected from the body bracket.*

6. Remove the wheel and tire assemblies.

7. Remove the brake drums.

8. Disconnect the rear flex hose.

9. Remove the carrier cover and gasket to drain the lubricant.

10. Remove the pinion lock screw using a metric allen wrench.

NOTE: *It may be necessary to shorten the short leg of the allen wrench to allow for clearance.*

11. Remove the pinion shaft and axle shaft "C" locks.

12. Reinstall the pinion shaft and lock screw to retain differental.

13. Remove both axle shafts.
14. Remove the brake lines at the wheel cylinder, backing plate retaining nuts, parking brake cables and backing plates.
15. Remove the lower control arm pivot bolts at the axle.
16. Lower the axle slowly until the coil spring tension is released then remove the axle from the vehicle.

To install:

1. Raise the axle into position.
2. Install the lower control arm pivot bolts and tighten to 33 ft. lbs.
3. Install the brake lines at the wheel cylinder, backing plate retaining nuts, parking brake cables and backing plates.
4. Install both axle shafts.
5. Install the axle shaft C-locks, differential pinion and pinion lock screw.
6. Install the carrier cover and gasket and fill to the bottom of the plug hole with lubricant. (See Chapter One, Fluids And lubricants).
7. Install the brake drums and wheel and tire assemblies.
8. Connect the stabilizer bar, tie rod and rear axle extension bracket.
9. Connect the propeller shaft and torque the strap bolts to 16 ft. lbs.
10. Connect the shock absorbers to the axle.
11. Remove the ajustable lifting device from under the axle.
12. Lower the vehicle.

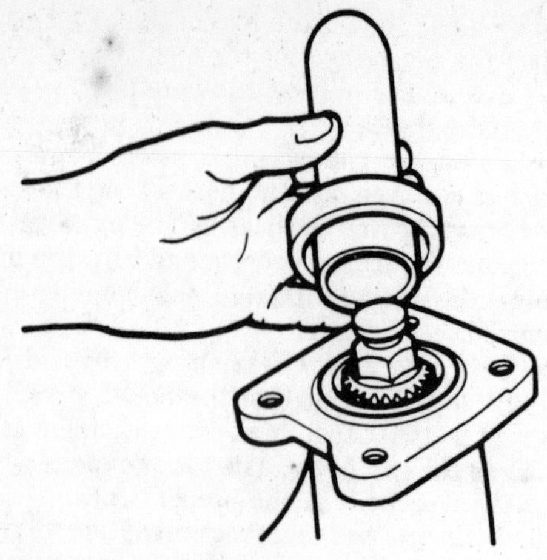

Pinion oil seal installation

Pinion Seal

REMOVAL AND INSTALLATION

1. Raise the car and support it safely.
2. Remove the axle extension assembly as outlined earlier.
3. Carefully pry out the pinion seal.
4. Lubricate and install the new seal with Tool J-25597.
5. Install the axle extension as outlined earlier.
6. Lower the vehicle.

Suspension and Steering

8

FRONT SUSPENSION

The Chevette and Pontiac 1000 front suspension is of conventional long and short control arm design with coil springs. The control arms attach with bolts and bushings at the inner pivot points and to the steering knuckle/front wheel spindle assembly at the outer pivot points. Lower ball joints are the wear indicator type. A front stabilizer bar is used.

Shock Absorber

REMOVAL AND INSTALLATION

1. Hold the shock absorber upper stem and remove the nut, upper retainer, and rubber grommet.
2. Raise the car.
3. Remove the bolt from the lower end of the shock absorber and remove the shock absorber.

To install

4. With the lower retainer and rubber grommet in position, extend the shock absorber stem and install the stem through the wheelhouse opening.

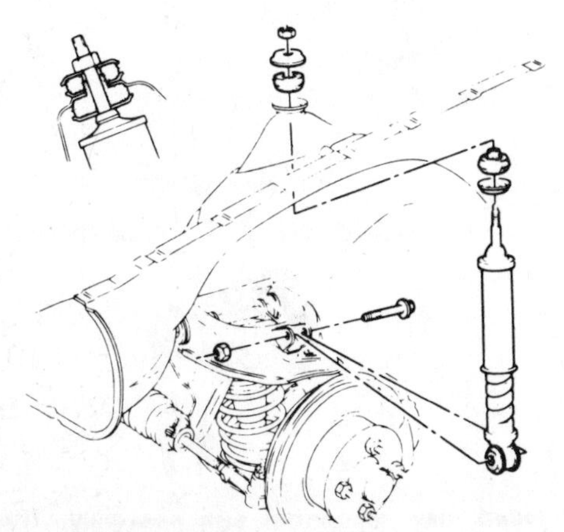

Front shock absorber mounting

The upper nut is 14 mm. Hold the shock absorber stem (arrow) while loosening the nut

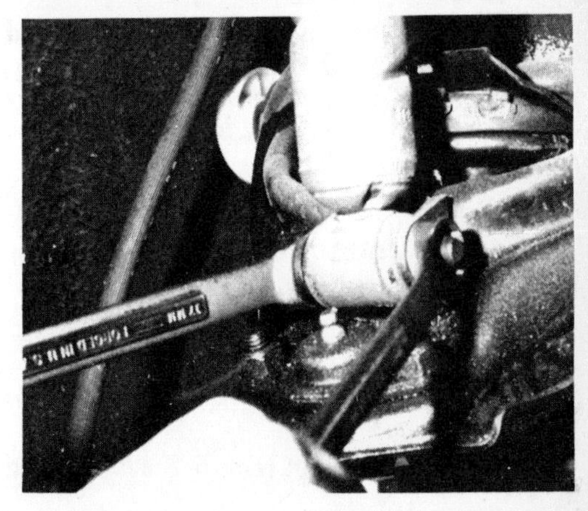

The lower bolt and nut will require two 17 mm wrenches

5. Install and torque the lower bolt to 35-50 ft. lbs.
6. Lower the car.
7. Install the upper grommet, retainer, and nut to the shock absorber stem.

Troubleshooting Basic Steering and Suspension Problems

Problem	Cause	Solution
Hard steering (steering wheel is hard to turn)	• Low or uneven tire pressure • Loose power steering pump drive belt • Low or incorrect power steering fluid • Incorrect front end alignment • Defective power steering pump • Bent or poorly lubricated front end parts	• Inflate tires to correct pressure • Adjust belt • Add fluid as necessary • Have front end alignment checked/adjusted • Check pump • Lubricate and/or replace defective parts
Loose steering (too much play in the steering wheel)	• Loose wheel bearings • Loose or worn steering linkage • Faulty shocks • Worn ball joints	• Adjust wheel bearings • Replace worn parts • Replace shocks • Replace ball joints
Car veers or wanders (car pulls to one side with hands off the steering wheel)	• Incorrect tire pressure • Improper front end alignment • Loose wheel bearings • Loose or bent front end components • Faulty shocks	• Inflate tires to correct pressure • Have front end alignment checked/adjusted • Adjust wheel bearings • Replace worn components • Replace shocks
Wheel oscillation or vibration transmitted through steering wheel	• Improper tire pressures • Tires out of balance • Loose wheel bearings • Improper front end alignment • Worn or bent front end components	• Inflate tires to correct pressure • Have tires balanced • Adjust wheel bearings • Have front end alignment checked/adjusted • Replace worn parts
Uneven tire wear	• Incorrect tire pressure • Front end out of alignment • Tires out of balance	• Inflate tires to correct pressure • Have front end alignment checked/adjusted • Have tires balanced

8. Hold the shock absorber upper stem and torque the nut to 60-120 in. lbs.

NOTE: *The required torque is produced by running the nut to the unthreaded part of the stud.*

Lower Ball Joint

REMOVAL AND INSTALLATION

1. Raise the car.
2. Remove the tire and wheel.
3. Support the lower control arm with a hydraulic floor jack.
4. Loosen, but do not remove the lower stud nut.
5. Install a ball joint removal tool with the cup end over the upper ball stud nut.
6. Turn the threaded end of the ball joint removal tool until the ball stud is free of the steering knuckle.
7. Remove the ball joint removal tool and remove the nut from the ball stud.
8. Remove the ball joint.

NOTE: *Inspect the tapered hole in the steering knuckle. Clean the area. If any out-of-roundness, deformation, or damage is found, the steering knuckle MUST be replaced.*

9. To install the lower ball joint, mate the

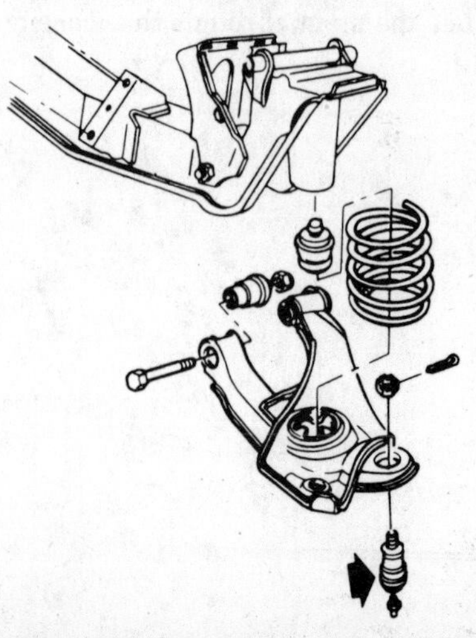

Exploded view of control arm assembly. The arrow points out the ball joints

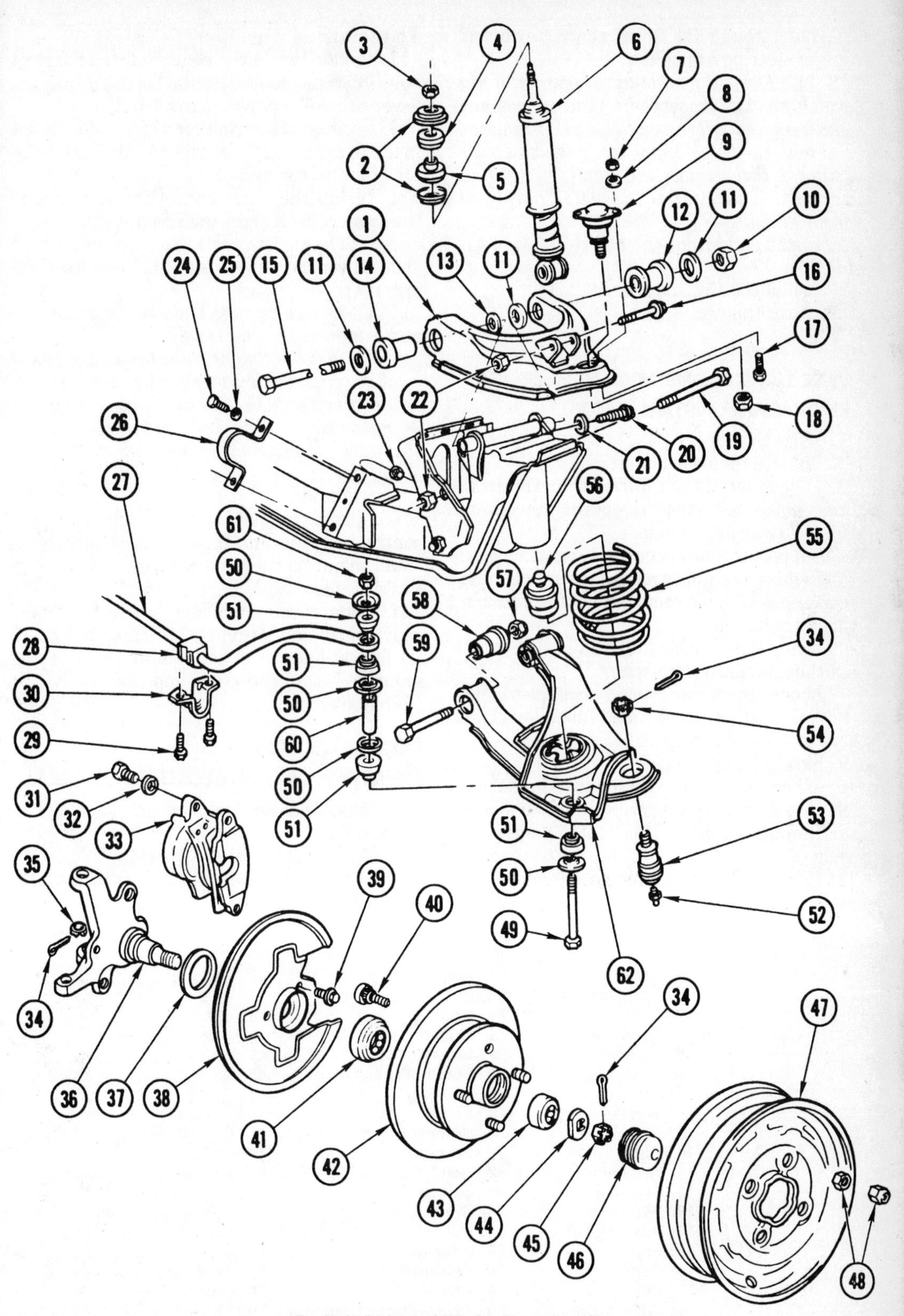

Exploded view of the front suspension

ball stud through the lower control arm and into the steering knuckle.

NOTE: *The ball joint studs use a special nut which must be discarded whenever loosened and removed. On assembly, use a standard nut to draw the ball joint into position on the knuckle, then remove the standard nut and install a new special nut for final installation.*

10. Install and torque the ball stud nut to 41-54 ft. lbs.
11. Install the tire and wheel.
12. Lower the car.

Lower Control Arm and Coil Spring

REMOVAL AND INSTALLATION

1. Raise the car.
2. Remove the wheel and tire.
3. Disconnect the stabilizer bar from the lower control arm and disconnect the tie rod from the steering knuckle.
4. Support the lower control arm with a jack.
5. Remove the nut from the lower ball joint, then use a ball joint removal tool to press out the lower ball joint.
6. Swing the knuckle and hub aside and attach them securely with wire.
7. Loosen the lower control arm pivot bolts.
8. As a safety precaution, install a chain through the coil spring.
9. Slowly lower the jack.
10. When the spring is extended as far as possible, use a pry bar to carefully lift the spring over the lower control arm seat. Remove the spring.
11. Remove the pivot bolts and remove the lower control arm.

To install:

12. Install the lower control arm and pivot bolts to the underbody brackets. Torque the lower control arm pivots to 40 ft. lbs.
13. Position the spring correctly and install it in the upper pocket. Use tape to hold the insulator onto the spring.
14. Install the lower end of the spring onto the lower control arm. An assistant may be necessary to compress the spring far enough to slide it over the raised area of the lower control arm seat.
15. Use a jack to raise the lower control arm and compress the coil spring.

NOTE: *The ball joint studs use a special nut which must be discarded whenever loosened and removed. On assembly, use a standard nut to draw the ball joint into position on the knuckle, then remove the standard nut and install a new special nut for final installation.*

16. Install the ball joint through the lower control arm and into the steering knuckle. Install the nut on the ball stud nut and torque to 41-54 ft. lbs.
17. Connect the stabilizer bar to the lower control arm and torque its attaching bolt to 15 ft. lbs. Connect the tie rod to the steering knuckle. Install the wheel and tire.
18. Lower the car.

Upper Ball Joint

REMOVAL AND INSTALLATION

1. Raise the car and support it safely on jackstands.
2. Remove the tire and wheel.
3. Support the lower control arm with a floor jack.

1. Steering arm
2. Retainer
3. Nut
4. Grommet
5. Grommet
6. Absorber
7. Nut
8. Washer
9. Ball joint
10. Nut
11. Washer
12. Bushing
13. Washer
14. Bushing
15. Bolt
16. Bolt
17. Bolt
18. Nut
19. Bolt
20. Bolt
21. Washer
22. Nut
23. Nut
24. Bolt
25. Washer
26. Bracket
27. Stabilizer shaft
28. Bushing
29. Screw
30. Bracket
31. Washer
32. Bolt
33. Caliper
34. Cotter pin
35. Nut
36. Knuckle
37. Washer
38. Shield
39. Screw and washer
40. Bolt
41. Bearing
42. Hub and bearing
43. Bearing
44. Washer
45. Nut
46. Nut
47. Wheel
48. Nut
49. Bolt
50. Retainer
51. Grommet
52. Fitting
53. Ball joint
54. Nut
55. Spring
56. Bumper
57. Nut
58. Bushing
59. Bolt
60. Spacer
61. Nut
62. Arm

Exploded view of the front suspension

4. Loosen, but do not remove the upper ball stud nut.

5. Install a ball joint removal tool with the cup end over the lower ball stud nut.

6. Turn the threaded end of the ball joint removal tool until the upper ball stud is free of the steering knuckle.

7. Remove the ball joint removal tool and remove the nut from the ball stud.

8. Remove the two nuts and bolts attaching the ball joint to the upper control arm and remove the ball joint.

NOTE: *Inspect the tapered hole in the steering knuckle. Clean the area. If any out-of-roundness, deformation, or damage is found, the steering knuckle MUST be replaced.*

9. To install the upper ball joint, install the nuts and bolts attaching the ball joint to the upper control arm. Torque the nuts to 20 ft. lbs. Then mate the upper control arm ball stud to the steering knuckle.

NOTE: *The ball joint studs use a special nut which must be discarded whenever loosened and removed. On assembly, use a standard nut to draw the ball joint into position on the knuckle, then remove the standard nut and install a new special nut for final installation.*

10. Install and torque the ball stud nut to 29-36 ft. lbs.

11. Install the tire and wheel.

12. Lower the car.

Upper Control Arm

REMOVAL AND INSTALLATION

1. Raise the car.

2. Remove the tire and wheel.

3. Support the lower control arm with a floor jack.

4. Remove the upper ball joint from the steering knuckle as previously described.

5. Remove the upper control arm pivot bolts and remove the upper control arm.

6. To install the upper control arm, install the upper control with its pivot bolts.

NOTE: *The inner pivot bolt must be installed with bolt head toward the front.*

7. Install the pivot bolt nut.

8. Position the upper control arm in a horizontal plan and torque the nut to 43-50 ft. lbs.

NOTE: *The ball joint studs use a special nut which must be discarded whenever loosened and removed. On assembly, use a standard nut to draw the ball joint into position on the knuckle, then remove the standard nut and install a new special nut for final installation.*

9. Install the ball joint to the upper control arm and to the steering knuckle as previously described. Torque the ball joint-to-upper control arm attaching bolts to 20 ft. lbs. Torque the ball stud nut to 29-36 ft. lbs.

10. Install the tire and wheel.

11. Lower the car.

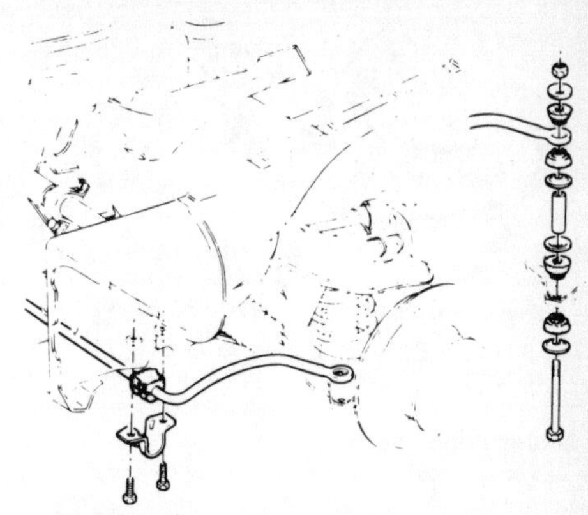

Front stabilizer bar mounting

Stabilizer Bar

REMOVAL AND INSTALLATION

1. Raise the car.

2. Remove the stabilizer bar nuts and bolts from the lower control arms.

3. Remove the stabilizer bar brackets and remove the stabilizer bar.

To install:

4. Hold the stabilizer bar in place and install the body bushings and brackets. Torque the bracket bolts to 14 ft. lbs.

5. Install the retainers, grommets, and spacer to the lower control arms and install the attaching nuts.

6. Lower the car.

7. Torque the attaching nuts to 15 ft. lbs.

NOTE: *The correct torque is produced by running the nuts to the unthreaded portions of the link bolts.*

Front End Alignment

CAMBER ADJUSTMENT

Camber angle can be increased by approximately 1 degree by removing the upper ball joint, rotating it ½ turn, and reinstalling it with the flat of the upper flange on the inboard side of the control arm.

CASTER ADJUSTMENT

Caster angle can be changed with a realignment of the washers located between the legs of the upper control arm. To adjust the caster angle, an adjustment kit consisting of one 3mm and one 9mm washer must be used. Install as shown in the illustration.

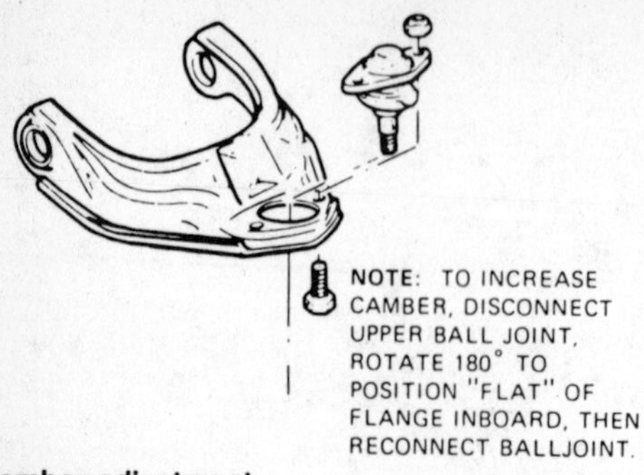

Camber adjustment

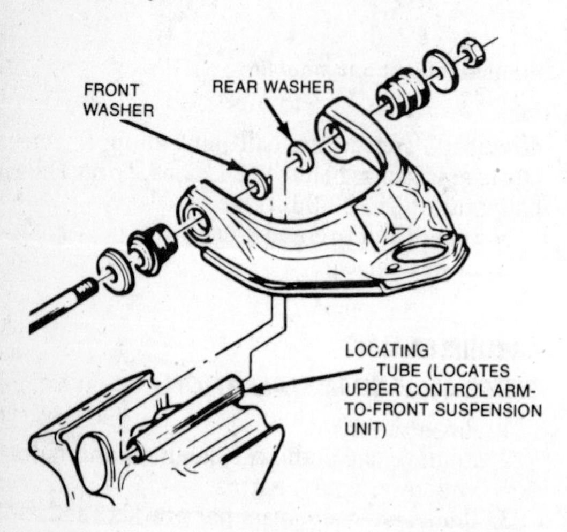

FRONT	REAR	NET CHANGE
3MM	9MM	+1°
9MM	3MM	−1°

Caster adjustment

NOTE: *You must always use two washers that total 12mm, with one washer at each end of the floating tube.*

TOE-IN ADJUSTMENT

Toe-in is controlled by the position of the tie rods. To adjust the toe, loosen the nuts at the steering knuckle end of the tie rod, and the rubber cover at the other end, then rotate the rod

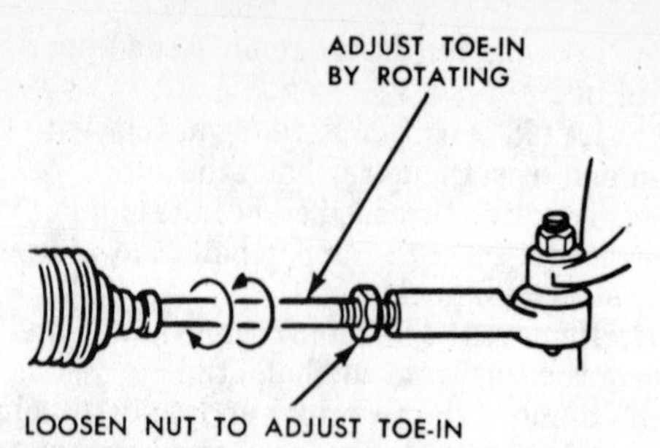

Toe-in—adjustment

as needed to adjust toe-in. Tighten the cover and the locknuts.

REAR SUSPENSION

Chevette and Pontiac 1000 models use a solid rear axle and coil springs. The axle is attached to the body by two tubular lower control arms, a straight track rod, two shock absorbers and a bracket at the front end of the rear axle extension.

The lower control arms maintain fore and aft relationship of the axle to the chassis. The coil springs are located between the brackets on the axle tube and the spring seats in the frame. They are held in place by the weight of the car and, during rebound, by the shock absorbers which limit axle movement. The shock absorbers are angle-mounted on brackets behind the axle housing and the rear spring seats in the frame. A rear stabilizer bar is used.

When using a hoist contacting the rear axle be sure that the stabilizer links and the track rod are not damaged.

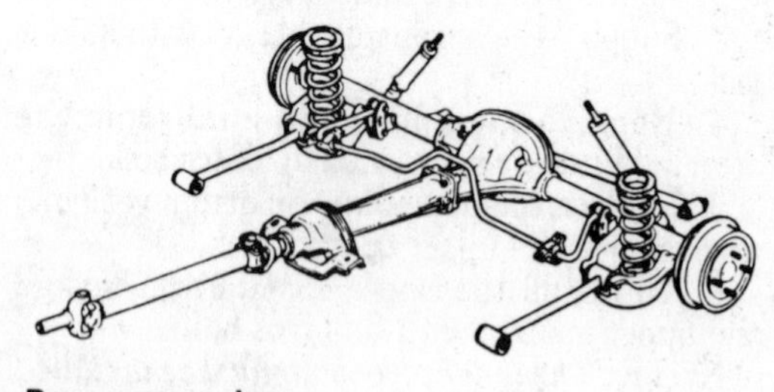

Rear suspension

Wheel Alignment Specifications

		Caster		Camber			
Year	Model	Range (deg)	Pref Setting (deg)	Range (deg)	Pref Setting (deg)	Toe-in (in.)	Steering Axis Inclination (deg)
1976–81	All	3½P to 5½P	4½P	¼N to ½P	¼P	1/16	7½
1982–87	All	4P to 6P	5P	¼P to ½P	¼P	1/16	—

N Negative
P Positive

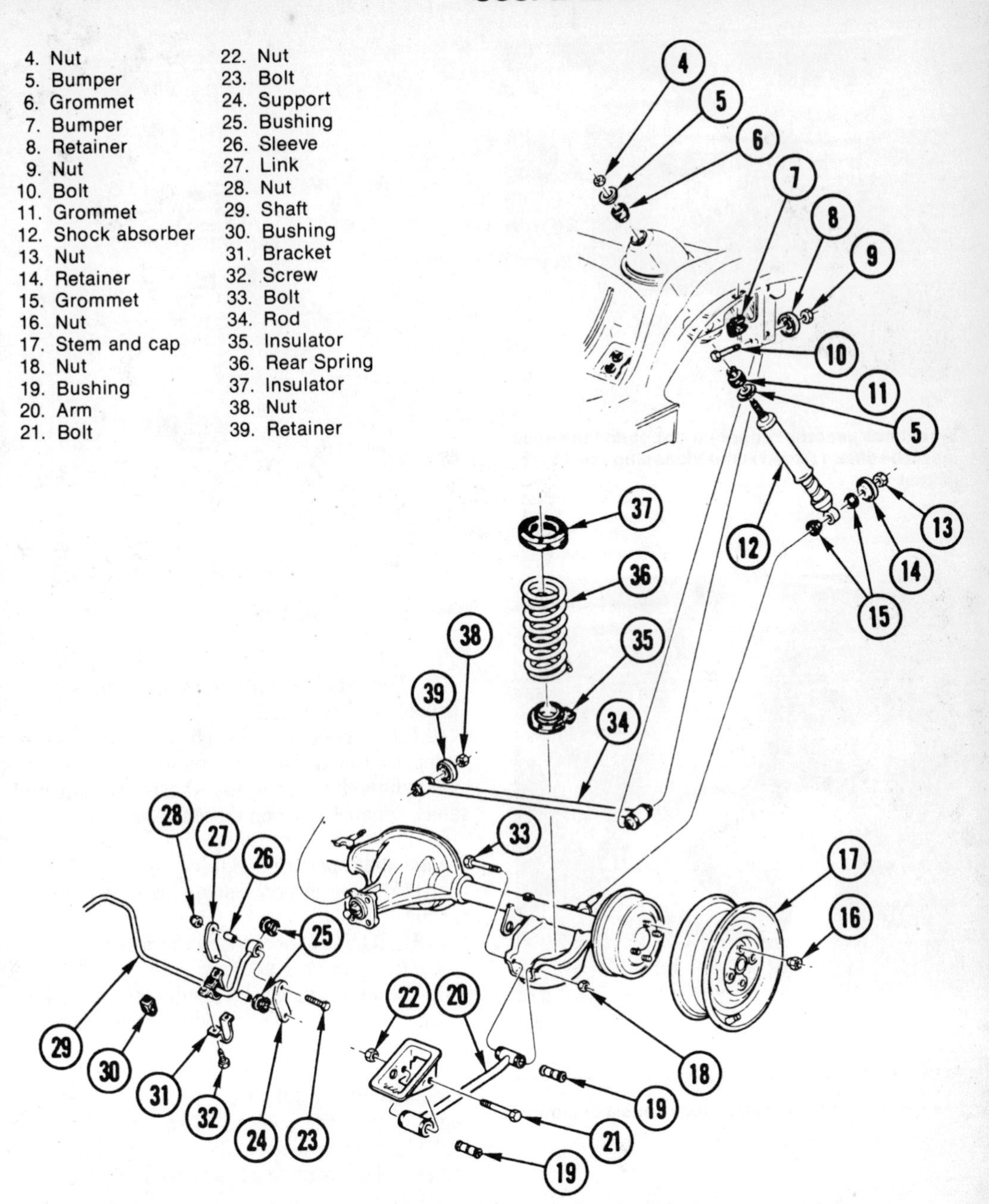

Exploded view of the rear suspension

Shock Absorber

REMOVAL AND INSTALLATION

1. Raise the car.
2. Support the rear axle.
3. Remove the shock absorber upper attaching nut and lower attaching bolt and nut, and remove the shock absorber.

To install:

4. Install the retainer and the rubber grommet onto the shock absorber.
5. Place the shock absorber into its installed position and install and tighten the upper retaining nut to 7 ft. lbs.
6. Install the lower shock absorber nut and bolt and torque to 33 ft. lbs.
7. Remove the rear axle supports and lower the car.

Springs

REMOVAL AND INSTALLATION

1. Raise the car.
2. Support the rear axle with a hydraulic jack.

Rear shock absorber upper mount. Hold the shock absorber stem (arrow) while loosening the 14 mm locknut

One nut retains the bottom shock absorber mount

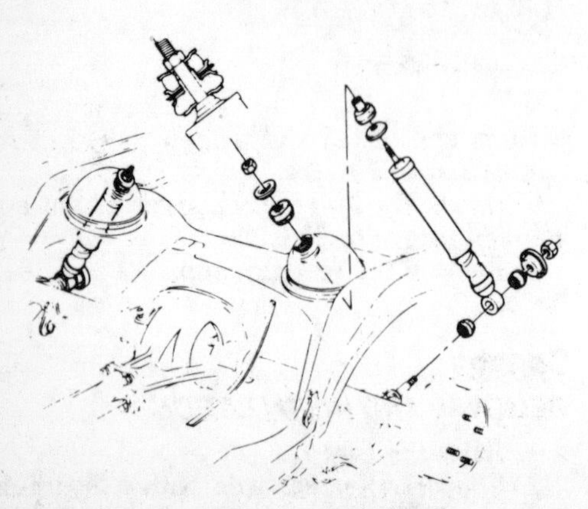

Rear shock absorber mounting detail

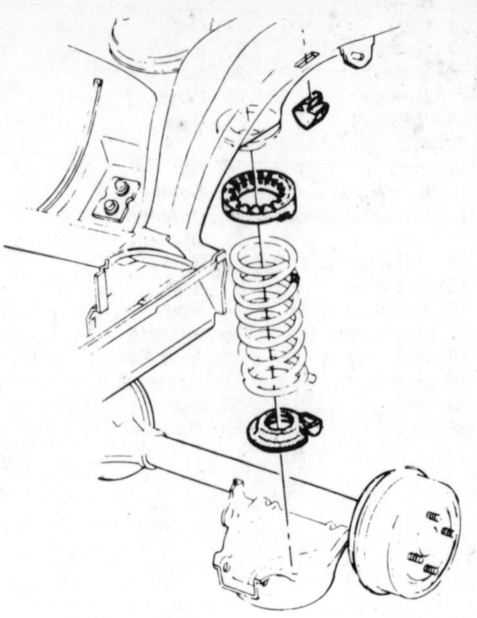

Rear spring installation

3. Disconnect both shock absorbers from their lower brackets.

4. Disconnect the rear axle extension center support bracket from the underbody. Use caution when disconnecting the extension and safely support it when disconnected.

5. Lower the rear axle and remove the springs and spring insulators.

NOTE: *One or both springs can be removed now.*

CAUTION: *Do not stretch the rear brake hoses when lowering the rear axle.*

6. To install, place the insulators on top and on the bottom of the springs and position the springs between the upper and lower seats.

7. Raise the rear axle. Connect the rear axle extension center support bracket to the underbody. Torque the bolts to 37 ft. lbs.

8. Connect the shock absorbers to their lower brackets. Torque the nuts to 33 ft. lbs.

9. Remove the hydraulic jack from the axle.

10. Lower the car.

Stabilizer Bar

REMOVAL AND INSTALLATION

1. Raise the car.

2. Remove the bolts attaching the stabilizer bar to its brackets and links. Remove the stabilizer bar.

3. To install, place the stabilizer bar in position and install the attaching bolts and nuts in the brackets and links. Torque both the bracket and link bolts to 15 ft. lbs.

4. Lower the car.

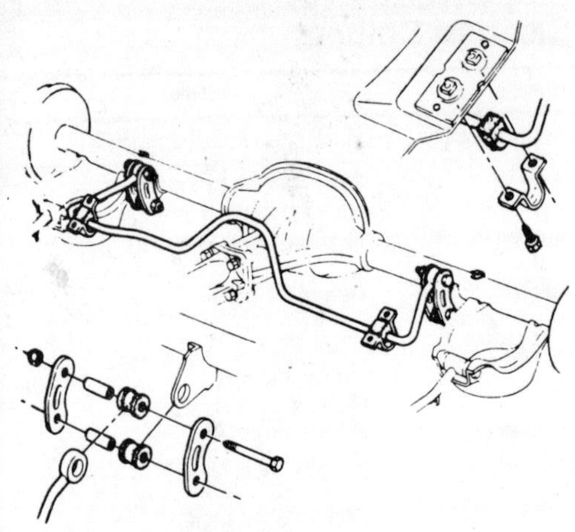
Rear stabilizer mounting

Lower Control Arm and Track Rod

REMOVAL AND INSTALLATION

CAUTION: *If both control arms are to be replaced, remove and replace one control arm at a time to prevent the axle from rolling or slipping sideways.*

1. Raise the car.
2. Support the rear axle.
3. Disconnect the stabilizer bar.
4. Remove the control arm front and rear attaching bolts and remove the control arm.
5. Remove the track rod attaching bolts and remove the track rod.
6. Press the rubber bushings out of the control arm and track rod with the proper tools. Inspect the private ends of the control arm and track rod for distortion, burrs, etc., and press new bushings into place.
7. To install, place the lower control arm into position and install and torque the front and rear attaching bolts to 49 ft. lbs.
8. Place the track rod in position and torque both the axle housing nut and body bracket bolt and nut to 49 ft. lbs.

NOTE: *The car must be at curb height when tightening pivot bolts.*

9. Connect the stabilizer bar. Torque all stabilizer bar attaching bolts to 15 ft. lbs.
10. Remove the support from the axle.
11. Lower the car.

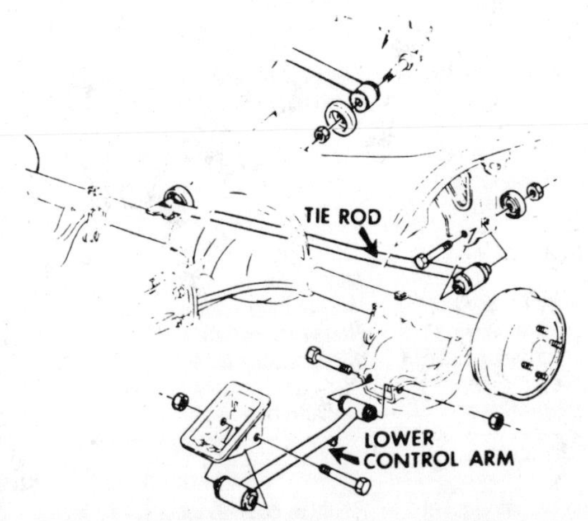

Lower control arm and track rod mounting

STEERING

All Chevette and Pontiac 1000 models use rack and pinion steering which encloses the steering gear and linkage in one unit. Power steering was available in 1981.

Rotary motion of the steering wheel is converted into linear motion to turn the wheels by the meshing of the helical pinion with the teeth of the rack. The pinion and a major portion of the rack are encased in a die cast aluminum housing. Inner tie rod assemblies are threaded and staked to the rack. The inner tie rods contain a belleville spring-loaded ball joint which permits both rocking and rotating tie rod movement. The outer tie rods thread onto the inners and are held in position by jam nuts. Two convoluted boots are secured by clamps to the housing and inner tie rods to prevent the entrance of dirt. The rack and pinion assembly is secured to the front suspension crossmember with two clamps and bushings.

The energy absorbing steering column has a "smart" switch which operates the turn signals (up and down movement), the headlight dimmer switch (front and back movement), the windshield wipers (rotation) and the windshield washers (by pushing the lever into the column).

Rack and Pinion Steering Assembly

REMOVAL AND INSTALLATION

NOTE: *On models with power steering it is necessary to disconnect and connect the two hydraulic lines.*

1. Raise the car and support it safely on jackstands.
2. Remove the retaining bolts and the shield.
3. Remove both tie rod cotter pins and nuts and remove the tie rods.
4. Remove the flexible coupling pinch bolt-to-shaft.
5. Remove the four bolts at the clamps and remove the rack and pinion steering assembly.
6. To install, position the assembly, install four new bolts into the clamps, and tighten the bolts to 14 ft. lbs.
7. Install the flexible coupling pinch bolt-to-shaft.

Troubleshooting the Steering Column

Problem	Cause	Solution
Will not lock	• Lockbolt spring broken or defective	• Replace lock bolt spring
High effort (required to turn ignition key and lock cylinder)	• Lock cylinder defective • Ignition switch defective • Rack preload spring broken or deformed • Burr on lock sector, lock rack, housing, support or remote rod coupling • Bent sector shaft • Defective lock rack • Remote rod bent, deformed • Ignition switch mounting bracket bent • Distorted coupling slot in lock rack (tilt column)	• Replace lock cylinder • Replace ignition switch • Replace preload spring • Remove burr • Replace shaft • Replace lock rack • Replace rod • Straighten or replace • Replace lock rack
Will stick in "start"	• Remote rod deformed • Ignition switch mounting bracket bent	• Straighten or replace • Straighten or replace
Key cannot be removed in "off-lock"	• Ignition switch is not adjusted correctly • Defective lock cylinder	• Adjust switch • Replace lock cylinder
Lock cylinder can be removed without depressing retainer	• Lock cylinder with defective retainer • Burr over retainer slot in housing cover or on cylinder retainer	• Replace lock cylinder • Remove burr
High effort on lock cylinder between "off" and "off-lock"	• Distorted lock rack • Burr on tang of shift gate (automatic column) • Gearshift linkage not adjusted	• Replace lock rack • Remove burr • Adjust linkage
Noise in column	• One click when in "off-lock" position and the steering wheel is moved (all except automatic column) • Coupling bolts not tightened • Lack of grease on bearings or bearing surfaces • Upper shaft bearing worn or broken • Lower shaft bearing worn or broken • Column not correctly aligned • Coupling pulled apart • Broken coupling lower joint • Steering shaft snap ring not seated • Shroud loose on shift bowl. Housing loose on jacket—will be noticed with ignition in "off-lock" and when torque is applied to steering wheel.	• Normal—lock bolt is seating • Tighten pinch bolts • Lubricate with chassis grease • Replace bearing assembly • Replace bearing. Check shaft and replace if scored. • Align column • Replace coupling • Repair or replace joint and align column • Replace ring. Check for proper seating in groove. • Position shroud over lugs on shift bowl. Tighten mounting screws.
High steering shaft effort	• Column misaligned • Defective upper or lower bearing • Tight steering shaft universal joint • Flash on I.D. of shift tube at plastic joint (tilt column only) • Upper or lower bearing seized	• Align column • Replace as required • Repair or replace • Replace shift tube • Replace bearings
Lash in mounted column assembly	• Column mounting bracket bolts loose • Broken weld nuts on column jacket • Column capsule bracket sheared	• Tighten bolts • Replace column jacket • Replace bracket assembly

Troubleshooting the Steering Column (cont.)

Problem	Cause	Solution
Lash in mounted column assembly (cont.)	• Column bracket to column jacket mounting bolts loose • Loose lock shoes in housing (tilt column only) • Loose pivot pins (tilt column only) • Loose lock shoe pin (tilt column only) • Loose support screws (tilt column only)	• Tighten to specified torque • Replace shoes • Replace pivot pins and support • Replace pin and housing • Tighten screws
Housing loose (tilt column only)	• Excessive clearance between holes in support or housing and pivot pin diameters • Housing support-screws loose	• Replace pivot pins and support • Tighten screws
Steering wheel loose—every other tilt position (tilt column only)	• Loose fit between lock shoe and lock shoe pivot pin	• Replace lock shoes and pivot pin
Steering column not locking in any tilt position (tilt column only)	• Lock shoe seized on pivot pin • Lock shoe grooves have burrs or are filled with foreign material • Lock shoe springs weak or broken	• Replace lock shoes and pin • Clean or replace lock shoes • Replace springs
Noise when tilting column (tilt column only)	• Upper tilt bumpers worn • Tilt spring rubbing in housing	• Replace tilt bumper • Lubricate with chassis grease
One click when in "off-lock" position and the steering wheel is moved	• Seating of lock bolt	• None. Click is normal characteristic sound produced by lock bolt as it seats.
High shift effort (automatic and tilt column only)	• Column not correctly aligned • Lower bearing not aligned correctly • Lack of grease on seal or lower bearing areas	• Align column • Assemble correctly • Lubricate with chassis grease
Improper transmission shifting—automatic and tilt column only	• Sheared shift tube joint • Improper transmission gearshift linkage adjustment • Loose lower shift lever	• Replace shift tube • Adjust linkage • Replace shift tube

Troubleshooting the Ignition Switch

Problem	Cause	Solution
Ignition switch electrically inoperative	• Loose or defective switch connector • Feed wire open (fusible link) • Defective ignition switch	• Tighten or replace connector • Repair or replace • Replace ignition switch
Engine will not crank	• Ignition switch not adjusted properly	• Adjust switch
Ignition switch wil not actuate mechanically	• Defective ignition switch • Defective lock sector • Defective remote rod	• Replace switch • Replace lock sector • Replace remote rod
Ignition switch cannot be adjusted correctly	• Remote rod deformed	• Repair, straighten or replace

Troubleshooting the Turn Signal Switch

Problem	Cause	Solution
Turn signal will not cancel	• Loose switch mounting screws • Switch or anchor bosses broken • Broken, missing or out of position detent, or cancelling spring	• Tighten screws • Replace switch • Reposition springs or replace switch as required

Troubleshooting the Turn Signal Switch (cont.)

Problem	Cause	Solution
Turn signal difficult to operate	• Turn signal lever loose • Switch yoke broken or distorted • Loose or misplaced springs • Foreign parts and/or materials in switch • Switch mounted loosely	• Tighten mounting screws • Replace switch • Reposition springs or replace switch • Remove foreign parts and/or material • Tighten mounting screws
Turn signal will not indicate lane change	• Broken lane change pressure pad or spring hanger • Broken, missing or misplaced lane change spring • Jammed wires	• Replace switch • Replace or reposition as required • Loosen mounting screws, reposition wires and retighten screws
Turn signal will not stay in turn position	• Foreign material or loose parts impeding movement of switch yoke • Defective switch	• Remove material and/or parts • Replace switch
Hazard switch cannot be pulled out	• Foreign material between hazard support cancelling leg and yoke	• Remove foreign material. No foreign material impeding function of hazard switch—replace turn signal switch.
No turn signal lights	• Inoperative turn signal flasher • Defective or blown fuse • Loose chassis to column harness connector • Disconnect column to chassis connector. Connect new switch to chassis and operate switch by hand. If vehicle lights now operate normally, signal switch is inoperative • If vehicle lights do not operate, check chassis wiring for opens, grounds, etc.	• Replace turn signal flasher • Replace fuse • Connect securely • Replace signal switch • Repair chassis wiring as required
Instrument panel turn indicator lights on but not flashing	• Burned out or damaged front or rear turn signal bulb • If vehicle lights do not operate, check light sockets for high resistance connections, the chassis wiring for opens, grounds, etc. • Inoperative flasher • Loose chassis to column harness connection • Inoperative turn signal switch • To determine if turn signal switch is defective, substitute new switch into circuit and operate switch by hand. If the vehicle's lights operate normally, signal switch is inoperative.	• Replace bulb • Repair chassis wiring as required • Replace flasher • Connect securely • Replace turn signal switch • Replace turn signal switch
Stop light not on when turn indicated	• Loose column to chassis connection • Disconnect column to chassis connector. Connect new switch into system without removing old. Operate switch by hand. If brake lights work with switch in the turn position, signal switch is defective.	• Connect securely • Replace signal switch

Troubleshooting the Turn Signal Switch (cont.)

Problem	Cause	Solution
Stop light not on when turn indicated (cont.)	• If brake lights do not work, check connector to stop light sockets for grounds, opens, etc.	• Repair connector to stop light circuits using service manual as guide
Turn indicator panel lights not flashing	• Burned out bulbs • High resistance to ground at bulb socket • Opens, ground in wiring harness from front turn signal bulb socket to indicator lights	• Replace bulbs • Replace socket • Locate and repair as required
Turn signal lights flash very slowly	• High resistance ground at light sockets • Incorrect capacity turn signal flasher or bulb • If flashing rate is still extremely slow, check chassis wiring harness from the connector to light sockets for high resistance • Loose chassis to column harness connection • Disconnect column to chassis connector. Connect new switch into system without removing old. Operate switch by hand. If flashing occurs at normal rate, the signal switch is defective.	• Repair high resistance grounds at light sockets • Replace turn signal flasher or bulb • Locate and repair as required • Connect securely • Replace turn signal switch
Hazard signal lights will not flash—turn signal functions normally	• Blow fuse • Inoperative hazard warning flasher • Loose chassis-to-column harness connection • Disconnect column to chassis connector. Connect new switch into system without removing old. Depress the hazard warning lights. If they now work normally, turn signal switch is defective. • If lights do not flash, check wiring harness "K" lead for open between hazard flasher and connector. If open, fuse block is defective	• Replace fuse • Replace hazard warning flasher in fuse panel • Conect securely • Replace turn signal switch • Repair or replace brown wire or connector as required

Troubleshooting the Manual Steering Gear

Problem	Cause	Solution
Hard or erratic steering	• Incorrect tire pressure • Insufficient or incorrect lubrication • Suspension, or steering linkage parts damaged or misaligned • Improper front wheel alignment • Incorrect steering gear adjustment • Sagging springs	• Inflate tires to recommended pressures • Lubricate as required (refer to Maintenance Section) • Repair or replace parts as necessary • Adjust incorrect wheel alignment angles • Adjust steering gear • Replace springs
Play or looseness in steering	• Steering wheel loose • Steering linkage or attaching parts loose or worn	• Inspect shaft spines and repair as necessary. Tighten attaching nut and stake in place. • Tighten, adjust, or replace faulty components

Troubleshooting the Manual Steering Gear (cont.)

Problem	Cause	Solution
Play or looseness in steering (cont.)	• Pitman arm loose • Steering gear attaching bolts loose • Loose or worn wheel bearings • Steering gear adjustment incorrect or parts badly worn	• Inspect shaft splines and repair as necessary. Tighten attaching nut and stake in place • Tighten bolts • Adjust or replace bearings • Adjust gear or replace defective parts
Wheel shimmy or tramp	• Improper tire pressure • Wheels, tires, or brake rotors out-of-balance or out-of-round • Inoperative, worn, or loose shock absorbers or mounting parts • Loose or worn steering or suspension parts • Loose or worn wheel bearings • Incorrect steering gear adjustments • Incorrect front wheel alignment	• Inflate tires to recommended pressures • Inspect and replace or balance parts • Repair or replace shocks or mountings • Tighten or replace as necessary • Adjust or replace bearings • Adjust steering gear • Correct front wheel alignment
Tire wear	• Improper tire pressure • Failure to rotate tires • Brakes grabbing • Incorrect front wheel alignment • Broken or damaged steering and suspension parts • Wheel runout • Excessive speed on turns	• Inflate tires to recommended pressures • Rotate tires • Adjust or repair brakes • Align incorrect angles • Repair or replace defective parts • Replace faulty wheel • Make driver aware of conditions
Vehicle leads to one side	• Improper tire pressures • Front tires with uneven tread depth, wear pattern, or different cord design (i.e., one bias ply and one belted or radial tire on front wheels) • Incorrect front wheel alignment • Brakes dragging • Pulling due to uneven tire construction	• Inflate tires to recommended pressures • Install tires of same cord construction and reasonably even tread depth, design, and wear pattern • Align incorrect angles • Adjust or repair brakes • Replace faulty tire

Troubleshooting the Power Steering Gear

Problem	Cause	Solution
Hissing noise in steering gear	• There is some noise in all power steering systems. One of the most common is a hissing sound most evident at standstill parking. There is no relationship between this noise and performance of the steering. Hiss may be expected when steering wheel is at end of travel or when slowly turning at standstill.	• Slight hiss is normal and in no way affects steering. Do not replace valve unless hiss is extremely objectionable. A replacement valve will also exhibit slight noise and is not always a cure. Investigate clearance around flexible coupling rivets. Be sure steering shaft and gear are aligned so flexible coupling rotates in a flat plane and is not distorted as shaft rotates. Any metal-to-metal contacts through flexible coupling will transmit valve hiss into passenger compartment through the steering column.

Troubleshooting the Power Steering Gear (cont.)

Problem	Cause	Solution
Rattle or chuckle noise in steering gear	• Gear loose on frame	• Check gear-to-frame mounting screws. Tighten screws to 88 N·m (65 foot pounds) torque.
	• Steering linkage looseness	• Check linkage pivot points for wear. Replace if necessary.
	• Pressure hose touching other parts of car	• Adjust hose position. Do not bend tubing by hand.
	• Loose pitman shaft over center adjustment **NOTE:** A slight rattle may occur on turns because of increased clearance off the "high point." This is normal and clearance must not be reduced below specified limits to eliminate this slight rattle.	• Adjust to specifications
	• Loose pitman arm	• Tighten pitman arm nut to specifications
Squawk noise in steering gear when turning or recovering from a turn	• Damper O-ring on valve spool cut	• Replace damper O-ring
Poor return of steering wheel to center	• Tires not properly inflated	• Inflate to specified pressure
	• Lack of lubrication in linkage and ball joints	• Lube linkage and ball joints
	• Lower coupling flange rubbing against steering gear adjuster plug	• Loosen pinch bolt and assemble properly
	• Steering gear to column misalignment	• Align steering column
	• Improper front wheel alignment	• Check and adjust as necessary
	• Steering linkage binding	• Replace pivots
	• Ball joints binding	• Replace ball joints
	• Steering wheel rubbing against housing	• Align housing
	• Tight or frozen steering shaft bearings	• Replace bearings
	• Sticking or plugged valve spool	• Remove and clean or replace valve
	• Steering gear adjustments over specifications	• Check adjustment with gear out of car. Adjust as required.
	• Kink in return hose	• Replace hose
Car leads to one side or the other (keep in mind road condition and wind. Test car in both directions on flat road)	• Front end misaligned	• Adjust to specifications
	• Unbalanced steering gear valve **NOTE:** If this is cause, steering effort will be very light in direction of lead and normal or heavier in opposite direction	• Replace valve
Momentary increase in effort when turning wheel fast to right or left	• Low oil level	• Add power steering fluid as required
	• Pump belt slipping	• Tighten or replace belt
	• High internal leakage	• Check pump pressure. (See pressure test)
Steering wheel surges or jerks when turning with engine running especially during parking	• Low oil level	• Fill as required
	• Loose pump belt	• Adjust tension to specification
	• Steering linkage hitting engine oil pan at full turn	• Correct clearance
	• Insufficient pump pressure	• Check pump pressure. (See pressure test). Replace relief valve if defective.
	• Pump flow control valve sticking	• Inspect for varnish or damage, replace if necessary

Troubleshooting the Power Steering Gear (cont.)

Problem	Cause	Solution
Excessive wheel kickback or loose steering	• Air in system	• Add oil to pump reservoir and bleed by operating steering. Check hose connectors for proper torque and adjust as required.
	• Steering gear loose on frame	• Tighten attaching screws to specified torque
	• Steering linkage joints worn enough to be loose	• Replace loose pivots
	• Worn poppet valve	• Replace poppet valve
	• Loose thrust bearing preload adjustment	• Adjust to specification with gear out of vehicle
	• Excessive overcenter lash	• Adjust to specification with gear out of car
Hard steering or lack of assist	• Loose pump belt	• Adjust belt tension to specification
	• Low oil level **NOTE:** Low oil level will also result in excessive pump noise	• Fill to proper level. If excessively low, check all lines and joints for evidence of external leakage. Tighten loose connectors.
	• Steering gear to column misalignment	• Align steering column
	• Lower coupling flange rubbing against steering gear adjuster plug	• Loosen pinch bolt and assemble properly
	• Tires not properly inflated	• Inflate to recommended pressure
Foamy milky power steering fluid, low fluid level and possible low pressure	• Air in the fluid, and loss of fluid due to internal pump leakage causing overflow	• Check for leak and correct. Bleed system. Extremely cold temperatures will cause system aeriation should the oil level be low. If oil level is correct and pump still foams, remove pump from vehicle and separate reservoir from housing. Check welsh plug and housing for cracks. If plug is loose or housing is cracked, replace housing.
Low pressure due to steering pump	• Flow control valve stuck or inoperative	• Remove burrs or dirt or replace. Flush system.
	• Pressure plate not flat against cam ring	• Correct
Low pressure due to steering gear	• Pressure loss in cylinder due to worn piston ring or badly worn housing bore	• Remove gear from car for disassembly and inspection of ring and housing bore
	• Leakage at valve rings, valve body-to-worm seal	• Remove gear from car for disassembly and replace seals

Troubleshooting the Power Steering Pump

Problem	Cause	Solution
Chirp noise in steering pump	• Loose belt	• Adjust belt tension to specification
Belt squeal (particularly noticeable at full wheel travel and stand still parking)	• Loose belt	• Adjust belt tension to specification
Growl noise in steering pump	• Excessive back pressure in hoses or steering gear caused by restriction	• Locate restriction and correct. Replace part if necessary.

Troubleshooting the Power Steering Pump (cont.)

Problem	Cause	Solution
Growl noise in steering pump (particularly noticeable at stand still parking)	• Scored pressure plates, thrust plate or rotor • Extreme wear of cam ring	• Replace parts and flush system • Replace parts
Groan noise in steering pump	• Low oil level • Air in the oil. Poor pressure hose connection.	• Fill reservoir to proper level • Tighten connector to specified torque. Bleed system by operating steering from right to left—full turn.
Rattle noise in steering pump	• Vanes not installed properly • Vanes sticking in rotor slots	• Install properly • Free up by removing burrs, varnish, or dirt
Swish noise in steering pump	• Defective flow control valve	• Replace part
Whine noise in steering pump	• Pump shaft bearing scored	• Replace housing and shaft. Flush system.
Hard steering or lack of assist	• Loose pump belt • Low oil level in reservoir **NOTE:** Low oil level will also result in excessive pump noise • Steering gear to column misalignment • Lower coupling flange rubbing against steering gear adjuster plug • Tires not properly inflated	• Adjust belt tension to specification • Fill to proper level. If excessively low, check all lines and joints for evidence of external leakage. Tighten loose connectors. • Align steering column • Loosen pinch bolt and assemble properly • Inflate to recommended pressure
Foaming milky power steering fluid, low fluid level and possible low pressure	• Air in the fluid, and loss of fluid due to internal pump leakage causing overflow	• Check for leaks and correct. Bleed system. Extremely cold temperatures will cause system aeriation should the oil level be low. If oil level is correct and pump still foams, remove pump from vehicle and separate reservoir from body. Check welsh plug and body for cracks. If plug is loose or body is cracked, replace body.
Low pump pressure	• Flow control valve stuck or inoperative • Pressure plate not flat against cam ring	• Remove burrs or dirt or replace. Flush system. • Correct
Momentary increase in effort when turning wheel fast to right or left	• Low oil level in pump • Pump belt slipping • High internal leakage	• Add power steering fluid as required • Tighten or replace belt • Check pump pressure. (See pressure test)
Steering wheel surges or jerks when turning with engine running especially during parking	• Low oil level • Loose pump belt • Steering linkage hitting engine oil pan at full turn • Insufficient pump pressure	• Fill as required • Adjust tension to specification • Correct clearance • Check pump pressure. (See pressure test). Replace flow control valve if defective.
Steering wheel surges or jerks when turning with engine running especially during parking (cont.)	• Sticking flow control valve	• Inspect for varnish or damage, replace if necessary
Excessive wheel kickback or loose steering	• Air in system	• Add oil to pump reservoir and bleed by operating steering. Check hose connectors for proper torque and adjust as required.

Troubleshooting the Power Steering Pump (cont.)

Problem	Cause	Solution
Low pump pressure	· Extreme wear of cam ring	· Replace parts. Flush system.
	· Scored pressure plate, thrust plate, or rotor	· Replace parts. Flush system.
	· Vanes not installed properly	· Install properly
	· Vanes sticking in rotor slots	· Freeup by removing burrs, varnish, or dirt
	· Cracked or broken thrust or pressure plate	· Replace part

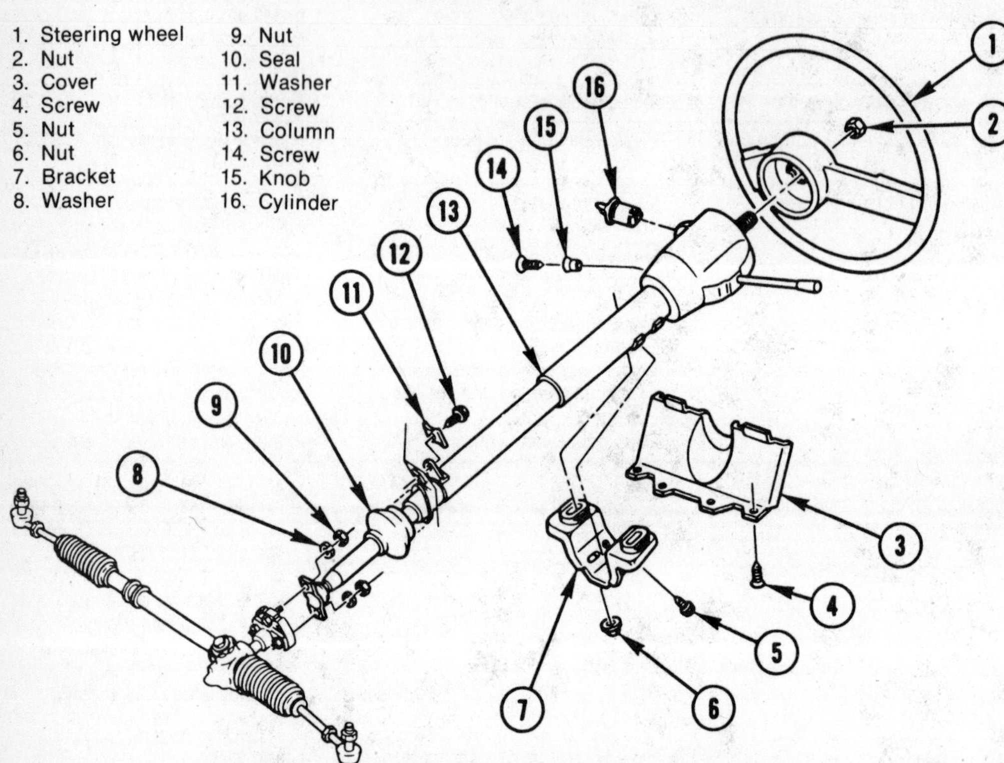

Exploded view of the manual rack and pinion steering system

8. Install the tie rods into the steering knuckles. Install the tie rod nuts. If the cotter pin holes do not align, tighten the nut until the cotter pin can be inserted, and install the cotter pins.

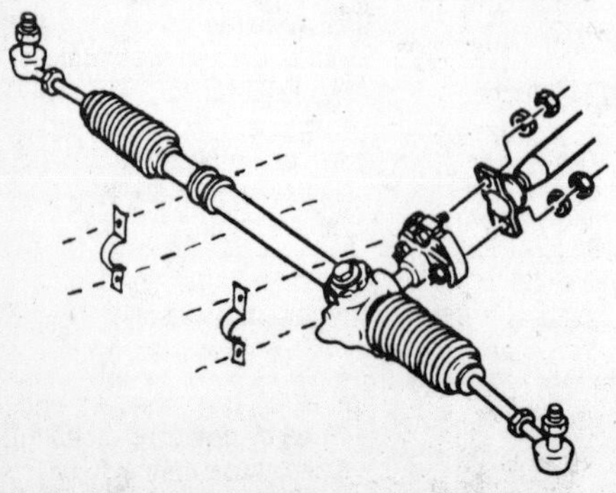

Installation of the rack and pinion assembly

9. Install the bolts and the shield.
10. Lower the car.

Power Steering Pump

REMOVAL AND INSTALLATION

1. Remove the upper adjusting bolt.
2. Remove the lower brace bolt-to-pump bracket.
3. Remove the LH crossmember brace-to-body.
4. Remove the pressure line and the reservoir line at the pump.
5. Remove the rear pump adjusting bracket.
6. Remove the front pivot bolt at the pump.
7. Remove the bolt that attaches the front bracket to the engine and remove the pump and bracket.

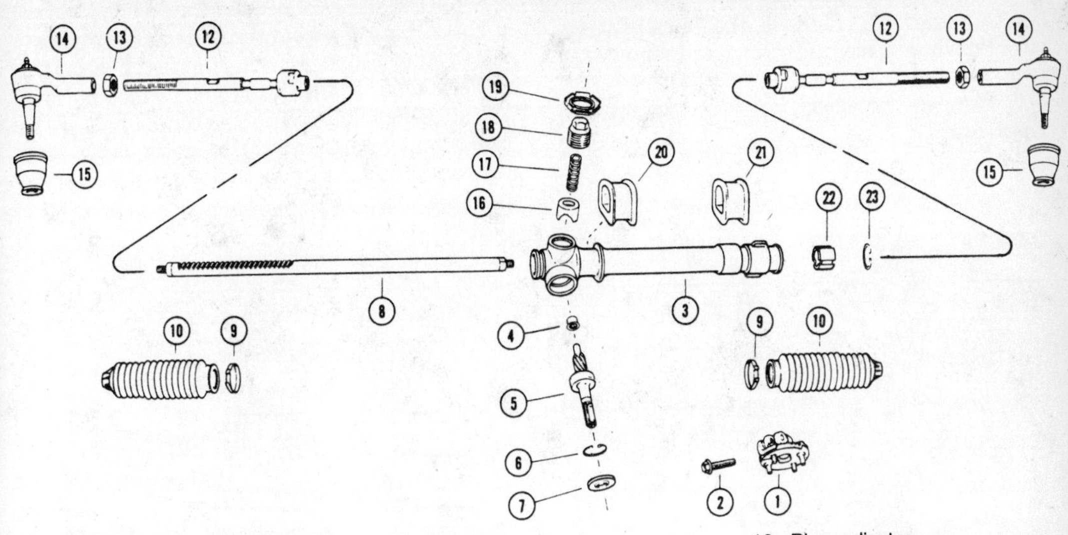

1. Flange assy, coupling & strg.
2. Bolt, pinch
3. Housing assy, rack & pinion
4. Bearing assy, roller
5. Pinion assy, bearing &
6. Ring, retaining
7. Seal, steering pinion
8. Rack, steering
9. Clamp, boot
10. Boot
12. Rod assy, inner tie
13. Nut, jam
14. Rod assy, outer tie
15. Seal, tie rod
16. Bearing, rack
17. Spring, adjuster
18. Plug, adjuster
19. Nut, adjuster plug lock
20. Grommet, gear mounting (LH)
21. Grommet, gear mounting (RH)
22. Bushing, rack
23. Ring, retaining

Exploded view of the manual rack and pinion assembly

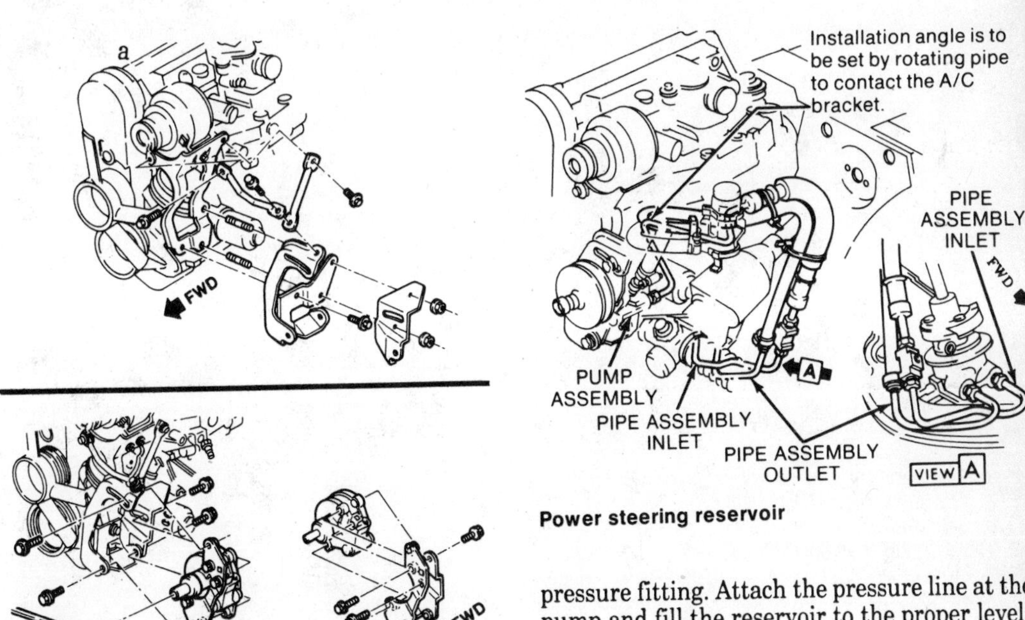

Power steering reservoir

Power steering pump mounting

8. Installation is the reverse of removal. Adjust the belt, fill the reservoir and bleed the system as follows: With the pressure line disconnected at the pump outlet add fluid to the reservoir until fluid begins leaving the pump at the pressure fitting. Attach the pressure line at the pump and fill the reservoir to the proper level.

Steering Wheel

REMOVAL AND INSTALLATION

1. Disconnect the negative battery cable.
2. On models through 1978, remove the two steering wheel shroud screws at the underside of the steering wheel and remove the shroud. On 1979 and later models, pull up on the horn

cap to remove it. Remove the horn ring-to-steering wheel attaching screws and remove the ring.

3. Remove the wheel nut retainer and the wheel nut.

CAUTION: *Do not overexpand the retainer.*

4. Using a steering wheel puller, thread the puller anchor screws into the threaded holes in the steering wheel. With the center bolt of the puller butting against the steering shaft, turn the center bolt clockwise to remove the steering wheel.

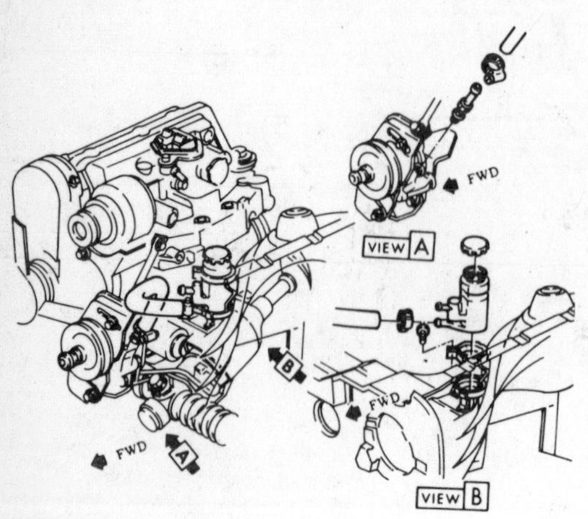

Power steering hoses

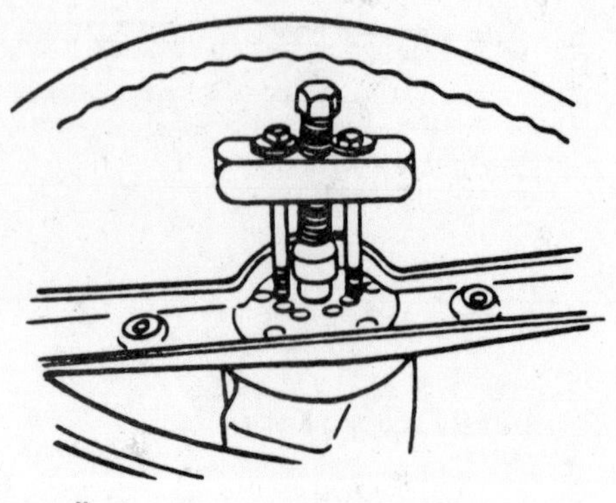

Use a puller to remove the steering wheel

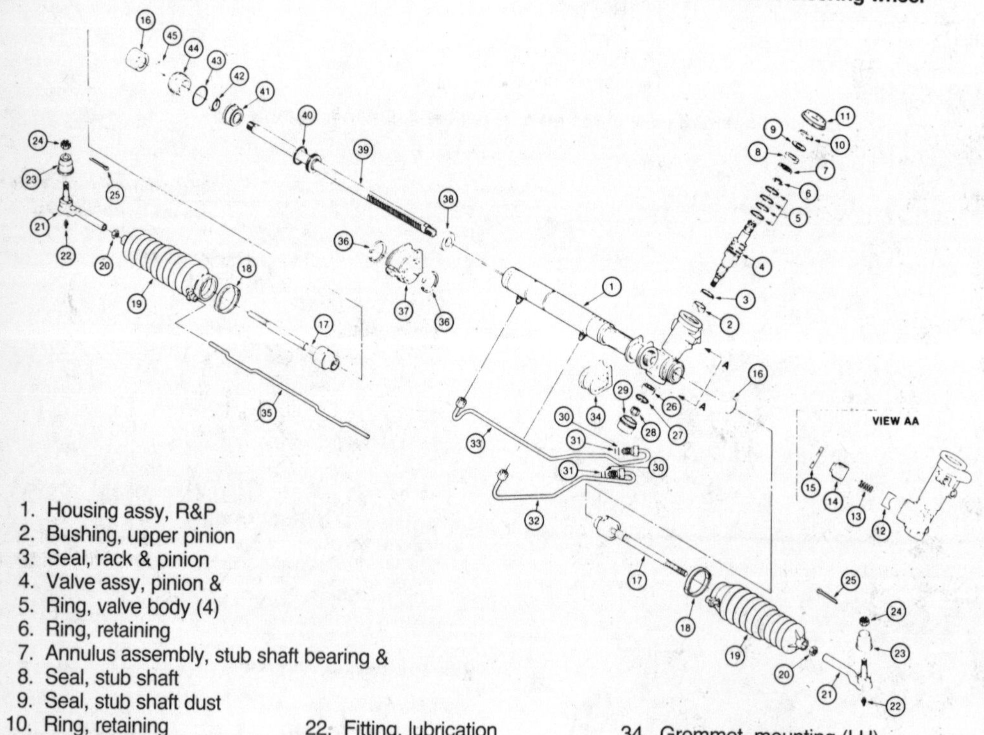

1. Housing assy, R&P
2. Bushing, upper pinion
3. Seal, rack & pinion
4. Valve assy, pinion &
5. Ring, valve body (4)
6. Ring, retaining
7. Annulus assembly, stub shaft bearing &
8. Seal, stub shaft
9. Seal, stub shaft dust
10. Ring, retaining
11. Adapter, shield
12. Bearing, rack
13. Spring, adjuster
14. Plug, adjuster
15. Nut, adjuster plug lock
16. Ring, shock dampener
17. Rod assy, inner tie
18. Clamp, boot
19. Boot, rack & pinion
20. Nut, hex jam
21. Rod assy, outer tie
22. Fitting, lubrication
23. Seal, tie rod
24. Nut, hexagon slotted
25. Pin, cotter
26. Bearing assy, ball
27. Ring, retaining
28. Nut, hex lock
29. Cover, dust
30. Seal, O-ring
31. Seal, O-ring
32. Line assy, cylinder (RT)
33. Line assy, cylinder (LT)
34. Grommet, mounting (LH)
35. Tube, breather
36. Ring, retaining
37. Grommet assembly, mounting (RH)
38. Seal, inner rack
39. Rack assy, piston & steering
40. Ring, piston
41. Bulkhead, cylinder inner
42. Seal, rack & pinion (bulkhead)
43. Seal, O-ring
44. Bulkhead, cylinder outer
45. Ring, bulkhead retaining

Exploded view of the power rack and pinion assembly

NOTE: *The puller centering adapter need not be used.*

5. To install, place the turn signal lever in the neutral position and install the steering wheel. Torque the steering wheel nut to 30. ft. lbs. and install the nut retainer.
6. Connect the negative battery cable.

Turn Signal Switch

REMOVAL AND INSTALLATION

1. Remove the steering wheel as previously described.
2. Position a screwdriver blade into one of the three cover slots. Pry up and out (at least two slots) to free the cover.
3. Place the U-shaped lockplate compressing tool on the end of the steering shaft and compress the lockplate. The full load of the spring should not be relieved because the ring will rotate and make removal difficult. Pry the round wire snapring out of the shaft groove and discard it. Remove the lockplate compressing tool and lift the lockplate off the end of the shaft.

WARNING: *If the steering column is being disassembled out of the car, with the snapring removed, the shaft could slide out of the lower end of the mast jacket and be damaged.*

4. Slide the turn signal cancelling cam, upper bearing preload spring, and thrust washer off the end of the shaft.
5. Remove the multi-function lever by rotating it clockwise to its top (off position), then pull the lever straight out to disengage it.
6. Push the hazard warning knob in and unscrew the knob.
7. Remove the two screws, pivot arm, and spacer.
8. Wrap the upper part of the connector with tape to prevent snagging the wire during switch removal.
9. Remove the three switch mounting screws and pull the switch straight up, guiding the wiring harness through the column housing.

This lockplate compressor is necessary for turn signal switch removal

CAUTION: *On installation it is extremely important that only the specified screws, bolts and nuts be used. The use of over-length screws could prevent the steering column from compressing under impact.*

10. Position the switch into the housing.
11. Install the three switch mounting screws. Replace the spacer and pivot arm. Be sure that the spacer protrudes through the hole in the arm and that the arm finger encloses the turn signal switch frame. Tighten the truss head screw (secures the spacer to the signal switch) to 20 in. lbs. and the flat head screw to 35 in. lbs.
12. Install the hazard warning knob.
13. Make sure that the turn signal switch is in the neutral position and that the hazard warning knob is out. Slide the thrust washer, upper bearing preload spring, and the canceling cam into the upper end of the shaft.
14. Place the lockplate and a NEW snapring onto the end of the shaft. Using the lockplate compressing tool, compress the lockplate as far as possible. Slide the new snapring into the shaft groove and remove the lockplate compressing tool.

CAUTION: *On assembly, always use a new snapring.*

15. Install the multi-function lever, guiding the wire harness through the column housing. Align the lever pin with the switch slot. Push on the end of the lever until it is seated securely.
16. Install the steering wheel as previously described.

Wiper/Washer Switch

REMOVAL AND INSTALLATION

The wiper/washer switch is located on the left side of the column under the turn signal switch.

1. Remove the steering wheel and turn signal switch as previously described. The ignition switch is mounted on top of the mast jacket near the front of the dash.
2. Remove the upper attaching screw on the ignition and dimmer switch; this releases the dimmer switch and actuator rod assembly.

NOTE: *Do not move the ignition switch. If this happens, refer to switch adjustment procedure in Ignition Switch and Dimmer Switch Removal and Installation.*

3. The wiper/washer switch and pivot assembly now can be removed from the column housing.
4. To install, place the wiper/washer switch and pivot assembly into the housing and guide the connector down through the bowl and shroud assembly.

5. Install the turn signal switch as previously described.

6. Fit the pinched end of the dimmer switch actuator rod into the dimmer switch. Feed the other end of the rod through the hole in the shroud into the hole in the wiper/washer switch and pivot assembly drive, but do not tighten the attaching screw. Depress the dimmer switch slightly to insert a $^3/_{32}$" drill bit to lock the switch to the body. Push the switch up to remove the lash between both the ignition and dimmer switches and the actuator rod. Install the wiper/washer switch mounting screw and tighten it to 35 in. lbs. Remove the drill and check dimmer switch operation with the actuating lever.

Ignition Key Buzzer Switch

REMOVAL AND INSTALLATION

1. Remove the steering wheel and turn signal switch as previously described.

2. Make a right angle bend in a short piece of small wire about ¼" from one end. The wire should be inserted in the exposed loop of the wedge spring, then a straight pull on the wire will remove both the spring and the switch.

CAUTION: *Do not attempt to remove the switch separately as the clip may fall into the column. If this happens, the clip must be found before assembly.*

NOTE: *The lock cylinder must be in the* **Run** position if it is in the housing. Also, if the lock cylinder is in place, the buzzer switch actuating button on the lock cylinder must be depressed before the buzzer switch can be installed.

3. Install the buzzer switch with the contacts toward the upper end of the steering column and with the formed end of the spring clip around the lower end of the switch. Push the switch and spring assembly into the hole with the internal switch contacts toward the lock cylinder bore.

4. Install the turn signal switch and the steering wheel as previously described.

Lock Cylinder

REMOVAL AND INSTALLATION

The lock cylinder is located on the right side of the steering column and should be removed only in the **Run** position. Removal in any other position will damage the key buzzer switch. The lock cylinder cannot be disassembled; if replacement is required, a new cylinder coded to the old key must be installed.

1. Remove the steering wheel and turn signal switch as previously described.

2. Do not remove the buzzer switch or damage to the lock cylinder will result.

3. On models through 1978, insert a small screwdriver or similar tool into the turn signal housing slot to the upper right of the steering shaft. Keep the tool to the upper right of the steering shaft. Keep the tool to the right side of the slot and depress the retainer at the bottom to release the lock cylinder. Remove the lock cylinder.

On 1979 and later models, place the lock cylinder in the RUN position. Remove the securing screw and remove the cylinder.

4. To install the lock cylinder, hold the cylinder sleeve in the left hand and rotate knob (key in) clockwise to stop. (This retracts the actuator). Insert the cylinder into the housing bore with the key on the cylinder sleeve aligned with the keyway in the housing. Push the cylinder in until it bottoms. On models through 1978, rotate the knob counterclockwise while maintaining a light pressure inward until the drive sec-

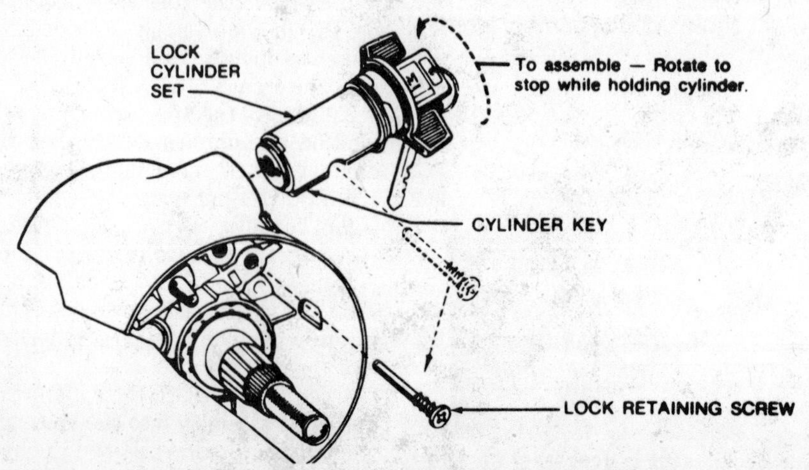

Lock cylinder removal and installation—1979 and later

Lock cylinder removal—through 1978

tion of the cylinder mates with the sector. Push the cylinder in fully until the retainer pops into the housing groove. On 1979 and later models, install the retaining screw.

5. Install the turn signal switch and the steering wheel as previously described.

Ignition Switch and Dimmer Switch

REMOVAL AND INSTALLATION

The ignition switch is mounted on top of the mast jacket near the front of the dash. The switch is located inside the channel section of

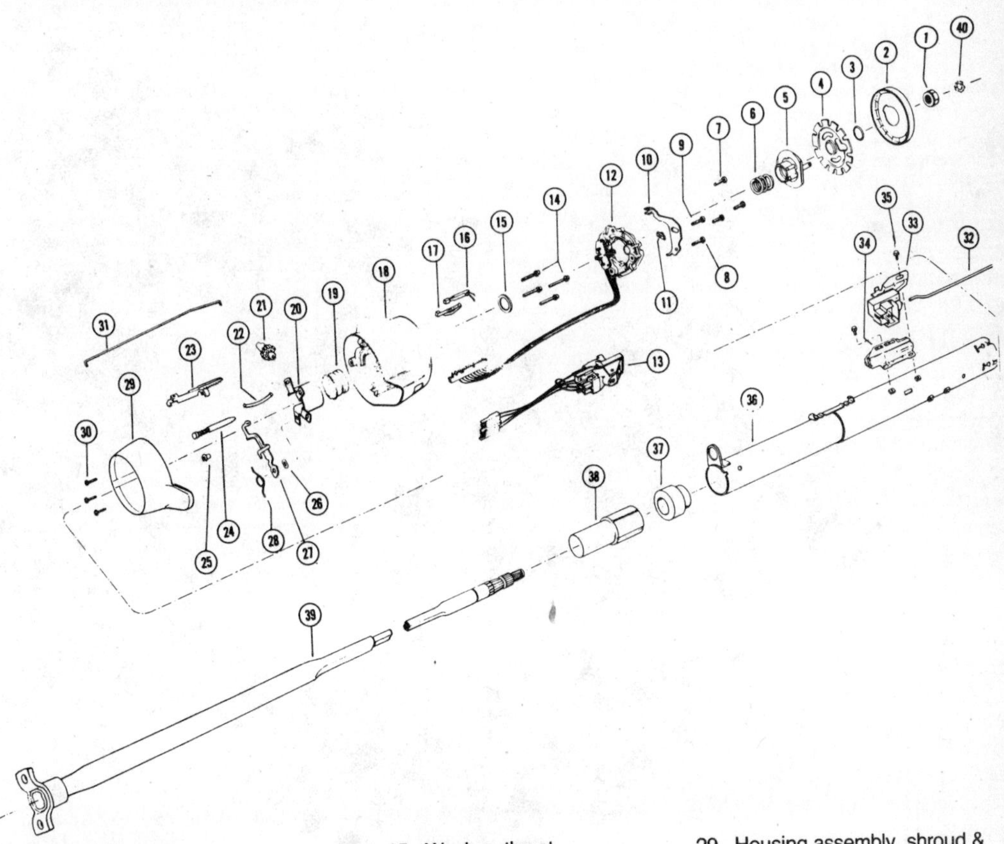

1. Nut, hexagon jam
2. Cover assembly, shaft lock
3. Ring, retaining
4. Lock, steering shaft
5. Cam assembly, turn signal cancelling
6. Spring, upper bearing
7. Screw, pan head cross recess
8. Screw, flat head cross recess
9. Screw, round head cross recess
10. Arm, pivot
11. Spacer, turn signal screw
12. Switch assembly, turn signal
13. Switch assembly, pivot &
14. Screw hex washer head tapping
15. Washer, thrust
16. Switch assembly, buzzer
17. Clip, buzzer switch retaining
18. Housing, steering column
19. Bearing assembly
20. Retainer, bearing
21. Sector, switch actuator
22. Spring, rack preload
23. Rack, switch actuator
24. Bolt assembly, spring &
25. Washer, spring thrust
26. Washer, wave
27. Lever, key release
28. Spring, lock inhibiter
29. Housing assembly, shroud &
30. Screw, pan head cross recess
31. Rod, switch actuator
32. Rod, dimmer switch actuator
33. Switch assembly, dimmer
34. Switch assembly, ignition
35. Screw, washer head
36. Jacket assembly, steering column
37. Seal, steering shaft
38. Bushing, steering column jacket
39. Shaft assembly, steering
40. Retainer

Exploded view of the standard steering column

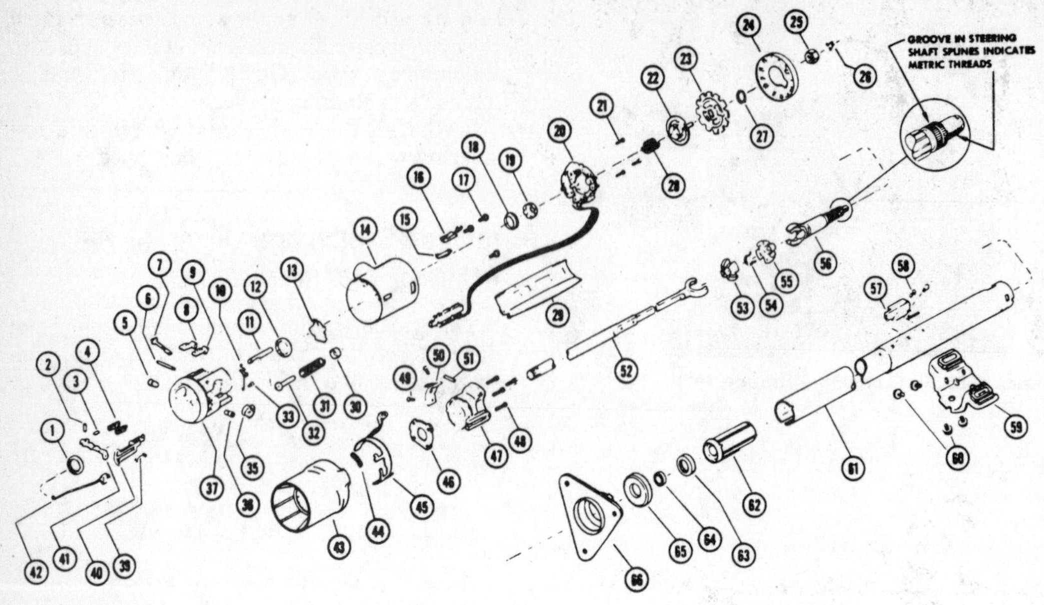

1. Bearing assy
2. Pin, release lever
3. Spring, release lever
4. Spring, shoe
5. Pin, pivot
6. Pin, dowel
7. Shaft, drive
8. Shoe, steering wheel lock
9. Shoe, steering wheel lock
10. Spring, lock bolt
11. Bolt, lock
12. Bearing assy
13. Shield, tilt lever opening
14. Cover, lock housing
15. Clip, buzzer switch retaining
16. Switch assy, buzzer
17. Screw, oval head cross recess
18. Race, inner
19. Seat, upper bearing inner race
20. Switch assy, turn signal
21. Screw, binding hd cross recess
22. Cam assy, turn signal cancelling
23. Lock, shaft
24. Cover, shaft lock
25. Nut, hexagon jam (9/16–18)
26. Retainer
27. Ring, retainer
28. Spring, upper bearing
29. Protector, wiring
30. Retainer, spring
31. Spring, wheel tilt
32. Guide, spring
33. Screw, hex. washer head
34. This number not used
35. Sector, switch actuator
36. Pin, pivot
37. Housing, steering column
38. This number not used
39. Spring, rack preload
40. Rack, switch actuator
41. Lever, shoe release
42. Actuator assy, switch
43. Shroud, column housing
44. Spring, key release
45. Lever, key release
46. Plate, lock
47. Support, steering column housing
48. Screw, support
49. Screw, oval head cross recess
50. Plate, shroud retaining
51. Pin, dowel
52. Shaft assy, lower steering
53. Sphere, centering
54. Spring, joint preload
55. Sphere, centering
56. Shaft assy, race & upper
57. Switch assy, ignition
58. Screw, washer head (#10-24 × .25)
59. Bracket assy, steering column support
60. Bolt, flanged hex head
61. Jacket assy, sleeve &
62. Bearing assy, adapter &
63. Bearing assy
64. Spacer, steering shaft
65. Seal, jacket & dash bracket
66. Bracket assy, column dash

Exploded view of the tilt wheel steering column

the brake pedal support and is completely inaccessible without first lowering the steering column.

1. Disconnect the negative battery cable.
2. Remove the steering wheel as previously described.
3. Move the driver's seat as far back as possible.
4. Remove the floor pan bracket screw.
5. Remove the two column bracket-to-instrument panel nuts and lower the column far enough to disconnect the ignition switch wiring harness.

CAUTION: *Be sure that the steering column is properly supported before proceeding.*

6. The switch should be in the **Lock** position before removal. If the lock cylinder has already been removed, the actuating rod to the switch should be pulled up until there is a definite stop, then moved down one detent which is the **Lock** position.
7. Remove the two mounting screws and remove the ignition and dimmer switch.
8. Refer to the installation procedure previously described in Lock Cylinder Removal and Installation.
9. Turn the cylinder clockwise to stop and then counterclockwise to the **Off-Unlock** position.
10. Place the ignition switch in the **Off-Unlock** position by positioning the switch as shown in the accompanying illustration. Move

Installing the dimmer switch

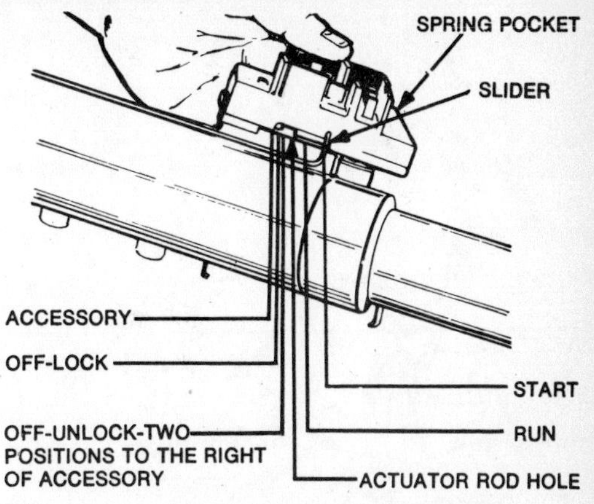

Positioning the ignition switch for installation

the slider two positions to the right from **Accessory** to the **Off-Unlock** position.

11. Fit the actuator rod into the slider hole and install the switch on the column. Be sure to use only the correct screws. Tighten only one bottom screw to 35 in. lbs. Be careful not to move the switch out of its detent.
12. Perform the dimmer switch adjustment procedure previously outlined in Wiper/Washer Switch Removal and Installation.
13. Connect the ignition switch wiring harness.
14. Loosely install the column bracket-to-instrument panel nuts to within 1mm ± ½mm of being tight.
15. Install the floor pan bracket screw and tighten it to 25 ft. lbs.
16. Tighten the column bracket-to-instrument panel nuts to 20 ft. lbs.
17. Install the steering wheel as previously outlined.
18. Connect the battery negative cable.

Steering Column

REMOVAL

1. Disconnect the negative battery cable.
2. If the column is to be repaired, remove the steering wheel.
3. Remove the bracket attaching bolts, coupling bolts and seal retainer screws as shown.

WARNING: *Use care when handling the steering column it is extremely susceptible to damage.*

INSTALLATION

With Power Steering

1. Attach bracket **A** to the jacket and install bolt **B** first, bolt **C** second and bolts **D** and **E** last. Tighten to 22 ft. lbs.
2. Attach seal **F** to retainer **G** by pulling (carrots) part of seal **F** through the holes of clamp **G**.
3. With the column through the front of the dash, assemble seal **F** and retainer **G** with bolt/screws **H**.
4. Install the steering coupling shield **S** over the column.
5. Position the splined shaft of the steering column into the coupling. Make sure no visible splines show between the coupling and the shaft.
6. Loose assemble the capsule nuts **J** to within 1.0 ± 0.5 of touching capsule surface.
7. Attach the column to the front of the dash with with screw **M** and washer **M**.
8. Tighten capusle nuts **J** at the instrument panel.
9. Tighten pinch bolt **T** to 30 ft. lbs.
10. Remove the alignment spacer **R**.
11. Position the steering coupling shield **S** over the adapter and secure with screw **U** and nut **V**.
12. After the vehicle is on wheels the minimum clearance between the O.D. of the shaft and the I.D. of the jacket lower bushing after installation is 2.5mm.

Without Power steering

1. Attach bracket **A** to the jacket and install bolt **B** first, bolt **C** second and bolts **D** and **E** last. Tighten to 22 ft. lbs.
2. Attach seal **F** to retainer **G** by pulling (carrots) part of seal **F** through the holes of clamp **G**.
3. With the column through the front of the dash, assemble seal **F** and retainer **G** with bolt/screws **H**.
4. Position the coupling flange to the coupling studs.
5. Loose assemble the capsule nuts to within 1.0 ± 0.5 of touching capsule surface.
6. Install the coupling flange to the coupling with lockwasher **K** and nuts **K** and tighten to 17 ft. lbs.

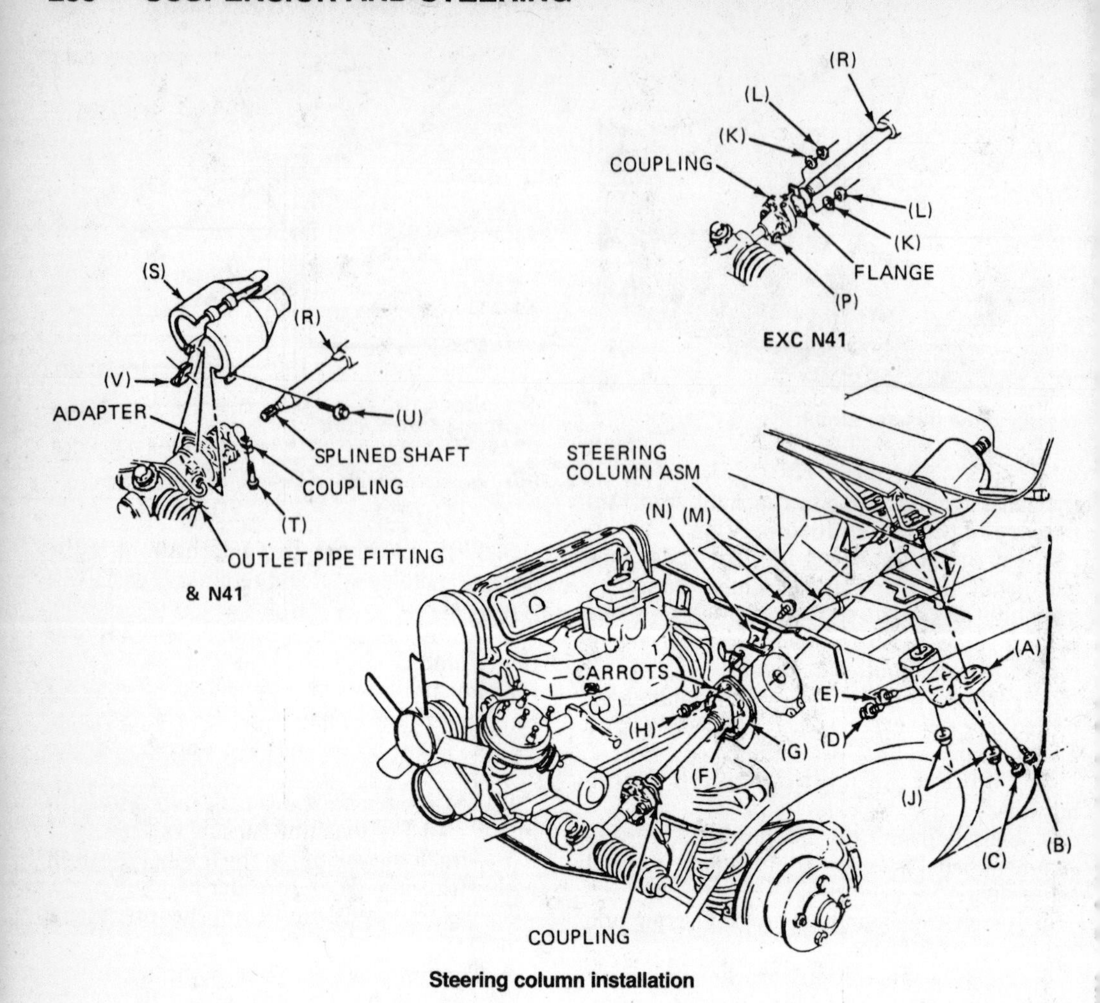

Steering column installation

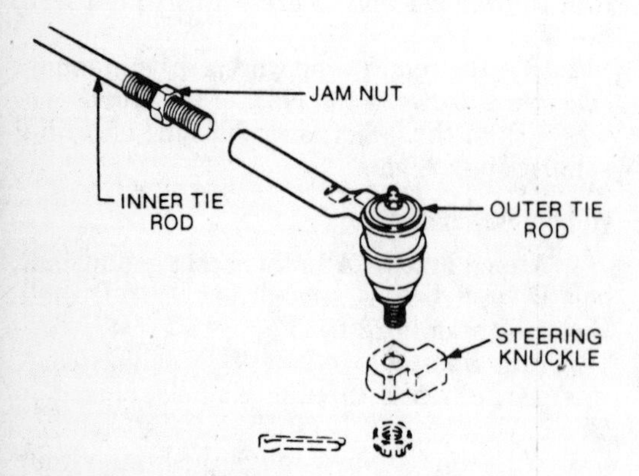

Outer tie rod installation

7. Attach the column to the front of the dash with screw **M** and washer **N**.

8. Tighten capusle nuts **J** at the instrument panel.

9. Tighten pinch bolt **P** to 30 ft. lbs.

10. Remove the alignment spacer **R**.

11. After the vehicle is on wheels the minimum clearance between the O.D. of the shaft and the I.D. of the jacket lower bushing after installation is 2.5mm.

Outer Tie Rod

REMOVAL AND INSTALLATION

1. Loosen the jam nut.

2. Using tool J-24319-01 or BT-7101 or equivalent, remove the tie rod from the knuckle.

3. Install all parts but do not tighten the jam nut.

4. Make the toe-in adjustment by turning the inner tie rod.

5. Torque the jam nut to 50 ft. lbs.

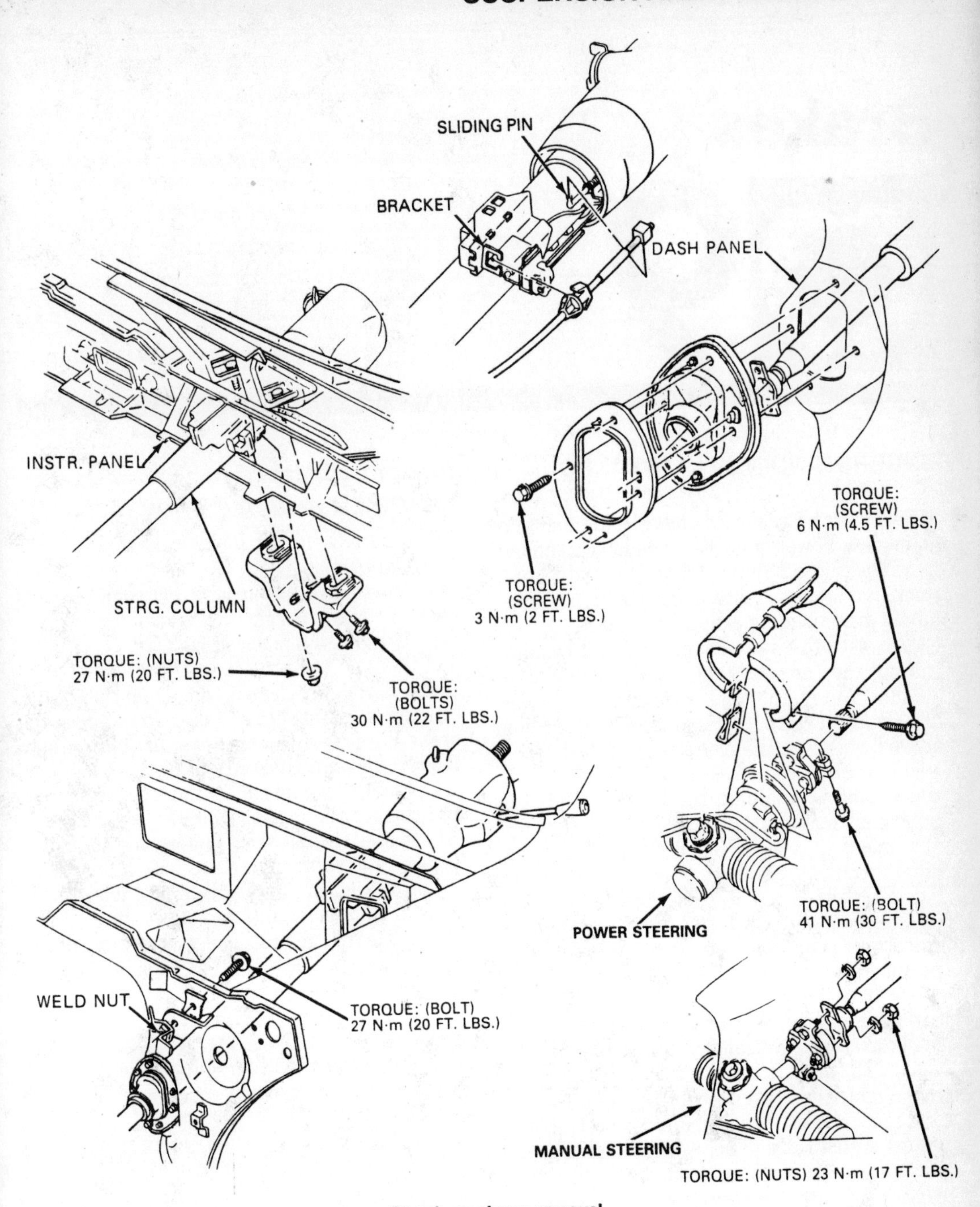

Steering column removal

Brakes

UNDERSTANDING THE BRAKES

Front disc brakes are standard equipment on all models. Power brakes are available as an option. The disc is 246mm in diameter and 13mm. thick and is a one piece casting with the hub. Single piston sliding calipers are used.

The rear brakes are of conventional leading/trailing shoe design. Brake drum diameter is 200mm. Automatic adjusters are used in the rear brakes which provide adjustment when needed whenever the brakes are applied.

The master cylinder is a two piece design: a cast housing containing the primary and secondary pistons and a stamped steel reservoir. The reservoir is attached to the cast housing with two retainers and sealed with two O-rings. The reservoir is not divided, however a dual braking system is used. The front (secondary) piston operates the rear brakes, while the rear (primary) piston operates the front brakes.

The front and rear brake lines are routed through a distributor and switch assembly located on the left hand engine compartment side panel. The switch is a pressure differential type which lights the brake warning light on the instrument panel if either the front or rear hydraulic system fails. The switch is nonadjustable and non-serviceable; it must be replaced if defective.

Brake Adjustment

All Chevettes and Pontiac 1000s are equipped with front disc brakes which require no adjustment. Rear brake adjustment takes place every time the brakes are applied through the use of an automatic brake adjuster. Only an initial adjustment is necessary when the brakes have been installed. This is done by depressing the brake pedal a few times until the pedal becomes firm. Check the fluid level in the master cylinder frequently during the adjustment procedure.

Master Cylinder

REMOVAL AND INSTALLATION

WARNING: *Never allow brake fluid to spill on painted surfaces.*

1. Disconnect the master cylinder pushrod from the brake pedal.
2. Remove the pushrod boot.
3. Remove the air cleaner.
4. Thoroughly clean all dirt from the master cylinder and the brake lines. Disconnect the brake lines from the master cylinder and plug them to prevent the entry of dirt.
5. Remove the master cylinder securing nuts and remove the master cylinder.
6. Install the master cylinder with its spacer. Tighten the securing nuts to 150 in. lbs.
7. Connect the brake lines to their proper ports. Tighten the nuts to 150 in. lbs.
8. Place the pushrod boot over the end of the pushrod. Secure the pushrod to the brake pedal with the pin and clip.
9. Fill the master cylinder and bleed the entire hydraulic system. After bleeding, fill the master cylinder to within ¼″ from the top of the reservoir. Check for leaks.
10. Install the air cleaner.
11. Check brake operation before moving the car.

OVERHAUL

If the master cylinder leaks externally, or if the pedal sinks while being held down, the master cylinder is worn. There are three ways to correct this situation:

a. Buy a new master cylinder;
b. Trade in the worn unit for a rebuilt unit;
c. Rebuild the old master cylinder with a rebuilding kit.

Your choice depends on the time and finances available. To rebuild the master cylinder:

1. Remove the old master cylinder from the car as previously outlined.

Troubleshooting the Brake System

Problem	Cause	Solution
Low brake pedal (excessive pedal travel required for braking action.)	• Excessive clearance between rear linings and drums caused by inoperative automatic adjusters	• Make 10 to 15 alternate forward and reverse brake stops to adjust brakes. If brake pedal does not come up, repair or replace adjuster parts as necessary.
	• Worn rear brakelining	• Inspect and replace lining if worn beyond minimum thickness specification
	• Bent, distorted brakeshoes, front or rear	• Replace brakeshoes in axle sets
	• Air in hydraulic system	• Remove air from system. Refer to Brake Bleeding.
Low brake pedal (pedal may go to floor with steady pressure applied.)	• Fluid leak in hydraulic system	• Fill master cylinder to fill line; have helper apply brakes and check calipers, wheel cylinders, differential valve tubes, hoses and fittings for leaks. Repair or replace as necessary.
	• Air in hydraulic system	• Remove air from system. Refer to Brake Bleeding.
	• Incorrect or non-recommended brake fluid (fluid evaporates at below normal temp).	• Flush hydraulic system with clean brake fluid. Refill with correct-type fluid.
	• Master cylinder piston seals worn, or master cylinder bore is scored, worn or corroded	• Repair or replace master cylinder
Low brake pedal (pedal goes to floor on first application—o.k. on subsequent applications.)	• Disc brake pads sticking on abutment surfaces of anchor plate. Caused by a build-up of dirt, rust, or corrosion on abutment surfaces	• Clean abutment surfaces
Fading brake pedal (pedal height decreases with steady pressure applied.)	• Fluid leak in hydraulic system	• Fill master cylinder reservoirs to fill mark, have helper apply brakes, check calipers, wheel cylinders, differential valve, tubes, hoses, and fittings for fluid leaks. Repair or replace parts as necessary.
	• Master cylinder piston seals worn, or master cylinder bore is scored, worn or corroded	• Repair or replace master cylinder
Decreasing brake pedal travel (pedal travel required for braking action decreases and may be accompanied by a hard pedal.)	• Caliper or wheel cylinder pistons sticking or seized	• Repair or replace the calipers, or wheel cylinders
	• Master cylinder compensator ports blocked (preventing fluid return to reservoirs) or pistons sticking or seized in master cylinder bore	• Repair or replace the master cylinder
	• Power brake unit binding internally	• Test unit according to the following procedure: (a) Shift transmission into neutral and start engine (b) Increase engine speed to 1500 rpm, close throttle and fully depress brake pedal (c) Slow release brake pedal and stop engine (d) Have helper remove vacuum check valve and hose from power unit. Observe for backward movement of brake pedal. (e) If the pedal moves backward, the power unit has an internal bind—replace power unit

Troubleshooting the Brake System (cont.)

Problem	Cause	Solution
Spongy brake pedal (pedal has abnormally soft, springy, spongy feel when depressed.)	• Air in hydraulic system	• Remove air from system. Refer to Brake Bleeding.
	• Brakeshoes bent or distorted	• Replace brakeshoes
	• Brakelining not yet seated with drums and rotors	• Burnish brakes
	• Rear drum brakes not properly adjusted	• Adjust brakes
Hard brake pedal (excessive pedal pressure required to stop vehicle. May be accompanied by brake fade.)	• Loose or leaking power brake unit vacuum hose	• Tighten connections or replace leaking hose
	• Incorrect or poor quality brakelining	• Replace with lining in axle sets
	• Bent, broken, distorted brakeshoes	• Replace brakeshoes
	• Calipers binding or dragging on mounting pins. Rear brakeshoes dragging on support plate.	• Replace mounting pins and bushings. Clean rust or burrs from rear brake support plate ledges and lubricate ledges with molydisulfide grease. **NOTE:** If ledges are deeply grooved or scored, do not attempt to sand or grind them smooth—replace support plate.
	• Caliper, wheel cylinder, or master cylinder pistons sticking or seized	• Repair or replace parts as necessary
	• Power brake unit vacuum check valve malfunction	• Test valve according to the following procedure: (a) Start engine, increase engine speed to 1500 rpm, close throttle and immediately stop engine (b) Wait at least 90 seconds then depress brake pedal (c) If brakes are not vacuum assisted for 2 or more applications, check valve is faulty
	• Power brake unit has internal bind	• Test unit according to the following procedure: (a) With engine stopped, apply brakes several times to exhaust all vacuum in system (b) Shift transmission into neutral, depress brake pedal and start engine (c) If pedal height decreases with foot pressure and less pressure is required to hold pedal in applied position, power unit vacuum system is operating normally. Test power unit. If power unit exhibits a bind condition, replace the power unit.
	• Master cylinder compensator ports (at bottom of reservoirs) blocked by dirt, scale, rust, or have small burrs (blocked ports prevent fluid return to reservoirs).	• Repair or replace master cylinder **CAUTION:** Do not attempt to clean blocked ports with wire, pencils, or similar implements. Use compressed air only.
	• Brake hoses, tubes, fittings clogged or restricted	• Use compressed air to check or unclog parts. Replace any damaged parts.
	• Brake fluid contaminated with improper fluids (motor oil, transmission fluid, causing rubber components to swell and stick in bores	• Replace all rubber components, combination valve and hoses. Flush entire brake system with DOT 3 brake fluid or equivalent.
	• Low engine vacuum	• Adjust or repair engine

Troubleshooting the Brake System (cont.)

Problem	Cause	Solution
Grabbing brakes (severe reaction to brake pedal pressure.)	• Brakelining(s) contaminated by grease or brake fluid	• Determine and correct cause of contamination and replace brakeshoes in axle sets
	• Parking brake cables incorrectly adjusted or seized	• Adjust cables. Replace seized cables.
	• Incorrect brakelining or lining loose on brakeshoes	• Replace brakeshoes in axle sets
	• Caliper anchor plate bolts loose	• Tighten bolts
	• Rear brakeshoes binding on support plate ledges	• Clean and lubricate ledges. Replace support plate(s) if ledges are deeply grooved. Do not attempt to smooth ledges by grinding.
	• Incorrect or missing power brake reaction disc	• Install correct disc
	• Rear brake support plates loose	• Tighten mounting bolts
Dragging brakes (slow or incomplete release of brakes)	• Brake pedal binding at pivot	• Loosen and lubricate
	• Power brake unit has internal bind	• Inspect for internal bind. Replace unit if internal bind exists.
	• Parking brake cables incorrrectly adjusted or seized	• Adjust cables. Replace seized cables.
	• Rear brakeshoe return springs weak or broken	• Replace return springs. Replace brakeshoe if necessary in axle sets.
	• Automatic adjusters malfunctioning	• Repair or replace adjuster parts as required
	• Caliper, wheel cylinder or master cylinder pistons sticking or seized	• Repair or replace parts as necessary
	• Master cylinder compensating ports blocked (fluid does not return to reservoirs).	• Use compressed air to clear ports. Do not use wire, pencils, or similar objects to open blocked ports.
Vehicle moves to one side when brakes are applied	• Incorrect front tire pressure	• Inflate to recommended cold (reduced load) inflation pressure
	• Worn or damaged wheel bearings	• Replace worn or damaged bearings
	• Brakelining on one side contaminated	• Determine and correct cause of contamination and replace brakelining in axle sets
	• Brakeshoes on one side bent, distorted, or lining loose on shoe	• Replace brakeshoes in axle sets
	• Support plate bent or loose on one side	• Tighten or replace support plate
	• Brakelining not yet seated with drums or rotors	• Burnish brakelining
	• Caliper anchor plate loose on one side	• Tighten anchor plate bolts
	• Caliper piston sticking or seized	• Repair or replace caliper
	• Brakelinings water soaked	• Drive vehicle with brakes lightly applied to dry linings
	• Loose suspension component attaching or mounting bolts	• Tighten suspension bolts. Replace worn suspension components.
	• Brake combination valve failure	• Replace combination valve
Chatter or shudder when brakes are applied (pedal pulsation and roughness may also occur.)	• Brakeshoes distorted, bent, contaminated, or worn	• Replace brakeshoes in axle sets
	• Caliper anchor plate or support plate loose	• Tighten mounting bolts
	• Excessive thickness variation of rotor(s)	• Refinish or replace rotors in axle sets
Noisy brakes (squealing, clicking, scraping sound when brakes are applied.)	• Bent, broken, distorted brakeshoes	• Replace brakeshoes in axle sets
	• Excessive rust on outer edge of rotor braking surface	• Remove rust

Troubleshooting the Brake System (cont.)

Problem	Cause	Solution
Noisy brakes (squealing, clicking, scraping sound when brakes are applied.) (cont.)	• Brakelining worn out—shoes contacting drum of rotor	• Replace brakeshoes and lining in axle sets. Refinish or replace drums or rotors.
	• Broken or loose holdown or return springs	• Replace parts as necessary
	• Rough or dry drum brake support plate ledges	• Lubricate support plate ledges
	• Cracked, grooved, or scored rotor(s) or drum(s)	• Replace rotor(s) or drum(s). Replace brakeshoes and lining in axle sets if necessary.
	• Incorrect brakelining and/or shoes (front or rear).	• Install specified shoe and lining assemblies
Pulsating brake pedal	• Out of round drums or excessive lateral runout in disc brake rotor(s)	• Refinish or replace drums, re-index rotors or replace

Master cylinder mounting

2. Remove the cover and drain all fluid from the reservoir. Pump the fluid from the cylinder bore by depressing the pushrod.
3. Position the master cylinder in a vise. Use soft wood or rags to protect the cylinder from the vise jaws.
4. Remove the snapring.
5. Remove the pushrod and retainer as a unit.
6. Remove the primary piston.

NOTE: *A new primary piston is included in the rebuilding kit, so it's unnecessary to disassemble the old piston.*

7. Remove the secondary piston (it's at the front), and spring by applying air pressure through the front outlet.
8. Make sure that your hands are clean and then use new brake fluid to clean all metal parts thoroughly.
9. Check the cylinder bore for pitting or corrosion. Clean the outlet ports of any dirt and then rewash all parts.
10. Place the parts on a clean rag and allow them to air dry.

Location of the brake master cylinder

NOTE: *Be sure you have the correct rebuilding kit by checking the identification marks on the old secondary piston with those on the new one in the kit.*

11. Install the new secondary piston seals in the grooves of the piston. The seal that is nearest the front end of the piston will have its lip facing toward that end. Be sure that the seal protector is in place. The front seal has the smallest inside diameter.
12. Install the seal retainer and spring seat after the seal is in place.
13. Install the seal on the rear of the secondary piston. The seal should face toward the rear of the piston.
14. Use new brake fluid to coat the bore of the master cylinder and the primary and secondary seals of the front piston.
15. Install the secondary piston spring over the nose of the piston and onto the spring seat.
16. Install the primary piston and pushrod and retainer into the cylinder bore. Hold pressure on the pushrod and install the snapring.
17. Fill the master cylinder reservoir with fresh brake fluid and stroke the pushrod several times to bench bleed the cylinder. Snap the retaining bails over the cylinder cover.
18. Install the master cylinder as previously described.
19. Bleed the brakes.

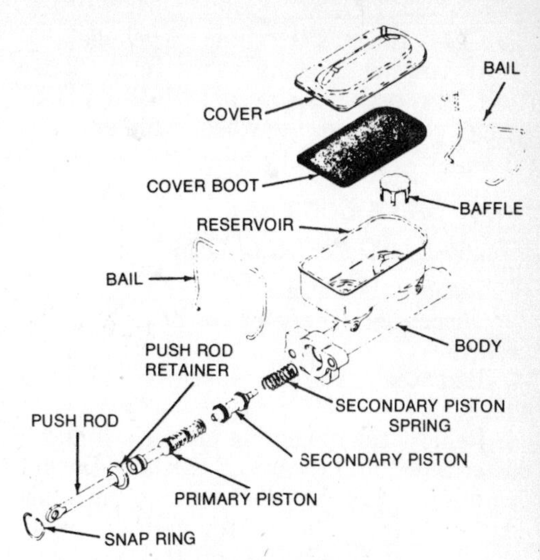

Exploded view of the master cylinder

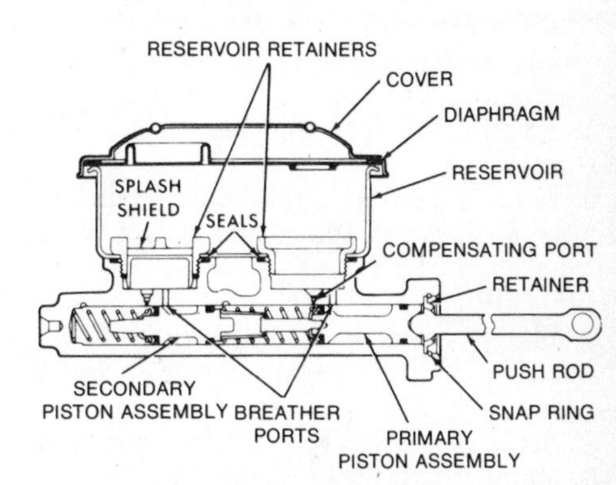

Cross-section of the master cylinder

BLEEDING

The hydraulic system must be bled whenever the pedal feels spongy, indicating that compressible air has entered the system. The system must be bled whenever any component has been disconnected or there has been a leak.

Brake fluid sometimes becomes contaminated and loses its original qualities. Old brake fluid should be bled from the system and replaced if any part of the hydraulic system becomes corroded or if the fluid is dirty or discolored.

1. Clean off the top of the master cylinder and remove the cover. Check that the fluid level in each reservoir is within ¼ in. of the top.
2. Attach a $^{7}/_{32}''$ inside diameter hose to the bleeder valve at the first wheel to be bled. Start at the wheel farthest from the master cylinder and work closer. Pour a few inches of brake fluid into a clear container and stick the end of the tube below the surface.

NOTE: *The tube and container of brake fluid are not absolutely necessary, but this is a very sloppy job without them.*

3. Open the bleed valve counterclockwise ⅓ turn. Have a helper slowly depress the pedal. Close the valve just before the pedal reaches the end of its travel. Have the helper let the pedal back up.
4. Check the fluid level. If the reservoir runs dry, the procedure will have to be restarted from the beginning.

Bleeder valve location on rear brake

5. Repeat Step 3 until no more bubbles come out of the hose.
6. Repeat the bleeding operation, Steps 3 to 5, at the other three wheels.

7. Check the master cylinder level again.

8. If repeated bleeding has no effect, there is an air leak, probably internally in the master cylinder or in one of the wheel cylinders.

Power Brake Booster

REMOVAL AND INSTALLATION

1. Remove the air cleaner.
2. Disconnect the vacuum hose from the check valve.
3. Remove the master cylinder/booster brace rod.
4. Remove the remaining master cylinder to booster nut. Pull forward on the master cylinder until it clears the booster mounting studs. Carefully move the master cylinder aside (brake lines attached). Support the master cylinder to avoid stress on the brake lines.

NOTE: *Move the master cylinder only enough to allow room for removal of the booster.*

5. Remove the nuts securing the booster to the dash.
6. Remove the push rod to pedal retainer and slip the push rod off the pedal pin. Remove the booster assembly.

To install:

7. Place the booster into position and attach the push rod to the pedal pin and install the retainer.
8. Secure the booster to the dash and torque the retaining nuts to 13 ft. lbs.
9. Attach the master cylinder to the booster and torque to 20 ft. lbs. Don't forget the booster brace rod.
10. Use a new check valve and grommet and connect the vacuum hose to the check valve.
11. Install the air cleaner.

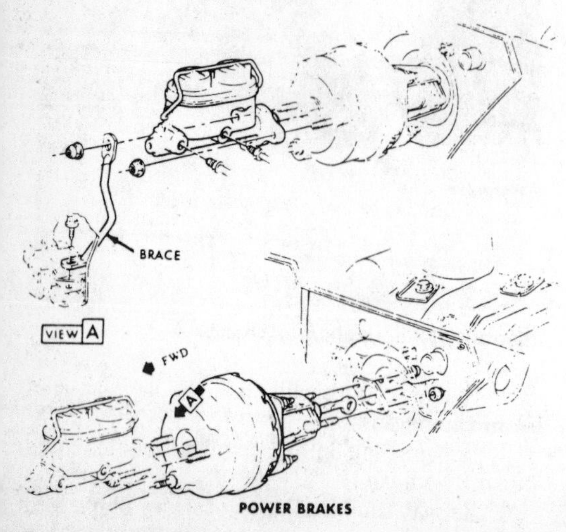

Booster mounting

Brake Distribution and Warning Switch Assembly

BRAKE WARNING LIGHT CHECKING

1. Disconnect the electrical lead from the switch terminal and use a jumper wire to connect the lead to a good ground.
2. Turn the ignition to the "On" position. The instrument panel warning lamp should light. If it does not light, either the bulb is burned out or the circuit is defective. Replace the bulb or repair the circuit as necessary.
3. When the warning lamp lights, turn the ignition off, remove the jumper wire, and connect the electrical lead to the brake line switch.

BRAKE WARNING LIGHT SWITCH TESTING

1. Raise the car on a hoist and attach a bleeder hose to a rear bleed screw. Immerse the other end of the hose in a container partially filled with clean brake fluid. Check the master cylinder reservoir to make sure that it is full.
2. Turn the ignition switch to "On." Open the bleed screw while an assistant applies heavy pressure to the brake pedal.
3. Repeat Step 2 on the front brake bleed screw. The warning lamp should light again. Turn the ignition off.
4. Lower the car. Check and fill the master cylinder reservoir to the correct level.

NOTE: *If the warning lamp does not light during Steps 2 and 3, but does light when a jumper wire is connected to ground, the warning light switch is defective and must be replaced.*

REMOVAL AND INSTALLATION

The distribution and warning switch assembly is nonadjustable and non-serviceable. It must be replaced if defective.

1. Disconnect the negative battery cable.
2. Clean the switch assembly thoroughly to remove dirt and foreign matter.
3. Disconnect the electrical lead from the switch.

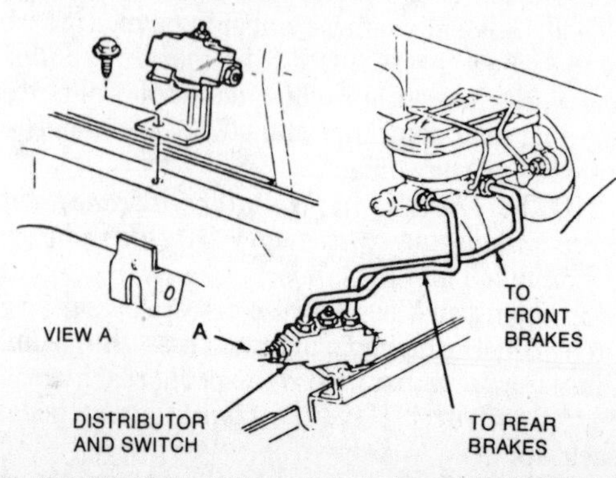

Brake distribution switch assembly mounting

4. Place dry rags below the switch to absorb any brake fluid which may be spilled.

5. Disconnect the hydraulic lines from the switch. If necessary, loosen the lines at the master cylinder to assist removal at the switch. Cover the open lines with a clean, lint-free material to prevent the entry of dirt.

6. Remove the mounting screw and remove the switch.

7. Make sure that the new switch is clean and free of dust and lint. If there is any doubt, wash the switch in clean brake fluid and dry with compressed air.

8. Place the switch in its installed position and install its mounting screws. Tighten the mounting screw to 100 in. lbs.

9. Remove the protective covering from the brake lines and connect the lines to the switch. If necessary, tighten the brake lines at the master cylinder. Tighten the brake line nuts at the switch and master cylinder to 150 in. lbs.

10. Connect the electrical lead to the switch.

11. Connect the negative battery cable.

12. Bleed the entire hydraulic system. Fill the master cylinder to within 1/4" from the top of the reservoir after bleeding. Check for proper brake operation and leaks before moving the car.

Brake Hose

REMOVAL AND INSTALLATION

Front

1. Separate the steel line from the hose using a back up wrench on the fitting.

2. Remove the clip retainer from the frame bracket.

3. Clean the dirt from the hose to the caliper connection and remove the bolt retaining the hose to the caliper.

4. Cover the open lines to prevent contamination.

To install:

5. Install the hose to the caliper using new gaskets. Torque the mounting bolt to 32 ft. lbs.

NOTE: *The hose must be positioned with the male fitting against the machined shoulder on the caliper to assure proper hose positioning.*

6. Insert the hose into the frame bracket. This end of the hose will properly mate to the bracket in one direction only.

NOTE: *The hose should enter the bracket with a slight twist of about 20° of the hose.*

7. Install the clip retainer.

8. Install the steel line to the hose using a back up wrench on the hose and torque to 18 ft. lbs.

9. Bleed all brakes.

Rear

1. Claen the dirt from both hose connections.

2. Separate the hose from the steel line by turning the double flare connector out of the hose fitting.

3. Remove the U-shaped retainer from the hose fitting and withdraw the hose from the support bracket.

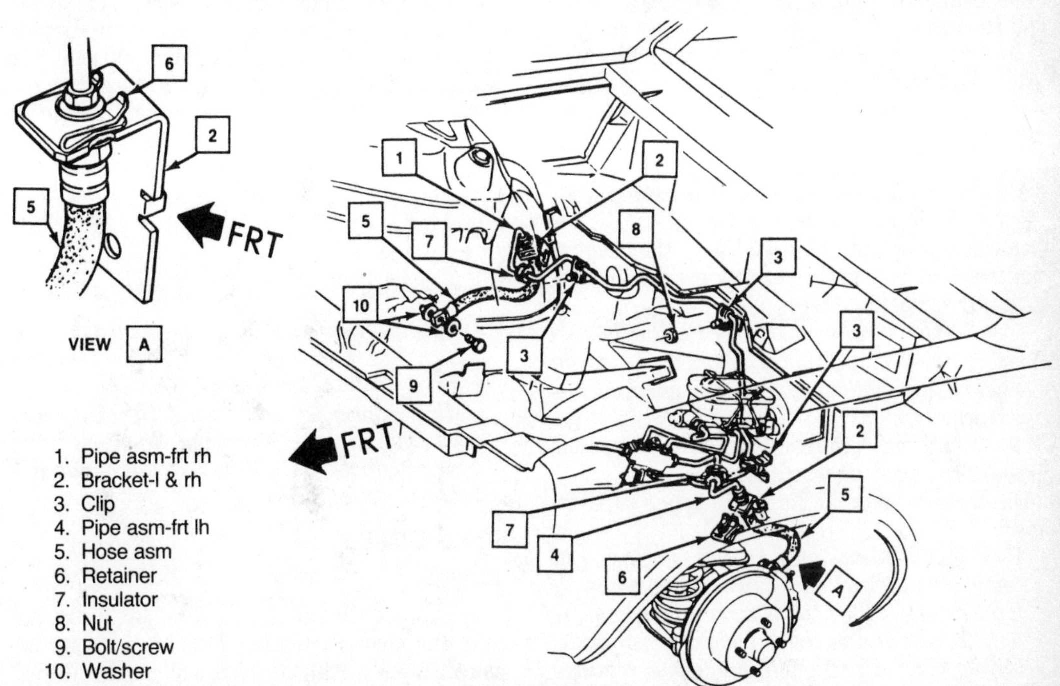

Front brake line routing

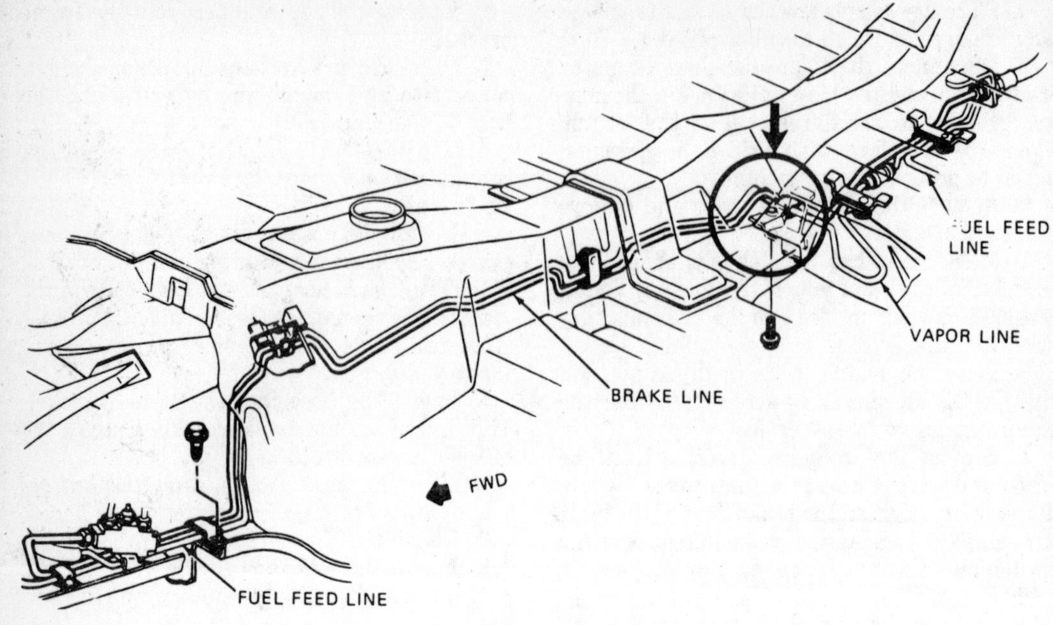

Rear brake line routing

4. Separate the rear brake lines from the hose connector (at axle) by turning the flare nuts out of the hose connector. Cover the open ports and lines.
5. Remove the axle cover bolt holding the hose connector and remove the hose.

To install:

6. Install the hose connector with the axle cover bolt and torque to 20 ft. lbs.
7. Install the brake lines to the hose connector and torque the flare nuts to 18 ft. lbs.
8. With the weight of the car on the wheels, pass the female end of the hose through the support bracket. The female fitting will fit the bracket in only one position. Insert the hose fitting into the hole in the support bracket in a position that has the least twist.

CAUTION: *Proper positioning of the hose is necessary to maintain correct hose-to-suspension clearance through full movement of the suspension.*

9. Install the U-shaped retainer to secure the hose in the support bracket.
10. Install the brake line and torque to 18 ft. lbs.

CAUTION: *Make sure the hose does not touch other parts during suspension travel. If it does remove the hose retainer and rotate the female hose end in the support bracket in the appropriate direction, replace the retainer and reinspect*

11. Bleed all brakes.

FRONT DISC BRAKES

Instead of the traditional expanding brakes that press outward against a circular drum, disc brake systems consist of two cast iron discs with brake pads positioned on either side. Braking action is achieved by the pads squeezing either side of the rotating disc. Dirt and water do not greatly affect braking action since they are thrown off the rotor by centrifugal action or scraped off by the pads. The equal clamping action of the pads tends to ensure uniform, straight stopping. All disc brakes are self-adjusting.

Disc Brake Pads and Caliper

CAUTION: *Brake shoes contain asbestos, which has been determined to be a cancer causing agent. Never clean the brake surfaces with compressed air! Avoid inhaling any dust from any brake surface! When cleaning brake surfaces, use a commercially available brake cleaning fluid.*

REPLACEMENT

1976-82

1. Siphon off about one half of the brake fluid in the master cylinder. This is necessary because the new, thicker pads will push the caliper pistons in farther and cause the master cylinder to overflow.

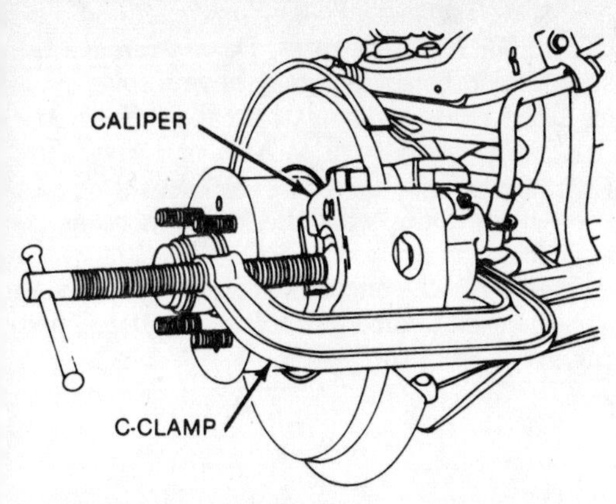

A 7 inch or larger C-clamp is necessary for pad replacement—1976–82

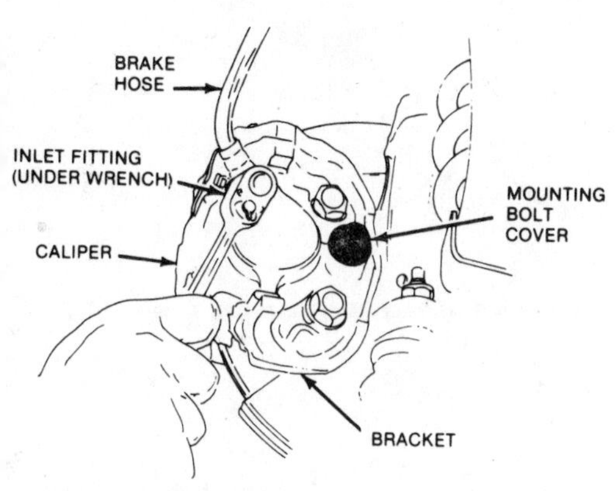

Disconnect the brake hose by removing the bolt at the inlet fitting—1976–82

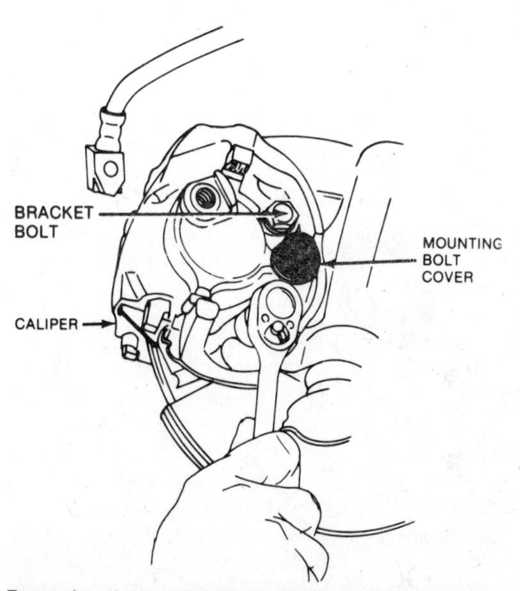

Removing the two bracket bolts. Do not remove the mounting bolt in the center—1976–82

2. Jack up the front of the car and support it safely on jackstands. Remove the wheels.

NOTE: *Always replace brake pads on both wheels. Never replace one pair. Replace pads when worn to within 1/32" of the metal pad backing.*

3. Mount a 7 in. C-clamp on the caliper with the solid end on the caliper housing and the

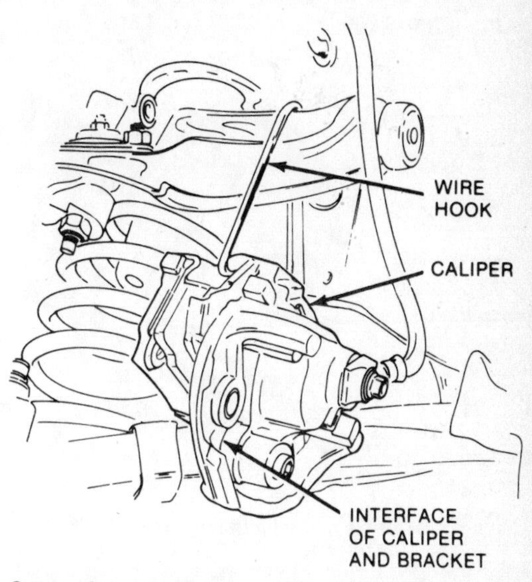

Supporting the caliper assembly from the front suspension—1976–82

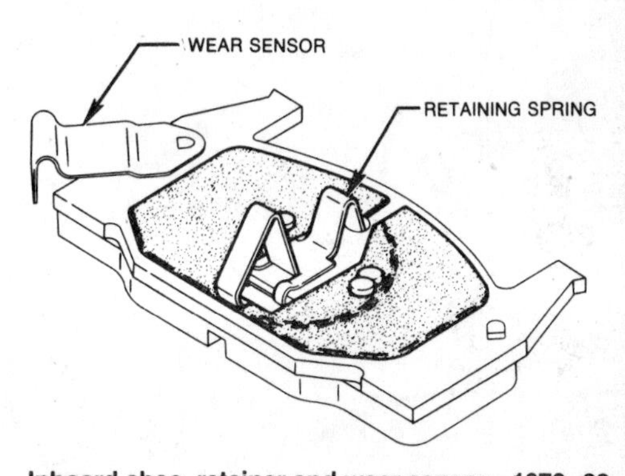

Inboard shoe, retainer and wear sensor—1976–82

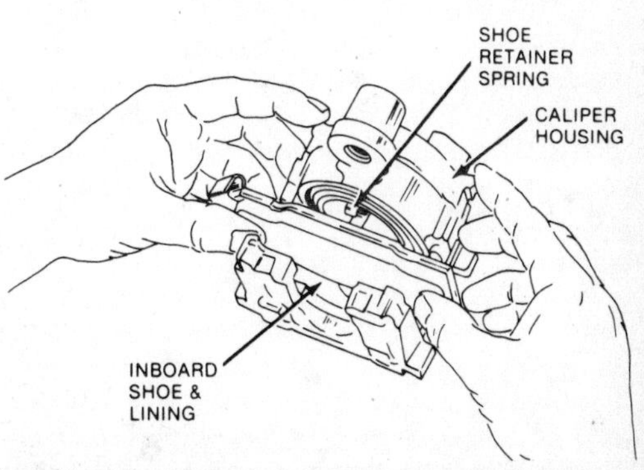

Installing the inboard shoe and lining—1976–82

screw end on the metal back of the outboard shoe (pad). Tighten the C-clamp to bottom the piston in the cylinder bore and remove the clamp.

4. If the caliper is to be removed for overhaul purposes disconnect the brake hose at the inlet fitting by removing the bolt and washers. If only the shoe and lining are to be replaced so not disconnect the brake hose.

5. Remove the two bracket bolts and remove the caliper from the rotor. Do not remove the socket head bolt which may have a cover on it on later models. Hang the caliper from the front suspension with a chain or heavy wire. Coat hanger wire should be sufficient. Don't let the caliper hang with the brake hose as its support.

6. Remove the old pads. If the shoe retaining spring doesn't come out with the inboard pad, remove it from the piston.

Cinching the brake pad tabs using pliers—1976–82

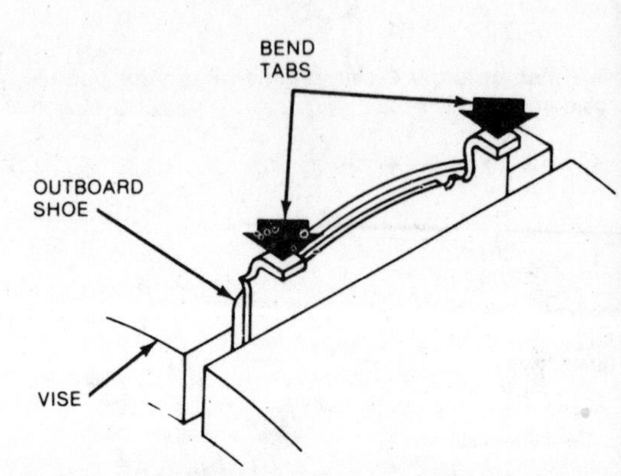

Bending the tabs on the shoe using a vise—1976–82

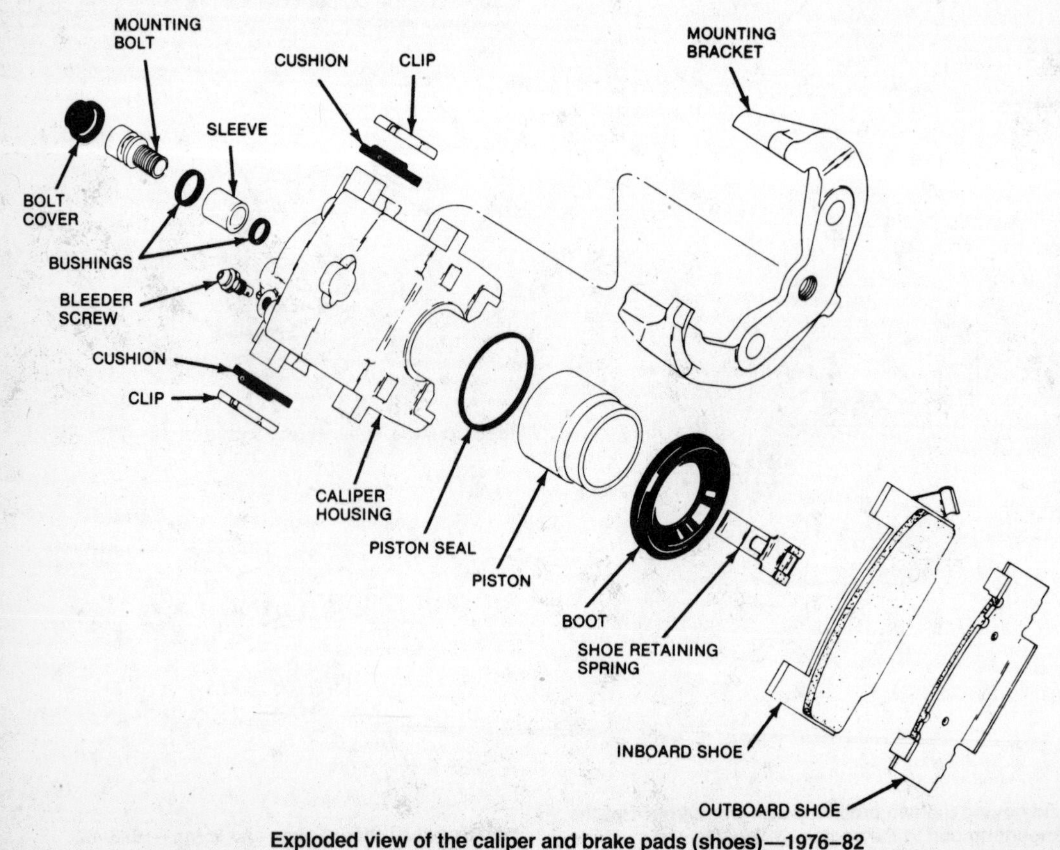

Exploded view of the caliper and brake pads (shoes)—1976–82

7. Blow any dirt out of the caliper and check that the piston boot isn't damaged or leaking fluid.

8. Install the new pads in the same locations as the old ones. Before installing the inboard pad, be sure that the retaining spring is properly positioned. Push the tab on the single leg end of the spring down into the pad hole, and then snap the other two legs over the edge of the pad notch.

9. Position the caliper over the rotor (disc). Install the two retaining bolts and tighten them to 70 ft. lbs.

10. Using a large pair of Channel Lock® pliers, cinch the outboard pad to the caliper. Position the lower jaw of the pliers on the bottom edge of the outboard pad. Place the upper jaw of the pliers on the outboard pad tab. Squeeze the pliers firmly to bend the tab. Cinch the other end of the outboard pad the same way. The tabs may also be bent by placing the shoe in a vise and bending slightly. The purpose is to have zero clearance between the shoe and the caliper.

11. Install the wheels and lower the car.

12. Refill the master cylinder with fresh fluid.

13. Pump the brake pedal several times to push the pads in on the rotor. Check the fluid level in the master cylinder after this has been done. Do not move the car until a firm pedal is obtained.

14. Carefully road test the car.

1983 and Later

1. Remove ⅔ of the brake fluid from the master cylinder assembly.

2. Raise the car and support with jackstands.

3. Mark the relationship of the wheel to the axle, then remove the wheel.

4. Position a C-clamp as shown in the illustration and tighten until the piston bottoms in the bore, then remove the C-clamp.

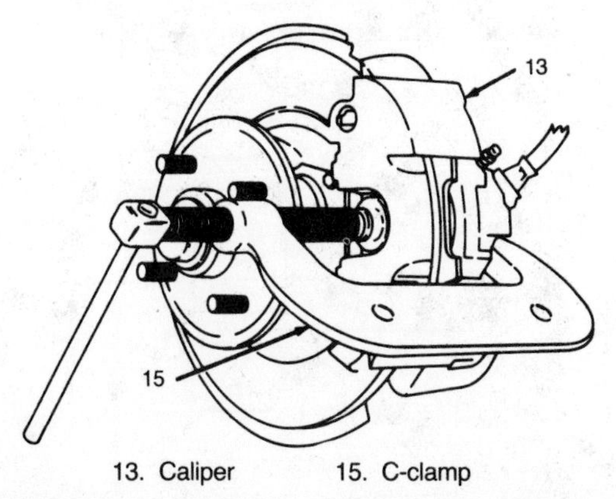

13. Caliper 15. C-clamp

Position a C-clamp to bottom the piston—1983 and later

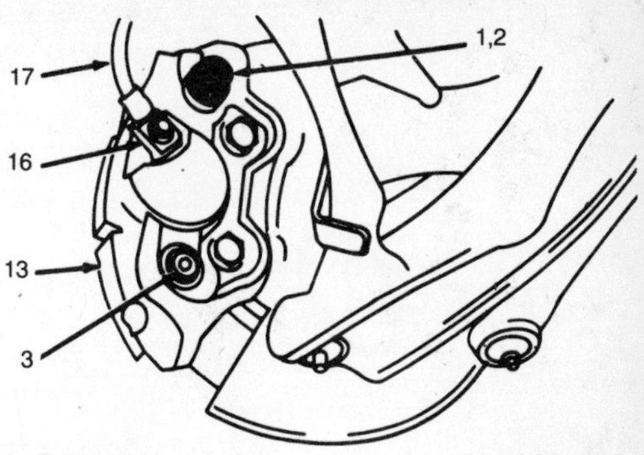

1. Bolt cover
2. Mounting bolt
3. Mounting bolt
13. Caliper
16. Inlet fitting
17. Brake hose

Mounting bolts and inlet fitting bolt—1983 and later

5. Remove the bolt holding the inlet fitting.

NOTE: *If only the shoe and lining are being replaced, do not remove the inlet fitting.*

6. Remove the two bolt covers and allen head mounting bolts.

NOTE: *If the mounting bolts show signs of corrosion replace them with new ones.*

7. If only the shoe and linings are being replaced, remove the caliper from the rotor and suspend it from the suspension so that there isn't any tension on the brake hose.

8. Remove the shoe and lining assemblies from the caliper. To remove the outboard shoe and lining, use 12 inch channel lock pliers to straighten bent over shoe tabs.

9. Remove the sleeves from the mounting bolt holes.

10. Remove the bushings from the grooves in the mounting bolt holes.

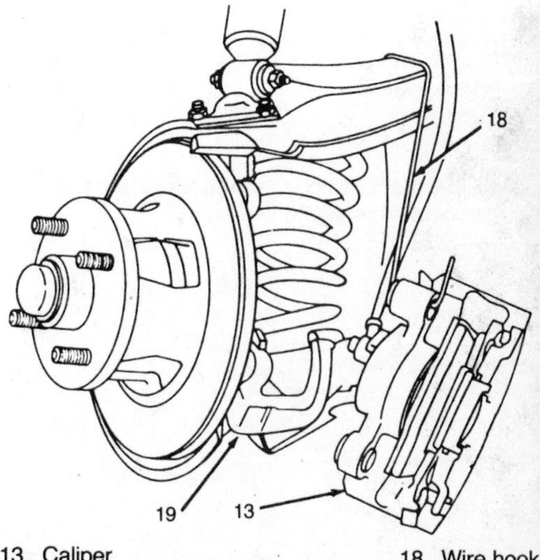

13. Caliper
18. Wire hook
19. Bracket

Suspending caliper assembly—1983 and later

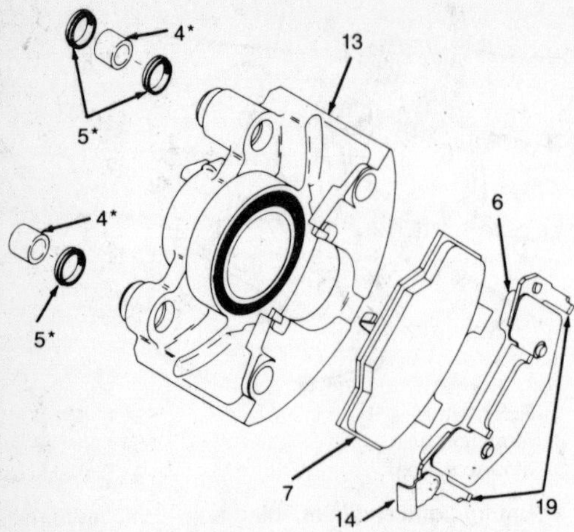

4. Sleeve
5. Bushing
6. Outboard shoe & lining
7. Inboard shoe & lining
13. Caliper housing
14. Wear sensor
19. Shoe tab

Lubricate the bushings and sleeves with silicone grease before installation—1983

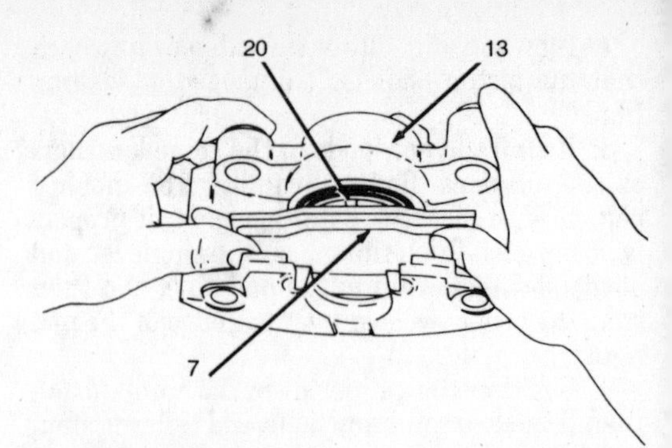

7. Inboard shoe & lining
13. Caliper housing
20. Shoe retainer spring

Installation of the inboard shoe—1983 and later

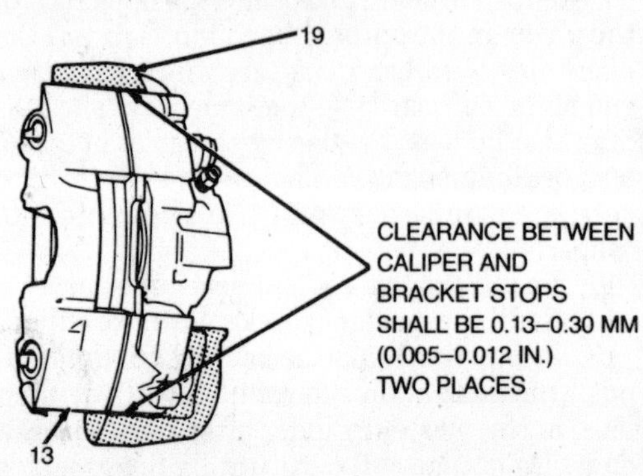

Check clearance between the caliper and the bracket stops—1983 and later

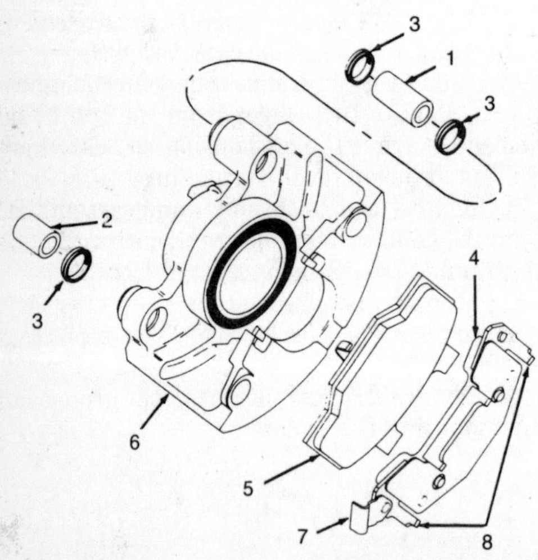

1. Sleeve (long)
2. Sleeve (short)
3. Bushing
4. Outboard shoe & lining
5. Inboard shoe & lining
6. Caliper housing
7. Wear sensor
8. Shoe tab

Lubricate the bushings and sleeves with silicone grease before installation—1984–87

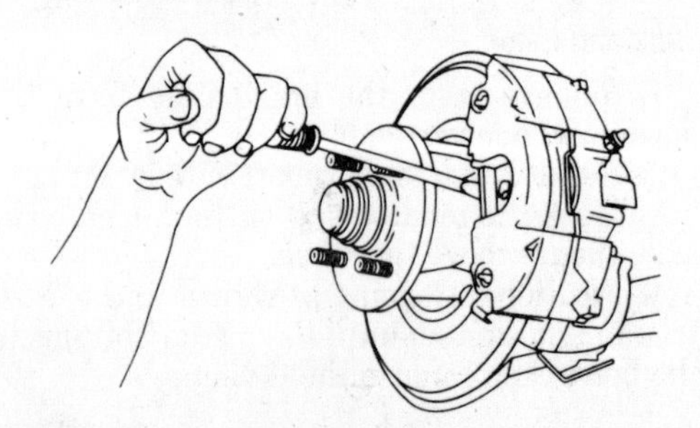

Wedge a large pry tool between the outboard shoe flange and the hat section of the rotor—1983 and later

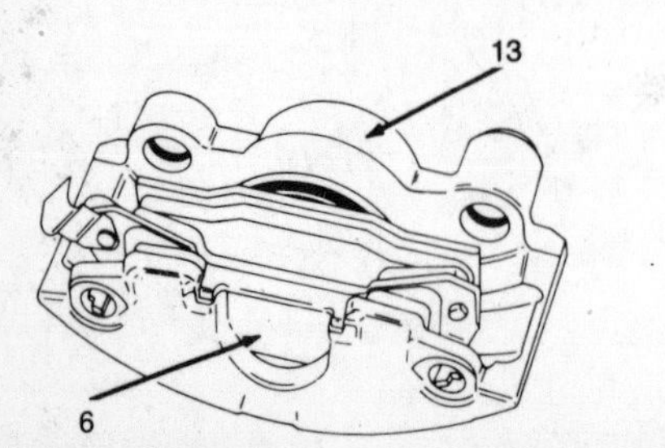

6. Outboard shoe & lining
13. Caliper housing

Installation of the outboard shoe—1983 and later

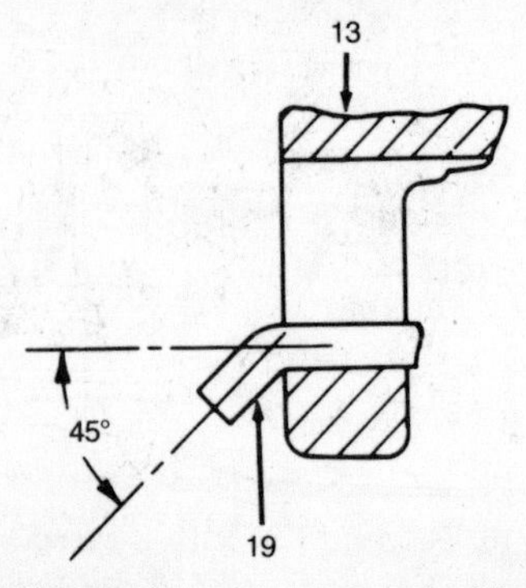

13. Caliper housing
19. Shoe tab

Check the angle of the shoe tabs—1983 and later

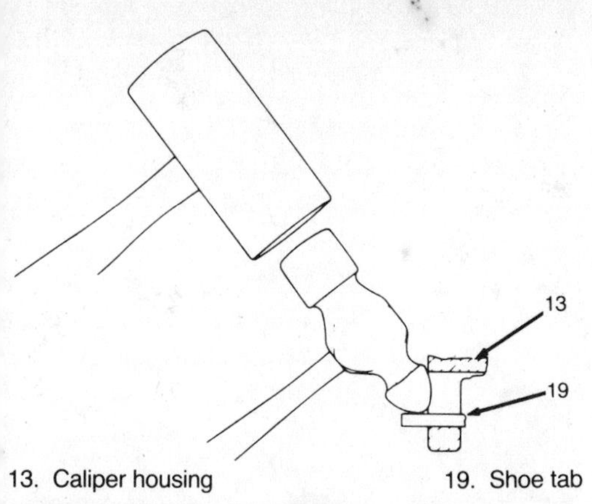

13. Caliper housing 19. Shoe tab

Bending the outboard shoe tabs with a hammer—1983 and later

11. Prior to installation, lubricate and install new bushings and sleeves.

12. Install the inboard shoe and lining positioning the shoe retainer spring into the piston.

13. Install the outboard shoe and lining with the wear sensor at the leading edge of the shoe during forward wheel rotation.

14. Position the caliper over the rotor in the mounting bracket.

15. Coat the threads and shoulder of the mounting bolts with silicone grease. Install the mounting bolts and torque to 21-25 ft. lbs.

16. Check the clearance between the caliper and bracket stops as shown in the illustration and if necessary, file the ends of the bracket to provide the proper clearance.

17. Install the inlet fitting if removed and torque to 18-30 ft. lbs.

18. Cinch the outboard shoe by performing the following steps:

a. Wedge a prying tool between the outboard shoe flange and the hat section of the rotor to seat the shoe flange in the caliper.

b. Have an assistant lightly press on the brake pedal to clamp the outboard shoe tightly to the caliper. Maintain pressure on the hydraulic system to keep the tool wedged in place during the remaining steps.

NOTE: *Make sure the master cylinder is filled to the proper level and the cover is in place before performing the previous step.*

c. Bend the outboard shoe tabs and cinch the shoe to the caliper by positioning an 8 ounce machinists hammer as shown in the illustration, then striking it with a 16 ounce brass hammer.

d. Check that the shoe tabs are bent to an angle of approximately 45 degrees. After both tabs are bent and hydraulic pressure released, check that the outboard shoe is locked tightly in position. If not, repeat steps a through c.

CAUTION: *Outboard shoe and linings that have been cinched as described in the preced-*

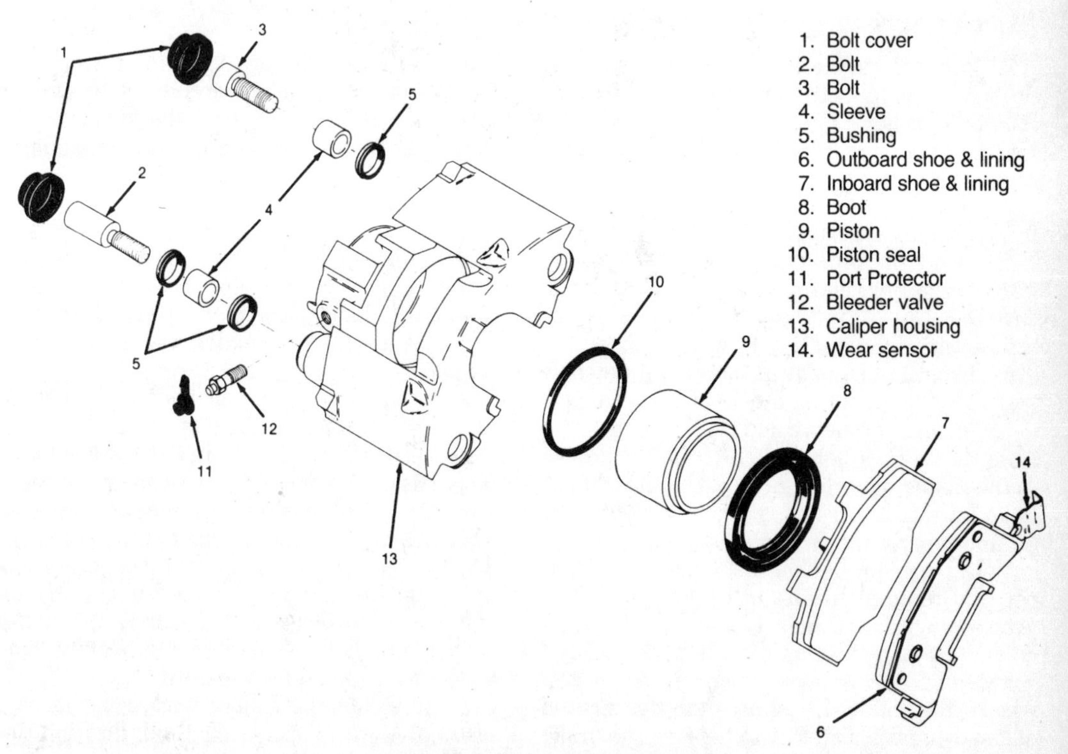

Caliper and shoe assembly—1983

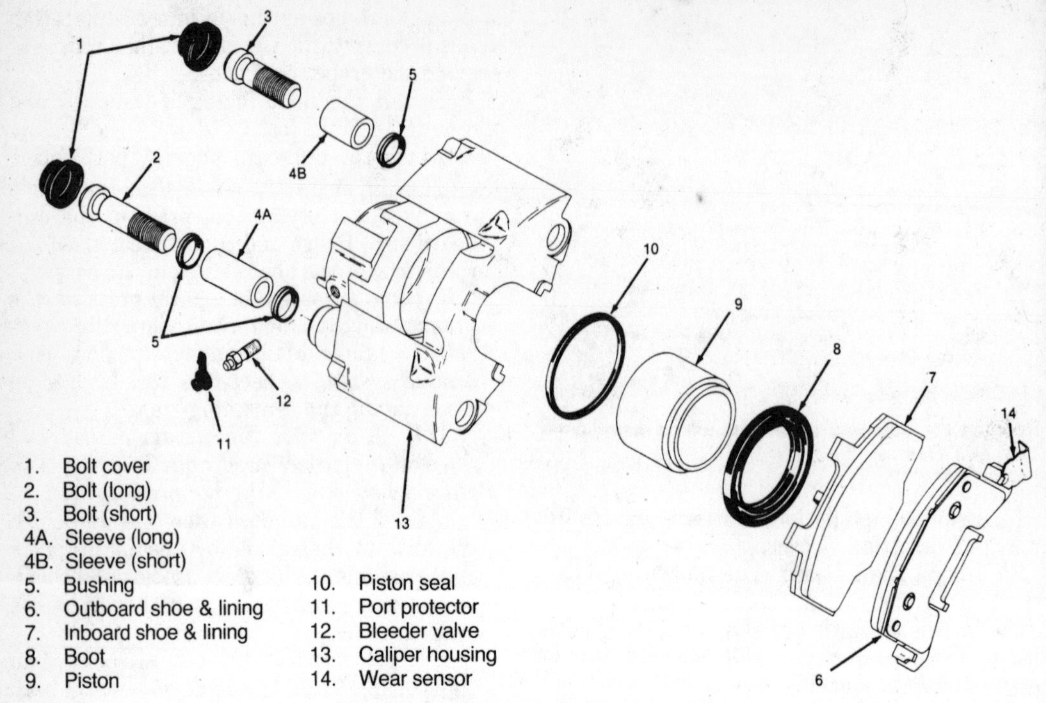

Caliper and shoe assembly—1984–87

ing steps should be replaced if uncinched for any reason. Bleed the system if the inlet fitting and hose were removed.

CALIPER OVERHAUL

1. Remove the caliper as previously described. Disconnect the brake line and remove the brake pads.
2. Clean all dirt from the brake hose-to-caliper connection.
3. Seal the brake line fitting to prevent dirt from entering the caliper.
4. Clean the outside of the caliper using fresh brake fluid and place it on a clean work surface.
5. Drain all brake fluid from the caliper.
6. Remove the mounting back cover and bolt and slide the mounting bracket off the caliper.
7. Remove the sleeve and two bushings, one from the retainer bolt and one from the groove in the caliper mounting hole. If the clips do not fall off when the bracket is removed, take them off and remove the cushions.
8. Use rags to cushion the inside of the caliper and remove the piston by applying compressed air into the caliper inlet hole. Use just enough pressure to ease out the piston; excessive pressure may cause damage to the piston when it flies out of the caliper. Another method of removing the piston is to depress the brake pedal slowly and gently with the hydraulic lines still connected. This will push the piston out of the caliper.

   CAUTION: *Never place your hands in the way of the piston as it can fly out with considerable force!*
9. Use a screwdriver to pry the piston boot out of the caliper being careful not to scratch the housing bore. Extend the screwdriver across the caliper bore, under the boot, and pry it up. Be careful not to gouge the cylinder bore, or the caliper will have to be replaced.
10. Use a piece of wood or plastic (a plastic knitting needle is perfect), to remove the seal from its groove in the caliper bore. Using a metal tool will damage the bore surface.
11. Remove the bleeder valve from the caliper.
12. Buy a high quality caliper rebuilding kit, preferably original equipment type.
13. Clean all metal parts in fresh brake fluid. Never use other solvents for cleaning, as gasoline or paint thinner will ruin the rubber parts.
14. Inspect all parts for rust or other damage. The caliper bore should be free from corrosion or nicks. Replace any suspect parts. Minor stains or corrosion can be polished out of the caliper bore with crocus cloth, but heavily damaged pieces should be discarded.
15. Lubricate the caliper bore and the new piston seal with fresh brake fluid. Position the seal in the caliper bore groove.

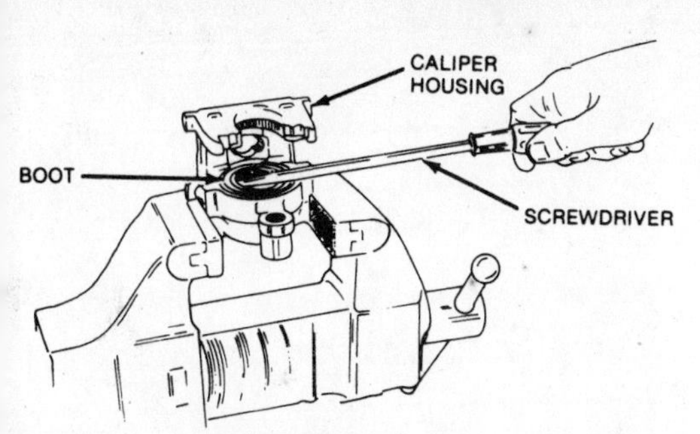

Removing the piston boot

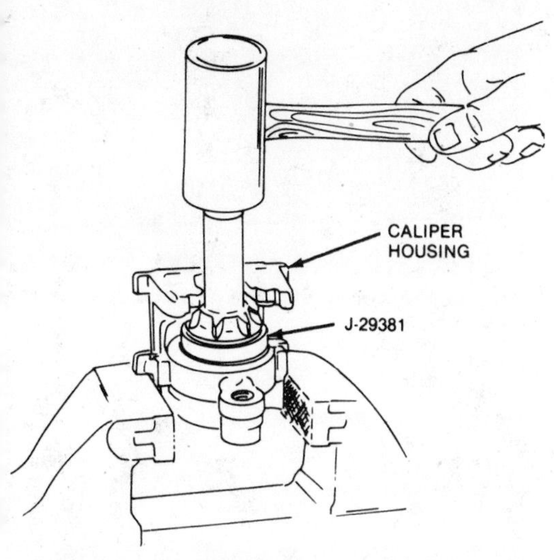

Installing the piston and boot into the caliper using a bushing driver. 1976–82 tool shown. Use tool J-29077 for 1983 and later models

16. Lubricate the piston with fresh brake fluid and assemble a new boot into the piston groove so that the fold faces the open end of the piston.
17. Insert the piston into the caliper being careful not to dislodge the seal. Force the piston down to the bottom in the bore. This requires about 50-100 lbs. of force.
18. Place the outside diameter of the boot in the caliper counterbore and seat it with a bushing driver of the same diameter as the boot.
19. Install the bleeder screw.
20. Fit new cushions on the caliper lugs. Stretch the cushions over the lugs, fitting the heavy section in the lug recess, with the sawtooth edges of the cushions pointing out.
21. Liberally lubricate the sleeve and bushings, inside and out, and the unthreaded portion of the retainer bolt with silicone lubricant.
22. Fit the larger bushing in the caliper mounting hole groove and install the sleeve.
23. Position the smaller bushing in the groove in the retainer bolt.
24. Clamp the caliper in a vise, mounting lug up, across the pad openings. Fit the clips over the cushions and squeeze the mounting bracket down over the clips, lining up the retainer bolt hole.
25. Move the bracket against the retainer boss on the caliper and install the retainer bolt. Tighten the bolt to 25 ft. lbs.

NOTE: *It may be very difficult to squeeze the bracket over the cushions and clips on the caliper. Start with the open end of the bracket over the ends of the clips near the boot and move the bracket towards the closed end of the piston housing.*

26. Install the caliper. Use new copper gaskets on the brake hose connection. Bleed the brakes.

Brake Disc

REMOVAL AND INSTALLATION

1. Jack up the front of the car and support it safely with jackstands.
2. Remove the wheel and tire.
3. Remove the brake caliper as previously described.
4. Remove the hub dust cap, cotter pin, spindle nut and washer, and remove the disc. Do not allow the bearing to fall out of the hub when removing the disc.
5. Remove the outer bearing with the fingers.
6. Remove the inner bearing by prying out the grease seal. Discard the seal.
7. Thoroughly clean all parts in solvent and blow dry.
8. Check the bearings for cracked separators or pitting. Check the races for scoring or pitting.

NOTE: *If it is necessary to replace either the inner or outer bearing it will also be necessary to replace the race for that bearing.*

9. Drive out the old race from the hub with a brass drift inserted behind the race in the notches in the hub.
10. Lubricate the new race with a light film of grease.
11. Use the proper tool to start the race squarely into the hub and carefully seat it.
12. Pack the inner and outer bearings with high melting point wheel bearing grease.
13. Place the inner bearing in the hub and install a new grease seal. The seal should be installed flush with the hub surface. Use a block of wood to seat the seal.
14. Install the disc over the spindle.
15. Press the outer bearing firmly into the hub by hand.
16. Install the spindle washer and nut. Adjust the wheel bearings as outlined in Front Wheel Bearing Adjustment, following.

17. Install the brake caliper. Tighten the brake caliper mounting bolts to 70 ft. lbs.
18. Install the wheel and tire.
19. Lower the car.

Front Wheel Bearings

INSPECTION

1. Raise the car and support it at the front lower control arm.
2. Spin the wheel to check for unusual noise or roughness.
3. If the bearings are noisy, tight, or excessively loose they should be cleaned, inspected, and re-lubricated before adjustment.
4. Grip the tire at the top and bottom and move the wheel assembly in and out on the spindle. Measure the movement of the hub, it should be 0.025-0.127mm. If not, adjust the bearings.

ADJUSTMENT

1. Raise the car and support it at the front lower control arm.
2. Remove the hub cap or wheel cover from the wheel. Remove the dust cap from the hub.
3. Remove the cotter pin from the spindle.
4. Spin the wheel forward by hand and tighten the spindle nut to 12 ft. lbs. This will fully seat the bearings.
5. Back off the nut to the "just loose" position.
6. Hand tighten the spindle nut. Loosen the spindle nut until either hole in the spindle aligns with a slot in the nut, but not more tha ½ flat.
7. Install a new cotter pin, bend the ends c the pin against the nut, and cut off any extr length to avoid interference with the dust cap
8. Measure the end-play in the hub. Prope bearing adjustment should give 0.025 0.127mm of end play.

Unbend the cotter pin and remove it from the spindle nut

Pry the dust cover off with a large, flat-bladed screwdriver

Hand-tighten (approx. 12 ft lbs), the spindle nut t seat the wheel bearings

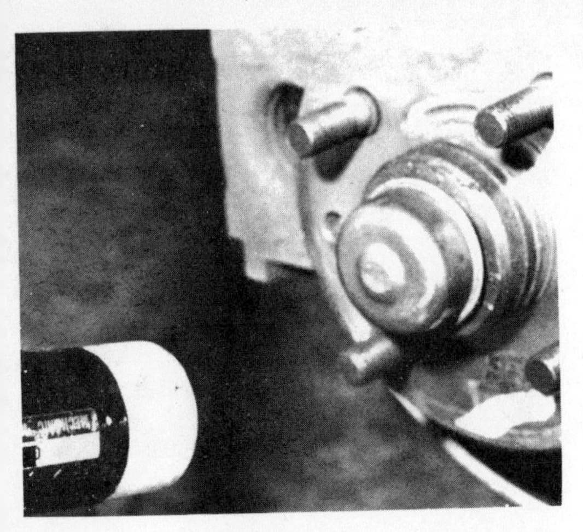

Tap the dustcover back on with a soft-faced hammer

9. Install the dust cap on the hub and the hub cap or wheel cover on the wheel.
10. Lower the car.
11. Adjust the opposite front wheel bearings in the same manner.

REMOVAL AND INSTALLATION

For wheel bearing removal and installation procedure see Brake Disc Removal and Installation.

REAR DRUM BRAKES

1976-79

Drum brakes employ tow brake shoes mounted on a stationary backing plate. These shoes are positioned inside a circular cast iron drum which rotates with the wheel assembly. The shoes are held in place by springs; this allows them to slide toward the drums (when they are applied) while keeping the linings and drums in alignment. The shoes are actuated by a wheel cylinder which is mounted at the top of the backing plate. When the brakes are applied, hydraulic pressure forces the wheel cylinder's two actuating links outward. Since these links bear directly against the top of the brake shoes, the tops of the shoes are then forced outward against the inner side of the drum. This action forces the bottoms of the two shoes to contact the brake drum by rotating the entire assembly slightly (known as servo action). When pressure within the wheel cylinder is relaxed, return springs pull the shoes back away from the drum.

Most modern drum brakes are designed to self-adjust themselves during application when the vehicle is moving in reverse. This motion causes both shoes to rotate very slightly with the drum, rocking an adjusting lever, thereby causing rotation of the adjusting screw by means of a star wheel.

The duo-servo brake with pin and slot adjusters is a new design used only on the Chevette through 1979.

1980 And Later

The rear drum brake system introduced in 1980 is a duo-servo and direct torque design. In the duo-servo design the force which the wheel cylinder applies to the shoes is supplemented by the tendency of the shoes to wrap into the drum during braking. With the direct torque design, torque from the brake shoes is transferred directly through the anchor pin to the control arm.

CAUTION: *Brake shoes contain asbestos, which has been determined to be a cancer causing agent. Never clean the brake surfaces with compressed air! Avoid inhaling any dust from any brake surface! When cleaning brake surfaces, use a commercially available brake cleaning fluid.*

Brake Shoes

REPLACEMENT

1976-79

1. Remove the brake drum.

NOTE: *If the brake drum is stubborn in coming off, rotate the adjusters on the back of the brake toward the axle tube to retract the shoes from the drum.*

2. Loosen the equalizer to let all tension from the parking brake cable.
3. Unhook the parking brake cable from the lever.
4. Use pliers to remove the long shoe pull back spring at the top.
5. Use pliers to remove the shoe holddown springs and retainers from the middle of each shoe.
6. Separate the shoes at the top and remove them.

NOTE: *Examine all parts for wear or stress and replace as necessary.*

7. Check that the adjusters work properly; it should take 29-36 ft. lbs. torque to turn the adjusters. The adjusters and backing plate must be replaced as an assembly.
8. Lubricate the shoe contact surfaces on the backing plate and all pivot points with brake lubricant. Lubricate the parking brake cable.
9. Lubricate the pivot end of the parking brake lever and attach the lever to the shoe.
10. Connect the shoes at the bottom with the retaining spring.
11. Place the shoes in position and fasten the

Remove the spring washers (arrows) before attempting to remove the drum

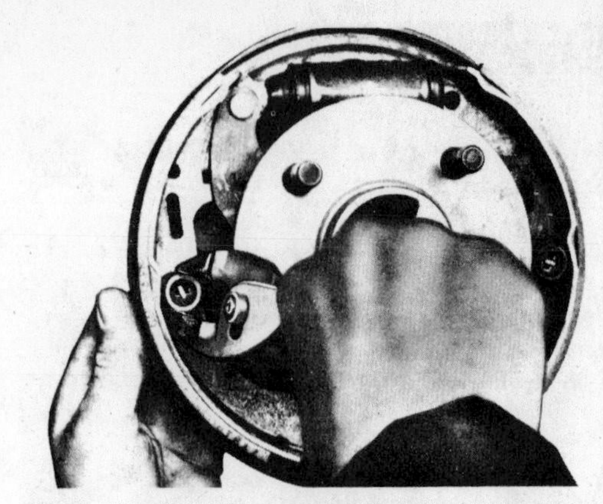

Removing the hold-down springs and retainers

Rotate adjuster bolts in direction of arrows to retract shoes

Removing the brake shoes (linings)

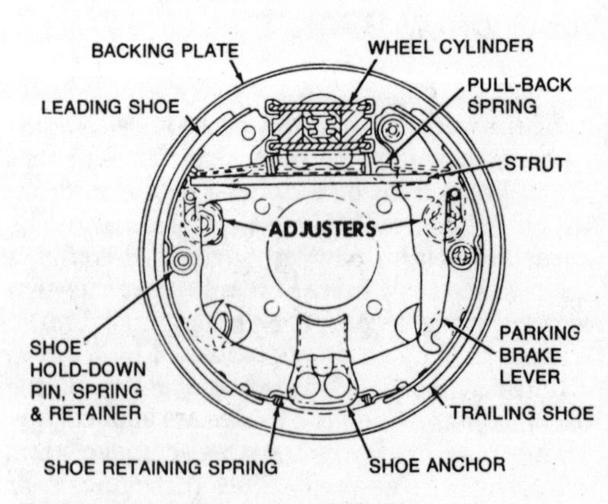

Rear brake components—1976–79

Unhooking the parking brake cable

front shoe with the holddown spring and retainer. Be sure that the adjuster peg is in the shoe slot.

12. Install the parking brake lever to front shoe strut. Fasten down the rear shoe with the holddown spring and retainer. Be sure that the adjuster peg is in the shoe slot.

13. Install the shoe pull back spring.

14. Attach the end of the parking brake cable to the lever.

15. Replace the drum, Adjust the brakes by applying the brake several times until the pedal is firm. Check the fluid level frequently. Adjust the parking brake.

1980 and Later

1. Jack up the car and support safely with jackstands.
2. Mark the relationship of the wheel to the axle and remove the wheel.
3. Mark the relationship of the drum to the axle and remove the drum.
4. Using a suitable tool remove the return springs, holddown springs, lever pivot and holddown pins.
5. Lift up on the actuator lever and remove the actuating link.
6. Remove the actuator lever, actuator pivot and return spring.
7. Remove the parking brake strut and spring by spreading the shoes apart.
8. Spread the shoe and lining assemblies to clear the axle flange. Disconnect the parking brake cable and remove the shoes, connected by a spring from the vehicle.

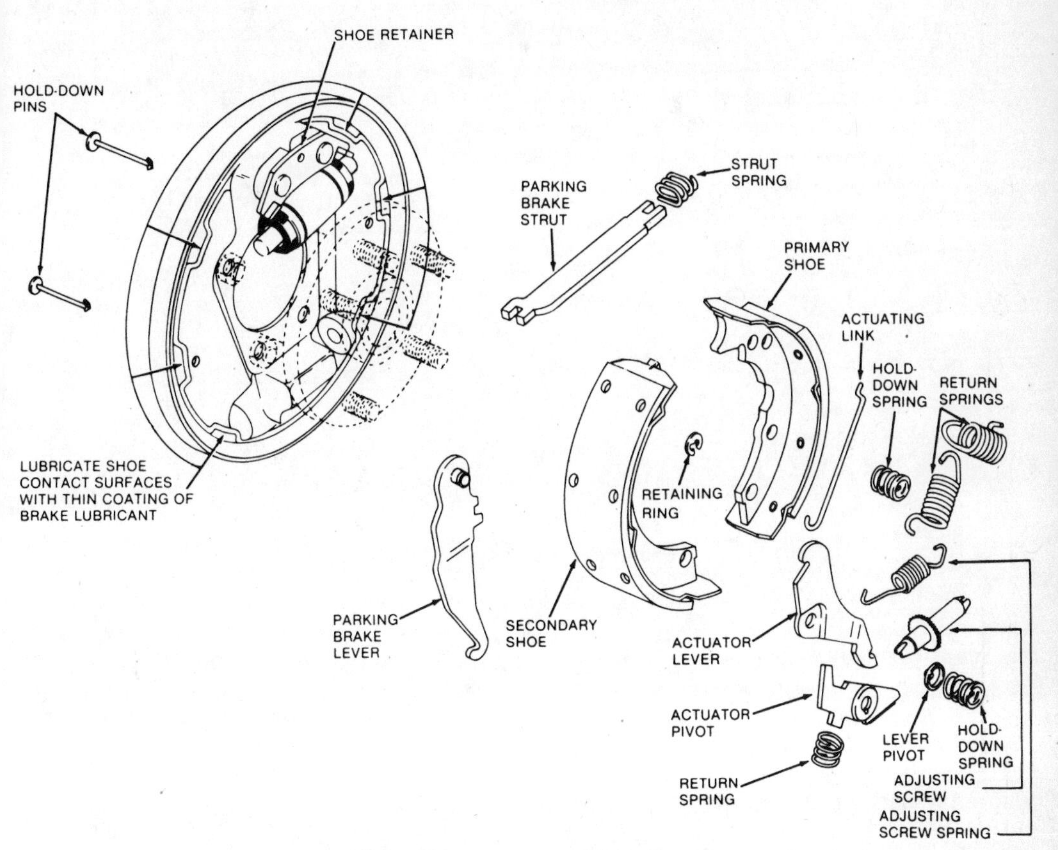

Rear brake assembly—1980–84

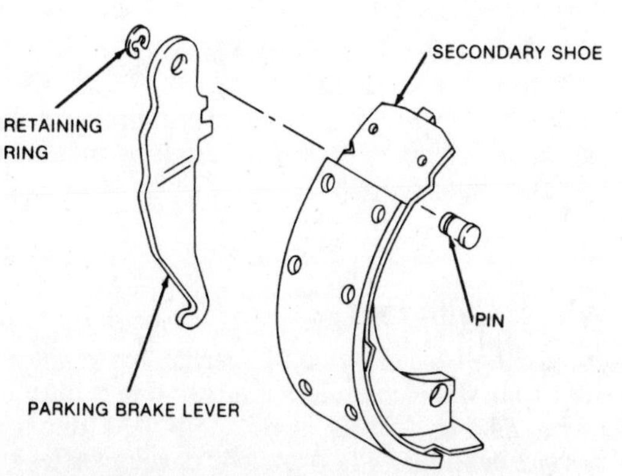

The parking brake lever is connected to secondary shoe by a retaining ring

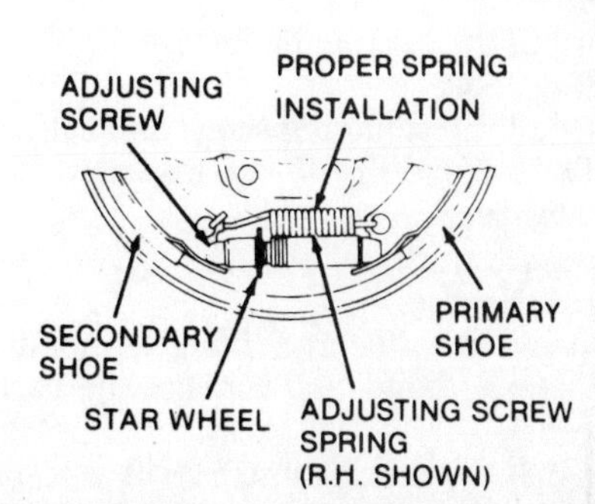

Proper installation of the adjusting screw and spring. Note that the coils of the spring are not over the star wheel

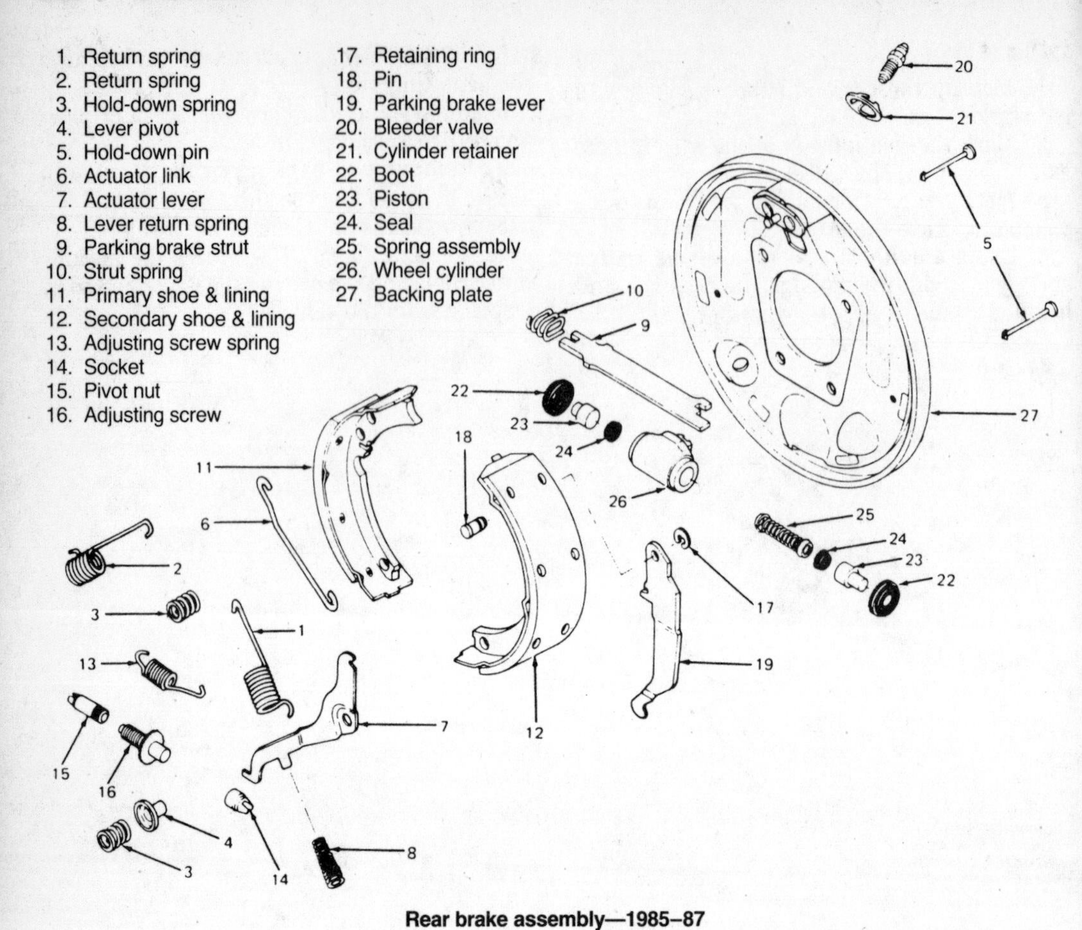

Rear brake assembly—1985–87

9. While noting the position of the adjusting spring, remove the adjusting screw and spring.

NOTE: *Do not interchange adjusting screws from RH and LH brake assemblies.*

10. Remove the retaining ring and pin then remove the parking brake lever from the secondary shoe.

NOTE: *Examine all parts for wear or stress and replace as necessary.*

INSTALLATION

1. Install the parking brake lever on the new secondary shoe.
2. Install the adjusting screw and spring.

NOTE: *The coils of the spring must not be over the star wheel. Left and right hand springs are different and must not be interchanged.*

3. Spread the shoe and lining assemblies to clear the axle flange and connect the parking brake cable.
4. Install the parking brake strut and spring by spreading the shoes apart.

NOTE: *The end of the strut without the spring engages the parking brake lever. The end with the spring engages the primary shoe.*

5. Install the actuator pivot, lever and return spring.
6. Install the actuating link in the shoe retainer.
7. Lift up on the actuator lever and hook the link onto the lever.
8. Install the holddown pins, lever pivot and holddown springs.
9. Install the shoe return springs.
10. Install the drum and wheel. Adjust the brakes by applying the brake several times until the pedal is firm. Check the fluid level and adjust the parking brake.

Wheel Cylinders

It is the best practice to overhaul or replace both rear wheel cylinders if either one is found to be leaking. If this is not done, the undisturbed cylinder will probable develop a leak soon after the first repair job. New wheel cylinders are available at a price low enough to make

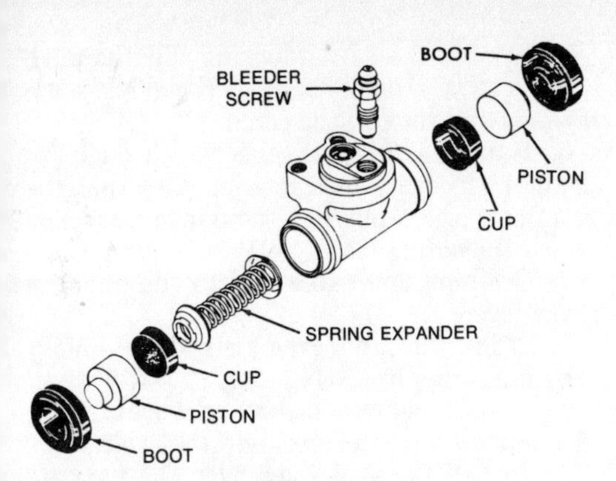

Exploded view of a wheel cylinder

overhaul impractical, except in emergency situations.

OVERHAUL

1. Disassemble the brake system as described under "Brake Shoe Replacement".
2. Unbolt the wheel cylinder from the backing plate.
3. Remove and discard the rubber boots, the pistons, and the cups.
4. Clean all parts in brake fluid or denatured alcohol.
5. If there are any pits or roughness inside the cylinder, it must be replaced. Polish off any discolored area by removing the cylinder around a piece of crocus cloth held by a finger. Do not polish the cylinder in a lengthwise direction. Clean the cylinder again after polishing. Air dry.
6. Replace the piston if it is scratched or damaged in any way.
7. Lubricate the cylinder bore with clean brake fluid and insert the spring and the expanders.
8. Install the new cups with the flat side to the outside. Do not lubricate them.
9. Install the new boot onto the piston and insert the piston into the cylinder with the flat surface towards the center of the cylinder. Do not lubricate the pistons before the installation.
10. Replace the cylinder and tighten the bolts evenly.
11. Reassemble the brake system and bleed the brake hydraulic system.

PARKING BRAKE

Cable

ADJUSTMENT

1. Raise the car.
2. Applying the parking brake 1-3 notches from the fully released position.
3. Tighten the parking brake cable, equalizer adjusting nut until a light drag is felt when the rear wheels are rotated forward. The equalizer adjusting nut should be tightened to 55 in. lbs. at its adjustment point.
4. Fully release the parking brake and rotate the rear wheels. There should be no drag.
5. Lower the car.

REMOVAL AND INSTALLATION

1. Raise the car.
2. Disconnect the parking brake equalizer spring and equalizer.

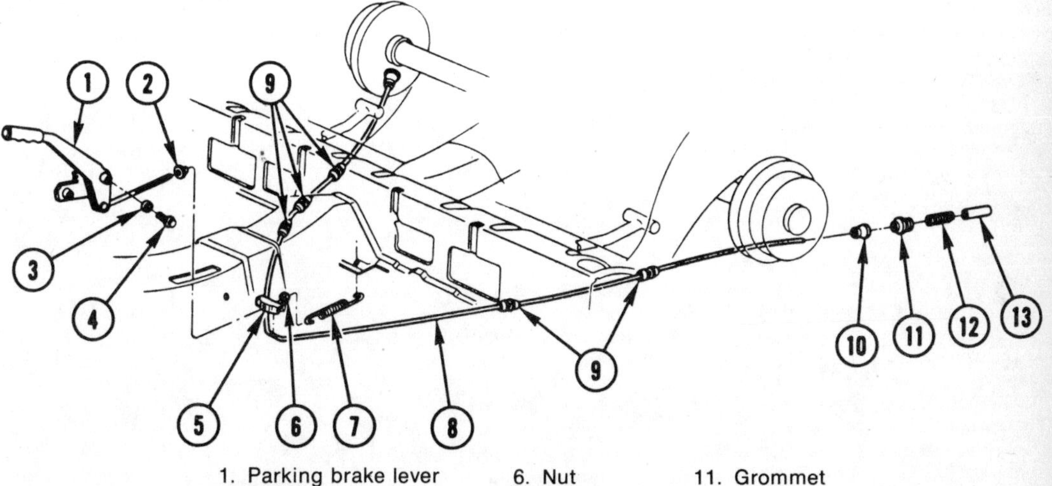

1. Parking brake lever
2. Grommet
3. Washer
4. Bolt and washer
5. Equalizer
6. Nut
7. Spring
8. Cable
9. Grommet
10. Boot
11. Grommet
12. Spring
13. Eye

Parking brake components

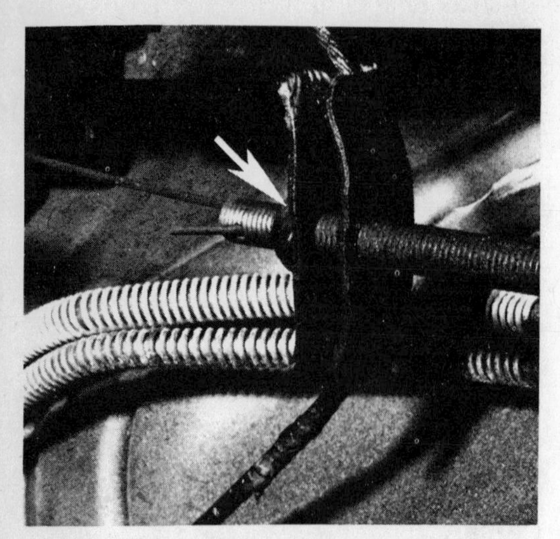

Parking brake cable is adjusted by turning the equalizer nut (arrow) in or out as necessary

3. Remove the cable from the underbody mounting brackets.
4. Remove the wheel and brake drum. With the rear brakes exposed, remove the parking brake cable from the parking brake lever.
5. Remove the spring locking clip and push out the cable grommets at the flange plate entry hole and remove the cable.
6. To install, pass the cable end through the flange plate entry hole making sure that the grommets are in place on the flange plate, and install the spring locking clips.
7. Connect the cable end to the parking brake lever.
8. Install the cable grommets at the underbody mounting brackets.
9. Install the brake drum and wheel.
10. Install the equalizer onto the cable.
11. Install the equalizer over the parking brake lever rod and install the equalizer nut. Install the cable return spring.
12. Pre-stress the cable by applying the parking brake two or three times with heavy handle pressure.
13. Adjust the parking brake as previously described.
14. Lubricate the cable at the equalizer and at all grommets.
15. Lower the car.

Brake Specifications

All measurements in mm, inches are given in parentheses

Year	Model	Master Cylinder Bore	Wheel Cylinder or Caliper Piston Bore		Brake Disc or Drum Diameter	
			Front	Rear	Front	Rear
1976–85	All	19.05 (.750)	47.625 (1.875)	19.05 (.750)	245.87 (9.68)	200.15 (7.88)
1986–87	All	22.2 (.874)	—	17.5 (.689)	245.87 (9.68)	200.15 (7.88)

NOTE: *Drums cannot be turned more than 0.632 mm (0.025 in.)*

Body

10

EXTERIOR

Doors

REMOVAL AND INSTALLATION

Front

1. Remove the door check link to support the attaching rivet by punching out the rivet center pin and then drilling out the rivet.
2. Pry out the plastic hinge pin plugs on the top and bottom of both hinges.
3. Support the door and drive out the hinge pins with tool J-21688 or equivalent.
4. Use tool J-21688 or its equivalent is designed to be used as follows:
   a. Remove the threaded collar from the pin.
   b. Insert the pin through the hinge pin (from the bottom for the upper hinge and from the top for the lower hinge) and reassemble the collar on the pin.
   c. Hammer on the handle of the tool near the pin to drive (pull) out the hinge pin.

To install

1. Position the door side hinges onto the body side hinges and drive the hinge pins using a hammer and a block.
2. Fill the hinge pins with a lubricant such as Lubriplate Auto Lube A® or equivalent and install the plastic plugs.
3. Assemble the door check link to the support with a steel rivet $^{3}/_{16}'' \times {^{9}/_{16}}''$.

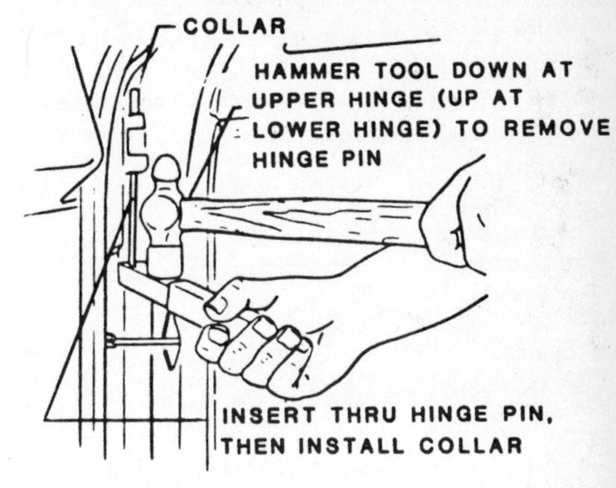

Removing the hinge pin

Rear

1. Tape the area (on the door and body pillars) below the upper hinge with cloth backed body tape.

If replacement hinge pin retaining clips or hinge pins are not available, save the clips as follows:

   a. Using a suitable tool, spread the clip enough to lift the clip above recess, toward the enough the pointed end of the pin.
   b. As the pin is removed, the clip will ride the shank of the pin and fall free.
   c. Reinstall the clips onto the pins before installing the door.

2. With the door in the full open position, place the flat side of a cold chisel on the pointed end of the upper hinge pin and strike with a hammer to loosen the pin. This will move the pin enough to force the serrated shank (near the head of the pin) out of hinge mating surface.
3. With the aid of a helper to support and work the door up and down., drive out the upper and lower hinge pins using a soft headed hammer and locking type pliers.
4. Carefully remove the door assembly from the body.

Before installing, replace the hinge pin retaining clips or reuse the old clips as outlined earlier. If clips are not available and the old clips are broken, replace the hinge pins. The upper hinge pin is installed with the pointed end up and the lower hinge pin is installed with the pointed end down.

Hood

REMOVAL AND INSTALLATION

1. Raise the hood and support with the rod.
2. Disconnect the under hood lamp wire, if so equipped.
3. Scribe the hinge bolt to hood location.
4. With an assistant, remove the hood to hinge bolts and remove the hood.
5. With an assistant, place the hood in position and install the hood hinge to hood bolts. Line up the scribe marks made during removal. Check hood alignment after tightening.

Rear Compartment Lid

REMOVAL AND INSTALLATION

1. Open the rear compartment lid to the full open position.
2. On models equipped with a rear window defogger, disconnect the wires from the terminals.

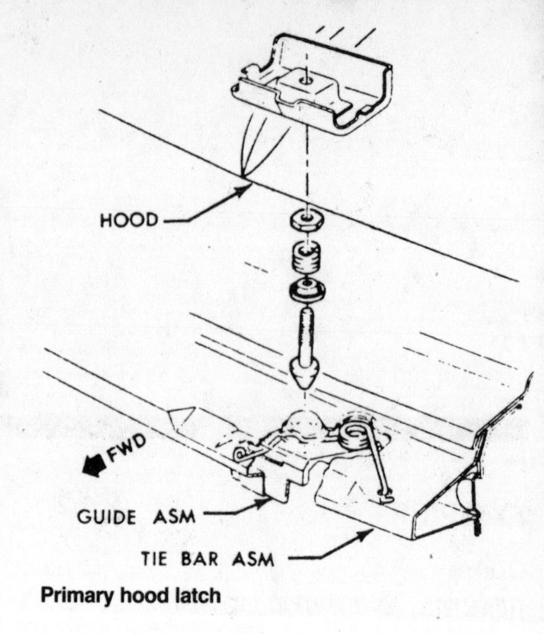

Primary hood latch

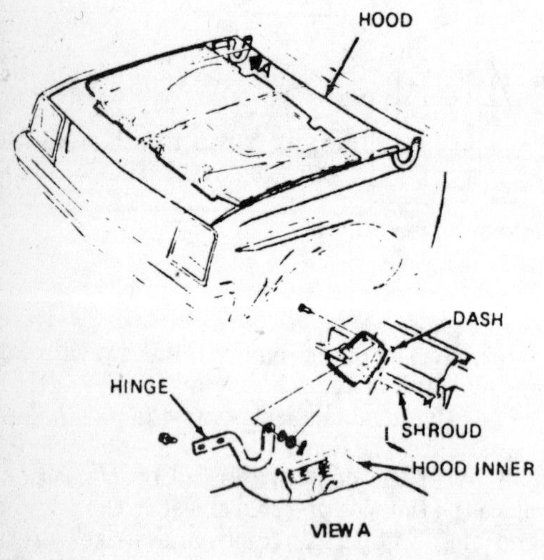

Hood assembly

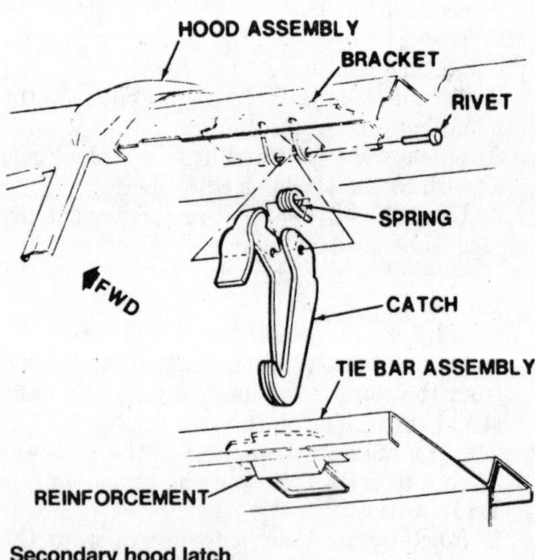

Secondary hood latch

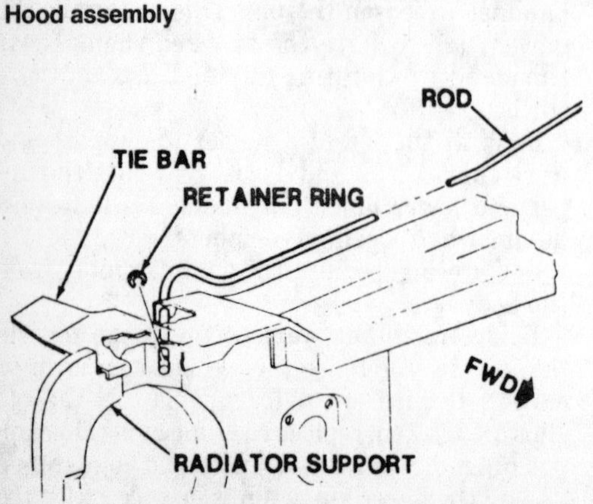

Hood support rod

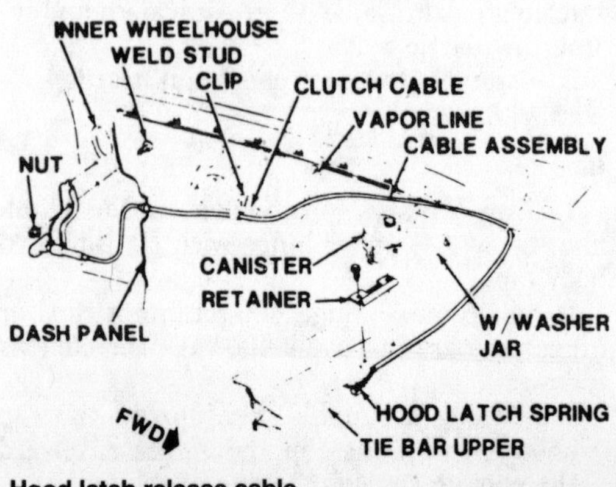

Hood latch release cable

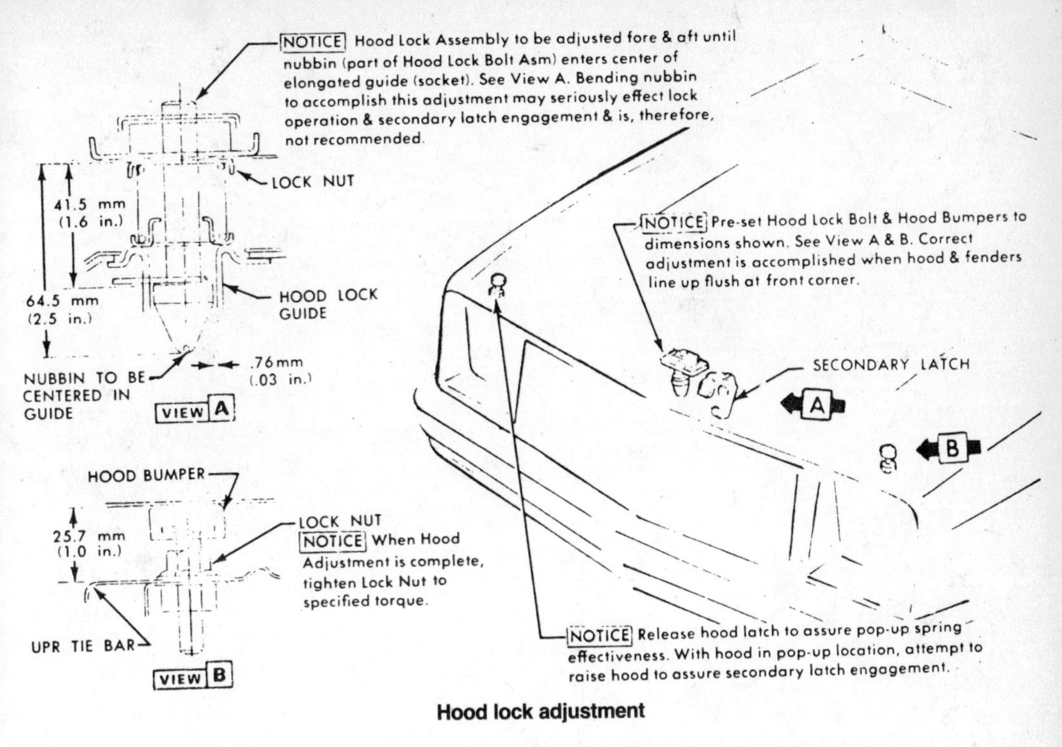

Hood lock adjustment

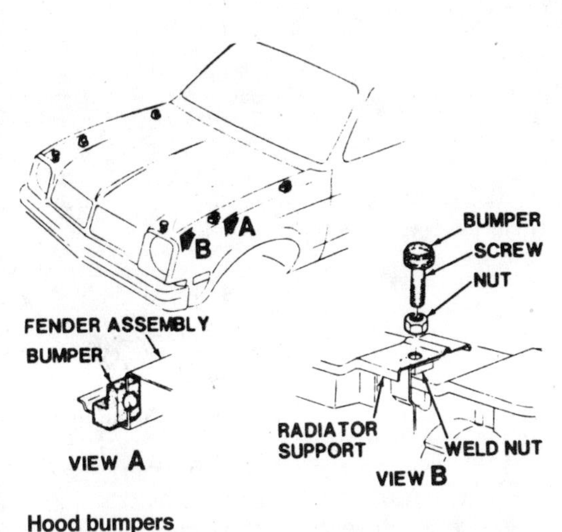

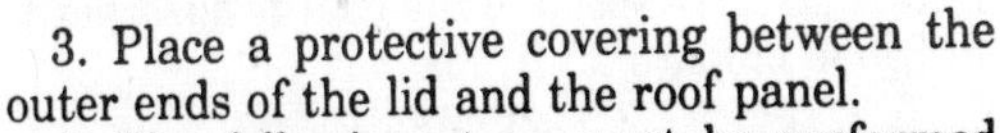

Hood bumpers

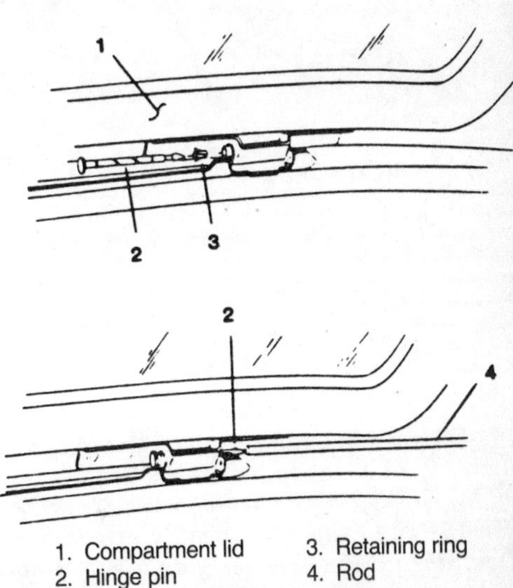

1. Compartment lid
2. Hinge pin
3. Retaining ring
4. Rod

Removing the rear compartment lid hinge pin

3. Place a protective covering between the outer ends of the lid and the roof panel.

4. The following steps must be performed while a helper supports the lid in the fully opened position.

CAUTION: *Do not attempt to remove or loosen the gas support assembly attachments with the lid in any other than the fully open position or personal injury may result.*

5. Remove the lid side retaining clip from the gas support assembly and detach the support assembly from the lid side attaching ball.

6. With a helper holding the lid, use a 5mm diameter rod to remove the hinge pins from the hinges. place the end of the rod against the pointed end of the hinge pin; then strike the end of the rod firmly to shear the retaining ring tabs and drive the pin through the hinge. Repeat the operation on the opposite side hinge and remove the lid from the body.

7. To install the lid, reverse the removal procedure. Prior to installing the hinge pins, install new retaining rings in the notches provided in pins. Position the retaining ring so that the tabs point toward the head of the pin.

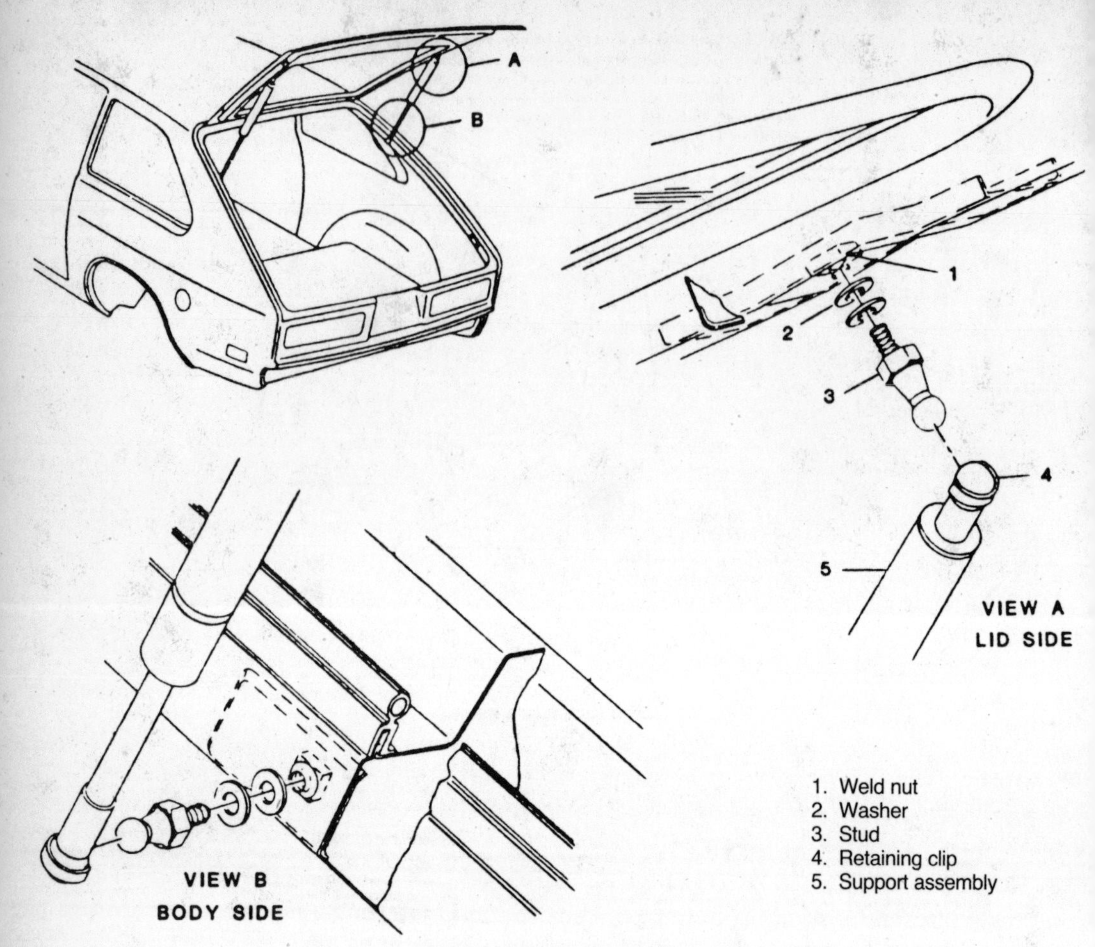

Attaching the rear compartment lid support assembly

Gas Support Assembly

REMOVAL AND INSTALLATION

1. Obtain a helper to support the rear compartment lid in the full open position.

CAUTION: *Do not attempt to remove or loosen the gas support assembly attachments with the lid in any other than the fully open position or personal injury may result.*

2. Remove the lid side retaining clip from the gas support assembly and detach the support assembly from the lid side attaching ball.
3. Detach the ball from the socket attachment at each end of the support and remove from the body.
4. Installation is the reverse of removal.

Front Bumper

REMOVAL AND INSTALLATION

1976-82

1. Disconnect the parking signal lamp bulbs.
2. Support the bumper and remove the four bumper to energy absorber nuts on each side of the bumper.
3. Remove the bumper guards and protective strips, if so equipped.
4. To remove the energy absorber, remove the rear nut on the energy absorber.
5. To install reverse the removal procedure and torque the energy absorber to to bumper nuts to to 25 ft. lbs. and the energy absorber to to frame bolts to 25 ft. lbs.

1983-87

1. Disconnect the parking signal lamp bulbs.
2. Remove the extensions and valance panel.
3. Support the bumper and remove the four bumper to energy absorber nuts on each side of the bumper.
4. Remove the bumper guards and protective strips, if so equipped.
5. To install reverse the removal procedure and torque the energy absorber to to bumper nuts to to 25 ft. lbs.

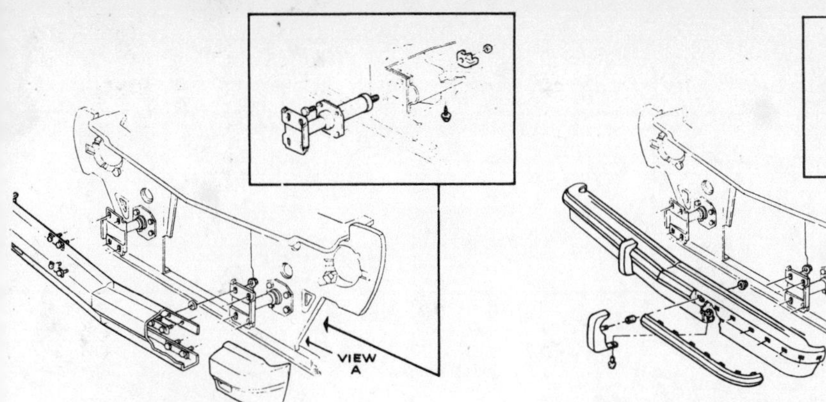

Front bumper assembly, 1976–78

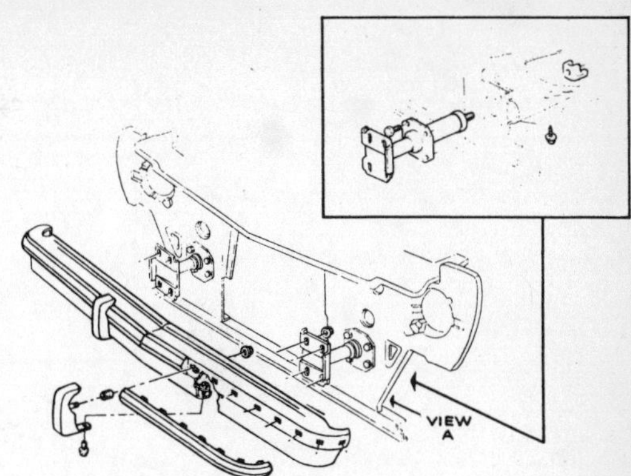

Front bumper assembly, 1979–82

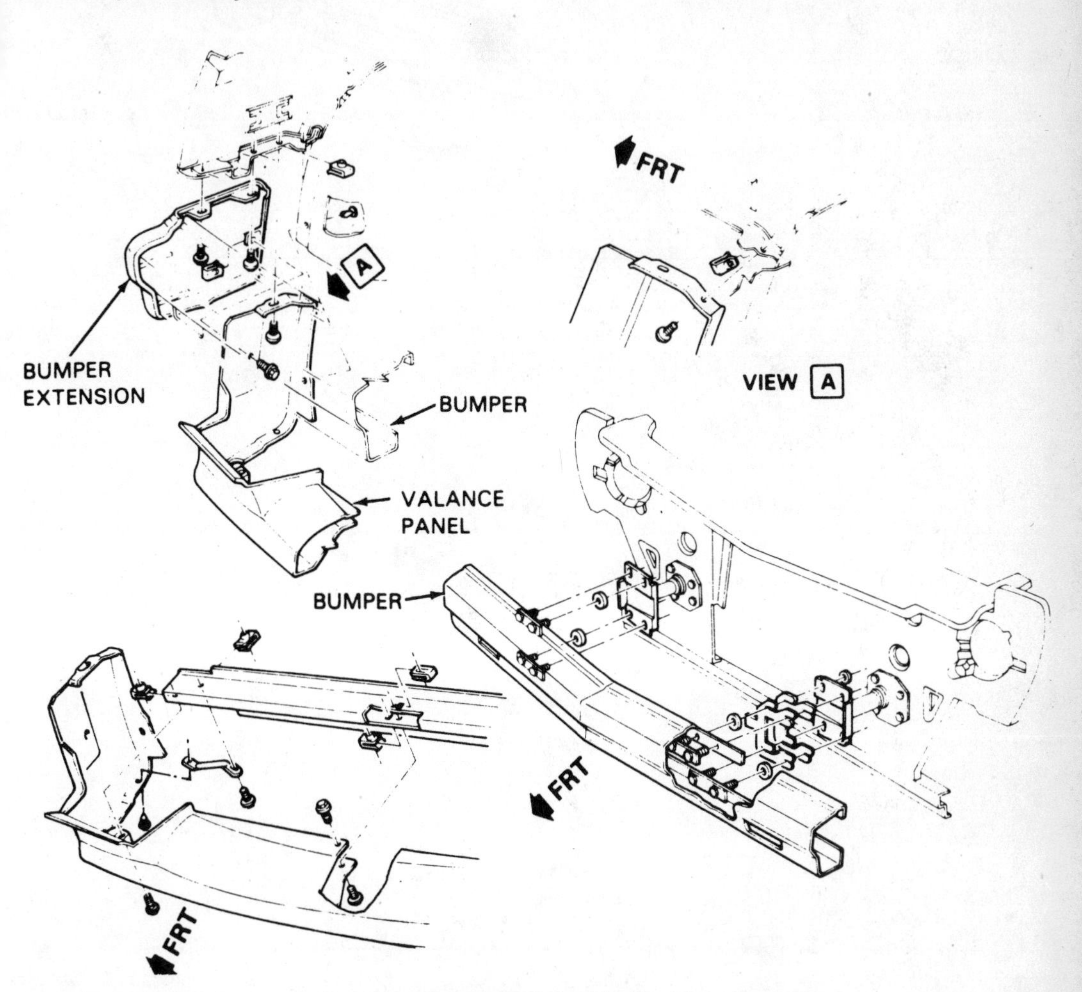

Front bumper assembly, 1983–87

Rear Bumper

REMOVAL AND INSTALLATION

1. Support the bumper and remove the four bumper to energy absorber nuts on each side of the bumper.

2. Remove the bumper guards and protective strips, if so equipped.

3. To install reverse the removal procedure and torque the energy absorber to to bumper nuts to to 25 ft. lbs.

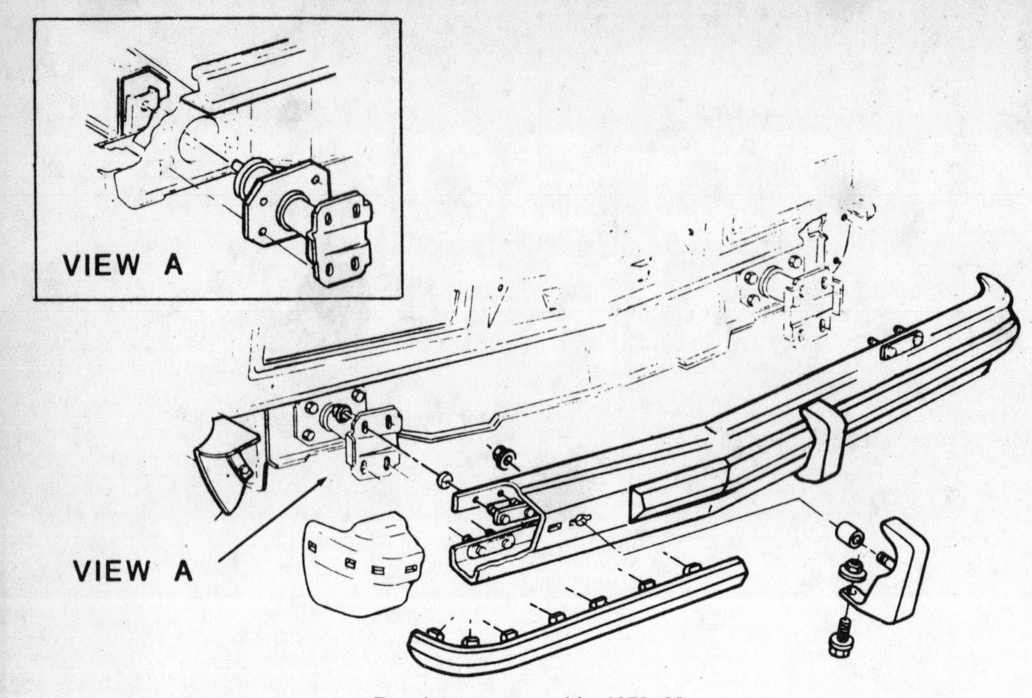

Rear bumper assembly, 1979–82

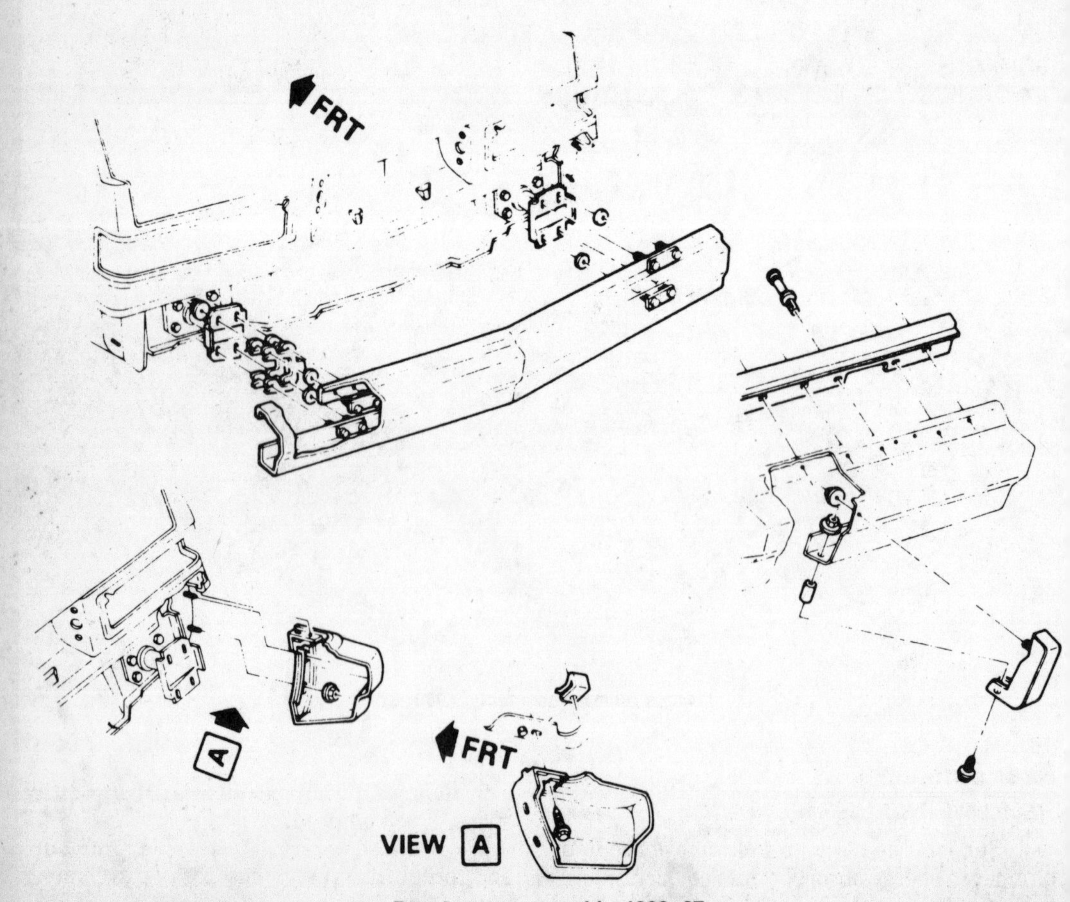

Rear bumper assembly, 1983–87

EASY STEP-BY-STEP TIPS FROM PROS

CHILTON'S AUTO BODY REPAIR TIPS

Tools and Materials • Step-by-Step Illustrated Procedures
How To Repair Dents, Scratches and Rust Holes
Spray Painting and Refinishing Tips

With a little practice, basic body repair procedures can be mastered by any do-it-yourself mechanic. The step-by-step repairs shown here can be applied to almost any type of auto body repair.

TOOLS & MATERIALS

You may already have basic tools, such as hammers and electric drills. Other tools unique to body repair — body hammers, grinding attachments, sanding blocks, dent puller, half-round plastic file and plastic spreaders — are relatively inexpensive and can be obtained wherever auto parts or auto body repair parts are sold. Portable air compressors and paint spray guns can be purchased or rented.

Auto Body Repair Kits

The best and most often used products are available to the do-it-yourselfer in kit form, from major manufacturers of auto body repair products. The same manufacturers also merchandise the individual products for use by pros.

Kits are available to make a wide variety of repairs, including holes, dents and scratches and fiberglass, and offer the advantage of buying the materials you'll need for the job. There is little waste or chance of materials going bad from not being used. Many kits may also contain basic body-working tools such as body files, sanding blocks and spreaders. Check the contents of the kit before buying your tools.

BODY REPAIR TIPS

Safety

Many of the products associated with auto body repair and refinishing contain toxic chemicals. Read all labels before opening containers and store them in a safe place and manner.

• Wear eye protection (safety goggles) when using power tools or when performing any operation that involves the removal of any type of material.

• Wear lung protection (disposable mask or respirator) when grinding, sanding or painting.

Sanding

1 Sand off paint before using a dent puller. When using a non-adhesive sanding disc, cover the back of the disc with an overlapping layer or two of masking tape and trim the edges. The disc will last considerably longer.

2 Use the circular motion of the sanding disc to grind *into* the edge of the repair. Grinding or sanding away from the jagged edge will only tear the sandpaper.

3 Use the palm of your hand flat on the panel to detect high and low spots. Do not use your fingertips. Slide your hand slowly back and forth.

WORKING WITH BODY FILLER

Mixing The Filler

leanliness and proper mixing and application are extremely impor-
nt. Use a clean piece of plastic or ass or a disposable artist's palette to ix body filler.

Allow plenty of time and follow directions. No useful purpose will be erved by adding more hardener to ake it cure (set-up) faster. Less hard-ner means more curing time, but the ixture dries harder; more hardener eans less curing time but a softer mix-re.

2

2 Both the hardener and the filler should be thoroughly kneaded or irred before mixing. Hardener should a solid paste and dispense like thin othpaste. Body filler should be nooth, and free of lumps or thick ots.

Getting the proper amount of hard-ner in the filler is the trickiest part of eparing the filler. Use the same nount of hardener in cold or warm eather. For contour filler (thick coats), bead of hardener twice the diameter of e filler is about right. There's about a % margin on either side, but, if in ubt use less hardener.

2

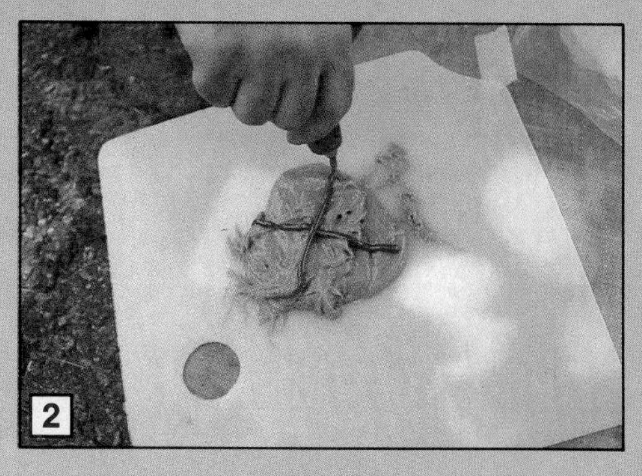

2

3 Mix the body filler and hardener by wiping across the mixing surface, picking the mixture up and wiping it again. Colder weather requires longer mixing times. Do not mix in a circular motion; this will trap air bubbles which will become holes in the cured filler.

3

Applying The Filler

1 For best results, filler should not be applied over 1/4" thick.

Apply the filler in several coats. Build it up to above the level of the repair surface so that it can be sanded or grated down.

The first coat of filler must be pressed on with a firm wiping motion.

Apply the filler in one direction only. Working the filler back and forth will either pull it off the metal or trap air bubbles.

REPAIRING DENTS

Before you start, take a few minutes to study the damaged area. Try to visualize the shape of the panel before it was damaged. If the damage is on the left fender, look at the right fender and use it as a guide. If there is access to the panel from behind, you can reshape it with a body hammer. If not, you'll have to use a dent puller. Go slowly and work the metal a little at a time. Get the panel as straight as possible before applying filler.

1 This dent is typical of one that can be pulled out or hammered out from behind. Remove the headlight cover, headlight assembly and turn signal housing.

2 Drill a series of holes 1/2 the size of the end of the dent puller along the stress line. Make some trial pulls and assess the results. If necessary, drill more holes and try again. Do not hurry.

3 If possible, use a body hammer and block to shape the metal back to its original contours. Get the metal back as close to its original shape as possible. Don't depend on body filler to fill dents.

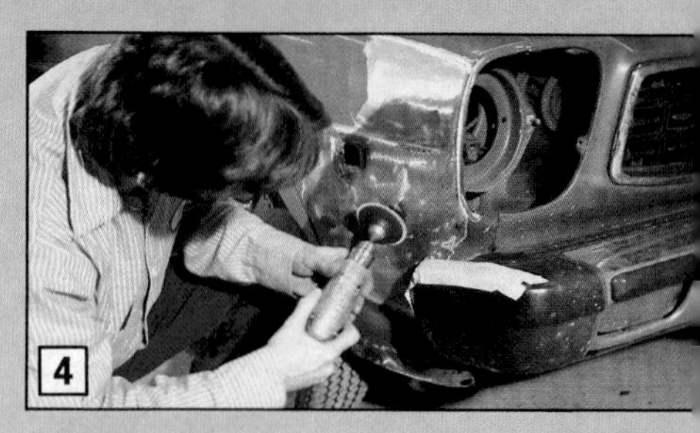

4 Using an 80-grit grinding disc on ar electric drill, grind the paint from th surrounding area down to bare meta Use a new grinding pad to prevent hea buildup that will warp metal.

5 The area should look like this wher you're finished grinding. Knock th drill holes in and tape over small open ings to keep plastic filler out.

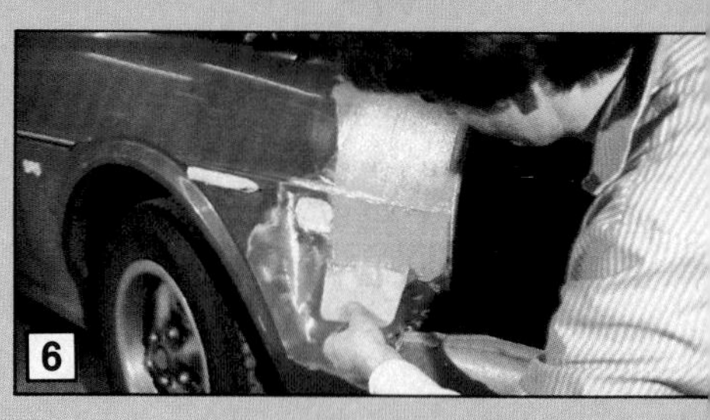

6 Mix the body filler (see Body Repai Tips). Spread the body filler evenl over the entire area (see Body Repai Tips). Be sure to cover the area com pletely.

7 Let the body filler dry until the sur face can just be scratched with you fingernail. Knock the high spots from the body filler with a body file ("Cheese grater"). Check frequently with the palm of your hand for high and low spots.

8 Check to be sure that trim pieces that will be installed later will fit ex- ctly. Sand the area with 40-grit paper.

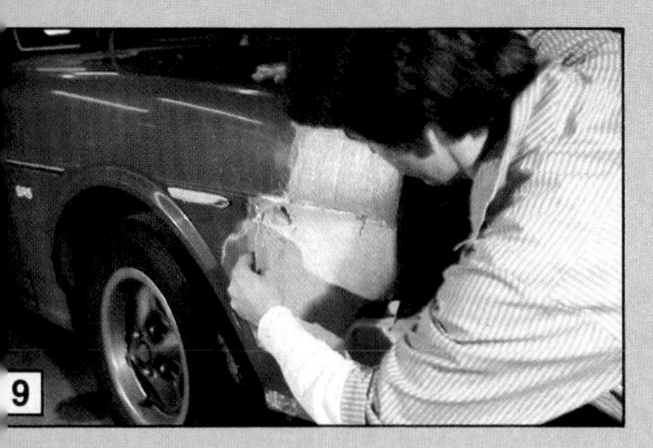

9 If you wind up with low spots, you may have to apply another layer of ller.

10 Knock the high spots off with 40-grit paper. When you are satisfied vith the contours of the repair, apply a ıin coat of filler to cover pin holes and cratches.

11 Block sand the area with 40-grit paper to a smooth finish. Pay par- cular attention to body lines and ridges ıat must be well-defined.

12 Sand the area with 400 paper and then finish with a scuff pad. The finished repair is ready for priming and painting (see Painting Tips).

Materials and photos courtesy of Ritt Jones Auto Body, Prospect Park, PA.

REPAIRING RUST HOLES

There are many ways to repair rust holes. The fiberglass cloth kit shown here is one of the most cost efficient for the owner because it provides a strong repair that resists cracking and moisture and is relatively easy to use. It can be used on large and small holes (with or without backing) and can be applied over contoured areas. Remember, however, that short of replacing an entire panel, no repair is a guarantee that the rust will not return.

1 Remove any trim that will be in the way. Clean away all loose debris. Cut away all the rusted metal. But be sure to leave enough metal to retain the contour or body shape.

2 Grind away all traces of rust with a 24-grit grinding disc. Be sure to grind back 3-4 inches from the edge of the hole down to bare metal and be sure all traces of paint, primer and rust are removed.

3 Block sand the area with 80 or 100 grit sandpaper to get a clear, shiny surface and feathered paint edge. Tap the edges of the hole inward with a ball peen hammer.

4 If you are going to use release film, cut a piece about 2-3″ larger than the area you have sanded. Place the film over the repair and mark the sanded area on the film. Avoid any unnecessary wrinkling of the film.

5 Cut 2 pieces of fiberglass matte to match the shape of the repair. One piece should be about 1″ smaller than the sanded area and the second piece should be 1″ smaller than the first. Mix enough filler and hardener to saturate the fiberglass material (see Body Repair Tips).

6 Lay the release sheet on a flat su face and spread an even layer c filler, large enough to cover the repai Lay the smaller piece of fiberglass clot in the center of the sheet and sprea another layer of filler over the fiberglas cloth. Repeat the operation for th larger piece of cloth.

7 Place the repair material over th repair area, with the release film fac ing outward. Use a spreader and worl from the center outward to smooth th material, following the body contours Be sure to remove all air bubbles.

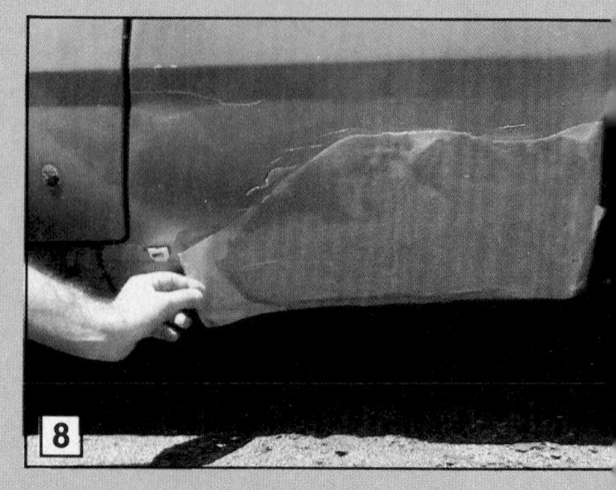

8 Wait until the repair has dried tack free and peel off the release sheet The ideal working temperature is 60° 90° F. Cooler or warmer temperatures o high humidity may require additiona curing time. Wait longer, if in doubt.

9

9 Sand and feather-edge the entire area. The initial sanding can be one with a sanding disc on an electric rill if care is used. Finish the sanding ith a block sander. Low spots can be lled with body filler; this may require everal applications.

10

10 When the filler can just be scratched with a fingernail, nock the high spots down with a body ile and smooth the entire area with 80-grit. Feather the filled areas into the surounding areas.

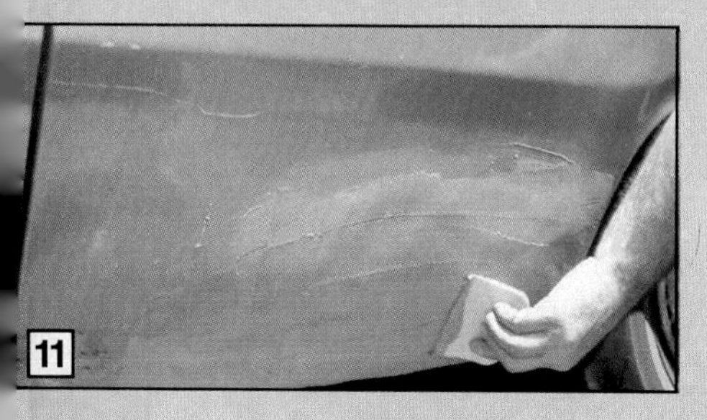

11

11 When the area is sanded smooth, mix some topcoat and hardener and apply it directly with a spreader. This will give a smooth finish and prevent the glass matte from showing through the paint.

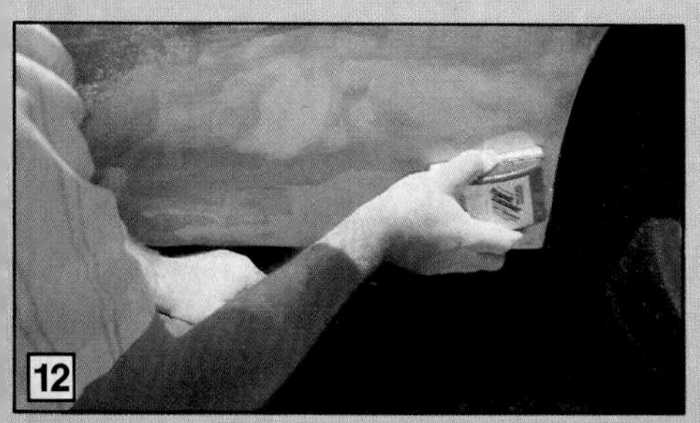

12

12 Block sand the topcoat smooth with finishing sandpaper (200 grit), and 400 grit. The repair is ready for masking, priming and painting (see Painting Tips).

Materials and photos courtesy Marson Corporation, Chelsea, Massachusetts

PAINTING TIPS

Preparation

1 SANDING — Use a 400 or 600 grit wet or dry sandpaper. Wet-sand the area with a 1/4 sheet of sandpaper soaked in clean water. Keep the paper wet while sanding. Sand the area until the repaired area tapers into the original finish.

2 CLEANING — Wash the area to be painted thoroughly with water and a clean rag. Rinse it thoroughly and wipe the surface dry until you're sure it's completely free of dirt, dust, fingerprints, wax, detergent or other foreign matter.

3 MASKING — Protect any areas you don't want to overspray by covering them with masking tape and newspaper. Be careful not get fingerprints on the area to be painted.

4 PRIMING — All exposed metal should be primed before painting. Primer protects the metal and provides an excellent surface for paint adhesion. When the primer is dry, wet-sand the area again with 600 grit wet-sandpaper. Clean the area again after sanding.

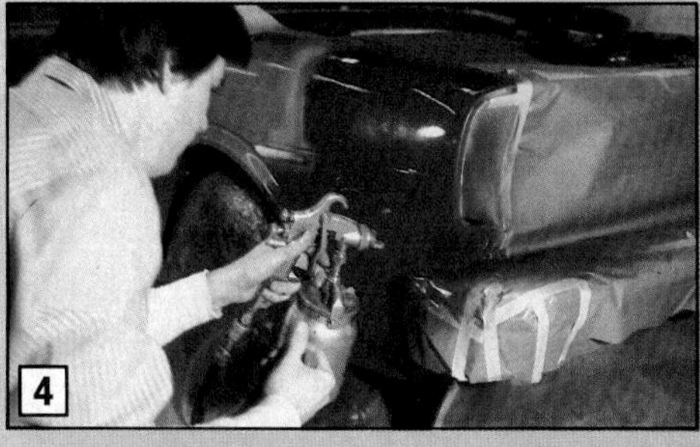

4

Painting Techniques

Paint applied from either a spray gun or a spray can (for small areas) will provide good results. Experiment on an old piece of metal to get the right combination before you begin painting.

SPRAYING VISCOSITY (SPRAY GUN ONLY) — Paint should be thinned to spraying viscosity according to the directions on the can. Use only the recommended thinner or reducer and the same amount of reduction regardless of temperature.

AIR PRESSURE (SPRAY GUN ONLY) — This is extremely important. Be sure you are using the proper recommended pressure.

TEMPERATURE — The surface to be painted should be approximately the same temperature as the surrounding air. Applying warm paint to a cold surface, or vice versa, will completely upset the paint characteristics.

THICKNESS — Spray with smooth strokes. In general, the thicker the coat of paint, the longer the drying time. Apply several thin coats about 30 seconds apart. The paint should remain wet long enough to flow out and no longer; heavier coats will only produce sags or wrinkles. Spray a light (fog) coat, followed by heavier color coats.

DISTANCE — The ideal spraying distance is 8″-12″ from the gun or can to the surface. Shorter distances will produce ripples, while greater distances will result in orange peel, dry film and poor color match and loss of material due to overspray.

OVERLAPPING — The gun or can should be kept at right angles to the surface at all times. Work to a wet edge at an even speed, using a 50% overlap and direct the center of the spray at the lower or nearest edge of the previous stroke.

RUBBING OUT (BLENDING) FRESH PAINT — Let the paint dry thoroughly. Runs or imperfections can be sanded out, primed and repainted.

Don't be in too big a hurry to remove the masking. This only produces paint ridges. When the finish has dried for at least a week, apply a small amount of fine grade rubbing compound with a clean, wet cloth. Use lots of water and blend the new paint with the surrounding area.

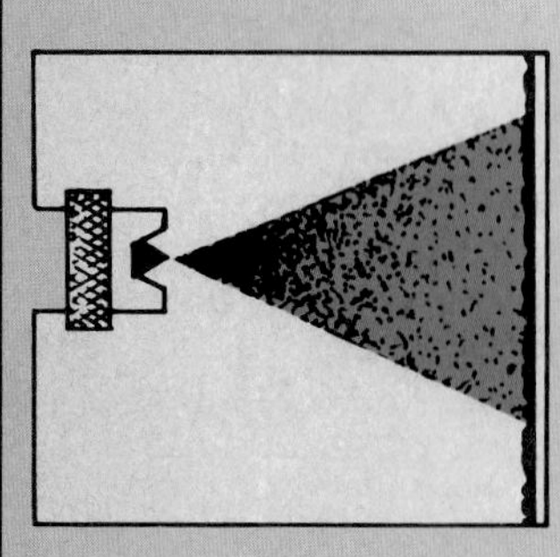

WRONG

Thin coat. Stroke too fast, not enough overlap, gun too far away.

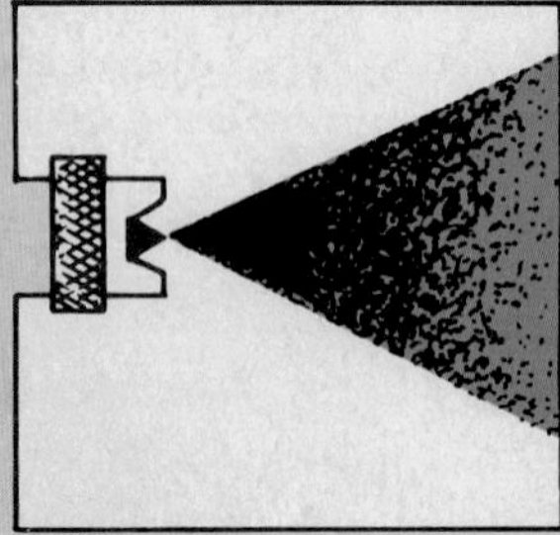

CORRECT

Medium coat. Proper distance, good stroke, proper overlap.

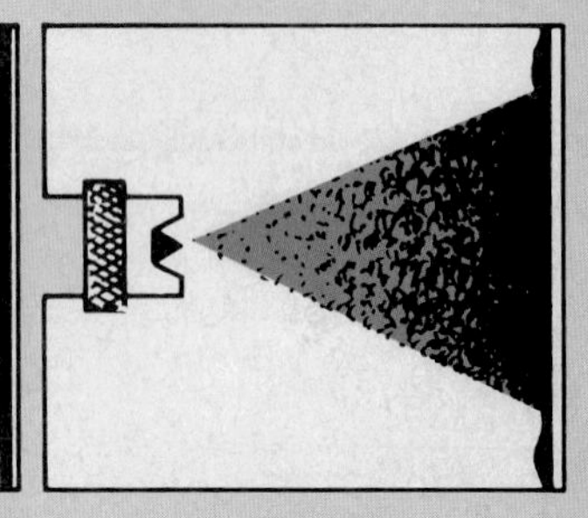

WRONG

Heavy coat. Stroke too slow, too much overlap, gun too close.

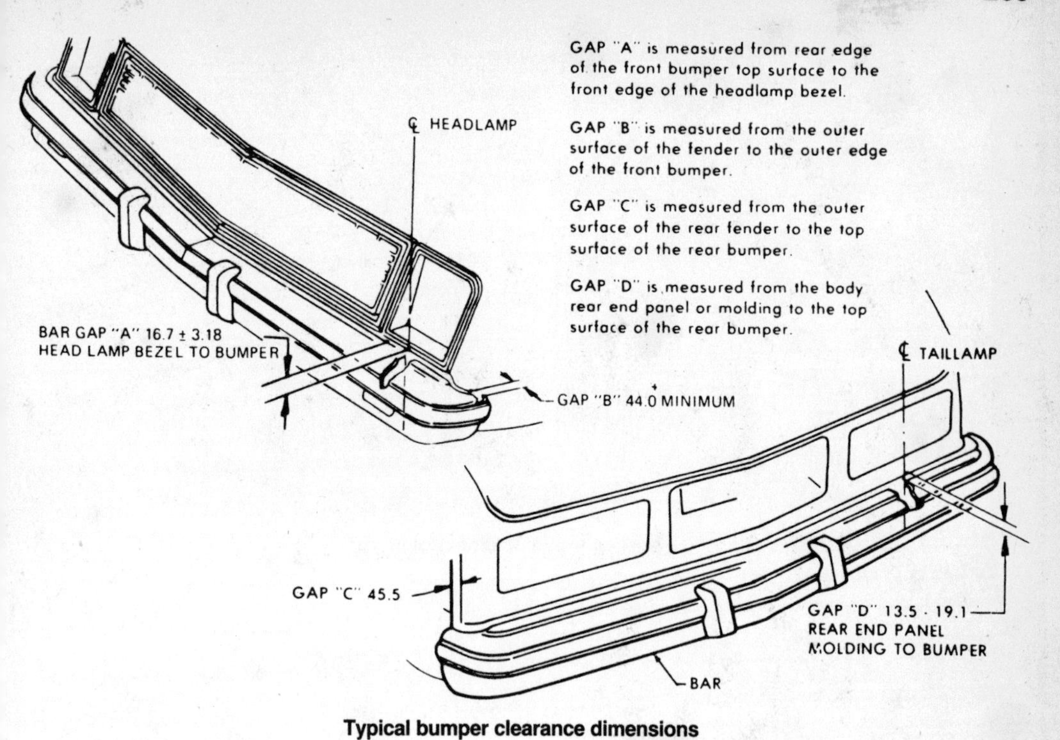

Typical bumper clearance dimensions

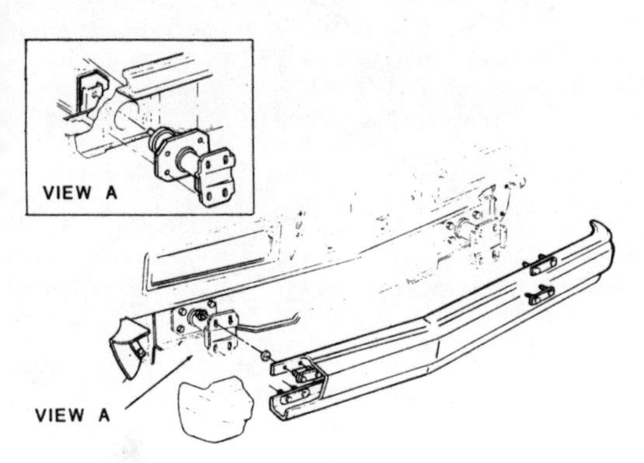

Rear bumper assembly, 1976–78

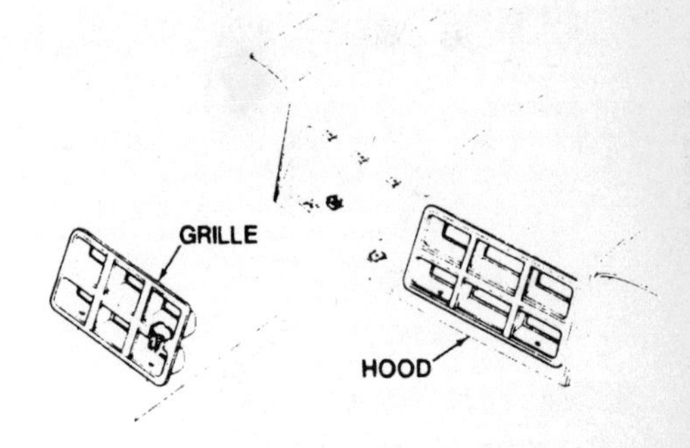

Grille assembly, 1978 shown, 1976–77 similar

Grille

REMOVAL AND INSTALLATION

The grilles are attached to the hood with sheet metal screws on models through 1978 and to the radiator support on 1979-87 models.

Outside Mirrors

The door outside mirrors are stud mounted to the door filler. The mirror glass face may be replaced by placing a piece of tape over the glass then breaking the mirror face. Adhesive back mirror faces are available. Left side flat and right side convex mirror faces must be replaced with the same type mirror face when surfaced.

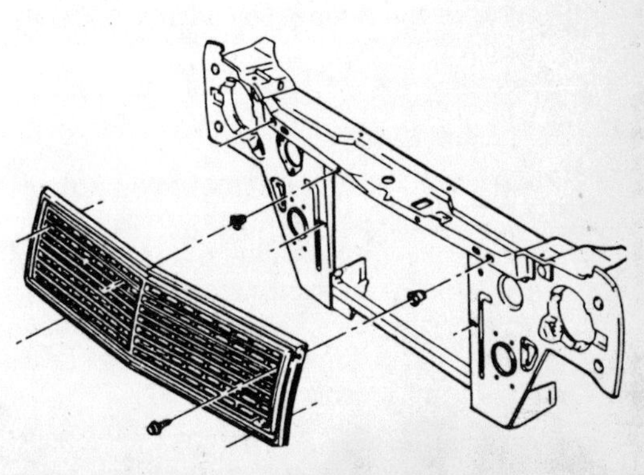

Grille assembly, 1979–87

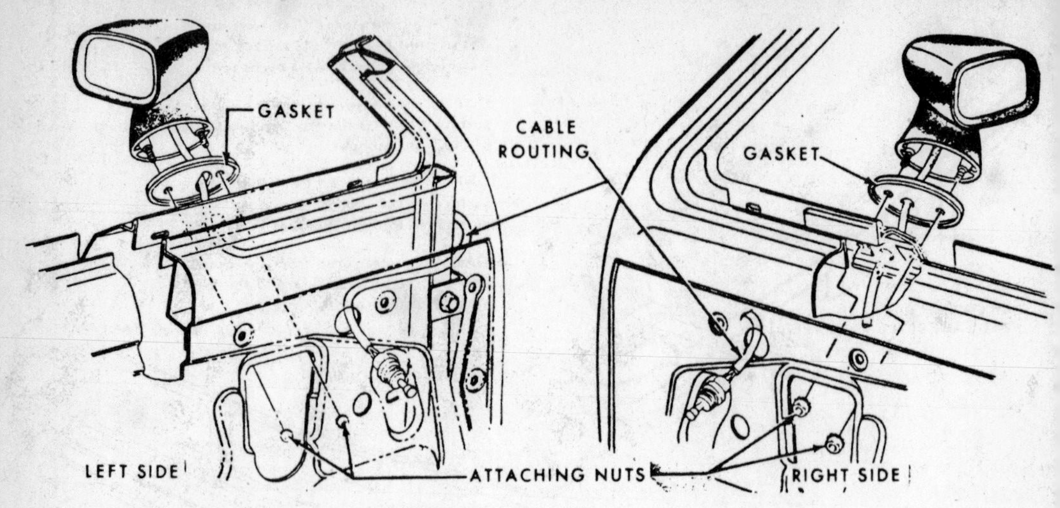

Installing the remote control mirror

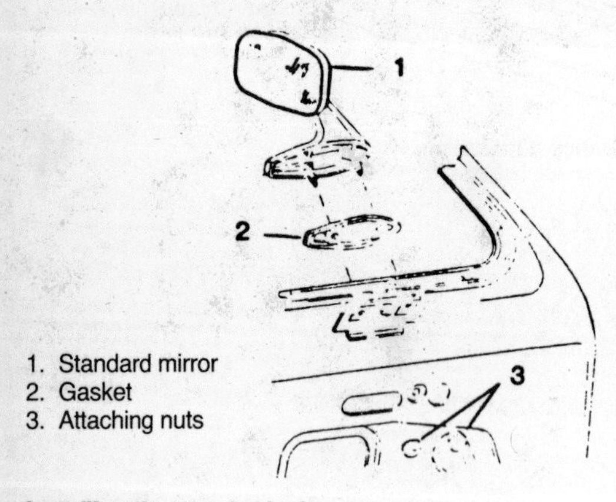

Installing the standard mirror

Antenna and cable installation

REMOVAL AND INSTALLATION

Standard Mirror

1. Remove the door trim panel and detach the inner panel water deflector enough to expose the front access hole.
2. Remove the attaching nuts from the mirror base studs and remove the mirror assembly from the door.
3. Installation is the reverse of removal.

Remote Control Mirror

1. Remove the mirror remote control escutcheon and the door trim panel.
2. Detach the inner panel water deflector enough to expose the front access hole.
3. Remove the mirror base to door outer panel stud nuts and remove the mirror and cable assembly from the door.
4. To install reverse the removal procedure. Be sure the cable is routed around the front glass run channel retainer

Antenna

REMOVAL AND INSTALLATION

1. Use a wrench to hold the cable assembly to prevent it from turning and use another wrench to remove the mast nut.
2. Remove the antenna by pulling the mast out of the cable assembly.
3. Installation is the reverse of removal.

INTERIOR

Door Trim Panels

REMOVAL AND INSTALLATION

Front

1. Remove the armrest pad (or armrest on the custom trim option), window regulator han-

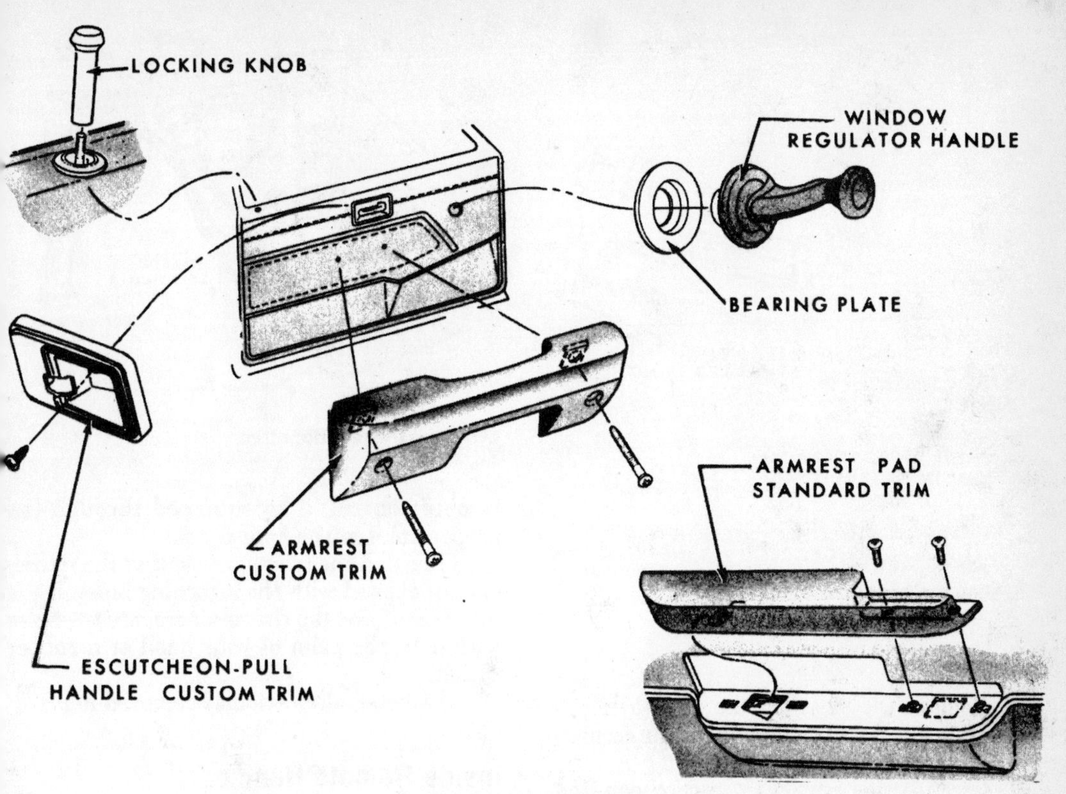

Door trim components

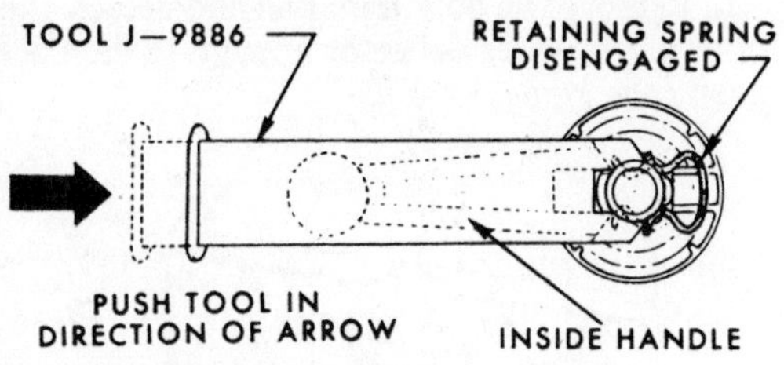

Removing the window regulator handle

dle, and the remote control mirror escutcheon (if so equipped).

2. Remove the screw in the remote handle pocket. Also remove the remote handle escutcheon on the custom trim option.

3. Remove the screw at the front lower corner on the standard trim left door.

4. With tool BT-7323A, J-24595B or equivalent inserted between the trim panel and the door inner panel, pry each trim retainer and trim panel away from the inner panel.

5. Before installing make sure that all the trim retainers are securely fastened and not damaged.

6. Insert the remote handle and the mirror remote control, if so equipped through the proper holes in the trim panel.

7. Position the trim panel so that the retainers are aligned with the attaching holes in the inner panel and tap the retainers into the holes with with the palm of your hand or a rubber mallet.

8. Reinstall the screws and other components.

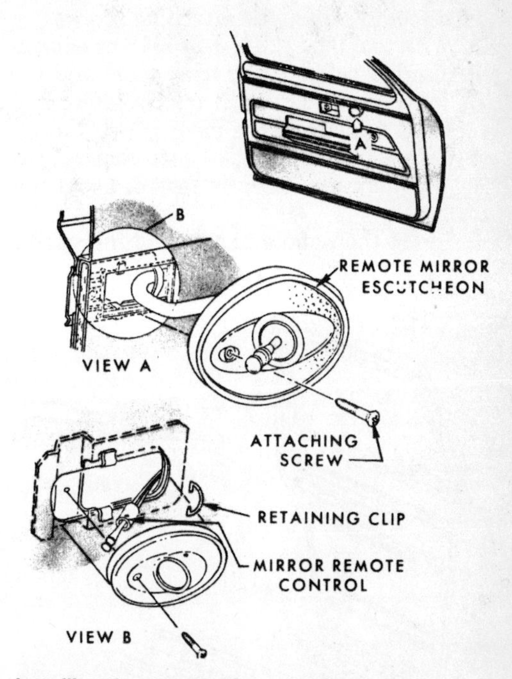

Installing the remote mirror escutcheon

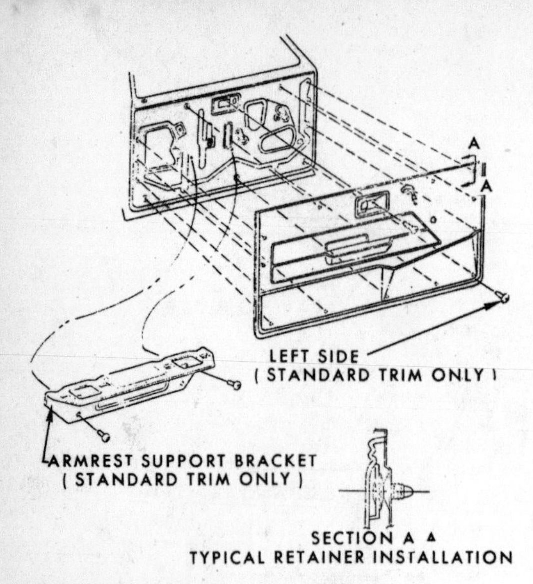

Installing the front door trim panel

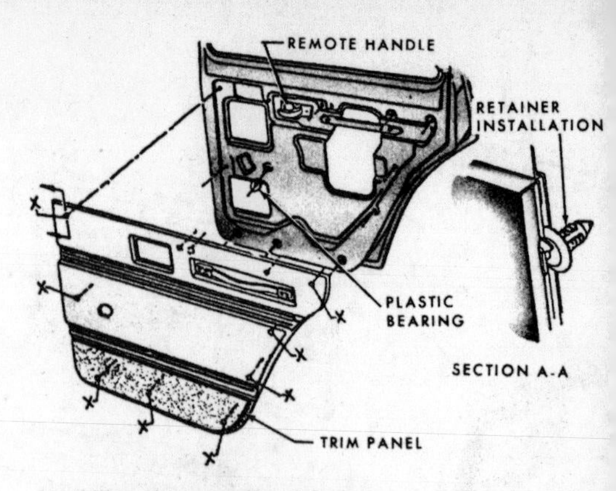

Installing the rear door trim

Rear

1. Remove the screw in the remote handle pocket. Also remove the remote handle escutcheon on the custom trim option.
2. Carefulley Disengage the escutcheon from the inside door pull handle retainer using a flat-bladed tool to expose the attaching screws.
3. With tool BT-7323A, J-24595B or equivalent inserted between the trim panel and the door inner panel, pry each trim retainer and trim panel away from the inner panel.
4. Before installing make sure that all the trim retainers are securely fastened and not damaged.
5. Insert the remote handle and the mirror remote control, if so equipped through the proper holes in the trim panel.
6. Position the trim panel so that the retainers are aligned with the attaching holes in the inner panel and tap the retainers into the holes with with the palm of your hand or a rubber mallet.
7. Reinstall all previously removed items.

Inside Remote Handle

REMOVAL AND INSTALLATION

1. Remove the door trim pad and detach the inner panel water deflector enough to gain access to the remote handle.

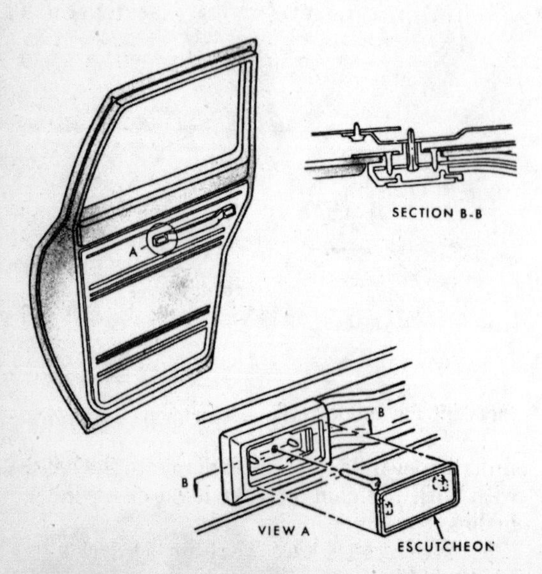

Attaching the rear door pull handle

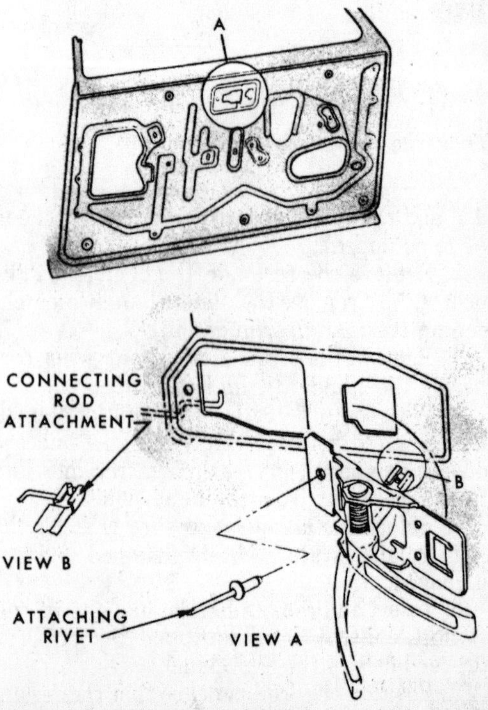

Inside remote handle installation

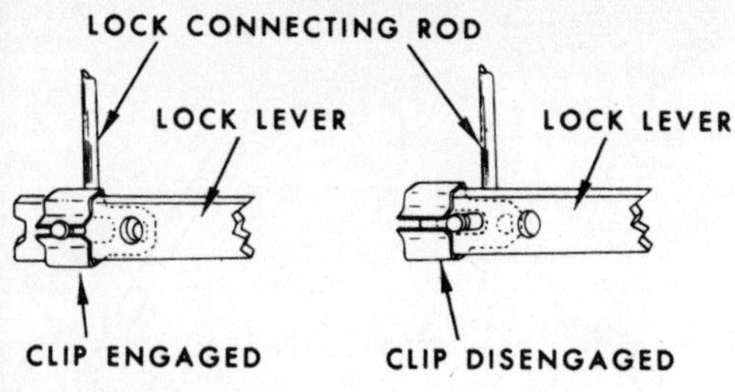

Spring clip removal

2. Disengage the connecting rod spring clip at the remote handle and disconnect the rod.
3. Punch out the center pin of the attaching rivet, then drill out the rivet using a $^3/_{16}$" drill.
4. Slide the remote handle forward to disengage the front retaining tab and remove.
5. To install, reverse the removal procedure. Use a steel rivet, $^3/_{16}$" × $^5/_{16}$", to attach the remote handle.

Outside handle

REMOVAL AND INSTALLATION

1. Raise the door window.
2. Remove the door trim panel and detach the inner panel water deflector enough to expose the rear access hole.
3. Remove the glass run channel by removing the lower attaching screw and pulling the retainer downward to disengage the upper attaching clip.
4. Remove the outside handle to lock rod by disengaging the spring clip on the lock lever.
5. Remove the two attaching nuts in the handle studs.
6. Slide the handle rearward and rotate up to disengage from the attaching holes.
7. Installation is the reverse of removal.

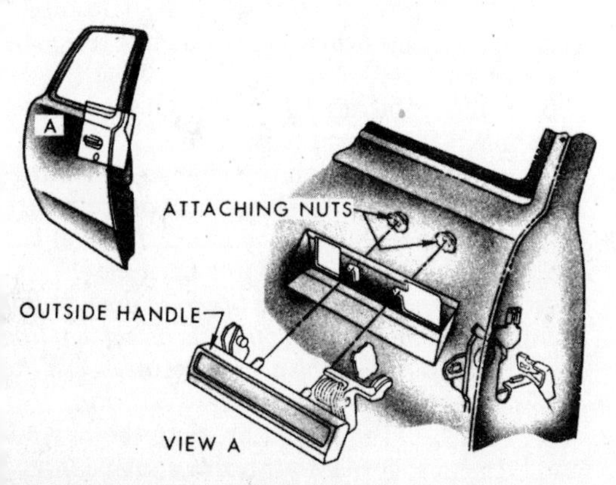

Outside handle installation

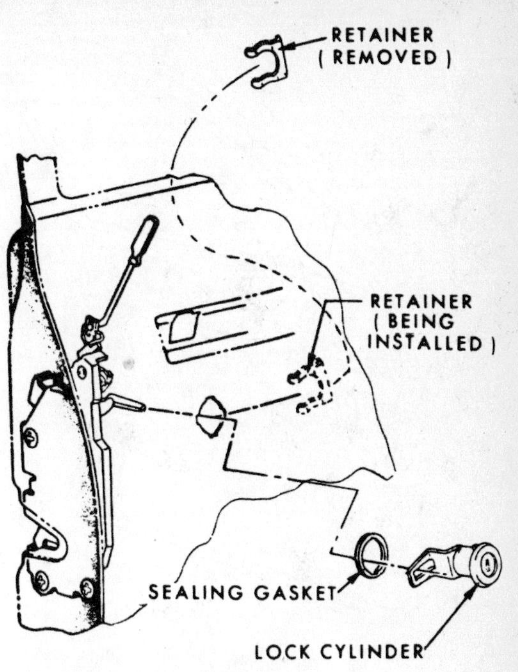

Installing the lock cylinder

Lock Cylinder

REMOVAL AND INSTALLATION

1. Raise the door window.
2. Remove the door trim panel and detach the inner panel water deflector enough to expose the rear access hole.
3. Using a suitable tool, slide the lock cylinder retaining clip (on the door outer panel) out of engagement and remove the lock cylinder pawl assembly from outside of the door.
4. Installation is the reverse of removal. Be sure to engage the lock cylinder pawl with the lock lever before engaging the the retaining clip.

NOTE: *Black lock cylinders should be lubricated with light oil. All other lock cylinders should be lubricated with a general purpose silicone.*

Door Locks

REMOVAL AND INSTALLATION

Front

1. Raise the door window.
2. Remove the door trim pad and detach the inner panel water deflector enough to expose the rear access hole.
2. Remove the rear glass run channel retainer by removing the lower attaching screw and pulling the retainer downward to disengage the upper attaching clip.

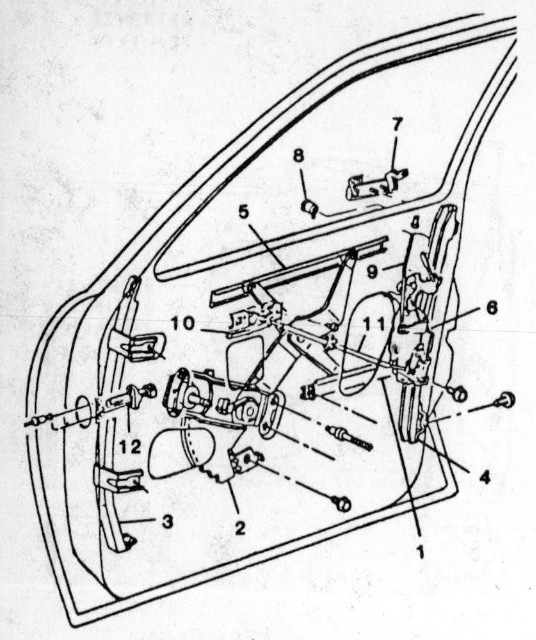

1. Inner panel cam
2. Window regulator
3. Front glas run channel retainer
4. Rear glass run channel retainer
5. Lower sash channel cam
6. Door lock
7. Outside handle
8. Lock cylinder
9. Inside locking rod
10. Inside remote handle
11. Handle to lock connecting rod
12. Door check link

Front door hardware, two door shown, four door similar

3. Disconnect the inside remote handle connecting rod and the inside lock button rod.
4. Remove the three attaching screws and disengage the lock from the outside handle and lock lever from the key cylinder pawl while removing the lock.
5. Installation is the reverse of removal. Tighten the door lock attaching screws to 80-100 in. lbs.

Rear

1. Raise the door window.
2. Remove the door trim pad and detach the inner panel water deflector enough to expose the rear access hole.
2. Remove the rear glass run channel retainer by removing the lower attaching screw and pulling the retainer downward to disengage the upper attaching clip.
3. Disconnect the inside remote handle connecting rod and bell crank to the lock rod.
4. Remove the three attaching screws and disengage the lock to outside handle rod from the outside handle.

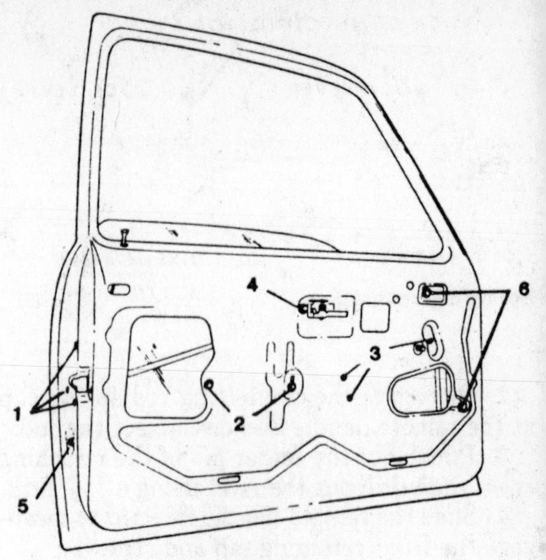

1. Door lock attaching screws
2. Inner panel cam attaching screws
3. Window regulator attaching rivets
4. Remote handle attaching rivets
5. Rear glass run channel retainer attaching screw
6. Front glass run channel retainer attaching screws

Front door hardware attachments, two door shown, four door similar

5. Installation is the reverse of removal. Tighten the door lock attaching screws to 80-100 in. lbs.

Door Window Regulator

REMOVAL AND INSTALLATION

Front

1. Remove the door trim pad and detach the inner panel water deflector.
2. Tape the glass in the up position with a fabric backed body tape.
3. Remove the inner panel cam.
4. Punch out the center pin of the three regulator attaching rivets; then drill out rivets using a ¼ in drill.
5. Slide the regulator fore and aft to disengage the balance arm and lift the arm from the glass cam.
6. Remove the regulator through the rear access hole, lift the arm first.
7. To install, position the U-clips on the regulator at the three attaching locations. Be sure to install the clips with the clinch nuts on the outboard side of the regulator backplate.

NOTE: *When replacing the four door sedan front door window regulator using U-clips and screws, it may be necessary to rework the U-clip at the front attachment position.*

8. To install the regulator, slide the balance and lift arm rollers into the lower sash channel cam on the glass; align the regulator attaching

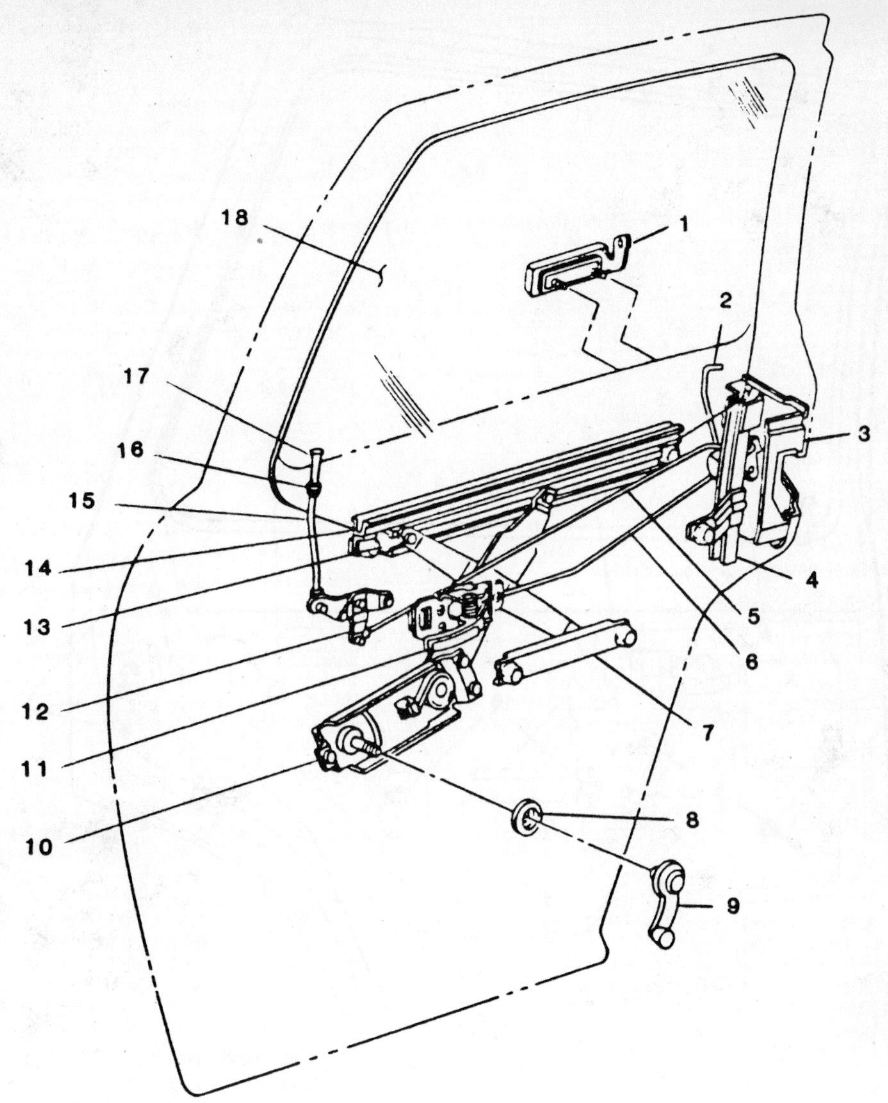

1. Outside handle
2. Outside handle to lock connecting rod
3. Door lock
4. Glass rear run channel retainer
5. Bell crank to lock connecting rod
6. Inside handle to lock connecting rod
7. Inner panel cam
8. Window regulator handle bearing plate
9. Window regulator handle
10. Window regulator
11. Remote inside handle
12. Bell crank
13. Lower sash channel cam
14. Lower sash channel
15. Inside locking rod
16. Inside locking rod ferrule (on inner panel)
17. Inside locking rod knob
18. Window glass

Rear door hardware

clips with the holes in the inner panel. Attach the regulator to the door using ¼-20 × 7⁄16″ or ¼-20 × ½″ screws or equivalent. Tighten the screws to 72 in. lbs.

Rear

1. Remove the door trim pad and detach the inner panel water deflector.

2. Tape the glass in the up position with a fabric backed body tape.

3. Remove the inner panel cam.

4. Remove the lower sash channel cam.

5. Punch out the center pin of the three regulator attaching rivets; then drill out rivets using a ¼ in drill.

6. Remove the regulator through the rear access hole, lift the arm first.

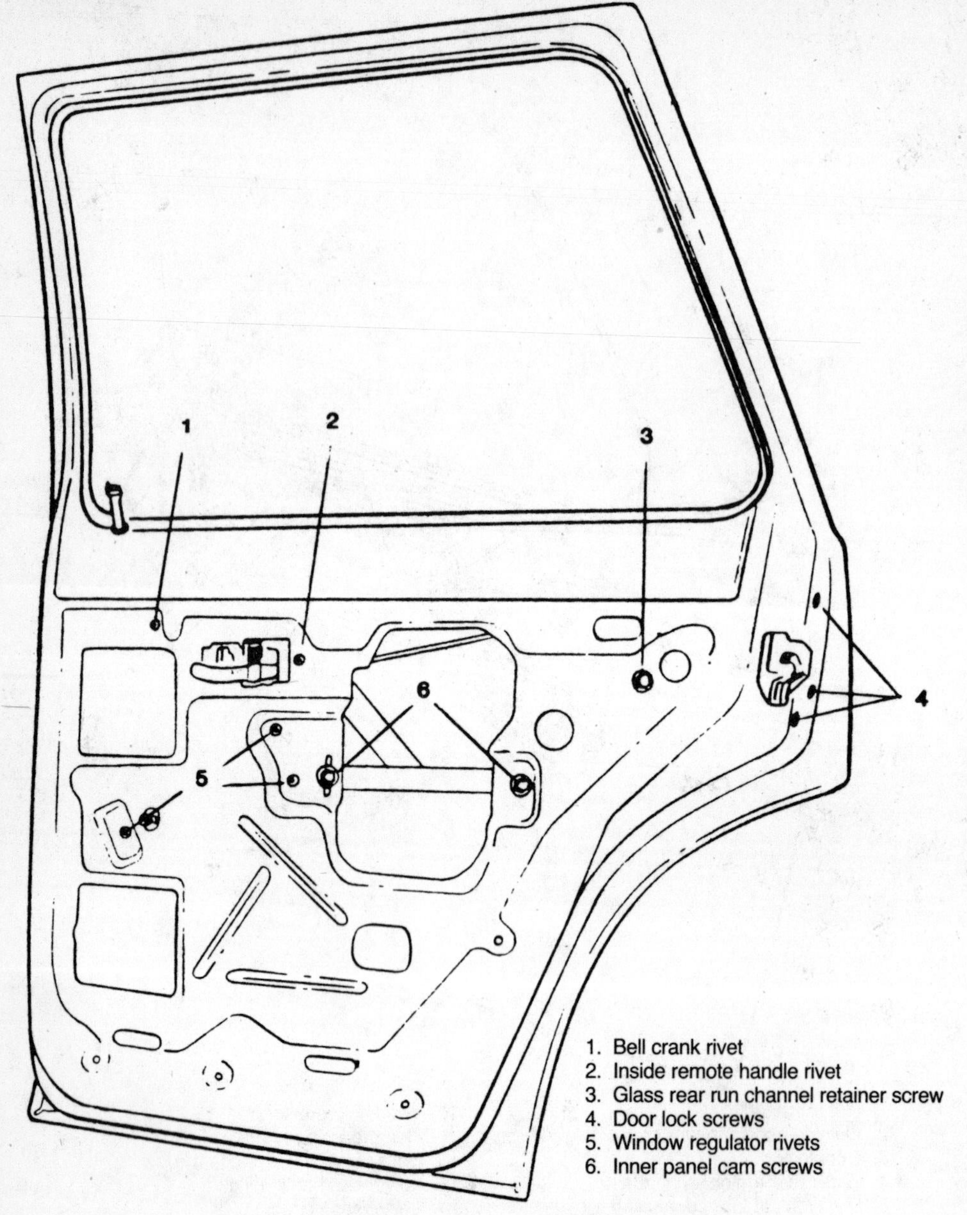

Rear door hardware attachments

7. To install, position the U-clips on the regulator at the three attaching locations. Be sure to install the clips with the clinch nuts on the outboard side of the regulator backplate.

NOTE: *When replacing the door window regulator using U-clips and screws, it may be necessary to rework the U-clip at the front attachment position.*

8. Align the attaching clips with holes in the inner panel.

9. Attach the regulator to the door using ¼-20 × $^{7}/_{16}$″ or ¼-20 × ½″ screws or equivalent. Tighten the screws to 72 in. lbs.

10. Install the lower sash channel cam to the regulator rollers. Install the cam attaching screws.

11. Install the inner panel cam and all other components.

Door Glass

REMOVAL AND INSTALLATION

Front

1. Remove the door trim pad and detach the inner panel water deflector.

2. Lower the glass and remove the outer belt sealing strip.

3. Remove the inner panel cam.

NOTE: *To aid glass removal, adjust the window regulator position as necessary.*

4. Starting with the window about half-up, tilt the glass forward about 45° and slide the glass rearward and up outside the door frame to disengage the balance arm roller.

5. Continue sliding the glass up and rearward to disengage the lift arm roller and lift the glass and cam assembly out of the door.

6. Reposition the glass in the door and reinstall all previously removed parts.

Rear

1. Remove the door trim pad and detach the inner panel water deflector.

2. Loosen the glass rear run channel retainer.

3. Remove the inner window belt sealing strips.

4. Remove the inner panel cam.

5. Remove the lower sash channel cam.

6. Raise the glass and tilt the glass forward about 45° and slide the glass rearward and up outside the door frame to disengage the balance arm roller. Remove the glass.

7. Reposition the glass in the door and reinstall all previously removed parts.

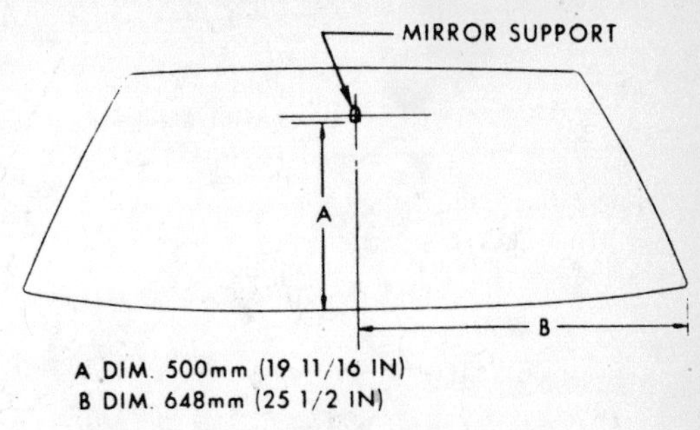

Rearview mirror support location on glass

Rearview Mirror

The rearview mirror is attached to a support which is secured to the windshield glass. The support is installed by the glass supplier using a plastic-polyvinyl butyl adhesive.

Front Seat

REMOVAL AND INSTALLATION

1. Operate the seat to the full-forward position.

2. At the rear of the adjusters, remove the adjuster-to-floor pan rear covers and nuts. Operate the seat to the full-rearward position. Remove the adjuster-to-floor pan front nuts.

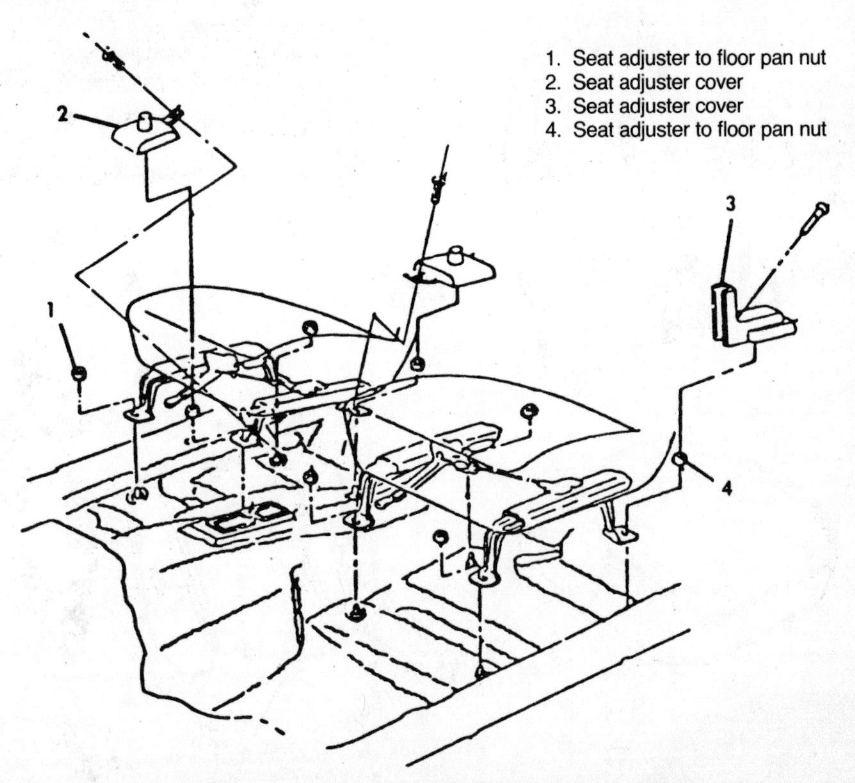

Front seat to floor pan installation—standard seats

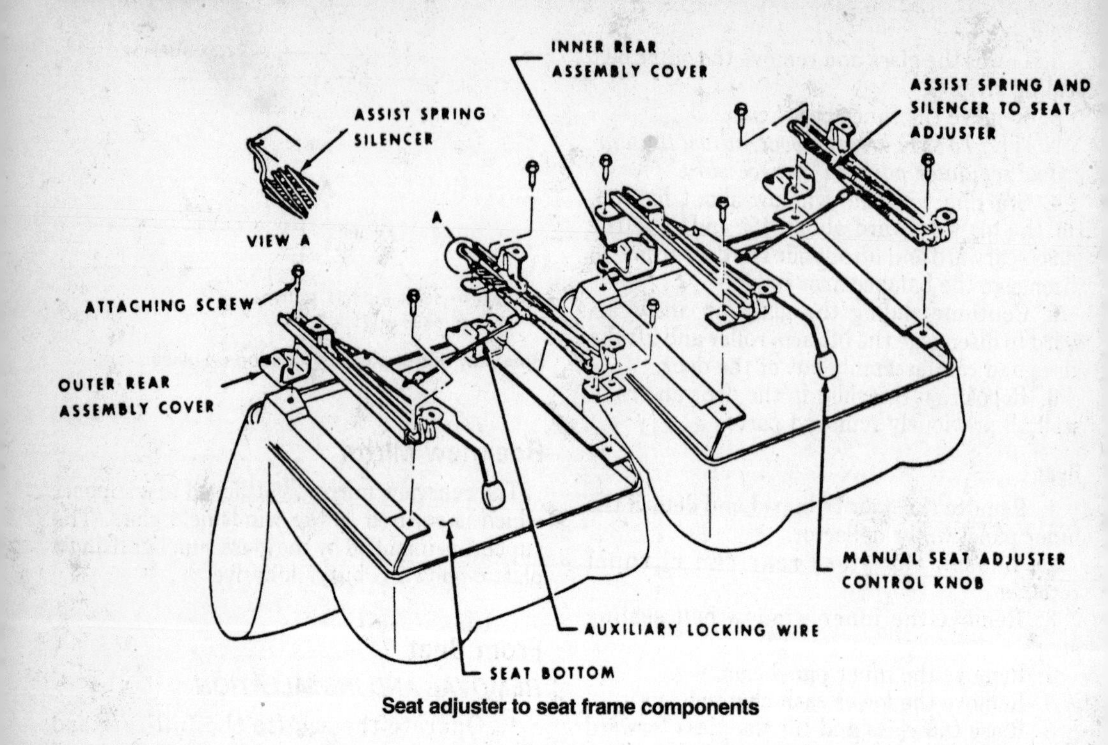

Seat adjuster to seat frame components

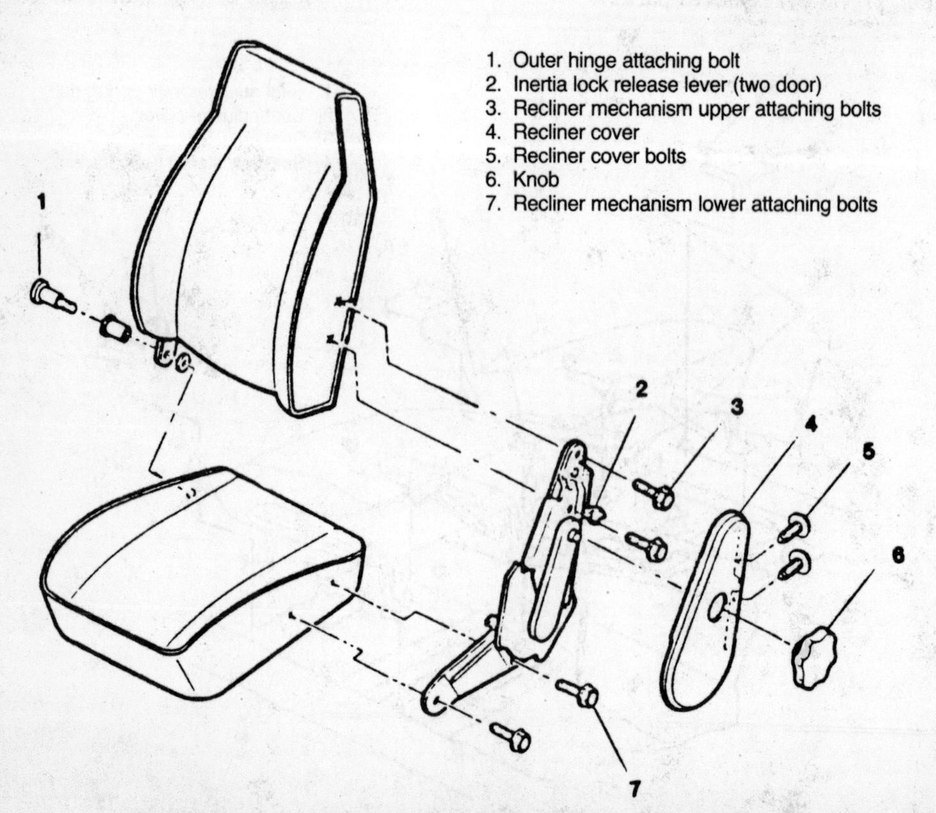

Recliner control mechanism (passenger seat shown, driver side similar)

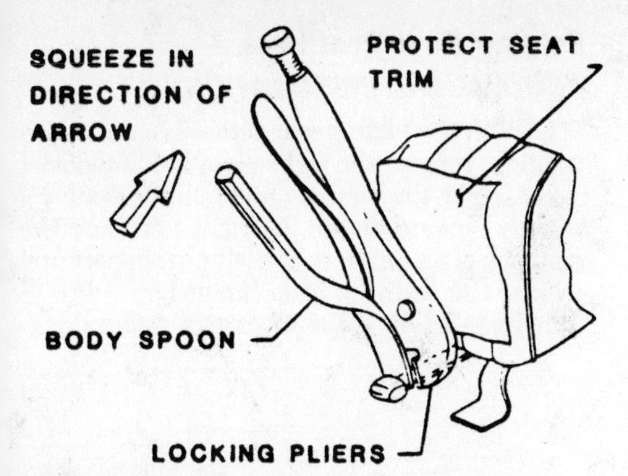

Front seat adjuster control knob removal and installation

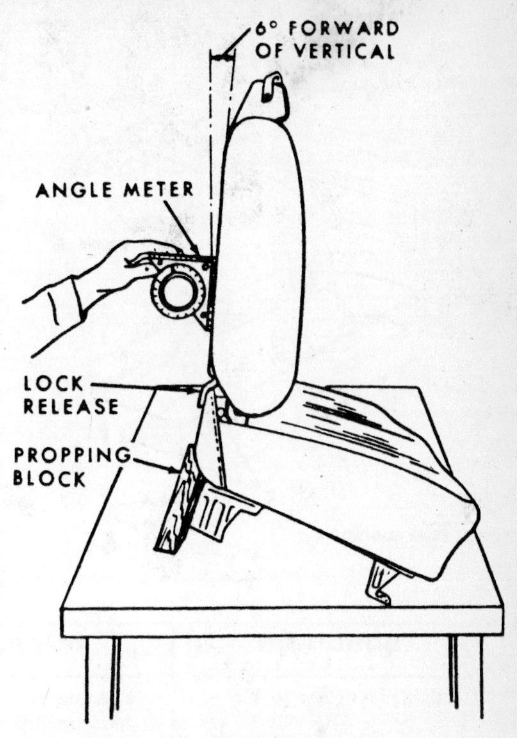

Front seatback inertia lock check (out of car)

3. Remove the seat from the car.
4. When installing the seat, tighten the seat adjuster-to-floor pan attaching nuts to 15-21 ft. lbs.

Rear Seat Cushion

REMOVAL AND INSTALLATION

The rear seat cushion is mounted directly to the floor pan and is retained by the seat cushion trim cover assembly.

1. Release the seat trim cover assembly from the front and side retainers.
2. Peel back the cover and slide the rear seat belt buckles back through the seat cushion, then remove the seat cushion.
3. Installation is the reverse of removal.

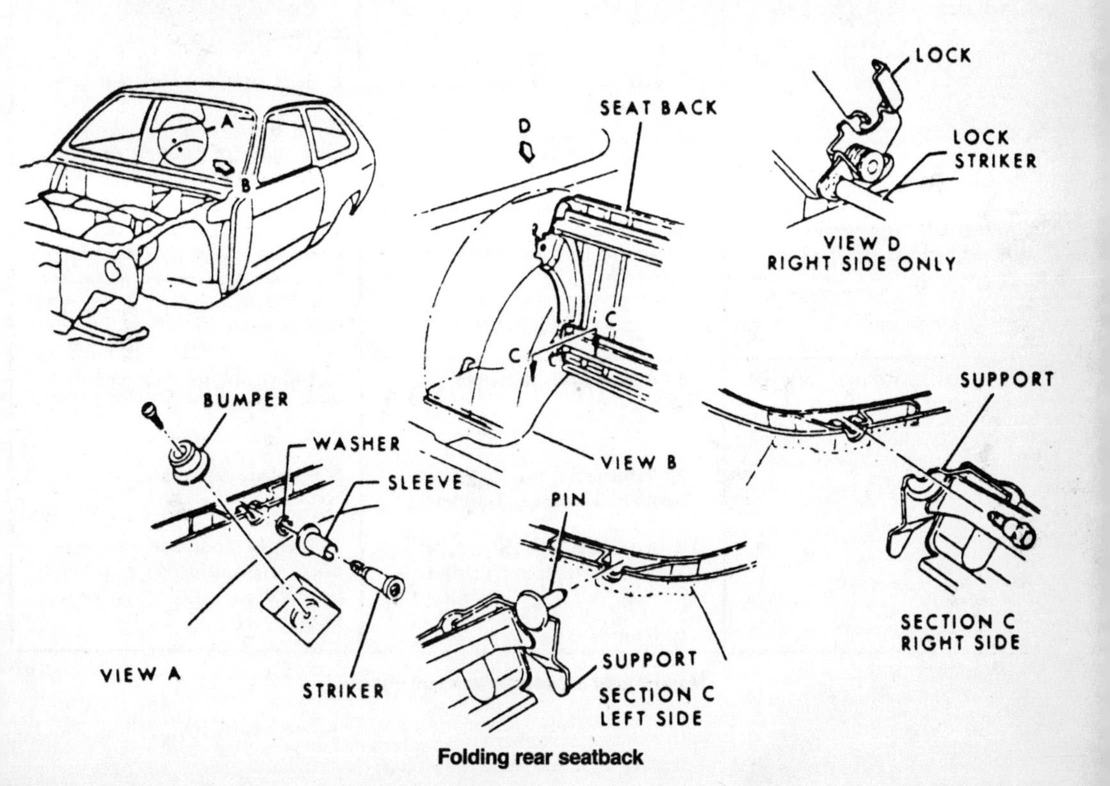

Folding rear seatback

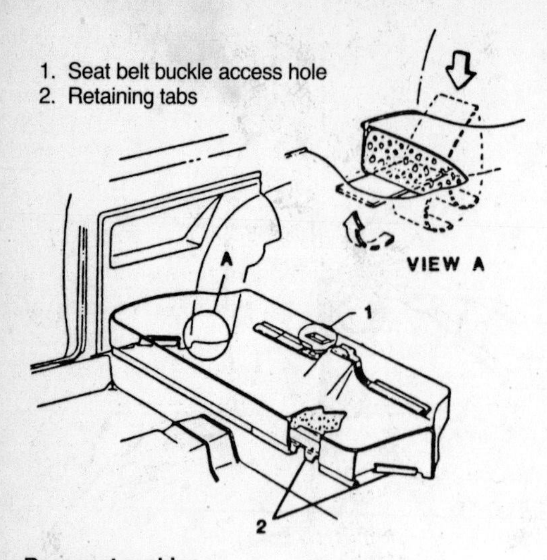

Rear seat cushion

Folding Rear Seat Back

REMOVAL AND INSTALLATION

1. With the folding rear setback in the raised position, remove the right pivot bolt support.
2. Unlock the seatback and pull the seatback slightly forward and to the right to release the seatback pivot pin from the left pin support and remove the seatback from the body.
3. Installation is the reverse of removal.

CONDITION	APPARENT CAUSE	CORRECTION
1. Adjuster will not lock.	1. Adjuster lock bar spring disconnected or broken	1. Connect spring or install new spring.(Fig. 9-16).
	2. Adjuster lock bar sticking or binding.	2. (a) Lubricate lock bar pivot. (b) If bar is binding, eliminate cause of binding or replace adjuster.
2. Adjuster will not unlock	1. Locking wire disconnected.	1. Connect locking wire to adjusters
	2. Adjuster lock bar sticking or binding.	2. (a) Lubricate lock bar pivot. (b) If bar is binding, eliminate cause of binding or replace adjuster.
3. When left adjuster locks, right adjuster is between lock positions.	1. Right adjuster either rearward or forward of left adjuster.	1. Loosen adjuster to floor pan nuts, move one adjuster forward or rearward as far as possible and the other adjuster the opposite direction.
4. Seat hard to move forward or rearward.	1. Adjuster(s) improperly lubricated	1. Lubricate adjuster channels with Lubriplate AAW or equivalent.
	2. Adjuster(s) binding due to bent or damaged channels.	2. Replace adjuster.
	3. Adjusters not in parallel alignment with each other.	3. Loosen floor pan attaching nuts, align adjusters parallel on floor pan and retighten nuts.

Manual seat adjuster diagnosis chart

How to Remove Stains from Fabric Interior

For rest results, spots and stains should be removed as soon as possible. Never use gasoline, lacquer thinner, acetone, nail polish remover or bleach. Use a 3′ x 3″ piece of cheesecloth. Squeeze most of the liquid from the fabric and wipe the stained fabric from the outside of the stain toward the center with a lifting motion. Turn the cheesecloth as soon as one side becomes soiled. When using water to remove a stain, be sure to wash the entire section after the spot has been removed to avoid water stains. Encrusted spots can be broken up with a dull knife and vacuumed before removing the stain.

Type of Stain	How to Remove It
Surface spots	Brush the spots out with a small hand brush or use a commercial preparation such as K2R to lift the stain.
Mildew	Clean around the mildew with warm suds. Rinse in cold water and soak the mildew area in a solution of 1 part table salt and 2 parts water. Wash with upholstery cleaner.
Water stains	Water stains in fabric materials can be removed with a solution made from 1 cup of table salt dissolved in 1 quart of water. Vigorously scrub the solution into the stain and rinse with clear water. Water stains in nylon or other synthetic fabrics should be removed with a commercial type spot remover.
Chewing gum, tar, crayons, shoe polish (greasy stains)	Do not use a cleaner that will soften gum or tar. Harden the deposit with an ice cube and scrape away as much as possible with a dull knife. Moisten the remainder with cleaning fluid and scrub clean.
Ice cream, candy	Most candy has a sugar base and can be removed with a cloth wrung out in warm water. Oily candy, after cleaning with warm water, should be cleaned with upholstery cleaner. Rinse with warm water and clean the remainder with cleaning fluid.
Wine, alcohol, egg, milk, soft drink (non-greasy stains)	Do not use soap. Scrub the stain with a cloth wrung out in warm water. Remove the remainder with cleaning fluid.
Grease, oil, lipstick, butter and related stains	Use a spot remover to avoid leaving a ring. Work from the outisde of the stain to the center and dry with a clean cloth when the spot is gone.
Headliners (cloth)	Mix a solution of warm water and foam upholstery cleaner to give thick suds. Use only foam—liquid may streak or spot. Clean the entire headliner in one operation using a circular motion with a natural sponge.
Headliner (vinyl)	Use a vinyl cleaner with a sponge and wipe clean with a dry cloth.
Seats and door panels	Mix 1 pint upholstery cleaner in 1 gallon of water. Do not soak the fabric around the buttons.
Leather or vinyl fabric	Use a multi-purpose cleaner full strength and a stiff brush. Let stand 2 minutes and scrub thoroughly. Wipe with a clean, soft rag.
Nylon or synthetic fabrics	For normal stains, use the same procedures you would for washing cloth upholstery. If the fabric is extremely dirty, use a multi-purpose cleaner full strength with a stiff scrub brush. Scrub thoroughly in all directions and wipe with a cotton towel or soft rag.

Mechanic's Data

General Conversion Table

Multiply By	To Convert	To	
	LENGTH		
2.54	Inches	Centimeters	.3937
25.4	Inches	Millimeters	.03937
30.48	Feet	Centimeters	.0328
.304	Feet	Meters	3.28
.914	Yards	Meters	1.094
1.609	Miles	Kilometers	.621
	VOLUME		
.473	Pints	Liters	2.11
.946	Quarts	Liters	1.06
3.785	Gallons	Liters	.264
.016	Cubic inches	Liters	61.02
16.39	Cubic inches	Cubic cms.	.061
28.3	Cubic feet	Liters	.0353
	MASS (Weight)		
28.35	Ounces	Grams	.035
.4536	Pounds	Kilograms	2.20
—	To obtain	From	Multiply by

Multiply By	To Convert	To	
	AREA		
.645	Square inches	Square cms.	.155
.836	Square yds.	Square meters	1.196
	FORCE		
4.448	Pounds	Newtons	.225
.138	Ft./lbs.	Kilogram/meters	7.23
1.36	Ft./lbs.	Newton-meters	.737
.112	In./lbs.	Newton-meters	8.844
	PRESSURE		
.068	Psi	Atmospheres	14.7
6.89	Psi	Kilopascals	.145
	OTHER		
1.104	Horsepower (DIN)	Horsepower (SAE)	.9861
.746	Horsepower (SAE)	Kilowatts (KW)	1.34
1.60	Mph	Km/h	.625
.425	Mpg	Km/1	2.35
—	To obtain	From	Multiply by

Tap Drill Sizes

National Coarse or U.S.S.

Screw & Tap Size	Threads Per Inch	Use Drill Number
No. 5	40	39
No. 6	32	36
No. 8	32	29
No. 10	24	25
No. 12	24	17
1/4	20	8
5/16	18	F
3/8	16	5/16
7/16	14	U
1/2	13	27/64
9/16	12	31/64
5/8	11	17/32
3/4	10	21/32
7/8	9	49/64

National Coarse or U.S.S.

Screw & Tap Size	Threads Per Inch	Use Drill Number
1	8	7/8
1 1/8	7	63/64
1 1/4	7	1 7/64
1 1/2	6	1 11/32

National Fine or S.A.E.

Screw & Tap Size	Threads Per Inch	Use Drill Number
No. 5	44	37
No. 6	40	33
No. 8	36	29
No. 10	32	21

National Fine or S.A.E.

Screw & Tap Size	Threads Per Inch	Use Drill Number
No. 12	28	15
1/4	28	3
6/16	24	1
3/8	24	Q
7/16	20	W
1/2	20	29/64
9/16	18	33/64
5/8	18	37/64
3/4	16	11/16
7/8	14	13/16
1 1/8	12	1 3/64
1 1/4	12	1 11/64
1 1/2	12	1 27/64

Drill Sizes In Decimal Equivalents

Inch	Decimal	Wire	mm	Inch	Decimal	Wire	mm	Inch	Decimal	Wire & Letter	mm	Inch	Decimal	Letter	mm	Inch	Decimal	mm
1/64	.0156		.39		.0730	49			.1614		4.1		.2717		6.9		.4331	11.0
	.0157		.4		.0748		1.9		.1654		4.2		.2720	I		7/16	.4375	11.11
	.0160	78			.0760	48			.1660	19			.2756		7.0		.4528	11.5
	.0165		.42		.0768		1.95		.1673		4.25		.2770	J		29/64	.4531	11.51
	.0173		.44	5/64	.0781		1.98		.1693		4.3		.2795		7.1	15/32	.4688	11.90
	.0177		.45		.0785	47			.1695	18			.2810	K			.4724	12.0
	.0180	77			.0787		2.0	11/64	.1719		4.36	9/32	.2812		7.14	31/64	.4844	12.30
	.0181		.46		.0807		2.05		.1730	17			.2835		7.2		.4921	12.5
	.0189		.48		.0810	46			.1732		4.4		.2854		7.25	1/2	.5000	12.70
	.0197		.5		.0820	45			.1770	16			.2874		7.3		.5118	13.0
	.0200	76			.0827		2.1		.1772		4.5		.2900	L		33/64	.5156	13.09
	.0210	75			.0846		2.15		.1800	15			.2913		7.4	17/32	.5312	13.49
	.0217		.55		.0860	44			.1811		4.6		.2950	M			.5315	13.5
	.0225	74			.0866		2.2		.1820	14			.2953		7.5	35/64	.5469	13.89
	.0236		.6		.0886		2.25		.1850	13		19/64	.2969		7.54		.5512	14.0
	.0240	73			.0890	43			.1850		4.7		.2992		7.6	9/16	.5625	14.28
	.0250	72			.0906		2.3		.1870		4.75		.3020	N			.5709	14.5
	.0256		.65		.0925		2.35	3/16	.1875		4.76		.3031		7.7	37/64	.5781	14.68
	.0260	71			.0935	42			.1890		4.8		.3051		7.75		.5906	15.0
	.0276		.7	3/32	.0938		2.38		.1890	12			.3071		7.8	19/32	.5938	15.08
	.0280	70			.0945		2.4		.1910	11			.3110		7.9	39/64	.6094	15.47
	.0292	69			.0960	41			.1929		4.9	5/16	.3125		7.93		.6102	15.5
	.0295		.75		.0965		2.45		.1935	10			.3150		8.0	5/8	.6250	15.87
	.0310	68			.0980	40			.1960	9			.3160	O			.6299	16.0
1/32	.0312		.79		.0981		2.5		.1969		5.0		.3189		8.1	41/64	.6406	16.27
	.0315		.8		.0995	39			.1990	8			.3228		8.2		.6496	16.5
	.0320	67			.1015	38			.2008		5.1		.3230	P		21/32	.6562	16.66
	.0330	66			.1024		2.6		.2010	7			.3248		8.25		.6693	17.0
	.0335		.85		.1040	37		13/64	.2031		5.16		.3268		8.3	43/64	.6719	17.06
	.0350	65			.1063		2.7		.2040	6		21/64	.3281		8.33	11/16	.6875	17.46
	.0354		.9		.1065	36			.2047		5.2		.3307		8.4		.6890	17.5
	.0360	64			.1083		2.75		.2055	5			.3320	Q		45/64	.7031	17.85
	.0370	63		7/64	.1094		2.77		.2067		5.25		.3346		8.5		.7087	18.0
	.0374		.95		.1100	35			.2087		5.3		.3386		8.6	23/32	.7188	18.25
	.0380	62			.1102		2.8		.2090	4			.3390	R			.7283	18.5
	.0390	61			.1110	34			.2126		5.4		.3425		8.7	47/64	.7344	18.65
	.0394		1.0		.1130	33			.2130	3		11/32	.3438		8.73		.7480	19.0
	.0400	60			.1142		2.9		.2165		5.5		.3445		8.75	3/4	.7500	19.05
	.0410	59			.1160	32		7/32	2188		5.55		.3465		8.8	49/64	.7656	19.44
	.0413		1.05		.1181		3.0		.2205		5.6		.3480	S			.7677	19.5
	.0420	58			.1200	31			.2210	2			.3504		8.9	25/32	.7812	19.84
	.0430	57			.1220		3.1		.2244		5.7		.3543		9.0		.7874	20.0
	.0433		1.1	1/8	.1250		3.17		.2264		5.75		.3580	T		51/64	.7969	20.24
	.0453		1.15		.1260		3.2		.2280	1			.3583		9.1		.8071	20.5
	.0465	56			.1280		3.25		.2283		5.8	23/64	.3594		9.12	13/16	.8125	20.63
3/64	.0469		1.19		.1285	30			.2323		5.9		.3622		9.2		.8268	21.0
	.0472		1.2		.1299		3.3		.2340	A			.3642		9.25	53/64	.8281	21.03
	.0492		1.25		.1339		3.4	15/64	.2344		5.95		.3661		9.3	27/32	.8438	21.43
	.0512		1.3		.1360	29			.2362		6.0		.3680	U			.8465	21.5
	.0520	55			.1378		3.5		.2380	B			.3701		9.4	55/64	.8594	21.82
	.0531		1.35		.1405	28			.2402		6.1		.3740		9.5		.8661	22.0
	.0550	54		9/64	.1406		3.57		.2420	C		3/8	.3750		9.52	7/8	.8750	22.22
	.0551		1.4		.1417		3.6		.2441		6.2		.3770	V			.8858	22.5
	.0571		1.45		.1440	27			.2460	D			.3780		9.6	57/64	.8906	22.62
	.0591		1.5		.1457		3.7		.2461		6.25		.3819		9.7		.9055	23.0
	.0595	53			.1470	26			.2480		6.3		.3839		9.75	29/32	.9062	23.01
	.0610		1.55		.1476		3.75	1/4	.2500	E	6.35		.3858		9.8	59/64	.9219	23.41
1/16	.0625		1.59		.1495	25			.2520		6.		.3860	W			.9252	23.5
	.0630		1.6		.1496		3.8		.2559		6.5		.3898		9.9	15/16	.9375	23.81
	.0635	52			.1520	24			.2570	F		25/64	.3906		9.92		.9449	24.0
	.0650		1.65		.1535		3.9		.2598		6.6		.3937		10.0	61/64	.9531	24.2
	.0669		1.7		.1540	23			.2610	G			.3970	X			.9646	24.5
	.0670	51		5/32	.1562		3.96		.2638		6.7		.4040	Y		31/64	.9688	24.6
	.0689		1.75		.1570	22		17/64	.2656		6.74	13/32	.4062		10.31		.9843	25.0
	.0700	50			.1575		4.0		.2657		6.75		.4130	Z		63/64	.9844	25.0
	.0709		1.8		.1590	21			.2660	H			.4134		10.5	1	1.0000	25.4
	.0728		1.85		.1610	20			.2677		6.8	27/64	.4219		10.71			

AIR/FUEL RATIO: The ratio of air to gasoline by weight in the fuel mixture drawn into the engine.

AIR INJECTION: One method of reducing harmful exhaust emissions by injecting air into each of the exhaust ports of an engine. The fresh air entering the hot exhaust manifold causes any remaining fuel to be burned before it can exit the tailpipe.

ALTERNATOR: A device used for converting mechanical energy into electrical energy.

AMMETER: An instrument, calibrated in amperes, used to measure the flow of an electrical current in a circuit. Ammeters are always connected in series with the circuit being tested.

AMPERE: The rate of flow of electrical current present when one volt of electrical pressure is applied against one ohm of electrical resistance.

ANALOG COMPUTER: Any microprocessor that uses similar (analogous) electrical signals to make its calculations.

ARMATURE: A laminated, soft iron core wrapped by a wire that converts electrical energy to mechanical energy as in a motor or relay. When rotated in a magnetic field, it changes mechanical energy into electrical energy as in a generator.

ATMOSPHERIC PRESSURE: The pressure on the Earth's surface caused by the weight of the air in the atmosphere. At sea level, this pressure is 14.7 psi at 32°F (101 kPa at 0°C).

ATOMIZATION: The breaking down of a liquid into a fine mist that can be suspended in air.

AXIAL PLAY: Movement parallel to a shaft or bearing bore.

BACKFIRE: The sudden combustion of gases in the intake or exhaust system that results in a loud explosion.

BACKLASH: The clearance or play between two parts, such as meshed gears.

BACKPRESSURE: Restrictions in the exhaust system that slow the exit of exhaust gases from the combustion chamber.

BAKELITE: A heat resistant, plastic insulator material commonly used in printed circuit boards and transistorized components.

BALL BEARING: A bearing made up of hardened inner and outer races between which hardened steel ball roll.

BALLAST RESISTOR: A resistor in the primary ignition circuit that lowers voltage after the engine is started to reduce wear on ignition components.

BEARING: A friction reducing, supportive device usually located between a stationary part and a moving part.

BIMETAL TEMPERATURE SENSOR: Any sensor or switch made of two dissimilar types of metal that bend when heated or cooled due to the different expansion rates of the alloys. These types of sensors usually function as an on/off switch.

BLOWBY: Combustion gases, composed of water vapor and unburned fuel, that leak past the piston rings into the crankcase during normal engine operation. These gases are removed by the PCV system to prevent the buildup of harmful acids in the crankcase.

BRAKE PAD: A brake shoe and lining assembly used with disc brakes.

BRAKE SHOE: The backing for the brake lining. The term is, however, usually applied to the assembly of the brake backing and lining.

BUSHING: A liner, usually removable, for a bearing; an anti-friction liner used in place of a bearing.

BYPASS: System used to bypass ballast resistor during engine cranking to increase voltage supplied to the coil.

CALIPER: A hydraulically activated device in a disc brake system, which is mounted straddling the brake rotor (disc). The caliper contains at least one piston and two brake pads. Hydraulic pressure on the piston(s) forces the pads against the rotor.

CAMSHAFT: A shaft in the engine on which are the lobes (cams) which operate the valves. The camshaft is driven by the crankshaft, via a belt, chain or gears, at one half the crankshaft speed.

CAPACITOR: A device which stores an electrical charge.

CARBON MONOXIDE (CO): a colorless, odorless gas given off as a normal byproduct of combustion. It is poisonous and extremely dangerous in confined areas, building up slowly to toxic levels without warning if adequate ventilation is not available.

CARBURETOR: A device, usually mounted on the intake manifold of an engine, which mixes the air and fuel in the proper proportion to allow even combustion.

CATALYTIC CONVERTER: A device installed in the exhaust system, like a muffler, that converts harmful byproducts of combustion into carbon dioxide and water vapor by means of a heat-producing chemical reaction.

CENTRIFUGAL ADVANCE: A mechanical method of advancing the spark timing by using flyweights in the distributor that react to centrifugal force generated by the distributor shaft rotation.

CHECK VALVE: Any one-way valve installed to permit the flow of air, fuel or vacuum in one direction only.

CHOKE: A device, usually a moveable valve, placed in the intake path of a carburetor to restrict the flow of air.

CIRCUIT: Any unbroken path through which an electrical current can flow. Also used to describe fuel flow in some instances.

CIRCUIT BREAKER: A switch which protects an electrical circuit from overload by opening the circuit when the current flow exceeds a predetermined level. Some circuit breakers must be reset manually, while other reset automatically

COIL (IGNITION): A transformer in the ignition circuit which steps of the voltage provided to the spark plugs.

COMBINATION MANIFOLD: An assembly which includes both the intake and exhaust manifolds in one casting.

COMBINATION VALVE: A device used in some fuel systems that routes fuel vapors to a charcoal storage canister instead of venting them into the atmosphere. The valve relieves fuel tank pressure and allows fresh air into the tank as fuel level drops to prevent a vapor lock situation.

COMPRESSION RATIO: The comparison of the total volume of the cylinder and combustion chamber with the piston at BDC and the piston at TDC.

CONDENSER: 1. An electrical device which acts to store an electrical charge, preventing voltage surges.

2. A radiator-like device in the air conditioning system in which refrigerant gas condenses into a liquid, giving off heat.

CONDUCTOR: Any material through which an electrical current can be transmitted easily.

CONTINUITY: Continuous or complete circuit. Can be checked with an ohmmeter.

COUNTERSHAFT: An intermediate shaft which is rotated by a mainshaft and transmits, in turn, that rotation to a working part.

CRANKCASE: The lower part of an engine in which the crankshaft and related parts operate.

CRANKSHAFT: The main driving shaft of an engine which receives reciprocating motion from the pistons and converts it to rotary motion.

CYLINDER: In an engine, the round hole in the engine block in which the piston(s) ride.

CYLINDER BLOCK: The main structural member of an engine in which is found the cylinders, crankshaft and other principal parts.

CYLINDER HEAD: The detachable portion of the engine, fastened, usually, to the top of the cylinder block, containing all or most of the combustion chambers. On overhead valve engines, it contains the valves and their operating parts. On overhead cam engines, it contains the camshaft as well.

DEAD CENTER: The extreme top or bottom of the piston stroke.

DETONATION: An unwanted explosion of the air fuel mixture in the combustion chamber caused by excess heat and compression, advanced timing, or an overly lean mixture. Also referred to as "ping".

DIAPHRAGM: A thin, flexible wall separating two cavities, such as in a vacuum advance unit.

DIESELING: A condition in which hot spots in the combustion chamber cause the engine to run on after the key is turned off.

DIFFERENTIAL: A geared assembly which allows the transmission of motion between drive axles, giving one axle the ability to turn faster than the other.

DIODE: An electrical device that will allow current to flow in one direction only.

DISC BRAKE: A hydraulic braking assembly consisting of a brake disc, or rotor, mounted on an axle, and a caliper assembly containing, usually two brake pads which are activated by hydraulic pressure. The pads are forced against the sides of the disc, creating friction which slows the vehicle.

DISTRIBUTOR: A mechanically driven device on an engine which is responsible for electrically firing the spark plug at a predetermined point of the piston stroke.

DOWEL PIN: A pin, inserted in mating holes in two different parts allowing those parts to maintain a fixed relationship.

DRUM BRAKE: A braking system which consists of two brake shoes and one or two wheel cylinders, mounted on a fixed backing plate, and a brake drum, mounted on an axle, which revolves around the assembly. Hydraulic action applied to the wheel cylinders forces the shoes outward against the drum, creating friction and slowing the vehicle.

DWELL: The rate, measured in degrees of shaft rotation, at which an electrical circuit cycles on and off.

ELECTRONIC CONTROL UNIT (ECU): Ignition module, module, amplifier or igniter. See Module for definition.

ELECTRONIC IGNITION: A system in which the timing and firing of the spark plugs is controlled by an electronic control unit, usually called a module. These systems have not points or condenser.

ENDPLAY: The measured amount of axial movement in a shaft.

ENGINE: A device that converts heat into mechanical energy.

EXHAUST MANIFOLD: A set of cast passages or pipes which conduct exhaust gases from the engine.

FEELER GAUGE: A blade, usually metal, of precisely predetermined thickness, used to measure the clearance between two parts. These blades usually are available in sets of assorted thicknesses.

F-Head: An engine configuration in which the intake valves are in the cylinder head, while the camshaft and exhaust valves are located in the cylinder block. The camshaft operates the intake valves via lifters and pushrods, while it operates the exhaust valves directly.

FIRING ORDER: The order in which combustion occurs in the cylinders of an engine. Also the order in which spark is distributed to the plugs by the distributor.

FLATHEAD: An engine configuration in which the camshaft and all the valves are located in the cylinder block.

FLOODING: The presence of too much fuel in the intake manifold and combustion chamber which prevents the air/fuel mixture from firing, thereby causing a no-start situation.

FLYWHEEL: A disc shaped part bolted to the rear end of the crankshaft. Around the outer perimeter is affixed the ring gear. The starter drive engages the ring gear, turning the flywheel, which rotates the crankshaft, imparting the initial starting motion to the engine.

FOOT POUND (ft.lb. or sometimes, ft. lbs.): The amount of energy or work needed to raise an item weighing one pound, a distance of one foot.

FUSE: A protective device in a circuit which prevents circuit overload by breaking the circuit when a specific amperage is present. The device is constructed around a strip or wire of a lower amperage rating than the circuit it is designed to protect. When an amperage higher than that stamped on the fuse is present in the circuit, the strip or wire melts, opening the circuit.

GEAR RATIO: The ratio between the number of teeth on meshing gears.

GENERATOR: A device which converts mechanical energy into electrical energy.

HEAT RANGE: The measure of a spark plug's ability to dissipate heat from its firing end. The higher the heat range, the hotter the plug fires.

HUB: The center part of a wheel or gear.

HYDROCARBON (HC): Any chemical compound made up of hydrogen and carbon. A major pollutant formed by the engine as a byproduct of combustion.

HYDROMETER: An instrument used to measure the specific gravity of a solution.

INCH POUND (in.lb. or sometimes, in. lbs.): One twelfth of a foot pound.

INDUCTION: A means of transferring electrical energy in the form of a magnetic field. Principle used in the ignition coil to increase voltage.

INJECTION PUMP: A device, usually mechanically operated, which meters and delivers fuel under pressure to the fuel injector.

INJECTOR: A device which receives metered fuel under relatively low pressure and is activated to inject the fuel into the engine under relatively high pressure at a predetermined time.

INPUT SHAFT: The shaft to which torque is applied, usually carrying the driving gear or gears.

INTAKE MANIFOLD: A casting of passages or pipes used to conduct air or a fuel/air mixture to the cylinders.

JOURNAL: The bearing surface within which a shaft operates.

KEY: A small block usually fitted in a notch between a shaft and a hub to prevent slippage of the two parts.

MANIFOLD: A casting of passages or set of pipes which connect the cylinders to an inlet or outlet source.

MANIFOLD VACUUM: Low pressure in an engine intake manifold formed just below the throttle plates. Manifold vacuum is highest at idle and drops under acceleration.

MASTER CYLINDER: The primary fluid pressurizing device in a hydraulic system. In automotive use, it is found in brake and hydraulic clutch systems and is pedal activated, either directly or, in a power brake system, through the power booster.

MODULE: Electronic control unit, amplifier or igniter of solid state or integrated design which controls the current flow in the ignition primary circuit based on input from the pick-up coil. When the module opens the primary circuit, the high secondary voltage is induced in the coil.

NEEDLE BEARING: A bearing which consists of a number (usually a large number) of long, thin rollers.

OHM: (Ω) The unit used to measure the resistance of conductor to electrical flow. One ohm is the amount of resistance that limits current flow to one ampere in a circuit with one volt of pressure.

OHMMETER: An instrument used for measuring the resistance, in ohms, in an electrical circuit.

OUTPUT SHAFT: The shaft which transmits torque from a device, such as a transmission.

OVERDRIVE: A gear assembly which produces more shaft revolutions than that transmitted to it.

OVERHEAD CAMSHAFT (OHC): An engine configuration in which the camshaft is mounted on top of the cylinder head and operates the valve either directly or by means of rocker arms.

OVERHEAD VALVE (OHV): An engine configuration in which all of the valves are located in the cylinder head and the camshaft is located in the cylinder block. The camshaft operates the valves via lifters and pushrods.

OXIDES OF NITROGEN (NOx): Chemical compounds of nitrogen produced as a byproduct of combustion. They combine with hydrocarbons to produce smog.

OXYGEN SENSOR: Used with the feedback system to sense the presence of oxygen in the exhaust gas and signal the computer which can reference the voltage signal to an air/fuel ratio.

PINION: The smaller of two meshing gears.

PISTON RING: An open ended ring which fits into a groove on the outer diameter of the piston. Its chief function is to form a seal between the piston and cylinder wall. Most automotive pistons have three rings: two for compression sealing; one for oil sealing.

PRELOAD: A predetermined load placed on a bearing during assembly or by adjustment.

PRIMARY CIRCUIT: Is the low voltage side of the ignition system which consists of the ignition switch, ballast resistor or resistance wire, bypass, coil, electronic control unit and pick-up coil as well as the connecting wires and harnesses.

PRESS FIT: The mating of two parts under pressure, due to the inner diameter of one being smaller than the outer diameter of the other, or vice versa; an interference fit.

RACE: The surface on the inner or outer ring of a bearing on which the balls, needles or rollers move.

REGULATOR: A device which maintains the amperage and/or voltage levels of a circuit at predetermined values.

RELAY: A switch which automatically opens and/or closes a circuit.

RESISTANCE: The opposition to the flow of current through a circuit or electrical device, and is measured in ohms. Resistance is equal to the voltage divided by the amperage.

RESISTOR: A device, usually made of wire, which offers a preset amount of resistance in an electrical circuit.

RING GEAR: The name given to a ring-shaped gear attached to a differential case, or affixed to a flywheel or as part a planetary gear set.

ROLLER BEARING: A bearing made up of hardened inner and outer races between which hardened steel rollers move.

ROTOR: 1. The disc-shaped part of a disc brake assembly, upon which the brake pads bear; also called, brake disc.

2. The device mounted atop the distributor shaft, which passes current to the distributor cap tower contacts.

SECONDARY CIRCUIT: The high voltage side of the ignition system, usually above 20,000 volts. The secondary includes the ignition coil, coil wire, distributor cap and rotor, spark plug wires and spark plugs.

SENDING UNIT: A mechanical, electrical, hydraulic or electromagnetic device which transmits information to a gauge.

SENSOR: Any device designed to measure engine operating conditions or ambient pressures and temperatures. Usually electronic in nature and designed to send a voltage signal to an on-board computer, some sensors may operate as a simple on/off switch or they may provide a variable voltage signal (like a potentiometer) as conditions or measured parameters change.

SHIM: Spacers of precise, predetermined thickness used between parts to establish a proper working relationship.

SLAVE CYLINDER: In automotive use, a device in the hydraulic clutch system which is activated by hydraulic force, disengaging the clutch.

SOLENOID: A coil used to produce a magnetic field, the effect of which is produce work.

SPARK PLUG: A device screwed into the combustion chamber of a spark ignition engine. The basic construction is a conductive core inside of a ceramic insulator, mounted in an outer conductive base. An electrical charge from the spark plug wire travels along the conductive core and jumps a preset air gap to a grounding point or points at the end of the conductive base. The resultant spark ignites the fuel/air mixture in the combustion chamber.

SPLINES: Ridges machined or cast onto the outer diameter of a shaft or inner diameter of a bore to enable parts to mate without rotation.

TACHOMETER: A device used to measure the rotary speed of an engine, shaft, gear, etc., usually in rotations per minute.

THERMOSTAT: A valve, located in the cooling system of an engine, which is closed when cold and opens gradually in response to engine heating, controlling the temperature of the coolant and rate of coolant flow.

TOP DEAD CENTER (TDC): The point at which the piston reaches the top of its travel on the compression stroke.

TORQUE: The twisting force applied to an object.

TORQUE CONVERTER: A turbine used to transmit power from a driving member to a driven member via hydraulic action, providing changes in drive ratio and torque. In automotive use, it links the driveplate at the rear of the engine to the automatic transmission.

TRANSDUCER: A device used to change a force into an electrical signal.

TRANSISTOR: A semi-conductor component which can be actuated by a small voltage to perform an electrical switching function.

TUNE-UP: A regular maintenance function, usually associated with the replacement and adjustment of parts and components in the electrical and fuel systems of a vehicle for the purpose of attaining optimum performance.

TURBOCHARGER: An exhaust driven pump which compresses intake air and forces it into the combustion chambers at higher than atmospheric pressures. The increased air pressure allows more fuel to be burned and results in increased horsepower being produced.

VACUUM ADVANCE: A device which advances the ignition timing in response to increased engine vacuum.

VACUUM GAUGE: An instrument used to measure the presence of vacuum in a chamber.

VALVE: A device which control the pressure, direction of flow or rate of flow of a liquid or gas.

VALVE CLEARANCE: The measured gap between the end of the valve stem and the rocker arm, cam lobe or follower that activates the valve.

VISCOSITY: The rating of a liquid's internal resistance to flow.

VOLTMETER: An instrument used for measuring electrical force in units called volts. Voltmeters are always connected parallel with the circuit being tested.

WHEEL CYLINDER: Found in the automotive drum brake assembly, it is a device, actuated by hydraulic pressure, which, through internal pistons, pushes the brake shoes outward against the drums.

ABBREVIATIONS AND SYMBOLS

A: Ampere

AC: Alternating current

A/C: Air conditioning

A-h: Ampere hour

AT: Automatic transmission

ATDC: After top dead center

μA: Microampere

bbl: Barrel

BDC: Bottom dead center

bhp: Brake horsepower

BTDC: Before top dead center

BTU: British thermal unit

C: Celsius (Centigrade)

CCA: Cold cranking amps

cd: Candela

cm^2: Square centimeter

cm^3, cc: Cubic centimeter

CO: Carbon monoxide

CO_2: Carbon dioxide

cu.in., in^3: Cubic inch

CV: Constant velocity

Cyl.: Cylinder

DC: Direct current

ECM: Electronic control module

EFE: Early fuel evaporation

EFI: Electronic fuel injection

EGR: Exhaust gas recirculation

Exh.: Exhaust

F: Fahrenheit

F: Farad

pF: Picofarad

μF: Microfarad

FI: Fuel injection

ft.lb., ft. lb., ft. lbs.: foot pound(s)

gal: Gallon

g: Gram

HC: Hydrocarbon

HEI: High energy ignition

HO: High output

hp: Horsepower

Hyd.: Hydraulic

Hz: Hertz

ID: Inside diameter

in.lb.; in. lb.; in. lbs: inch pound(s)

Int.: Intake

K: Kelvin

kg: Kilogram

kHz: Kilohertz

km: Kilometer

km/h: Kilometers per hour

kΩ: Kilohm

kPa: Kilopascal

kV: Kilovolt

kW: Kilowatt

l: Liter

l/s: Liters per second

m: Meter

mA: Milliampere

mg: Milligram

mHz: Megahertz

mm: Millimeter

mm^2: Square millimeter

m^3: Cubic meter

MΩ: Megohm

m/s: Meters per second

MT: Manual transmission

mV: Millivolt

μm: Micrometer

N: Newton

N-m: Newton meter

NOx: Nitrous oxide

OD: Outside diameter

OHC: Over head camshaft

OHV: Over head valve

Ω: Ohm

PCV: Positive crankcase ventilation

psi: Pounds per square inch

pts: Pints

qts: Quarts

rpm: Rotations per minute

rps: Rotations per second

R-12: A refrigerant gas (Freon)

SAE: Society of Automotive Engineers

SO_2: Sulfur dioxide

T: Ton

t: Megagram

TBI: Throttle Body Injection

TPS: Throttle Position Sensor

V: 1. Volt; 2. Venturi

μV: Microvolt

W: Watt

∝: Infinity

‹: Less than

›: Greater than

Index

D

E

F

R

S

T

U

V

W

continued on next page